# PASS TRAK® 7

Review

# General Securities Representative

9th Edition

Dearborn Financial Publishing, Inc.

---

At press time, this 9th edition of PassTrak Series 7 contains the most complete and accurate information currently available for the NASD Series 7 license examination. Owing to the nature of securities license examinations, however, information may have been added recently to the actual test that does not appear in this edition.



Executive Editor: Kimberly K. Walker-Daniels
Senior Technical Editor: Kenneth R. Walker-Daniels
Managing Editor: Nicola Bell
Development Editor: Laura Schlachtmeyer
Product Editor: Brian K. Fauth


Published by Dearborn Financial Publishing, Inc.®



Printed in the United States of America.

96 97 98 10 9 8 7 6 5 4 3 2 1

**Library of Congress Cataloging-in-Publication Data**

PassTrak series 7, General securities representative. Review. — 9th ed.
p. cm.
ISBN 0-7931-1737-2 (pbk.)
1. Securities—United States—Examinations, questions, etc.
2. Stockbrokers—United States—Examinations, questions, etc.
I. Dearborn Financial Publishing.
HG4928.5.P3534 1996
332.63'27'076—dc20 96-12281
CIP

# Contents

Introduction to PassTrak Series 7 ix

1. Equity Securities 1
   - Corporate Ownership and Common Stock 1
   - Preferred Stock 7
   - Return on Investment 10
   - Transferability of Ownership 13
   - Rights and Warrants 15
   - American Depositary Receipts 19

2. Debt Securities 21
   - Characteristics of Bonds 21
   - Bond Yields 28

3. Corporate Debt Securities 35
   - Characteristics of Corporate Bonds 35
   - Convertible Securities 40

4. U.S. Government and Agency Securities 45
   - Marketable Government Securities 45
   - Nonmarketable Government Securities 49
   - Agency Issues 51

5. Money-market Securities and Interest Rates 55
   - The Money Market 55
   - Interest Rates 59
   - Eurodollars and the Foreign Currency Markets 61

6. Issuing Securities 65
The Regulation of New Issues 65
The Underwriting Process 70
The Underwriting Syndicate 74
Types of Underwriting Commitments 76
Exemptions from the Securities Act of 1933 78
Freeriding and Withholding: Hot Issues 81

7. Trading Securities 85
The Regulation of Trading 85
Securities Markets and Broker-Dealers 88
The New York Stock Exchange 91
The Specialist 95
Types of Orders 97
Long and Short Sale Rules 102
The Over-the-Counter Market 104
Quotations 106
NASD 5% Markup Policy 108
NASD Automated Quotation System 111
Computerized Order Routing 114
The Consolidated Tape 115

8. Customer Accounts 119
New Accounts 119
Types of Accounts 127
Uniform Gifts to Minors Act Accounts 133

9. Brokerage Office Procedures 137
Brokerage Support Services 137
Accrued Interest Calculations 145
Rules of Good Delivery 149

10. Margin Accounts 153
Extension of Credit in the Securities Industry 153
Margin Accounting 155

| | | |
|---|---|---|
| | Special Memorandum Account | 164 |
| | Pledging Customer Securities for Loans | 168 |
| 11. | Economics and Analysis | 171 |
| | Economics | 171 |
| | Government Economic Policy | 177 |
| | Technical Analysis | 181 |
| | Fundamental Analysis | 184 |
| | Financial Statements | 185 |
| | Financial Ratios | 190 |
| 12. | Ethics, Suitability and Recommendations | 195 |
| | Ethics in the Securities Industry | 195 |
| | Know Your Customer | 199 |
| | Analyzing Financial Risks and Rewards | 202 |
| | Portfolio Analysis | 205 |
| | Federal and State Taxation | 207 |
| 13. | U.S. Government and State Rules and Regulations | 213 |
| | Insider Trading Act of 1988 | 213 |
| | Securities Investor Protection Corporation | 214 |
| | Other Federal and State Legislation | 217 |
| 14. | Other SEC and SRO Rules and Regulations | 221 |
| | Registration and Regulation | 221 |
| | NASD Bylaws | 223 |
| | Codes of Procedure and of Arbitration Procedure | 228 |
| | NYSE Constitution and Rules | 231 |
| | Communications with the Public | 234 |
| 15. | Municipal Securities | 239 |
| | Municipal Bond Characteristics | 239 |
| | Issuing Municipal Securities | 246 |
| | Municipal Trading and Taxation | 255 |

Analysis of Municipal Securities 262
Municipal Securities Rules and Regulations 267

16. Option Contracts 277
Introduction to Options 277
Equity Options 281
Option Trading and Strategies 287
Multiple Option Strategies 296
Introduction to Nonequity Options 309
Tax Rules for Options 316

17. Investment Company Products 319
Investment Company Offerings 319
Characteristics of Mutual Funds 324
Investment Company Registration 328
Management of Investment Companies 332
Mutual Fund Marketing, Pricing and Valuation 335
Mutual Fund Purchase and Withdrawal Plans 343
Mutual Fund Distributions and Taxation 346
Real Estate Investment Trusts 350

18. Retirement Planning 351
Individual Retirement Accounts 351
Keogh (HR-10) Plans 357
Corporate Retirement Plans 360
Nonqualified Corporate Retirement Plans 361
Annuity Plans 362
Qualified Annuity Plans 367
Employee Retirement Income Security Act 368

19. Direct Participation Programs 369
Characteristics of Limited Partnerships 369

20. Key Facts and Figures 373

References in *Review* for Q&A Exams 379

Glossary 397

Index 453

## Acknowledgments

Special thanks to the following persons for their efforts in reviewing this book:

Randy Bauer

Trace Fasano

Phil Keener

Gib Larson

Amy Morgan

Richard Smith

Curt Wild

# Introduction to PassTrak® Series 7

Welcome to PassTrak® Series 7. Because you probably have a lot of questions about the course and the exam, we have tried to anticipate some of them and provide you with answers to help you on your way.

## The Course

### How is the course structured?

PassTrak Series 7 consists of three books: a comprehensive textbook, a concise review book and an exam book. The textbook, *Principles & Practices*, contains 20 chapters. Each of the first 19 chapters is devoted to a particular area of general securities sales and regulation that you will need to know in order to pass the General Securities Registered Representative Exam (the Series 7). Chapter 20 helps you answer questions relating to securities quotations as they appear in the financial press. Each chapter is divided into study sections devoted to more specific areas with which you need to become familiar.

The *Review* book also contains 20 chapters. The first 19 chapters cover the same topics as the corresponding chapters in *Principles & Practices,* but present the material in a concise format, omitting much of the explanatory material contained in *Principles & Practices*. Chapter 20 contains mnemonics and study aids designed to help you review some of the important facts you need for the exam.

The exam book, *Questions & Answers,* contains review exams that test the topics covered in *Principles & Practices* and *Review,* and concludes with two final exams composed of questions similar to those you will encounter on the Series 7 exam.

If you have purchased a self-study PassTrak set, you will have received three books: *Principles & Practices*, *Review* and *Questions & Answers*. If you will be attending a Series 7 class, you will have received the special classroom set, which consists of two books: *Review* and *Questions & Answers*.

### What topics are covered in this course?

The information needed to pass the Series 7 exam is covered in PassTrak Series 7 through the following chapters:

Chapter 1: Equity Securities
Chapter 2: Debt Securities
Chapter 3: Corporate Debt Securities

Chapter 4: U.S. Government and Agency Securities
Chapter 5: Money-market Securities and Interest Rates
Chapter 6: Issuing Securities
Chapter 7: Trading Securities
Chapter 8: Customer Accounts
Chapter 9: Brokerage Office Procedures
Chapter 10: Margin Accounts
Chapter 11: Economics and Analysis
Chapter 12: Ethics, Suitability and Recommendations
Chapter 13: U.S. Government and State Rules and Regulations
Chapter 14: Other SEC and SRO Rules and Regulations
Chapter 15: Municipal Securities
Chapter 16: Option Contracts
Chapter 17: Investment Company Products
Chapter 18: Retirement Planning
Chapter 19: Direct Participation Programs

**How much time should I spend studying?**

You should plan to spend about 90 to 120 hours reading the material and working through the questions. Your actual time, of course, may vary depending on your reading rate, comprehension, professional background and study environment.

Spread your study time over the six to eight weeks prior to the date on which you are scheduled to take the Series 7 exam (or, if you will be attending a Series 7 class, over the two to four weeks before the first day of class). Select a time and place for studying that will allow you to concentrate your full attention on the material at hand. You have a lot of information to learn and a lot of ground to cover. Be sure to give yourself enough time to learn the material.

**What is the best way to approach the exams?**

Approach each review and final exam as if you were preparing to take the actual Series 7 test. Read each question carefully and write down your answer. Then check your answers against the key and read the accompanying rationale. Making yourself go through all of these steps (rather than simply reading each question and skipping directly to the rationale) will greatly increase your comprehension and retention.

At the end of each rationale, you will find a page reference that directs you to the page in *Principles & Practices* where the information is covered. If you are using the classroom set, you will find a special section at the back of the *Review* book that lists the question numbers for each review and final exam, and directs you to the page in *Review* where the information is covered.

**Do I need to take the final exams?**

The final exams test the same knowledge you will need in order to answer the questions on the Series 7 exam. By completing these exams and checking your answers against the rationale, you should be able to pinpoint any areas with which you are still having difficulty. Review any questions you miss, paying particular attention to the rationale for those questions. If any subjects still seem troublesome, go back and review those topics.

## The Exam

### Why do I need to pass the Series 7 exam?

Your employer is a member of the New York Stock Exchange (NYSE) or another self-regulatory organization that requires its members and employees of its members to pass a qualification exam in order to become registered. To be registered as a representative qualified to sell all types of securities (except commodities), you must pass the Series 7 exam.

### What is the Series 7 exam like?

The Series 7 is a two-part, six-hour, 250-question exam administered by the National Association of Securities Dealers (NASD). The exam is given in two three-hour sessions, each covering different areas of general securities sales and regulation. It is offered as a computer-based test at various testing sites around the country. A paper-and-pencil exam is available to those candidates who apply to and obtain permission from the NASD to take a written exam.

### What topics will I see covered on the exam?

This course covers the wide range of topics that the NASD has outlined as being critical functions of the general securities registered representative. The NYSE exam is divided into seven broad function areas:

| Critical Function | No. of Questions | Percentage of Exam |
|---|---|---|
| Prospecting for and qualifying customers | 9 | 3.6 % |
| Evaluating customer needs and objectives | 4 | 1.6 % |
| Providing customers with investment information and making suitable recommendations | 123 | 49.2 % |
| Handling customer accounts and account records | 27 | 10.8 % |
| Understanding and explaining the securities markets, their organization and their participants to customers | 53 | 21.2 % |
| Processing customer orders and transactions | 13 | 5.2 % |
| Monitoring economic and financial events, performing customer portfolio analysis and making suitable recommendations | 21 | 8.4 % |
| | 250 | 100.0 % |

### What score must I achieve in order to pass?

You must answer correctly at least 70% of the questions on the Series 7 exam in order to pass and become eligible for NYSE registration as a general securities representative.

### How long does the exam take?

You will be allowed six hours, in two three-hour sessions, in which to finish the exam. If you are taking the computerized version of the exam, you will be given additional time before the test to become familiar with the PROCTOR® terminal.

If English is your second language, you may be entitled to additional time in which to complete the exam. Before scheduling your appointment with the certification center, your firm must send a fax or letter to the NASD in Washington, D.C. stating your name, the exam you are taking and the test location, along with a statement that English is not your first language. The NASD coordinator then authorizes the test location to set the PROCTOR® terminal to reflect additional time. For the Series 7, you will receive an additional 30 minutes per session.

### Are there any prerequisites I have to meet before taking the exam?

There are no prerequisite exams you must pass before sitting for the Series 7.

### How do I enroll for the exam?

To obtain an admission ticket to the Series 7 exam, your firm must file the proper application form with the NASD along with the appropriate processing fees. The NASD will send you a directory of Certification and Training Service Centers and a PROCTOR® enrollment valid for a stated number of days. To take the exam during this period, make an appointment with a Certification and Training Service Center as far in advance as possible of the date on which you would like to sit for the test.

### What should I take to the exam?

Take one form of personal identification that bears your signature and your photograph as issued by a government agency. You are not allowed to take reference materials or anything else into the testing area. Calculators will be available upon request; you will not be allowed to use your personal calculator.

Scratch paper and pencils will be provided by the certification center, although you will not be permitted to take them with you when you leave.

### What is PROCTOR®?

The Series 7 exam, like many professional licensing examinations, is administered on the PROCTOR® computerized testing system. PROCTOR® is a nationwide, interactive computer system designed for the administration and delivery of qualifications examinations. Included with your PROCTOR® enrollment, you will receive a brochure describing how the exam is formatted and how to use the computer terminal to answer the questions. When you have completed the exam, the PROCTOR® system promptly scores your answers and within minutes displays your grade for the exam on the terminal screen.

### How well can I expect to do on the exam?

The examinations administered by the NASD are not easy. You will be required to display considerable understanding and knowledge of the topics presented in this course in order to pass the Series 7 exam and qualify for registration. If you study and complete all of the sections of this course, and consistently score at least 80% on the review and final exams, you should be well prepared to pass the Series 7 exam.

# 1 Equity Securities

## Corporate Ownership and Common Stock

### What Is Stock?

- **Ownership**. Shares of stock represent individual pieces of ownership (or equity) in a corporation. The property a business owns (assets) less the claims of its creditors (liabilities) belongs to the stockholders.
- **Diversified ownership, centralized management**. Each share carries with it the same rights and privileges as every other share. Most corporations are organized in such a way that the holders of their common stock vote for and elect a board of directors. Stockholders, therefore, have a say in the management of the company, but are not responsible for day-to-day operations.
- **Different types, different rights**. Preferred stockholders acquire equity in the corporation, but usually do not have the same voting rights as the holders of common stock.

#### Classifying Stock by Its Holder

- **Authorized stock** is the number of shares that the state has permitted the corporation to issue.
- **Issued stock** is the number of shares that have actually been sold (or otherwise distributed) to stockholders. Stock is issued to:
  - raise new capital for expansion;
  - pay stock dividends;
  - provide stock purchase plans for employees or stock options for officers;
  - exchange common stock for outstanding convertible bonds or preferred stock; and
  - redeem outstanding stock warrants.
- **Unissued stock** is any authorized stock that has not been sold or distributed.
- **Treasury stock** is stock that has been repurchased and is being held by the company.
  - The corporation has the right to hold this stock indefinitely, retire it or reissue it to fund stock option plans or other employee bonus arrangements, or could distribute it to holders of record in the form of a stock dividend.
  - Treasury stock does *not* carry voting rights and the right to receive dividends.
  - A corporation will buy back its stock for a number of reasons, such as to: increase earnings per share (by reducing the number of shares outstanding); have an inventory of stock available to distribute as stock options, employee pension plans, and so on; or use for future acquisitions.
- **Outstanding stock** represents all shares still in the hands of investors.

### Putting a Value on Common Stock

**Par value.** Par value is the arbitrary dollar value given to the stock by the company in its articles of incorporation and normally bears little or no relationship to its market price ($1 par, $5 par, and so on). Par value may change in the event of a stock split.

When stock is sold, the amount of money received in excess of the par value is recorded on the corporate balance sheet as capital in excess of par (also called *paid-in surplus, capital surplus* or *paid-in capital*). The following illustrates a portion of a balance sheet reflecting stock that was assigned a par value of $1.00 and was initially sold for $5.00 per share:

TCBS Balance Sheet
December 31, 1995

| Net Worth | |
|---|---|
| Capital stock<br>TCBS was authorized to sell 2,500,000 shares. It issued 2 million of those shares with a par value of $1 per share. | $ 2,000,000 |
| Paid-in surplus<br>TCBS received $4.00 per share in excess of the $1 par value. | $ 8,000,000 |
| Total | $10,000,000 |

**Book value.** Book value per share is how much a holder of common stock could expect to receive for each share if the corporation were to be liquidated. Book value is the difference between the value of a corporation's assets and its liabilities divided by the number of shares outstanding.

**Market value.** Market value reflects supply and demand. There is no direct relationship between the market value and the book value of a stock.

The market value of a stock is quoted in whole dollars plus fractions of a dollar (3/4 point = 3/4 of a dollar, or $.75; 1/8 point = 1/8 of a dollar, or $.125). In the brokerage world, however, the term "dollars" is not used; brokers quote stocks in points. If a stock is quoted at 35, this means that the market price for that stock is $35 per share. A stock quoted at 42 1/2 is selling for $42.50 per share.

Normally, stock prices are quoted in 1/8ths of a point. Some low-priced stocks (known as **penny stocks**) are quoted in fractions as small as 1/256th. You should become familiar with these fractions and their decimal conversions. You can do this either by memorizing the conversions or using your calculator.

Think of 1/8 as the "bit" in "two bits," and it will help make conversions from fractions into dollars and cents easier. Because "two bits" is 25 cents, one bit equals 12 1/2 cents. A quote of 5 1/8 equals $5 plus 12.5 cents, or $5.125 per share of stock, and a round lot of 100 shares would cost $512.50.

## The Rights of Corporate Ownership

### Voting Rights

Stockholders are entitled to vote on:

- directors for the board;
- issuance of senior securities or additional common stock;
- stock splits; and
- substantial changes in the corporation's business.

Stockholders do not vote on either the timing or the amount of cash or stock dividends.

**Statutory voting.** Under the statutory voting system, a stockholder may cast one vote per share owned for each position. If four directors are to be elected, the stockholder with 500 shares may cast from 0 to 500 votes for each of the four positions. In the event that the stockholder casts fewer than 500 votes for a candidate for one of the available seats, the remainder of those 500 votes may not be cast for another candidate for the same seat.

**Cumulative voting.** Cumulative voting entitles the stockholder to the same total number of votes as the statutory system, but places no restriction upon allocation of those votes. If four directors are to be elected, the stockholder has a total of 2,000 votes (one vote per share times four candidates). Under a cumulative voting system, those 2,000 votes could be cast in any manner the stockholder chooses. The stockholder could cast all 2,000 votes for a single candidate or split them between two or more candidates.

### Proxies

A proxy is a written authorization for someone other than the stockholder to vote the stockholder's shares for directors and on other corporate issues. If a vote will determine control of the company (a **proxy contest**):

- All persons involved in the contest must register with the SEC as participants in the proxy contest.
- A participant in a proxy contest is anyone who gives unsolicited advice to stockholders about how they should vote in a contest.
- There are criminal penalties for not registering with the SEC as a participant.
- Giving advice that is asked for is not considered participation.
- A stockholder may revoke a proxy at any time until the final tabulation of the votes at the company's annual meeting.

### Voting Trust Certificates

Management responsibilities may be temporarily transferred to an outside *voting trust*. Stockholders' voting rights may be relinquished to this trust, and they are issued voting trust certificates in place of their stock certificates. All of the benefits of ownership except the power to vote are retained by the stockholders.

### Nonvoting Common Stock

Companies can choose to issue both Class A (voting) and Class B (nonvoting) stock.

### Preemptive Rights

When a corporation raises capital through the sale of common stock (or securities convertible into common stock), it may be required by law or by its corporate charter to offer the securities to its common stockholders before it offers them directly to the public; this is known as an **antidilution agreement**. Stockholders then have what is known as a preemptive right to purchase enough newly issued shares to protect their proportionate ownership in the corporation.

To illustrate, a person who already owns 6% of the stock of Flibinite, Inc. will have a preemptive right to purchase 6% of any new stock issue.

### Other Stockholder Rights

- **Limited liability**. Stockholders cannot lose more than they have invested in the stock of a particular corporation.
- **Inspection of corporate books**. Stockholders have the right to obtain lists of stockholders, receive annual reports, and so on.
- **Protection of the corporation**. Stockholders may take the company's management to court if they believe that it has committed wrongful acts that could harm the corporation.
- **Restraint of illegal acts**. Stockholders may take action against the board of directors of a corporation to restrain it from acting in a manner inconsistent with the corporate charter.
- **Residual claims to assets**. When a corporation ceases to exist (liquidates), the stockholder, as owner, has a residual right to corporate assets.

## Benefits and Risks of Common Stock

Benefits of owning stock include:

- growth
- income

Risks of owning stock include:

- decreased or no income
- low priority at dissolution
- fall in price

# Questions

1. TCBS just issued 100,000 shares of common stock. If a pension plan manager purchased 3,000 shares of TCBS for the plan's portfolio, to how many votes would he be entitled?

______________________

2. What percentage of TCBS would its holdings represent?

______________________

3. At its next annual meeting, TCBS will be electing five directors to its board. One of your clients owns 200 shares of TCBS common stock and intends to cast his votes at the meeting. Under the statutory voting system, what is the maximum number of votes he is entitled to cast for each director?

______________________

4. Under the statutory voting system, how many votes can he cast in total for all directors?

______________________

5. If TCBS was using the cumulative voting system, what is the maximum number of votes he is entitled to cast for each director?

______________________

6. What is the minimum number of votes he is entitled to cast for each director?

______________________

7. How many votes can he cast in total for all directors?

______________________

8. Which of the following represent ownership (equity) in a company?

   I. Corporate bonds
   II. Common stock
   III. Preferred stock
   IV. Mortgage bonds

   A. I and IV only
   B. II only
   C. II and III only
   D. I, II, III and IV

9. Which of the following statements about treasury stock are true?

   I. It has voting rights and is entitled to a dividend when declared.
   II. It has no voting rights and no dividend entitlement.
   III. It has been issued and repurchased by the company.
   IV. It is authorized but unissued stock.

   A. I and III
   B. I and IV
   C. II and III
   D. II and IV

10. Hybrid Technologies is authorized to issue 1 million shares of common stock. It has issued 600,000 shares. Of this amount, 40,000 shares are treasury shares. Hybrid Technologies declares a dividend of $2 per share. How many shares of common stock does Hybrid Technologies have outstanding?

    A. 40,000
    B. 560,000
    C. 600,000
    D. 1,000,000

11. Limited liability regarding ownership in a large, publicly held U.S. corporation means all of the following EXCEPT
    A. investors might lose the amount of their investment
    B. investors might lose their investment plus the difference between their investment and par value
    C. investors' shares are nonassessable
    D. investors are not liable to the full extent of their personal property

## Answers

1. If the plan manager purchased 3,000 shares of TCBS common stock, each of those shares would entitle the plan (the owner of the shares) to one vote, for a total of 3,000 votes.

2. The plan's 3,000 votes represent a 3% ownership of TCBS (3,000 ÷ 100,000 = .03, or 3%).

3. The stockholder with 200 shares may cast from zero to 200 votes for each of the five positions under the statutory voting system. In the event that your client elects not to cast all 200 votes for a particular director, he cannot carry them over and cast them for one of the others.

4. Under the statutory voting system, he can cast from zero up to 1,000 votes in this director election (five positions times 200 votes each).

5. If he were allocating his votes for director at the TCBS annual meeting under the cumulative voting system, the client who owns 200 shares would have a total of 1,000 votes (one vote per share times the number of positions on which he will be casting his votes). Under the cumulative voting system, those 1,000 votes could be cast in any manner he chooses. He could cast all 1,000 votes for a single candidate and none for the others. He could cast 400 votes for his two top choices, 100 for each of two others and none for the last. Or he could choose to cast no votes at all.

6. Under any voting system, the stockholder is entitled to not vote for any candidate.

7. He is entitled to cast 1,000 votes, and can allocate them in any manner he desires.

8. **C.** Common and preferred stock represent ownership in a corporation; corporate and mortgage bonds are debt securities.

9. **C.** Treasury stock has no voting rights and no dividend entitlement, having been origi-

nally issued by the company and subsequently repurchased by the company.

10. **B.** Treasury stock is stock that has been reacquired by the corporation. Stock issued minus stock reacquired equals the amount of stock outstanding.

11. **B.** Investors never lose more than their investment.

# Preferred Stock

## What Is Preferred Stock?

Preferred stock:

- is an equity security;
- does not provide all of the privileges of ownership of common stock;
- is often issued as a fixed income security with a stated dividend; and
- price fluctuations tend to be affected more by changes in interest rates than by supply and demand.

Preferred stock does not typically have the same growth potential as common stock. The owners of preferred stock generally have an advantage over common stockholders in two ways:

1. when dividends are declared by the board of directors, owners of preferred stock receive their dividends first; and
2. if a corporation goes bankrupt after paying off creditors, preferred stockholders have a prior claim on the remaining assets.

Other characteristics of preferred stock include:

- **Dividend preference over common stock.** Dividends must be paid to preferred stockholders before they can be paid to common stockholders.
- **Stated (fixed) rate of return.** Preferred stock has a fixed dividend (a few preferred stocks are issued with variable dividends exist). A preferred stock with a par value of $100 that pays $6 in annual dividends would be known as a 6% preferred. No-par value preferred stock has a dividend stated in a dollar amount. A $6 no-par preferred would pay a $6 annual dividend.
- **Adjustable-rate preferred.** Some preferred stocks are issued with an *adjustable* (or *variable*) dividend rate tied to the rate of some other interest rate and can be adjusted as often as quarterly.
- **Prior claims to assets.** Preferred stock has a higher claim against the assets of the corporation than common stock.
- **Limited ownership privileges.** Preferred stocks usually do not carry either voting rights or preemptive rights.
- **No maturity date or set maturity value.** Preferred stock has no preset date at which it matures or is scheduled for redemption.

### Classes of Preferred Stock

**Prior preferred.** Prior preferred stock has a prior claim over other preferred stock in receiving dividends, as well as in the distribution of assets in the event of liquidation.

**Cumulative preferred.** Cumulative preferred stock is entitled to any and all dividends due that accumulate on the company's books until such time as the corporation is able to pay them. When the company is able to resume full payment of dividends, holders of cumulative preferred stock will receive the current preferred dividend plus the total accumulated dividends (dividends in arrears) before any dividends are distributed to common stockholders.

To illustrate the advantage of owning cumulative preferred stock, suppose that one of your investors owns 100 shares of $100 par Nitco 8% Cumulative Preferred. Two years ago, the company paid out only $4 per share in dividends (a $100 par value 8% preferred should have paid a total of $8 in dividends for the year). Last year, payment of the dividend was suspended entirely.

This year, the board of directors finally believes that the corporation has enough cash to pay dividends to both preferred stockholders (including all dividends in arrears) and common stockholders. Before dividends are paid to the common stockholders, however, the holders of the 8% cumulative preferred must be paid a total of $20 ($8 for this year, plus $8 for last year, plus $4 for the first year of suspended payments).

**Participating preferred.** Participating preferred stockholders receive a share of any corporate profits that remain after all dividends due other securities are paid. If a preferred stock is described as "COD 6% Preferred Participating to 9%," the company will pay its holders up to 3% in additional dividends in profitable years. Owners of participating preferred stock do not participate in a corporation's profits until the company has paid:

- interest to bondholders
- dividends to other preferred stockholders
- the basic dividend rate
- dividends to common stockholders

**Convertible preferred.** Convertible preferred stock gives the holder the right to convert its shares into shares of common stock at some future point in time.

To illustrate, a convertible preferred stock with a $100 par value might be convertible into common stock at $25 per share. For each share of $100 par value preferred an investor owns, she can exchange it for four shares of common stock. As long as the price of the common stock in this example remains below $25 per share, the preferred stockholder would have little incentive to take advantage of the conversion feature. If the market price of this corporation's common stock were to move above $25 per share, however, the preferred stockholder could profit by converting her shares into common stock at the preset below-market conversion price. Because the value of convertible preferred is linked to the value of common stock in this way, it tends to fluctuate more in price than do other fixed income securities.

**Callable preferred.** Callable preferred stock gives the issuer the right to call (buy back) the stock from investors. Stockholders do not have to surrender their stock when it is called by the corporation, but most will because dividend payments and conversion rights generally cease on the call date.

**Combinations.** A single preferred issue can include participating, cumulative, convertible and/or callable features.

# Questions

1. All of the following statements are true of a callable convertible preferred issue EXCEPT that

   A. the convertible is issued with a lower stated dividend rate than a nonconvertible preferred
   B. the convertible preferred can increase in price because of the underlying security
   C. the stockholder must surrender the preferred when called or lose the right to par value
   D. dividend payments stop after the preferred is called

2. Brunswick issues a Series A $2.40 cumulative convertible preferred voting stock. This stock

   I. is convertible into common stock
   II. pays back dividends
   III. receives excess dividends on a pro rata basis with common stock

   A. I only
   B. I and II only
   C. I and III only
   D. I, II and III

3. In a period of stable interest rates, which of the following securities is MOST likely to fluctuate in value?

   A. Cumulative preferred stock
   B. Participating preferred stock
   C. Senior preferred stock
   D. Convertible preferred stock

4. A corporation has 7% $100 par cumulative convertible preferred stock outstanding. The preferred dividend was paid until two years ago, when 6% was paid. Last year, 5% was paid. This year, the corporation wishes to declare a common dividend. How much in preferred dividends must first be paid on each preferred share outstanding?

   A. $3
   B. $7
   C. $10
   D. $15

5. Amalgamated Widget has outstanding an issue of 6% callable preferred stock. Which of the following situations would induce Amalgamated to call the stock?

   A. Earnings increase by 6% or more.
   B. Dividends are withheld on common stock.
   C. Interest rates increase to 9%.
   D. Interest rates drop to 5%.

# Answers

1. **C.** Owners of callable preferred don't have to surrender the shares if called. The par value doesn't change, but the conversion privilege and the right to dividends end. Investors want convertibles because they participate in increased value of the common. The dividend rate on convertibles will be less than on nonconvertibles.

2. **B.** Cumulative convertible preferred stock can be converted into common stock and will pay any back dividends. Only participating preferred can pay excess dividends.

3. **D.** Because interest rate movement affects the price of preferred stock, preferred stocks will not fluctuate as much in value during stable interest rates. Convertible preferred stocks will fluctuate with movements in the price of the common stock.

4. **C.** In order to pay this year's common dividend, the corporation must pay preferred stockholders the 1% dividend not paid two years ago, the 2% from last year and this year's 7% dividend. Therefore, 10%, or $10, must be paid.

5. **D.** When interest rates drop below the stock's stated dividend rate, the company will want to issue stock at the lower rate.

# Return on Investment

## Dividends

Stockholders are entitled to dividend distributions only if the company board of directors votes to make such a distribution. Stockholders are automatically sent any dividends to which their shares entitle them.

- **Cash dividends** are normally distributed by corporations quarterly to stockholders in the form of checks representing the stockholders' share of the companies' profits.
- **Stock dividends** are issued by companies that want to use their available cash for other purposes. The company issues shares of its common stock as a dividend and all common stockholders receive the same percentage of stock, retaining their proportionate share of ownership in the company. The market price of the stock tends to decrease after a stock dividend, but the total market value of the position remains the same.
- **Property dividends** are distributions by a corporation of securities it owns in other companies (e.g., a parent corporation may divest itself of a subsidiary by distributing the stock it owns in the subsidiary to the stockholders as a dividend).

## Calculating Return on Investment

To determine the **current yield**, divide the yearly dividend by the current market price of the stock.

If, for example, the yearly dividend paid by TCBS on its common stock is $1.00 (a quarterly dividend of $.25) and the market price of the stock is $20, the current yield for TCBS would be 5%. If TCBS paid $.25 for the first quarter of the year and then raised its dividend to $.35 for each of the last three quarters, at a current market value of $20, TCBS's current yield would be 6.5% ($1.30 ÷ $20 = .065, which equals 6.5%).

## Stock Splits and Reverse Splits

### Stock Split

To reduce a stock's the price without placing current stockholders at a disadvantage, a company can declare a **stock split**.

The board of directors of ICBS has decided that ICBS common stock is selling for too much at $100 per share, so the company declares a 4-for-1 stock split. Each share of stock currently worth $100 will be replaced by four shares worth $25 each. Every stockholder will receive three new shares of ICBS for each share held before the split. The original outstanding shares have been split into four shares, each valued at one-fourth as much as before. A client who owned 100 shares before the split worth $10,000 (100 shares × $100 dollars = $10,000) will own 400 shares worth $25 each after the split.

To calculate the effect of a 4:1 split (4:1 is shorthand for "4-for-1"), multiply the number of shares by 4/1 and the price by 1/4. The stockholder's position doesn't change because he will hold stock of the same value both before and after the split.

Let's look at other possible splits. If DWAQ Corporation decides that its stock is overpriced when it reaches $90 per share and splits the stock 3-for-2 (shorthand: "3:2"), an investor with 100 shares before the split has 150 shares worth $60 per share after the split. To calculate the effect of a 3:2 split, multiply the number of shares by 3/2 and the price by 2/3. You can check your arithmetic because you know that the dollar value of the position will remain the same before and after the split.

If DWAQ Corporation decides that its stock is overpriced when it reaches $100 per share and splits the stock 5:4, an investor with 100 shares before the split has 125 shares worth $80 per share after the split. To calculate the effect of a 5:4 split, you multiply the number of shares by 5/4 and the price by 4/5. Check your arithmetic, and you will find that the dollar value of the position is the same before and after the split.

### Reverse Split

After a reverse split, investors own fewer shares that are now worth more per share. After a 1:4 reverse split, for example, a stockholder who owned 500 shares with a market value of $17 per share now owns 125 shares worth $68 per share.

## Questions

1. Datawaq has 10,000 shares outstanding and declares a 30% stock dividend. One of your clients owns 100 shares of DWAQ, and another owns 1,200. How many shares will the client who owns 100 shares receive as a dividend?

   ______________________________

2. How many shares will the client who owns 1,200 shares receive as a dividend?

   ______________________________

3. Common stock of ICBS, Inc. (I Can't Believe It's Sushi, a top competitor of TCBS) has a current market price of $30 per share and pays a yearly dividend of $3 (a quarterly dividend of $.75). An investor in ICBS's common stock would realize a current yield for that stock of 10% ($3 ÷ $30 = .10, or 10%). If ICBS stock rose to $40 and the company declared a $6 annual dividend, how much would an owner of 100 shares receive each quarter?

   ______________________________

4. What would that investor's current yield be on her ICBS stock?

   ______________________________

5. In which of the following ways may a company declare dividends?

   I. Cash
   II. Stock
   III. Stock of another company

   A. I only
   B. I and II only
   C. I and III only
   D. I, II and III

6. ALFA Enterprises currently has earnings of $4 and pays a $.50 quarterly dividend. The market price of ALF is $40. What is the current yield?

    A. 1.25%
    B. 5%
    C. 10%
    D. 15%

7. Mountain Brewing is currently paying an $.80 quarterly dividend. The stock is $10 par value and is selling in the market for $50 per share. What is its current yield?

    A. 1.6%
    B. 6.4%
    C. 8%
    D. 32%

8. If the ICBS board of directors voted a 5:1 split, how many shares would your client, who owns 150 shares at $100 each, own after the split?

    ______________________________

9. What would each of those shares be worth after the split?

    ______________________________

10. How much will the total value of the investor's shares change after the split?

    ______________________________

# Answers

1. An investor who owns 100 shares will receive 30 additional shares of Datawaq stock.

2. An investor who owns 1,200 shares would receive 360 new shares as a dividend.

3. An annual dividend of $6 would equal four $1.50 quarterly dividends. The owner of 100 shares of ICBS would be entitled to $150 each quarter, or $600 per year.

4. Her current yield would be 15% ($6 ÷ $40 = .15, or 15%).

5. **D.** A company may pay a dividend that it has declared in any of the three ways shown: cash, stock or stock in another company such as a subsidiary. The last method is also known as a *property dividend.*

6. **B.** The quarterly dividend is $.50 as stated, paying $2 annually. $2 annually divided by $40 equals a 5% current yield.

7. **B.** The quarterly dividend is $.80; therefore, the annual dividend is $3.20. $3.20 ÷ $50 = 6.4% current yield.

8. To calculate the effect of this split, multiply the number of shares your client owns by 5/1. You should get 750.

9. Multiply the dollar value of the original shares by 1/5 (the same as dividing by 5). $100 times 1/5 (or divided by 5) equals $20. Your client owned $15,000 worth of ICBS before the split (150 × $100), and still owns $15,000 worth after the split (750 × $20).

10. The investor's shares are worth the same amount both before and after the split.

# Transferability of Ownership

### The Stock Certificate

A stock certificate is physical evidence of a person's share in the ownership of a corporation, and individual stock certificates may be issued for any number of shares.

### CUSIP Numbers

Each issue of common stock, preferred stock, corporate bonds and municipal bonds has its own CUSIP number, which helps identify and track the certificate in the event that it becomes lost or stolen.

### Negotiability

To transfer ownership of any stock, the registered owner must:

- either sign (endorse) the stock certificate on the back in the place designated for the owner's signature; *or*
- sign a stock power; *and*
- an exchange member, an authorized person of a broker-dealer or an officer of a national bank must guarantee the signature.

### Transfer Procedures

**Transfer agent.** The transfer agent for a corporation:

- sees that stock and bond certificates are issued in the correct owner's name;
- distributes additional shares in the event of a stock split, or new certificates in the event of a reverse split;
- cancels and issues certificates;
- maintains records of ownership for the corporation;
- handles problems relating to lost, stolen or destroyed certificates;
- has the certificates signed by the appropriate officer(s);
- affixes the corporate seal;
- delivers them to the new owner; and
- destroys the original certificates registered in the seller's name.

For each registered stockholder, the transfer agent records:

- his name
- his full address
- his Social Security number
- the total number of shares he owns

**Registrar.** The responsibilities of the registrar include:

- keeping records relating to the stock and bond certificates issued by a corporation (but not a list of the names of the owners of the issuer's securities);
- ensuring that a corporation does not have more stock outstanding than can be accounted for on the company's books; and
- certifying that a bond represents a legal debt of the issuer.

## Questions

1. Who is responsible for issuing new certificates for a publicly held corporation?

   A. Registrar
   B. Trader
   C. Transfer agent
   D. Broker-dealer

2. Who is responsible for handling problems relating to lost, stolen or missing coupons or certificates?

   A. Registrar
   B. Trader
   C. Transfer agent
   D. Broker-dealer

3. Who is responsible for ensuring that a corporation does not have more stock outstanding than it has been authorized to issue?

   A. Registrar
   B. Trader
   C. Transfer agent
   D. Broker-dealer

## Answers

1. **C.** The transfer agent is responsible for issuing certificates and for recording the number of shares owned, and the stockholder's name, address and Social Security number.

2. **C.** The transfer agent is responsible for all matters relating to the physical certificates, their safekeeping and their transfer.

3. **A.** The registrar is responsible for keeping careful accounts of the number of shares a company is authorized to issue and the number it has outstanding.

# Rights and Warrants

## Issuance

**Preemptive right** refers to the right of an existing stockholder to purchase shares of a new issue of stock in proportion to the number of shares the investor already owns.

The rights entitle the stockholder to purchase common stock below the current market price. Rights are valued separately and trade in the secondary market during the subscription period. A stockholder who receives rights may take one of the following actions:

- exercise the right
- sell the right
- let the right expire

## Characteristics of Rights

- **Subscription right certificate**. A rights offering is a short-term privilege a stockholder receives from a corporation, and a subscription right is the actual certificate representing that privilege. One right is issued for each share of common stock the investor owns.
- **Terms of the offering**. The rights describe the new shares to which the stockholder is entitled to subscribe, the price, the date the new stock will be issued, the name of the rights agent that will send the subscription and the final date for exercising those rights.
- **Significant trading dates and prices**. When a corporation declares a rights offering (on the **offering date**) it will specify a date on which the rights will expire and from that date a **record date** will be determined. Stock is traded **cum rights** until the ex-date. An investor who purchases the stock cum rights is entitled to receive the right. Beginning on the day after the registration's effective date, common stock trades **ex-rights**. An investor who purchases the stock ex-rights does not receive a right. Rights are traded on a when issued basis until the issuance date. Investors who do not intend to exercise their rights may sell them separately. Between the offering date and the expiration date the stock tables will show two different entries:
  - the price of the stock itself, either with rights (**cum rights**) or, after the ex-date, without them (**ex-rights**); and
  - the price of the rights, either on a **when issued** basis or, after they have been issued, at the current market price.

The following is an example of a rights offering. On September 1st, Amalgamated Featherbedders, Inc. declares a rights offering. Holders of the common stock as of October 1st will be able to subscribe to one new share at $30 for each ten shares already owned. The stock is currently trading at $41. The rights expire November 15th.

Assume Amalgamated Featherbedders, Inc. has 20 million shares outstanding and wants to issue another 2 million shares. Each existing share is entitled to one right, so there will be 20 million rights issued. Those rights entitle stockholders to only 2 million shares, so 20 million rights divided by 2 million new shares means that it will require ten rights to buy one new share.

The corporation will issue rights October 8th to any stockholder of record October 1st. Stock is traded cum rights until the ex-date. An investor who purchases the stock cum rights is also entitled to receive the right.

### The Rights Agent

The **rights agent** keeps a record of who owns each right. When a right is sold, the rights agent records the name of the new owner.

### Standby Underwriting

If in the initial offering current stockholders do not subscribe to all the rights, the unsold rights may be offered through a broker-dealer in a standby underwriting. This will be done on a firm commitment basis.

## Value of Rights

**Theoretical**. Rights have a theoretical value based on the savings investors will be able to realize by exercising the subscription rights to purchase securities below market price.

**Prior to ex-date**. To compute the value of a right when the stock is trading cum rights, we will use the Amalgamated Featherbedders, Inc. example. The market price (M) of the stock cum rights is $41; the subscription price (S) is $30. The investor needs ten rights and $30 to buy one new share. The ten rights, therefore, earn the investor an $11 discount on a share of stock ($41 market price – $30 subscription price).

To determine the value of one right, divide the savings it represents (M – S) by the number of rights needed to purchase one share (N), plus one right (N + 1). ($41 – $30) ÷ 11 = $1.

**After ex-date**. On the day the stock first trades ex-rights, the market price typically drops by the value of the right. For the stock selling without rights, the divisor, in this case, is the same as the number of rights needed to purchase one share.

To determine the value of one right when the stock is ex-rights, divide the savings it represents (M – S) by the number of rights needed to purchase one share (N). In the previous example, the stock is now at $40. ($40 – $30) ÷ 10 = $1.

## Warrants

A warrant is usually a long-term instrument, affording the investor the option of buying shares at a later date at the subscription price, subject to the warrant's expiration date.

Warrants may be detachable from the underlying security, or they may be nondetachable. If detachable, they trade in the market. The exercise price is set above the market price of the stock when the warrant is first issued. The investor can:

1. exercise the warrant and buy the stock below the price he would have to pay in the market; or
2. sell the warrant in the market at a price based on the benefit the purchaser can get by exercising the warrant and buying the stock below market price.

### Origination of Warrants

Warrants are usually offered to the public as a sweetener in connection with other securities (usually debentures) to make these securities more attractive.

As an example, Amalgamated Featherbedders may make an offering of 4,000,000 shares of new preferred stock, bundling it into units of 4 shares of preferred and two warrants for 1/4 of a share of common stock exercisable at a specific price. An investor who purchases 100 units will receive 400 shares of preferred stock and warrants redeemable for 50 shares of common (100 units times two warrants for 1/4 of a share of common per unit).

# Questions

1. A corporation issues new stock with a subscription price of $25. The stock is currently selling for $29. Under the terms of the offering, four rights are needed to subscribe to one new share. Using the ex-rights formula, what is the value of one right?

   A. $.80
   B. $1.00
   C. $4.00
   D. The value cannot be determined from the information given.

2. A corporation issuing stock has informed its stockholders that they can buy the newly issued stock for $21.50 per share with 20 rights. The outstanding stock is currently trading at $40. To purchase a share of the stock at the subscription price takes

   A. $21.50 with 20 rights
   B. $21.50 with 21 rights
   C. one right with $21.50
   D. one right with $40

3. Kelptek, Inc. wishes to sell additional shares to its existing stockholders through a rights offering. The market price of KLP is currently $42 and the subscription price has been set at $28. The terms of the offering are that 20 rights are necessary to purchase one new share. If an investor wishes to buy the rights before the ex-date, the price per right will be approximately

   A. $.67
   B. $.70
   C. $1.00
   D. $1.12

4. Which of the following instruments does NOT receive dividends?

   A. Warrants
   B. Common stock
   C. Preferred stock
   D. Convertible preferred stock

5. Which of the following statements is true of warrants?

   A. Warrants give the holder a perpetual interest in the issuer's stock.
   B. Warrants are shorter term than rights.
   C. Warrants are issued to make a security offering more attractive.
   D. Warrants are safer than corporate bonds.

6. Which of the following statements about rights is true?

   A. Common stockholders do not have the right to subscribe to rights offerings.
   B. Preferred stockholders do not have the right to subscribe to rights offerings.
   C. Both common and preferred stockholders have the right to subscribe to rights offerings.
   D. Neither common nor preferred stockholders have the right to subscribe to rights offerings.

# Answers

1. **B.** Use the formula:

$$\frac{\text{Market value (M)} - \text{Subscription price (S)}}{\text{Number of rights (N)}}$$

$$\frac{\$29 - \$25}{4} = \$1$$

2. **A.** The subscription price of the new stock is \$21.50 plus the 20 rights required to exercise. The 21 rights will be used only in calculating the theoretical value of the rights on a cum rights basis.

3. **A.** Using the cum rights formula, the price per right is \$.67.

$$(M - S) \div (N + 1) = (42 - 28) \div (20 + 1)$$

$$= 14 \div 21 = \$.67$$

4. **A.** Warrants do not pay dividends under any circumstance. The other instruments listed will pay dividends when dividends are declared by the board of directors.

5. **C.** Warrants are issued with primary common stock or bond offerings as a "sweetener." Warrants are long-term options to buy common stock.

6. **B.** Preferred stockholders have a preference as to liquidation, distribution or income, but they have no right to maintain a percentage of ownership.

# American Depositary Receipts

## Facilitate Trading in Foreign Securities

An ADR is a negotiable security and represents a receipt for a given number of shares of stock in a non-U.S. corporation. The ADR itself is an instrument that can be bought and sold in the U.S. securities markets on an exchange or over the counter.

### Rights of ADR Owners

Rights of holders of ADRs include:

- voting rights
- right to receive dividends when declared
- delivery of foreign security

### Custodian Bank

ADRs are issued by foreign branches of large commercial U.S. banks. The shares of foreign stock that the ADR represents are held by a custodian (typically a foreign bank in the home country of the issuer). The stock must remain on deposit as long as the ADR is outstanding, because the ADR is the depository bank's guarantee that it holds the stock.

**Registered owner**. ADRs are registered on the books of the U.S. bank that issued them and dividends are sent to the bank as registered owner. The custodian bank collects any dividends paid by the foreign issuer, converts the payments into U.S. funds for U.S. owners and withholds any required payments of foreign taxes.

**Bank responsibilities**. The bank must provide information to the ADR holders about any developments in the foreign corporation or the country of registry that could affect the ADR.

ADR holders do not have preemptive rights. When the bank receives the rights or warrants from the issuer, it sells the rights and warrants in a market of the issuer's own country and distributes the sale proceeds in cash to the ADR owners.

## Currency Risk

ADR investors are subject to currency risk, which is the risk arising from fluctuations in currency exchange rates. Suppose a Russian company declares a dividend to be paid in Russian rubles. By the time the ADR holder receives the dividend, the value of the ruble may have changed in relation to the U.S. dollar, causing a gain or a loss.

## Questions

1. ADRs are used to facilitate the

   A. foreign trading of domestic securities
   B. foreign trading of U.S. government securities
   C. domestic trading of U.S. government securities
   D. domestic trading of foreign securities

## Answers

1. **D.** ADRs are tradable securities issued by banks, with the receipt's value based on the underlying foreign securities held by the bank.

# 2 Debt Securities

## Characteristics of Bonds

Bondholders:

- do not have ownership interest in the issuer;
- do not have a voice in management;
- receive the issuer's promise to repay principal and pay interest; and
- receive preferential treatment over common and preferred stockholders in the event of a liquidation.

### Issuers

Bonds are issued by:

- **Municipalities.** Municipal securities are issued to raise capital to finance public works and construction projects that benefit the general public.
- **Corporations.** Corporate bonds are issued to raise money for working capital or for capital expenditures and are also known as *funded debt*.
- **U.S. government and government agencies.** The federal government is the nation's most secure credit risk and its debt obligations are backed by its full faith and credit and almost unlimited powers of taxation.

### Interest

The bond issuer promises to pay investors interest for that loan at a fixed rate and on particular dates. Interest accrues daily and is paid semiannually. An investor who owns a $20,000 bond that pays 6% interest will receive $1,200 ($20,000 × 6% = $1,200) in income each year in the form of two $600 semiannual installments.

An investor who owns $50,000 of a 6% bond receives $3,000 ($50,000 × 6% = $3,000) each year in two $1,500 payments. The final interest payment will be made on the date the bond is scheduled to mature, and is normally combined with repayment of the principal amount: this bondholder will receive a check for $51,500.

### Maturities

There are three basic bond maturity structures:

1. **Term** bonds mature all at once.
2. **Serial** bonds mature at set intervals over a period of time.
3. **Balloon** bonds mature at intervals, but most of the issue matures on the final maturity date.

A bond issuer that spreads its bond sales over several years is issuing them in separate **series**.

### Bond Certificate

Each bond certificate contains the following information:

- name of issuing company
- type of bond
- principal amount
- date of issue
- maturity date
- call feature(s)
- interest rate and payment date
- where interest is payable
- reference to trust indenture

### Registration of Bonds

- **Coupon (bearer) bonds**. Coupon bonds are not registered. Whoever is currently in possession of those bonds is entitled to collect interest (by clipping the coupons and delivering them to the issuer's paying agent), trade the bonds or deliver them for redemption.
- **Registered bonds**. There are two types:
  - **Fully registered**. When bonds are registered as to both principal and interest, the transfer agent maintains a list of bondholders. Interest payments are automatically sent to bondholders of record in the transfer agent's books. Most corporate and municipal bonds are currently being issued in fully registered form.
  - **Registered as to principal only**. Bonds registered as to principal only have the owner's name printed on the front. The coupons are in bearer form.
- **Book-entry bonds**. The transfer agent maintains a list of bondholders. The owner of a book-entry bond does not receive a certificate—the owner of a registered bond does.

### Debt Service

Debt service is the amount of money required to make payments of principal and interest to bondholders.

### Pricing

Par represents the dollar amount of the contract between the issuer and the investor and is the amount repaid to investors per bond when the bond is due.

Either before or after bonds begin to trade in the secondary market, they may sell at par, below par (that is, at a **discount**) or above par (at a **premium**). A bond's **premium** is the difference between par and its higher market value. A bond's discount is the difference between par and its lower market value. Affecting a bond's market value are the market's perception of the investment quality of the bond and overall interest rates.

Quotes on bonds are stated as percentages of the principal amount of the bond. For example, a bid of 100 means 100% of par, or $1,000. A bond point is equal to $10 (1% of $1,000). A bond quote of 98 1/8 means 98 and 1/8th percent (98.125%) of $1,000.

## Rating and Analyzing Bonds

Standard & Poor's and Moody's rate both corporate and municipal bonds; Fitch's rates corporate bonds, municipal bonds and commercial paper. Standard & Poor's, Moody's and Fitch's base their bond ratings primarily on the issuer's creditworthiness—that is, the ability of the issuer to make interest and principal payments as they come due.

A plus or minus sign in a Standard & Poor's rating indicates that the bond falls within the top or bottom of that particular category. A1 and Baa1 are used by Moody's to indicate the highest quality bonds within those two categories. Moody's also provides ratings for short-term municipal notes, designating MIG-1 as the highest quality and MIG-4 as the lowest.

### Basis for Bond Ratings

Specific criteria used to rate corporate and municipal bonds include:

- the amount and composition of existing debt;
- the stability of the issuer's cash flow;

- the ability of the issuer to meet scheduled payments of interest and principal on its debt obligations;
- asset protection; and
- management ability.

**Investment grade.** Investment grade is a rating of BBB/Baa or higher and is also known as *bank grade.*

### Relationship of Rating to Yield

Generally, the higher the bond rating, the lower the yield. Some bonds will sell at deep discounts, producing high yields (these are often referred to as **junk** bonds). These bonds may have low ratings or may be selling at deep discounts because they have low coupons.

If interest rates decline, the bonds that will appreciate most in price are long-term bonds.

### Comparative Safety of Debt Securities

- **U.S. government securities.** When comparing the safety of different types of securities, a person should know that the *highest safety* is found in securities backed by the U.S. government.

- **Government agency securities.** The *second highest degree of safety* is found in securities that, although not backed by the U.S. government, are issued by government agencies and government-sponsored corporations.

- **Municipal issues.** Generally, the next highest degree of safety is found in securities issued by municipalities.

- **Corporate issues.** The next highest category of safety is found in corporate debt securities.

These rankings simply provide rough guidelines. For example, some AAA rated corporate bonds are safer than many municipal bonds.

### Marketability and Liquidity

Many factors work together to determine a bond's marketability and liquidity. Chief among these factors are:

- quality
- rating
- maturity
- call features
- coupon rate and current market value
- issuer
- existence of a sinking fund
- type of registration

## Debt Retirement

### Redemption

**Sinking fund.** A *sinking fund* is operated by the bonds' trustees, who act to protect the interests of the investors holding the bonds. A sinking fund is part of the trust indenture and may be used to call bonds, pay bonds off at maturity or buy back bonds from investors in the open market.

### Calling Bonds

During periods of high interest rates, a number of bonds will be issued with what is known as a *call feature* (or *call option*). A call feature in a bond's trust indenture allows the issuing company to call (buy back) the bond from investors before its final maturity date. The issuer does this by notifying bondholders that it is willing to buy the bonds back from them at a specified price on a particular date (frequently preset at the time the bond is issued).

**Call premium.** In return for the call privilege, the issuer usually pays the bondholder a *call premium* over the bond's par value at the time of the call.

**Advantages of a call option.** Callable bonds can be advantageous to the issuer for the following reasons:

- If general interest rates decline, the issuer can call in bonds on which it must pay a high rate of interest and replace them with a new issue of bonds with a lower coupon.
- The issuer can call in bonds to reduce its debt whenever it chooses (once it has passed the initial call date).

- The issuer can replace short-term debt issues with long-term issues, and vice versa.
- The issuer can call bonds as a means of forcing the conversion of convertible corporate securities.

**Call protection.** Call protection is an initial noncallable period following the issuance of the bonds. Once the call protection period has expired, the issuer may elect to call any or all of the bonds. A call protection feature in a trust indenture can be an advantage to bondholders during periods of declining interest rates.

**Risks to bondholders.** A callable bond paying a high rate of interest may be called when prevailing interest rates drop. If this occurs, the investor may be unable to obtain a similar yield. This disadvantage is referred to as *call risk.*

**Effects of a call on trading.** After a call notice is issued and before the specified call date has arrived, bonds that are called continue to trade in the open market. The bonds will trade at a slight discount to the call price during this period.

### Notice of Redemption

Notice by a company that it intends to call back an issue of bonds usually is given in newspapers and other financial publications 30 to 90 days prior to the call. *The Bond Buyer*, a trade paper published Monday through Friday for the municipal securities industry, publishes a called bond list.

### Refunding Bonds

**Refunding** an issue means retiring an outstanding issue of bonds using the money generated by the sale of a new offering. Refunding, like redemption, can be done in full or in part.

### Prerefunding

In a prerefunding (*advance refunding*), a new issue is sold at a lower coupon than the original bond issue prior to the first call date on the original issue. The proceeds from the new issue are placed in an escrow account and invested in U.S. government securities or are held in cash equivalents, with the interest received from the investment used to pay the interest on the outstanding prerefunded bonds. The original bonds are then called at the first call date, and the escrowed securities are used to redeem them.

Rating services rate prerefunded bonds highly—often as high as AAA (or Aaa), the highest rating available.

### Tender Offers

Companies may also redeem bonds and replace them with securities paying a lower rate by making a tender offer to investors for their bonds. Bondholders are not likely to tender their securities to the issuer unless the offer includes a promise to pay them a substantial cash bonus.

### Put Bonds

Bonds issued with a put option and are known as **put** (or **puttable**) **bonds.** In return for accepting a slightly lower interest rate, the investor receives the right to put (sell) the bond back to the issuer at some point before the ultimate maturity for the full face value of the bond.

# Questions

1. What is the face value of most bonds?

 ______________________________

2. How much would an investor pay (excluding commissions and fees) for a bond being sold at par?

 ______________________________

3. How much annual interest will the owner of a $1,000 5% bond receive?

 ______________________________

4. How much will the semiannual interest payments be on a $1,000 9% bond?

 ______________________________

5. A trust indenture is a contract between the

 A. issuer and investor
 B. issuer and trustee
 C. trustee and underwriter
 D. issuer and underwriter

6. Bonds that mature with a smaller amount in the earlier years and a greater amount in later years are called

 A. series bonds
 B. term bonds
 C. balloon bonds
 D. callable bonds

7. Which of the following statements are true of bonds?

 I. Bonds represent a loan to the issuer.
 II. Bonds give the bondholder ownership in the entity.
 III. Bonds are issued to finance capital expenditures or to raise working capital.
 IV. Bonds are junior securities.

 A. I and II only
 B. I and III only
 C. II and III only
 D. I, II, III and IV

8. Which of these bond features is the most attractive to a corporate issuer?

 A. Low call premium
 B. High interest rate
 C. Nonrefundable
 D. High sinking fund requirement

9. An investor purchased a 5 1/2% bond to yield 6 1/2%. If the company calls the bond at par before maturity, the effective yield would be

 A. less than 5 1/2%
 B. 5 1/2%
 C. 6 1/2%
 D. greater than 6 1/2%

10. A new convertible bond contains a provision that it cannot be called for five years after the date of issuance. This call protection would be most valuable to a recent purchaser of the bond if interest rates are

 A. falling
 B. rising
 C. stable
 D. fluctuating

11. A bond with a high coupon rate is selling at a premium and is called at par. The party that benefits from the call provision is the

 A. bondholder
 B. issuer
 C. trustee
 D. broker-dealer

12. 30-year term bonds have an average life of 21 years and 6 months to maturity. This probably means that the

    A. buyer has the option to redeem the bonds early
    B. issuer has the option to redeem the bonds in 21 years and 6 months
    C. bonds are callable at a future date
    D. bonds are sinking fund instruments

13. Which of the following are characteristics of bearer bonds?

    A. They come in registered form.
    B. They pay interest quarterly.
    C. They have interest coupons attached.
    D. They do not have interest coupons attached.

# Answers

1. The face value of most bonds sold is $1,000. An issue is made up of many hundreds to thousands of these $1,000 bonds.

2. A bond sold at par, whether as part of an initial offering or in the secondary market, is being sold for $1,000.

3. The annual interest payment per $1,000 on a 5% bond is $50.

4. A $1,000 9% bond pays $90 per year in interest in two $45 semiannual payments.

5. **B.** A trust indenture is an agreement between the issuer and a trustee appointed to protect the interests of the bondholders.

6. **C.** A balloon maturity is one in which bonds mature serially with the vast majority of the issue maturing in the later years.

7. **B.** Bonds are debt securities; as such, they represent loans to the issuer. They are senior securities, taking precedence over common and preferred stock in claims against an issuer.

8. **A.** A low call rate means that the bond may be *called* or redeemed at a low premium before maturity. This feature is attractive to corporations because it increases the flexibility of their capital structure. For example, it allows a corporation to discontinue debt financing or to replace it with equity financing. The other answers would place burdens on a corporation and, therefore, are not attractive.

9. **D.** The bond with a 5 1/2% coupon is priced to yield 6 1/2% and is selling at a discount. If the bond is called before maturity, the discount will be earned in a shorter period of time, increasing the yield to greater than 6 1/2%.

10. **A.** Call protection is most valuable to a purchaser when interest rates are falling because

the attractive coupon will increase the market price of the bond. In the meantime, the holder is assured the higher return even though interest rates generally fall below the bond interest rate.

11. **B.** When a bond is called, the party that benefits is the issuer. The call provisions are established for the benefit of the issuer, not for the benefit of the holder.

12. **C.** The fact that 30-year bonds have an average life of 21 years and 6 months indicates that the bonds have a sinking fund that allows the issuer to call bonds before their maturity.

13. **C.** Bearer bonds, also known as *unregistered bonds*, must have interest coupons attached.

# Bond Yields

## Comparing Yields

Bonds frequently are quoted and traded by their yields rather than by dollar amounts.

### Nominal Yield

A bond's nominal yield is a fixed percentage of the bond's par value. It is set at issuance and printed on the face of the bond. A coupon of 3 1/4%, for instance, means the issuer will pay $32.50 interest per $1,000 of par value every year until the bond matures.

### Current Yield

Current yield is a measure of the return an investor receives compared to the current price of the security:

$$\frac{\text{Annual interest}}{\text{Current market price}} = \text{Current yield}$$

**Relationship of yield to price.** A bond traded at par will have identical nominal and current yields. An investor who pays $1,000 for a 5% bond will receive a 5% return on investment, or $500 per year.

A bond purchased at a discount will have a current yield that is higher than its nominal yield. For example, a 5% coupon bond trading at a discounted price of $800 has an annual interest payment of $50 and a current yield of 6.25% ($50 ÷ $800 = 6.25%).

A bond purchased at a premium will have a current yield that is lower than its nominal yield. An investor who buys a 5% coupon bond trading at a premium of $1,100 receives an annual interest payment of $50 and a current yield of 4.5% ($50 ÷ $1,100 = 4.5%).

Current yield does not take into account a gain or loss on the sale of the bond or whether the bond is held to maturity.

**Summary of current yield.** As a rule, when a bond is traded:

- **at a discount**, the current yield is greater than the nominal yield;
- **at a premium**, the current yield is less than the nominal yield; and
- **at par**, the current yield equals the nominal yield.

### Yield to Maturity

A bond's yield to maturity (YTM) is a measure of the annual return on investment from purchase until maturity and accounts for the difference between the amount an investor pays for the bond and the amount the investor receives at the time the bond matures.

**Premium bonds.** YTM on a premium bond will always be lower than the nominal yield, as illustrated by the following equations:

$$\text{Annual interest} \begin{array}{c} + \text{ Prorated discount} \\ \text{or} \\ - \text{ Prorated premium} \end{array} = \text{Annual ROI}$$

$$\frac{\text{Purchase price} + \text{Par value}}{2} = \text{Average price}$$

$$\frac{\text{Annual ROI}}{\text{Average price}} = \text{YTM}$$

**YTM calculations for premium bonds.** The following formulas can be used to approximate the yield to maturity of a bond investment.

1. Calculate the **prorated premium**:

$$\frac{\text{Premium paid}}{\text{Years to maturity}} = \text{Prorated premium}$$

2. Calculate the **annual ROI**:

$$\text{Annual interest} - \text{Prorated premium}$$
$$= \text{Annual ROI}$$

3. Calculate the **average price**:

$$\frac{\text{Purchase price} + \text{Maturity price}}{2} = \text{Avg. price}$$

4. Calculate the **YTM**:

$$\frac{\text{Annual ROI}}{\text{Average price}} = \text{YTM}$$

The yield to maturity on a 6% bond purchased at 110 ($1,100 per bond, a $100 premium) and maturing in 10 years would be calculated as follows:

1. Calculate the **prorated premium**:

   $100 premium paid ÷ 10 years = $10

2. Calculate the **annual ROI**:

   $60 annual interest – $10 prorated premium = $50

3. Calculate the **average price**:

$$\frac{\$1{,}100 \text{ purchase price} + \$1{,}000 \text{ maturity price}}{2}$$

   = $2,100 ÷ 2 = $1,050

4. Calculate the **YTM**:

   $50 ÷ $1,075 = .0476
   (a 4.76% yield to maturity)

**YTM calculations for par bonds.** The yield to maturity of a bond bought at par will be the same as its current and coupon yields. Yield to maturity will differ from current yield whenever the price paid for the security differs from par value.

**YTM calculations for discount bonds.** The YTM of discount bonds is higher than the coupon rate because the investor realizes a capital gain when the bond is redeemed at par. Suppose an investor purchases a bond with a 6% coupon at a discounted price of 90 ($900 per $1,000 face value bond). She will receive $60 a year in interest plus a gain of $100 (the difference between the $1,000 value at redemption and the $900 purchase price) if she holds the bond to maturity.

Two discount bonds with the same current yields may have different yields to maturity. As an example, two investors purchase two different 6% bonds, one maturing in ten years, one maturing in 20. Each pays 80 for his bond. The bonds will have different YTMs because they have a different number of years remaining until maturity. The investor with the 20-year bond has to wait a longer time to recoup the value of the $200 discount. Prorating the $200 discount over 20 years is the equivalent of an additional $10 per year in income (a 1% increase in return). Prorating the same $200 discount over ten years means an additional yield of $20 per year (a 2% increase in return).

**Summary of yield to maturity.** As a rule, for a bond purchased:

- **at a discount**, yield to maturity will be greater than nominal yield and greater than current yield;
- **at a premium**, yield to maturity will be lower than nominal yield and lower than current yield; and
- **at par**, yield to maturity will be equal to nominal yield and equal to current yield.

### Yield to Call

A bond may be called any time after a **call date** set at the time of issuance. A bond is said to have **call protection** before that date.

**Premium bonds.** An investor who buys a callable bond at a premium stands to lose money if the bond is called at par before maturity. The yield to call will be lower than the nominal yield, current yield or yield to maturity if the bond is called at par.

Suppose an investor bought a 6% bond for 120 that is scheduled to mature in ten years but is callable at any time (that is, it has passed its call protection date). If the bond is not called and is redeemed by the issuer in ten years at $1,000, the investor realizes a loss of $200 ($1,200 paid minus $1,000 received). Prorating the $200 over the ten years decreases yield by $20 per year—the equivalent of reducing yield by 2%. The investor received an annual yield of 4% for the time he held the bond (6% coupon minus 2% prorated premium).

Now suppose the issuer called the bonds in only five years at $1,000. The investor would prorate the $200 loss over the five years, which would equal a loss of $40 per year—a 4% reduction in yield. The investor's annual yield would be just 2% (6% coupon minus 4% prorated premium). An investor who buys a callable bond at a premium is at a disadvantage when the bond is called.

**Par bonds**. The yield of a bond bought at par and called away before its maturity date will remain unchanged. An investor who buys a 7% bond for $1,000 receives a 7% return on the bond for however long it is held. That fact is not changed when the issuer calls the bond and repays the $1,000 original investment. Because an issuer receives no substantial economic benefit from calling bonds selling at par, these bonds are unlikely to be called before maturity.

**Discount bonds**. When a bond bought at a discount is called before its maturity date, the discount will accrue faster and result in a higher yield to the bondholder (yield to call higher than yield to maturity). However, the bond is not likely to be called, because the issuer would receive no economic benefit. A bond sells at a discount when its coupon rate is lower than prevailing interest rates. Because the issuer is able to make relatively low interest payments, the issuer is not likely to call a bond selling at a discount.

**Calculating yield to call**. Prorate the discount or premium over the time remaining to the **first call date**. The call price is used instead of the par value:

$$\text{Annual interest} + \frac{\text{Discount from call price}}{\text{Years to call}} = \text{Annual ROI}$$

$$\frac{\text{Purchase price} + \text{Call price}}{2} = \text{Average price}$$

$$\frac{\text{Annual return on investment}}{\text{Average price}} = \text{Yield to call}$$

**Summary of yield to call**. As a rule, for a bond purchased:

- **at a discount**, yield to call will always be greater than yield to maturity (but the issuer is unlikely to call the bond);
- **at a premium**, yield to call may be greater or less than the yield to maturity depending on the relationship between the purchase price and the call price. If the purchase price of the bond is lower than the call price, the yield to maturity will be lowest; if the purchase price is higher than the call price, the yield to call will be the lowest; and
- **at par**, the yield to call will be the same as the yield to maturity (but the issuer is unlikely to call the bond).

### Yield to Price Relationship

Bond prices and yields have an inverse relationship. As bond prices go up, yields go down (and vice versa). If a bond is trading at a discount, the current yield increases; if a bond is trading at a premium, the current yield decreases.

Generally speaking, when comparing two discount bonds, the bond with the interest rate that is farther away from the current market rates will be more volatile in price.

### Short-term and Long-term Yields

A positive yield curve is referred to as a *normal curve* due to the fact that most investors are willing to pay a higher price (and, therefore, receive a lower yield) for the benefit of liquidity.

Changing interest rates have a greater effect on bonds with long maturities than on those with short maturities. As interest rates rise, the price of long-term bonds drops more quickly than the price of short-term bonds.

When a yield curve is inverted it is said to have a *negative* (or downward) slope. An inverted curve is one in which bonds with shorter maturities have higher yields than bonds of longer terms.

When the yields of bonds with short maturities are the same as those of bonds with long maturities the yield curve is said to be *flat* or *even*.

## Questions

1. What is the nominal yield of a bond paying $130 in interest every year?

    ______________________

2. What is the coupon rate of a bond paying $42.50 in interest semiannually?

    ______________________

3. What is the nominal rate of a bond paying $80 in interest annually that is currently being offered for $800?

    ______________________

4. What is the current yield of a bond paying $95 per year and trading at par?

    ______________________

5. What is the current yield of a bond paying $85 per year and trading at $700?

    ______________________

6. What is the current yield of a bond paying $110 per year and trading at $1,100?

    ______________________

7. A bond has a current yield of 12% and is trading at $1,000. What is its coupon rate?

    ______________________

8. A bond has a current yield of 12% and is trading at $800. What is its coupon rate?

    ______________________

9. A bond has a current yield of 12% and is trading at $1,600. What is its coupon rate?

    ______________________

10. An investor receives $37.50 in semiannual interest payments on a bond for which he paid $1,200. What is the bond's current yield?

    ______________________

11. An investor receives $37.50 in semiannual interest payments on a bond for which he paid $1,200. What is the bond's coupon rate?

    ______________________

12. An 8% bond is purchased at 110 and matures in 20 years. What is the prorated premium?

    ______________________

13. A bond at par has a coupon rate

    A. less than current yield
    B. less than yield to maturity
    C. the same as current yield
    D. greater than current yield

14. What is the calculation for determining the current yield on a bond?

    A. Annual interest ÷ Par value
    B. Annual interest ÷ Current market price
    C. Yield to maturity ÷ Par value
    D. Yield to maturity ÷ Current market price

15. A customer purchased a 5% U.S. government bond yielding 6%. A year before the bond matures, new U.S. government bonds are being issued at 4%, and the customer sells the 5% bond. The customer probably

    I. bought it at a discount
    II. bought it at a premium
    III. sold it at a discount
    IV. sold it at a premium

    A. I and III
    B. I and IV
    C. II and III
    D. II and IV

16. Which yield to maturity would be higher?

    A. 10% nominal yield bond with a premium price
    B. 10% nominal yield bond with a discount price
    C. 10% nominal yield bond with a price at par
    D. 10% nominal yield bond with a zero coupon

17. A corporation issues 9% Aaa rated debentures at par. Two years later, similar Aaa issues are being offered in the primary market at 9 1/2%. Which of the following statements are true regarding the outstanding 9% issue?

    I. The current yield on the issue will be higher.
    II. The current yield on the issue will be lower.
    III. The dollar price per bond will be higher than par.
    IV. The dollar price per bond will be lower than par.

    A. I and III
    B. I and IV
    C. II and III
    D. II and IV

18. An investor has purchased three municipal issues quoted at 7% yield, with 5-, 10- and 15-year maturities, respectively. If municipal yields drop by ten basis points, which of the following will show the greatest dollar price movement?

    A. 5-year maturity
    B. 10-year maturity
    C. 15-year maturity
    D. All will move equally.

19. In a comparison of long-term bonds with short-term bonds, all of the following are characteristics of long-term bonds EXCEPT that they

    A. usually have higher yields than short-term bonds
    B. usually provide greater liquidity than short-term bonds
    C. are more likely to be callable
    D. will fluctuate in price more than short-term bonds in response to interest rate changes

20. When interest rates are falling or rising, the price fluctuations of which of the following will be the greatest?

    A. Short-term bonds
    B. Long-term bonds
    C. Money-market instruments
    D. Common stock

21. Interest payments on a bond are based on the bond's

    A. par value
    B. discount value
    C. market value
    D. book value

22. A 5% bond is issued at par. It is now selling at 90 and is redeemable at par. What is its annual income?

    A. $20
    B. $50
    C. $500
    D. $5,000

# Answers

1. The nominal yield of a bond that pays an investor $130 in annual interest is $130 divided by $1,000, which is 13%.

2. A bond that pays $42.50 every six months pays $85 per year. $85 ÷ $1,000 = 8.5%.

3. The nominal rate is always calculated by using the par value. Even though the bond is currently selling for $800, to calculate its nominal yield you must divide $80 by $1,000. The bond has a nominal yield of 8%.

4. To find the current yield of a bond paying $95 per year and trading at par, divide $95 by $1,000. The bond's current yield is 9.5%.

5. To find the current yield of a bond paying $85 per year and trading at $700, divide $85 by $700. The bond's current yield is 12.14%.

6. The current yield of a bond paying $110 per year and trading at $1,100 is 10%. $110 ÷ $1,100 = 10%.

7. $1,000 times 12% equals $120. A bond with a current yield of 12% trading at $1,000 is paying $120 in annual interest. This bond's current yield equals its coupon yield because the bond is trading at par ($1,000).

8. A bond with a current yield of 12% that is trading at $800 is paying $96 in annual interest ($800 × 12% = $96). $96 in annual interest divided by $1,000 par value is a coupon rate of 9.6%.

9. A bond trading for $1,600 with a current yield of 12% is paying $192 in interest annually to the investor ($1,600 × 12% = $192). To find its coupon rate, divide $192 by $1,000 to get 19.2%.

10. $37.50 in semiannual interest payments on a bond represents $75 in annual interest. $75 divided by the current price of $1,200 equals a current yield of 6.25%.

11. $75 in annual interest on a bond ($37.50 in semiannual interest payments times 2) divided by the bond's $1,000 par value represents a 7.5% coupon.

12. The investor paid a $100 premium for the bond. $100 prorated over 20 years is $5 per year.

13. **C.** A bond at par has a coupon rate equal to current yield. All yields will be the same as the coupon yield when the bond is at par.

14. **B.**

$$\frac{\text{Annual interest}}{\text{Current market price}} = \text{Current yield}$$

15. **B.** The customer purchased the 5% bond when it was yielding 6%, therefore at a discount. The customer sold the bond when other bonds of like kind, quality and maturity were yielding 4%. The bond is now at a premium because the 5% coupon is attractive to other investors. The customer, therefore, made a capital gain on the investment.

16. **B.** With the same nominal yield, the discount bonds will generate higher yields because the discount will be received in addition to coupon interest.

17. **B.** Because interest rates in general have risen since the issuance of the 9% bond, the bond's price will now be discounted to give a higher current yield on the bond—making it competitive with new issues now being sold at 9 1/2%.

18. **C.** For a given change in interest rates, bonds with the longest maturity will show the greatest change in dollar price.

19. **B.** Long-term bonds are not as liquid as short-term obligations.

20. **B.** Long-term debt prices will fluctuate more than short-term debt prices as interest rates rise and fall. Common stock prices are not directly affected by interest rates.

21. **A.** Interest on bonds is always based on the bond's par value.

22. **B.** Regardless of current market price, the coupon is based on par value of $1,000. The bondholder receives 5% on $1,000, or $50, annually.

# 3 Corporate Debt Securities

## Characteristics of Corporate Bonds

### Types of Bonds

#### Secured Bonds

When the issuer has set aside certain identifiable assets as collateral for the prompt payment of interest and the repayment of principal the bond issue is known as *secured*. In a default, bondholders can lay claim to the assets.

**Mortgage bonds**. In reorganization or liquidation, mortgage bonds have absolute priority among claims on the assets pledged to secure them and are sometimes called **senior debt securities** (senior lien). First claim on the pledged property goes to first-mortgage bonds, second claim to second-mortgage bonds and so on.

**Closed-end indentures**. In a closed-end mortgage arrangement, a corporation issues the maximum number of bonds authorized in the trust indenture as first-mortgage bonds. Any subsequent issue will have subordinated claims on the property.

**Open-end indentures**. In an open-ended trust indenture, the corporation can issue more bonds of the same class later. Subsequent issues will be secured by the same collateral backing the initial issue and will have equal liens on the property.

**Prior lien bonds**. Mortgage bonds that take precedence over first-mortgage bonds are known as prior-lien bonds. Before issuing prior lien bonds, a corporation must have the consent of first-mortgage bondholders.

**Collateral trust bonds**. Collateral trust bonds are usually issued by corporations that own securities of other companies and issues bonds secured by a pledge of these investment securities as collateral.

**Equipment trust certificates**. Equipment trust certificates are used to finance the purchase of transportation equipment.

#### Unsecured Bonds

Unsecured bonds have no specific collateral backing.

**Debentures**. Debentures are backed by the general credit of the issuing corporation. The owner of a debenture is considered a general creditor of the corporation.

**Subordinated debentures**. Subordinated debentures are so called because the claims of their owners are subordinated to the claims of other general creditors, including owners of ordinary debentures.

#### Guaranteed Bonds

With guaranteed bonds, a company other than the issuer has guaranteed payment of principal and interest.

### Income Bonds

Income bonds pay interest on the bond only if the corporation's earnings are sufficient to meet the interest payment and if the payment is declared by the board of directors.

### Zero-coupon Bonds

**Issuing zero-coupon bonds.** Zero-coupon bonds are debt obligations of the issuer. The issuers of zero-coupon bonds do not make interest payments to the owners of zeros. They sell these debt obligations to investors at a deep discount from the face value with a promise to redeem the bonds at face value when they mature. The difference between the deeply discounted purchase price and the full face value at maturity is the return (interest) the investor receives.

Zero-coupon bonds are issued by corporations, municipalities and the U.S. Treasury (e.g., Separate Trading of Registered Interest and Principal of Securities—STRIPS), and they may be created by broker-dealers from other types of securities, including those issued by the federal government.

### Advantages and Disadvantages of Zero-coupon Bonds

An advantage of an investment in zero-coupon bonds is that there is *no reinvestment risk* for the purchaser. A disadvantage of an investment in zeros is that they are *more subject to market risk* than are interest-paying debt obligations. Zero-coupon bond prices tend to be extremely volatile because of their deep discount and zero interest rate.

### Taxation of Zero-coupon Bonds

The investor who owns corporate or government zeros owes income tax each year on a portion of that amount, just as though it had been received in cash (interest from municipal obligations, including municipal zeros, is generally federally tax-exempt). The annual interest is not prorated on a straight-line basis and the investor is apportioned a different amount each year.

### Liquidation Priority

In order of priority, liquidation occurs as follows:

1. unpaid wages;
2. IRS (taxes);
3. secured claims (mortgages);
4. secured liabilities (bonds);
5. unsecured liabilities (debentures) and general creditors;
6. subordinated debt;
7. preferred stockholders; and
8. common stockholders.

## The Trust Indenture

The trust indenture is a legal contract between the bond issuer and a trustee that represents the bondholders. Within the trust indenture, covenants identify the bondholders' rights and name the entity that will act as trustee. The trustee ensures compliance with the covenants of the indenture and acts on behalf of the bondholders in the event of a default by the issuer.

### The Trustee

The trustee helps prepare the issue. In the trust indenture the corporation agrees to abide by certain covenants.

### Exemptions

Federal and municipal governments are exempt from the provisions of the Trust Indenture Act. The act also exempts securities not issued under an indenture, as long as the total dollar amount of securities issued by a single entity does not exceed $5 million in a twelve-month period.

### Protective Covenants of the Indenture

The debtor corporation agrees to:

- pay the interest and principal of every bond;
- specify the places bonds or coupons can be presented for payment;
- defend the legal title to the property;
- maintain the property to ensure that business can be conducted profitably;
- do nothing that will diminish the claims of the bonds;
- insure the mortgaged property against fire and other losses;
- pay all taxes and assessments (property, income, franchises);
- maintain its corporate structure and the right to do business; and
- record the mortgage and pay any recording fees.

### Remedies of Bondholders

If a corporation is judged to be bankrupt, liquidated or failing to meet its promises in the indenture, the trustee and bondholders have access to the following remedies:

- right of entry;
- right to sell property to the highest bidder;
- right to foreclose;
- right to bring suit; and
- right to declare the principal due prior to the maturity date.

Also included in the provisions of the indenture are:

- acceleration of maturity in cases of default;
- release of mortgaged property; and
- protection for bondholders in consolidations and mergers.

Unless the trust indenture specifies otherwise, changes in the indenture cannot be made without the unanimous consent of the bondholders.

## Questions

1. Ted Thompson bought five $1,000 corporate bonds. All of the following statements are true EXCEPT that
   A. Ted's bonds represent ownership in the corporation
   B. the bonds are debt securities
   C. Ted is a creditor of the corporation
   D. if the corporation goes bankrupt, Ted will receive company assets before corporate stockholders receive them

2. Which of the following is commonly referered to as funded debt?
   A. Corporate bonds
   B. Municipal bonds
   C. Preferred stock
   D. Government bonds

3. Equipment trust certificates would most commonly be issued by
   I. airline companies
   II. railroad companies
   III. farm equipment companies
   IV. automobile manufacturers

   A. I and II
   B. II
   C. III
   D. III and IV

4. Bonds that are secured by other securities placed with a trustee are called
   A. mortgage bonds
   B. collateral trust bonds
   C. debenture bonds
   D. guaranteed bonds

5. When a person owns a convertible bond, he is
   A. a creditor of the issuer
   B. an owner of the issuer
   C. neither a creditor nor an owner of the issue
   D. both a creditor and an owner of the issue

6. In case of bankruptcy, debentures rank on a par with

   A. first-mortgage bonds
   B. equipment trust certificates
   C. unsecured debts of private creditors
   D. collateral trust bonds

7. An indenture has a closed-end provision. This means that

   A. additional issues will have junior liens
   B. the bonds must be called before maturity
   C. a sinking fund must be established
   D. no additional bonds may be issued

8. An investor purchasing 2 GMAC ZR 12's at 53 1/2 would receive annual interest of

   A. $0
   B. $12
   C. $53.50
   D. $120

9. A customer who bought 10 Ogden 5's at 93 would receive annual interest of

   A. $50
   B. $93
   C. $500
   D. $930

10. A first-mortgage bond is issued by ABC Sewer Company. The bond is backed by the

    A. mortgages of cities serviced by the sewer company
    B. liens on the property of the sewer company
    C. customers' mortgages
    D. collateral of investments owned by the sewer company

11. A corporate bond valued at $1,012.50 is shown in the bond guide as

    A. 101.25
    B. 101 8/32
    C. 101 4/16
    D. 101 1/4

12. An investor buys $1 million of 10% corporate bonds at par. At the end of the day, the bonds close up 1/2 point. The investor has a gain of

    A. $2,500
    B. $5,000
    C. $25,000
    D. $50,000

## Answers

1. **A.** Bonds, unlike stocks, do not represent ownership of the corporation. Instead, bonds represent corporate debt. The corporation owes money ($5,000 in Ted's case) to the bondholder, who is a creditor of the corporation. In bankruptcy, the corporation pays the debts (including bonds) before distributing assets to stockholders.

2. **A.** *Funded debt* is the term used to describe long-term corporate debt.

3. **A.** Equipment trust certificates can be issued only by companies that actually use the equipment (the equipment is collateral for the loan). Manufacturers do not issue equipment trust certificates.

4. **B.** Collateral bonds or collateral trust bonds are used frequently in railroad financing where securities owned by the parent are pledged as collateral for a loan. The pledged collateral for common stock is generally deposited in a trust, especially when money is raised publicly.

5. **A.** A bondholder is a creditor (whether or not the bond is convertible). Only after the bondholder converts is he considered an owner.

6. **C.** A debenture is an unsecured debt, backed only by the corporation's promise to pay. Therefore, of the answers offered, A, B and D are backed by specific assets and have preference before debentures.

7. **A.** The indenture may include a restriction on the sale of additional bonds—this is a "closed-end" provision. If any additional bonds are issued, their owners' claims on the mortgaged property will be subordinated to the claims of bondholders owning the original issue.

8. **A.** The GMAC bond is a zero-coupon bond (ZR) with no interest payments. These bonds sell at a deep discount, and the tax law requires annual accretion of the discount.

9. **C.** "Ogden 5's" means 5% bonds. 5% of $1,000 par equals $50 of interest per bond annually. For ten bonds, the annual interest is $500. The investor paid $930 for each bond.

10. **B.** A mortgage bond is evidence of indebtedness that is secured by a mortgage or other lien on some underlying real property of a corporation.

11. **D.** Corporates are quoted in fractions of 1/8th and 1/4th. The quote of 101 1/4th equals $1,012.50. This represents $1,010 (101% of par) plus $2.50 (1/4th of $10). Each point in a corporate bond is equal to $10.

12. **B.** The investor owns $1 million face value of bonds. An increase of 1/2 point is an increase of 1/2 of 1% of $1,000,000, or $5,000.

# Convertible Securities

### Why Corporations Issue Convertibles

A corporation will add a conversion feature to its bonds and preferred stock issues to make them more marketable. When the bond market is strong, convertible debentures are frequently issued as a means of raising equity capital on a postponed basis. When (and if) the debentures are converted, the corporation's capitalization changes from debt to equity.

### Advantages to Issuer

Corporations issue convertible securities for a number of reasons:

- Convertibles can be sold with a lower coupon rate than nonconvertibles.
- The company can eliminate a fixed interest charge as conversion takes place.
- A rapid increase in the number of shares in the market is unlikely because conversions take place over a longer period of time.
- The corporation avoids immediate dilution of primary earnings per share.

### Disadvantages to Issuer

Possible disadvantages of issuing convertibles to the corporation and its stockholders:

- When bonds are converted, shareholders' equity is diluted.
- A substantial conversion could cause a shift in the control of the company.
- Reducing corporate debt through conversion means a loss of leverage.
- The resulting decrease in (deductible) interest costs raises the corporation's taxable income.

There is no way of knowing when and how many of the bonds will be converted.

### The Market for Convertible Securities

The convertible bondholder has both the investment safety of the fixed income market and the potential appreciation of the equity market. This leads to several advantages:

- As a debt security, a convertible debenture pays interest at a fixed rate and will be redeemable for its face value at maturity.
- The convertible bondholder has priority over common stockholders in the event of a corporate liquidation.
- The market price of a convertible debenture will tend to be more stable during market declines than the price of common stock.
- The market price of convertibles tends to move upward if the stock price moves up.
- No tax liability is incurred on the conversion transaction.
- The conversion ratio is adjusted in the event of a stock dividend, a stock split or an additional stock issue.

### Conversion Price and Conversion Ratio

**Conversion price**. Conversion price is the amount of par value of the convertible bond that can be converted into one share of common stock. If a convertible debenture has a conversion price of $125, each $125 worth of par value will be converted into one share of common stock. For every bond a holder converts, the bondholder would receive eight shares of stock (an 8-to-1 conversion ratio).

**Conversion ratio**. Conversion ratio expresses the number of shares of common stock obtainable by converting $1,000 par value of the bonds. A conversion price of $125 has a conversion ratio of 8 to 1 ($1,000 ÷ $125 = 8).

### Fixed or Variable

Convertible debentures are normally issued with a schedule of different conversion prices incorporated into the indenture agreement. The schedule usually calls for higher conversion prices as the debenture nears maturity because the issuer anticipates that the price of the common stock will increase in the future. Factors that affect the initial conversion rate or price are the:

- price of the stock at the time the bonds are issued;
- earnings prospect of the issuing company and its effect on the stock price;
- market trend;
- conversion period; and
- amount of interest the corporation is willing to pay.

### Subscription Rights for Stockholders

Because convertibles can dilute shareholders' equity, stockholders often have a preemptive right to purchase any new security issue that is convertible to stock, usually at a subscription price below the market value of the bond.

### Protective Features

- **Stock splits and dividends.** Conversion prices may be adjusted if stock splits and stock dividends are declared on the underlying common stock during the life of the debenture.
- **Changes in class of conversion securities.** If outstanding common shares are converted into the same number of shares of another class, the conversion privilege would apply to an equal number of new shares.
- **Additional shares.** The indenture fixes both the maximum number of additional shares the corporation can issue while convertible bonds are outstanding and the minimum price at which they can be issued.

## Calculating Conversion Parity

Parity means that two securities are of equal dollar value. If a corporation issues a convertible preferred stock that has a par value of $100 and is convertible at $50, the conversion ratio is 2 to 1. The investor can receive two shares of common stock for one share of the preferred.

Suppose that a convertible preferred is selling in the market at $88 and is convertible into four shares of common stock. The market price of the common would have to be about $22 to be at parity with the convertible preferred. Four shares of common stock at $22 per share are equal in value to one share of the preferred at $88 per share.

If you know that the common is trading at $18 and that the convertible preferred has a conversion ratio of 5 to 1, you can multiply $18 by 5 to calculate that the preferred's parity price is $90.

Use the following formulas to calculate the parity prices of convertible securities and their underlying common shares:

$$\frac{\text{Market price of convertible}}{\text{Conversion ratio}} = \text{Parity price of common}$$

$$\text{Market price of common} \times \text{Conversion ratio} = \text{Parity price of convertible}$$

### Investment Value and Conversion Value

The estimated investment value of a convertible debenture is the market price at which the security would sell if it were not convertible into common stock. The conversion value of a debenture is the total market value of common stock into which the debenture is convertible.

Take the example of a convertible debenture selling at 110 that can be converted into 20 shares of common stock. If the market value of each share is $60, the conversion value of the debenture is $1,200 ($60 × 20).

### Forced Conversion

A corporation can call convertible bonds when market conditions are such that bondholders will find it more profitable to convert the bonds than to submit them for redemption at the call price. This will happen when the parity price is above the call price.

Suppose, for example, that an issue of bonds is convertible into common stock at $50 (a conversion ratio of 20 to 1) and is called at 110. The stock is currently trading at $60 per share, so by converting a bond, an investor can become the owner of 20 shares of common worth $1,200. The parity price of the bond would be 120 ($1,200 for a $1,000 par value bond). The parity price, in other words, is above the call price. The bond owner is better off converting and selling the 20 shares of common for $1,200 than she is tendering the bond for redemption at $1,100.

As the call date nears, the shares will trade closer and closer to the call price and will eventually trade at a market price that reflects only a slight discount from the call price.

# Questions

1. Which of the following statements concerning convertible bonds is(are) true?

    I. Coupon rates are usually lower than nonconvertible bonds of the same issuer.
    II. Convertible bondholders are creditors of the corporation.
    III. If the underlying common stock should decline to the point where there is no advantage to convert the bonds into common stock, the bonds will sell at a price based on their inherent value as bonds, disregarding the convertible feature.

    A. I only
    B. I and III only
    C. III only
    D. I, II and III

Use the following tombstone to answer questions 2 and 3.

This announcement is neither an offer to sell nor a solicitation of an offer to buy these securities. The offer is made only by Prospectus.

New Issue — July 27, 1997

**Tippecanoe Ferry Company**

12% Convertible Subordinated Debentures
Due November 15, 2001

Convertible into Common Stock
at $12.50 per Share, unless previously redeemed.

**Price 100%**

Copies of this Prospectus may be obtained in any State in which this announcement is circulated only from such of the undersigned as may legally offer these securities in such State.

Moneyflow and Cash Co.
Millon, Billon, Dillon & Co. — Simpson, Sampson, Sobriquet
Dullard Securities Inc. — Fleecem Runn Skippe

2. The bonds are convertible into how many shares of common stock?

    A. 80
    B. 95
    C. 100
    D. 105

3. On December 3, 1994, the Tippecanoe debentures were trading at 102. Therefore, the parity price of the common stock on that date was approximately

   A. 12 1/4
   B. 12 1/2
   C. 12 3/4
   D. 13

4. A bond is convertible to common stock at $20 per share. If the market value of the bond falls to $800, what is the new parity price of the stock?

   A. $12
   B. $16
   C. $25
   D. $40

5. A convertible bond is purchased at its face value and convertible at $125.00. What is the conversion ratio?

   A. 2
   B. 8
   C. 12
   D. 20

6. All of the following are advantages of convertible debentures EXCEPT that the

   A. holder shares in the growth of the common stock
   B. holder receives a higher rate of interest
   C. issuer pays a lower rate of interest
   D. holder has a fixed rate of interest

# Answers

1. **D.** All three choices are true of convertible bonds. Coupon rates are lower because of the value of the conversion feature; bondholders are creditors; and if the stock price falls, its value as an income and debt security will be maintained.

2. **A.** Because the debentures are convertible at $12.50, they are convertible into 80 shares ($1,000 ÷ 12.50).

3. **C.** $1,000 (par) ÷ $12.50 = 80 shares. $1,020 bond price ÷ 80 conversion ratio = $12.75 = 12 3/4.

4. **B.** The calculations are: $1,000 ÷ $20 = 50 shares for one bond. $800 bond price ÷ 50 shares = $16 parity price.

5. **B.** $1,000 par ÷ $125 conversion price = 8 shares per bond.

6. **B.** Because of the possibility of participating in the growth of the common stock through an increase in the market price of the common, the convertible can be issued with a lower rate of interest. This is an advantage to the issuing company.

# 4 U.S. Government and Agency Securities

## Marketable Government Securities

### Treasury Bills

- **Issuance and trading**. T bills are issued at a discount from par in a **competitive bid** auction. Competitive tenders are submitted with the price that reflects the interest rate the bidder wishes to receive. Competitive bids are submitted for amounts of $500,000 and up and settle in federal funds. T bills trade at a discount and do not pay interest (that is, they are traded **flat**).
- **Book entry**. Treasury bills are issued in book-entry form.
- **Maturities and denominations**. Treasury bills:
  - have maturities of one year or less;
  - are issued in denominations of $10,000 to $1 million (in $5,000 increments); and
  - mature in 13 weeks, 26 weeks or 52 weeks.
- **Pricing**. Treasury bills are quoted at a discount from par. A quote of 5.50%, for example, means a 52-week T bill is selling at 5 1/2% less than its face value, or $9,450.

### Treasury Notes

- **Issuance and trading**. T notes pay interest every six months. They are issued in book-entry form only.
- **Maturities and denominations.** T notes are issued in denominations of $1,000 to $1 million maturing in one to ten years.
- **Pricing**. T notes are issued, quoted and traded in 1/32nds of a percent of par. A quote of 98.24 (which can also be expressed as 98-24 or 98:24) on a $1,000 note means that the note is selling for 98 and 24/32% of its par value of $1,000, or $987.50.
- **Redeemable at face value**. At maturity, T notes can be redeemed for cash at par or they can be refunded.

### Treasury Bonds

- **Issuance and trading**. Interest is payable every six months. T bonds are sold in book-entry form only.
- **Callable**. Some T bonds have optional call dates, ranging from three to five years before maturity.
- **Maturities and denominations**. Treasury bonds are issued in denominations of $1,000 to $1 million, and with maturities of ten years or more.
- **Pricing**. T bonds are issued, quoted and traded in 1/32nds of a percent of par. A quote

of 98.04 means that the bond is selling for 98 and 4/32% of its par value of $1,000, or $981.25.

- **Flower bonds**. Flower bonds can be purchased at a discount from face value and, after the investor's death, her heirs can redeem the bonds at face value to pay federal estate taxes. The last issue matures in 1998.

### Treasury Receipts

- Broker-dealers buy Treasury securities, place them in trust at a bank, and then sell receipts against the principal and coupon payments separately to investors.
- Treasury receipts are not backed by the full faith and credit of the U.S. government.
- Treasury receipts against interest payments are issued with maturities at six-month intervals.
- Treasury receipts against the principal amount are priced at a discount from face value.
- With Treasury receipts and other zero-coupon bonds, investors are not subject to **reinvestment risk.**

**STRIPS**. The Treasury department has designated certain Treasury issues as suitable for stripping into interest and principal components. STRIPS stands for "Separate Trading of Registered Interest and Principal of Securities." STRIPS are issued as book-entry securities.

The securities underlying Treasury STRIPS are the direct obligation of the U.S. government, but the STRIPS themselves are not.

## Questions

1. Government bonds and notes are quoted

   A. in 1/8ths
   B. as a percentage of par
   C. on a yield to maturity
   D. as a percentage of par on a discounted annualized basis

2. The maximum maturity on a Treasury note is how many years?

   A. One
   B. Three
   C. Five
   D. Ten

3. Which of the following statements are true regarding T bills?

   I. T bills trade at a discount to par.
   II. T bills have one year or less maturity.
   III. Most T bill issues are callable.
   IV. T bills are a direct obligation of the U.S. government.

   A. I and II only
   B. I, II and III only
   C. I, II and IV only
   D. I, II, III and IV

4. Which of the following U.S. government securities states a rate of interest on its face?

   I. Treasury bond
   II. Treasury note
   III. Treasury bill

   A. I and II only
   B. I and III only
   C. II and III only
   D. I, II and III

5. Which of the following is an original issue discount obligation?

   A. GNMA certificate
   B. T bill
   C. Corporate bond
   D. FNMA bond

6. If you invest $10,000 in T bills over a period of years, which of the following statements are true?

   I. The principal is stable.
   II. The interest is volatile.
   III. The interest is stable.
   IV. The principal is volatile.

   A. I and II
   B. I and III
   C. II and IV
   D. III and IV

7. Consider the following T bills:

| Maturity | Bid | Asked |
|---|---|---|
| 8-2 | 6.36 | 6.20 |
| 8-16 | 6.42 | 6.26 |

   The T bills maturing August 2nd (8-2) are being offered at par

   A. plus a premium to yield 6.20%
   B. less a discount to yield 6.20%
   C. plus a premium to yield 6.36%
   D. less a discount to yield 6.36%

8. A U.S. Treasury bond is listed as "4's of 88/94." This means that the bond

   A. is callable at par between 1988 and 1994
   B. matures between 1988 and 1994
   C. stops paying interest between 1988 and 1994
   D. sells at a premium between 1988 and 1994

9. The bid price of a Treasury bond is $875. It would appear in *The Wall Street Journal* as

   A. 87:12
   B. 87:16
   C. 87:5
   D. 87:8

10. Auctions for twelve-month Treasury bills are held every

   A. day
   B. week
   C. 4 weeks (monthly)
   D. 13 weeks (quarterly)

11. You purchase ten 8% T notes at 101–16. What is the dollar amount of this purchase?

   A. $1,001.50
   B. $1,011.60
   C. $10,150.00
   D. $10,812.00

# Answers

1. **B.** The notes, bonds and certificates are all quoted at a percentage of par. Only bills are quoted on an annualized discount basis.

2. **D.** Treasury notes have maturities that run from one to ten years.

3. **C.** T bills trade at a discount to par, are one year or less to maturity and are a direct obligation of the U.S. government. T bills are noncallable.

4. **A.** Bonds and notes are long-term government securities and show a stated rate of interest on their face. Bills, on the other hand, are short-term securities that are sold at a discount from face and redeemed at face, with the difference being the interest. T bills, therefore, do not carry a coupon rate.

5. **B.** T bills are auctioned weekly and are issued at a discount from par. At maturity, the holder receives par value with the earned discount treated as interest income.

6. **A.** Because T bills have a fixed principal amount, a \$10,000 T bill will always be worth \$10,000 at maturity—the price will not fluctuate a great deal when the maturity is so near. Interest rates, however, may well fluctuate from auction to auction; therefore, the interest is volatile.

7. **B.** T bills are being offered at a discount of 6.20%. This will result in a yield somewhat higher than 6.20, but this is the closest answer.

8. **A.** A listing with two apparent maturities means that the bond is callable after the first date and reaches maturity on the second. Treasury bonds are callable at par, never at a premium.

9. **B.** A bond selling at 875 equals 870 plus 16/32 (\$5 = a half a point, or 16/32). The quote is 87:16.

10. **C.** Auctions for twelve-month T bills are held every 4 weeks; 3-month and 6-month T bill auctions are held weekly.

11. **C.** Government notes and bonds are quoted in 1/32nds. Therefore, a quote of 101–16 means 101 16/32nds. 101.5 × 10 = \$1,015; \$1,015 × 10 bonds = \$10,150.

# Nonmarketable Government Securities

### Savings Bonds

Savings bonds are **nonmarketable securities** that:

- cannot be used as collateral;
- are not negotiable;
- are nontransferable;
- are not bought and sold on an exchange or over the counter;
- are purchased from the Treasury department through various issuing agents, including commercial banks and post offices;
- can be redeemed by only the purchaser or a beneficiary;
- are exempt from state and municipal taxation; and
- are subject to federal taxation.

**Series EE bonds**. Series EE bonds are discount bonds. Bondholders earn the discount over the life of the bond, and can continue to accrue interest for up to thirty years. Series EE bonds:

- can be redeemed for the face value at maturity;
- may be redeemed before they mature;
- are issued at 50% of their face value in denominations from $50 to $10,000; and
- will receive a lower rate of return if redeemed before maturity.

The tax on accrued interest on EE bonds can be paid annually or deferred until the bond matures. Tax can be deferred further by trading EE bonds for HH bonds.

**Series HH bonds**. Series HH bonds:

- pay interest semiannually;
- are designed for investors who want regular income;
- can be purchased only by trading in Series EE bonds at maturity;
- come in denominations of $500 to $10,000; and
- mature in ten years.

## Questions

1. All of the following are true of Series EE and Series HH bonds EXCEPT that

   I. EE bonds do not generate interest income whereas HH bonds have a fixed coupon
   II. HH bonds can be borrowed against
   III. EE bonds are registered whereas HH bonds are bearer bonds
   IV. EE bonds are issued at a discount whereas HH bonds are issued at par

   A. I and II
   B. I and IV
   C. II
   D. II and III

## Answers

1. **D.** Series EE and HH bonds are nonnegotiable and cannot be borrowed against. Both are issued in registered form.

# Agency Issues

**Authorization**. Congress authorizes certain agencies of the federal government to issue marketable debt securities:

- Federal Farm Credit System (FFCS);
- Government National Mortgage Association (GNMA or Ginnie Mae); and
- Inter-American Development Bank (IADB).

Other agency-like organizations that are operated by private corporations include:

- Federal Home Loan Mortgage Corporation (FHLMC or Freddie Mac);
- Federal Home Loan Banks (FHLBs);
- Federal National Mortgage Association (FNMA or Fannie Mae); and
- Student Loan Marketing Association (SLMA or Sallie Mae).

**Yields and maturities**. Agency issues:

- sell at higher yields than do direct obligations of the federal government;
- sell at lower yields than those available on corporate debt;
- have maturities that vary from very short to relatively long term;
- are quoted at a percentage of par; and
- are traded on the secondary market prior to their maturity.

**Backing**. Agency issues are backed by:

- the credit of the issuer;
- collateral, such as cash, U.S. Treasury securities and the debt obligations;
- a U.S. Treasury guarantee;
- the right of the agency to borrow from the Treasury; or
- the full faith and credit of the government (GNMAs only).

**Taxation**. Interest on government agency issues is:

- sometimes exempt from state and local income taxes; and
- always subject to federal income tax.

### Federal Farm Credit Bank

Federal Farm Credit Banks securities are:

- not directly backed by the faith and credit of the U.S. government;
- discount notes, six- and nine-month notes, mortgage-backed securities and longer term bonds;
- issued only in book-entry form;
- federally taxed; and
- exempt from local and state taxes.

### Federal Intermediate Credit Banks

The FICBs make loans to credit companies, agricultural institutions and commercial banks, which in turn lend that money to farmers. FICBs are private corporations and, as such, issue both common and preferred stock in themselves. FICB securities are:

- short- and long-term debentures
- federally taxable
- exempt from local and state taxes

### Federal Home Loan Bank

The Federal Home Loan Bank operates as a credit reserve system for the nation's savings and loan institutions, which in turn provide credit for residential mortgages. FHLB securities are:

- issued in book-entry form;
- noncallable;
- short-term discount notes;
- interest-bearing notes;
- bonds;
- available in denominations of $10,000, $25,000, $100,000 and $1 million;
- backed by mortgages, cash and other bank assets;
- federally taxable; and
- exempt from local and state taxes.

### Federal Home Loan Mortgage Corporation

The Federal Home Loan Mortgage Corporation is a corporation that promotes the development of a nationwide secondary market in mortgages by purchasing residential mortgages from financial institutions insured by an agency of the federal government and selling its interest in them through mortgage-backed securities. FHLMC securities are:

- pass-through certificates, which include
  - mortgage participation certificates (PCs); and
  - guaranteed mortgage certificates (GMCs); and
- subject to full state and federal income taxation.

### Federal National Mortgage Association

The Federal National Mortgage Association is a publicly held corporation (not a government agency) that provides mortgage capital. FNMA purchases conventional and insured mortgages from agencies such as the Federal Housing Administration (FHA) and the Department of Veterans Affairs. The securities are backed by FNMA's general credit. FNMA securities are:

- debentures (issued in denominations from $10,000 up in increments of $5,000);
- short-term discount notes (issued in denominations of $5,000, $25,000, $100,000, $500,000 and $1 million);
- mortgage-backed securities;
- set up to pay semi-annual interest;
- issued in book-entry form only; and
- taxed at federal, state and local levels.

### Government National Mortgage Association

The Government National Mortgage Association is a wholly U.S. government-owned corporation. Ginnie Maes are:

- backed by the full faith and credit of the government;
- pass-through certificates that provide monthly principal and interest payments;
- issued in minimum denominations of $25,000; and
- fully taxable at federal, state and local levels.

### Student Loan Marketing Association

The SLMA is a publicly owned corporation that purchases student loans from the originating financial institutions and packages them for sale in the secondary market, guaranteeing the payment of principal and interest.

## Collateralized Mortgage Obligations

CMOs are:

- mortgage-backed securities;
- pass-through obligations;
- not guaranteed;
- not backed by the federal government;
- collateralized by a pool of a very large number of mortgages; and
- affected by changes in interest rates (which affect the rate of early payoff of mortgages, which in turn affects the flow of principal repayment to the CMO investor).

A series of CMO securities is often divided into maturity classes called *tranches*. The particular tranche an investor owns determines the schedule, and security, of his receipt of principal repayment.

### Classes of CMOs

- **Principal-only CMOs (POs)**. For POs the income stream comes from principal payments on the underlying mortgages. POs typically sell at a deep discount; the difference between the discounted price and the principal value is the investor's return. The value of POs rises as interest rates drop and prepayments accelerate, and falls when interest rates rise and prepayments decline.
- **Interest-only CMOs (IOs)**. IOs exist as a by-product of POs. Whereas POs receive the principal stream from underlying mortgages, IOs receive the interest. IOs sell at a discount. IOs increase in value when interest rates rise and decline when interest rates fall.
- **Accrual bond or Z tranche CMOs** are similar to zero-coupon securities. Holders of a Z

tranche receive no cash payments for much of the life of the security, but the security increases in value as interest is accrued (though not received).

- **Planned amortization class CMOs (PACs)** have established (planned) maturity dates; they are retired first and have no prepayment risk because prepayments are transferred to TACs.
- **Targeted amortization class CMOs (TACs)** are a class of CMOs to which the risk of prepayment is transferred (targeted); TACs investors accept the extension risk in exchange for a slightly higher interest rate. Typically TACs are the last tranches to mature.

### CMO Characteristics

- **Yields**. CMOs typically yield more than Treasury securities.
- **Taxation**. CMOs are fully taxable by federal and state governments.
- **Liquidity**. There is a secondary market for CMOs; thus they are considered liquid.
- **Safety**. Because CMOs are backed by mortgages, they are relatively safe. CMOs carry several kinds of risk:
  - the rate of receipt of principal may vary;
  - reinvestment risk; and
  - the holding period may be longer than anticipated.

## REMICs

Real estate mortgage investment conduits:

- pool investors' money;
- purchase fixed portfolios of real estate mortgages;
- pass interest and gains through to investors;
- qualify for conduit treatment of passed-through income;
- provide significant tax benefits for the investors; and
- do not pass through deductions to investors.

# Questions

1. The function of the Federal National Mortgage Association is to

   A. purchase FHA-insured, VA-guaranteed and conventional mortgages
   B. issue conventional mortgages
   C. provide financing for government-assisted housing
   D. guarantee the timely payment of interest and principal on FHA and VA mortgages

2. How frequently do GNMA pass-through certificates pay interest?

   A. Monthly
   B. Quarterly
   C. Semiannually
   D. Annually

3. Federal Farm Credit Systemwide bonds are obligations of which of the following?

   I. Federal Land Banks
   II. Banks for Cooperatives
   III. Federal Intermediate Credit Banks

   A. I only
   B. I and II only
   C. I and III only
   D. I, II and III

4. The function of the FICB is to

   A. fund loans for farm expenses
   B. fund loans for international credit
   C. manage intermediate credit for the Federal Reserve Board
   D. insure commercial banks

5. All of the following are backed directly by the full faith and credit of the U.S. government EXCEPT
   A. Federal Intermediate Credit Bank issues
   B. Government National Mortgage Association issues
   C. Treasury notes
   D. New Housing Authority bonds

6. Which of the following statements are true regarding U.S. government agency obligations?
   I. They are direct obligations of the U.S. government.
   II. They generally have higher yields than yields of direct U.S. obligations.
   III. The Federal National Mortgage Association is a publicly traded corporation.
   IV. Securities issued by GNMA trade on the NYSE floor.

   A. I and II
   B. I and III
   C. II and III
   D. II and IV

7. CMOs are backed by which of the following?
   A. Mortgages
   B. Real estate
   C. Municipal taxes
   D. Full faith and credit of U.S. government

# Answers

1. **A.** FNMA buys FHA, VA and conventional mortgages and uses them to back the issuance of debt securities. Currently, FNMA issues debentures, mortgage-backed securities and certificates.

2. **A.** Ginnie Mae pass-through certificates are backed by single-family home mortgages. The home owner making a mortgage payment pays both principal and interest monthly into the pool. The pass-through certificates, therefore, pay interest and principal monthly.

3. **D.** Federal Land Banks (FLBs), the Banks for Cooperatives (COOPs) and Federal Intermediate Credit Banks (FICBs) compose the Federal Farm Credit System.

4. **A.** Securities issued by the FICB are used to obtain funds to make short-term loans to farmers for farm expenses.

5. **A.** FICB issues are an obligation of a U.S. government-sponsored agency; the other answers are obligations of U.S. government, agencies or municipalities that are backed by the full faith and credit of the U.S. government.

6. **C.** U.S. government agency debt is an obligation of the issuing agency. This causes agency debt to trade at higher yields reflecting this greater risk. FNMA was created as a government agency but was spun off in 1968 and is now an NYSE-listed corporation. GNMA pass-through certificates trade OTC.

7. **A.** Collateralized mortgage obligations are collateralized by mortgages on real estate. They do not own the underlying real estate, so they are not considered to be backed by it.

# 5 Money-market Securities and Interest Rates

## The Money Market

Money-market instruments provide ways for businesses, financial institutions and governments to meet their short-term obligations and cash requirements yet avoid the time and expense of SEC registration of securities (required for maturities of 270 days and greater).

**Moving money**. The money market shifts funds from institutions with temporary excesses of money to institutions with temporary deficiencies.

**Liquidity and safety**. Money-market instruments are:

- fixed income securities with short-term maturities;
- highly liquid; and
- provide investors with a relatively high degree of safety.

### Issuers

Money-market securities are issued by a number of different entities. The U.S. government and its agencies issue:

- T bills that have begun trading in the secondary market;
- FFCB short-term notes and bonds maturing in one year;
- FHLB short-term discount notes and interest-bearing notes; and
- FNMA short-term discount notes.

**Municipalities**. Municipalities issue:

- bond anticipation notes (BANs)
- tax anticipation notes (TANs)
- revenue anticipation notes (RANs)
- construction loan notes (CLNs)
- project notes (PNs)

**Corporations and banks**. Corporations and banks issue:

- repurchase agreements (repos)
- reverse repurchase agreements
- bankers' acceptances (time drafts)
- commercial paper (prime paper)
- negotiable certificates of deposit
- federal funds
- brokers' and dealers' loans

## Money-market Instruments

### Repurchase Agreements

A transaction in which a broker-delare raises cash by finding a temporary buyer for some of the securities it holds and signing a contract with that party in which the dealer agrees to buy the securities back at a later date is called a **repurchase agreement** (**repo**).

A repo is a fully collateralized loan. The effective rate at which the loan is made is negotiated between the two parties involved. In the event the dealer defaults on the agreement to buy back the securities, the lender can sell the securities (but not the repo) in the secondary market.

Repos are used by:

- U.S. government and municipal securities dealers financing their inventories;
- commercial banks raising short-term funds; and
- the Federal Reserve effecting short-term changes in member bank reserves (fine tuning the monetary supply).

### Reverse Repurchase Agreements

In a **reverse repurchase agreement** (**reverse repo**), a dealer agrees to buy securities from an investor and then sells them back to the investor later at a higher price.

### Bankers' Acceptances

A **banker's acceptance** (**BA**):

- is a short-term time draft with a specified payment date drawn on a bank—essentially a postdated check or line of credit;
- can be used by American corporations as a means of financing international trade (imports and exports of goods and services);
- normally matures between 1 and 270 days after it is written;
- is considered one of the few secured money-market instruments because the holder has a lien against the trade goods in the event the accepting bank fails; and
- can be used by banks as collateral against Federal Reserve Bank (FRB) loans.

### Commercial Paper

- Corporations issue short-term, unsecured **commercial paper** as a means of raising the cash.
- Commercial paper is a less expensive alternative to borrowing from banks when corporations need short-term funds.
- Securities with maturities of less than 270 days are exempt from registration under the 1933 act and are therefore less expensive to issue.
- Both the maturities and the rates of commercial paper are negotiable.
- Commercial paper issues have fixed maturities that range from 1 to 270 days.
- Commercial paper normally is issued in bearer form and at a discount from face value.
- Commercial paper is issued primarily by large, well-known companies with excellent credit ratings and is considered a very safe investment.

**Direct paper**. "Direct paper" or "finance company paper" is the term given to commercial paper sold directly to the public without the use of dealers. High-quality commercial paper is sometimes called *prime paper*.

**Dealer paper**. Dealer paper is commercial paper sold by the issuer through a dealer, rather than directly to the public.

### Certificates of Deposit

Certificates with fixed interest rates and minimum face values of $100,000 are issued and guaranteed by banks and can be traded in the secondary market.

**Nonnegotiable CDs** are those time deposits offered by banks and savings and loans with set maturities and fixed interest rates. The interest paid on these time accounts generally reflects the level of interest rates at the time of their issuance. The Federal Deposit Insurance Corporation (FDIC) guarantees deposits placed with its member banks, generally up to $100,000.

**Negotiable CDs**:

- are time deposits of funds with a bank at a specified rate of interest for a specified period of time;
- must have a minimum face value of $100,000 (most are issued for $1 million or more);

- are unsecured promissory notes guaranteed by the issuing bank;
- are issued with maturities of one year or less,
- can have negotiated maturity dates;
- can be bought and sold in the secondary market before their maturity;
- trade at a price depending on the prevailing interest rates; and
- trade with accrued interest.

# Questions

1. All of the following are money-market instruments EXCEPT

   A. Treasury bills
   B. municipal notes
   C. commercial paper
   D. newly issued Treasury bonds

2. Which of the following is a money-market instrument?

   A. Short-term debt
   B. Long-term debt
   C. Short-term equity
   D. Long-term equity

3. The maximum maturity of commercial paper is how many days?

   A. 90
   B. 180
   C. 270
   D. 360

4. Which of the following statements are true of negotiable certificates of deposit?

   I. The issuing bank guarantees them.
   II. They are callable.
   III. Minimum denominations are $1,000.
   IV. They can be traded in the secondary market.

   A. I, II and III only
   B. I and IV only
   C. II and III only
   D. I, II, III and IV

5. Commercial paper is

   A. a secured note issued by a corporation
   B. a guaranteed note issued by a corporation
   C. a promissory note issued by a corporation
   D. none of the above

6. Which of the following money-market instruments finances imports and exports?

   A. Eurodollars
   B. Bankers' acceptances
   C. ADRs
   D. Commercial paper

7. A banker's acceptance is a

   A. promissory note
   B. capital-market instrument
   C. time draft
   D. means to facilitate the trading of foreign securities

8. Which of the following money-market instruments is a time draft?

   A. Commercial paper
   B. CD
   C. Banker's acceptance
   D. Treasury bill

9. A U.S. government bond dealer sells bonds to another dealer with an agreement to buy back the securities in a specified period of time. This is a(n)

   A. repurchase agreement
   B. reverse repurchase agreement
   C. open market certificate
   D. open market note

# Answers

1. **D.** Newly issued Treasury bonds have a minimum maturity of ten years. Money-market instruments have a maximum maturity of one year.

2. **A.** A money-market instrument is short-term debt with one year or less to maturity.

3. **C.** Commercial paper is normally issued for a maximum period of 270 days.

4. **B.** Negotiable certificates of deposit are issued primarily by banks and are backed by (guaranteed by) the issuing bank.

5. **C.** Commercial paper is a short-term promissory note issued by a corporation.

6. **B.** Bankers' acceptances are used in international trade to finance imports and exports. Eurodollars are not money-market instruments.

7. **C.** A banker's acceptance is a time draft. It facilitates imports and exports, not the trading of foreign securities.

8. **C.** A banker's acceptance is a time draft—that is, a check payable in the future.

9. **A.** The question defines a repurchase agreement.

# Interest Rates

- **Prime rate.** The base rate on corporate loans at large U.S. money center commercial banks. The prime rate is relatively stable and moves only when the major money center banks react to changes in the money supply.
- **Federal funds rate.** The interest rate charged on reserves traded among member banks for overnight use in amounts of $1 million or more. The federal funds rate is the most volatile of the interest rates, changing daily in response to the needs of the borrowing banks, and represents a daily average of the rates charged by the lending banks. The rate fluctuates hourly.
- **Discount rate.** The charge on loans to depository institutions by the New York FRB.
- **Call money rate.** The charge on loans to brokers on stock exchange collateral.
- **Commercial paper.** The rate on commercial paper placed directly by GMAC or the rate on high-grade unsecured notes sold through dealers by major corporations.
- **Certificates of deposit.** Average top rates paid by major New York banks on new issues of negotiable CDs, usually on amounts of $1 million or more. The minimum unit is $100,000. Although the CD rate can fluctuate with market rates, it is normally the least volatile of the interest rates.
- **Bankers' acceptances.** Negotiable, bank-backed business credit instruments typically financing an import order.
- **London Interbank Offered Rate (LIBOR).** The average of interbank offered rates for dollar deposits in the London market based on quotations at five major banks.
- **Treasury bills.** Results of the auction of short-term U.S. government bills sold at a discount from face value in units of $10,000 to $1 million.

# Questions

1. The effective federal funds rate quoted in the business news represents the average rate for the previous
   A. hour
   B. day
   C. week
   D. two weeks

2. The federal funds rate is calculated from the
   A. daily average rate charged by the largest money center banks
   B. daily average rate charged by the national Federal Reserve member banks
   C. weekly average rate charged by the largest money center banks
   D. weekly average rate charged by the national Federal Reserve member banks

3. Which of the following interest rates is considered the MOST volatile?
   A. Discount rate
   B. Federal funds rate
   C. Prime rate
   D. LIBOR

4. The MOST volatile fluctuations in money-market rates would be found in the
   A. prime rate
   B. long-term interest rate
   C. federal funds rate
   D. discount rate

# Answers

1. **B.** The effective federal funds rate as published is a daily average calculated from the rates negotiated between the various banks.

2. **B.** The federal funds rate reflects the rate charged by member banks lending funds to member banks that need to borrow funds overnight to meet reserve requirements.

3. **B.** The federal funds rate is the interest rate that banks with excess reserves charge other banks that are associated with the Federal Reserve System and that need overnight loans to meet reserve requirements. Because the federal funds rate is set daily, it is the most sensitive indicator of interest rate direction.

4. **C.** The federal funds rate is the rate at which banks lend money overnight to each other to maintain reserve requirements. It is the most volatile rate and can fluctuate widely even during a business day. The effective federal funds rate is considered to be the average rate each day throughout the country.

# Eurodollars and the Foreign Currency Markets

## Eurodollars

When U.S. dollars are deposited in banks in countries outside the United States and the deposits remain denominated in U.S. dollars those deposited dollars are known as **Eurodollars**.

## Eurosecurities

**Eurobonds** are any long-term debt instrument that is issued and sold outside the country of the currency in which it is denominated. A U.S. dollar-denominated Eurobond *(Eurodollar bond)* is a bond issued and sold outside the United States, but for which the principal and interest is stated and paid in U.S. dollars. Eurodollar bonds can be issued by foreign corporations, foreign governments, domestic corporations and domestic governments (including municipalities).

The Eurobond market is unregulated and investors usually demand a higher return because there are fewer safeguards. Investors add investments in Eurosecurities to their portfolios to increase diversification.

## Foreign Currencies and the Interbank Market

As a means of handling, transacting business in, trading, lending and consolidating these deposits of foreign currencies, the **interbank market** developed.

**Regulation**. The interbank market is an unregulated, decentralized international market that deals in the various major currencies of the world.

**Exchange stabilization**. The U.S. Treasury department can and does buy and sell U.S. dollars in an attempt to influence the dollar's exchange rate in the interbank market. The money for these transactions comes from the Treasury's **exchange stabilization fund**.

If Treasury officials decide that the U.S. dollar is priced too high in the interbank market, it can sell U.S. dollars in the market. As the supply of dollars in the market increases, the price should decrease and the exchange rate should drop. Conversely, if the Treasury decides that exchange rates for the U.S. dollar are too low, it can buy dollars in the market. Stabilization of a currency through the purchase and sale of a country's currency by its central bank is sometimes known as **pegging**.

**Trading**. The interbank market for foreign currencies functions efficiently as a telephone/telex market conducting international monetary business and exchange from individual bank trading rooms around the world.

- **Spot trades** settle and are delivered in one or two business days (sometimes referred to as the **cash market** or **spot market**).
- **Forward trades** settle in more than two business days (sometimes referred to as the **forward market**).

# Exchange Rates

An **exchange rate** is the rate at which one currency (such as U.S. dollars) can be converted into another (such as Swiss francs or Japanese yen). Exchange rates change daily, affected by hundreds of market-influencing factors (including political, economic, social and market conditions). Exchange rates are usually quoted in terms of the currency of the country in which the quote is published.

**Appreciation**. A currency is said to be appreciating if it is rising in value compared to other securities on the foreign exchange market.

**Depreciation**. If currency falls in value compared to other securities on the foreign exchange market it is depreciating.

## Valuation

**Devaluation**. Devaluation occurs when the value of a currency drops substantially in comparison to the value of gold or to the value of another country's currency.

**Revaluation**. Revaluation is a change in the relative value of a country's currency and can represent either an increase or a decrease in that value. The revaluation of a currency usually occurs as the result of a decision by the government of that country and is implemented by its central bank.

### Speculating in Foreign Currencies

Foreign currencies provide speculative opportunities for sophisticated investors. Risks of foreign currency speculation include:

- the interbank market is unregulated;
- the interbank market is decentralized;
- there does not exist any facility or institution that can provide investors with reliable, timely quotations on foreign currency values; and
- changes in a country's economic, governmental and social policies could have great impact on the current price of its currency in the market.

## Questions

1. Which of the following statements would constitute a valid reason for investing in Eurobonds?

   A. Eurobonds can provide diversification to a portfolio.
   B. Eurobonds can be purchased more inexpensively than comparable U.S. bonds.
   C. Eurobonds are traded in an unregulated market free from government intervention.
   D. Eurobonds can provide an exchange rate hedge against a fall in the U.S. dollar.

2. An international, unregulated, decentralized market for trading currencies as well as debt obligations, and in which prices are affected by economic policies and conditions, is the

   A. Federal Reserve Board
   B. interbank system
   C. London Stock Exchange
   D. International Monetary Fund

## Answers

1. **A.** Eurobonds may provide a sophisticated investor with a means of adding diversification to her portfolio. All of the other answers are either untrue statements or represent disadvantages of investing in Eurobonds.

2. **B.** The interbank system is an international, unregulated, decentralized market involved in trading currencies and debt obligations. As with any market, changes in economic policies and conditions will influence prices.

# 6 Issuing Securities

## The Regulation of New Issues

### The Legislation

**The Securities Act of 1933.** The act of 1933 requires issuers of securities to provide sufficient information for investors to make fully informed buying decisions. This information must be registered with the federal government and published in a prospectus. The act outlaws fraud committed in connection with the underwriting and issuing of all securities (including exempt securities).

**The Glass-Steagall Act (Banking Act) of 1933.** The Glass-Steagall Act forbids commercial banks to underwrite securities (except municipal general obligation bonds) and denies investment bankers the right to open deposit accounts or make commercial loans.

**The Securities Exchange Act of 1934.** The act of 1934 addresses secondary trading of securities, personnel involved in secondary trading and fraudulent trading practices. It also created the Securities and Exchange Commission (SEC) to oversee the industry.

In 1938, the act was amended by the **Maloney Act**, which provides for the establishment of a self-regulatory body to help police the industry. Under the Maloney Act, the National Association of Securities Dealers (NASD) regulates over-the-counter (OTC) trading.

**The Trust Indenture Act of 1939.** The Trust Indenture Act of 1939 was created to provide the same sort of protection to the purchasers of debt securities as is afforded to investors in equities. The act prohibits the sale of any corporate debt security unless it has been issued under a **trust indenture**, the contract that gives the appointed trustee the powers necessary to enforce the issuer's obligations and the debt holders' rights.

### Registration of Securities

The Securities Act of 1933 ( which is also referred to as the *Full Disclosure Act*, the *New Issues Act*, the *Truth in Securities Act* and the *Prospectus Act*) regulates new issues of corporate securities sold to the public by ensuring that the investing public is fully informed about a security and its issuing company when the security is first sold (**primary offerings**). The act requires the registration of new issues of nonexempt securities with the SEC if the mails or any other means of interstate commerce are used to offer or sell the security to the public. It also requires that a prospectus be given to buyers.

The 1933 act protects the investor by:

- requiring registration of new issues that are to be distributed interstate;
- requiring the issuer to provide full and fair disclosure about itself and the offering;
- requiring the issuer to make available all material information necessary for the investor to judge the merit of the issue;

- regulating the underwriting and distribution of primary and secondary new issues; and
- providing *criminal penalties* for fraud in the issuance of new securities.

When a corporation wants to issue its securities to the public, the SEC requires it to:

- supply detailed information about itself and its securities to the SEC; and
- supply the relevant portion of that information to the general investing public.

A **registration statement** must contain:

- a description of the issuer's business;
- the names and addresses of key people in the company, officers and directors, their salaries and a five-year business history of each;
- the amount of corporate securities owned by these key people and by owners of 10% or more of the company;
- the company's capitalization, including its equity and the amount of funded debt;
- a description of how the proceeds will be used; and
- whether the company is involved in any legal proceedings.

### The Prospectus

**The preliminary prospectus.** After an issuer files a registration statement with the SEC:

- a 20-day **cooling-off** period begins (during which the SEC reviews a security's registration statement and can issue a **stop order** if the prospectus does not contain all of the required information);
- the SEC reviews a security's registration statement;
- a registered rep may discuss the new issue with clients and provide them with a **preliminary prospectus (red herring)**; and
- the underwriters and selling group members can use the preliminary prospectus to gather **indications of interest**.

A registered rep *may not* send anything with the preliminary prospectus, including:

- research reports
- *Value Line* sheets
- marketing letters
- other material

A red herring:

- need not include the final price of the securities, commissions, dealer discounts or net proceeds to the company; and
- must carry a legend to the effect that a registration statement has been filed with the SEC, but is not yet effective.

SEC rules prohibit the sale of public offering securities other than by prospectus—no sales are allowed unless and until the buyer is furnished with a final prospectus (securities may be *sold by prospectus only*).

**The final prospectus.** A copy of the final prospectus must precede or accompany all sales confirmations. The prospectus should include all of the following information:

- description of the offering;
- price of the offering;
- selling discounts;
- date of the offering;
- use of the proceeds;
- description of the underwriting, but not the actual contract;
- statement of the possibility that the issue's price may be stabilized;
- history of the business;
- risks to the purchasers;
- description of management;
- material financial information;
- legal opinion concerning the formation of the corporation; and
- SEC disclaimer.

**SEC review.** The SEC reviews the prospectus but does not:

- guarantee the accuracy of the disclosures;
- approve the issue; or
- pass judgment on the investment merit of the issue.

### Delivery of Prospectus by Dealers

- A **preliminary prospectus** must be made available to any customer who expresses interest in the securities about to be distributed in a public offering from the SEC registration filing date to the effective date.
- **The 48-hour rule.** If the issuer is *not* an SEC-reporting company, a preliminary prospectus must be sent to all interested customers and must arrive at least 48 hours prior to mailing a customer purchase confirmation.
- **Aftermarket sales by prospectus.** All sales of public offering stock listed on an exchange or traded on Nasdaq must be accompanied by a final prospectus during the period beginning with the effective date through to:
  - 90 days for an IPO;
  - 40 days for an additional issue not listed on an exchange or quoted on Nasdaq; and
  - 25 days for an additional issue listed on an exchange or quoted on Nasdaq.

### Advertising a New Issue

Advertising and sales literature include any:

- notice;
- circular;
- advertisement;
- letter; or
- other communication published or transmitted to any person.

The only advertising allowed during the cooling-off period is a **tombstone**. Advertising copy and other sales materials will qualify as tombstones and will not be deemed a prospectus if the body copy is limited to the following:

- the name of the issuer of the securities being offered;
- a brief description of the business of the person making the offer;
- the date, time and place of the meeting at which stockholders are to vote on or consent to the proposed transaction;
- a brief description of the planned transaction (material facts and financial information); and/or
- any legend or disclaimer statement required by state or federal law.

Any advertising copy in a tombstone *must* contain the following disclaimers:

- that the registration statement has been filed by the issuer but is not yet effective;
- that the communication does *not* represent an offer to sell the securities described—securities are **sold by prospectus only**;
- the name and address of the person (or firm) to contact for a prospectus; and
- that a response to this advertisement does not obligate the prospect to a buying commitment of any kind (i.e., that it represents only an *indication of interest*).

Open-end investment company securities being sold on a continuous new-issue offering basis are also covered by this rule. Issuers are not required under federal law to publish tombstones.

## Civil Liabilities under the Act of 1933

### Untruths in Registration Statement

If a registration statement contains untrue statements of material fact or omits material facts, any person acquiring the security may sue:

- those who signed the registration statement;
- directors and partners of the issuer;
- anyone named in the registration statement as being or about to become a director or partner of the company;
- accountants, appraisers and other professionals who contributed to the registration statement; and
- the underwriters.

### Untruths in Prospectus or Communication

To avoid civil liability, the seller must prove that he did not know of the misstatements or omissions and that reasonable care was exercised at the time of the sale to prevent communicating any untrue or misleading information of a material nature.

# Questions

1. Which of the following can a registered representative do regarding an underwriting that is in the registration process?

    I. Take an order.
    II. Accept an indication of interest.
    III. Promise a specific number of shares.
    IV. Do a private transaction for a customer.

    A. I and II
    B. I and III
    C. II
    D. II and IV

2. Which of the following statements are true of the Securities Act of 1933?

    I. It requires the registration of exchanges.
    II. It is called the *Truth in Securities Act.*
    III. It requires full and fair disclosure.
    IV. It requires that debt securities be issued with a trust indenture.

    A. I and II
    B. I, II and IV
    C. I and III
    D. II and III

3. Which of the following statements is(are) true?

    I. The SEC controls the release of new issues by approving or disapproving them.
    II. The prospectus contains all of the information that the registration statement contains, including all supporting documents.
    III. It is a criminal offense to imply that the SEC has approved a new issue.

    A. I and II
    B. I and III
    C. II and III
    D. III

4. Which of the following are considered to be nonexempt offerings according to the Securities Act of 1933?

    I. Government securities
    II. Private placement
    III. Public offering of $6,000,000 by a brokerage firm
    IV. Sale of corporate bonds of $10,000,000

    A. I and II
    B. I and III
    C. II, III and IV
    D. III and IV

# Answers

1. **C.** When an issue is in the registration process (during the cooling-off period), sale of the security is prohibited. The registered representative may distribute red herrings (preliminary prospectuses) and take indications of interest. A registered rep may never do private securities transactions.

2. **D.** The Securities Act of 1933 provides for registration of new issues, not for the registration of exchanges. The reason for registering the new issues is to give full and fair disclosure of all material facts for new issues sold to the public.

3. **D.** The SEC neither approves nor disapproves the issue of any security. Any representation to the contrary is a criminal offense. The prospectus is very similar to the registration statement, but it does not contain the documentation that the registration statement has.

4. **D.** The Securities Act of 1933 exempts U.S. government bonds and private placements from registration. Public offerings of less than $5 million are also exempt (under Reg A), so choices III (an offering of $6 million) and IV (corporate) are not exempt. They must be registered with the SEC before they are issued.

# The Underwriting Process

## Underwriting Corporate Securities

### Investment Banking

An investment banker's functions may include:

- advising corporations on the best ways to raise long-term capital;
- raising capital for issuers by distributing new securities;
- buying securities from an issuer and reselling them to the public; and
- distributing large blocks of stock to the public and to institutions.

## Participants in a Corporate New Issue

**Securities and Exchange Commission**. SEC is responsible for:

- reviewing the registration statement filed for the offering;
- sending a deficiency letter to the issuer if the review uncovers problems; and
- declaring the registration statement effective.

**The issuer**. The issuer's duties include:

- filing the registration statement with the SEC;
- filing a registration statement with the states in which it intends to sell securities; and
- negotiating the price of the securities and the amount of the spread with the underwriter.

**National Association of Securities Dealers**. The NASD reviews the underwriting spread to determine fairness and reasonableness of underwriting compensation.

**The individual states**. *Blue-sky laws* require state registration of new issues, broker-dealers and registered reps.

**The underwriter**. The underwriter will assist with registration by advising the corporate issuer on:

- whether to offer stock or bonds;
- tax consequences of the offering; and
- whether to go to the money market for short-term funds or to the capital market for long-term funds.

## Types of Offerings

### Securities Markets

New issue securities are also known as **initial public offering (IPO)** securities. The **additional issue market** is made up of new securities issues from companies that are already publicly owned.

- **Primary offering**. A primary offering is one in which the proceeds of the underwriting go to the **issuing corporation**.
- **Secondary offering**. A secondary offering is one in which underwriting proceeds are paid to the stockholders rather than to the corporation itself.
- **Split offering (combined distribution)**. A split offering is a combination of a primary and a secondary offering.
- **Shelf offering (Rule 415)**. In a **shelf offering**, the issuer can sell limited portions of a registered offering over a two-year period without having to reregister the security or incurring penalties, but it must file a supplemental prospectus prior to each sale.

## Buying Groups

- **Present stockholders**. Present stockholders of the issuing corporation may have a preemptive right to retain their current percentage of ownership of a new issue.
- **The general public**. Securities that are not subscribed to in a rights offering by present

stockholders are next offered to public investors. An investment banker will stand by to underwrite these securities in a transaction known as a **standby underwriting** or **standby offering**.

## Public Offerings and Private Placements

- In a public offering, securities are distributed (sold) to the investing public-at-large through a network of broker-dealers.
- Private placements occur when the institutional buyer, using an investment banker, purchases securities from the issuing corporation.

## Time Line for an Underwriting

- **Forming the syndicate**. In competitive bidding, the syndicate is assembled first and syndicate members work together to arrive at the bid. In a negotiated underwriting, the syndicate may be formed after the issuer and underwriting manager have negotiated the terms of the offering.
- **Preparing documents**. The underwriter may assist the issuer in preparing and filing the registration statement and prospectus.
- **Cooling-off period**. After the issue is filed with the SEC, a cooling-off period ensues. The registration can become effective as soon as the 20th calendar day following the date the SEC receives it.
- **Blue-skying the issue**. The syndicate manager takes the preliminary registration packet to the various states in which it plans to offer the securities. If the issue meets the registration requirements of a particular state brokers within that state can sell the security to state residents. Most states will exempt securities from individual registration if they are listed on a regional or national stock exchange or qualify as a Nasdaq or NNM stock.
  - *Registration by filing* is available to companies that file a registration statement with the SEC, meet certain requirements and notify the state administrator of the intent to offer or sell the security. It is a commonly used method for registering shares that are already trading in the secondary market.
  - If an application to register a security with the SEC under the Securities Act of 1933 currently is pending, *registration by coordination* may be used and the security may be registered simultaneously with the state administrator of the USA.
  - *Registration by qualification* involves the filing of all required registration statements with a state administrator in order to qualify an issue of securities.
- **Other state registration requirements**. A person or broker-dealer must usually be registered in any state in which he sells or attempts to sell securities.
- **Due diligence**. The preliminary studies, investigations, research, meetings and compilation of information about a corporation and a proposed new issue that go on during an underwriting are known collectively as **due diligence** (the exercise of reasonable effort and care).
- **Pricing the new issue**. The price of an issue is determined by the effective date of the registration. It is based on such factors as:
  - indications of interest from the underwriter's book;
  - prevailing market conditions;
  - price the syndicate members will accept
  - price-earnings ratios of similar companies; and
  - company's dividend payment record and financial health.
- **Pricing factors**. Pricing new issues takes into account the following factors:
  - company's present PE
  - recent offerings
- **Hot issues**. A hot issue is any security that sells at an immediate premium in the public offering aftermarket.

- **Effective date**. The effective date of an issue is the first date on which the securities can be sold to the public.
- **Final prospectus**. The final prospectus must be delivered with each sale of a newly issued security and must contain all the information that is found in Part I of the registration statement.
- **Selling the securities**. The syndicate sells the securities to the public.
- **Stabilizing and sticky issues**. Sticky issues are those for which there is considerably less demand than supply. The underwriter has the option of *stabilizing* the security by bidding for shares in the open market until the end of the offering period.
  - Stabilizing bids must *not* be made at a price higher than the public offering price. This is called *pegging* (or *fixing*) and is prohibited by the SEC.
  - The syndicate manager has the option of increasing the selling concession if the issue is selling poorly.

# Questions

1. A standby underwriting is used

   A. for a company going public for the first time
   B. in a secondary offering
   C. in a best efforts underwriting
   D. in a rights offering

2. ALFA Enterprises has filed an offering of 425,000 shares of common stock. One-third of the shares are being sold by existing stockholders, and the balance are new shares. Which of the following statements are true?

   I. ALFA will receive the proceeds from the entire sale.
   II. This offering is a combined distribution.
   III. The selling stockholders will receive some of the proceeds.
   IV. This offering is an exchange distribution.

   A. I and II
   B. I and IV
   C. II and III
   D. II, III and IV

3. The principal functions of an investment banker are to

   I. distribute securities to the public
   II. provide a secondary market
   III. provide financing for the individual
   IV. advise the issuer about alternatives in raising capital

   A. I and II
   B. I and IV
   C. II and III
   D. III and IV

4. The underwriting manager is the
   A. employee who supervises the underwriting activities of an investment banker
   B. broker-dealer that supervises the activity of the issuer on authority of the SEC
   C. broker-dealer that publishes the offering prospectus
   D. broker-dealer that supervises the activity of the underwriting syndicate and selling group

5. Which of the following are considered by an underwriter when establishing the offering price?
   I. Projected earnings for the company
   II. Likely dividends to be paid over the coming years
   III. Demand for the security by the investing public
   IV. Earnings multiples for other companies in the market in the same industry

   A. I and II only
   B. I, II and III only
   C. I, II and IV only
   D. I, II, III and IV

# Answers

1. **D.** The standby underwriter acts as a guarantor to the corporation, promising that the securities not purchased through a rights offering will be purchased by the underwriter. The underwriter then distributes the remaining shares on a firm commitment basis.

2. **C.** This is a combined primary and secondary distribution. The corporation receives the proceeds from the shares it sells and the selling stockholders receive the proceeds from the remainder.

3. **B.** The principal functions of the underwriter are to advise the issuer about the type of securities and the timing of the issue and to sell securities to the public.

4. **D.** The underwriting manager supervises the activity of the syndicate and selling group. The issuer publishes the prospectus.

5. **D.** The underwriter would consider all the factors listed when pricing a new issue.

# The Underwriting Syndicate

## Forming the Underwriting Syndicate

- **Underwriting manager**. The investment banker that negotiates with the issuer is known as the *underwriting manager* or *syndicate manager*.
- **Syndicate**. In a firm commitment offering, syndicate members make a commitment to distribute an agreed-on amount of the issue (their participation or bracket).
- **Selling group**. Selling group members act as agents with no commitment to buy securities.

### Syndicate Structure

Corporate underwriting is negotiated between the issuer and investment banker. This negotiated agreement is known as the **underwriting agreement**. The following are responsibilities of the syndicate manager:

- Execute the underwriting agreement with the issuer.
- Formulate the agreement among underwriters (also known as the *syndicate letter*), which establishes the underwriters' liability (Western/divided or Eastern/undivided) and compensation.
- Obtain from each member of the syndicate a commitment to underwrite a specific amount of the issue.
- Determine how many shares from its bracket each firm will sell.
- Reallocate any securities not sold by a member of the syndicate to other syndicate members with excess demand or to members of the selling group.
- Determine whether or not to establish a selling group.
- Form the selling group to assist in the distribution of the offering.

## Forming the Selling Group

Selling group members have no financial responsibility to the issuer, nor to anyone else, because they are not underwriters. Members of the selling group are under contract with the underwriters as to how, when and at what price the securities in question will be distributed to the public. The **selling group agreement** typically contains the following terms:

- statement that the manager acts for all the underwriters;
- amount of securities each selling group member will be allotted and the tentative POP at which the securities will be sold;
- provisions as to how and when payment for shares allotted to each selling group member is to be made to the managing underwriter; and
- legal provisions limiting each selling group member's liability in conjunction with the underwriting.

## Underwriting Compensation

The price to the issuer is referred to as the **underwriting proceeds**, and the price to the buying investors as the **public offering price**. The underwriting spread consists of:

1. manager's fee
2. underwriting fee
3. selling concession

### Industry Standard Practices

The following percentages are representative of the spread components when corporate equity issues are being underwritten:

- Syndicate manager's fee, 10% to 20%
- Underwriting fee, 20% to 30%
- Selling concession (takedown), 50% to 60%

## Questions

1. The compensation that the selling group receives is called the

   A. concession
   B. allowance
   C. discount
   D. spread

2. In a public offering at $9 per share, the underwriting spread is $1. The issuer receives how much per share?

   A. $7
   B. $8
   C. $9
   D. $10

Use the following information to answer questions 3 and 4. A corporation is offering 300,000 shares to the public at $15 per share. The manager's fee is $.15 per share, the underwriter's fee is $.20 per share, and the concession is $.65 per share.

3. How much does the public pay per share?

   A. $13.75
   B. $14.00
   C. $15.00
   D. $16.00

4. The total amount received by the issuer is

   A. $4,000,000
   B. $4,200,000
   C. $4,500,000
   D. $5,000,000

## Answers

1. **A.** The selling group receives a concession or reallowance. The underwriting spread or discount is the total amount due the syndicate.

2. **B.** If the offering is $9 per share and the underwriting spread is $1, the net to the issuer is $9 minus the $1, or $8 per share.

3. **C.** The corporation is issuing the stock at $15 per share, and that's the price the public pays.

4. **B.** The underwriting spread is composed of the $.15 management fee, the $.20 underwriting fee and the $.65 selling concession, for a total of $1. The issuer will receive $14 per share ($15 POP minus the $1 spread) times 300,000 shares, which is $4,200,000.

# Types of Underwriting Commitments

**Firm commitment.** The underwriter contracts with the issuing corporation to buy the securities described in the contract, within a defined price and quantity range, on or about a given date.

- **Allocation of losses.** If part of an issue that is being distributed under a firm commitment contract goes unsold, any losses incurred are prorated among the underwriting firms according to their participation.
- **Negotiated underwritings.** In a negotiated underwriting, the issuer and the investment banker *negotiate* the terms of the offering.
- **Competitive bid underwritings.** In a competitive bid, a state or municipal government unit will invite investment bankers to bid for the bonds and will award the securities to the underwriter that submits the highest bid price.
- **Risks beyond the underwriter's control.** Underwriters may exercise "market-out" provisions (suspend or abort the offering) if a *material, adverse event* occurs that affects the issuing corporation and impairs the investment quality of the securities to be offered.
- **Risks that the underwriter must assume.** Underwriters may not exercise market-out provisions if a *nonmaterial, adverse event* occurs that affects the issuing company but does not impair the investment quality of the securities to be offered.

**Best efforts.** The **best efforts** arrangement calls for the underwriter to buy securities as agent from the issuer contingent on the underwriter's ability to sell them.

**All or none.** In an **all or none (AON)** underwriting, all shares must be sold or the underwriting is canceled. Any purchase amounts collected from investors during the offering period must be held in **escrow**, pending final disposition of the underwriting.

**Mini-max.** A **mini-max** offering is a best efforts underwriting with a floor and a ceiling on the amount of securities the issuer is willing to sell.

**Standby underwritings.** When a publicly held corporation proposes to issue additional common stock and is obliged to protect the *proportional ownership interest* of the current stockholders, a standby underwriting comes into play. The company must first offer any additional issue of the same class of stock to the existing stock owners before offering the securities to the general public.

**Eastern and Western underwritings.** The agreement among underwriters details each underwriter's commitment and liability—particularly for any shares that remain unsold at the termination of the underwriting syndicate.

- **Eastern (undivided) account.** In an Eastern (or undivided) underwriting, every firm shares the risk that one or more underwriters will not be able to dispose of their full allotments of stock. If this happens, the cost of the unsold stock is spread and assessed *pro rata* to all of the underwriters.
- **Western (divided) account.** In a Western (or divided) underwriting, if one or more of the syndicate members is unable to sell its allotment in full, those shares remain that firm's responsibility.

# Questions

1. Which of the following are types of underwritings?

   I. Firm commitment
   II. All or none
   III. Standby
   IV. Best efforts

   A. I and II only
   B. I, III and IV only
   C. II and III only
   D. I, II, III and IV

2. In a best efforts offering, an underwriter

   A. makes no guarantee that an offering will be sold
   B. makes a best efforts attempt to reduce the underwriting spread
   C. guarantees a minimum price and makes a best efforts attempt to increase that price
   D. makes a best efforts attempt to bring the security to market within the cooling-off period

3. When an underwriter is NOT responsible for unsold securities, it is engaged in which type of underwriting?

   A. Best efforts
   B. Firm commitment
   C. Negotiated
   D. Standby

4. An underwriting that is canceled by the issuing corporation if the issue is not 100% subscribed for is a(n)

   A. firm commitment
   B. best efforts
   C. all or none
   D. mini-max agreement

# Answers

1. **D.** All of the choices listed are types of underwritings.

2. **A.** In a best efforts underwriting, the underwriter acts as an agent. It makes its best effort to sell the entire issue but is not responsible for unsold securities.

3. **A.** In a best efforts underwriting, the broker-dealer is an agent for the issuer and has no responsibility for purchasing unsold securities.

4. **C.** An all or none offering is a type of best efforts. If the securities are not 100% sold, the entire issue is aborted and the money returned to each prospective purchaser.

# Exemptions from the Securities Act of 1933

## Exempt Issuers and Securities

The following issuers and securities are not required to be registered with the SEC:

- U.S. government securities;
- state and municipal bonds;
- commercial paper and bankers' acceptances;
- insurance policies and fixed annuities;
- national and state bank securities;
- building and loan (S&L) securities;
- common carrier (e.g., trucking, airline and railroad) securities;
- farmers' cooperative securities;
- small business investment company (SBIC) securities;
- charitable, religious, educational and nonprofit association issues; and
- private transactions in securities if they do not involve the use of the U.S. mail or other means of interstate commerce.

## Exempt Transactions

The following transactions are not required to be registered with the SEC:

- **Regulation A: small offerings**. The Reg A exemption permits issuers to raise up to $5 million capital in a twelve-month period without full registration by filing an abbreviated notice of sale (**offering circular**) with the regional office of the SEC.
- **Regulation D: private placements (Rule 506)**. The SEC does not require registration of an offering privately placed with:
  - officers or other insiders of the issuer;
  - financial institutions or other similar investors that do not need SEC protection (accredited investors); or
  - a maximum of 35 individual (nonaccredited) investors.
  - An accredited investor is generally accepted to be one who has a net worth of $1 million or more; or has had an annual income of $200,000 or more in each of the two most recent years (or $300,000 jointly with a spouse) and who has a reasonable expectation of reaching the same income level in the current year.
- **Rule 144**. *Control* securities are owned by directors, officers or persons who own 10% or more of any type of outstanding securities of the company. Persons who have a control relationship with an issuer are considered **affiliated persons**. *Restricted* securities are those acquired through some means other than a registered public offering (most restricted securities are acquired through private placements).
  - **Sales volume restrictions**. Rule 144 limits the amount of stock control persons can sell over any 90-day period to the greater of 1% of the total outstanding shares of the same class at the time of sale (as reported by the issuing corporation), or the average weekly trading volume in the stock over the past four weeks on all exchanges (all markets), or as reported through Nasdaq.
  - **Sales by control persons** in amounts not exceeding 500 shares or $10,000 in sale proceeds are permitted without filing a Form 144.
- **Rule 144a**. Rule 144a covers nonregistered domestic and foreign securities sold to institutional investors in the United States. Securities acquired in a Rule 144a transaction are considered restricted securities.
- **Rule 145**. The transactions covered by Rule 145 are categorized as:
  - **Reclassifications**. When one class of securities is to be exchanged internally for another class this is considered a reclassification and is covered by Rule 145.
  - **Merger or consolidation**. Stockholders in a target company are offered securities

in another company in exchange for the surrender of their stock.
  - **Transfer of assets**. All or a portion of one company's business assets are exchanged for another company's securities.

- **Rule 147: intrastate offerings**. Rule 147 exempts offerings from registration under the following conditions:
  - The issuer of the securities has its principal office and receives at least 80% of its income within that state.
  - At least 80% of its assets are located within that state.
  - At least 80% of the proceeds of the offering are used within that state.
  - The broker-dealer acting as underwriter is a resident of that state and has an office in the state.
  - All of the purchasers are residents of that state (as verified by voter registration or drivers licenses).

## Antifraud Regulations of the Acts of 1933 and 1934

Although a security might be exempt from the registration requirement, *no offering is exempt from the antifraud provisions* of the Securities Act of 1933.

Securities that are exempt from registration under the act of 1933 are not subject to most of the Securities Exchange Act of 1934's rules and regulations. No security is exempt from the act of 1934's antifraud and market manipulation regulations.

# Questions

1. A Regulation A exemption applies to
   A. the minimum margin requirements of $5,000 for an underwriter
   B. the minimum net capital of $5,000 for an underwriter
   C. a new issue of $5,000,000 or more
   D. a new issue of $5,000,000 or less

2. SEC Rule 147 provides exemption from registration for
   A. small issues
   B. securities issued by banks
   C. intrastate issues
   D. private placements

3. Under the intrastate offering rule, when may a resident purchaser of the securities resell them to a nonresident?
   A. Three months after the first sale made in that state
   B. Six months after the last sale made in that state
   C. Nine months after the first sale made in that state
   D. None of the above

4. The private placement rule states that the person to whom the offer of securities is made must be an informed person
   A. but the person need not have access to the same type of information contained in a registration statement
   B. who has a net worth of $2 million
   C. who either has access to the same type of information contained in a registration statement or is furnished such information
   D. or a person who signs a statement testifying that he will not hold the broker-dealer responsible for any losses

# Answers

1. **D.** Regulation A is the exemption for small issues with a maximum size of $5,000,000.

2. **C.** Rule 147 exempts intrastate issues from registration with the SEC. To qualify:

- The issuer must have its principal office and at least 80% of its assets in the state.
- At least 80% of the proceeds must be used within the state.
- The underwriter must be a state resident.
- All purchasers must be state residents.
- Purchasers may not resell the securities to a resident of another state for at least nine months.

3. **D.** If you chose answer C, you were close but not quite correct. Purchasers of an intrastate offering may sell their securities to residents of another state no sooner than nine months after the last sale of the issue.

4. **C.** In a private placement, securities can be offered to any number of accredited investors (net worth $1,000,000 or more; income of $200,000 per year). Any investor must have access to information about the issuing company and the issue.

# Freeriding and Withholding: Hot Issues

**Hot issues.** Hot issues are public offering securities that sell at an *immediate premium* over the public offering price (POP) in the secondary market.

**Freeriding and withholding.** A member's failure to make a bona fide offering at the POP is considered *freeriding and withholding*. Any NASD member firm engaged in the distribution of a stock that proves to be a hot issue must make a bona fide public offering of the securities at the announced POP.

**Restricted accounts.** Hot issues may not be sold to any individual listed below:

- the underwriters;
- any NASD member broker-dealer;
- any person associated with an NASD member (including officers, directors, general partners, registered representatives, employees and agents of the member firm that is underwriting the hot issue, as well as any other member firm or persons associated with another member firm, such as officers, owners and employees);
- supported family members of a person associated with an NASD member; or
- any person financially dependent on a person associated with an NASD member.

**Exceptions for normal investment practice.** Under certain circumstances, limited amounts of a hot issue may be sold to:

- **Nonsecurities persons associated with the underwriting.** People in this category (finders, accountants, attorneys, financial consultants or others performing a fiduciary service for the managing underwriter) should not be allowed to purchase hot issues unless it can be proved that they regularly and routinely buy public offering securities of the same type (normal investment practice).
- **Bank trust officers.** These officers and similar senior officers of financial institutions would be in a position to direct their firms' securities business to the broker-dealer; therefore, they may not be sold shares of a hot issue.
- **Family members.** Relatives of the above and nonsupported family members of any classified accounts and members of the family of any securities industry personnel who are supported to a material extent by that person may not buy a hot issue. Any person, including a spouse, child, parent or in-law, to whom the securities industry person contributes direct, material financial support is considered immediate family.

**Nonsupported family members.** A family member who is *not* materially supported by any securities industry personnel may buy a hot issue if it can be proved that the person buys similar types of securities regularly and routinely or is purchasing from a broker-dealer that does not employ the restricted person.

### Sales to Restricted Accounts

The NASD concerns itself with three measurements when monitoring sales of hot issues to people in the restricted categories defined above (except for securities industry personnel) and when determining whether a violation of the freeriding and withholding rule has occurred.

**Normal investment practice.** A hot issue can be sold to a restricted individual if that type of security is consistent with the individual's investment patterns in terms of:

- the frequency with which similar securities have been purchased;
- the dollar amounts of these previous investments; and
- a clear history of buying new issue securities, provided that the normal investment practice includes buying new issues that are not considered hot.

**Disproportionate allocation.** An underwriter or a selling group member will not be accused of a rule violation if no more than 10% of the firm's allotment of hot issues is sold to restricted accounts.

**Insubstantiality**. Sales to restricted accounts that total less than 10% of the member firm's allotment should not be concentrated in only one or a few accounts.

## Hot Issue Sales Supervision

- **Sales to banks and other investment intermediaries**. *Directed sales* of hot issue stock to these accounts are not allowed unless inquiry is made as to who the end investors are and verification is made that they are not in the restricted account category.
- **Violations by members and associated persons**. If an NASD member firm or associated person sells to or otherwise places a hot issue with another member firm or associated person, this is a violation.

# Questions

1. "Freeriding and withholding" refers to

   A. distributing new issues valued at amounts exceeding the cost
   B. purchasing securities with the intent of selling them before the settlement date
   C. a member of an underwriting or selling group failing to make a public offering of a security at the public offering price
   D. none of the above

# Answers

1. **C.** "Freeriding and withholding" is the failure of an NASD member to make a bona fide public offering at the public offering price of a hot issue. A hot issue, of course, is an issue that sells at a premium on its first trading day. An example would be when a securities firm sees that a new issue is selling at a premium and decides not to sell it to the public, but instead keeps a substantial portion of the shares in its own investment account to benefit the owners of the firm.

# 7 Trading Securities

## The Regulation of Trading

### The Securities Exchange Act of 1934

The intent of the Securities Exchange Act of 1934 is to maintain a fair and orderly market for the investing public. The act of 1934 addresses the:

- creation of the SEC;
- regulation of exchanges;
- regulation of credit by the FRB;
- registration of broker-dealers;
- regulation of insider transactions, short sales and proxies;
- regulation of trading activities;
- regulation of client accounts ;
- customer protection rule;
- regulation of the OTC market; and
- net capital rule.

#### The Securities and Exchange Commission

The SEC has the responsibility and authority to regulate the securities markets. The SEC has established rules regarding:

- net capital requirements for broker-dealers;
- hypothecation of customers' securities;
- commingling of broker-dealer securities with those of customers;
- the use of manipulative and deceptive devices; and
- broker-dealer recordkeeping.

#### Registration of Exchanges and Firms

The national securities exchanges must file a registration statement. When they register, the exchanges agree to comply with and help enforce the rules of this act and institute and enforce disciplinary procedures for members who do not use just and equitable practices.

Companies that list securities on those exchanges must register with the SEC. Each listed company must file quarterly reports and annual reports informing the SEC of its financial status and other information.

Exchange members who do business with the public must register as well as broker-dealers that do business OTC or that use the mail (or telephone, TV, radio, etc.) to conduct OTC business. There are some exemptions from registration, including any broker-dealer that deals only on an intrastate basis. An *intra*state firm, however, cannot use the mail or other instruments of *inter*state commerce and still qualify for the exemption from registration.

#### Financial Statements Sent to Customers

Every broker-dealer must furnish financial statements to customers. A **customer** is any person for whom the broker-dealer holds funds or securities or anyone who has made a securities transaction at any time up to one month before the date of the financial statement. Excluded from the definition of "customer" are other broker-dealers, partners or officers of the broker-dealer, and subordinated lenders. NASD rules require a broker-dealer to provide a copy of its current balance sheet to any active customer who makes a written request for one.

**Audited financial statements.** Audited financials must be furnished to customers within 105 days of the annual audit report required by the SEC. This report is actually a part of the FOCUS reporting system and is prepared as of the broker-dealer's year end. If the year end is December 31st, financial statements must be sent to customers no later than April 15th of the following year. The audited financial statement must contain:

- a balance sheet;
- the amount of net capital computed under SEC Rule 15c3-1;
- a statement of changes in subordinated loans;
- whether the audit disclosed any material inadequacy in the broker-dealer's records; and
- a statement to the effect that the most recent audited full statement of financial condition is available for inspection either at the broker-dealer's office or at the SEC.

# Questions

1. The Securities Exchange Act of 1934 has some sections that deal with

    I. the regulation of investment companies
    II. trading activities such as short sales, stabilizing and the registration of over-the-counter brokers and dealers
    III. the form and content of the prospectus that must be given to all prospective purchasers of a security
    IV. the registration of persons engaged in the business of advising others about investment company transactions

    A. I and II only
    B. II only
    C. II and IV only
    D. I, II, III and IV

2. Under the Securities Exchange Act of 1934, the Securities and Exchange Commission does all of the following EXCEPT

    A. regulate the extension of credit by broker-dealers
    B. regulate the activities of members of national securities exchanges
    C. regulate the solicitation of proxies
    D. provide rules for the segregation of securities owned by clients

## Answers

1. **B.** Choice II is the only correct answer. The others are dealt with under other securities legislation: choice I, the Investment Company Act of 1940; choice III, the Securities Act of 1933; choice IV, the Investment Advisers Act of 1940.

2. **A.** The Securities Exchange Act of 1934 does speak to the regulation of credit by broker-dealers—but it delegates this responsibility to the Federal Reserve Board, not the SEC.

# Securities Markets and Broker-Dealers

## Securities Markets

The market in which securities are bought and sold is also known as the *secondary* market (as opposed to the *primary* market for new issues).

- **Exchange market**. The NYSE and other exchanges on which *listed* securities are traded compose the exchange market.
- **Over-the-counter market**. The dealer market in which *unlisted* securities (securities not listed on any exchange) are traded is called the *over-the-counter (OTC) market.*
- **Third market (OTC-listed)**. The third market is a trading market for institutional investors in which *exchange-listed* securities are bought and sold (usually in large blocks) in the OTC market.
- **Fourth market**. The fourth market is a market for institutional investors in which stock changes hands between banks, mutual funds, pension managers and other types of institutions, usually through the INSTINET service.

### Trading Hours

- **Exchange business hours**. Both the NYSE and AMEX begin trading at 9:30 am EST each business day and close trading at 4:00 pm EST.
- **OTC business hours**. Normal hours for retail OTC trading are the same as those of the NYSE: 9:30 am to 4:00 pm EST, Monday through Friday.

### Listed Markets

- **Location**. Listed markets (such as the NYSE or AMEX) have a central marketplace and trading floor facilities.
- **Pricing system**. Listed markets operate as **double-auction markets**. Floor brokers compete among themselves to execute trades at prices most favorable to the public.
- **Major force in the market**. The **specialist** is charged with maintaining an orderly market and providing price continuity. The specialist fills limit and market orders for the public and trades for his own account to either stabilize or facilitate trading when serious supply and demand imbalances occur.

### OTC Markets

- **Location**. There is no central marketplace for OTC trading. Trading takes place over the phone, over computer networks and in trading rooms across the country.
- **Pricing system**. The OTC market works through an **interdealer network**. Registered market makers compete among themselves to post the best bid and ask prices. The OTC market is a *negotiated* market.
- **Major force in the market**. The **market makers** are broker-dealers that post the current bid and ask prices and buy and sell securities in transactions with the public. The best price at which the public can buy (best ask) and the best price at which the public can sell (best bid) are called the **inside market**.

### Trading Halts

In the event that a trading halt is called for a particular security in a particular market or exchange, all trading in that security stops. During the halt, however, open orders may be canceled and options may be exercised. Moreover, a trading halt in a particular security in one market does not automatically affect trading of that security in other markets. Whenever a market halts or suspends trading in an eligible security, NASD members may continue to conduct trading in the OTC market in that security during the halt or suspension and to report all last sale prices for display on the Consolidated Tape.

## Role of the Broker-Dealer

**Brokers**. Brokers are agents that arrange trades for clients and charge them a commission.

**Dealers**. When firms act as dealers (principals), they buy and sell securities for their own accounts (inventory). A broker-dealer that is buying and selling for its own account is sometimes said to be **position trading**. Taking a position in a security also can be referred to as being *in control* of that amount of the security.

- When selling from their inventory, dealers charge their clients a markup rather than a commission. A markup is the difference between the current interdealer offering price and the actual price charged the client. When a price to a client includes a dealer's markup, it is called the *net price*.

**Broker-dealer role in transactions**. A firm is prohibited from acting as both a broker and a dealer in the same transaction.

# Questions

1. The over-the-counter market is a(n)

   A. negotiated market
   B. auction market
   C. transfer market
   D. double-auction market

2. Which of the following statements are true regarding the OTC market?

   I. It facilitates the trading of stock not listed on an exchange.
   II. It is a connection of broker-dealers via computers and phones.
   III. Stocks of banks and insurance companies typically trade in the OTC market.

   A. I and II only
   B. I and III only
   C. II and III only
   D. I, II and III

3. Which of the following can make a market?

   I. Broker
   II. Dealer
   III. Floor broker
   IV. Principal

   A. I and II
   B. II and III
   C. II and IV
   D. III and IV

4. When a firm "position trades," it

   I. makes a market in securities
   II. trades for the firm's account
   III. sells short in all transactions
   IV. executes agency trades for customers

   A. I and II only
   B. I, II and IV only
   C. II and III only
   D. I, II, III and IV

# Answers

1. **A.** The OTC is a *negotiated* market. The exchanges are *auction* markets. The new issue market is the *primary* market. There is no such thing as the "transfer market."

2. **D.** All of the statements are true regarding the OTC market.

3. **C.** Making markets involves buying and selling for one's own account, which are principal activities. Dealers act as principals in trades; brokers do not.

4. **A.** "Position trading" is simply trading as principal for the firm's inventory. Position trading may involve short or long positions.

# The New York Stock Exchange

The NYSE provides a central location for the transaction of its members' business and maintains high standards of integrity among its members, who are governed by a comprehensive set of rules that promote principles of fair trade. The Exchange itself does not buy and sell stocks.

## Exchange Listing Requirements

**Listing**. The initial requirements for any corporation that wants its stock listed on the NYSE are as follows:

- The market value of its publicly held shares must be at least $18 million.
- At least 1.1 million shares must be publicly held.
- Two thousand stockholders must each hold 100 shares or more (2,000 round-lot owners).
- Corporate earnings before federal income tax must be at least $2.5 million for the latest fiscal year and at least $2 million for each of the two preceding years.

Consideration is also given to:

- whether there is national interest in the company
- the market for its products (size, diversification, etc.)
- the strength and stability of the company
- prospects for maintaining position in an expanding industry
- the company's prospective earnings

**Delisting**. The NYSE may delist companies:

- if the number of stockholders, shares outstanding or total market value of outstanding shares falls below certain levels
- that engage in activities adverse to investors' interests, including failure to disclose financial statements or to solicit proxies for all meetings.

In order to receive the Exchange's permission to delist, a company must have approval from its stockholders. A decision by the board of directors alone is not sufficient justification for delisting, and the Exchange will not approve the security's removal from the list.

## Trading on the Floor of the Exchange

Only NYSE members (the individual owners of seats) can trade on the floor. These traders are of four types:

1. commission house brokers
2. two-dollar brokers
3. registered traders
4. specialists

### Auction Market

Exchange securities are bought and sold in an **auction (or double auction) market.**

**Priority, precedence and parity**. When more than one broker enters the crowd with the same bid or offer, the specialist awards the trade in the following order:

1. priority—first order in
2. precedence—largest order of those submitted
3. parity—random drawing

### Volatile Market Conditions

**Circuit breaker rules**. If the Dow Jone Industrial Average increases or decreases by 50 points within one day, the NYSE restricts program trading and index arbitrage transactions by professional traders.

If the DJIA falls 250 points wihin one day, trading on the Exchange halts for one hour. If the DJIA continues to decline by 400 points, trading halts for an additional two hours.

## Nine Bond Rule

Orders for fewer than ten bonds must be shown on the floor of the Exchange before being traded OTC.

## Arbitrage

- **Market arbitrage**. A trade that takes advantage of price differences between markets is known as a market arbitrage.
- **Convertible security arbitrage**. A trade that takes advantage of price differences between securities (such as convertibles) is known as a convertible securities arbitrage.
- **Risk arbitrage**. A trade that takes advantage of price changes due to extraordinary events is known as risk arbitrage.

# Questions

1. The New York Stock Exchange serves investors by

   A. offering securities for sale
   B. buying securities for members
   C. both A and B
   D. neither A nor B

2. Which of the following statements about the NYSE are true?

   I. The NYSE is a corporation operated by a board of directors.
   II. Membership on the Exchange is fixed at 1,000.
   III. Allied members can trade on the floor of the Exchange.
   IV. NYSE auction procedures are based on rules of priority, precedence and parity.

   A. I and II
   B. I and IV
   C. II and III
   D. III and IV

3. A company whose stock is listed on the NYSE may also have its stock listed on the

   A. American Stock Exchange
   B. Chicago Stock Exchange
   C. Chicago Board Options Exchange
   D. Chicago Board of Trade

4. Which of the following brokers would be allowed to trade on the NYSE?

   I. Registered representative
   II. Specialist
   III. Registered trader
   IV. Commission broker

   A. I and II only
   B. II and III only
   C. II, III and IV only
   D. I, II, III and IV

5. All of the following are used in awarding trades on the NYSE EXCEPT

   A. priority
   B. parity
   C. premium
   D. precedence

6. On the NYSE, specialists act as

   I. brokers for the public
   II. brokers for other brokers
   III. dealers

   A. I and III only
   B. II only
   C. II and III only
   D. I, II and III

7. Who is permitted to transact business on the floor of the Exchange?

   A. Members
   B. Allied members
   C. Floor clerks
   D. Floor officials

8. In order to be considered for listing on the NYSE, a corporation must meet which of the following requirements?

   I. At least 2,000 stockholders must each own at least 100 shares.
   II. At least 4,000 stockholders must each own at least 100 shares.
   III. A national interest in trading the stock must be present.
   IV. Voting by stockholders must be allowed through the solicitation of proxies.

   A. I, III and IV
   B. II and III
   C. II, III and IV
   D. II and IV

9. A company's stock is listed on the NYSE. Which of the following could result in the company's being delisted?

   I. The company files for bankruptcy under Chapter 11.
   II. The company issues nonvoting common stock.
   III. Public interest in the stock declines considerably.
   IV. The company does not mail out proxy statements.

   A. I and III only
   B. I and IV only
   C. II and IV only
   D. I, II, III and IV

# Answers

1. **D.** The NYSE provides facilities for trading. The members, not the Exchange, buy and sell securities.

2. **B.** Membership is fixed at 1,366. Only members can trade on the Exchange floor.

3. **B.** Stock listed on the NYSE can also be listed on regional exchanges, but not on the American Stock Exchange. The Chicago Board of Trade is a commodities exchange, and the Chicago Board Options Exchange is an options exchange.

4. **C.** Only members can trade on the floor of the Exchange. Registered reps may not.

5. **C.** Priority, precedence and parity are used for breaking ties on the floor of the NYSE. Priority goes to the first bid or offer. If priority cannot be established, the largest bid or offer takes precedence. If neither priority nor precedence can be established, parity exists and the trade is awarded by drawing straws or tossing a coin.

6. **C.** Specialists trade only with other members of the Exchange, not with the public. They act as dealers for their own accounts and as brokers for other members.

7. **A.** Only members of the Exchange are permitted to trade securities on the floor of the Exchange.

8. **A.** To be NYSE-listed, a corporation must have at least 2,000 stockholders; it must allow stockholders to vote; there must be a national interest in trading the stock; and minimum earnings and asset tests must be met.

9. **D.** The NYSE takes many factors into consideration when determining whether a company should be delisted. Among the factors are all the choices given: the company files for bankruptcy; the company issues nonvoting common stock; public interest in the company declines considerably; or the company does not mail out proxy statements. However, if the question said, "Which would definitely cause delisting?" answer C would be correct. Issuing nonvoting common stock or not mailing out proxy statements are more serious events than the other choices.

# The Specialist

## Role of the Specialist on the Exchange

**Agent and principal.** On the floor of the Exchange, specialists can act in two capacities:

- As agents (or brokers' brokers), executing all orders left with them by other brokers.
- As principals (dealers), buying and selling for their own accounts.

**Responsibilities of the specialist.** Specialists are required to abide by certain NYSE floor rules in the daily conduct of their business:

- The specialist must work to maintain a fair and orderly market.
- The specialist is expected to transact business for his own account in such a way as to maintain price continuity and depth and to minimize temporary price disparities attributable to differences in supply and demand.
- The specialist must avoid transacting business for his own account at the opening or reopening of trading in a stock if this would upset the public balance of supply and demand.
- The specialist must file the reports and keep the books and records required by the Exchange.

### Limit Order Book

**The specialist's book.** A specialist's most important tool is his **limit order book**, a record of limit and stop orders the specialist holds for execution (as well as market orders that are received after the close of the market). The book's contents are confidential; the entries need not be disclosed by the specialist to anyone.

**Quote.** The current quotation always states the best (highest) bid and the best (lowest) offer and includes limit orders. No stop orders are included in the quote because no order has been triggered yet and therefore it cannot be executed.

**Size.** The specialist is allowed to reveal the number of shares available in a current quote, but is not allowed to reveal the number of shares or prices above or below the current quote. The specialist continuously provides a *quote and size*. The quote and size (Q&S) are good only for the moment they are given; however, they provide some indication of the current price.

### Stopping Stock

A specialist can guarantee that a market order will be filled at the current bid or offer by **stopping stock**. The commission house broker who originated the order has time to go into the crowd and try to find a better price.

A specialist may stop stock only for the benefit of a public order and does not require the Exchange's permission to do so. In the event the price in the crowd moves beyond the stopped price, the specialist automatically executes the order.

## Questions

1. Stopping stock is permitted only if the specialist
   - A. receives the permission of an NYSE floor governor
   - B. is executing an order for another member
   - C. has not guaranteed the price
   - D. is executing a public order

## Answers

1. **D.** A specialist may not stop stock for her own account, for the account of a competing specialist in the same stock or for the account of another member of the Exchange. The privilege of stopping stock is limited to public orders.

# Types of Orders

Clients who want to buy or sell securities can enter several types of orders.

**Market order**. A market order is executed immediately at the market price.

- As long as the security is trading, a market order guarantees execution. No other type of order offers that guarantee.

**Limit order**. A limit order sets a limit on the amount paid or received for the securities.

- A sell order at a limit sets a minimum price at which the client is willing to sell the stock.
- A limit order to buy sets a maximum purchase price.
- Limit orders are left with the specialist so that they can be executed if and when price conditions meet the order limitation.
- Customers who enter limit orders risk missing the chance to buy or sell, especially if the market moves rapidly away from the limit.
- If a limit order is not executed, even if the limit price is met, the explanation could be that there is **stock ahead** (i.e., another order at the same price took precedence) or there has not been a **plus-tick** (i.e., a trade at a price higher than the last trade).

**Stop order**. A stop order is an order instructing the broker-dealer to enter a market order if the stock reaches the stop price (or the trigger price if the order is a stop limit order).

- A stop order is designed to protect a profit or prevent further loss if the stock begins to move in the wrong direction.
- The stop order becomes a market order once the stock trades at or moves through a certain price, known as the stop price.
- Stop orders are usually left with and executed by the specialist.
- There is no guarantee that the executed price will be as favorable as the stop price. In this way, a stop order differs from a limit order, which does guarantee execution at the limit price or better.
- The stop price *triggers* (or *elects*) the order, which is then normally entered as a market order. A stop order takes two trades to execute: the **trigger transaction** activates the trade (the trigger transaction must be at or through the stop price) and the **execution transaction** completes the trade (the stop order has become a market order and is executed at the best market price).
- A large number of stop orders on the specialist's book may accelerate the advance or decline of the stock price.

**Buy stop order**. A buy stop order is always entered at a price above the current offering price and is triggered when the market price touches or goes through the buy stop price. Buy stop orders are usually made to limit the risk of short sales.

**Sell stop order**. A sell stop order is always entered at a price below the current offering price and is triggered when the market price touches or drops through the sell stop price. Sell stop orders are made (1) to protect a profit; and (2) to stop losses.

**Stop limit order**. A stop limit order is an order instructing the broker-dealer to enter a limit order if the stock hits the trigger price.

- Once the limit is reached, the order then becomes a market order, and shares are sold at the next available price.
- The buy stop, buy stop limit and sell limit orders are entered at or above the current market price. The buy limit, sell stop and sell stop limit orders are entered below the current market price.
- Stop limit orders are not allowed OTC unless the stop price and the limit price are the same.

**Day order**. A day order expires if not filled by the end of the day.

- Unless marked to the contrary, an order is assumed to be a day order, valid only until the close of trading on the day it is entered by the customer.
- If the order has not been filled, it will be canceled at the close of the day's trading.
- Day orders are executed in the order in which they are received.

**Good till canceled order.** A GTC order does not expire until filled or canceled.

- Regardless of the day the orders are entered, the specialist will cancel them on the last business day of April or October (that is, every six months) unless the customer renews them at that time.
- A GTC order that has been properly renewed or confirmed retains its original position on the specialist's book.

**At-the-opening and market-on-close order.** This order is executed at the opening of trading the day after the order is placed or as close as possible to the close of trading on the day the order is placed.

- If an at-the-opening or market-at-close order does not reach the post in time, the order is canceled.

**Not held order.** An NH order gives the floor broker discretion on price and time of execution.

- Market not held orders may not be placed with the specialist.

**Reducing order.** A reducing order automatically drops in price under certain conditions.

- *All orders entered below the market* are reduced on the ex-date. On the ex-date, the price of the stock drops by the amount of the distribution. Orders reduced include buy limits, sell stops and sell stop limits.
- The stop or limit price is reduced by the next greatest increment of trading; that is, the amount of the dividend is rounded to the next highest 1/8th.
- **Do not reduce (DNR)** orders will not be reduced by an ordinary cash dividend but will be reduced for other distributions, such as after a stock dividend or when a stock trades ex-rights.
- **Reductions for stock splits (proportional reductions).** To calculate the reduction in the price of an open buy order or an open stop order after a stock split, divide the market price by the fraction that represents the split. For example, if a buy stop order has been entered for a stock at $100 and a 5-for-4 stock split has been announced, the $100 order price is divided by the fraction 5/4 to find the adjusted order price of $80.

Order price: $100
Stock split: 5 for 4
5/4 = 1.25
$100 ÷ 5/4 = $80
Adjusted order price = $80

Order price: $100
Stock split: 2 for 1
2/1 = 2.00
$100 ÷ 2/1 = $50
Adjusted order price = $50

Order price: $100
Stock split: 3 for 2
3/2 = 1.50
$100 ÷ 3/2 = $66.67
Adjusted order price = $66.625 (66 5/8)

- If a calculation results in a price that cannot be converted exactly into 1/8ths, the order price is rounded *down* to the nearest 1/8th.

**Fill or kill order.** An FOK order must be executed immediately in full or be canceled.

- The commission house broker will not leave the order with the specialist.

**Immediate or cancel order.** An IOC order must be executed immediately in full or in part—any part of the order that remains unfilled will be canceled.

**All or none order.** An AON order must be executed in full, but not immediately.

**Alternative order.** This order provides two alternatives, such as sell a stock at a limit or sell it on stop.

**Contingent order.** This order cannot be executed until another specified order has been executed.

# Questions

1. An order that instructs the specialist not to adjust the limit (or stop) price when a stock goes ex-dividend is designated

   A. DNA
   B. DNR
   C. FOK
   D. EX

2. Which of the following orders would NOT be reduced by the specialist on the ex-dividend date?

   I. Buy limit order
   II. Open sell stop order
   III. Buy stop order
   IV. Sell limit order

   A. I and II
   B. I and IV
   C. II, III and IV
   D. III and IV

3. An order to sell at 38 5/8 Stop, 38 5/8 Limit is entered before the opening. The subsequent trades are 38 7/8, 38 1/2, 38 3/8. The order

   A. was executed at 38 1/2
   B. was executed at 38 5/8
   C. was executed at 38 7/8
   D. has not yet been executed

4. A "not held" order means

   A. that the commission house broker will not be held responsible if he does not get an immediate execution of the market order
   B. the same as "stock ahead" and refers to an unexecuted limited order
   C. the order cannot be found by the member firm
   D. the order has expired

5. A sell stop order is entered

   A. above the current market price
   B. below the current market price
   C. either above or below the current market price
   D. at the current market price

6. A company is about to pay a dividend of $.70. On the ex-dividend date, an open order to sell at 46 stop would

   A. be automatically adjusted to 45 1/4 Stop
   B. be automatically adjusted to 45 3/8 Stop
   C. be automatically adjusted to 45 1/2 Stop
   D. remain 46 Stop

7. Which of the following statements are true concerning stop orders?

   I. They can limit a loss in a declining stock.
   II. They become market orders when there is a trade at, or the market passes through, a specific price.
   III. They are the same as limit orders.
   IV. They can affect the price of the stock when the specific stop price is reached.

   A. I and II
   B. I, II and IV
   C. I, III and IV
   D. II and III

8. A customer enters an order that must be effected at once, either in full or in part, and asks that any unfilled portion of the order be canceled. This is a(n)

   A. good till canceled order
   B. immediate or cancel order
   C. all or none order
   D. fill or kill order

9. A day order is entered to buy 500 ALF at 24 3/8. By the close, the firm has 100 shares at 24 1/4 and 200 at 24 3/8. The remainder is unfilled. What is the outcome?

   A. The customer may reject the incomplete order unless the broker can guarantee filling the remainder by the end of the day.
   B. The customer may reject the incomplete order unless the remainder can be filled within three business days.
   C. The customer may demand that the firm deliver the remaining shares at 24 3/8.
   D. The customer must accept the execution for 300 shares, and the remainder of the order is canceled after the close.

10. A customer tells a broker to buy 1,500 shares of ALF at 33 5/8 immediately or else to cancel the whole order. This is a(n)

    A. good till canceled order
    B. immediate or cancel order
    C. all or none order
    D. fill or kill order

11. The price range on a particular day for the stock of ALFA Enterprises is shown below:

    ALF Co. High 26 Low 24 1/4 Close 25 1/2

    If a customer had placed a day order to buy 100 ALF at 24 before the market opened, at what price would he buy the stock?

    A. 23 7/8
    B. 24
    C. 24 1/4
    D. The order was not filled.

# Answers

1. **B.** The qualifying price on a do not reduce (DNR) order will not be reduced by ordinary cash dividends on the ex-dividend date. DNRs do not apply to other distributions, such as rights or stock dividends.

2. **D.** When a stock goes ex-dividend, the specialist will reduce open buy limit orders and open sell stop orders because they are placed below the market price and could be triggered when the market price is reduced for the loss of dividend. The specialist will not reduce open sell limit orders and open buy stop orders.

3. **D.** A stop limit order is a stop order that becomes a limit order once the stop price has been triggered. When the limit price is the same as the stop price on a stop limit order, the order can be executed only at or better than the limit price. In this case, the order has not yet been executed because no transaction has occurred at or above 38 5/8 since the stop was triggered at 38 1/2.

4. **A.** When a market order with an NH code is used, the customer agrees not to hold the floor broker responsible for the time and price of execution.

5. **B.** Sell stop orders are always entered below the market price. A sell stop order is triggered when a transaction occurs at or below the price specified on the order. A buy stop order is always entered at a price above the current offering price.

6. **A.** When a stock goes ex-dividend, the price of the stock falls by the amount of the dividend. If the dividends are not equivalent to a round eighth, the dividend is rounded to the next highest fraction. A dividend of $.70 would reduce the stock price by $.75, or 3/4ths of a point. The specialist also reduces open buy limit orders and open sell stop limit orders by the amount of the dividend.

7. **B.** A stop order becomes a market order once the market price reaches or passes the specific

stop price. An investor in a long position can use the sell stop order for protection against a market decline. When a large number of stop orders are triggered at a particular price, the advance or decline of the market at that point can be magnified. Stop orders are not the same as limit orders because there is no guarantee of a specific execution price or better for a stop order.

8. **B.** Under an immediate or cancel order, the commission house broker is instructed to fill immediately as much of the order as possible at the limit price or better. The remaining unexecuted part of the order is canceled. A fill or kill order must be executed in its entirety or it is canceled. An all or none order must be executed in its entirety, but does not have to be executed immediately.

9. **D.** A customer must accept partial fulfillment of a limit order.

10. **D.** Under a fill or kill order, the commission house broker is instructed to fill the entire order immediately at the limit price or better. If this cannot be done, he will cancel it and notify the originating branch office. An immediate or cancel order is similar except that partial execution is acceptable.

11. **D.** An order that can be executed only at a specified price or better is a limit order. A buy limit order can be executed only at or below the price specified on the order. Because the stock of ALFA Enterprises never traded at or below 24, the order was not filled.

# Long and Short Sale Rules

**Long sale**. By purchasing the securities of a company, an investor is *going long* those securities. The sale of those securities is a *long sale*.

**Short sale**. The customer takes a short position by selling shares of stock he does not own. The short-selling investor initially borrows stock from a broker-dealer, then sells the stock at the market. The investor anticipates that the price of the stock will go down enough to allow him to replace the borrowed stock at a lower price at a later date. The seller is obligated to buy the stock and replace the borrowed shares in order to close the short position.

- Short sales are always executed and accounted for in a customer's margin account and are subject to Reg T 50% initial margin requirements.
- Short sales always entail the delivery of borrowed stock to the buy side of the trade.
- Short sales are subject to higher NASD/NYSE minimum margin maintenance requirements than long purchases in a margin account.

### Exchange Short Sale Rules

Orders to sell a listed security short on an exchange may be executed only on a *plus tick* or *zero-plus tick*. A plus tick is a price higher than the last different price. A zero-plus tick occurs when the last trade for the security was made at the same price as the trade before, but that trade was higher than the previous trade. The plus tick or minus tick carries over from the previous day's trading to the next day's opening.

### OTC Short Sale Rules

Nasdaq's short sale rule prohibits member firms from entering short sales in Nasdaq National Market (NNM) securities at or below the current inside bid whenever that bid is lower than the previous inside bid.

A short sale on a "down bid" is permitted if the sale is at least 1/16th above the current inside bid. An opening bid is a down bid if it is lower than the previous day's closing bid, or the same as the previous day's closing bid if that closing bid was a down bid.

### Sell Order Tickets

A person is considered to be long (own) a security if he (or his agent):

- has title to it;
- has purchased the security or has entered into an unconditional contract to purchase the security, but has not yet received it;
- owns a security convertible into (or exchangeable for) the security and has tendered such security for conversion or exchange; or
- has an option to purchase the security and has exercised that option.

**Sell orders must be identified**. The SEC requires that all sell orders be identified as either "long" or "short." No sale can be marked "long" unless the security to be delivered is in the account of the customer or is owned by the customer and will be delivered to the broker by the settlement date. If securities owned by the customer are not to be delivered to complete the sale, the customer is going *short against the box.*

### Shorting Bonds

Bonds are not usually shorted. It is difficult to cover shorts for most municipal and many corporate bonds because the limited number of bonds available in each issue could make it very difficult to buy in the short position.

## Questions

1. Which of the following reasons is appropriate justification for selling a stock short?
   A. To cut losses on a long position.
   B. To benefit from a decline in the price of the stock.
   C. To benefit from a rise in the price of the stock.
   D. To seek a modest potential reward with limited risk.

2. ALFA Enterprises stock was traded as shown below:

| Open | 25 1/4 | 25 | 25 1/4 | 25 1/8 | 25 1/4 | 25 1/4 |
|---|---|---|---|---|---|---|
| | | I | II | III | IV | V |

   On which transactions can short sales be made?
   A. I, II, IV and V
   B. I, III, IV and V
   C. II, IV and V
   D. II and V

3. A customer is short against the box. He now sells the stock that he owned in the long position. The order will be marked
   A. long
   B. short
   C. round lot long exempt
   D. short exempt

## Answers

1. **B.** Selling short does not reduce the risk of a long position: the investor is selling borrowed, not owned, stock. The appropriate time to sell short is when one suspects that the stock price is about to drop. The investor wants to sell at a high price, buy later at a lower price. Both the reward and risk potential of selling short are high. If the stock price moves down dramatically, the investor can reap a large gain. If it moves up dramatically, the investor can lose a great deal of money.

2. **C.** Short sales can be made only on upticks or zero-plus ticks. An uptick occurs when the stock is traded at a price higher than the last different price. A zero-plus tick occurs when there is no change in price but the last time the price changed it was an uptick. Choices II and IV are upticks. Choice V is a zero-plus tick.

3. **B.** In the initial sale, to establish the short against the box, the order must be marked "short," and the security can be sold only on an uptick. The owner does not plan to deliver his own security. He is borrowing a certificate to complete the transaction. When the account is both long and short a security, it is said to be in a "zero net" position. Because he is selling long the securities he owns, the transaction is not exempt from the uptick rule. Only the short position will remain.

# The Over-the-Counter Market

The computerized information system that keeps track of much of the OTC trading is called **Nasdaq—the National Association of Securities Dealers Automated Quotation service.** Securities that can be traded in the OTC market include, but are not limited to:

- American depositary receipts (ADRs)
- bank stocks and insurance company stocks
- most corporate bonds
- municipal bonds
- U.S. government securities
- common and preferred stock
- equipment trust certificates
- closed-end investment companies

Mutual funds and other new issues are initially issued OTC.

### Negotiated Market

The OTC market is a *negotiated* market in which market makers may bargain during a trade. A negotiated market is competitive.

## OTC Market Makers

The OTC market maker takes a position in the security by purchasing it or selling it (called **position trading**). Because a broker-dealer acting as a market maker buys and sells for its own account rather than arranging trades, it acts as a principal and not an agent.

The NASD requires market makers to:

- provide continuous two-sided quotations for that security;
- be able and willing to execute a trade for at least a normal trading unit (round lot) at its quote;
- file monthly trading data and other information as required by NASD rules;
- file daily volume reports for those securities in which it makes a market; and
- perform these functions during normal business hours.

**Loss of market-maker status.** Market makers may be prohibited from entering quotations in the Nasdaq system if they:

- are experiencing financial or operational difficulties to the point where investors might be jeopardized; or
- have been suspended or expelled from NASD membership or membership in a national securities exchange.

***Pink Sheets***. Interdealer quotations sent to the National Quotation Bureau are published and printed as the ***Pink Sheets***:

1. They are devoted exclusively to OTC stocks.
2. The prices are quotes, not actual transaction prices.
3. The quotes are between dealers (*interdealer*—that is, not retail).
4. The quotes are subject, not firm.
5. For Nasdaq system stocks, the Nasdaq symbol appears right after the name of the stock.
6. An "M" preceding the stock's name means the stock is marginable.

*Pink Sheet* quotes are subject. A dealer that publishes a quote on a security in the *Pink Sheets* must be ready to quote a firm price for 100 shares of that security. The *Pink Sheets* are published daily by the National Quotation Bureau and list all OTC market makers' quotes from the previous day.

***Yellow Sheets***. The National Quotation Bureau also publishes corporate bond quotations called the *Yellow Sheets*.

# Questions

1. A firm that is making a market in a security is permitted to do which of the following?

    I. Sell short without regard to the plus tick rule.
    II. Take either a long position or a short position in a stock.
    III. Charge a markup.
    IV. Charge both a markup and a commission on the same trade if both the markup and the commission are reasonable in size and related to the current market price of the stock.

    A. I, II and III
    B. I and III
    C. II, III and IV
    D. II and IV

2. When a broker-dealer maintains a firm market in a stock, that broker-dealer is committed to

    A. buying back any security it sells
    B. buying or selling the normal trading unit of that stock at the quoted price
    C. maintaining a continuous subject market
    D. working out the amount of the markup or commission on each OTC transaction

3. The *Pink Sheets* reflect

    A. retail securities prices
    B. quotes between dealers
    C. actual transactions between dealers
    D. firm quotes

4. A quote in the *Pink Sheets* indicates that a dealer is

    A. giving a firm quote for 100 shares
    B. prepared to make a firm quote for 100 shares
    C. quoting a firm market either way for 1,000 shares
    D. recommending the stock

# Answers

1. **A.** Market makers may take either a long position or a short position in a stock in which they make a market. They may also sell these securities short without regard to the plus tick rule. As a dealer, a market maker may charge a markup, but is prohibited from also acting as a broker (charging a commission) on the same transaction.

2. **B.** When a broker-dealer maintains a firm market in the stock, that broker-dealer has issued a firm quote on that stock and, therefore, is committed to buying or selling one trading unit of that stock at the quoted price.

3. **B.** Quotes listed on the *Pink Sheets* are quotes between dealers, not actual transaction prices. They are subject quotes.

4. **B.** Although a *Pink Sheets* quote is subject, its inclusion signifies that the broker-dealer is willing to make a firm quote upon request. If a dealer places a quote in the *Pink Sheets* and then refuses to give a firm quote, the dealer is said to have *backed away.*

# Quotations

## Bids, Offers and Quotes

A dealer's current bid represents the highest price at which that dealer will buy, and the current offer represents the lowest price at which that dealer will sell. The difference between the bid and ask is known as the **spread**.

## Quotation Requirements

### Firm Quote

A firm quotation is the price at which a market maker or broker-dealer stands ready to do business (i.e., to buy or sell at least one trading unit—100 shares of stock or five bonds—at the quoted price) with other NASD member firms in the interdealer market.

**Recall quotes**. In a recall quote, a market maker can give another broker-dealer a quote that is firm for an hour with five-minute recall. This is a firm quote that remains good for an hour. If, within that hour, the market maker receives another order for the same security, the trader will call the broker-dealer back and give it five minutes to confirm its order or lose its right to buy that security at the price it was quoted.

**Backing away**. A market maker that revises a firm quote without apparent cause, or that otherwise refuses to do business at the price(s) quoted, is said to be *backing away* from the quote, a practice inconsistent with the just and equitable principles of trade held by members of the NASD.

**Recognized quotation**. A recognized quotation under NASD/NYSE rules is any public bid or offer for one or more round lots. Any bid for less than a round lot must state the amount of the security for which it is good.

### Subject Quote

A subject quote is one in which the price is tentative, subject to reconfirmation by the market maker.

### Qualified Quotes

- **Workout quote**. A workout quote is an approximate figure used to provide the buyer or seller with an indication of price, not a firm quote.
- **Nominal quote**. A nominal quote is someone's assessment of where a stock might trade if there were an active market.

## Quotation Spread and Size

**Spread**. The difference between the bid and the asked prices of a security is known as the quotation's *spread*. Factors that influence the size of a spread include:

- size of the issue;
- financial condition of the issuer;
- amount of interest (market activity) in the issue; and
- market conditions.

**Size**. Unless otherwise specified, a firm quote is always good for one round lot for the standard unit of trading for the security in question.

# Questions

1. An over-the-counter trader attempting to buy stock is given a quote of "16–17 work-out." This indicates that the quote is

   A. $16 with a suggested broker-dealer markup of $1
   B. firm
   C. bona fide
   D. approximate

2. If an over-the-counter trader gives the quote, "My market is 12 to 12 5/8," this is

   A. a firm quote, and the trader must be willing to trade 100 shares at that quote
   B. subject to approval
   C. subject to confirmation
   D. an unacceptable quote

3. Assume that Quantum Rapid Search, Inc. is quoted at 25–25 1/4 and Tippecanoe Ferry Co. is quoted at 24–27. Which of the following is MOST likely?

   A. QRS is more actively traded.
   B. TIP is more actively traded.
   C. QRS is quoted on a work-out basis.
   D. TIP has more market makers.

# Answers

1. **D.** A *workout* quote is an approximate quote that is not firm. The trader giving the quote gives a range and will work out the final quote.

2. **A.** If a quote begins, "My market is . . . ," it is a firm quote and the trader must be willing to trade 100 shares at the specified price.

3. **A.** Dealers are very cautious about making a market in stocks that are traded inactively. A dealer may find it very difficult to liquidate a sizable position in such stocks. For protection, a dealer will open up or widen the spread on such stocks. If a stock is very actively traded, the spread will be relatively small.

# NASD 5% Markup Policy

The 5% markup policy is considered *a guideline only* and is not a firm rule for markups and markdowns. A firm charging a customer less than a 5% markup could be in violation of fair and equitable trade practices if the markup is considered excessive once all of the relevant factors are taken into account. Conversely, a markup of greater than 5% could be considered fair and reasonable if the costs involved in the transaction justify it.

If the firm makes a market in the security, it can, as principal, buy from or sell to the customer. If the firm does not make a market in the security, it will contact a broker-dealer that is making a market and, acting either as agent or as principal, fill the customer's order.

### Markup Applies to all OTC Transactions

The NASD 5% markup policy applies to all transactions in nonexempt securities in the OTC market regardless of whether the transactions are executed as agency transactions or principal trades.

### Fixed Public Offering Price Securities

The 5% markup policy does not apply to mutual funds, variable annuity contracts or securities sold in public offerings and accompanied by a prospectus.

### Representative Market Prices

In OTC principal transactions, the base for computing the markup and testing for compliance with the 5% policy is the price *representative of prevailing (inside) market prices* at the time of the customer transaction.

### Dealer's Inventory Costs

If a customer's buy order is filled from the broker-dealer's inventory, the net price to the customer is based on the prevailing market price.

The price at which the broker-dealer acquired stock that is now being sold to the customer has no bearing on the net price to the customer.

### Riskless and Simultaneous Transactions

The dealer has two options for filling the riskless and simultaneous transaction order:

- as agent for the customer, it could go to the market maker, buy or sell on the customer's behalf and charge a commission; or
- it could go to the market maker, buy or sell for its own account and then buy or sell to the customer as principal, charging a markup or markdown (as the case may be) subject to the 5% policy.

### Proceeds Transactions

When a customer sells securities and uses the proceeds to purchase other securities, this is called a *proceeds transaction*. The buy and sell sides may each show a commission or markup, but *when combined* the 5% policy is used as a guideline to determine the fairness of the markup.

### Relevant Factors

In assessing the fairness of a broker-dealer's commission and markup practices, the NASD considers the following factors.

- **Type of security**. The more risk a broker-dealer must assume, the greater the justification for higher markups.
- **Inactively traded stocks**. A broker-dealer is justified in charging higher markups on inactively traded stocks.
- **Selling price of security**. Commission and markup rates should decrease as the selling price of a stock or another security increases.
- **Dollar amount of transaction**. Transactions involving relatively small dollar amounts generally warrant higher markups than large-dollar-amount transactions.

- **Nature of the broker-dealer's business**. A general securities broker-dealer may be able to justify higher commissions and markups than an introducing broker. On the other hand, a discount broker that does not offer research and other services may be able to justify only a small markup.
- **Pattern of markups**. A single incident could be considered an unfair markup.
- **Disclosure**. Disclosure of its fee in advance of the transaction does not relieve the broker-dealer of the obligation to keep such fees reasonable and fair.

# Questions

1. A customer wants to sell $10,000 worth of Barnett Banks and use those funds to buy $10,000 worth of Bay Banks. Assuming that your firm acts as a dealer in both transactions, which of the following statements is(are) true?

   I. This set of trades is called a *proceeds transaction.*
   II. Your firm must consider each transaction separately in determining the fairness of the markup.
   III. Your firm must consider the combined markups charged by the firm in determining a fair markup on the securities purchased.
   IV. Your firm has acted illegally: it may act as a broker in only one of the transactions.

   A. I
   B. I and II
   C. I and III
   D. IV

2. A broker-dealer holds in its inventory an OTC stock for which it paid an average price of $12 a share, and the stock is currently quoted at 9 3/8. The broker-dealer quotes its client a price of 12–12 1/2 for 100 shares. This price

   A. is reasonable because its markup is less than 5% of its original cost
   B. would violate the Rules of Fair Practice
   C. should reveal the amount of its commission
   D. would be justified only if the market were thin

# Answers

1. **C.** A *proceeds transaction* occurs when a client sells securities to a dealer and uses the proceeds to buy other securities from the same dealer; for markup purposes, this is viewed as one transaction. The combined markups on the securities must be considered when determining the fairness of the markup.

2. **B.** The stock is currently quoted at 9 3/8. If the broker-dealer quotes that stock to a client at 12–12 1/2, this price would violate the Rules of Fair Practice. Remember, markups must be based on the current market, not on the member's original cost.

# NASD Automated Quotation System

## Scope of Nasdaq Service

The Nasdaq National Market (NNM) package is the most popular with NASD member firm subscribers. In total, the Nasdaq system includes current price quotations from more than 500 market makers on more than 5,300 actively traded securities.

### Levels of Quotation Service

The Nasdaq system provides three levels of stock quotation service to the securities industry. Level 1 is designed for registered representatives, Level 2 is for the use of retail and institutional traders, and Level 3 has special features for market makers. Level 3 includes all the features of Level 2, and Level 2 includes all the features of Level 1.

- **Level 1**. Nasdaq Level 1 is available to registered reps. Level 1 displays the **inside market only**: the highest bid and the lowest ask for securities authorized for inclusion in the system. Because of normal market price fluctuations, a Level 1 quote as it appears on the screen may or may not be accurate, and the registered rep cannot guarantee a Level 1 price to a customer.
- **Level 2**. Nasdaq Level 2 is available to NASD approved subscribers only and provides the **current quote and the size of the quote** available from *each* market maker in that security.
- **Level 3**. Nasdaq Level 3 provides subscribers with all of the services of Levels 1 and 2 and allows registered market makers to **update their quotes** on any security in which they make a market.

Generally, the Nasdaq system does not provide up-to-the-minute volume in each security, nor does it provide the price of the last sale in each security. It does, however, give the volume in each security at the end of the day.

## Nasdaq Market Maker Requirements

### Market Maker Reports

**90-second reporting**. Registered market makers are required to transmit reports of last sales made during designated transaction-reporting hours. All of this information must be reported *within 90 seconds* after the execution of the transaction.

**Volume reports**. Registered market makers must make daily reports to Nasdaq of their total daily volume (purchases and sales) in each security for which they are registered market makers. If there has been no activity in a security that day, the market maker must report "zero volume."

### The Inside Market

The inside market is the best bid (highest) price at which stock can be sold in the interdealer market and the best ask (lowest) price at which the same stock can be bought.

## Nasdaq Authorized Securities

In order to be quoted on Nasdaq, a company must meet certain minimum qualifications in:

- total assets;
- capital and surplus;
- outstanding principal value of convertible debt securities;
- publicly held shares;
- number of stockholders; and
- registered and active market makers.

**Minimum of two market makers**. In order for a security to be listed on any Nasdaq quotation service, the security must have at least *two registered and active market makers* able and willing to enter firm quotations in the system.

### Nasdaq National Market Issuer Qualifications

Nasdaq National Market (NNM) securities are the largest and most active securities quoted on Nasdaq. To be accepted as an NNM security, a company must meet minimum standards in:

- annual net income;
- number of market makers registered for its security;
- price per share; and
- market value of the outstanding shares.

Issuers of securities designated as NNM securities must meet higher minimum conditions for:

- number of publicly held shares
- available capital and surplus

### Suspension or Termination of a Listing

A Nasdaq listing may be pulled if any of the following situations occur:

- the issuer of the security files for bankruptcy;
- the issuer's independent accountants issue a disclaimer opinion on the issuer's financial statements; or
- the NASD decides it is necessary to prevent fraud or to protect the public interest.

# Questions

1. Level 2 of the Nasdaq system provides which of the following?

   I. Firm quotes
   II. Names of the firms making markets
   III. Actual prices of transactions
   IV. Cumulative, up-to-the-minute volume in the security

   A. I only
   B. I and II only
   C. II and III only
   D. I, II, III and IV

2. Level 1 of the Nasdaq system provides which of the following?

   A. Highest bid and lowest offer for each security
   B. Price of the last sale for each security
   C. Current bid and asked price of each market maker for each security
   D. Current representative bid and asked prices for each security

## Answers

1. **B.** Level 2 on the Nasdaq system provides the current quote and the name of each market maker in each security.

2. **A.** Level 1 on the Nasdaq system is the inside quote—the highest bid and lowest offer on a stock.

# Computerized Order Routing

Each exchange has its own system for routing orders electronically.

### New York Stock Exchange SuperDot

The NYSE's computerized trading and execution system is called **SuperDot** (Super Designated Order Turnaround). An order can be routed directly to the appropriate specialist or it can be sent to the brokerage firm's house booth for handling by the Exchange member. Once the order is received by the specialist or commission broker, it is presented in the auction market. If the order is executed, the same automated routing system can be used to send an execution report back to the firm, which then notifies the registered representative, who notifies the customer that the order was executed. Orders executed through SuperDot are often confirmed back to the broker in less than 60 seconds.

All NYSE-listed stocks are eligible for trading on SuperDot, subject to the following limits:

- preopening market orders—up to 30,099 shares per order;
- postopening market orders—up to 2,099 shares per order; and
- pre- and postopening limit orders—up to 99,999 shares per order.

### National Association of Securities Dealers SOES

The NASD's **Small Order Execution System (SOES)** is an automatic order execution system designed to facilitate the trading of small public market and executable limit orders of up to 1,000 shares.

- **Market-maker registration**. All NNM market makers are required to also participate in SOES.
- **Clearance and settlement**. Small orders may be aggregated if the total is less than the maximum 1,000-share limit, but broker-dealers may not split up large customer orders for the purpose of avoiding the 1,000-share limit.
- **Restrictions**. Institutions and broker-dealers may not use the system to trade for their own accounts or for other NASD members. Only public market and executable limit orders are acceptable.

### Intermarket Trading System/Computer Assisted Execution System

ITS/CAES offers a computerized link between market makers and specialists on the various exchanges who make a market in the same security. Quotations entered into the system by market makers are considered irrevocable for *two minutes*, unless the market maker specifically states that it will honor the quote for one minute only.

### Consolidated Quotation System

The NASD's **Consolidated Quotation System (CQS)** is used by market makers willing to stand ready to buy and sell the securities for their own accounts on a continuous basis, but who do not wish to do so through an exchange.

NASD members that are registered market makers may enter quotes into CQS through the Nasdaq system.

**CQS securities**. Securities eligible for quotation on CQS include all NYSE- and AMEX-listed securities, designated securities listed on regional exchanges and any securities registered for unlisted trading on the national exchanges.

**Trading hours**. CQS is open for quotations from 9:30 am to 4:00 pm EST.

### INSTINET

The **INSTINET Corporation** is a privately operated computerized system to facilitate fourth market trades (institution-to-institution direct trades). Institutional investors subscribing to the service can enter bids and offers and trade directly with other institutions.

# The Consolidated Tape

### How the Tape Works

The Consolidated Tape system (also known as the *Consolidated Ticker Tape*) is a NYSE service designed to deliver real-time reports of securities transactions to subscribers as they occur on the various exchanges. Subscribers to the Tape can choose to receive transaction reports in either of two ways: over the high-speed, electronic line (linked directly to their quote terminals); or through the low-speed ticker (visible report) line—the type of report commonly seen as quotes racing across a sign at a brokerage counter.

- **Network A** reports transactions in NYSE-listed securities wherever they are traded.
- **Network B** carries reports of AMEX-listed securities transactions as well as reports of transactions in regional exchange issues that *substantially meet* AMEX listing requirements. Transactions in these securities must be reported within 90 seconds for inclusion on the Consolidated Tape.

## How to Read the Consolidated Tape

### Market Identifier

The Tape prints volumes and prices of securities transactions within seconds of their execution on the floor of the NYSE and other exchanges. On the high-speed line, the transactions are reported with a **market identifier**, a letter identifying the exchange or market on which the transaction took place. The market identifiers currently used on the high-speed line are as follows:

| | | | | | |
|---|---|---|---|---|---|
| AMEX | A | Boston | B | Cincinnati | C |
| Chicago | M | NYSE | N | INSTINET | O |
| Pacific | P | NASD | T | Philadelphia | X |

### Quotations and Administrative Messages

**Number of shares.** The Tape reports numbers of shares as follows:

- A sale of a single round lot of stock is indicated by listing the trading symbol and the price at which the transaction occurred but with no quantity.
- Sales of multiples of a round lot are indicated by printing the number of round lots followed by the letter "s" and the price.
- If a transaction is executed for 10,000 shares or more, the entire amount will be printed.
- Stocks sold in 10-share units report the number of units, followed by the symbol $\frac{S}{S}$.
- If two similar trades for the same security occur consecutively, the report prints them under the same trading symbol and separates them with a dot.

**Error reports.** In the event that an error is made in printing the report of a transaction, the Tape will report any necessary correction preceded by the letters "CORR." If the symbols "ERR" or "CXL" appear on the Tape, they indicate that a printed report is to be erased or disregarded.

**Active markets.** If activity in the markets and exchanges that report to the Tape is so high that it becomes difficult to report all of the information from every trade accurately, several **delete information** modes can be used.

- DIGITS & VOL DELETED. When this message appears, the first digit of the price and the volume will be dropped.
- REPEAT PRICES OMITTED. This message indicates that the Tape will be showing only transactions that differ in price from the previous report.
- MINIMUM PRICE CHANGES OMITTED. If necessary, the Tape will print only those trades that differ by more than 1/8 point from the last report printed.

**Other messages.** Other messages that appear on the Tape are as follows:

- SLD indicates that the exchange did not report a sale on time, so it is out of sequence on the Tape.
- OPD announces the initial transaction in a security for which the opening has been delayed.
- HALT means that trading in that security has been halted.
- $\frac{W}{I}$ indicates when issued stock resulting from a stock split or stock trading when issued.
- $\frac{R}{T}$ indicates rights.
- WS indicates warrants.
- Pr indicates preferred stock.

# Questions

1. Based on the following sample Tape, how many shares of Federal Paper Board (FBO) preferred were sold and at what price?

| FBOpr | T | ADM |
|---|---|---|
| 50$^{S}_{S}$24 1/8 | 42 1/2 | 2s17 3/8 |

A. 5,000 at 24 1/8
B. 100 at 24 1/8
C. 500 at 24 1/8
D. 50 at 24 and 50 at 24 1/8

2. Because ABC Company split its stock 2 for 1, both old and new shares are trading on the floor of the NYSE. The old stock was priced at 70, the new stock at 35. If a client bought 300 of the new shares of ABC stock, how would this be reported on the Tape?

A. ABC 300s35
B. ABC 3s35
C. ABC 150s70
D. ABC 3s35$^{W}_{I}$

3. A registered rep places an order for a client to buy 1,600 shares of RCA at 36 3/4 and sees the following trades on the Tape. Assuming he was the only bidder, how many shares did he buy and at what price(s)?

| GE | RCA | TX | RCA |
|---|---|---|---|
| 52 1/2 | 5s36 1/2 | 2s23 1/2 | 10s36 1/2.3/4 |

A. 500 at 36 1/2
B. 1,000 at 36 1/2
C. 100 at 36 3/4
D. 500 at 36 1/2, 1,000 at 36 1/2, 100 at 36 3/4

## Answers

1. **C.** Inactive stocks that trade in round lots of 10 shares are recognizable on the Tape because they are reported this way: Volume $\genfrac{}{}{0pt}{}{\text{S}}{\text{s}}$ Price.

2. **D.** If a stock trades at a certain price and then splits and new shares are being issued, these new shares are traded "when issued," and they will be identified on the Tape by $\genfrac{}{}{0pt}{}{\text{W}}{\text{I}}$.

3. **D.** Two separate entries for RCA appear on the Tape. The first indicates that the registered rep was able to partially fill the order by picking up 500 shares at 36 1/2; he then filled the remainder of the order by buying 1,000 shares at 36 1/2 plus the final 100 shares at 36 3/4.

# 8 Customer Accounts

## New Accounts

### Classification of Accounts

**Account ownership**. The principal types of ownership are:

- individual
- joint
- corporate
- partnership

**Trading authorization**. The primary types of trading authorization are:

- **Discretionary**. After receiving written authority from the customer, the registered representative enters trades without having to consult the customer before each trade.
- **Fiduciary**. The individual given fiduciary responsibility enters the trades for the account.
- **Custodial**. The custodian for the beneficial owner enters all trades.

**Payment method**. In cash accounts, customers must pay the full purchase price of securities. In margin accounts, customers may borrow part of the purchase price of a security from the broker-dealer.

### Opening New Accounts

**Required information**. According to NYSE Rule 405 ("Know Your Customer"), registered reps should interview each customer in order to obtain an inventory of the customer's present holdings and discover the customer's financial situation, needs and objectives.

**Payment and delivery instructions**. Payment and delivery instructions can include:

- **Transfer and ship**. Securities are transferred into the name of the customer and shipped to him.
- **Transfer and hold in safekeeping**. Securities are transferred into the customer's name, but are held by the broker-dealer.
- **Hold in street name**. Securities are transferred into the broker-dealer's name and held by the broker-dealer. The broker-dealer is the nominal owner of the securities. The customer is the beneficial owner.
- **Delivery vs. payment**. Securities are delivered to a bank or depository against payment.

For *sell* orders, the customer will give one of two instructions: hold the cash at the broker-dealer or forward the cash balance upon the completion of the transaction.

### Approval and Acceptance of an Account

Every new account must be approved by a partner or a principal of the firm, in writing on the account form, prior to or promptly after the completion of the first transaction in that account. The principal may initial the new account form to indicate that the account is approved and the firm has accepted the account.

## Documenting New Accounts

### New Account Form

The registered rep must fill out a new account form (account card) and enter certain details regarding customer identification and information concerning suitability. The firm must record the following information about each customer who will have access to the account:

- full name;
- address and telephone number;
- Social Security or tax identification number;
- occupation, employer and type of business;
- citizenship;
- whether the customer is of legal age;
- financial information;
- investment objectives;
- bank and brokerage references;
- whether the customer is an employee of a member broker-dealer;
- how the account was acquired;
- name and occupation of the person(s) with authority to make transactions in the account; and
- signatures of the *representative* opening the account and a *principal* of the firm (the customer's signature is *not* required on a new account form).

The MSRB requires the registered rep to ask about the customer's tax status. MSRB rules also state that the broker-dealer must make a reasonable effort to obtain the customer's Social Security number (or tax ID) before the settlement of a transaction. If, for whatever reason, it cannot do so, it must keep a record of that fact.

If the customer refuses to disclose or provide all of the financial information requested by the firm, the firm may still open the account if it determines by other means that the customer has the financial resources to carry the account and that whatever trades the customer seeks to enter are suitable.

Customer information should be updated periodically as situations change. Transactions placed by the customer and judged unsuitable by the registered rep may still be entered by the customer.

### Signature Cards

Although many firms request it, the customer is not legally required to fill out a signature card for a cash account.

### Mailing Instructions

Statements and confirms may be sent to someone who holds power of attorney for the customer (his agent or attorney, for example) if the customer requests it in writing or if duplicate confirms are also sent to the customer. A member firm may hold the customer's mail for up to two months if the customer is traveling in the United States, and for up to three months if the customer is abroad.

## Cash Accounts

In a cash account, a customer is expected to pay in full for any securities purchased. Accounts that may be opened *only* as cash accounts include:

- personal retirement accounts (IRAs, Keoghs and TSAs);
- corporate retirement accounts; and
- custodial accounts (UGMAs).

## Margin Accounts

The term "margin" refers to the minimum amount of cash or marginable securities that a customer is required to deposit on the purchase of securities.

### The Federal Reserve Board's Regulation T

The Securities Exchange Act of 1934 grants the Federal Reserve Board (FRB) authority to regulate credit extended in the purchase of securities. The FRB established Regulation T, which sets forth the equity or margin required in a purchase of securities in a margin account. Regulation T stipulates which securities may be purchased on margin. The board establishes the rules and regulations governing margin accounts, and then delegates the enforcement of them to the SEC.

### Opening a Margin Account

The customer is allowed to place orders for investments and is asked to deposit only a percentage of their cost (and to pay interest on the unpaid balance at the broker call rate). The securities purchased are held for the customer in the account in street name.

When the investor decides to make an investment, the firm will calculate the amount of money that he will have to deposit (the margin requirement) for the purchase. The FRB requires the investor first to meet certain minimum deposit requirements, and then bases the amount he has to pay on a percentage of the total market value of the security. When a brokerage firm lends money for any new securities purchase, the firm takes into consideration the total amount of money that the customer already owes on securities in the account.

The margin account also serves as a potential source of cash. If the customer has fully paid securities in the account and needs some cash, the firm can lend money against those securities (or margin them) up to the current margin limits set by the FRB.

**Documenting a margin account.** When opening a margin account, the customer signs a **margin agreement** disclosing the terms under which credit will be extended. The margin agreement contains the:

- **credit agreement**, which discloses the terms under which credit is extended;
- **hypothecation agreement**, which gives the firm permission to pledge (or hypothecate) securities held on margin; and
- **loan consent agreement**, which gives the firm permission to lend the customer's securities held in a margin account to other broker-dealers.

## Options Accounts

When opening an options account, the customer signs a customer options agreement, acknowledging having read the OCC Options Disclosure Document, and understanding the risks associated with trading options.

Initial approval for options accounts may come from the branch manager. If the manager is not a ROP (registered options principal), the manager's signature must be approved by either a ROP, Senior ROP (SROP) or Compliance ROP (CROP) within a reasonable time. When opening an options account, a registered rep must:

- ascertain the customer's investment history and financial status;
- ascertain the customer's investment objectives and needs;
- give or send the customer the OCC Options Disclosure Document; and
- within 15 days of approval, obtain the customer's signature on a customer options agreement, which states that the investor will abide by OCC guidelines and option exchange regulations.

The customer's account information must be updated within 15 days of a change in either the customer's financial status or objectives.

Additional approval may be required if the customer wishes to engage in writing options (including writing covered calls), uncovered option writing, ratio writing, spreads and straddles.

## Penny Stock Trading

The **Penny Stock Reform Act of 1990** was adopted to protect unsophisticated investors from unsuitable high-risk investments. Penny stocks are:

- non-Nasdaq-listed equity securities;
- traded in the OTC market;
- for prices of less than $5 per share; and
- quoted on the NASD's OTC Bulletin Board Service and in the *Pink Sheets*.

**Penny Stock Rules**. A potential investor must be approved by the broker-dealer to make penny stock transactions. The broker-dealer must have the following documents on file:

- **Suitability statement**, signed by the customer, describing the customer's financial condition, investment objectives and investment experience;
- **Risk disclosure document**, signed by the customer, prior to the customer's first penny stock transaction; and
- **"Important Information on Penny Stocks"** with a signed acknowledgement of receipt by the customer. The document defines the term "penny stock," describes the market for penny stocks, the risks of investing in penny stocks, the broker-dealer's responsibilities and the investor's legal rights.

Before making a penny stock trade for a customer, the broker-dealer must obtain a signed transaction agreement containing:

- the name of the penny stock;
- the number of shares to be purchased;
- a current quotation; and
- the amount of commission received by the firm and by the representative.

Established customers are exempt from the Penny Stock Rules. Established customers are those who have an account open with the broker-dealer *and:*

- have made a securities transaction previous to the last year; *or*
- have made at least three penny stock purchases from different issuers on different days.

## Business Accounts

When a registered rep opens a business account of any type, it is necessary to establish three items:

1. the business's legal right to open an investment account;
2. any limitations that the owners, stockholders, a court or any other entity has placed on the investments in which the business will be allowed to invest; and
3. who will be allowed to represent the business in transactions involving the account.

## Trading Authorization/ Power of Attorney

Any time a power of attorney or a discretionary power to the broker has been established for an investment account, a signed copy of that document must be kept on file.

## Special Account Situations

**Numbered accounts**. If a customer account is identified by only a number or symbol, the customer must sign a form certifying that she owns the account(s) identified by the number or symbol.

**Account transfers**. In transferring a customer's account from one broker-dealer to another, if any of the assets in the account cannot be transferred (for example, because they are proprietary products or available only through a business relationship with a third party), the customer must provide directions as to whether they should be liquidated, retained for the customer by the original broker-dealer or transferred directly to the customer. The transfer instructions are validated when the current firm returns them to the new firm together with an attachment detailing the customer's securities positions, securities held in street name, cash balances and outstanding Regulation T calls. The account transfer must be completed within *four business days after validation.*

## Account Records

Books or records for each customer's account are maintained at both the branch and the main office and include the following:

- customer's name, address and phone number
- type of account and account number
- investment objective
- list of all securities deposited with the firm
- list of all transactions

**Signatures**. When a customer opens an individual cash account or a custodial account, the customer's signature is not required. For all other types of accounts, the customer's signature must be included in the account records.

## Opening Accounts for Employees of Other Brokers

Permission from or written notification to some other broker-dealer regarding the establishment of the account may be required for:

- employee of a broker-dealer; and
- spouse or minor child of an employee of a broker-dealer.

**NASD requirements**. NASD rules require the firm opening the account to notify the customer's employer. The employee is responsible for disclosing that she is an associated person of an NASD member when opening the account. Duplicate confirmations and statements must be sent to the employer broker-dealer only if the employer requests them.

**NYSE requirements**. The NYSE requires prior written approval from the employer broker-dealer before an employee of a member firm can open a cash or margin account with another firm. Duplicate statements and confirmations must be sent by the transacting firm to the employer broker-dealer.

**MSRB requirements**. The employer must be notified in writing that the account is being opened and must be mailed duplicate confirmations, unless requested in writing not to do so.

# Questions

1. When a registered rep receives instructions from a customer to *transfer and ship*, the rep will instruct the margin department to transfer ownership into the
   A. customer's name and deliver the securities to the customer
   B. brokerage firm's name and deliver the securities to the customer
   C. brokerage firm's name and deliver the securities to the brokerage firm's commercial bank for safekeeping
   D. customer's name and deliver the securities to the customer's bank for safekeeping

2. A brokerage firm can open an account for all of the following EXCEPT a(n)
   A. pension fund
   B. insurance company
   C. estate
   D. third party without written authorization to do so

3. An employee of another broker-dealer would like to open an account with your firm. All of the following statements regarding the employee and the account are true EXCEPT that the
   A. employer must receive duplicate copies of all transactions made in the account if requested
   B. employer must be notified of the opening of the account
   C. opening member must notify the employee, in writing, that the employer will be notified of the employee's intent to open the account
   D. broker-dealer holding the account must approve each transaction made by the person before entry of the order

4. A customer wants her account designated by number, not by her name. The registered rep
   A. cannot open the account in this manner
   B. can open the account with a written statement of ownership from the customer
   C. can open this account with a written statement of ownership and approval from an authorized delegate of the customer
   D. can open this account without additional documentation

5. Which of the following must sign a new account form?
   I. Principal
   II. Registered representative
   III. Customer
   IV. Spouse of the customer

   A. I and II only
   B. I, II and III only
   C. II and III only
   D. I, II, III and IV

6. All of the following are required on a new account form EXCEPT the customer's
   A. name
   B. date of birth
   C. Social Security number
   D. occupation

7. All of the following need permission to open margin accounts with an NYSE member firm EXCEPT an employee of a(n)
   A. communications company
   B. bank
   C. broker-dealer
   D. insurance company

8. An NYSE member firm must notify or receive prior permission of the employer of a customer in all of the following situations EXCEPT when opening a

   A. margin account for a bank teller
   B. margin account for the president of an insurance firm
   C. margin account for an employee of the NYSE
   D. cash account for an employee of an NYSE firm

9. Confidential or numbered accounts may be opened provided that the customer

   A. has a regular account at the firm already
   B. signs a power of attorney form
   C. signs a form stating he is the owner of the numbered account
   D. is of legal age

10. A customer is going on a trip and wishes to have his brokerage firm stop sending mail. The firm can do all of the following EXCEPT

   A. hold it for two months if he is traveling domestically
   B. hold it for three months if he is traveling internationally
   C. send the mail to a post office box
   D. send the mail to his registered representative's office

# Answers

1. **A.** "Transfer and ship" means to *transfer* the securities into the name of the customer and *ship* (deliver) the securities to the customer. *Hold in street name* would require the securities to be transferred into the name of the broker-dealer and held for safekeeping.

2. **D.** An account cannot be opened for a third party without proper authorization. For example, John Jones cannot open an account for his brother Fred. But Fred can open an account and authorize John to trade in it. Fred may also sign a power of attorney, which grants John the right to open an account and trade for Fred.

3. **D.** The NASD does not require prior approval of individual transactions by the broker-dealer at which the account has been opened.

4. **B.** For numbered accounts, the customer must sign a document attesting to ownership.

5. **A.** To open a cash account, only the signatures of the registered rep introducing the account and the principal accepting the account are required. For margin accounts, the signature of the customer is required on the margin agreement. The signature of the spouse is required only for a joint account.

6. **B.** Although the date of birth is often obtained, it is not required. All that is required is information stating that the customer is of age.

7. **A.** Under NYSE rules, employees of other broker-dealers or employees of other financial institutions must have permission in hand to open a margin account. The rules do not apply to an employee or someone outside the financial industry. The communications company is outside the financial industry.

8. **B.** NYSE rules require that if an NYSE employee or an employee of a member firm opens either a cash or margin account at another member firm, the employer must be notified in writing. If

an employee of an institution wished to open a margin account (not a cash account), the employer must also be notified in writing. An officer of an institution is not an employee—no written notification is required for this individual to open a margin account.

9. **C.** A numbered account gives the customer a degree of anonymity in the securities traded. The name of the customer in a numbered account is not public knowledge, but someone in the member firm must know who owns the account. So, the customer must sign a form attesting to the fact that he owns the account.

10. **D.** Customer mail may not be sent to a customer's registered representative's office. If this were done, there is no assurance that the mail would be forwarded to the customer. It could also provide a way for a registered representative to withhold information from the customer.

# Types of Accounts

## Single Accounts

In a single account, there is only one beneficial owner, the only person who can:

- control the investments within the account; and
- request distributions of cash or securities from the account.

## Joint Accounts

If the names of two or more adults appear on the account and each will be allowed some form of control over the account, it is called a **joint account**. Any or all tenants may transact business in the account. Checks must be made payable to the name(s) in which the account is registered, although mail need only be sent to a single address. To be in good delivery form, securities sold from a joint account must be signed by all tenants.

- **Joint tenants in common**. JTIC ownership provides that a deceased tenant's fractional interest in the account is retained by that tenant's estate and is not passed to the surviving tenant(s), if any.
- **Joint tenants with right of survivorship**. JTWROS ownership stipulates that a deceased tenant's interest in the account passes to the surviving tenant(s).

## Partnership Accounts

The partnership is required to provide a partnership agreement stating which of the partners can make transactions for the account. If a margin account is opened, the partnership must disclose any investment limitations.

## Corporate Accounts

The corporation must submit a corporate resolution for a cash account. The resolution, signed by the secretary of the corporation, identifies officers authorized to make transactions. In addition to the documentation required for all margin accounts, corporate margin accounts require a certified copy of the corporate charter and bylaws authorizing a margin account. A *certificate of incumbency*, which empowers the officers to trade the account, must be obtained within 60 days of opening the account.

## Fiduciary and Custodial Accounts

In a fiduciary account, the investments exist for the beneficial interest of the owner, yet the owner has little or no legal control over them. The fiduciary makes all of the investment, management and distribution decisions, and is required by law to manage the account in the best interests of the owner. The contents of the account may never be used by the fiduciary for his own benefit, although the fiduciary may be reimbursed for reasonable expenses incurred in the management of the account.

Securities bought in a fiduciary or custodial account must be registered in such a way that the relationship is evident. The *beneficial owner's Social Security number* would be used to open the account and would appear on the account statements.

Fiduciaries include:

- **trustees** designated to administer a trust;
- **executors** who are designated in a decedent's will to manage the affairs of the estate;
- **administrators** appointed by the courts to liquidate the estate of a person who died intestate (without a will);
- **guardians** designated by the courts to handle the affairs of a minor until that minor reaches the age of majority or to handle the affairs of an incompetent;

- **custodians** of a Uniform Gifts to Minors Act (UGMA) account;
- **receivers** in a bankruptcy; and
- **conservators** for incompetents.

Fiduciaries may need special permission to trade certain securities in a custodial account. In general, the trust agreement will state whether there are restrictions or prohibitions that the fiduciary must abide by (such as no option trades or no trading on margin). In addition, any trades that are entered by the fiduciary must be compatible with the trust's investment objectives.

**Opening a fiduciary account.** Opening a fiduciary account requires:

- completion of a new account form for fiduciaries; and
- acquisition of a court certificate or another acceptable document to certify the individual's appointment and authority.

No documentation of custodial rights is required for an UGMA. Fiduciary account rules include:

- **Authorization.** Proper authorization must be given (the necessary court documents must be filed with and verified by the broker-dealer).
- **Speculation.** Speculative transactions are generally not permitted.
- **Margin trading.** Margin accounts are permitted only if the legal documents establishing the fiduciary account authorize them.
- **Prudent man rule.** The prudent man rule requires fiduciaries to make prudent (wise and safe) investments.
- **Legal list.** Many states publish a legal list of securities approved for fiduciary accounts.
- **Power of attorney.** No authority may be delegated (a power of attorney cannot be accepted for the account).
- **Compensation.** The fiduciary may not share in the profits of the account, but may charge a reasonable fee for services.

## Power of Attorney

If an individual wants another person to have trading authority in (access to or control of) her investment account and that person is not named on the account as an owner, custodian, trustee or some other form of legal account manager, then the customer must file written authorization with the broker-dealer giving that person access to the account.

### Full Power of Attorney

A full power of attorney allows someone who is not the beneficial owner of an account to:

- deposit or withdraw cash and/or securities; and
- make investment decisions for the owner of the account.

Custodians, trustees, guardians and other people filling similar legal duties typically have been given full power of attorney.

### Limited Power of Attorney

A limited power of attorney gives someone other than the beneficial owner some (but not total) control over the account.

## Discretionary Accounts

Customers who want to give a registered rep the authority to make transactions on their behalf without having to ask for specific approval each time set up a *discretionary account*. "Discretion" is defined as the *authority to decide*:

- the security
- the number of shares (or units)
- whether to buy or sell

Discretion *does not* apply to decisions regarding only the *timing* of the investment or the *price* at which it is acquired.

**Discretionary authority**. There are a number of rules and regulations regarding discretionary accounts of which the registered rep must be aware. A customer can give a registered rep discretionary power over his account(s) only by filing a trading authorization or a limited power of attorney with the registered rep's broker-dealer. No transactions of a discretionary nature can take place without this document on file. Once trading authorization has been given, the customer is legally bound to accept the registered rep's decisions, although the customer may continue to enter orders on his own.

The power of attorney remains in force for no more than three years, at which point it can be renewed at the discretion of the customer.

On every discretionary account the registered rep needs to record whether the customer is of legal age and the occupation of the customer, as well as the signature of each person authorized to exercise discretion in the account. The account file must also include the signature of the registered rep who introduced the account and the signature of the member, partner or other company officer who accepted the account for the firm.

Discretionary accounts are subject to the following:

- Each discretionary order must be *identified* as such at the time it is entered for execution.
- Each order must be *approved promptly* and in writing by an officer or partner of the brokerage house.
- A *record* must be kept of all transactions.
- There must *not be excessive trading* in the account.
- A designated supervisor or manager (registered principal) must *review all trading activity* frequently and systematically.
- If a firm has a control relationship with an issuer, the customer's specific permission is required before the issuer's securities can be sold to a discretionary account.

## Death or Incompetence of an Account Holder

In the event a customer dies or is declared incompetent by a court, the necessary legal documents must be obtained (e.g., death certificate, affidavit of domicile and letters testamentary).

### Powers of Attorney

All trading authorizations cease upon the death or declaration of incompetency of the account owner.

### Single Account

If the owner of a single account dies or is declared incompetent, the account must be frozen, which means all pending transactions and outstanding orders must be *immediately canceled*. The registered rep may need to obtain a copy of the death certificate, of the document appointing the executor of the estate or a copy of the certificate of incompetency. The executor of the estate will then instruct the registered rep as to how the account should be handled or distributed.

### Joint Tenants with Right of Survivorship (JTWROS)

Each owner of the JTWROS form of account has an **equal and undivided interest** in the cash and securities in the account. On the death or declaration of incompetency of any or all of the account owners, all pending transactions and outstanding orders must be canceled immediately. Account ownership passes to the survivor(s)—there is a "right of succession."

### Joint Tenants in Common (JTIC)

Each owner of the JTIC form of account has a **separate title** but an **undivided interest** in the cash and securities in the account. At the death or declaration of incompetency of one of the owners of the account, all pending transactions and outstanding orders must be canceled immediately. That person's proportionate share of the cash and securities in the account is distributed according to the instructions in the decedent's will to his heirs.

### Custodial Account

If the beneficial owner of a custodial account dies, all pending transactions and outstanding orders must be immediately canceled and any securities or cash in the account go to the owner's estate, not to the custodian or the custodian's estate. If the custodian dies, a new custodian must be named to manage the account.

### Partnership Account

If one of the partners in a partnership account dies or is declared incompetent, all pending transactions and outstanding orders must be immediately canceled and the account frozen.

## Questions

1. An account is owned by three partners, one of whom dies. The registered rep

   A. may continue to trade the account once a letter stating that the partner has died is received
   B. must freeze the account's assets
   C. must close out the account and all outstanding orders because the death of a partner dissolves the partnership
   D. may continue to trade the account only after receiving a certified copy of the partner's death certificate

2. A brokerage firm carrying an account managed by an investment adviser requires all of the following EXCEPT

   A. a written statement of the investment adviser's authority to manage the account
   B. a written statement from the customer as to where the confirmations of transactions are to be sent
   C. the name, address and other essential information concerning the customer
   D. a list, including addresses and phone numbers, of all of the investment adviser's customers

3. All of the following can grant third-party trading authorizations EXCEPT a(n)

   A. corporation
   B. partnership
   C. individual
   D. custodian

4. Which of the following are considered fiduciaries?

   I. Executor of an estate
   II. Administrator of a trust
   III. Custodian of an UGMA account
   IV. Registered rep granted the authority to choose the security, quantity and action in a customer's account

   A. I and II only
   B. I, II and III only
   C. II, III and IV only
   D. I, II, III and IV

5. A customer of an NYSE firm asks her registered rep to exercise discretion over her account. To do so, the rep must

   I. obtain written authorization from the customer for the discretionary account
   II. obtain evidence of written acceptance of the account by a registered principal of the firm
   III. have a principal promptly initial each order
   IV. effect no transaction beyond the customer's financial capability

   A. I only
   B. I and III only
   C. II and IV only
   D. I, II, III and IV

6. The NASD Rules of Fair Practice state that

   I. the member or designated person must approve in writing each discretionary order entered and must frequently review all discretionary accounts to detect excessive trading
   II. a registered representative must have the customer's prior written authorization before exercising any discretionary power
   III. transactions in discretionary accounts cannot be excessive in size

   A. I and II only
   B. I and III only
   C. II and III only
   D. I, II and III

7. Which of the following would be considered discretionary?

   A. Order that specifies the size of the security but leaves the choice of price and time up to the registered rep
   B. Account in which the broker has the power to decide when and what to trade, without specific customer authorization for those trades
   C. Account in which the customer has power of attorney over another individual's account
   D. Account in which an investment adviser has power of attorney over another individual's account

# Answers

1. **B.** The partnership assets will be frozen until receipt of appropriate documentation. The partnership is dissolved, and the other partners cannot trade without a reformation of the partnership.

2. **D.** The adviser does not have to disclose his customer list to the broker-dealer. What is required when opening a separate customer account is a new account card, a trading authorization and a statement from the customer as to who will receive the confirmations.

3. **D.** A custodian is a fiduciary and may not assign a power of attorney or trading authorization to another. The custodian may only resign the position of custodian.

4. **D.** Each of these has a fiduciary relationship to the customer or entity involved.

5. **D.** The requirements for a discretionary account include a written authorization from the customer, a written acceptance by the firm, and close supervision of each transaction to ensure suitable transactions in light of the customer's objectives and financial situation.

6. **D.** According to the Rules of Fair Practice, no member or registered representative can exercise discretionary authority over a customer's account without prior written authorization. The account must be approved by the member. Discretionary orders must be promptly approved in writing by the member, and the account must be reviewed frequently to prevent excessive trading (churning).

7. **B.** An order is *discretionary* when it is placed by the member firm or its representative for a customer's account without the customer's express authorization for that order. Also, for the order to be considered discretionary, the firm must choose more than just the price or time of execution; that is, the size of the trade, whether to buy or sell, and/or the security must be chosen by the firm.

# Uniform Gifts to Minors Act Accounts

UGMA and UTMA accounts require an adult (or bank trust department) to act as custodian for a minor (the beneficial owner). Any kind of security—cash, life insurance, annuity contracts and other forms of property—may be given, and there is no limitation on the dollar amount of the gift.

### Donating Securities

A gift to a minor through an UGMA gives the minor what is known as **indefeasible title**; that is, title that cannot be made null or void. The minor is considered the beneficial owner of the account and its contents. The gift is *irrevocable*: the donor may not take back the gift, nor may the minor return the gift until she has reached the age of majority or the age that the laws of her state have set as the age when the custodianship will terminate. When the minor reaches the specified age, the property in the accounts is transferred into her name.

### Custodian

Securities given in an UGMA account are managed by a custodian until the minor attains the age of majority. The custodian may be either the donor or a person appointed by the donor. The custodian has full control over the minor's account and can:

- buy or sell securities
- exercise rights or warrants
- liquidate, trade or hold securities

The custodian may also use the property in the account in any way that person deems proper for the support, education, maintenance, general use or benefit of the minor. The account may *not* be used to discharge the liabilities normally associated with raising the child, such as for payment of food, shelter, and so on.

Restrictions governing the custodial relationship in a minor's account include:

- For each account, there may be only one custodian and one minor or beneficial owner.
- One person may not be the custodian for two minors in a joint account, nor can there be two people sharing custodial duties for one minor.
- A minor can be the beneficiary of more than one account and a person may serve as custodian for more than one UGMA as long as each account benefits only one minor.
- The donor of the securities can act as custodian or can appoint someone else to the responsibility.
- Parents, unless acting as custodians for a minor's account, have no legal control over, or recourse to, the account or any of the securities in it.

The registered representative is not responsible for determining whether the appointment is valid or whether the custodian's activities are actually within his authority.

### Opening an UGMA Account

When opening an UGMA account for a customer, the rep must ensure that the account application contains the custodian's name, the minor's name and Social Security number, and the state in which the UGMA is registered.

### Registration of UGMA Securities

Any securities in an UGMA account are registered in the name of the custodian for the benefit of the minor; they cannot be registered *in street name*. When the minor reaches the age of majority, all of the securities in the account will be registered in her name.

### Fiduciary Responsibility

Restrictions placed on what is deemed to be proper handling of the investments in an UGMA include:

- UGMAs may only be opened and managed as cash accounts.

- Securities in the account may not be purchased on margin or pledged by the custodian as collateral for a loan.
- All cash proceeds, dividends and interest must be reinvested by the custodian within a reasonable period of time. Cash proceeds from sales or dividends may be held in a noninterest-bearing custodial account for a reasonable period.
- Investment decisions must take into account the age of the minor and the custodial relationship; commodities futures, naked options and other high-risk securities are examples of inappropriate investments. Options may not be placed or purchased in a custodial account because no evidence of ownership is issued to an option buyer.
- Stock subscription rights or warrants must be either exercised or sold.
- A custodian for an UGMA may not grant trading authority to a third party.
- A custodian may loan money to the account, but may never borrow from it.

The custodian may be reimbursed for any reasonable expenses incurred in the management of the account (unless the custodian is also the donor).

### Taxation

The minor's Social Security number appears on the account, and the minor must file an annual income tax return and pay taxes on any income produced by the UGMA at *the parent's top marginal tax rate*, regardless of the source of the gift, until the minor reaches the age of 14. Exclusions are available, and they are indexed for inflation. For example, in 1995 the first $650 of a minor's earnings is tax free and the next $650 is taxed at the minor's rate, usually 15%, for a total of $1,300; earnings in excess of $1,300 are taxed at the parent's top rate.

When the minor reaches age 14, any taxes incurred by the account will be charged at the minor's rate, rather than at the parent's rate.

### Death of the Minor, Custodian or Donor

If the minor beneficiary of an UGMA dies, the securities in the account pass to the minor's estate, not to the parents' or custodian's estates.

## Questions

1. Securities owned by a donor and given to a minor under the Uniform Gifts to Minors Act become the property of the minor

   A. when the securities are paid for by the minor
   B. on the settlement date
   C. when the securities are registered in the custodian's name for the benefit of the minor
   D. when the donor decides to give the securities to the minor

## Answers

1. **C.** Transfer of securities into the custodial account completes the gift. At that time the minor becomes the owner of the securities.

# 9 Brokerage Office Procedures

## Brokerage Support Services

### Processing an Order

Orders and order tickets are routed as follows:

- order department (wire room, order room)
- purchases and sales department
- margin or credit department
- cashiering department

A clearing corporation (such as the National Securities Clearing Corporation—NSCC) totals all trades on a daily basis for each of its participating firms and balances the books of one firm against those of another.

Other departments involved in client transactions include:

- reorganization department
- dividend department
- proxy department
- stock record department
- controller's department

### Transactions and Trade Settlement

#### Receipt and Delivery of Securities

When a representative accepts a buy order from a customer, the representative must inquire of and be assured that the customer agrees to receive the securities and will pay for them at the agreed upon price. For a sell order, the rep must be assured that the customer has the security (in a long position) and can deliver it within three business days of the trade date (T+3). If the customer claims the security is being held in street name at another firm, the rep must verify this before executing a sell transaction for the customer.

#### Order Memorandum

The order memo must be prepared by the registered rep and approved by a principal on the day of the trade.

The following information is required on the order ticket:

- client identification number;
- registered rep identification number;
- description of the security (symbol);
- number of shares or bonds to be traded;
- where the security is traded;
- action (buy, sell long, sell short);
- options (buy, write, covered, uncovered, opening, closing);
- price qualifications (at market, GTC, day order, stop order, price limit);
- type of account (cash, margin);
- settlement instructions (if not established when account was opened);
- security instructions;
- payment instructions; and
- location of certificates sold.

### Report of Execution

If there is any error that appears to be due to either an incorrect ticket or a mistaken execution, the error should be reported immediately to a supervisor or manager. A registered rep should never try to correct an error by making additional trades without approval from a principal of the firm.

**Erroneous reports**. Whether or not the details of a trade are reported to a customer incorrectly, the actual trade is binding on the customer.

### Trade Confirmations

A confirmation is a printed document that confirms the trade, settlement date and amount of money due from or owed to the client. For each transaction, a client must be sent or given a written confirmation of the trade *at or before the completion of the transaction* (known as the **settlement date**). An exception to this rule is made for wire order purchases of mutual funds for which confirmation may be sent by the selling agent as late as the day after the settlement date.

Components of the trade confirmation include the following:

- trade date
- customer account number
- registered rep's identification number
- the notation "BOT" (bought) or "SLD" (sold)
- number (or quantity) of securities
- description of securities, such as:
  - yield to call, if applicable
  - CUSIP number
- price, including odd-lot differential, if applicable
- amount
- commission
- interest or tax
- registration fee
- net amount

**Timely mailing of confirmations**. Customer confirmations must be sent no later than *at or before the completion of the transaction*.

### Customer Account Statements

Firms are required to send each customer who has a securities position (or whose account has seen any activity) a quarterly statement showing positions and entries in that account. The statement shows:

- all activity in the account since the previous statement;
- securities positions, long or short; and
- account balances, debit or credit.

If a *free credit balance* exists in a customer's account, the statement must advise the customer that these funds are available on request.

### Charges for Services Performed

A member broker-dealer's fees and charges (for services, safekeeping, securities transfers, securities redemptions and dividend and interest collection) must:

- be reasonable;
- relate to the work performed, transaction entered or advisory services given; and
- not be unfairly discriminatory between customers.

## Transaction Settlement Dates and Terms

**Settlement date** is the date on which ownership changes between buyer and seller. It is the date on which a customer is expected to pay for securities bought and make delivery on securities sold.

### Regular Way Settlement

The SEC sets the *standard securities settlement cycle* in the United States, and this settlement cycle is used to determine various settlement and payment dates. **Regular way settlement** for most securities transactions (with the notable exceptions of transactions in U.S. government securities and money-market instruments) is the *third business day* following the trade date (also known as *T+3*). As an example, if a trade occurs on a Tuesday (trade date), it would settle regular way on Friday (T+3). If a trade takes place on a Thursday, it would settle the following Tuesday.

If the seller delivers prior to the settlement date, the buyer may either accept the security or refuse it without prejudice.

For U.S. government notes and bonds, regular way settlement is the *next business day*. For money-market securities (commercial paper, bankers' acceptances, negotiable certificates of deposit and U.S. Treasury bills), settlement is the *same day* (small retail transactions are sometimes billed for next day settlement).

### Cash Settlement

Cash settlement requires delivery of securities from sellers and payment from buyers on the *same day* the trade is executed.

### Seller's Option Contracts

A seller's option contract allows the seller to settle the trade up to *60 calendar days* from the trade date. Or, if the seller elects to settle earlier than originally specified, the trade can be settled on any date from the *fourth business day* (one day beyond regular way settlement) through the *sixtieth calendar day*, provided the buyer is given a one-day written notice.

A buyer's option contract works the same way, except the option rests with the buyer as to when settlement will take place.

### When-, As- and If-issued Contracts

When issued trades come about mainly in two ways: through corporate stock splits and through new issue municipal bonds. The final settlement date of when issued trades is determined by the NASD's Uniform Practice Committee, and normally is *three business days* after issuance.

### Reg T Payment

The Reg T payment date is the day the broker-dealer must collect payment from the customer (payment is due from the customer). Under Reg T, the *payment period* is defined as the number of days in one standard securities settlement cycle *plus two business days*. When the standard securities settlement cycle is three business days, as it is now, the Reg T payment period is five business days.

**Extensions**. If for good reason a buyer is unable to pay for a trade within five business days from the trade date, the broker-dealer may request an extension from its designated examining authority (DEA) prior to the fifth business day. The broker-dealer has the option of ignoring amounts of less than $1,000 without violating Reg T requirements.

**Frozen accounts**. If a customer buys securities in a cash account and sells them before paying for the buy side in full by the fifth business day, or fails to meet a Reg T call, the account is *frozen*—any additional transactions must be on a cash-and-carry basis. Frozen account status continues for a period of *90 calendar days*. If a customer buys and sells as described previously but pays for the buy side not later than the fifth business day, frozen account status is lifted.

## Dividend Department

### Dividend Disbursing Agent

The stockholder does not have to do anything in order to receive cash, property or stock dividends, or new shares after a split or a reverse split. If the securities are held at the broker-dealer's in street name, the **dividend disbursing agent** (in the case of dividends) or the **transfer agent** (in the case of stock splits) will make the appropriate distributions or transfers directly to the broker-dealer.

### Dividend Disbursing Process

**Declaration date**. A company's board of directors approves the payment of a dividend, announcing the amount, payment date and date on which it will be determined who is and who is not a registered stockholder (known as the *dividend record date*).

**Ex-dividend date**. Based on the dividend record date announced previously, an **ex-date** will be posted for trading and price continuity purposes. The ex-date is *two business days* before the announced record date. Because most trades settle regular way—three business days after the trade date—a customer would have to purchase the stock three business days before the record date in order to qualify for the dividend.

On the ex-date, the opening price of the stock drops to compensate for the fact that customers who buy the stock that day or later will not qualify for the dividend. The customer who buys the stock before the ex-date receives the dividend, but pays a higher price for the stock (and is said to have *bought the dividend*). The customer who buys the stock after the ex-date does not receive the dividend, but pays a lower price for the stock.

**Cash trades**. Cash trades settle the same day—cash trades go ex-dividend on the day after the record date.

**Dividend record date**. The date selected by a corporation that is used to determine who is and who is not stockholder of record for dividend payment or rights distribution purposes.

**Payable date**. The date the dividend disbursing agent (or another company-authorized entity) cuts dividend checks and mails them to all stockholders whose names appear on the books as of the record date.

### Rights and Warrant Distributions

**Rights** are distributed in connection with stock subscription offerings. The ex-rights date is the first business day after the effective date of the SEC registration statement. **Warrant distributions** are treated in the same manner as dividends. The ex-warrant date is the same as the ex-dividend date, which is the second business day preceding the record date.

### Stock Dividends and Splits

Normal stock dividends (such as 2% or 5%) are handled exactly the same as cash dividends. But any stock distribution (including a stock split) that amounts to 25% or more of the shares outstanding is subject to special handling. The ex-date on stock dividends in excess of 25% and stock splits of 5 for 4 or better is the *first business day* following the payable date.

### Ex-dates for Bonds Traded Flat

Bonds that are traded "flat" will have an ex-date and record date if the issuer declares an interest payment.

## Proxy Department

**The proxy**. A proxy is a *limited power of attorney* given by a stockholder to another person with which the stockholder gives that person the right to vote on behalf of the stockholder. The exchanges require listed companies to solicit proxies from stockholders, which ensures that all stockholders will have input into major company decisions. Proxies must be in printed or written form, are valid only for the specified meeting and are intended to be used to cast votes only on matters addressed at that meeting.

The voting authorization given through a proxy is revocable by the stockholder in the event she later chooses to attend the meeting. A stockholder who signs a proxy and sends it in without specifying a vote is indicating that she wishes the broker-dealer holding her certificates to vote her shares in the same manner as any others the firm has. All proxies become invalid at the death of the stockholder.

Proxy material, annual reports and other information sent by corporations to member firms that hold stock in street name for their customers must be forwarded to the beneficial owners at the issuing corporation's expense.

## Tender Offers

A tender is an offer to buy securities, often used in the takeover of a corporation. The buyer may want an unlimited amount of stock (an unlimited tender) or just enough stock to gain control. When stock is tendered, there is no guarantee of purchase. The offer could be canceled for a number of reasons. An **exchange offer** is one type of tender offer. One party is interested in exchanging its own securities for those of another party.

# Questions

1. Which department in a brokerage firm would handle all credit transactions for a client?

   A. Margin
   B. Cashiering
   C. Purchases and sales
   D. Reorganization

2. Once received, orders flow through a brokerage firm in which sequence?

   I. Wire room
   II. Purchases and sales department
   III. Margin department
   IV. Cashiering department

   A. I, II, III, IV
   B. I, IV, II, III
   C. II, I, IV, III
   D. III, IV, II, I

In questions 3 through 5, write T (True) or F (False) next to each statement.

3. ___ A client must be sent or given a written confirmation at or before the completion of every transaction (the settlement date).

4. ___ The cashiering department handles all credit activities.

5. ___ If there are any errors in the execution of a transaction, you should try to correct them yourself only if it happens in one of *your* client's accounts.

6. Mr. Jones buys 200 shares of RCA at 34 1/2. Later the same day his broker tells him that the report he received was in error and, in fact, the shares were bought for 34 3/4. Mr. Jones

   A. must pay 34 1/2 per share
   B. must pay 34 3/4 per share
   C. may cancel the order
   D. may require that his broker pay the difference

7. According to the 1934 act, an individual or a firm becomes a *participant* in a proxy contest if the individual or firm

   A. gives unsolicited advice to one or more stockholders
   B. gives advice (either solicited or not) to six or more stockholders
   C. gives advice (either solicited or not) to twelve or more stockholders
   D. votes 1,000 or more stocks against the management

8. A customer has an inactive account at a broker-dealer firm. The account does have a few dollars remaining in it as a free credit balance. The firm must report to the customer

   A. monthly
   B. quarterly
   C. semiannually
   D. annually

9. If a registered rep volunteers advice to her clients about how to vote in a proxy contest, she

   A. has acted illegally
   B. may do so only on listed securities
   C. may do so only if her firm specializes in that stock
   D. may have to file under SEC proxy contest rules as a participant

10. When a "contest" condition exists, a member firm can vote stock held *in street name*

    A. if the beneficial owner requests it
    B. only in favor of management
    C. only to oppose management
    D. only if the member firm owns less than 10% of the voting stock of the corporation

11. A sell-out is when

    A. the buyer of a security fails to complete the contract to buy according to its terms and the broker-dealer closes the contract by selling the security for the account of the buyer
    B. the seller of a security fails to complete the contract to sell according to its terms and the buyer closes the contract by buying the security in the best available market and charging the seller
    C. the party who requests the transfer of securities fails to pay the transfer agent's service charges and the transfer agent sells off the securities to cover the deficit
    D. a season ticketholder gives a single game's ticket to a client

12. NASD rules make it clear that any service charges (other than commissions) have to be

    A. limited to less than 1% a year
    B. based on the size and the amount of activity in a client's account
    C. standardized across the board at 5% a year
    D. reasonable and not unfairly discriminatory between clients

13. In a cash transaction on the record date, when is the ex-dividend date?

    A. Record date
    B. Business day following the record date
    C. Two days following the record date
    D. Second business day preceding the record date

14. According to NYSE rules, the delivery date for regular way transactions is
    A. the day of the contract
    B. the third business day following the day of the contract
    C. within the time specified, but not less than four business days or more than 60 calendar days
    D. the business day following the day of the contract

# Answers

1. **A.** The margin department deals with credit transactions.

2. **A.** Once received, the order flows from the order department (wire room), to the purchases and sales department, to the margin department, to the cashiering department.

3. True. A client must be sent or given (not necessarily receive) a written confirmation at or before the completion of every transaction.

4. False. The margin department handles credit transactions.

5. False. You should never try to correct an error through later executions without approval from a principal.

6. **B.** If an error has been made in the notice of execution and reported to a customer, the customer must pay for the shares at the correct price.

7. **A.** Giving any unsolicited advice to a stockholder makes one a *participant* in a proxy contest. Answering customers' questions, however, is allowed and does not mean one is a participant.

8. **B.** A broker-dealer firm must send reports to customers about their accounts at least quarterly.

9. **D.** If the client asks for advice, the registered representative may give it without registering as a participant. But if the registered representative volunteers the information without being asked, she must register as a participant.

10. **A.** It would be preferable if the beneficial owner—the customer—would vote the stock he owns. But if the customer requests it, the member firm may vote the stock.

11. **A.** If a buyer fails to accept delivery of securities as stipulated in the contract and does not provide a properly completed reclamation or rejec-

tion form, the broker-dealer can sell out in the best available market and hold the buyer liable for the price of the securities and the resulting transaction costs.

12. **D.** According to the NASD Rules of Fair Practice, charges for services performed, such as the collection of dividends, safekeeping of securities held in street name, etc., must be reasonable and not unfairly discriminating between clients.

13. **B.** In a cash transaction on the record date, the purchaser's trade date and settlement occur on the record date. Therefore, the first date on which the purchaser would not receive the dividend is the business day after the record date.

14. **B.** Settlement (regular way) is the third business day after the trade date.

# Accrued Interest Calculations

The majority of bonds trade "and interest,"—the buyer pays the seller the market price of the bond plus any interest accrued since the previous interest payment. Because the buyer will receive the full amount of the next interest payment (including interest that accrued while the seller still owned the bond), the seller will be reimbursed for that portion of interest.

Most bonds pay interest every six months on either the lst or the 15th of specified months. The payment dates are known as *coupon dates* and help identify the bond. For example:

| Interest Dates | Description |
|---|---|
| Jan. 1 and Jul. 1 | J&J bonds |
| May 1 and Nov. 1 | M&N bonds |
| Feb. 15 and Aug. 15 | F&A 15 bonds |
| Jun. 15 and Dec. 15 | J&D 15 bonds |

Accrued interest affects bond transactions when settlement occurs between coupon dates. For example, if a J&J bond trades in March, the buyer will collect six months of interest in July from the issuer even though he owned the bond for only three months of that period. The buyer and seller settle this by adding the accrued interest to the cost of the buy transaction (as well as to the sales proceeds). Therefore, the buyer pays the accrued interest to the seller and receives the full interest payment on the next coupon date.

**Accrued interest and the dated date.** The date from which interest accrual begins is called the **dated date.**

## Corporate and Municipal Bonds

Unless the settlement date on a bond transaction coincides with the bond's most current interest payment date, the cost of the bond to the buyer will include **accrued interest**. By the same token, the bond proceeds to the seller will include accrued interest.

Accrued interest is calculated from the last interest payment date up to but not including the settlement date.

### Accrued Interest Calculation: 360-day Year

Accrued interest on corporate and municipal bonds is calculated for a 360-day year of 30-day months:

$$\frac{\text{Principal} \times \text{Int. rate} \times \text{Elapsed days}}{360 \text{ days}}$$

$$= \text{Accrued bond interest}$$

For example, if an F&A corporate or municipal bond were traded regular way on Monday, March 5th, the number of days of accrued interest would be:

| | | |
|---|---|---|
| February | 30 days | |
| March 5th trade | 7 days | (settles March 8th) |
| | 37 days | |

Therefore, interest would accrue up to, but not including, the settlement date of March 8th (5 + 2).

If an A&O corporate or municipal bond is bought or sold in a cash trade on August 16th, the number of days of accrued interest would be:

| | | |
|---|---|---|
| April | 30 days | |
| May | 30 days | |
| June | 30 days | |
| July | 30 days | |
| August | 15 days | (day before trade date) |
| | 135 days | |

Assume that a particular corporate bond issue pays interest on January 1st and July 1st at an annual rate of 8%. On Tuesday, July 5th, a customer sells $10,000 worth of these bonds for regular way settlement, which will take place Friday, July 8th, the third business day from the July 5th trade date.

The selling customer is entitled to seven days' accrued interest (July 1st through July 7th). Using the 360-day-year interest formula presented earlier, accrued interest on this transaction is $15.55:

$$\$10{,}000 \times 8\% \times 7 \text{ days} \div 360 \text{ days} = \$15.55$$

## U.S. Government Bonds

### Accrued Interest Calculation: 365-day Year

For calculating time elapsed since the most recent interest payment on a government bond, an actual-days-elapsed method is used instead of the 30-day-month, 360-day-year method used for corporate and municipal bonds:

$$\frac{\text{Principal} \times \text{Int. rate} \times \dfrac{\text{Actual days}}{\text{Actual days in period}}}{2}$$

= Accrued bond interest

For example, if an F&A government bond is traded regular way on Monday, March 5th, the number of days of accrued interest would be:

| | |
|---|---|
| February | 28 days |
| March | 5 days |
| | 33 days (up to, but not including, March 6th—next day settlement date) |

If an A&O government bond is traded for cash on August 16th, the number of days of accrued interest would be:

| | |
|---|---|
| April | 30 days |
| May | 31 days |
| June | 30 days |
| July | 31 days |
| August | 15 days |
| | 137 days (actual days elapsed) |

Assume that a particular U.S. government bond carries an 8% coupon interest rate, paid semiannually on January 1st and July 1st. Using the calendar below, assume that today's date is May 14th and that a customer has entered an order to sell $10,000 worth of these bonds for regular way settlement.

The transaction will settle on Monday, May 17th, which is the next business day after Friday, May 14th. Remember that regular way settlement for government securities is the next business day, not the third business day, after the trade date.

Once again, accrued interest runs up to *but does not include* the settlement date, which, in this case, is through Sunday, May 16th. (If the customer had sold the bonds for cash settlement on May 14th, the interest would run to May 13th, a difference of three days.)

The next step is to find the actual number of calendar days from the last coupon interest date (January 1st) to May 16th. It is necessary to count the actual number of days in the bond's full interest period, which runs from January 1st to July 1st.

| Month | Actual Days | Coupon Period |
|---|---|---|
| January | 31 | 31 |
| February | 28 | 28 |
| March | 31 | 31 |
| April | 30 | 30 |
| May | 16 | 31 |
| June | | 30 |
| | 136 | 181 |

The dollar amount of accrued interest on the sell transaction is $300.55:

($10,000 × 8% × 136 days ÷ 181 days) ÷ 2 = $300.55

For government securities, a half-year's interest is used to calculate accrued interest.

# Questions

1. Sara Long purchased a 7% J&J 15 municipal bond on Thursday, March 18th, in a regular way trade. How much accrued interest will she pay?

   A. $12.83
   B. $13.22
   C. $13.61
   D. $15.36

2. A customer purchased a T bond in a regular way transaction on Monday, April 4th. Settlement will be on

   A. Monday, April 4th
   B. Tuesday, April 5th
   C. Wednesday, April 6th
   D. Thursday, April 7th

3. A customer purchased a T bond in a regular way transaction on Monday, April 4th. The bond is a J&J bond. How many days of accrued interest will the seller receive?

   A. 79
   B. 80
   C. 94
   D. 95

4. A J&J Treasury bond with a 10 1/4% coupon due July 1, 1999, is purchased in a cash transaction with a settlement date of February 24th. What is the number of days of accrued interest?

   A. 53
   B. 54
   C. 55
   D. 63

5. A bond is dated June 1, 1995. The first interest payment is on January 1, 1996. How many months will the first and second interest payments cover?

   A. one month for the first, five months for the second
   B. one month for the first, six months for the second
   C. seven months for the first, five months for the second
   D. seven months for the first, six months for the second

# Answers

1. **B.** Interest was paid up to but not including January 15th when the last payment was made. This leaves 16 days of interest accrual in January (30 – 14). Settlement on the trade is March 23rd (18 + 5, three business days plus the weekend). Interest accrues for the seller, then, through March 22nd. Interest accrues, therefore, for 68 days (Jan 16 + Feb 30 + Mar 22). The amount of accrued interest is calculated as follows: $70 (annual interest) times 68 divided by 360 (the portion of the year accrued) equals $13.22.

2. **B.** Regular way settlement on government securities is the next business day.

3. **C.**

| | |
|---|---|
| January | 31 days |
| February | 28 days |
| March | 31 days |
| April | 4 days |
| Total | 94 days |

Remember that government obligations accrue interest for the actual number of days (up to but not including settlement).

4. **B.** A coupon bond starts accruing interest on the payment date of the previous coupon (January 1st) and accrues up to but not including the settlement date (February 24th) because it was a cash settlement. Because accrued interest on government bonds is computed actual days, actual year, 31 for Jan plus 23 for Feb equals 54 days.

5. **D.** Because the bond is dated June 1st with the first interest payment the following January 1st, the initial payment covers seven months of interest. Thereafter, the bond will pay interest semiannually, as bonds normally do.

# Rules of Good Delivery

It is the registered rep's responsibility to inquire of a customer who calls with a sell order as to whether the security:

- is negotiable,
- is in compliance with the contract of sale,
- can be delivered to the broker-dealer within three business days, and
- is ready to be transferred from seller to purchaser.

"**Good delivery**" describes the physical condition, signatures, attachments and denomination of the certificates involved in a securities transaction. The transfer agent is the final arbiter of whether a security meets the requirements of good delivery.

- **Round lots: stocks**. A round lot for common stock is 100 shares or any multiple thereof. Odd lots are units of fewer than 100 shares or a combination of a round lot with an odd lot.
- **Round lots: bonds**. A round lot for bonds is $1,000 face amount or multiples thereof.
- **Registered and bearer form**. Normal delivery is $1,000 or $5,000 bearer bonds. If nothing is said and registered bonds are delivered, the delivery is not good.

**Overdelivery and underdelivery**. If the customer overdelivers or underdelivers, the transaction is not good delivery.

**Partial delivery**. A broker-to-broker partial delivery must be accepted if the remainder of the delivery constitutes a round lot or multiple thereof.

**Good delivery clearing rule (100-share uniform units)**. Odd lot certificates can be used to clear round lot trades provided the odd lot certificates add up to single round lots (100 shares).

For example, if a broker-dealer is attempting to clear a 200-share trade using the following certificate denominations, which combinations can be added together to equal 100-share units and meet the requirements of good delivery?

| No. of certificates | 5 | 10 | 2 and 1 |
|---|---|---|---|
| Denomination | 40 | 20 | 90 and 20 |
| 100-share units? | No | Yes | No |
| Good delivery | No | Yes | No |

In a transaction involving round lots with an odd lot, the odd lot must be separate. For example, on a 450-share trade, one certificate for 400 shares and one certificate for 50 shares would be good delivery; five certificates for 90 shares would not.

**Missing coupons**. When coupon bonds have missing interest coupons, the broker-dealer deducts the cash value of the coupons in question from the sale proceeds to the customer.

**Partially called bonds**. If a bond issue has been partially called, no bonds in that issue are good delivery between brokers. If the entire bond issue has been called, normal good delivery rules apply.

### Certificate Negotiability

The final authority on certificate negotiability is the transfer agent.

**Assignment**. All stock and bond certificates must be **assigned** (endorsed by signature) by the owner(s) whose name is registered on the face of the certificate. Certificates registered in joint name require the signatures of all owners. The physically challenged or illiterate investor may sign with an "*X*" mark witnessed by a notary public.

Endorsement by the customer may be made on the back of the certificate on the assignment (signature) line or by signing a detached (separate) assignment (also known as a **stock power** or a **power of substitution**).

If there has been an alteration or correction to the assignment, a full explanation of the change signed by the person or firm who executed the correction must be attached.

**Signature guarantee**. All customer signatures must be guaranteed by a party acceptable to the transfer agent, such as a member of the NYSE (or another exchange) or a national bank.

**Signature requirements**. The customer's signature must match exactly the name registered on the face of the security, without abbreviation or enlargement. The only exception is for certificates registered in corporate name, in which case the following interchangeable endorsements are acceptable: "Company" or "Co." and "and" or "&" (ampersand).

**Legal transfer items**. For corporate securities, a corporate resolution naming the person signing the certificate is typically required. For fiduciaries, either a certified copy of a trust agreement or a copy of a court appointment may be needed, depending on the type of fiduciary involved.

**Invalid signatures**. Deceased persons cannot sign their names to certificates. The executor or administrator of the estate must either endorse the certificate or furnish stock power and must transfer the securities to the name of the estate before they can be sold.

Minors' signatures are invalid for securities registration purposes. Although minors can enter into contracts at will, those contracts are not binding on them should they elect not to honor their obligations. An adult who contracts with a minor does so at great risk.

**Good condition of security**. If a certificate is mutilated or appears to be counterfeit, appropriate authentication (by the transfer agent, registrar, trustee, paying agent or issuer) must be obtained before the transfer agent can accept the security for replacement.

## NASD CUSIP Regulations

The Committee on Uniform Securities Identification Procedures (CUSIP) number is used in all trade confirmations and correspondence regarding specific securities. A separate CUSIP number is assigned to each issue of securities.

## Legal Opinion: Municipal Securities

In municipal bond trading, unless the bond is traded and stamped "ex-legal" (which means without the legal opinion), the legal opinion must be printed on or attached to the bond as evidence of the validity of the bond. Securities traded ex-legal are in good delivery condition without the legal opinion.

## Fail to Deliver

A **fail to deliver** situation occurs when the broker-dealer on the sell side of a contract does not deliver the securities in good delivery form to the broker-dealer on the buy side on or before settlement. As long as a fail to deliver exists, the seller will not receive payment.

## Questions

1. To be considered in good delivery form, certificates must be
   A. accompanied by a preliminary prospectus
   B. called for redemption by the issuing body
   C. accompanied by an assignment or a stock power
   D. in the name of the deceased person, if he died after the trade date

2. Your client has a certificate registered in his own name. To be a good delivery, the certificate must be accompanied by
   A. a properly executed assignment to the brokerage firm, on the reverse side of the certificate
   B. the promise that it has not been called for redemption
   C. a buyer's option
   D. the legal opinion, unless the client is selling municipal bonds

3. Which of the following would be considered good delivery for a sale of 600 shares of MCS?
   A. 3 certificates for 100 shares each and 8 certificates for 25 shares each
   B. 2 certificates for 100 shares each and 4 certificates for 50 shares each
   C. 6 certificates for 75 shares each and 6 certificates for 25 shares each
   D. 8 certificates for 75 shares each

## Answers

1. **C.** To be considered in good delivery form, certificates must be accompanied by an assignment or a stock power.

2. **A.** If the certificate is registered in your client's name, a stock power and a properly executed assignment to the brokerage firm must appear on the reverse side of the certificate.

3. **C.** Each certificate for 25 shares can be matched to a certificate for 75 shares to make a round lot; with six round lots, these certificates would be considered good delivery. Answer A is only 500 shares; Answer B includes only 400 shares; and Answer D cannot be bunched into round lots.

# 10 Margin Accounts

## Extension of Credit in the Securities Industry

### Margin Accounts

By borrowing a portion of the purchase price, the customer can **leverage** an investment. For example, compare the return on investment received by a customer who purchases 1,000 shares of KLP at $16 per share in a cash account and then purchases an additional 1,000 shares in a margin account.

- **Cash account.** If the price of 1,000 shares of KLP, purchased for $16,000 ($16 per share), increases to $24 per share, the customer's equity in a cash account will be $24,000, representing a 50% return ($24,000 less the initial outlay of $16,000 equals $8,000; $8,000 divided by $16,000 is 50%).
- **Margin account.** If the purchase is made in a margin account, the customer's equity will be $16,000 ($24,000 less the loan of $8,000 on the initial purchase price that is still owed to the firm), representing a return of 100% on the initial cash outlay of $8,000.
  - If the market turns down, a customer with a margin account would experience a magnified loss.

**Relationship between customer and broker.** All securities purchased on margin are registered in street name. The brokerage firm is called the *nominal owner* of the securities. The customer is known as the *beneficial owner.*

### Regulation T

- The Federal Reserve Board (FRB) sets the minimum amount a customer must **deposit** when purchasing securities or when selling securities short.
- The current required minimum deposit is **50%** of the market value of the marginable securities. Therefore at 50% margin, for every $100,000 worth of securities purchased, the customer must deposit $50,000 and the broker-dealer advances the other $50,000 as a loan against the securities.

Securities **exempt** from Reg T are:

- U.S. Treasury bills, notes and bonds;
- government agency securities;
- municipal securities; and
- corporate straight debt (nonconvertible) securities.

**Purchases in cash accounts**. Customers making purchases in cash accounts must make payment in full not later than the fifth business day after the trade date (two business days after settlement date).

**Purchases in margin accounts**. Customers making purchases in margin accounts must meet initial margin calls on new commitments not later than the fifth business day after the trade date (two business days after settlement date).

### Marginable Securities

Marginable securities include:

- stocks and bonds listed on an exchange;
- stocks listed as eligible for trading in the Nasdaq National Market (NNM); and
- certain OTC securities designated by the FRB.

### Nonmarginable Securities

Nonmarginable securities cannot be used as collateral for loans and must be paid for in full. They include:

- put and call options;
- common and preferred OTC stocks not designated by the FRB;
- rights;
- insurance contracts; and
- new issues (first 30 calendar days).

## Initial Requirements

The initial deposit requirement is called the **Reg T call,** *initial margin requirement, initial call* or *federal call.* To meet a Reg T call, a customer can:

- deposit cash
- deposit marginable securities
- liquidate securities

### When Issued Securities

- Purchases of when issued (when distributed) securities are subject to the same Reg T and NASD/NYSE requirements as other securities purchases.
- If the when issued security is part of a *new issue* (within the first 30 days of the issue), 100% of the purchase price must be deposited.
- If the when issued security is not part of a new issue, Reg T margin requirements apply.
- When issued exempt securities (such as municipal bonds) are not subject to these credit requirements, and individual firms may set their own requirements.

### Failure to Meet Reg T Calls

**Payment extensions for margin customers.** A broker-dealer may apply to its designated examining authority for permission to extend credit beyond the fifth business day to margin account customers.

**Forced sell-outs**. The following rules apply:

- If a margin customer does not meet a Reg T call by the fifth business day and no extension has been applied for, the broker-dealer must liquidate enough securities in the account to satisfy the call in full.
- The firm must *freeze the account for 90 days.*
- No credit may be extended to the customer during this 90 days.
- For amounts less than $1,000, the broker-dealer can choose to take no action.
- If payment is received for the buy side within five business days from trade date, the account is unfrozen.

# Margin Accounting

## Calculating Initial Requirements

A customer with a margin account has:

- current market value;
- debt (the loan from the firm) on which he pays interest; and
- equity (the difference between the market value and the loan balance).

A customer opens a margin account and purchases 1,000 shares of COW at $64 per share.

### Buy $64,000 COW Stock

| CMV | – | DR | = | EQ |
|---|---|---|---|---|
| $64,000 | – | $64,000 | = | $0 |

Reg T initial margin call: $32,000 (50% of the cost of the stock). The customer promptly deposits the required margin in cash.

### Deposit $32,000 Cash

| CMV | – | DR | = | EQ |
|---|---|---|---|---|
| $64,000 | – | $32,000 | = | $32,000 |

The equity in an account represents that portion of the securities fully owned by the customer.

The equation for a long position in a margin account is CMV minus DR equals customer EQ.

### Using Fully Paid Securities to Meet Margin Requirements

A customer may deposit securities with a loan value equal to the debit in the account (in this case, securities with a loan value of $32,000 would be required). The loan value of a stock is the complement of Reg T. In other words, 100% minus the Reg T percentage equals the loan value percentage.

The Reg T loan value of stock is currently 50% of its CMV. The above customer must therefore deposit $64,000 worth of stock ($2 of fully paid securities for each $1 of debt).

If the customer buys $64,000 worth of COW and deposits $64,000 worth of fully paid KLP stock in the account, 50% of the COW in the account is paid for, thus meeting the Reg T requirement. The formula for calculating the dollar amount of stock necessary to meet a Reg T call is:

$$\frac{\text{Reg T call in \$}}{100\% - \text{Reg T\%}} = \text{\$ Amount of stock}$$

### Excess Equity

Excess equity (EE) is the amount by which customer equity exceeds the Reg T requirement; it generates **buying power**.

- A customer can use the excess equity to buy more securities or he can withdraw the excess equity in cash.
- To determine buying power, multiply the dollar amount of excess equity by 2.

$$\text{EQ} - \text{Reg T} = \text{EE}$$

$$\text{EE} \times 2 = \text{Buying power}$$

### Nonrequired Cash Deposits

- Any deposit of cash that is not needed to meet a margin call is used to pay off part of the debit balance.
- Anything that reduces the debit balance increases equity.
- Any nonrequired cash deposit is always available for the customer to withdraw.

### Increase in Market Value

As the market value of a stock goes up, equity in the account increases. The debit balance stays the same until cash is either deposited to or withdrawn from the account.

The customer purchased 1,000 shares of COW. If COW appreciates from $64 to $72 per share:

- The CMV of the account rises $8,000, to $72,000.
- The debit remains $32,000.

- The equity increases by $8,000, to $40,000.
- The increase in CMV increases equity dollar for dollar.
- The Reg T requirement is 50% of the CMV (which is now $72,000), or $36,000.

| | |
|---|---|
| $ 72,000 | CMV |
| – 32,000 | DR |
| $ 40,000 | EQ |
| – 36,000 | Reg T |
| $ 4,000 | EE |

### $6,000 Market Increase

Assume the DJIA is up 20 points and the customer's account shows a $6,000 gain in market value (a $6 per share increase from $72 to $78):

| | |
|---|---|
| $ 78,000 | CMV |
| – 32,000 | DR |
| $ 46,000 | EQ |
| – 39,000 | Reg T 50% |
| $ 7,000 | EE |

### Using Excess Equity to Purchase Stock

The customer now has excess equity of $7,000, which can be used to purchase $14,000 of stock. (When Reg T is 50%, $7,000 meets the initial deposit requirement for a $14,000 purchase.)

### $14,000 Stock Purchase

| | |
|---|---|
| $ 92,000 | CMV |
| – 46,000 | DR |
| $ 46,000 | EQ |
| – 46,000 | Reg T 50% |
| $ 0 | EE |

### Withdrawing Excess Equity

- A customer can withdraw cash equal to the excess equity.
- The withdrawal will increase the customer's debit by the amount withdrawn.
- Withdrawing the excess equity results in a fully margined account.

### Decrease in Market Value

If stock decreases in value:

- The equity in the account will fall dollar for dollar with the market value of the stock.
- The debit balance will not change.

CMV – DR = EQ

Reg T does not require that the account be kept at a 50% margin; it requires the 50% deposit only for the initial purchase. A decrease in market value that brings equity below the Reg T requirement does not necessarily require an additional deposit of cash or securities. If declining market value reduces equity below 50% of CMV, and no deposit is made, the account becomes a **restricted account**.

## Restricted Accounts

A restricted account is a margin account in which the equity is less than the Reg T initial requirement. For example, assume that Reg T is 50% and a customer's account has the following balances:

| | |
|---|---|
| $ 90,000 | CMV |
| – 46,000 | DR |
| $ 44,000 | EQ |

The customer's $44,000 equity is less than 50% of the CMV of the securities. When equity falls between the 50% Reg T initial margin requirement and the 25% minimum maintenance, the account becomes restricted. The Reg T *retention requirement* mandates that the customer may not withdraw securities without depositing cash equal to 50% or securities equal to 100% of whatever is withdrawn.

### Transactions in a Restricted Account

**Purchasing additional shares.** To purchase additional shares in a restricted margin account, a customer must deposit either cash or securities with a loan value equal to 50% of the purchase price.

**Selling securities.** The proceeds of any sale are credited to the investor's debit balance, decreasing the amount the investor owes to the broker-dealer. An amount equal to 50% of those sale proceeds must be made available to the investor for withdrawal.

To determine how much of the proceeds from a sale is available to a customer who wishes to make a cash withdrawal from a restricted account, the following calculation is made.

50% × Proceeds of sale =
Amount available to client

As an example, assume an investor with a restricted account sells $10,000 worth of securities. The investor may withdraw cash up to 50% of $10,000, which means $5,000 is available for withdrawal.

## Withdrawals Not Involving Securities Transactions

### Cash Withdrawals

- Whether or not the account is restricted, a customer is entitled to withdraw cash dividends and interest.
- For any other cash withdrawal, a customer with a restricted account must either deposit additional marginable securities with a loan value equal to the amount of the cash withdrawal or have SMA.

### Stock Withdrawals

- If the customer wants to withdraw stock from his account, he must deposit cash equal to the retention requirement (cash equal to half—50%—of the value of the securities withdrawn).
- A customer can also withdraw stock and meet the retention requirement with fully paid stock held elsewhere (he will have to deposit new stock with a loan value equal to 50% of the value of the stock withdrawn).

## Calculating Maintenance Requirements

### NASD and NYSE Requirements

- **$2,000 minimum deposit.** Overriding all initial margin requirements (Reg T included) is the NASD/NYSE margin rule requiring that each new margin account be opened subject to a minimum deposit of $2,000. An investor must meet the larger of either the 50% Reg T requirement or the NASD/NYSE requirement of $2,000.
- **Total cost of transaction.** If the initial transaction in a margin account is for less than $2,000, the investor is not required to deposit more than the total cost of the transaction.

### Minimum Maintenance Requirements

The NASD/NYSE maintenance requirement for long common stock is *25% of the current market value (CMV).*

### Maintenance Calls

- A maintenance call is sent to a customer whose account falls below the minimum required equity level.
- If the equity in the account falls below $2,000 due to a change in market value, no maintenance call will be issued.
- The NASD/NYSE requirement prevents a brokerage firm from lending money to a customer or permitting withdrawals of cash or securities by a customer whose account equity is $2,000 or less.

### Change in Market Value

If an account drops below the required minimum maintenance level, the firm will *mark to the market* (i.e., calculate the difference between the maintenance margin and the current equity in the account) and the client will receive a maintenance call. The following is an example of the change in status of an account in which the market value of 100 shares of stock initially purchased at $60 falls to $36.

**Stock Is at $60 Per Share:**

| | | |
|---|---|---|
| $ 6,000 | (100%) | CMV |
| – 3,000 | (50%) | DR |
| $ 3,000 | (50%) | EQ |
| $ 1,500 | (25%) | NASD/NYSE requirement |

**Stock Drops to $36 Per Share:**

| | | |
|---|---|---|
| $ 3,600 | (100%) | CMV |
| – 3,000 | (83.3%) | DR |
| $ 600 | (16.7%) | EQ |
| $ 900 | (25%) | NASD/NYSE requirement |

Because the equity in the account is less than the required minimum maintenance, the customer will receive a maintenance call.

To calculate the SRO-required minimum maintenance equity, multiply the current market value by 25%. A maintenance call must be met by depositing cash, depositing any security acceptable to the firm or liquidating securities in the account *promptly*.

### Calculating Market Value at Minimum Maintenance

The following formula can be used to calculate how low the value of securities can go in the market before a client is sent a maintenance call.

DR ÷ 75% = CMV at minimum maintenance

When equity reaches the allowable minimum of 25% of current market value, the debit balance represents the remaining 75%. If the debit exceeds 75% of CMV, equity will be below maintenance and the customer will receive a maintenance call.

### Purchasing Bonds in a Margin Account

**Initial requirement.** Nonconvertible bonds are subject to the NASD/NYSE $2,000 initial margin requirement.

Convertible corporate bonds are subject to the same Reg T requirements as marginable (nonexempt) stocks (50%).

## House Maintenance Requirements

Broker-dealers can set house requirements higher than either Reg T initial or NASD/NYSE initial and minimum maintenance requirements, *but never lower.* House maintenance calls are due promptly.

On long positions, the typical **house maintenance** is 30%.

## Short Sales and Margin Requirements

### Reg T Margin Requirements on Short Sales

- The Reg T initial margin deposit requirement on short sales is 50% of the sale proceeds.
- Reg T uses the phrase "150% of the current market value of the security" to indicate that the full amount (100%) of the sale proceeds *plus* an additional 50% initial margin on the position must be deposited in the account.
- The deposit is expected promptly, but is required within five business days.
- Reg T initial margin on short sales can be met either with cash or through the deposit of marginable securities with a loan value equal to the amount of the call.

As an example, a customer sells short 100 shares of MTN at $60. To calculate the margin deposit requirement, use the following:

| | |
|---|---|
| $ 6,000 | Proceeds (100%) |
| + 3,000 | Reg T (50%) |
| $ 9,000 | CR (150%) |

### NASD/NYSE Minimum Deposit on Short Sales

When establishing a short margin account, a client must always deposit a minimum of $2,000. Even if a client sells short only $100 worth of stock, she must still deposit at least $2,000.

### Margin Maintenance Calls on Short Sales

NASD/NYSE margin maintenance requirements on short positions (30%) are higher than on long positions (25%), and house maintenance requirements on short positions might be higher still.

When a short sale position moves adversely, under minimum requirement rules, there must be enough credit in the account to cover 100% of the now-higher current market value, and 30% of the now-higher current market value must also be on deposit as margin. The equation for determining a customer's equity in a short position is:

CR – SMV = EQ

To illustrate, assume that a customer sells short 1,000 shares of stock at 64 for proceeds of $64,000, which is credited to his margin account. He then deposits the 50% Reg T initial margin requirement of $32,000 for a total of $96,000, which equals 150% of the market value.

| | |
|---|---|
| $ 64,000 | (100%) |
| + 32,000 | (50%) |
| $ 96,000 | CR (150%) |
| – 64,000 | SMV |
| $ 32,000 | EQ |

To determine the maximum market value to which a short sale position can advance before a margin maintenance call will be issued, the following formula is used:

Total credit balance ÷ 130% = Maximum market value

**Low-priced stock**. The NASD/NYSE margin maintenance requirement on short positions in stocks under $5 per share is the greater of 100% of market value or $2.50 per share.

### Short Against the Box

Selling short against the box is the same as a regular short sale except that the client already owns securities identical to the securities that she borrows to sell short.

- **Tax benefits**. Clients borrow a stock they already own to sell short against the box primarily for tax deferral.
- **No Reg T deposit**. For margin purposes, the short against the box position is treated as a net-zero position. There is no Reg T initial requirement when an investor establishes the short against the box position.
- **Maintenance.** The investor must leave on deposit the greater of *5% of the market value* of the long side or $2,000.
- **Closing out**. A short-against-the-box transaction is closed out when the customer instructs the broker-dealer to release the box stock and pair off the offsetting long and short positions. A customer can close a short against the box position in either of two ways: by delivering the long position to the lender or by buying stock to deliver to the lender.

### Summary of Short Accounts

- **Credit balance**. Clients sell securities short and they make margin deposits to cover their risk. The credit balance represents actual cash, which is available when a client wants to purchase the securities to close the short position.
- **Equity**. Equity equals the amount by which the credit balance exceeds the current market value of the securities short in the account.
- **Buying power**. A decline in the current market value of a security below the original short sale price may produce excess equity in a client's margin account.
- **Restricted accounts**. In a short account, restriction can take place when a stock appreciates above the selling price.

## Combined Accounts

To compute the equity in an account that combines long and short positions, add the equity on the long position to the equity on the short position.

- **Reg T margin requirement**. To calculate the Reg T requirement for a combined account, calculate the Reg T requirement for the long and short accounts separately and then combine them.
- **SRO maintenance requirement**. To calculate the SRO maintenance requirement for a combined account, calculate the long and short positions separately. For a long position, the NASD/NYSE requirement is 25% of the CMV. For a short position, the NASD/NYSE requirement is 30% of the CMV.
- **Buying power**. When Reg T is 50%, any excess equity in the account has a purchasing power of 2 to 1.

# Questions

1. A customer's margin account contains the following registered nonexempt securities:

   100 shares of COD, CMV $40 per share
   100 shares of AMF, CMV $50 per share
   100 shares of KLP, CMV $80 per share

   The account has a debit balance of $10,800, and the initial margin requirement is 50%. How much equity is in the account?

   A. $4,030
   B. $6,200
   C. $11,050
   D. $17,000

2. In the account described in the preceding question, the excess equity is

   A. $0
   B. $2,300
   C. $6,200
   D. $8,500

Use the following information to answer questions 3 through 6. With the initial margin requirement at 50%, a customer purchased 100 shares of Consolidated Codfish (COD) at $100 per share and deposited $5,000. COD then increases in value to $150 per share.

3. With COD at $150 per share, the customer's equity in the account is

   A. $5,000
   B. $7,500
   C. $10,000
   D. $15,000

4. What is the excess equity in the account?

   A. $2,500
   B. $5,000
   C. $7,500
   D. $10,000

5. How much more COD can the customer purchase without depositing additional cash?

   A. $2,500
   B. $5,000
   C. $7,500
   D. $10,000

6. How much cash can the customer withdraw from the account without selling any COD?

   A. $2,500
   B. $5,000
   C. $7,500
   D. $10,000

7. When stock held in a margin account appreciates, which of the following increase(s)?

   I. Current market value
   II. Debit balance
   III. equity

   A. I only
   B. I and III only
   C. II only
   D. I, II and III

8. A client chooses to leave a dividend payment in a margin account; as a result, the

   I. equity increases
   II. equity decreases
   III. debit balance increases
   IV. debit balance decreases

   A. I and III
   B. I and IV
   C. II and III
   D. II and IV

9. A client has a margin account with $23,000 in securities and a debit of $12,000. Which of the following statements are true? (Reg T is 50%.)

   I. The account is restricted.
   II. The client will receive a margin call for $500.
   III. The client may withdraw securities if he deposits 50% of the securities' value.
   IV. The account has excess equity of $5,250.

   A. I and II only
   B. I and III only
   C. II, III and IV only
   D. I, II, III and IV

10. A client has a margin account with $23,000 in securities and a debit of $12,000. The stock increases in value to $26,000. How much money may the client withdraw from the account?

    A. $1,000
    B. $2,000
    C. $3,000
    D. $4,000

11. Sandy Bruin has a margin account with a market value of $8,000 and a debit of $4,200. She would like to withdraw $4,000 of the securities and deposit other securities to satisfy the retention requirement. What dollar value of securities must she deposit?

    A. $2,000
    B. $3,000
    C. $4,000
    D. $4,200

12. A customer sells short against the box 100 shares of MTN at 50. Four months later, when MTN is at 40, the customer delivers the long shares to cover his short position. How much can be withdrawn from the account?

    A. $1,000
    B. $4,000
    C. $5,000
    D. $7,500

13. A customer sells short 100 shares of Mountain Brewing at $80 per share and meets the minimum Reg T requirement. Two months later, she covers her short position by buying Mountain Brewing at $70 per share. This was her only transaction in the account. What is the maximum amount she can withdraw from the account after closing the short position? (Reg T is 50%.)

A. $1,000
B. $4,000
C. $5,000
D. $12,000

# Answers

1. **B.** The total market value in the account is $17,000. CMV – DR = EQ; $17,000 CMV – $10,800 DR = $6,200.

2. **A.** The required equity is $8,500 (50% × $17,000 CMV). The account has no excess equity. It is, in fact, restricted—that is, it is below the Reg T amount.

3. **C.** The account now looks like this:

| | |
|---|---|
| $15,000 | CMV |
| – 5,000 | DR |
| $10,000 | EQ |

4. **A.** The account now looks like this:

| | |
|---|---|
| $10,000 | EQ |
| – 7,500 | Reg T |
| $ 2,500 | EE |

5. **B.** The purchasing power is $5,000 ($2,500 EE ÷ 50% Reg T).

6. **A.** The customer could withdraw cash equal to the excess equity.

7. **B.** The debit balance changes only when money is borrowed or deposited. A withdrawal of cash is borrowing against the loan value of the securities in the account and increases the debit balance. A deposit of cash into the account reduces the debit balance.

8. **B.** Any cash deposit lowers the debit balance. A lower debit balance with no change in market value results in higher equity.

9. **B.** The account is restricted by $500. The client will not, however, receive a margin call for the $500 because Reg T applies only to the initial purchase. Because the account is restricted, any withdrawal of securities requires a cash deposit of 50% or a deposit of securities with a loan value of 50% of the value of the securities withdrawn. The

account is $5,250 above the required minimum, but this amount is not considered excess equity.

10. **A.** The account now has equity of $14,000. The Reg T requirement is $13,000. This leaves $1,000 in excess equity that may be withdrawn.

| | |
|---|---|
| $ 26,000 | CMV |
| – 12,000 | DR |
| $ 14,000 | EQ |
| – 13,000 | Reg T |
| $ 1,000 | EE |

11. **C.** A withdrawal of $4,000 of securities from a restricted account would require a cash deposit of $2,000 ($4,000 × 50%). If securities are deposited, they must have a loan value of $2,000. Loan value is currently 50%, so Sandy must deposit $4,000 in securities ($2,000 ÷ 50%, or $2,000 × 2).

12. **C.** Although the question tells us that the stock was at $40 when the customer delivered the long shares, we do not know what the customer actually paid for the stock. We do know how much the stock was sold for. As soon as the customer delivers the long shares against the short position, he is free to withdraw the sale proceeds. This is virtually the same as if he had bought the stock and then sold it, except that he does not deliver the shares until some time after the sale date.

13. **C.** The customer sold the stock at $80 per share and deposited $4,000 per the Reg T requirement ($8,000 × 50%). She now has an SMV of $8,000 and a credit balance of $12,000 ($8,000 sale proceeds + $4,000 deposit). The market value of the stock is now down to $7,000 and the customer uses $7,000 of her credit balance to purchase the shares and close the short position. The remaining credit balance is all excess equity because she no longer has any short position and the entire amount may be withdrawn. A second way to look at the account is to see that after the short position is closed, the customer may withdraw the Reg T deposit and the $1,000 profit ($8,000 sale proceeds – $7,000 purchase price).

# Special Memorandum Account

## The Role of Excess Equity

- A margin account in which the customer's equity is more than 50% of the CMV of the securities in the account has *excess equity*.
- Excess equity is normally the result of market value advances.
- The customer may withdraw excess equity, leave it in the account to be applied against the debit balance or use it to purchase additional securities.
- When excess equity exists, it can be credited to the **special memorandum account** (**SMA**).

### SMA Characteristics

- No real funds, cash or securities are actually transferred to an SMA. It is a line of credit, a limit on the amount of money a client can borrow now or in the future.
- The firm does not charge interest on SMA because it is not considered money until the client uses it.
- When a client withdraws or uses SMA, she is actually borrowing more money from the broker-dealer, thereby increasing the debit balance in her account.
- Clients may always use the balance in their SMAs unless the use (either withdrawing cash or securities or purchasing securities) will cause the account equity to drop below the minimum maintenance (or the $2,000 minimum) requirement.
- Once SMA is credited to a client's account, only the client's use of it can deplete it. Market or broker actions cannot take away the SMA line of credit.
- SMA *increases* as the excess equity in a margin account increases.
- SMA *does not decrease* as the result of market value decreases.
- SMA may be more than excess equity or may exist even if there is no excess equity in the account.

### Generating SMA

An SMA balance can be generated when excess equity is credited to SMA or by any of the following means:

- nonrequired cash deposits
- dividends and interest earned
- loan value of nonrequired stock deposits

### Increase in Market Value

Suppose a client buys 200 shares of stock at $100 and deposits cash to meet the 50% Reg T requirements. Her margin account will look like this:

| | |
|---:|---|
| $ 20,000 | CMV (200 × $100) |
| – 10,000 | DR |
| $ 10,000 | EQ |
| 10,000 | Reg T (50%) |
| $ 0 | EE |
| $ 0 | SMA |

If the stock increases in market value to $110 per share, this creates excess equity in the client's account. Excess equity can be borrowed, used to purchase additional securities or left in the account to be credited to SMA.

### Stock Is at $110 per Share:

| | |
|---:|---|
| $ 22,000 | CMV (200 × $110) |
| – 10,000 | DR |
| $ 12,000 | EQ |
| 11,000 | Reg T |
| $ 1,000 | EE |
| $ 1,000 | SMA |

If the stock subsequently drops to $95, the CMV declines, the debit remains unchanged, equity decreases and excess equity decreases, but SMA remains the same.

**Stock Drops to $95 per Share:**

| | |
|---|---|
| $ 19,000 | CMV |
| – 10,000 | DR |
| $ 9,000 | EQ |
| 9,500 | Reg T |
| $ 0 | EE |
| $ 1,000 | SMA |

**Selling securities.** When stock is sold in a margin account, you can calculate the new SMA balance by adding 50% of the sale proceeds to the existing amount of the SMA.

## Depleting SMA

An SMA balance is depleted by all of the following:

- cash withdrawals
- new margin purchases
- withdrawing securities

**Using SMA to buy stock.** The following equation calculates the buying power of SMA:

SMA ÷ Reg T requirement = Buying power

For every dollar of SMA, the investor can purchase two dollars of securities when Reg T is at 50% ($1 ÷ 50% = $2).

The entire purchase price of any new security purchased with SMA is borrowed from the firm. The SMA is used to meet the Reg T call, but because it does not represent an actual cash deposit, it does not lower the debit when used. Because the investor has put no more cash in, her equity remains the same as before the purchase.

**Withdrawing cash.** Customers also may use SMA to withdraw money from their margin accounts. If a customer withdraws cash equal to the entire SMA balance:

- the customer's CMV would remain unchanged;
- the debit balance would increase by the amount borrowed;
- equity would decrease by the amount borrowed; and
- the SMA would be depleted.

A withdrawal may not be made if it would bring the equity below $2,000 or the minimum maintenance requirement (whichever is greater). SMA may not be used to meet a maintenance call.

## SMA and Restricted Accounts

**Withdrawing securities.** When withdrawing securities from a restricted account, a client must meet the 50% Reg T retention requirement. This can be done with SMA unless doing so violates maintenance requirements.

To calculate how much market value of securities the client can withdraw, divide the SMA balance by the retention requirement (50%).

SMA ÷ Retention requirement =
CMV of withdrawable securities

**Same-day substitution of stock.** A client with a margin account can sell one stock and buy an equivalent amount of another stock without incurring a Reg T call, resulting in a same-day substitution.

# Questions

1. A customer's margin account contains securities with a market value of $50,000, a debit balance of $30,000 and no SMA balance. After the value of the securities increases to $70,000, the customer sells $20,000 worth of securities. What is SMA after the sale? (Reg T is 50%.)

   A. $0
   B. $5,000
   C. $10,000
   D. $15,000

2. A customer has a margin account with $50,000 in securities and a debit of $26,000. SMA is $4,000. How much cash can the customer withdraw from the account?

   A. $0
   B. $2,000
   C. $4,000
   D. $24,000

3. Which of the following can change the balance in SMA?

   I. Sale of securities in the account
   II. Market appreciation of securities in the account
   III. Interest and cash dividends deposited in the account
   IV. Decrease in value of securities in the account

   A. I only
   B. I and II only
   C. I, II and III only
   D. I, II, III and IV

4. A customer has a short account with $25,000 short market value, $37,000 credit balance and SMA of $500. What is the maximum short market value for this account before the customer will incur an NYSE maintenance call?

   A. $28,462
   B. $33,020
   C. $33,500
   D. $48,100

# Answers

1. **D.** After the value of the securities in the account increased to $70,000, the customer had equity of $40,000. Because Reg T requires equity of $35,000, the customer had $5,000 in excess equity after the increase in market value. The new excess equity was credited to SMA. When the customer sold $20,000 worth of securities, half of the sale proceeds were automatically released to SMA, as prescribed by retention requirements. The $10,000 in sale proceeds released to SMA increased SMA to $15,000.

2. **C.** The customer may withdraw SMA from the account. SMA may always be withdrawn in cash unless doing so will bring the account below the minimum margin requirements. The minimum market value in this case is $12,500 ($50,000 × 25%). Withdrawal of $4,000 will increase the debit to $30,000, leaving an equity of $20,000—well above the minimum requirements.

3. **C.** The sale of securities in the account (choice I) results in an automatic release of funds to SMA. Nonrequired cash deposits, such as interest and dividends (choice III), will also be automatically credited to SMA. An increase in the value of the securities (choice II) will increase SMA if the excess equity becomes greater than existing SMA. A decrease in the market value of the securities (choice IV) will not increase or decrease SMA.

4. **A.** When the account is at minimum maintenance level, the equity will be 30% of market value. Because the formula to compute equity for a short account is CR minus SMV, the credit balance will be 130% of market value when the account is at minimum maintenance. The credit balance will be the only number that is constant as the market increases, so we must use the credit balance to calculate the maximum value the securities can be before a call is issued:

$$\frac{\text{CR}}{130\%} = \frac{\$37{,}000}{1.30} = \$28{,}461.54$$

# Pledging Customer Securities for Loans

## Hypothecation of Customer Securities—Rule 15c2-1

- **Hypothecation.** When a customer purchases securities in a margin account using money borrowed from the broker-dealer, the securities are pledged to the broker-dealer as collateral for the loan. This process is called *hypothecation* of the securities.
- **Rehypothecation.** When a broker-dealer borrows money from a bank using customer securities to finance customer debit balances, the process is called *rehypothecation.*

**Commingling of customer securities.** Broker-dealers are prohibited from commingling one customer's securities with another customer's securities, unless the customers specifically give written authorization. The standard margin agreement carries a *customer hypothecation agreement* providing for this authorization.

**Liens.** Broker-dealers are prohibited from commingling customer securities with firm securities. Loans entered into by a broker-dealer for firm business may be collateralized by securities owned by the firm *only*. The lending bank (or other firm) cannot place a lien on customer securities that may be pledged separately (a **cross lien**).

### Customer Securities

The SEC's **customer protection rule** (Rule 15c3-3) requires that a customer's fully paid securities and excess margin securities (those securities valued in excess of 140% of the customer's debit balance) must be **segregated** (actually physically set aside) and kept safely, and that each firm must keep a reserve bank account for customers' funds.

- **Fully paid securities.** Fully paid securities are securities held for customers in accounts in which the customer has no debit balance. The broker-dealer must inform the customer that all fully paid securities are available to the customer upon request.
- **Margin securities.** Those securities in a margin account that have a market value of up to 140% of the account's net debit balance are known as *margin securities.*
- **Excess margin securities.** All of the securities in a margin account more than 140% of the account's debit balance are known as *excess margin securities.*

### Calculating Hypothecation Limits

For example, if a customer has a net debit balance of $10,000 in a margin account and $20,000 CMV of securities, the firm may rehypothecate up to $14,000 worth of the customer's margined securities ($14,000 is 140% of $10,000). The other $6,000 worth of securities ($20,000 – $14,000) are considered excess margin securities and must be segregated and not used as loan collateral.

# Questions

1. All of the following are true statements according to NYSE regulations EXCEPT that

   A. proxies must be forwarded to beneficial owners of the securities held *in street name*
   B. with NYSE approval, member firms may lend client securities without specific client authorization
   C. a corporate margin account can be opened only after it is established that such accounts are not contrary to the firm's charter and bylaws
   D. in order to open an account for an allied member of another member firm, written permission from the person's employer (a general partner, principal executive or supervisory person) must be given

# Answers

1. **B.** Clients' securities may never be lent unless they have signed the consent to loan agreement. Fully paid securities must be segregated from the broker-dealer's securities.

# 11 Economics and Analysis

## Economics

### Business Cycles

Long-term business cycles go through four stages:

- **Expansion**. Also known as **recovery**, expansion is characterized by increases in business activity throughout the economy.
- **Peak**. When these activity increases reach a peak, economists call the stage **prosperity**.
- **Contraction**. As business activity begins an overall period of decline, the economy is said to be going through a contraction. Mild short-term contractions that last two to six consecutive quarters are known as **recessions**. More severe contractions of longer duration may be deemed **depressions**.
- **Trough**. At the bottom of a contraction is a period in which business activity stops its decline and begins the long road back through expansion to prosperity. This bottom of the business cycle is known as a *trough.*

Some of the signs of expansion that an economist will look for include:

- increases in industrial production;
- bullish (rising) stock markets;
- rising property values;
- increased consumer demand for goods and services; and
- increasing GDP.

Downturns in the business cycle tend to be associated with:

- rising numbers of bankruptcies and bond defaults;
- higher consumer debt;
- bearish (falling) stock markets;
- rising inventories (a sign of slackening consumer demand in hard times); and
- decreasing GDP.

### Gross Domestic Product

The annual economic output of a nation (all of the goods and services produced by the workers and capital located within it) is known as its *gross domestic product.* In periods of recession, the GDP decreases. During periods of expansion, the GDP increases.

| | |
|---|---|
| C | Consumption |
| + G | Government spending |
| + I | Gross investment |
| GDP | Gross domestic product |

Economists adjust GDP figures to **constant dollars**, rather than attempting to compare actual dollars. This allows economists and others who use GDP figures to compare the actual purchasing power of the dollars, rather than the dollars themselves.

### Price Levels

**Inflation**. Inflation is a persistent and measurable rise in the general level of prices and generally is associated with periods of expansion and high levels of employment. Increases in the inflation rate tend to drive up the rate of interest on new fixed income securities; this, in turn, drives down the prices of existing debt securities. Decreases in the inflation rate have the opposite effect: as the inflation rate drops, new debt is issued at lower rates and the prices of existing debt rise.

**Deflation**. Deflation is a persistent and measurable fall in the general level of prices. During periods of deflation, the production of goods and services exceeds the demand for them. Deflation usually occurs during recessions, when unemployment is on the rise.

**Stagflation**. Stagflation is used to describe those periods of high unemployment (stagnation) coupled with rising prices (inflation).

**Consumer Price Index**. The CPI measures the rate of increase or decrease in consumer prices for such things as food, housing, transportation, medical care, clothing, electricity, entertainment and services.

### Economic Indicators

**Leading indicators**. Leading indicators are those factors that appear to reliably *predict* trends in the economy. Leading indicators that economists use most often include:

- average work week in manufacturing;
- average weekly initial claims for state unemployment compensation;
- new orders for consumer goods;
- slowdowns in deliveries by vendors;
- contracts and orders for plant and equipment;
- building permits (housing starts);
- changes in inventories of durables;
- changes in sensitive materials prices;
- stock prices;
- money supply (M2, which includes M1); and
- changes in business and consumer borrowing.

Positive changes in any of these leading indicators (such as a bull market, expansion of the money supply, issuance of more building permits and increases in orders for consumer goods or plant and equipment) lead economists to believe that there will be more spending, production and employment in days to come. Negative changes in leading indicators give rise to a more pessimistic outlook among economists and politicians, as possible downturns and recessions loom.

**Coincident indicators**. Coincident indicators are those measurable factors that vary directly and simultaneously with the business cycle. Coincident indicators include:

- nonagricultural employment
- personal income
- industrial production
- manufacturing and trade sales

**Lagging indicators**. Lagging indicators are those factors that change after the economy already has started to follow a pattern or trend. Lagging indicators include:

- average duration of unemployment (in months between periods of employment);
- ratio of deflated inventories to sales, manufacturing and trade;
- labor cost per unit of output (manufacturing);
- commercial and industrial loans outstanding;
- corporate profits; and
- ratio of consumer installment credit to personal income.

## Economic Theories and the Business Cycle

### Keynesian Theory

Keynes held that active government intervention was vital to the health, well-being and stability of a nation's economy. In his 1935 book *The General Theory of Employment, Interest and Money*, he explained his philosophy that *demand* was the factor that controlled employment and prices. Keynes believed that it was the government's right and responsibility to manipulate aggregate demand (and therefore manipulate the economy) by changing its own levels of spending and taxation.

Keynesian economists teach that the most important determinant of consumer spending and saving levels is how much income is received and how much is available to spend. When income and spending reach equilibrium, the economy is stable. To a Keynesian, it is the government's job to make sure that the economy stabilizes at a high level of prosperity, ensuring jobs for all.

Several special terms are used by Keynesian economists:

- **Consumption** is any spending done by household units to purchase newly produced consumer goods and services.
- **Marginal propensity to consume** is the marginal change in current household consumption per dollar change in current household income. A marginal change is that fraction of any increase or decrease in income that is spent rather than saved by the household.
- **Savings** is any personal income not spent on taxes or goods.
- **Investment** refers to planned or intended investment and not to actual or realized investment.

**Economic phases**. Keynesian economics established three economic phases:

- **Equilibrium** occurs when the private market's aggregate demand is in balance with (or equal to) aggregate supply.
- **Falling production** is that stage during which aggregate demand falls short of aggregate supply and production is reduced to better match the lower demand.
- **Rising production** is taken as an indication that aggregate demand is *greater* than aggregate supply. As demand exceeds supply, production is increased to meet that demand.

### The Government's Role in Keynesian Economics

If a government decides that it is necessary to reduce consumer and business demand and spending, it can do so in several ways, including:

- raising taxes
- reducing the money supply
- reducing government spending

Each of these activities serves to remove money from the country's economic system (a condition known as *tight money*), which discourages demand and spending. On the other hand, if government economists decide it would be beneficial to increase demand and spending, the government can do this by:

- reducing taxes
- increasing the money supply
- increasing government spending

These activities inject money into the economy (a condition known as *easy money*) and, as a result, encourage consumer demand and spending.

# Questions

1. An improvement in economic conditions is indicated by an increase in all of the following EXCEPT

   A. industrial production
   B. inventories
   C. Standard & Poor's 500
   D. consumer orders

2. Gross domestic product is the sum of all the

   A. goods and services produced by a country
   B. goods produced by a country
   C. household goods of a country
   D. manufactured and nonmanufactured goods of a country

3. A six-month decline in business activity, employment and stock prices is

   A. a depression
   B. a recession
   C. inflation
   D. stagflation

4. The Consumer Price Index is based on which of the following?

   A. Prices of all items in the GDP
   B. Selected goods in selected cities
   C. Average price of goods and services per person for three months
   D. Cost of food and utilities

5. Which of the following is NOT one of the normal economic phases?

   A. Expansion
   B. Stagflation
   C. Inflation
   D. Recession

6. Which of the following economists is(was) a supporter of demand-side economics?

   A. Adam Smith
   B. John Maynard Keynes
   C. Arthur Laffer
   D. Milton Friedman

7. Which of the following economists is(was) a supporter of monetarist economics?

   A. Adam Smith
   B. John Maynard Keynes
   C. Arthur Laffer
   D. Milton Friedman

8. According to monetarist economic theory, an economy's health can be ensured if the government

   A. cuts taxes for businesses and the wealthy
   B. increases aggregate demand
   C. increases the money supply
   D. leaves the economy alone

9. According to Keynesian economic theory, an economy's health can be ensured if the government

   A. cuts taxes for businesses and the wealthy
   B. increases aggregate demand
   C. increases the money supply
   D. leaves the economy alone

10. What term do economists use to describe a downturn in the economy that lasts more than two consecutive quarters?

    A. Inflation
    B. Stagflation
    C. Depression
    D. Recession

11. What term do economists use to describe a downturn in the economy that lasts several years and is accompanied by extremely high unemployment?

    A. Inflation
    B. Stagflation
    C. Depression
    D. Recession

12. What term do economists use to describe a downturn in the economy characterized by increasing price levels?

    A. Inflation
    B. Stagflation
    C. Depression
    D. Recession

13. What term do economists use to describe a downturn in the economy that is characterized by both unemployment and rising prices?

    A. Inflation
    B. Stagflation
    C. Depression
    D. Recession

14. New orders for durable goods is what kind of economic indicator?

    A. Leading
    B. Coincident
    C. Coterminous
    D. Lagging

15. Changes in the money supply is what kind of economic indicator?

    A. Leading
    B. Coincident
    C. Coterminous
    D. Lagging

16. Initial state unemployment claims is what kind of economic indicator?

    A. Leading
    B. Coincident
    C. Coterminous
    D. Lagging

17. Changes in which industry would be considered a *leading indicator* for economic growth trends?

    A. Personal income
    B. Natural gas
    C. Retailing
    D. New housing

# Answers

1. **B.** Increasing inventories means that consumer demand is slackening. Thus, disposable income is dropping and economic conditions are deteriorating.

2. **A.** The GDP is the sum of all goods and services produced in the United States.

3. **B.** Two or more consecutive quarters of decline are termed a *recession.*

4. **B.** The CPI is a composite of selected items (housing, food, clothing, transportation) in selected cities. Answer C is incorrect because the CPI is an index of average prices paid during a one-month period, not a three-month period.

5. **B.** Economists consider expansion (recovery) as the beginning of the business cycle, followed by the peak (prosperity), the contraction (recession or deflation) and the trough. Stagflation is an unusual situation combining characteristics of expansion (inflation) with contraction (unemployment).

6. **B.** John Maynard Keynes was the first demand-side economist and believed that by increasing the income available for spending and saving, a government could increase demand and improve the country's economic well-being.

7. **D.** Milton Friedman is probably the best known monetarist; he supports the theory that the determining factor of an economy's health is the size and rate of growth of its money supply.

8. **C.** Monetarists theorize that a controlled, gradually increasing money supply will result in the healthiest economy.

9. **B.** Keynesians theorize that government efforts to increase aggregate demand by increasing its own purchases of goods and services will result in the healthiest economy.

10. **D.** An economic downturn that lasts for more than two consecutive quarters (six months) is known as a *recession.*

11. **C.** A long-term economic downturn with unemployment reaching 15% or more is known as a *depression.*

12. **A.** Inflation is the overall increase of price levels that occurs when spending is increasing faster than the supply of goods on the market.

13. **B.** "Stagflation" is the term used to describe the unusual combination of inflation and unemployment (stagnation).

14. **A.** New orders for durable goods is a leading economic indicator.

15. **A.** Changes in the money supply is a leading economic indicator.

16. **A.** Initial state unemployment claims is a leading economic indicator.

17. **D.** A leading indicator is one that predicts future growth trends. The usual indicators involve increases in basic productive processes such as steel shipments and housing starts. Durable goods (autos, home appliances) tend to be leading indicators. Natural gas usage and retail sales are generally noncyclical.

# Government Economic Policy

**Fiscal policy**. The President's and the federal government's policies on taxation and spending make up the country's fiscal policy.

**Monetary policy**. The FRB's policies on the size, movement and growth of the money supply compose its monetary policy.

## Monetary Policy

### Money and Banking

**Demand deposit**. A demand deposit is money left with a bank that the depositing customer has the right to withdraw on demand.

**Time deposit**. A time deposit, in contrast, is a deposit of money that the depositing customer has agreed not to withdraw for a specified period of time or without sufficient advance notice to the depository bank.

### Creating Money

By granting loans to establish demand deposits, banks actually can create money. As an example, assume that a commercial bank lends a customer $7,000 for a home improvement loan. The bank will credit the customer's checking account with $7,000, instantly creating money that can be spent. As the customer makes her planned home improvements, she writes checks against that $7,000 to various merchants, contractors, suppliers and workers. The recipients of her payments take those checks and deposit them in other banks. The banks receiving this inflow of money make new loans based on those deposits, which eventually are deposited in other banks, and so on in a chain broken only when someone withdraws cash from an account.

### Definition of Money

Economists divide money into four categories, depending on the type of account in which it is kept.

1. **M1**. M1 consists of currency and demand deposits that can be converted to currency immediately.
2. **M2**. M2 includes M1 and some time deposits that are fairly easy to convert into demand deposits.
3. **M3**. M3 includes M1 and M2 and time deposits of more than $100,000 and repurchase agreements with terms longer than one day.
4. **L**. L includes M1, M2 and M3 plus other long-term liquid assets, including T bills, savings bonds, commercial paper, bankers' acceptances and Eurodollar holdings of U.S. residents.

### The Federal Reserve Board

The Fed performs the following functions:

- acts as an agent of the U.S. Treasury;
- regulates the U.S. money supply;
- sets reserve requirements for members;
- supervises the printing of currency;
- clears fund transfers throughout the system; and
- examines members to ensure their compliance with federal regulations.

The FRB affects the money supply through its use of three monetary tools:

1. changes in reserve requirements;
2. changes in the discount rate (on loans to member banks); and
3. open-market operations (buying and selling bonds).

### Federal Funds

Commercial banks are required by the Federal Reserve Board to keep on deposit an amount of cash equal to a certain percentage of their depositors' money (called the **reserve requirement**). The term "**federal funds**" commonly is used to describe all money deposited by commercial banks at a Federal Reserve Bank, including any money in excess of the reserve requirement.

When a bank falls short of its reserve requirement, it may borrow the excess reserves (federal funds) of another member bank, normally as an overnight loan. Interest on these unsecured, overnight loans is computed at an annualized rate (360-day year) and paid by the borrower to the lender daily. The effective rate of interest is the daily average rate of interest costs as negotiated between the banks through the Federal Reserve System and is called the **federal funds rate**. The federal funds rate fluctuates daily and is one of this country's most volatile rates.

### Reserve Requirements

- **Percentage of deposits**. The FRB requires member banks to have reserves equal to a certain percentage of their deposits, a percentage that can vary from 7% to 22%. The reserve requirements are greater for demand deposits (checking accounts) than they are for time deposits (savings accounts).
- **Lowering requirement**. The FRB can expand credit during a deflationary period by lowering the reserve requirement percentage.
- **Raising requirement**. The FRB can tighten credit during a deflationary period by raising the reserve requirement percentage.
- **Multiplier effect**. The amount of money available to businesses and consumers (the money supply) multiplies rapidly when banks lend because banks can lend more money than they take in. This expansion of the money supply is called the *multiplier effect.*
- **Rarely used**. Although changing reserve requirements can have a major impact on the nation's economy, it is the Fed's least frequently used tool for combating inflation. A small change in the reserve requirement has a comparatively large influence on the money supply.
- **Borrowing**. When banks must borrow to meet reserve requirements, they can borrow money directly from the Fed at its **discount rate**, or they can borrow **excess reserves** from another member bank at the **federal funds rate**.
- **Volatility**. The federal funds rate is the economy's most volatile interest rate.

### Discount Rate

The Fed's second most important tool for affecting the money supply is raising and lowering the **discount rate**—the interest rate the Fed charges its members for certain very short-term loans. If a member has a reserve deficiency, it can borrow funds from its Federal Reserve district bank. This borrowing process is sometimes called **going to the discount window.**

- **Lowering** the discount rate tends to counteract a recessionary trend by making it easier for banks to increase their reserve funds.
- **Raising** the discount rate tends to counteract inflation by making it more difficult for member banks to increase their reserves.

### Open-market Operations

The Federal Reserve's most important and flexible tool is **open-market operations**. When engaging in open-market operations, the Federal Open Market Committee (FOMC) buys and sells U.S. government securities in the open market in order to expand and contract the money supply.

- **Buying securities**. When credit is tight and the Fed wants to expand (or *loosen*) the money supply, it buys securities. By buying securities, the Fed has pumped money into the banking system, expanding the money supply.
- **Selling securities**. In times of inflation, when the Fed wants to contract (or *tighten*) the money supply, it sells some of its securities. By selling securities, the Fed has pulled money out of the system, contracting the money supply.

- **Regulation U**—covers bank loans to brokers, dealers or customers
- **Regulation G**—governs loans of other lenders

The effect of changing margin requirements is more limited than that of changing reserve requirements. Higher margin requirements tend to slow down the purchase of securities, thus putting a brake on inflation. Lower margin requirements make investing easier, thus helping to invigorate a flagging economy.

The FRB can use **moral suasion** by suggesting to member banks that its unofficial policies and banking directives be followed. If moral suasion is not effective, the FRB may have to make official policies it can enforce.

## Fiscal Policy

"Fiscal policy" refers to governmental budget decisions, which can include increases or decreases in:

- federal spending
- money raised through taxation
- federal budget deficits or surpluses

The government can:

- reduce the rate of inflation by reducing aggregate demand for goods and services if price levels are excessive; or
- increase the rate of inflation by increasing aggregate demand if low inflation is causing unemployment and economic stagnation.

### Interest Rates

The cost of credit (interest rates) depends on supply and demand. In periods of easy money, when the credit supply exceeds demand, interest rates fall. Conversely, interest rates tend to rise when the FRB is tightening the money supply and demand exceeds supply. By influencing the money supply, the FRB affects interest rates.

### Disintermediation

**Disintermediation** is the flow of money from low-yielding accounts in traditional savings institutions (financial intermediaries) to higher yielding investments in the marketplace. Disintermediation occurs when the FRB tightens the money supply and interest rates rise.

## International Monetary Factors

### Balance of Payments

The **balance of payments** may run a surplus (more money entering the country than leaving it) or a deficit (more money leaving the country than entering it). A deficit may occur when high interest rates in another country attract savings dollars of U.S. citizens or corporations. Because of this deficit, citizens of other countries accumulate more dollars than they need for their payments to the United States, and there is an excess supply of U.S. dollars abroad.

The largest component of the balance of payments is the **balance of trade**. On the U.S. credit side are:

- foreign spending in the United States
- foreign investments in the United States

On the debit side are:

- U.S. spending abroad
- U.S. investments abroad
- U.S. bank loans abroad
- U.S. foreign aid

A favorable balance of trade is the result of more exports than imports. An unfavorable balance of trade is the result of more imports than exports.

# Questions

1. The short-term effect of the Federal Reserve's buying and selling securities in the marketplace is to

   A. check inflation
   B. stop a recession
   C. make credit more or less available
   D. do all of the above

2. Of the following, the item the Federal Reserve Board changes most often is the

   A. federal funds rate
   B. prime rate
   C. discount rate
   D. reserve rate

3. Which of the following actions by the Federal Reserve would result in a decrease in the money supply?

   A. Selling securities in the open market
   B. Changing the federal income tax rates
   C. Decreasing the discount rate
   D. Decreasing the reserve requirement

# Answers

1. **C.** The short-term effect is to make credit more or less available. The long-term effect is to check inflation or to create a situation where the economy can recover from a recession.

2. **C.** Of the items listed, the FRB changes the discount rate most frequently. It seldom changes the reserve rate. It does not change the federal funds rate or the prime rate. These rates are both market rates and are changed by market forces and by banks.

3. **A.** When securities are sold by the Fed, money is being taken out of circulation by purchasers who buy the securities. Tax changes are not used to control the money supply. Increasing discount rates and reserve requirements, not decreasing them, contracts the money supply.

# Technical Analysis

For the technical analyst, the decision to buy or sell depends almost entirely on market activity and overall market trends.

## Market Averages and Indexes

Stock prices tend to move (**trend**) together. Any given stock will tend to go up in a bull market and down in a bear market.

- **Trading volume.** If volume of trading is significantly higher or lower than average, technicians consider the market strong or weak.
- **Advances/declines.** The **breadth of the market** is the number of issues being traded up or down during a specific day. When declines exceed advances, the market is bearish. In bull markets, advances exceed declines. By plotting advances and declines on a graph, technical analysts can produce an *advance/decline line.*

**Dow Jones averages.** The Dow Jones averages are based on the prices of a limited number of stocks from four categories:

1. Industrial Average (30 stocks);
2. Transportation Average (20 stocks);
3. Utilities Average (15 stocks); and
4. Composite Average (the 65 stocks from the three other averages).

The Dow Jones averages are price weighted.

**Standard & Poor's 500.** Standard & Poor's 500 stock index (S&P 500) is based on the prices of 400 industrials, 20 transportation stocks, 40 financial stocks and 40 public utility stocks. Each stock is weighted according to the aggregate value of shares outstanding.

The S&P 100 index is a value-weighted index of 100 blue chip stocks, such as IBM, General Motors and Xerox.

**NYSE index.** The NYSE Composite Index is based on the prices of all common stocks listed on the Exchange. It is weighted by the total value of shares outstanding for each stock.

***Value Line.*** The *Value Line* Composite Index consists of 1,700 NYSE, AMEX and OTC stocks.

**Wilshire 5,000 Equity Index.** The Wilshire 5,000 is the broadest measure of the market. It is a value-weighted index composed of 5,000 NYSE, AMEX and OTC common stocks.

## Charting Stocks

### Trendlines

A trendline connects the reaction lows in an uptrend and the rally highs in a downtrend. Once established, trendlines are not easily halted or reversed.

**Consolidation.** If a market is staying within a narrow price range, it is said to be *consolidating.* When viewed on a graph, the trendline is horizontal and is said to be moving sideways, neither up nor down.

**Reversals.** A reversal indicates that an upward or a downward trendline has halted and the stock's price is moving the other way. In between the two trendlines there is usually a period of consolidation, a leveling off. A trendline that forms a "head and shoulders top" pattern indicates a bearish trend. When reversed, this pattern is called a "head and shoulders bottom" (also known as an *inverted* head and shoulders) and indicates a bullish reversal.

**Support and resistance levels.** When stock prices hover in a narrow range for an extended period, the bottom of this trading range is known as the **support level**; the top of the trading range is called the **resistance level**.

If the price on a particular stock penetrates either the support or the resistance level, the change is considered significant and is known as a **breakout**. Breakouts usually signal the beginning of a new upward or downward trend.

## Technical Market Theories

- **Dow theory**. According to the Dow theory, the primary trend in a bull market is a series of higher highs and higher lows. In a bear market, the primary trend is a series of lower highs and lower lows. Daily fluctuations are considered irrelevant.
- **Odd-lot theory**. When odd-lot traders are buying, odd-lot theorists are bearish. When odd-lot traders are selling, odd-lot theorists are bullish.
- **Short-interest theory**. High short interest is a bullish indicator, and low short interest is a bearish indicator.
- **Confidence theory**. *Barron's Confidence Index* is based on comparisons of the yields of a group of high-grade bonds with the yields of lower ranked bonds.
- **Modern portfolio theory**. Adherents to MPT say that securities markets are efficient markets, meaning that securities prices react so quickly to most investment information that no analyst is likely to outsmart the market as a whole.
- **Random walk theory**. Some analysts believe that the past movement or direction of a stock's price cannot be used to predict its future movement or direction. They subscribe instead to the **random walk theory**—that is, that the direction in which a stock's or market's price will move is no more predictable than the direction of a drunkard's walk.

# Questions

1. Which of the following is the narrowest measure of the market?

   A. NYSE Composite Index
   B. *Value Line* Index
   C. Dow Jones Industrial Average
   D. Standard & Poor's 100

2. The NYSE Composite Index consists of

   A. common stocks
   B. preferred stocks
   C. certain listed bonds
   D. all of the above

3. The stock index that contains the securities of 400 industrial corporations is the

   A. Dow Jones Composite Index
   B. Nasdaq Index
   C. NYSE Index
   D. Standard & Poor's 500

4. The value of the Dow Jones averages would be most affected by a change in the value of which of the following stocks?

   A. Utility
   B. Industrial
   C. Transportation
   D. Growth

5. What is the largest component of the NYSE Composite Index?

   A. Transportation
   B. Industrial
   C. Utilities
   D. Finance

6. A fundamental analyst would be interested in all of the following EXCEPT

   A. statistics of the U.S. Department of Commerce on disposable income
   B. daily trading volumes on the NYSE
   C. corporate annual reports
   D. innovations within the automotive industry

# Answers

1. **C.** Of those listed, the *Value Line* Composite, consisting of approximately 1,700 NYSE, AMEX and OTC stocks, is the broadest index. The second broadest is the NYSE Composite, containing all of the common stocks on the NYSE (about 1,500). The third broadest is the Standard & Poor's 100, made up of 100, mostly NYSE-traded, industrial stocks, for which options are available on the CBOE. The Dow Jones Industrial Average, containing 30 actively traded blue chip stocks, is the narrowest measure of the market.

2. **A.** The NYSE Composite Index is composed of only common stocks.

3. **D.** The Standard & Poor's 500 contains 400 industrials. The other 100 stocks are divided among financials, utilities and transportation stocks.

4. **B.** The Dow Jones Composite Index consists of 65 stocks: 30 industrial, 20 transportation and 15 utilities issues. Because industrials are the largest component, changes in their prices have the greatest effect on the averages.

5. **B.** Industrial stocks are the largest component of the NYSE Composite Index, the Standard & Poor's 500 and the Dow Jones Composite Index.

6. **B.** Trading volume interests the technical analyst, who looks at fluctuations in the market, not at fundamental economic values.

# Fundamental Analysis

## Industry Analysis

- **Defensive industries**. Defensive industries are those industries that are least affected by normal business cycles. Stock in companies in these defensive industries offers investors some protection against the inevitable downturns in the economy. Most defensive industries involve the production of nondurable consumer goods such as food, insurance, pharmaceuticals, tobacco and energy. Investment in defensive industries tends to involve less risk and, consequently, less opportunity for a high return on investment.
- **Cyclical industries**. Cyclical industries are highly affected by business cycles and price changes. Most cyclical industries produce durables such as capital goods, raw materials (such as steel, cement, aluminum and paper) and heavy equipment. **Counter-cyclical industries**, on the other hand, are those that tend to turn down as the economy heats up and to rise when the economy turns down.
- **Growth industries**. An industry is considered in its growth phase if the industry is growing faster than the economy as a whole. Because most companies in their growth phases retain nearly all of their earnings for expansion, stocks in these industries usually pay little or no dividends.

## Corporate Analysis

To ascertain a company's ability to compete in its industry, analysts examine the company's current and probable future market share, whether it is a leader within its industry and whether it is introducing new product lines that might increase its market share.

Fundamental analysts are concerned with the growth and stability of a company. They look at the quality of the firm's management and historical earnings trends. They plot how its projected growth compares with that of its competitors and whether its growth is stable or erratic. Analysts also examine a corporation's capitalization and use of working capital. They try to pinpoint stocks that afford the investor maximum potential for growth, stability and profits.

# Financial Statements

## Balance Sheet

A balance sheet shows what the company owns (its assets), what it owes (its liabilities) and the excess of the book value of assets over the book value of liabilities (its equity), as shown in the following equation:

Assets = Liabilities + Shareholders' equity

### Assets

- **Current assets** include the following:
  - cash and equivalents
  - accounts receivable
  - inventory
  - prepaid expenses
- **Fixed assets** cannot be easily liquidated. They can be **depreciated** and their cost deducted from taxable income in annual installments to compensate for loss in value.
- **Other assets** include intangible assets, such as patents, trademarks and goodwill.

### Liabilities

- **Current liabilities** include the following:
  - accounts payable
  - accrued wages payable
  - current long-term debt
  - notes payable
  - accrued taxes
- **Long-term liabilities**. Long-term debts are financial obligations due for payment after twelve months. Funded debt is any long-term debt that is payable in five years or more.

### Shareholders' Equity

Shareholders' equity is equal to total assets less total liabilities and is represented by three items:

1. capital stock at par;
2. capital in excess of par—often called **additional paid-in capital**, this is the amount of money over par value that the company received for selling stock; and
3. retained earnings—profits that have not been paid out in dividends.

### Liquidity

The formula for working capital is:

Current assets − Current liabilities = Working capital

## Changes that Affect the Balance Sheet

### Valuing Inventories

- **First in, first out**. FIFO is based on the assumption that items acquired first are sold first.
  - FIFO assigns the highest possible value to inventory because it assumes that the latest received (and most expensive) items remain unsold.
  - FIFO assigns the lowest possible value for cost of goods sold because it assumes the first (and cheapest) items are sold first.
- **Last in, first out**. LIFO is based on the assumption that goods acquired last are sold first.

## Capital Structure

Capital structure has four elements:

1. long-term debt
2. capital stock
3. capital in excess of par
4. earned surplus

The following have an effect on capital structure:

- **Issuing securities**. Net worth increases. Cash assets increase.
- **Convertible securities**. Liabilities decrease. Equity increases.
- **Bond redemption**. Liabilities decrease. Cash assets decrease.
- **Dividends**. Retained earnings are lowered.
- **Stock splits**. The par value and number of shares outstanding change.

### Financial Leverage

As a rule of thumb, industrial companies with a debt-to-equity ratio of 30% are said to be highly leveraged. Utilities, with their relatively stable earnings and cash flow, can be more highly leveraged without subjecting stockholders to undue risk.

## Income Statement

- **Net sales**. Net sales are gross sales minus returns.
- **Cost of goods sold**. Cost of goods sold are subtracted from net sales to calculate operating income.
- **Operating costs**. Operating costs are subtracted from net sales to arrive at operating income.
- **Operating profit**. Operating profit is a company's profit from the year's business operations.
- **Nonoperating income**. Other sources of revenue are listed separately on the income statement.
- **Interest expenses**. Interest payments on outstanding debt are not considered part of operating expenses nor part of the corporation's taxable income. The corporation reduces operating income by the amount of interest charges.
- **Net income after taxes**. Dividends are paid to stockholders out of net income.
- **Earnings per share**. Earnings per share is calculated after payment of interest on debt securities, taxes and the payment of preferred dividends. Earnings per share are computed by dividing the earnings available to common by the number of shares of common stock outstanding.
- **Retained earnings**. Earnings not paid out in interest, dividends to preferred and common stockholders, or taxes are called *retained earnings* or *earned surplus.*
- **Extraordinary items**. Extraordinary items are listed separately on the income statement.

### Summary of Income Statement

The following example illustrates typical entries on an income statement:

| | |
|---|---|
| | Net sales |
| *minus* | Cost of goods sold |
| *minus* | Operating costs |
| *equals* | Operating profit |
| *minus* | Nonoperating income |
| *equals* | Earnings before interest and taxes |
| *minus* | Interest expenses |
| *equals* | Taxable income |
| *minus* | Taxes |
| *equals* | Net income after taxes |
| *minus* | Preferred dividends |
| *equals* | Earnings available to common |
| *minus* | Common dividends |
| *equals* | Retained earnings |

# Questions

1. As a result of corporate transactions, a company's assets remain the same and its equity decreases. Which of the following statements is true?

   A. Prepaid expenses decrease.
   B. Total liabilities increase.
   C. Accrued expenses decrease.
   D. Net worth increases.

2. A company has been experiencing increased earnings but has kept its dividend payments constant. Due solely to this, the company's balance sheet would reflect

   A. decreased net working capital
   B. decreased net worth
   C. decreased retained earnings
   D. increased shareholders' equity

3. The difference between current assets and current liabilities is called

   A. net worth
   B. working capital
   C. cash flow
   D. quick assets

4. Earned surplus is

   A. net profits
   B. operating income
   C. cumulative earnings after dividends have been paid from net income
   D. cumulative earnings paid in dividends

5. All of the following can be said of accumulated depreciation EXCEPT that it

   A. provides funds for the actual cost of replacement
   B. is accumulated against liabilities
   C. is used to reduce the carrying value of fixed assets
   D. is a balance sheet item

6. During an inflationary period, FIFO will

   A. decrease profits
   B. decrease tax liabilities
   C. increase costs of goods sold
   D. increase profits and value of inventory on hand

7. Which of the following is NOT affected by the issuance of a bond?

   A. Assets
   B. Total liabilities
   C. Working capital
   D. Shareholders' equity

8. If a company redeems an outstanding debenture, working capital

   A. increases
   B. is not affected because debentures are long-term debts
   C. is not affected because cash and liabilities decrease equally
   D. decreases

9. Under what circumstances will a dilution of equity occur?

   A. Stock dividend
   B. Stock split
   C. Conversion of convertible bonds into common stocks
   D. Issue of mortgage bonds to replace debentures

10. A company that is highly leveraged has as the smallest portion of its capitalization

    A. preferred stock
    B. common stock
    C. debentures
    D. convertible debentures

11. A corporation that is highly leveraged is generally MORE attractive to

    A. secured bondholders
    B. general creditors
    C. preferred stockholders
    D. common stockholders

12. Which of the following statements is(are) true?

    I. The higher the bond rating, the lower the yield.
    II. Deep discount bonds have a high degree of safety.
    III. Interest rates can affect the discount on bonds.

    A. I
    B. I and III
    C. II
    D. II and III

13. Quantitative measures for corporate bonds include all of the following EXCEPT

    A. yields
    B. debt ratios
    C. net fixed assets per bond
    D. industry stability

14. When analyzing the investment quality of a mortgage bond, which of the following would be LEAST useful?

    A. Rating assigned the obligation by a nationally recognized rating service
    B. Information pertaining to the collateral that backs the obligation
    C. Name of the trustee that holds title to the collateral
    D. General trends in the economic cycle

# Answers

1. **B.** The formula for the balance sheet is: assets = liabilities + shareholders' equity. If assets stay the same and equity (net worth) decreases, liabilities must increase. Answer A is incorrect because prepaid expenses are assets; answer C is incorrect because accrued expenses are liabilities.

2. **D.** If earnings increase, retained earnings also increase. If the increased retained earnings are not paid out as dividends, shareholders' equity increases.

3. **B.** Working capital (or net working capital) is, by definition, the difference between current assets and current liabilities.

4. **C.** Earned surplus (also called *retained earnings)* is created by earnings of the company that have not been paid out in the form of dividends.

5. **B.** Accumulated depreciation offsets the value of fixed assets (not liabilities) on the balance sheet. The depreciation deduction reduces tax liability, keeping the balance sheet in balance. Depreciation expense is a deduction representing the decline in value of a fixed asset as it wears out. The deduction is based on a percentage of the asset's actual cost—not its current market value. The deduction reduces taxable income each year, which reduces taxes. Because of this income reduction, depreciation deductions are said to provide funds for the asset's replacement when it wears out.

6. **D.** When FIFO is used during periods of inflation, inventory purchased some time ago at a lower price is continually being charged against current sales. This practice results in higher profits on the income statement. The remaining inventory is valued at the latest price paid. In an inflationary economy, this inventory will be priced higher than the inventory charged against sales. Thus, the cost of inventory carried on the balance sheet has been increased.

7. **D.** On the issuance of a bond, cash is received (thus increasing current assets) and long-

term debt increases (increasing total liabilities) Because there is no corresponding increase in current liabilities, working capital will increase. It would have no effect on shareholders' equity.

8. **D.** The debenture, representing long-term debt, is part of the capitalization of a company. Cash is paid out to redeem the long-term debt. Therefore, cash, a current asset, has been reduced without a corresponding reduction of current liabilities. Consequently, working capital (current assets minus current liabilities) will decrease.

9. **C.** Dilution of equity occurs when each existing stockholder is affected by a change in capital structure that reduces his percentage interest in the company. A stock dividend or stock split does not change a stockholder's percentage of ownership. Refunding debts (answer D) has no effect on stockholders. However, if bonds are converted, more common shares are issued and the shareholder's equity is diluted.

10. **B.** The question defines a highly leveraged company. With a substantial amount of debt outstanding, highly leveraged companies have relatively little common stock. Remember: total capitalization = long-term debt + equity. So, if a company increases its long-term debt, a smaller percentage of its total capital will represent shareholders' equity.

11. **D.** High leverage tends to benefit common stockholders by magnifying the effect of increasing sales and earnings upon returns on common equity. Creditors, bondholders and preferred stockholders receive a fixed return. Any earnings above the amount necessary to pay that fixed return will apply to common stockholders' accounts.

12. **B.** Deep discount bonds may have a degree of uncertainty surrounding the safety of the investment and the ability of the issuer to continue interest payments.

13. **D.** Industry stability is a qualitative factor.

14. **C.** Rating services evaluate risk. The value of pledged collateral affects the safety of a bond investment. Economic trends affect the ability of an issuer to pay debt service and interest rates that, in part, determine the resale value of a bond. The trustee named in the bond indenture, however, assumes no liability for repaying the bond issuer's debt and does not guarantee repayment.

# Financial Ratios

### Capitalization Ratios

**Risk of bankruptcy**. Analysts assess the risk that a company will go bankrupt by studying its capitalization and its degree of leverage.

**Ratios**. When assessing a company's capitalization, analysts use ratios that express the percentage of capitalization composed of long-term debt, common stock and preferred stock. Bond analysts use the following three capitalization ratios to assess the degree of safety of a corporation's bonds.

$$\frac{\text{Long-term liabilities}}{\text{Total capitalization}} = \text{Bond ratio}$$

$$\frac{\text{Common shareholders' equity}}{\text{Total capitalization}} = \text{Common stock ratio}$$

$$\frac{\text{Preferred stock}}{\text{Total capitalization}} = \text{Preferred stock ratio}$$

The **bond ratio** measures the percentage of total capitalization that is provided by long-term debt financing. It is sometimes called the **debt ratio.** The **common stock ratio** measures the percentage of total capitalization contributed by common stockholders. The **preferred stock ratio** measures the percentage of total capitalization that is in preferred stock.

**Leverage**. The **debt-to-equity ratio** provides a common measure of leverage:

$$\frac{\text{Total long-term debt}}{\text{Total shareholders' equity}} = \text{Debt-to-equity ratio}$$

### Liquidity Ratios

Liquidity ratios measure the firm's ability to meet its current obligations. Working capital is the amount of liquid assets available to meet new short-term obligations.

$$\text{Current assets} - \text{Current liabilities} = \text{Working capital}$$

The **current ratio** measures the amount of current assets in relation to current liabilities.

$$\frac{\text{Current assets}}{\text{Current liabilities}} = \text{Current ratio}$$

**Quick assets** takes into account the size of the company's unsold inventory. Analysts use quick assets instead of current assets in the **acid-test ratio**. Most accountants believe that the acid-test ratio is a better measure of a company's liquidity than is the current ratio.

$$\text{Current assets} - \text{Inventory} = \text{Quick assets}$$

$$\frac{\text{Quick assets}}{\text{Current liabilities}} = \text{Acid-test ratio}$$

The final liquidity ratio, the **cash assets ratio,** measures only the cash assets (including marketable securities) in relation to current liabilities.

### Profitability Ratios

Ratios that demonstrate how high a company's profits are in relation to its sales include the **margin of profit ratio**, **operating ratio** and **net profit ratio.**

$$\frac{\text{Operating profit}}{\text{Net sales}} = \text{Margin of profit ratio}$$

$$\frac{\text{Operating expenses}}{\text{Net sales}} = \text{Operating ratio}$$

$$\frac{\text{Net income (after taxes)}}{\text{Net sales}} = \text{Net profit ratio}$$

Profitability is also reflected in a firm's return on assets, which analysts measure with the following ratios:

$$\frac{\text{Net income (after taxes)}}{\text{Shareholders' equity}} = \text{Return on equity}$$

### Asset Coverage and Safety of Income

**Debt service ratio.** An issuer's ability to meet principal and interest payments on bonds can be calculated by including principal payments in the denominator of the bond interest coverage ratio. This modified version of the ratio is called the *debt service ratio.*

$$\frac{\text{EBIT}}{\text{Annual interest} + \text{Principal payments}} = \text{Debt service ratio}$$

**Book value per share.** The book value of a company's assets is determined by deducting all liabilities and the value of any preferred stock from the company's tangible assets. Dividing this by the number of outstanding shares of common stock shows how far a company's assets might go toward reimbursing stockholders for their losses in bankruptcy.

$$\frac{\text{Assets} - \text{Liabilities} - \text{Intangible assets} - \text{Par value pref. stock}}{\text{No. of shares of common stock outstanding}}$$

$$= \text{Book value per share}$$

### Valuation Ratios

**Earnings per share.** Earnings per share (EPS), measures the value of one share against the earnings of the company. EPS is calculated after payment of interest on debt securities, taxes and payment of preferred dividends.

$$\frac{\text{Earnings available to common}}{\text{Number of common shares outstanding}} = \text{EPS}$$

The concept of EPS applies only to common stock. Preferred stockholders have no claims to earnings beyond the stipulated preferred stock dividends.

**Earnings per share after dilution.** If a corporation has rights, stock options, warrants, convertible preferred stock or convertible bonds, the EPS after dilution is used. EPS after dilution assumes that all convertible securities have been converted.

**Dividends per share.** The dividends per share is simply the dollar amount of cash dividends paid on each common share during the year.

$$\frac{\text{Annual dividends}}{\text{No. of common shares outstanding}} = \text{Dividends per share}$$

**Price-earnings ratio.** The price-earnings (PE) ratio formula is:

$$\frac{\text{Current market price of com. stock}}{\text{EPS}} = \text{PE ratio}$$

**Current yield.** The current yield of a common stock expresses the annual return on the investment as a percentage of the market value.

$$\frac{\text{Ann. dividends per com. share}}{\text{Market value per com. share}} = \text{Current yield}$$

**Dividend payout ratio.** The dividend payout ratio is used to measure the proportion of common earnings actually paid to common stockholders as dividends.

$$\frac{\text{Ann. dividends per com. share}}{\text{EPS}} = \text{Dividend payout ratio}$$

### Analyzing Corporate Debt

**Times interest earned ratio.** The likelihood that a company will have sufficient earnings to cover its interest payments can be measured by the number of times earnings before interest and taxes (EBIT) exceeds annual interest on the company's outstanding bonds.

$$\frac{\text{EBIT}}{\text{Annual interest payable to bonds}} = \text{Times interest earned}$$

The times interest earned ratio is also called the *interest coverage ratio, bond interest coverage ratio, fixed charge coverage ratio* and *times fixed charges earned ratio.*

**Credit risk.** To measure the credit risk of a company, use the ratio of total debt to net tangible assets.

# Questions

1. The times interest earned ratio is

   A. sales ÷ inventory
   B. receivables ÷ sales
   C. total debt ÷ net worth
   D. net income before taxes and interest ÷ interest expense

2. A corporation has annual sales of $15,000,000, operating expenses of $9,000,000, interest expense of $2,000,000 and principal payments on bonds totaling $1,000,000. What is the company's debt service ratio?

   A. 2 to 1
   B. 3 to 1
   C. 4 to 1
   D. 5 to 1

3. Mountain Brewing has total current assets of $40,000,000, $20,000,000 in inventory, total assets of $110,000,000, current liabilities of $10,000,000 and long-term debts totalling $50,000,000. What is the current ratio for Mountain Brewing?

   A. 1 to 2
   B. 2 to 1
   C. 4 to 1
   D. 8 to 1

4. Which of the following is the most stringent test of liquidity?

   A. Assets ÷ Current liabilities
   B. Current assets ÷ Current liabilities
   C. (Current assets − Inventory) ÷ Current liabilities
   D. (Cash + Marketable securities) ÷ Current liabilities

5. A corporation has $12,000,000 net income after taxes, 5,000,000 common shares outstanding and $10,000,000 of 6% preferred stock ($100 par). What is the corporation's earnings per share?

   A. $1.20
   B. $2.15
   C. $2.28
   D. $2.40

6. Which of the following would increase earnings per share?

   I. Tax loss carryover
   II. Cash dividends paid
   III. Bond interest received
   IV. Retirement of debt

   A. I, III and IV only
   B. I and IV only
   C. III and IV only
   D. I, II, III and IV

# Answers

1. **D.** The times interest earned ratio is operating income divided by interest expense. Operating income can also be described as *net income before taxes and before interest.*

2. **A.** The corporation has operating income before taxes and interest of $6,000,000 ($15,000,000 in sales less $9,000,000 operating expenses). The debt service ratio is: operating income of $6,000,000 divided by interest plus principal of $3,000,000, which equals a debt service ratio of 2 to 1.

3. **C.** The current ratio is: current assets of $40,000,000 divided by current liabilities of $10,000,000, which equals a current ratio of 4 to 1.

4. **D.** Of the answers given, answer D, the cash assets ratio, is the most stringent because it excludes inventories and accounts receivable.

5. **C.** Begin by calculating how much of the net income is available for common stockholders: net income after taxes minus preferred dividends equals earnings for common. The preferred stockholders receive $600,000 in dividends ($10,000,000 × 6% preferred stock = $600,000). To compute earnings per share: net income after taxes of $12,000,000 minus preferred dividend of $600,000, divided by the number of shares of common outstanding (5,000,000) equals $2.28 EPS.

6. **A.** When net income after taxes increases (for example, if there is a tax loss carried forward or bond interest is received), EPS will increase. Retirement of debt ends interest payments, thereby increasing net income and EPS. Payment of cash dividends has no effect on earnings, so choice II is incorrect.

# 12 Ethics, Suitability and Recommendations

## Ethics in the Securities Industry

### Ethical Business Practices

#### Corporate Ethics and Responsibility

The rules that guide relationships between members of the securities industry and all of the other participants are set by the states, NASAA, the NASD, the SEC, the MSRB and other regulatory bodies and exchanges throughout the country. The federal securities acts, state laws, NASAA's *Statement of Policy on Unethical Business Practices of Investment Advisers*, *NASD Manual*, *NYSE Constitution and Rules* and various other legislative acts governing securities all contain guidelines for what is and is not acceptable behavior. It is the responsibility of broker-dealers, investment advisers, registered reps and others in the securities industry to be familiar with and follow these guidelines.

#### Employee Ethics and Responsibility

Many firms view the regulations as minimum standards, and set stricter policies for internal behavior. Employees are responsible for knowing their firm's particular policies as these relate to the job they do. Even a well-intentioned employee of a broker-dealer can sometimes run afoul of the regulations. For example, a customer might suggest that an employee deliver a security in person, saving the firm the time and expense of registration and registered-mail delivery. But in most firms, delivering securities in this fashion is strictly against policy, and any person doing so could be subject to dismissal.

#### Customer Ethics and Responsibility

Practices that would tend to give select investors an unfair advantage over the general public are prohibited by regulations; a prime example of such practices is insider trading. It is the responsibility of the individual investor to abide by these regulations.

### Prohibited Practices

#### Manipulative and Fraudulent Devices

NASD member firms are strictly prohibited from using manipulative, deceptive or other fraudulent tactics or methods to effect a transaction or in an attempt to induce the sale or purchase of a security. The statute of limitations under the act of 1934 is three years from the alleged manipulation and within one year of discovering it. There is no dollar limit placed on damages in lawsuits based on allegations of manipulation.

### Outside Business Activity (Private Securities Transactions)

Associated persons are prohibited from being employed by any business other than their own member firm or engaging in private securities transactions without the knowledge and consent of their employing broker-dealers. Violations of the private securities transaction regulations are often referred to as **selling away**.

**Notification.** If an associated person wishes to enter into such a transaction or into outside employment, that person must:

- provide prior written notice to his employer;
- describe in detail the proposed transaction;
- describe in detail his proposed role in the transaction; and
- disclose whether he has or may receive compensation for the transaction.

If the transaction or business activity is to be entered into for compensation, the employing member may approve or disapprove the associated person's participation. If the member approves the participation, it is required to treat the transaction as if it is being done on its own behalf by entering the transaction on its own books and supervising the associated person during the transaction. If the member disapproves the transaction, the associated person may not participate in it.

## Recommendations to Customers

### Suitability and Investment Recommendations

Investment recommendations must be in keeping with customer needs, financial capability and objectives.

### Fair Dealing

The following activities are considered violations of the rules regarding fair dealing:

- recommending speculative securities without finding out the customer's financial situation and being assured that the customer can bear the risk;
- short-term trading of mutual funds;
- setting up fictitious accounts to transact business that otherwise would be prohibited;
- making unauthorized transactions or use of funds;
- recommending purchases that are inconsistent with the customer's ability to pay; and
- committing fraudulent acts (such as forgery and the omission or misstatement of material facts).

### Excessive Trading: Churning

The practice of engaging aggressively or excessively in trading a customer's account primarily to generate commissions, rather than to help achieve the customer's stated investment objectives, is an abuse of fiduciary responsibility known as *churning*.

As one method of preventing such abuses, self-regulatory organizations require that all accounts in which a registered rep or investment adviser has discretionary authority be reviewed frequently by a principal of the member firm.

### Selling Dividends

A registered rep is forbidden to encourage an investor to purchase mutual fund shares prior to a distribution because this increases tax liability, and doing so is known as **selling dividends**.

### Breakpoint Sales

**Breakpoint sales** are those in which a customer unknowingly buys investment company shares in an amount just under a dollar bracket amount that would qualify the investment for a reduction in sales charges. Encouraging a customer to make purchases in such a manner is unethical and a violation of the Rules of Fair Practice.

### Borrowing and Lending

**Borrowing money or securities from a customer.** Registered reps and investment advisers are prohibited from borrowing money or securities from a customer *unless* the customer is a bank, broker-dealer or other financial institution that is in the business of lending money.

**Loaning money or securities to a customer.** Registered reps and investment advisers also are prohibited from lending money or securities to a customer. This prohibition against lending money does not include broker-dealers making margin loans or investment advisers lending money as part of their normal business practices.

### Misrepresentations

Registered reps and investment advisers are prohibited from misrepresenting themselves or their services to clients or potential clients. Included in this prohibition are misrepresentations covering:

- qualifications, experience and education
- nature of services offered
- fees to be charged

It would also be considered a misrepresentation to either inaccurately state or fail to state a material fact regarding any of the above.

## Guarantees and Sharing in Customer Accounts

Broker-dealers and registered reps must not guarantee any customer against a loss or guarantee that a gain will be achieved in his account. Except in limited circumstances, members, advisers and representatives are also prohibited from sharing in any profits or losses in a customer's account. An exception will be made if a joint account has received the *prior* written approval of the member firm, and the registered representative shares in the profits and losses only to the extent of his *proportionate contribution* to the account.

If the member firm authorizes such a **shared account**, any or all such sharing must be directly proportionate to the financial contributions made by each party. However, in the case of an account being shared by a member or associated person and a member of that person's immediate family, directly proportionate sharing of profits and losses is not mandatory.

Immediate family members include parents, mother- or father-in-law, husband or wife, children, or any relative to whom the officer or employee in question contributes financial support.

## Other Unethical Trading Practices

**Front-running.** "Front-running" refers to situations in which a broker-dealer holds a customer order to buy or sell (typically a large block of stock that is very likely to move the market up or down) and buys or sells for the firm's own account on the same side of the market as the customer before showing the customer's order to the market. A broker-dealer, when holding a customer order to buy, is prohibited from buying stock for its own account at or below the price at which the customer's order is subsequently filled. Similarly, when holding a customer's order to sell, a broker-dealer is prohibited from selling stock for a firm trading account at or above the price at which the customer's order is subsequently filled.

**Capping.** Any attempt to place selling pressure on a stock in order to keep a price low or move it lower is known as *capping* and is prohibited by the NASD's Rules of Fair Practice.

## Criminal Penalties

The criminal penalties for violations of securities laws were increased through an amendment to the act of 1934. If a person is convicted of willfully violating federal securities regulations, or of *knowingly* making false or misleading statements in a registration document, that person can be fined up to $1,000,000, sentenced to prison for not more than ten years, or both; the maximum fine is $2,500,000 for other than a natural person.

## Questions

1. According to the Securities Exchange Act of 1934, which of the following statements is(are) true?

   A. Matching is prohibited.
   B. Pegging or fixing is not allowed.
   C. Using any means to create the appearance of active trading in a security is prohibited.
   D. All of the above statements are true.

2. Under the Securities Exchange Act of 1934, it is unlawful to

   I. enact a series of trades in a security to make it appear as if it is actively traded
   II. induce the sale of a security through misleading statements
   III. give out information about the actions of a person or a group that might affect the price of a security

   A. I only
   B. I and III only
   C. II only
   D. I, II and III

## Answers

1. **D.** *Matching* is entering identical orders to buy and sell a security. It would be done to create the illusion of high activity in a particular stock. It is prohibited activity. *Pegging* is entering bids for a security that is above the offering price. Broker-dealers are prohibited from pegging. Anything that creates an appearance of activity in a stock when it is not really there is considered to be market manipulation and is prohibited by the act of 1934.

2. **D.** All of the activities listed are manipulative or deceptive devices. They are prohibited by the act of 1934.

# Know Your Customer

## Financial Profile

The more you know about your customer, the better will be your recommendations. The more your customer knows, the better will be his investment decisions.

### Customer's Balance Sheet

Determine the status of your customer's balance sheet by asking questions similar to those following:

- What kinds of assets do you own? Do you own your home? A car? Collectibles? A second home?
- What are your liabilities? Do you make mortgage payments on your home? Do you make car payments? Do you have any other outstanding loans or regular financial commitments?
- Do you own any marketable securities? What types of investments do you currently hold?
- Have you established any long-term investment accounts? Do you have an IRA, a Keogh or a corporate pension or profit-sharing plan? Are you contributing to any annuities? What is the cash value of your life insurance?

### Customer's Income Statement

Determine the status of your customer's income statement by asking questions similar to those following:

- What is your total gross income? What is your total family income? How stable is this income? Do you see major changes taking place over the next few years?
- How much do you pay in expenses each month? Is this a relatively stable figure? Do you anticipate any change in this amount over the next few years?
- What is your net spendable income after expenses? How much of this is available for investment?
- What is your net worth? How much of it is liquid?

### Other Financial Elements

You will also want to learn:

- whether the person owns his own home;
- how much and what type of insurance he has;
- what his tax bracket is and what changes may occur in it over the next few years; and
- whether he has experienced any credit problems.

## Nonfinancial Investment Considerations

Some of the items you will want to ask your customer about his nonfinancial status include:

- age
- marital status
- number and ages of dependents
- employment
- employment of family members
- current and future family educational needs
- current and future family health care needs

To understand better a customer's aptitude for investment, ask questions similar to the following:

- What kind of risks can you afford to take?
- How liquid must your investments be?
- How important are tax considerations?
- Are you seeking long-term or short-term investments?
- What is your investment experience?
- What types of investments do you currently hold?
- How would you react to a loss of 5% of your principal? 10%? 50%?
- What level of return do you consider good? Poor? Excellent?
- What combination of risks and returns would you feel comfortable with?
- What is your investment temperament?

- Do you get bored with stable investments?
- Can you tolerate market fluctuations?

**Customer Investment Outlook**

- Preservation of capital
- Current income
- Capital growth
- Tax advantages
- Portfolio diversification
- Liquidity
- Speculation

# Questions

1. Which of the following considerations must you take into account when recommending suitable investments for clients?

   A. Client's age and marital status
   B. Current investment portfolio
   C. Investment objectives
   D. All of the above

2. "Growth" refers to

   A. the value of the investment increasing over time
   B. increasing principal and accumulating interest and dividends over time
   C. investments that appreciate tax-deferred
   D. all of the above

3. Credit risk involves

   A. safety of principal
   B. fluctuations in overall interest rates
   C. the danger of not being able to sell the investment at a fair market price
   D. inflationary risks

4. Bonds with long maturities offer

   I. stability of income
   II. stability of market value
   III. fluctuation of income
   IV. fluctuation of market value

   A. I and II
   B. I and IV
   C. II and III
   D. III and IV

5. Which of the following investments is LEAST appropriate for a client who is concerned primarily with liquidity?

   A. Preferred stock
   B. Municipal bond mutual funds
   C. Bank savings accounts
   D. Direct participation programs

6. Which of the following securities generates the greatest current return with moderate risk?
   A. Common stock of a new company
   B. Security convertible into the common stock of a company
   C. Fixed-income security
   D. Income bond

## Answers

1. **D.** A thorough investigation of a customer's situation, needs and objectives would take all of these factors into account before making an investment recommendation.

2. **A.** The term "growth" refers to an increase in the value of a product, not to an accumulation of undistributed interest or dividends.

3. **A.** This is the danger of losing all or part of one's invested principal. Answer B is market risk; answer C is marketability risk; and answer D is purchasing power risk.

4. **B.** If you buy one $1,000 bond with an 8% nominal (or coupon) yield, you will receive stable income: $80 every year. However, your principal (the current market value of the bond) will fluctuate, depending on the prevailing interest rates.

5. **D.** Clients who are concerned about liquidity risk should not invest in products like DPPs that do not have an active secondary market and, therefore, are not considered liquid investments.

6. **C.** Of the answers offered, in order to generate the greatest return a fixed-income security (a bond) is most suitable. Common stock is definitely not suitable; convertibles (either bonds or preferred) generally pay out a lower income rate than nonconvertibles because the investors receive benefit from the conversion feature; income bonds pay interest only if the corporation meets targeted earnings levels.

# Analyzing Financial Risks and Rewards

## Suitability

As an investment adviser, one of your key tasks is to recommend suitable investments that best match your clients' unique characteristics.

### Unsuitable Trades

Occasionally a customer will ask a registered rep to enter a trade for a corporate security that the rep feels is unsuitable. It is the rep's responsibility to discuss the trade with the customer, and explain why that particular trade might not be suitable. If the customer insists on entering the transaction, the registered rep should have the customer sign a statement acknowledging that the rep recommended against the trade, and the rep should mark the order ticket "unsolicited." The account belongs to the investor to do with as he pleases—while the rep may attempt to counsel the customer against unsuitable trades, the customer has the right to enter into any transaction he chooses and to be given good service on all transactions.

If the transaction that is determined to be unsuitable for the customer is in municipal securities, however, the MSRB prohibits the registered rep or broker-dealer from entering the trade, despite any customer requests to the contrary.

## Investment Risks

- **Inflation risk**. Also known as **purchasing power risk**, inflation risk measures the effects of continually rising prices on investments.
- **Capital risk**. Capital risk is the potential for an investor to lose all of her money or capital under circumstances unrelated to the financial strength of the issuer.
- **Selection risk**. This is the risk that when all other factors have been accounted for and an investor chooses (or has recommended to her) an investment, there is always the possibility that the choice will be a poor one.
- **Timing risk**. This is the risk to an investor of buying or selling at the wrong time and incurring losses or lower gains.
- **Interest rate risk**. This refers to the sensitivity of the price or value of an investment to fluctuations in the current level of interest rates.
- **Reinvestment risk**. This is the risk of not being able to reinvest interest income or principal at the same rate.
- **Market risk**. Also known as **systematic risk**, market risk is the risk that investors may lose some of their principal due to price volatility in the overall market.
- **Credit risk**. Also called **financial risk** or **default risk**, credit risk involves the danger of losing all or part of one's invested principal through failure of the issuer.
- **Liquidity risk**. Also known as **marketability risk**, this is the risk that a client might not be able to liquidate her investment at a time when she needs cash.
- **Legislative risk**. Also known as **legislative risk** or **political risk**, this is the risk that a change in law might affect an investment adversely.
- **Call risk**. Call risk is the risk that a bond might be called before maturity and investors will be unable to reinvest their principal at the same (or a higher) rate of return.

## Analyzing Investment Returns

- **Holding period return**. The HPR is a calculation of total return from capital gains and dividend income without taking into consideration how long the investment was held.

- **Present value**. Present value calculates today's value of a future payment or stream of payments, discounted at a given compound interest rate.
- **Internal rate of return**. The IRR is the discount rate at which the present value of future cash flows of an investment equals the cost of that investment.

# Questions

1. Geographical diversification of municipal investments can protect against all of the following EXCEPT

   A. adverse legislation in one area
   B. economic decline in one region
   C. increasing interest rates
   D. default by a particular issuer

2. Which of the following securities carries the highest degree of purchasing power risk?

   A. Short-term note
   B. Blue chip stock
   C. Long-term, high-grade bond
   D. Convertible cumulative preferred stock

3. Bondholders risk the value of their bonds falling as interest rates rise. This is known as what type of risk?

   A. Credit
   B. Reinvestment
   C. Marketability
   D. Market

# Answers

1. **C.** Geographical diversification cannot protect an investor against a loss in the value of an investment due to rising interest rates.

2. **C.** The longer you hold a fixed-income investment, the more vulnerable you are to purchasing power risk from inflation. Although preferred stock is also a fixed-income investment, convertible preferred will increase in value with the underlying common stock.

3. **D.** Among the different forms of market risk is the risk that fixed-income securities prices will drop as interest rates rise.

# Portfolio Analysis

## Portfolio Management Strategies

### Aggressive Investment Strategies

Aggressive investors pursue aggressive policies to buy and sell securities, including:

- selecting stocks with high betas
- buying securities on margin
- using put and call option strategies
- employing arbitrage techniques

### Defensive Investment Strategies

Defensive investors are willing to accept potentially lower total returns in order to minimize investment risk and preserve their capital. These investors place a high percentage of their investable capital in bonds, cash equivalents and stocks in defensive industries.

### Balanced Investment Strategies

An investor who creates a balanced portfolio will have securities that provide a hedge against the market no matter what its course.

## Modern Portfolio Theory

### Systematic and Nonsystematic Risk

- **Systematic risk**. The tendency for security prices to move together is known as systematic risk (also known as **market risk**). Investors who hold securities in their portfolio cannot avoid this risk, not even through diversification.
- **Nonsystematic risk**. Nonsystematic risk is associated with the underlying investment itself. The larger and more diversified an investor's portfolio, the less subject it is to nonsystematic risk.

### Risk Management Techniques

**Diversification**. A portfolio can be diversified in many ways, including:

- type of instrument (equity, debt, packaged and so on);
- industry;
- companies within an industry;
- length of maturity;
- investment rating; and
- geography.

**Dollar cost averaging**. An investor makes periodic purchases of a fixed dollar amount in one or more common stocks or mutual funds. In a fluctuating market, the average *cost* of the stock purchased in this manner is always less than the average market *price*.

**Constant ratio plan**. The investor initially sets an equity-to-debt ratio. Purchases and sales are then made as necessary to maintain the ratio.

**Constant dollar plan**. This strategy's primary goal is to buy and sell securities so that a set dollar amount remains invested at all times.

### Measuring Stock Price Volatility

**Beta coefficient**. A stock's beta coefficient quantifies the degree to which the stock's price changes in comparison to changes in the market.

| If the beta coefficient is: | The stock's return will probably: |
|---|---|
| exactly 1 | move exactly with the market |
| less than 1 | move less than the market moves |
| greater than 1 | move more than the market moves |

## Questions

1. Which of the following constitutes a constant dollar plan?
   A. 60% equities, 40% fixed income
   B. 40% equities, 60% fixed income investments
   C. Fixed amount in the portfolio regardless of market price
   D. Fixed amount in fixed-income investments regardless of market price

2. An investor who makes transactions once a month using dollar cost averaging would
   A. buy the same dollar amount of a stock
   B. buy the same number of shares of a stock
   C. put 70% of the money in a bond fund and buy stocks with the rest
   D. buy equal amounts of speculative and blue chip securities

3. Mr. Smith is pursuing an aggressive stock buying strategy. Which of the following is most suitable for him?
   A. ABC stock with a beta coefficient of 1.0
   B. DEF stock with a beta coefficient of .93
   C. GHI stock with a beta coefficient of 1.04
   D. Convertible bonds of a blue chip company

## Answers

1. **C.** In a constant dollar plan, a fixed dollar amount is invested in the portfolio. If the market value rises, the excess is sold. If the market value falls, the securities are purchased to restore the "constant" dollar position.

2. **A.** Because the dollar amount remains constant, the investor will automatically buy more shares when the price is low, thus reducing the average cost.

3. **C.** Beta coefficients over 1 signify that the stock will fluctuate more than the market as a whole. In general, the higher the beta, the greater the risk. Such risk-taking is appropriate for investors who seek aggressive stock-buying strategies and have both the financial ability and the temperament to withstand downturns in the market.

# Federal and State Taxation

## Regressive and Progressive Taxes

Regressive taxes fall the hardest on the poorest people; progressive taxes are felt more by the rich. Sales, excise, payroll, property and gasoline taxes are regressive taxes.

- **Gift tax**. A gift tax is imposed on gifts of cash, real property, securities and other valuables that one individual gives to another. The tax is paid by the donor. A $10,000 gift tax exemption is allowed annually ($20,000 for a married couple). This means that $10,000 in cash or other assets can be given each year to each of a person's children or to anyone else free of any gift tax.
- **Estate taxes**. Estate taxes are imposed by a state or the federal government on assets willed to others. Federal law allows a $600,000 exclusion on assets left to beneficiaries.

### Income Taxes

- **Earned income**. Earned income includes salary, bonuses and income derived from active participation in a trade or business.
- **Passive income**. Passive income and losses come from rental property, limited partnerships and enterprises in which the individual is not actively involved. Passive income is netted against passive losses in order to determine net taxable income. Passive losses may be used to offset passive income only.
- **Portfolio income**. Portfolio income includes dividends, interest and net capital gains derived from the sale of securities. It is taxed in the year in which it is received.

### Individual Federal Income Taxes

The basic design of the tax return is:

| | |
|---|---|
| | Earned income |
| *plus* | Passive income (net against passive losses) |
| *plus* | Interest and dividends |
| *plus/minus* | Net capital gains/losses |
| *equals* | Adjusted gross income (AGI) |
| *minus* | Itemized or standard deductions |
| *minus* | Personal exemptions |
| *equals* | Taxable income |
| *times* | Tax rate |
| *equals* | Tax liability |

### Income Tax Brackets

U.S. income tax tables are structured so that successively earned portions of one's income are taxed at progressively higher rates.

## Taxation and Investment Portfolios

### Interest Income

Based on the **doctrine of reciprocal immunity** (also known as the **doctrine of mutual reciprocity**), there is a reciprocal agreement between governments. The federal government does not tax state and municipal issues. In turn, state and local governments usually do not tax federal securities. Furthermore, the debt obligations of U.S. territories and political subdivisions (Puerto Rico, Guam, the Virgin Islands) are fully exempt from all taxation.

- **Corporate bonds**. Interest income on corporate bonds is taxable by federal, state and some local governments.
- **U.S. government securities**. Interest income on direct federal debt is exempt from state and local taxes, but is federally taxable.
- **Agency issues**. The interest income on most federal agency debt, like that on Treasury securities, is taxable by the federal govern-

ment. Federally taxable agency issues include:

- mortgage-backed securities of the Government National Mortgage Association (GNMA—Ginnie Maes);
- securities issued by the Federal National Mortgage Association (FNMA—Fannie Maes); and
- securities of the Inter-American Development Bank (IADB).

- **Accrued interest**. Interest income includes accrued interest received when bonds are sold between interest payment dates. Accrued interest is taxable income to the seller.

### Tax-exempt Interest Income

**Municipal securities**. Interest on municipal bonds issued before August 7, 1986, and on municipal bonds with a public purpose issued after that date is exempt from federal taxes.

### Dividend Income

**Dividend income from mutual funds**. Under Subchapter M of the Internal Revenue Code (IRC), a **regulated investment company** may gain exemption from taxation on income if 90% of that income is passed on to shareholders.

- Municipal bond mutual funds or unit investment trusts (UITs) distribute federally tax-free dividends to shareholders.
- Dividend distributions from taxable mutual funds (for example, a corporate bond fund or stock fund) are taxable in the year they are received by the investor. Reinvested dividends are considered constructively received and also are taxable in the year they are distributed.

### Foreign Securities

The interest and dividend income from a foreign investment is taxed by the country in which the investor is a citizen.

If foreign tax has been withheld on a distribution of dividends or interest from a foreign security, a U.S. citizen is eligible for a 15% income tax credit for the amount withheld.

### Taxable on Receipt

Interest and dividends are taxable only in the year they are *received*. Investors do not owe taxes on dividends or interest declared or accrued until the year in which they actually receive the money.

### Capital Gains (Losses)

A capital gain occurs when the difference between a capital asset's purchase price and its selling price is positive. If the difference is negative, it is a capital loss.

### Adjusting Cost Basis

The cost basis of an investment is used to determine whether there is a taxable gain or tax-deductible loss when the asset is sold. The IRS allows the cost basis to be adjusted for such things as stock splits and stock dividends.

- **Capital gains**. A capital gain occurs when capital assets (securities, real estate and tangible property) are sold at prices that exceed the adjusted cost basis.
- **Capital losses**. A capital loss occurs when capital assets are sold at prices that are less than the adjusted cost basis.
- **Net capital gains and losses**. To calculate tax liability, taxpayers must first add all short-term capital gains and losses for the year. Then, they separately add all long-term capital gains and losses. Finally, they offset the totals to determine the net capital gain or loss for the year. Net capital losses are deductible against earned income to a maximum of $3,000 per year. Any capital losses not deducted in a taxable year may be carried forward indefinitely to lower taxable income in future years.

### Taxable on Trade Date

Net capital gains are taxable (and losses are deductible) *only* in the year in which the trade date occurs. A trade done at the end of a year and that settles the following year is taxable (or deductible) in the year in which it is executed.

**Determining which shares to sell.** An investor holding identical securities with different acquisition dates and cost bases may determine which shares to sell by electing one of three accounting methods: first in, first out (FIFO), last in, first out (LIFO) or share identification. If the investor fails to choose, the IRS assumes the investor is liquidating shares on a FIFO basis.

### Wash Sales

Capital losses may not be used to offset gains or income if the investor sells a security at a loss and purchases the same (or a substantially identical) security within 30 days before or after the trade date establishing the loss. The sale at a loss and the repurchase within this period is a wash sale.

Substantially identical securities include stock rights, call options, the exercise of short-term deep in-the-money puts, warrants and convertible securities of the same issue.

### Bonds Purchased at a Discount

**Original issue discount.** If an original issue discount (OID) bond is sold before it matures, the cost basis of the bond is adjusted by **accreting** the amount of the discount annually as determined by the issuer (normally on a straight-line basis). Each year, owners of corporate and government OID bonds are taxed on the amount of the discount accreted during the year. The amount accreted on a municipal OID bond is exempt from federal income tax.

If an OID bond is held until maturity, 100% of the discount will have been accreted and the investor will have no taxable capital gain.

**Secondary market discount.** The cost basis of a bond bought at a discount in the secondary market is not adjusted.

### Donated (Gifted) and Inherited Securities

- **Gifts.** When a donor makes a gift of securities, the cost basis to the recipient (the *donee*) is the donor's cost basis.
- **Inherited securities.** When a person dies and securities the person owned are passed on to heirs (either by will or by law), the cost basis to the recipient is the fair market value on the date of the owner's death.

### Margin Expenses

Interest paid for securities margin loans is a tax-deductible expense, unless it is incurred in the purchase of municipal securities.

## Alternative Minimum Tax

**AMT for individuals.** The AMT is 26% or 28%. To determine whether an individual is subject to the AMT:

1. Add all preference items to taxpayer's AGI.
2. From this amount, subtract $45,000 (married, filing jointly), $33,750 (single) or $22,500 (married, filing separately).
3. Of the remaining amount, the first $175,000 (single filers) or $87,500 (married, filing separately) is taxed at 26%; and the remainder at 28%.

**Tax preference items.** Certain items receive favorable tax treatment; these must be added back into taxable income for the AMT. They include:

- accelerated depreciation on property placed in service after 1986;
- certain costs associated with DPPs, such as research and development costs and intangible drilling costs;
- local tax and interest on investments that do not generate income;
- tax-exempt interest on private purpose municipal bonds issued after August 7, 1986; and
- incentive stock options in excess of their fair market value.

## Corporate Taxes

The 1993 tax law reduced or eliminated some of the techniques that corporations used to reduce their tax burden, including:

- repealing the investment tax credit (ITC);
- lengthening depreciation schedules; and
- eliminating the favorable treatment of capital gains.

**Provisions affecting corporate taxes.** Some of the IRC provisions affecting corporations as investors include:

- **Dividend exclusion rule.** Dividends paid from one corporation to another are 70% exempt from taxation.
- **Municipal securities.** Like individual taxpayers, corporations do not pay federal taxes on income received from municipal obligations.

# Questions

1. A couple who file a joint tax return has $275 in corporate preferred dividends. According to the tax law, this couple can exclude how much of this dividend income?

   A. $0
   B. $100 on a joint return
   C. $200 on a joint return
   D. All of it

2. Which of the following bonds is totally tax exempt?

   A. Hawaii GO bond
   B. U.S. government bond
   C. Puerto Rico GO bond
   D. U.S. Steel bond

3. Dr. Nichols invests $5,000 in the following new issue:

   | Ohio General Telephone Company |
   |---|
   | $20,000 9% debentures |
   | Price 97 |
   | To yield 9.2% |

   The bonds listed above are

   A. federal and state tax exempt
   B. state tax exempt
   C. federal and state tax exempt if purchased by an Ohio resident
   D. fully taxable

4. A customer owns five 6% U.S. government bonds. The customer is in the 28% federal tax bracket and the 14% state tax bracket. What is her income tax liability on the interest?

   A. $0
   B. $42
   C. $84
   D. $126

5. The income from all of the following securities is fully taxable at the federal, state and local levels EXCEPT

   A. Ginnie Maes
   B. Treasury bonds
   C. reinvested mutual fund dividends
   D. IADB securities

6. Assuming that each of the bonds under consideration has the same maturity, place the following bonds in order of their pretax yields, from highest to lowest.

   I. U.S. government bonds
   II. AAA municipal bonds
   III. AA corporate bonds

   A. I, II, III
   B. II, I, III
   C. III, I, II
   D. III, II, I

7. A corporation announces a redemption call on March 15th for its $9 cumulative convertible preferred stock. The redemption is to be made at 100 plus a $.80 accrued dividend. The preferred stock, which is trading at 98, is convertible into 1.4 shares of common trading at 73 1/2. If the customer buys 100 shares of the preferred stock, converts the stock into common and sells the common at the market, what would be the resulting gain or loss?

   A. $490 profit
   B. $2,500 loss
   C. $7,790 loss
   D. $10,290 profit

8. Which of the following statements are true concerning the tax treatment of mutual funds?

   I. Dividend payments and capital gains distributions will not be subject to taxation as long as they are reinvested in the fund.
   II. Dividend payments and capital gains are both taxed at the same rate.
   III. The IRS treats exchanging shares within the same family of funds as a sale and repurchase of securities.

   A. I and II only
   B. I and III only
   C. II and III only
   D. I, II and III

9. Losses from direct participation programs can be used to offset

   A. earned income from salary or commissions
   B. portfolio income
   C. income from limited partnerships
   D. none of the above

10. Interest expense incurred to purchase which of the following types of securities is NOT federally tax deductible?

   A. Corporate bonds
   B. Treasury securities
   C. Municipal bonds
   D. Common stocks

# Answers

1. **A.** Individual taxpayers must pay taxes on the full amount of their dividend income.

2. **C.** Bonds issued by territories and political subdivisions of the United States (Puerto Rico, Guam and the U.S. Virgin Islands) are exempt from federal, state and local taxes.

3. **D.** These bonds are issued by General Telephone, a publicly held corporation located in the state of Ohio. Like all corporate bonds, the interest income is fully taxable.

4. **C.** U.S. government bonds are exempt from state and local taxes, but the interest is taxed by the federal government. The customer earned $300 annual interest ($5,000 × 6%). The federal tax liability is $84 ($300 × 28%).

5. **B.** Dividends (whether reinvested or not), Ginnie Maes, Fannie Maes and IADB securities are all fully taxable. U.S. government securities are exempt from state and local taxes.

6. **C.** Normally, the greater the risk, the higher the yield that must be offered to potential investors. Therefore, government securities yield less than corporate securities. In this problem, you must also take into account the difference in taxable bonds (corporate and governments) versus tax-free bonds (municipals). This difference in taxation causes the pretax yield of municipals to be lower than that of corporate and government bonds.

7. **A.** One hundred preferred shares cost $9,800 (100 × $98). These 100 shares convert into 140 shares of common (100 × 1.4). The 140 shares of common stock are worth $10,290 (140 × $73.50). The profit is the sale proceeds on the common stock less the cost of the preferred, or $490 ($10,290 – $9,800).

8. **C.** Both dividend payments and capital gains distributions are taxed at ordinary income tax rates (choice II). Investors must report and pay taxes on all such distributions even if they are automatically reinvested in the fund (so choice I is false). The exchange of mutual fund shares within a family of funds is treated as a sale and repurchase of securities, so taxable capital gains or losses are incurred when shares are exchanged.

9. **C.** Passive losses can be used only to offset passive gains.

10. **C.** Interest expense incurred to purchase a security that offers federally tax exempt income cannot be deducted.

# 13 U.S. Government and State Rules and Regulations

## Insider Trading Act of 1988

### Policies and Procedures

- An insider is any person who has access to nonpublic information about a corporation.
- Insiders may not use inside information as a basis for personal trading until that information has been made public.
- The SEC can levy a civil penalty of up to three times the amount of profit made (or loss avoided) if inside information is used.
- Inside information is any information that has not been disseminated to, or is not readily available to, the general public.

**SEC investigations.** The SEC has the right to investigate any person who has violated or is suspected of violating any of the provisions of the Insider Trading Act.

### Civil Penalties

The person controlling the incident may be liable for civil penalties of up to the greater of $1 million or 300% of profits made (or losses avoided). Any person who knowingly violates these rules can be imprisoned for up to ten years.

**Profits gained and losses avoided.** When determining how much profit was made (or loss avoided), the Commission looks at the market price of the security a reasonable period after the information becomes general public knowledge.

### Criminal Penalties

If a person is convicted of willfully violating federal securities regulations or of knowingly making false or misleading statements in any registration document, that person can be fined up to $1 million, sentenced to prison for up to ten years, or both.

### Insider Trading Rules

- Does the *tipper* owe a *fiduciary duty* and has he breached it?
- Does the *tipper* meet the *personal benefits test*?
- Does the *tippee know or should the tippee have known* that the information was inside or confidential?
- Is the *information material and nonpublic*?

### Chinese Wall Doctrine

Those departments or branches of a broker-dealer that have access to material nonpublic information may not disseminate this information to anyone who could conceivably trade on it.

# Securities Investor Protection Corporation

The **Securities Investor Protection Corporation (SIPC)** is an independent government-sponsored corporation. All broker-dealers registered with the SEC must be SIPC members. Exempt from membership are:

- broker-dealers handling exclusively open-end investment company shares or unit trusts;
- broker-dealers handling exclusively variable annuities or insurance; and
- investment advisers.

**The SIPC fund.** SIPC collects from its members an annual assessment based on a percentage of a member's gross revenues from the securities business.

## Liquidation Proceedings

The court-appointed trustee in a liquidation proceeding is required to *promptly*:

- deliver securities that are registered in a customer's name back to the customer;
- assign ownership and distribute street name securities to customers;
- sell or transfer branches or other offices of the failed broker-dealer to raise capital; and
- liquidate the business of the broker-dealer.

**Notification.** The appointed trustee must notify by mail all customers of the firm during the preceding twelve months about the liquidation proceedings. Each customer must then file a statement of claim with the trustee.

Customer claims are based on the customers' net equity as of the valuation date of their accounts. The valuation date is generally the day customer protection proceedings commence. In the case of customer margin accounts, net equity is the market value of all securities in the accounts as of the valuation date less the debit balances.

**Payment of customers.** At this point, the trustee will distribute the securities held by the broker-dealer according to the following guidelines:

- Securities registered in customer name are returned to the owners without dollar limit. If there are liens against the securities attributable to a customer, the debt must be paid before the distribution.
- Securities held in street name and cash are distributed to customers on a pro rata basis.
- After the distribution of street name securities and cash, SIPC funds are available to meet remaining claims of each customer up to a *maximum of $500,000*, with *cash claims* not to exceed *$100,000* of the $500,000 total.
- For claims in excess of $500,000, the customers become general creditors of the broker-dealer and share pro rata with all other general creditors.

## Account Coverage

- **Individuals.** Under SIPC rules, each *separate customer account* is entitled to coverage up to SIPC limits. In general, "separate customer accounts" are defined as those accounts with *unique beneficial owners*. Usually, if the account name is different it is considered a different customer and is entitled to full and separate coverage.

- **Broker-dealers.** Claims by broker-dealers, general partners of broker-dealers, officers of broker-dealers, subordinated lenders, control persons of broker-dealers and owners of more than 5% of the equity of firms are not allowed.

- **Coverage limits.** Customer accounts are covered to a *maximum of $500,000*, with *cash claims* not to exceed *$100,000*. Only claims for securities and cash are covered; claims resulting from open positions in commodity futures contracts do not fall under SIPC coverage. Each customer may enter a claim up to the $500,000 coverage limit. This limit is applied to all accounts in that customer's name (for instance, John Doe's cash account and his margin account would be considered one account).

### Advertising SIPC Membership

Broker-dealers that are members of SIPC may not advertise their membership in such a way as to imply that this coverage represents more or less than it actually is.

### Fidelity Bonds

Every member firm required to join SIPC must purchase and maintain a blanket fidelity bond that indemnifies against losses due to acts such as check forgery, lost securities or fraudulent trading.

## Questions

1. Which of the following is NOT true of SIPC?

   A. It is a nonprofit corporation designed to protect the public in the event a broker-dealer fails.
   B. It is a government agency designed to protect the public.
   C. It is funded by broker-dealers.
   D. It is subject to an SEC overview.

2. Under SIPC, each customer's account is insured for

   A. $100,000 in cash
   B. $500,000 in bonds
   C. $500,000, with cash not to exceed $100,000
   D. $600,000 in bonds and cash

3. Claims for more than the maximum allowable coverage are settled under SIPC in which of the following manners?

   A. Rejected in whole
   B. Paid to the maximum coverage, with the excess rejected
   C. Paid to the maximum coverage, with the excess becoming the claim of a general creditor
   D. Paid to the maximum coverage, with the excess becoming a subordinated claim paid after the general creditors are paid

4. If a SIPC member corporation were to go bankrupt, the trustee appointed would be responsible for all of the following EXCEPT

   A. informing the firm's clients about the liquidation
   B. distributing identifiable customer-owned securities held by the firm
   C. supervising the distributions for commodity accounts
   D. supervising the liquidation of the firm and seeing that it is done methodically

## Answers

1. **B.** Answer B is untrue. The other answers are true. SIPC is a private organization that was set up as a nonprofit corporation. It was designed by Congress to protect the public even if the broker-dealer fails. SIPC is funded by broker-dealers and is subject to SEC overview.

2. **C.** SIPC insures accounts for a total of $500,000 with maximum coverage of $100,000 in cash.

3. **C.** Any claim exceeding the maximum coverage becomes a claim as a general creditor. The amount that is covered by SIPC insurance will be paid in full by SIPC.

4. **C.** SIPC does not cover commodity accounts.

# Other Federal and State Legislation

### Maloney Act

The Maloney Act provided for the creation and registration with the SEC of a national securities association to regulate brokers and dealers not affiliated with an exchange. Under the provisions of this amendment, the NASD was formed.

### Trust Indenture Act of 1939

The Trust Indenture Act of 1939 specifies that any corporate bond issue of more than $5 million and a maturity date more than nine months in the future must be issued with a trust indenture (a written agreement between the corporate issuer and a trustee who represents the investors). An independent trustee is appointed to ensure that the protective covenants are carried out. Each investor does not receive a copy of the indenture, but is entitled to review a copy at the custodian bank, where it is usually held.

## State Securities Regulations

In addition to federal securities regulations, each state has laws that pertain to the issuance of securities and to the trading of securities in the secondary market. State securities laws are known as **blue-sky laws**. The name "blue-sky" comes from a statement made by a U.S. Supreme Court justice who referred to "speculative schemes that have no more basis than so many feet of blue sky." The **Uniform Securities Act (USA)** serves as model legislation that each state may follow or adapt to its own needs.

Most states require broker-dealers that do business in a particular state to register with that state's securities commission. Salespeople associated with a broker-dealer must also be registered in the state(s) where they do business.

In most states, securities must be registered before they can be sold to the public. There are three ways to register a security in a state:

1. Coordination
2. Filing
3. Qualification

The types of securities and transactions exempt from state securities registration requirements include:

- securities listed on SEC-registered stock exchanges;
- nonprofit organizations;
- insurance companies;
- banks;
- building and loan associations;
- public utilities and railroads;
- cooperative associations; and
- private placements.

# Questions

1. Which of the following is(are) objectives of the Investment Company Act of 1940?
   A. To ensure that the individual investor is fully informed about the affairs of the investment company and is treated fairly by its management
   B. To require minimum financial and accounting standards of all broker-dealers engaged in interstate commerce
   C. To control the size of individual investment companies and their impact on securities markets
   D. All of the above

2. All of the following statements are true of blue-sky laws EXCEPT that
   A. they attempt to protect the public from the fraudulent sale of securities within a particular state
   B. the Securities Act of 1933 sets forth certain standard provisions that must appear in all blue-sky laws
   C. an issuer that intends to offer securities for sale in several states must comply with the provisions of the Securities Act of 1933 and all securities laws of the appropriate states
   D. a state securities division has the power to revoke the license of any securities salesperson for violation of its laws

3. A state requires registration for which of the following?
   I. In-state salesperson
   II. In-state broker-dealer
   III. Out-of-state salesperson doing business in that state
   IV. Out-of-state broker-dealer doing business in that state

   A. I and II only
   B. II and IV only
   C. III and IV only
   D. I, II, III and IV

4. In which of the following circumstances can a registered representative purchase a security for a client who lives in a certain state when the security is not registered in the state?
   I. The security is NYSE listed.
   II. The security is exempt from registration.
   III. The security is listed on the Canadian Stock Exchange.
   IV. The security has been publicly traded for at least twelve months.

   A. I and II only
   B. I, II and IV only
   C. II only
   D. I, II, III and IV

5. In some states, registration of securities with the state securities division may be accomplished through
   I. filing
   II. substitution
   III. qualification
   IV. coordination

   A. I and II
   B. I, II and IV
   C. I, III and IV
   D. II and III

6. Which of the following legislative acts exclusively regulates debt securities?
   A. Securities Act of 1933
   B. Securities Exchange Act of 1934
   C. Trust Indenture Act of 1939
   D. Investment Advisers Act of 1940

# Answers

1. **A.** A "rules and regulations" question tempts one to pick "all of the above." But, in this case, answers B and C do not apply to the Investment Company Act of 1940.

2. **B.** The Securities Act of 1933 is a federal statute—the federal government does not dictate state law. Blue-sky laws protect the public from securities fraud in each state and must be complied with by issuers and by broker-dealers.

3. **D.** A broker-dealer or salesperson doing business in the state must be registered in that state.

4. **A.** To sell a security in a given state, the security must be registered in the state. This is required unless the security is exempt. Most states exempt listed securities from state registration (a *blue chip* exemption). In addition, exempt securities under the act of 1933 are also exempt from state registration.

5. **C.** "Substitution" is not a method of registering securities with a state securities administrator. The other answers are methods by which a security can be registered.

6. **C.** The Trust Indenture Act of 1939 protects investors in corporate bonds in the case of the default of the issuing company.

# 14 Other SEC and SRO Rules and Regulations

## Registration and Regulation

### Securities Exchange Act of 1934

Broker-dealers that transact securities business with customers or with other broker-dealers must apply and be approved for registration with the SEC.

#### SEC Sanctions Against Broker-Dealers

The SEC is entitled to:

- censure
- limit activities, functions or operations
- suspend
- revoke registration
- fine
- seek civil monetary penalties

An associated person also can be suspended, censured, restricted in his activities, fined or barred from association with a broker-dealer. If the SEC has barred an associated person, no broker-dealer may allow that person to associate with it without the express permission of the Commission.

#### Fingerprinting

Registered broker-dealers are required to have fingerprint records made for all of their employees, directors, officers and partners. Exempt from the fingerprinting requirement are employees who:

- are not involved in securities sales;
- do not handle or have access to cash or securities; and
- do not supervise other employees engaged in these activities.

# Questions

1. Under the Securities Exchange Act of 1934, the SEC does which of the following?

   I. Regulates securities exchanges.
   II. Requires the registration of brokers and dealers.
   III. Prohibits inequitable and unfair trade practices.
   IV. Regulates over-the-counter markets.

   A. I and II only
   B. I and IV only
   C. II, III and IV only
   D. I, II, III and IV

# Answers

1. **D.** Although the SEC has delegated some of the responsibility of overseeing the OTC markets to the NASD, it is still ultimately responsible for their regulation.

# NASD Bylaws

Each SRO is accountable to the Commission for enforcing federal securities laws, as well as supervising securities practices within an assigned field of jurisdiction.

- **National Association of Securities Dealers (NASD).** Regulates all matters related to investment banking (securities underwriting) and trading in the OTC market and the conduct of NASD member firms and associated persons.
- **New York Stock Exchange (NYSE).** Regulates all matters related to trading in NYSE-listed securities and the conduct of NYSE member firms and associated persons.
- **Municipal Securities Rulemaking Board (MSRB).** Regulates all matters related to the underwriting and trading of state and municipal securities (the MSRB regulates but does not have enforcement powers—it depends on other SROs for the enforcement of its rules).
- **Chicago Board Options Exchange (CBOE).** Regulates all matters related to writing and trading standardized options and related contracts listed on that exchange.

## Administration of the NASD

### Purposes and Objectives

The purposes and objectives of the NASD are to:

- promote the investment banking and securities business, to standardize principles and practices, to promote high standards of commercial honor and to encourage the observance of federal and state securities laws;
- provide a medium for communication among its members, and between its members, the government and other agencies;
- adopt, administer and enforce the NASD's Rules of Fair Practice and rules designed to prevent fraudulent and manipulative practices, as well as to promote just and equitable principles of trade; and
- promote self-discipline among members and to investigate and adjust grievances between the public and members and between members.

### *NASD Manual*

The *NASD Manual* describes the following four sets of basic rules and codes by which the OTC market is regulated:

1. **Rules of Fair Practice.** This sets out fair and ethical trade practices that must be followed by member firms and their representatives when dealing with the public.
2. **Uniform Practice Code.** This established the Uniform Trade Practices, including settlement, good delivery, ex-dates, confirmations, don't know (DK) procedures and other guidelines for broker-dealers to follow when they do business with other member broker-dealer firms.
3. **Code of Procedure.** This describes how the NASD hears and handles member violations of the Rules of Fair Practice.
4. **Code of Arbitration Procedure.** This governs the resolution of disagreements and claims between members, registered reps and the public; it addresses monetary claims, not violations of the Rules of Fair Practice.

## NASD Membership and Registration

### Broker-Dealer Registration

Application for membership in the NASD specifically carries the applying firm's agreement to:

- comply with the rules and regulations of the Association;
- comply with federal securities laws; and

- pay dues, assessments and other charges in the manner and amounts fixed by the Association.

### Branch Offices

**Registration.** For those broker-dealers that maintain and staff branch office systems, each such office must be registered with the NASD. In addition, the NASD must be notified promptly in writing of the opening or closing of any branch.

**Nonbranch offices.** If a nonbranch office of a broker-dealer is not an office of supervisory jurisdiction (OSJ), it must identify the name, address and telephone number of its OSJ on letterheads, business cards, telephone directory listings and advertisements, and on signage prominently displayed at the site at which business (such as accepting customer accounts and taking customer orders) is conducted.

### Associated Person Registration

Any person who is or becomes associated with an NASD member firm and who intends to engage in the investment banking or securities business must be registered with the NASD as an associated person. Anyone applying for registration with the NASD as an associated person must have a member firm as a sponsor.

### Registration Rules and Regulations

**Qualifications investigated.** Prior to submitting an application (a U-4 Form) to enroll any person with the NASD as a registered representative, the member firm is obligated to investigate and ascertain the person's business reputation over the previous ten years, good character, educational institutions attended, qualifications and experience.

### Post-registration Rules and Regulations

**Registered persons changing firms.** NASD registration is *nontransferable*. If a registered person leaves one member firm to join another firm, he must terminate registration at the first firm on a U-5 Form and reapply for registration with the new employing member firm on a U-4 Form. If a person terminates his registration with one firm, he must register with another firm within two years or he will be required to requalify for his license.

**Continuing commissions.** Persons not registered may not receive commissions on securities sales. A registered rep who leaves a member firm (upon retirement, for example) may continue to receive commissions on business he placed while employed. There must, however, be a contract to this effect before the representative leaves the firm.

### Exemptions from Registration

Certain people in the securities industry and some employees of members are not required to register with the Association as associated persons; these include:

- foreign associates;
- clerical and ministerial personnel and corporate officers; and
- employees in other specific functions.

### Investment Adviser Registration

A broker-dealer that receives special compensation for giving investment advice must register as an investment adviser. It is unlawful for any person to transact business as an investment adviser in a state unless the person is registered as an investment adviser under the Uniform Securities Act or is exempt from registration.

**Exemptions from investment adviser registration.** Under the USA, a person does not have to register as an investment adviser in a state if he has no place of business in that state and does not direct business communications to more than five clients in that state in any twelve-month period (known as a *de minimis exemption*), or if he has no place of business in the state and his clientele is limited to:

- other investment advisers
- broker-dealers
- financial or institutional investors

## Qualifications Examinations

### Registered Representatives

For NASD registration, examination and licensing purposes, all associated persons engaged in the investment banking and securities business are considered registered representatives, including any:

- assistant officer who does not function as a principal;
- individual who supervises, solicits or conducts business in securities; and
- individual who trains people to supervise, solicit or conduct business in securities.

Anyone who is not already registered as a principal and who is not engaged strictly in clerical work or brokerage office administration must register as a representative and pass the appropriate licensing examination. In addition to registering with the NASD, registered reps and broker-dealers must register with the state securities administrator in each state in which they intend to do business.

### General Securities Representative License (Series 7)

A Series 7 general securities license allows a registered representative to sell all types of securities products, including corporate stocks and bonds, government and municipal securities, options, direct participation programs, investment company products and most other types of securities. The only product that a general securities rep cannot sell is commodities futures (which requires a Series 3 license).

### Limited Representative Licenses

**Series 6**. The Series 6 Investment Company/Variable Contract Products Limited Representative license entitles a representative to sell mutual funds and variable annuities and is used by many firms that are engaged primarily in the sale of insurance-related products.

**Series 11**. The Series 11 Assistant Representative—Order Processing license allows a registered sales assistant to take unsolicited orders, enter order tickets, update client information, fill out client new account forms and provide customers with quotes and other pro forma information relating to securities. This registration does not permit the assistant rep to determine suitability, make recommendations of transactions or provide advice to customers.

A broker-dealer must pay an assistant representative/order processor (AROP) a salary or an hourly wage. Compensation (including bonuses and commissions) cannot be related to completed transactions or finders fees or be based on the number of accounts opened. The rule prohibiting bonuses does not preclude an AROP from participating in a company's profit-sharing plan, however.

**Series 63**. In order to sell an issue in any state, the broker-dealer, the registered reps and the security itself must each be registered in that state. In order to sell securities in any of the 41 states that currently require state-level representative registration, a registered rep must pass the Series 63 Uniform Securities Agent State Law Exam and be registered in that state. The typical blue-sky laws have provisions for revoking the license of a broker-dealer or salesperson.

### Registered Principals

Anyone associated with a member who will be managing or supervising any part of the member's investment banking or securities business must be registered as a principal with the NASD. Unless the member firm is a sole proprietorship, there must be at least two registered principals per firm, one of whom must be registered as a general securities principal.

## Ineligibility and Disqualifications

**Statutory disqualification**. A broker-dealer or an individual applying for registration as an associated person will be rejected and must be treated as a nonmember if the firm or person:

- has been and is expelled or suspended from membership or participation in any other SRO;
- is under an SEC order revoking the broker-dealer's registration or barring the individual from association with a broker-dealer; or
- has been found to be the cause of another broker-dealer or associated person being expelled or suspended by another SRO or by the SEC.

Any of the following also will disqualify an applicant for registration:

- misstatements willfully made in an application for membership or registration as an associated person;
- a felony conviction within the previous ten years or a misdemeanor charge involving securities or money within the past ten years—misdemeanor charges involving securities or money include a range of white-collar crimes, such as larceny, extortion, forgery, counterfeiting, embezzlement, bribery and misappropriation of funds and securities, in addition to violations of federal securities laws, securities fraud, public deceptions and market manipulation; and
- court injunctions prohibiting the firm or individual from acting as an investment adviser, an underwriter or a broker-dealer or in other capacities aligned with the securities and financial services industry.

# Questions

1. A person who has just passed the Series 7 examination (NASD/NYSE exams) is now
   - A. registered to sell securities to residents of all states
   - B. registered to sell securities to residents of her state
   - C. allowed to sell securities to residents of her state after she has registered with the securities department of that state
   - D. allowed to sell securities in her NASD district

2. You are a registered representative and you are resigning from a member firm. In order to join another firm as a registered rep, you should
   - A. transfer your registration
   - B. take the Series 7 exam again immediately and reapply for membership when you pass
   - C. resign in writing, notify the NASD and file a new application form with the firm you are joining
   - D. notify the NASD and serve a 90-day apprenticeship with your new firm

3. The NASD Uniform Practice Code was established to
   - A. require that practices in the investment banking and securities industry be just, reasonable and nondiscriminatory between investors
   - B. eliminate advertising and sales literature the SEC considers to be in violation of standards
   - C. provide a procedure for handling trade complaints from investors
   - D. maintain similarity of business practices among member organizations in the securities industry

## Answers

1. **C.** A person who passes the Series 62 or Series 7 examination must register with the securities commission in each state in which she wants to do business. Most states require that a person passes the Series 63 (blue-sky) examination.

2. **C.** You cannot transfer your registration. You must terminate employment with your present employer by filling out a U-5 Form, and then you must reapply for registration with the new employer.

3. **D.** The Uniform Practice Code is designed to make uniform the customs, practices and trading techniques employed in the investment banking and securities business.

# Codes of Procedure and of Arbitration Procedure

## Code of Procedure

The NASD's Code of Procedure was developed as a guide to settling complaints that arise between and among members and associated persons. It is the task of the District Business Conduct Committees (DBCCs) of the NASD to determine whether a charge or complaint is valid, and if so to take appropriate disciplinary action against the offending member firm or associated person.

### Regular Complaint Procedure

1. **Sources of complaints**. When a customer, another member firm or one of the NASD's own committees lodges a complaint, an NASD examiner investigates the accused member's premises and inspects the books in an effort to substantiate or discredit the complaint.
2. **Complaint resolution process**. The DBCC notifies the accused member in writing, advising it as to the specifics of the complaint, identifying who has filed the complaint and requesting a response from the accused member within 20 calendar days of the date of receipt.
3. **Decision of the committee**. The presiding DBCC will pass on the merits of the charge, either upholding a rule violation or dismissing the complaint. The DBCC will issue a written decision and announce the sanctions being imposed on the member firm or associated person as disciplinary action.
4. **Decision becomes final**. The DBCC's decision becomes final after 45 calendar days (the first business day after expiration of the 45-calendar-day period).

**Penalties**. If the DBCC finds that a rule violation has occurred, one or more of the following sanctions may be imposed once the decision becomes final:

- censure
- fine
- suspension
- expulsion
- barring

**Appeal to NASD**. A respondent in receipt of the DBCC's findings in favor of the complainant has 15 calendar days from the date of receipt to appeal the decision to the NASD Board of Governors.

**Appeal to SEC**. If either the complainant or the respondent feels aggrieved by the decision of the NASD Board of Governors, application can be made to the SEC for a review.

### Summary Complaint Procedure

In a summary complaint, the complainant usually has sufficient evidence on hand to support the complaint that a violation has occurred.

If amenable to the settlement terms stated in a summary complaint, the member firm or associated person named in the complaint signs and returns a *letter of acceptance, waiver and consent*. The maximum penalty that can be imposed under a summary complaint is $2,500 per respondent, plus public censure.

## Code of Arbitration Procedure

The Code of Arbitration Procedure is geared primarily towards resolving problems and financial losses that usually can be traced to misunderstandings and faulty communications or to Uniform Practice Code violations.

- **Advantages**. Arbitration is a valuable process in that it offers participants a relatively easy method of settling disputes at a cost that is usually significantly lower than the cost of settling a dispute through the courts.
- **Statement of claim**. Any dispute or controversy may be submitted to the NASD's National Arbitration Committee for resolution

and settlement. The claimant files a statement of claim, a signed **submission agreement** and any supporting documents.

- **Statute of limitations**. A dispute or controversy eligible for arbitration must be submitted within six years of its occurrence.
- **Internal disputes**. Internal disputes between member firms and between associated persons must be submitted for resolution and settlement via arbitration.
- **Arbitration involving customers**. Customers are under no obligation to submit any matter of dispute or claim to the NASD's National Arbitration Committee. For them, arbitration is strictly optional.
- **No redress through the courts**. All parties to an NASD arbitration proceeding must understand that they are forfeiting the freedom to bring suit against one another in the civil courts while the arbitration proceeding is in progress, unless otherwise directed by law.
- **Simplified industry arbitration**. Disputes not involving customers can be submitted for resolution under simplified industry arbitration procedures provided the dollar amount of the claim does not exceed $10,000.
- **Simplified customer arbitration**. Disputes involving customers can be submitted under simplified customer arbitration; the dollar amount in dispute must not exceed $10,000.

## Amendments to the Code of Arbitration

The NASD has implemented amendments that make the Code of Arbitration Procedures uniform with those of other SROs. The major changes are as follows:

- Disputes subject to arbitration include the business of members (excluding insurance), as well as securities-related disputes.
- All parties have the right to challenge arbitrators, and arbitrators have the obligation to convey potential conflicts of interest.
- When the amount in dispute exceeds $30,000, the number of arbitrators increases from one arbitrator to no fewer than three nor more than five arbitrators.
- Parties may agree to arrange private settlements or to withdraw from arbitration without panel approval.

## Questions

1. An associated person of an NASD member firm can take a final appeal of disciplinary action to the

   A. Board of Governors
   B. SEC
   C. civil district court
   D. Supreme Court

2. If a case has gone to the Board of Arbitration of the NASD or NYSE, the decisions made are

   A. not binding on a client but are binding on the member
   B. binding only if the two parties agree on the decision
   C. not binding if the two parties decide not to accept the decision
   D. always binding on all parties to the arbitration

## Answers

1. **D.** The District Business Conduct Committee and the Board of Governors are the two bodies that are empowered to hear and pass upon all complaints concerning the Rules of Fair Practice. The District Business Conduct Committee has first jurisdiction over these complaints, and the Board of Governors acts as an appellate body. A decision by the Board of Governors can be appealed to the SEC, and an SEC decision can be appealed through the federal court system to the Supreme Court.

2. **D.** The decisions of the board of arbitration are final and are binding on the parties involved. There is no appeal of these decisions.

# NYSE Constitution and Rules

## Organization

The NYSE board of directors is responsible for setting policy, supervising Exchange and member activities, listing securities, overseeing the transfer of members' seats on the Exchange and judging whether an applicant is qualified to be a specialist.

## Membership

The number of memberships, or **seats**, on the NYSE is fixed at 1,366. Only individuals can own seats on the Exchange.

## Member Firms

- A member organization must keep its main office open for business every day that the Exchange is open for business.
- Each office must display its certificate of membership with the NYSE.
- Every branch must be supervised by a principal who has passed the appropriate principal's examination.

The principal's supervisory duties include:

- approving new accounts;
- reviewing all correspondence, trade blotters and registered representatives' client statements;
- reviewing all transactions with clients and representatives' accounts of clients; and
- initialing all of the above items.

## Registration of Employees

All employees of NYSE member firms must be registered through their firms with the NYSE.

- **Prerequisites**. Registered reps must sign statements agreeing to abide by certain regulations. A person who wishes to become a registered rep must give the Exchange a history of employment and other information. She must agree to read the NYSE constitution and regulations and abide by them.
- **Employment standards**. Registered reps who work for a member firm must exhibit high standards of business conduct and integrity, must pass an examination and must have reached the age of majority.
- **Bona fide employee**. A registered rep cannot be employed in name only. The rep must have the intention of building a real clientele.
- **Transfer**. Transfer of registration is not permitted; a rep must resign from one employer and reapply for registration with the new firm.
- **Termination**. The NYSE jurisdiction over a registered rep continues for one year after a termination.
- **Outside employment**. A registered rep must have her firm's written permission before taking a second job.
- **Compensation**. The representative can receive compensation for securities transactions only from her employer.

## Arbitration

The NYSE Board of Arbitration hears and settles disagreements between members, allied members, member organizations and their employees. Nonmembers (customers) may voluntarily submit to arbitration in a dispute with members or employees.

## Discipline

**Penalties and review**. If a member, allied member or associated person of a member is found guilty in any disciplinary hearing, the hearing panel may impose on that member any of the following penalties:

- censure
- fine
- suspension
- expulsion
- barring

# Questions

1. The objectives of the NYSE include which of the following?

    I. To maintain high standards of commercial honor
    II. To promote just principles of trade
    III. To provide a place for the transaction of a member's business

    A. I only
    B. I and III only
    C. II and III only
    D. I, II and III

2. An NYSE registered representative

    A. can, at his discretion, give evidence to an investigating body at the request of the Exchange
    B. must give evidence on any subject under investigation but is not required to produce relevant documents or records
    C. must produce relevant documents or records but is not required to give oral testimony
    D. must not fail to give evidence on any subject under investigation and must produce, on request of the Exchange, all relevant records or documents

3. All of the following statements are true EXCEPT that

    A. unless Exchange permission is granted, registered representatives cannot devote less than full time to the duties of their member employers
    B. the term *registered representative* applies to someone who solicits orders for the purchase or sale of securities for her employer's clients
    C. testimonials are representative of the experience of one or a few clients and are not necessarily indicative of future market performance
    D. compensations by members to an employee of another member firm are acceptable as long as they don't exceed the limit of $150

4. The NYSE requires a general partner or an officer of the member organization to

    A. supervise diligently all accounts handled by registered representatives of the organization
    B. use due diligence to learn the essential facts relative to every client
    C. specifically approve the opening of any account prior to or promptly after the completion of any transaction for the account of a client
    D. do all of the above

5. As a means of protecting the investing public from possible member organization financial failure, the NYSE

    A. charges a large price for membership
    B. requires an annual audit of the books of member firms by outside certified auditors
    C. insists that margin accounts be maintained at 50% of market value
    D. requires all of the above

6. How does one become an NYSE-registered representative?

   A. Fill out an application and pay a fee to the New York Stock Exchange.
   B. Pass an exam.
   C. Be sponsored by a member broker-dealer firm, exhibit high standards of integrity and pass an exam.
   D. Serve a 90-day apprenticeship.

# Answers

1. **D.** The NYSE maintains high standards of honor, promotes fair trade and provides the location for the trading of securities.

2. **D.** When a person becomes a registered representative, he agrees to appear before Exchange committees and to produce documents as requested by the Exchange.

3. **D.** Gifts by member firms to employees of another member firm are limited to $100 in any year.

4. **D.** All of the answers seem to be protective of the client. So, if you were in doubt about any of them, you could be quite sure that statements that protect the client are probably true.

5. **B.** SIPC protects investors from actual financial failure of member firms, but an annual audit might avert a failure before it happens.

6. **C.** Answers A and B are incorrect because there are more requirements than passing the exam and paying fees. The rep, moreover, is not a member of the Exchange; the rep is associated with the member firm.

# Communications with the Public

## Advertising and Sales Literature

**Advertising**. "Advertising" includes copy and support graphics and/or other support materials intended for:

- publication in newspapers, magazines or other periodicals;
- radio or television broadcast;
- prerecorded telephone marketing messages and tape recordings;
- videotape displays;
- signs or billboards;
- motion pictures and filmstrips;
- electronic (computer) communication devices;
- telephone directories; or
- *any other use of the public media.*

**Sales literature**. "Sales literature" is *any written communication distributed to customers* (or to the public in general) or available to people upon request and that does not meet the definition of "advertising." Sales literature includes materials such as:

- circulars;
- research reports;
- market letters;
- form letters;
- options worksheets;
- performance reports and summaries;
- text prepared and used for educational seminars;
- telemarketing scripts;
- prepared scripts for public-interest radio and television interviews; and
- reprints and excerpts from any advertisement, sales literature or published news item or article.

Sales literature can be distributed in written, oral or electronic form. It must always be preceded or accompanied by a prospectus.

**Form letters**. A **form letter** is a sales letter that contains sections or statements that are identical in essence to statements made or contained in other sales letters. These must be approved in advance by the principal.

**Generic advertising (Rule 135a)**. Generic advertising promotes securities as an investment medium but does not make reference to any particular security. Generic (institutional) advertising uses general terms and phrases and often includes information about:

- the securities offered by investment companies;
- the nature of investment companies;
- services offered in connection with the described securities;
- explanations of the various types of investment companies;
- descriptions of exchange and reinvestment privileges; and
- where the public can write or call for further information.

**Tombstones**. It is unlawful to solicit stockholders unless a prospectus accompanies the solicitation. Under Rule 134, advertising copy and other sales materials will not be deemed a prospectus if the body copy is limited to the following:

- the name of the issuer of the securities being offered;
- a brief description of the business of the person making the offer;
- the date, time and place of the meeting at which stockholders are to vote on or consent to the proposed transaction;
- a brief description of the planned transaction; or
- any legend or disclaimer statement required by state or federal law.

Advertisements that meet these restrictions are more commonly known as *tombstones*. Any advertising copy in a tombstone must also contain the following disclaimers:

- that the registration statement has been filed by the issuer but is not yet effective;

- that the communication does *not* represent an offer to sell the securities described—securities are **sold by prospectus only**;
- the name and address of the person (or firm) to contact for a prospectus; and
- that a response to this advertisement does not obligate the prospect to a buying commitment of any kind (i.e., that it represents only an **indication of interest**).

## Approval and Filing Requirements

### Approval

- Each advertisement and piece of sales literature must be approved *prior to use* and *prior to filing with the NASD* by the signature or initial of a registered principal of the member.
- For advertisements or sales literature specific to options, the advertisement or sales literature must be approved by a registered options principal (ROP) or compliance ROP (CROP).
- Research reports must be approved by a *supervisory analyst* acceptable to the NYSE.

### Filing Requirements

A separate file containing all advertisements and sales literature must be maintained by the member for a period of *three years;* for the first two years, the file must be kept in an easily accessible place.

**Investment company**. Advertisements and sales literature relating to investment company securities must be filed with the NASD's advertising department within ten days of first use or publication by the member. If the advertisement or sales literature refers to investment company products solely as part of a listing of services or products offered, the filing requirement will not apply.

**Options**. Any options advertisements sent to a customer must be preceded or accompanied by a current **OCC Options Disclosure Document**. If the advertisement or sales literature refers to options solely as part of a listing of services or products offered (a tombstone), the filing requirement will not apply.

## NASD Rules Concerning Public Communications

- All communications from a member to the public must be based on principles of fair dealing and good faith.
- The communication should provide sound basis for evaluating the facts in regard to the product, service or industry promoted.
- Exaggerated, unwarranted or misleading statements are strictly prohibited.
- Sales literature must identify: the name of the member firm; the person or firm that prepared the material if copy was prepared outside; and the date the material was first used.
- If the literature cites price or market performance data that are not current, that fact should be stated in the material.

### Customer Recommendations

- A proposal or written presentation that includes a specific recommendation must have a reasonable basis to support the recommendation.
- The member firm must provide these in the proposal or other document, or offer to furnish them upon request.
- If the recommendation includes a purchase of stock, the firm must also provide the current price of the stock.
- The member should have reasonable grounds for believing that a security is a suitable investment for a customer before recommending its purchase.
- A firm must disclose any potential conflicts of interest, including:
  - whether the firm intends to buy or sell any of the recommended security for its own account;
  - whether the firm is a market maker in the recommended security;
  - whether the firm or its officers or partners own options, rights or warrants to buy the recommended security; and
  - whether the firm managed or co-managed a public offering of the recommended

security or any other of the same issuer's securities during the past three years.

When a firm uses material referring to the performance of past recommendations, it must reveal certain information. In particular, it must disclose:

- the price (or price range) of the recommended security at the date and time that the recommendation is made;
- the general direction of the market;
- the availability of information supporting the recommendation;
- any recommendations made of similar securities within the past twelve months (including the nature of the recommendations—buy, sell or hold); and
- all recommendations (gainers and losers) made by the firm over the period of time in question.

The time span covered in the list of recommendations must run through consecutive periods, without skipping periods in an attempt to hide particular recommendations or negative price performance data.

**Restrictions**. The firm making the recommendation must not:

- imply that there are any guarantees accompanying the recommendation;
- compare the recommended security to dissimilar products;
- make fraudulent or misleading statements about the recommended security; or
- make any predictions about the future performance or potential of the recommended security.

### Recommending Investment Company Products

When recommending mutual funds to clients as investments and when using advertisements or sales literature developed for those investments the broker-dealer should:

- use charts or graphs showing the fund's performance covering a period of time long enough to reflect variations in value under different market conditions, generally a period of at least ten years;
- reveal the source of the graphic;
- separate dividends from capital gains when making statements about the fund's cash returns;
- not state that a mutual fund is similar to or safer than any other type of security (including government bonds, insurance policies or annuities, or corporate bonds);
- reveal the fund's highest sales charge, even if the client appears to qualify for a breakpoint; and
- not make any fraudulent or misleading statements or omissions of facts.

### Other Communication Prohibitions

- **Claims and opinions couched as facts and conclusions**. It is a violation of these regulations to pass off opinions, projections and forecasts as guarantees of performance or as scientific evidence.
- **Testimonials**. Testimonials and endorsements by celebrities must not be misleading or suggest that past performance is an indication of future performance.
- **Research facilities**. A communication must not state or imply that research facilities are more extensive than they actually are.
- **Misleading clauses**. Hedge clauses, caveats and disclaimers must not be used if they are misleading or inconsistent with the content of the material.
- **References to SROs**. Ambiguous references to the NASD or other SROs must not be made with the aim of leading people to believe that a broker-dealer is acting with the endorsement and approval of the Association (or one of the other SROs).
- **Recruitment advertising**. Recruitment advertisements must be truthful, informative and fair in representing the opportunities in the industry and must not contain exaggerated or unwarranted claims.

### Legal Recourse of Customers

The Securities Exchange Act of 1934, and the acts of 1933 and 1940, make it unlawful for any person to use the mails or any facilities of interstate commerce to "... employ, in connection with the purchase or sale of any security ... any manipulative or deceptive device ... in contravention of such rules and regulations as the Commission may prescribe as necessary."

## Telephone Communications with the Public

The Telephone Consumer Protection Act of 1991 (TCPA) was enacted to protect consumers from unwanted telephone solicitations. The act requires an organization that performs telemarketing to:

- maintain a "do-not-call list" of customers who do not want to be called;
- institute a written policy on maintenance procedures for the "do-not-call list";
- train reps on usage of the list;
- ensure that reps acknowledge and immediately record the names and telephone numbers of customers who ask to not be called again;
- ensure that anyone making cold calls for the firm informs the customer of the name and telephone number or address of the firm;
- ensure that telemarketers do not call customers who have made a do-not-call request; and
- ensure that telephone solicitations occur only between the hours of 8:00 am and 9:00 pm of the time zone in which the customer is located.

The act exempts calls:

- made to parties with whom the caller has an established business relationship or where the caller has prior express permission or invitation;
- made on behalf of a tax-exempt nonprofit organization;
- not made for a commercial purpose; and
- made for legitimate debt collection purposes.

# 15 Municipal Securities

## Municipal Bond Characteristics

Municipal securities are considered second only to U.S. government and U.S. government agency securities in safety.

### Tax Benefits

- The interest paid by most municipal securities is exempt from federal income taxation.
- The interest paid by federal securities is exempt from municipal taxation.
- This is known as the **doctrine of reciprocal immunity**, also known as the **doctrine of mutual reciprocity**.
- States also exempt from taxation bonds issued by a territory of the United States.
- Interest from municipal bonds is also exempt from state taxation in most states if the bond:
  - is issued by a municipality in that state, and
  - is sold to an investor who lives in that state.
- Municipalities can raise money at a lower cost than can corporations.
- Municipalities are able to offer tax-exempt bonds at lower interest rates than offered by similar taxable bonds.
- Municipal securities are more attractive to investors in high tax brackets than to those in lower brackets.
- Municipal bonds, like most other bonds, pay interest semiannually on a schedule set at issuance.

### Issuers

The three primary entities legally entitled to issue municipal debt securities are:

- territorial possessions of the United States (such as Puerto Rico, the U.S. Virgin Islands and Guam);
- state governments; and
- legally constituted taxing authorities.

### Maturity Structures

The three types of maturity schedules are called:

- serial
- balloon
- term

### Types of Issues

- **General obligation bonds** are backed by the full faith, credit and taxing powers of the municipal borrower.
- **Revenue bonds** are backed by revenues generated by the financed facility.

## Municipal Security Registration Documents

- **Bond contract**. The bond contract is a collection of legal documents that includes the bond resolution, the trust indenture, applicable state and national law, and any other legal document that pertains to that particular issue and issuer.
- **Bond resolution**. The bond resolution contains a description of the issuer's obligations to and duties regarding the holders of its bonds.
  - The **authorizing resolution** authorizes the issuance of the bonds.
  - The **award resolution** authorizes the bonds' sale.
- **Trust indenture**. The trust indenture serves as a contract between the bond's issuer and an appointed trustee on behalf of the bond's investors.
- **Official statement**. The official statement (OS) is the municipal securities industry's equivalent to the corporate prospectus. The official statement serves as a disclosure document and contains any material information an investor might need about an issue.
- **Preliminary official statement**. The preliminary official statement discloses most of the same material information as the official statement, with the exception of the interest rate(s) and offering price(s) of the issue.
- **Legal opinion**. Attached to every bond certificate (unless the bond is specifically stamped "**ex-legal**") is a **legal opinion** written and signed by the **bond counsel** stating that the issue conforms with applicable laws, the state constitution and established procedures.
  - If the legal opinion is issued as a **qualified opinion**, the bond counsel that issued the opinion has reservations about the issue or wants it known that certain conditions exist.
  - If the legal opinion is issued as an **unqualified opinion**, it is issued by the bond counsel unconditionally.

## General Obligation Bonds

- GOs are used to raise funds for municipal capital improvements that do not produce revenues.
- The financial support for city and county bonds is **ad valorem taxes**.
- Sales and income taxes are the support for state bonds.
- GOs are also known as *full faith and credit bonds*.

### Sources of Funds

GOs are backed by taxes.

- State-issued debt securities are backed by income taxes, license fees and sales taxes.
- Cities, towns and counties issue debt securities backed by property taxes, license fees, fines and all other sources of revenue to the municipality.
- School, road and park districts issue municipal bonds that are backed by property taxes.

### Legal Limitations

**Statutory or constitutional limits on municipal debt**. The amount of debt municipal governments are allowed to incur may be subject to:

- **Voter approval**. GOs must be approved by vote of the taxpayers in a referendum.
- **Tax limits**. Property taxes are limited by some states to a certain percentage (expressed in **mills**: one mill equals 1/10th of one cent—$.001) of the assessed property value or to a certain percentage increase in any single year. These bonds are frequently called **limited tax bonds**.
- **Overlapping debt**. If debt can be issued by several taxing authorities that draw from the same taxpayers, it is known as overlapping debt. Municipal entities that have overlapping boundaries are often described as **coterminous**, and their debt as **coterminous debt**.

## Revenue Bonds

Revenue bonds can be used to finance any municipal function that generates income. Debt service on a revenue bond is payable only from the earnings of a specific revenue-producing enterprise.

An analysis of the quality of revenue bonds would include:

- sources of revenue,
- feasibility studies,
- maturity structure,
- call provisions,
- application of revenues,
- protective covenants of the indenture, and
- construction period costs.

Revenue bonds are subject to no statutory debt limits and require no voter approval.

### Sources of Revenue

Revenue-producing facilities include:

- utilities
- housing
- transportation
- education
- health
- industrial

### Protective Covenants

The trust indenture usually includes provisions for the following protective covenants:

- **rate covenant**—a promise to maintain rates sufficient to pay expenses and debt service;
- **maintenance covenant**—a promise to maintain the equipment and facility(ies);
- **insurance covenant**—a promise to insure any facility(ies) built;
- **additional bonds test**—whether the indenture is open ended or closed ended;
- **sinking fund**—to pay off interest and principal obligations;
- **catastrophe clause**;
- **flow of funds**; and
- **call features**.

### Special Revenue Bonds

- **Industrial development revenue bonds**. Industrial revenue bonds (IDRs or IDBs) are issued by a municipal authority to construct facilities or purchase equipment, which is then leased to a corporation. The authority uses money from lease payments to cover the principal and interest on the bonds. The ultimate responsibility for the payment of principal and interest rests with the corporate lessee.
- **Lease rental bonds**. Under a typical lease-rental arrangement, a municipality might create an authority or agency to construct a new building or other new construction beneficial to the state, municipality or community. The authority issues bonds to raise money for construction of the building, then leases the finished building to the user. Backing for the bond is provided by the lease payments.
- **Special tax bonds**. Special tax bonds are issued for specific projects and are payable only from the proceeds of a special tax (tobacco, alcohol or hotel room rentals, for example).
- **New Housing Authority bonds**. New Housing Authority bonds (NHAs), are backed by the full faith and credit of the U.S. government. Because of this, they are considered the most secure revenue bonds.

**Double-barreled bonds**. Interest and principal are paid from the earnings of the facility. The bonds are also backed by the taxing power of the state or municipality. Double-barreled bonds are rated and traded as GOs.

- **Moral obligation bonds**. If revenues backing the bond are not sufficient to meet debt service requirements, the state has the authority to authorize payment on the debt through legislative appropriation. The state's obligation is not established by law; it is a moral obligation only.

## Municipal Notes

Municipal notes fall into several categories:

- tax anticipation notes (TANs)
- revenue anticipation notes (RANs)
- project notes (PNs)
- bond anticipation notes (BANs)
- construction loan notes (CLNs)
- grant anticipation notes (GANs)
- variable-rate demand notes

### Tax-exempt Commercial Paper

These promissory notes of a municipality are very similar to corporate commercial paper, are issued in both registered and bearer form and are usually issued with the backing of a line of credit from a bank.

# Questions

1. Municipal bonds are issued for all of the following EXCEPT

   A. sewers
   B. GNMAs
   C. hospitals
   D. capital improvements

2. Municipal bonds pay interest

   A. monthly
   B. quarterly
   C. semiannually
   D. annually

3. In safety of principal, municipal bonds are considered second only to

   A. preferred stock
   B. common stock
   C. U.S. government agency bonds
   D. FNMA securities

4. Which of the following is(are) a type of municipal bond?

   I. Collateral trust
   II. Revenue
   III. General obligation
   IV. Income

   A. I, II and III
   B. I, II and IV
   C. II and III
   D. III

5. A general obligation bond is backed by

   A. tolls
   B. special taxes
   C. public housing
   D. the full faith and credit of the issuing municipality

6. A bond issue backed by both net revenue rentals and the full faith and credit of the U.S. government is a

   A. Fannie Mae
   B. Ginnie Mae
   C. T bill
   D. New Housing Authority bond

7. A legal opinion on a municipal bond is prepared by

   A. the underwriter
   B. the trustee
   C. the municipality
   D. an independent bond attorney

8. All of the following would be found in the legal opinion of a municipal revenue bond EXCEPT

   A. the statutory, constitutional and other legal authority required to issue the bonds
   B. any call provisions
   C. a guarantee that revenue generated will be sufficient to pay the interest when due and the principal at maturity
   D. a description of the bonds

9. All of the following are examples of short-term, tax-exempt municipal issues EXCEPT

   A. BANs
   B. PNs
   C. AONs
   D. TANs

10. Short-term municipal notes normally have all of the following characteristics EXCEPT that they

    A. mature in less than one year
    B. are issued in anticipation of a bond sale
    C. pay interest every six months
    D. pay interest that is exempt from federal taxation

11. Revenue bonds are backed by all of the following EXCEPT

    A. tolls
    B. rental fees
    C. federal revenue sharing
    D. tuitions

12. Which of the following are characteristics of revenue bonds?

    I. They are usually free from debt limitations.
    II. They usually contain a rate covenant.
    III. They can be issued by interstate port authorities.

    A. I only
    B. I and II only
    C. II and III only
    D. I, II and III

13. To fund debt service on a general obligation bond, a municipality may use

    I. direct taxes
    II. special assessments
    III. fines
    IV. collection of delinquent funds

    A. I and II only
    B. I, III and IV only
    C. III and IV only
    D. I, II, III and IV

14. Special assessment bonds are backed by

    A. property taxes
    B. unlimited property claims
    C. charges against benefitted property
    D. gasoline, liquor and similar taxes

15. The taxing power of an issuer of a limited-tax bond is limited to a specified

    A. minimum rate
    B. maximum rate
    C. tax source
    D. method of taxation

16. All of the following statements are true of industrial revenue bonds EXCEPT that

    A. they may be deemed federally taxable by the IRS
    B. they are issued by municipalities to provide local industries with funds to purchase plants and equipment
    C. interest is paid from rental payments received from corporations that lease the property or equipment from the municipality
    D. the credit rating of the bonds is dependent on the credit rating of the municipality

17. A municipal bond is issued with a covenant that the state legislature has the authority to appropriate funds necessary to meet payments if revenue collections are not sufficient to do so. This bond is a

    A. contingent liability bond
    B. moral obligation bond
    C. general obligation bond
    D. double-barreled bond

18. A double-barreled municipal bond is backed by municipal

    A. revenues
    B. taxes
    C. taxes and revenues
    D. taxes and U.S. government taxes

19. A municipal bond issued to finance the construction of a new office complex will most likely be serviced and retired from

    A. a special tax
    B. a moral obligation
    C. lease payments from pooled rentals
    D. refunding

# Answers

1. **B.** GNMAs are federal obligations.

2. **C.** Most municipal bonds, like most debt instruments, pay interest semiannually.

3. **C.** Municipal bonds are second only to U.S. government bonds in safety.

4. **C.** Municipal bonds include revenue and general obligation bonds. Corporate bonds include the income or adjustment bond and the collateral trust bond. The question requires only that you distinguish between the types of bonds issued by municipalities and those issued by corporations.

5. **D.** General obligation bonds are, as the name indicates, general obligations of the municipality. They are not tied to specific revenue sources, such as tolls, special taxes or properties.

6. **D.** New Housing Authority bonds (NHAs) are backed by the U.S. government, as well as by the issuing municipality's rental revenue from the facility. Federal backing makes them especially safe from default risk.

7. **D.** The legal counsel must be independent of the issuer.

8. **C.** The legal counsel cannot guarantee that the project will go as planned or that the city will remain solvent. The legal opinion examines only the legal aspects of the bond issue. The official statement, which is similar to a prospectus, contains among other things information about the issuer's financial status.

9. **C.** An all or none (AON) is a type of order; the term has nothing to do with short-term tax-exempt notes.

10. **C.** Short-term notes normally pay interest at maturity. The other answers are true of short-term municipal notes.

11. **C.** Revenue bonds are backed by revenues from the facility (such as tolls, rentals or tuition), not by federal revenue sharing.

12. **D.** All of the characteristics listed are true of revenue bonds. They are not subject to debt limits; they are free from debt limitations; they contain a rate covenant requiring that revenues be high enough to provide operation, maintenance and debt service; and they are issued by interstate port authorities (such as the Milwaukee Port Authority).

13. **B.** General obligation bonds may be funded by tax revenues, fines or collections of delinquent obligations. Special assessments are used to pay off special assessment bonds—a type of revenue bond.

14. **C.** Municipalities finance the installation of streets, curbs and gutters, sidewalks and similar amenities by issuing special assessment bonds. Property holders are assessed for the increased value of their property and the money from assessments is used to repay bondholders.

15. **B.** A limited-tax municipal bond is issued under statutory or constitutional limitations on the maximum tax that a government entity can charge.

16. **D.** Industrial revenue bonds are a primary obligation of the corporation—the municipality acts as a conduit in issuing the bonds. The bond's credit rating, therefore, is dependent on the corporation's rating.

17. **B.** The legislature has the authority and a moral obligation (but not a legal obligation) to appropriate any additional funds necessary to pay off the issue if revenues are insufficient. A double-barreled bond would be a GO; that is, the municipality is obligated to back the bond.

18. **C.** A double-barreled bond is a bond backed by two different sources—income from a revenue-producing facility plus the full faith and credit of a municipal issuer with taxing power.

19. **C.** Office buildings are often financed with lease rental bond issues. This is a revenue bond backed by lease payments to the issuing authority.

# Issuing Municipal Securities

## The Bidding Process

### Negotiated Underwriting

In a negotiated underwriting, an investment banker works with the issuer to establish an interest rate and a purchase price that are both satisfactory to the issuer and likely to ensure the underwriter a profit. Most revenue bonds are issued through a negotiated underwriting

### Competitive Bidding

Municipal GOs are normally awarded to an underwriter through competitive bidding. A municipality publishes an invitation to bid (which is a part of the **official notice of sale**) on the issue to the investment banking community.

Using the information from the notice of sale and from *The Bond Buyer* about the 30-day visible supply, other municipal issues currently being offered and the placement ratio, investment bankers form **syndicates** to prepare bids for the securities. Syndicates can obtain *new issue (bid) worksheets* from *The Bond Buyer*.

On the date indicated in the notice of sale, the syndicate submits a bid outlining proposed interest rates and other conditions for conducting the underwriting. The municipality awards the bond issue to the bidder offering to sell the bonds at the lowest net cost to the issuer. The price at which the bonds are then sold to the public is known as the **reoffering price**.

**Official notice of sale**. The notice of bond sale (published in *The Bond Buyer*) includes the following information:

- date, time and place of sale;
- name and description of issuer;
- type of bond;
- interest payment dates;
- dated date, interest accrual date and first coupon payment date;
- maturity structure;
- call provisions (if any);
- name of the firm (sometimes called the *bond counsel*) providing the legal opinion; and
- criteria for awarding the issue.

Two key pieces of information not included in a notice of sale are the bond's rating and the name of the underwriter because they have not yet been determined.

## Functions of a Municipal Bond Counsel

The bond counsel (or bond attorney) is a disinterested party offering certain legal assurances to the issuer and investor, including assurances that the issuer is authorized to issue the bonds, that the bonds have been properly announced and that the bond certificates are properly printed.

**The legal opinion**. The legal opinion contains a description of the bonds, statements concerning the statutory basis for bond issuance, any tax limitation of the issuer and any call provision of the issue. The legal opinion is a bond attorney's written opinion that the issue of bonds is exempt from federal taxes, is a binding debt of the issuer and can be legally issued by the municipal authority. The legal opinion must be attached to or (more commonly) printed on the back of each bond certificate. A municipal bond certificate that does not have a legal opinion on or attached to it is referred to as *ex-legal*. Without the legal opinion attached, a bond certificate is not in good delivery form (unless identified as "ex-legal" prior to the transaction).

- **Unqualified legal opinion**. An unqualified legal opinion is the most desirable because it states that the opinion is given without question or restriction.
- **Qualified legal opinion**. A qualified legal opinion expresses reservations about the issue.

## Municipal Securities Publications

### Market and Index Information

*The Blue List* Total is a measure of the total par value of all municipal securities offered for sale in *The Blue List*. The number is considered an accurate reflection of the status of the secondary market for municipals.

*The Bond Buyer* weekly indexes that show average price levels for different groups of municipals include the:

- 11 Bond GO Index
- 20 Bond GO Index
- 30 Year Revenue Index

*The Bond Buyer* Municipal Bond Index is published daily and is a composite of the prices of 40 issues.

### Sources of Information on Proposed Issues

- ***The Bond Buyer*** is published every business day and is a source of information on new municipal bonds. *The Bond Buyer* publishes the **30-day visible supply** and the **placement ratio** indexes. *The Bond Buyer* also publishes a series of **new issue worksheets** for the municipal industry.
- ***Munifacts*** is a subscription wire service of *The Bond Buyer* that supplies prices, information about proposed new issues and general news relevant to the municipal bond market.
- ***The Blue List*** is a daily publication lists the par value, issuer, interest rate, maturity date, price or yield and offering dealer for current municipal bond secondary offerings of banks and brokers across the nation. *The Blue List* also contains a limited amount of information about new-issue delivery dates. Underwriters and issuers often consult *The Blue List* to determine current yields and prices.

## Formation of the Underwriting Syndicate

To spread the risk of underwriting a municipal issue, underwriters usually form an underwriting syndicate.

Participants formalize their relationship by signing a syndicate letter (in a competitive bid) or a **syndicate contract** or **agreement among underwriters** (in a negotiated underwriting). Syndicate letters include the following information:

- level of participation of each member firm;
- priority of order allocation;
- fee for the managing underwriter and breakdown of the spread; and
- other obligations, such as member expenses, good faith deposits, observance of offering terms and liability for unsold bonds.

### Types of Accounts

**Western account**. The Western account is a **divided account**. Each underwriter is responsible for its own underwriting allocation. For example, if the underwriter is allocated 10% of the issue to sell, its financial liability ends once it has sold its 10% participation.

**Eastern account**. An Eastern account is an **undivided account**. Each underwriter is allocated a portion of the issue. If there are any bonds unsold, each underwriter is then allocated additional bonds representing its proportionate share of any remaining undistributed bonds. For example, an underwriter that has successfully distributed its 10% allocation is still liable for 10% of any bonds or shares that remain unsold by other underwriters. If a 10% underwriter of a $10 million bond issue has sold its 10%, but bonds worth $5 million remain unsold by other members of the syndicate, the underwriter is responsible for 10% of the unsold bonds—in this case, $500,000 worth of bonds.

### Due Diligence

With revenue bonds, as with corporate securities, a **due diligence** investigation is conducted through a **feasibility study**, which focuses on information such as the projected revenues and costs associated with the project and on an analysis of competing facilities.

## Establishing the Syndicate Bid

A syndicate arrives at its competitive bid over a series of meetings, during which member dealers discuss the proposed price scale and spread for the underwriters. A final price for the bond is set at a meeting conducted just before the bid is due. Their goal is to arrive at the best price to the issuer (that is, the highest possible price with the lowest possible interest cost) while still making a profit for themselves.

The process of establishing the **reoffering yield** (or **price**) for each maturity is called **writing a scale**. The underwriters also determine the premium, or discount, at which the bonds are to be offered.

**Firm commitment**. Competitive bids are submitted as firm commitments. Bids must be competitive in the marketplace, as well as with the issuer. Although a low bid might win, it might also result in unsold bonds and a loss of capital for the underwriter.

### Awarding the Issue

All of the syndicates bidding on the issue send their sealed **bid worksheets (forms)** and a **good faith deposit** to the issuer. The issuer analyzes each bid and then awards the municipal bond issue to the syndicate that offers to underwrite the bonds at the lowest **net interest cost** (NIC), or **true interest cost (TIC)**, to the issuer.

### Syndicate Account

All sale proceeds are deposited to the syndicate account, and all expenses are paid out of the account.

## Breakdown of the Spread

The syndicate's compensation for underwriting the new issue is the **spread**. The spread is the difference between the price the syndicate pays to the issuer and the reoffering price at which the syndicate offers the bonds to the public.

- **Syndicate manager's fee**. The syndicate manager receives from the spread a per-bond fee for its work in bringing the new issue to market.
- **Underwriting fee**. Each syndicate member receives a share of the underwriting fee (or syndicate fee) according to its designated bracket or percentage of commitment. The managing underwriter would be entitled to its percentage of the syndicate fee *in addition to* the management fee it receives.
- **Takedown**. The percentage of the spread that remains after subtracting the manager's and syndicate fees is called the *takedown*. The takedown is the discount at which a syndicate member buys bonds from the syndicate. Members are said to buy the bonds from the syndicate *at the takedown*.
  - A member that has purchased bonds at the takedown can then either sell its bonds to customers at the POP or sell them to a dealer in the selling group at something less than full price.
- **Selling concession and reallowance**. A syndicate member can buy bonds from the syndicate for a discount from the face value, sell them to the public for the face value and earn the difference. If the firm chooses instead to sell bonds to another dealer in the selling group, it will do so at a price less than the face value. The discount the selling group dealer receives from the syndicate member is called the **concession**. Dealers are said to buy bonds from syndicate members *at the concession*.

## Order Allocation

Municipal bond orders are allocated according to priorities set by the syndicate. The syndicate may include a provision in its agreement that allows the syndicate manager to deviate from the established priority on a case-by-case basis, but this exception is made *only* if such action is in the best interest of the syndicate. The burden of proof for these exceptions to the stated order lies with the syndicate manager.

### Allocation Priorities

The normal priority is as follows:

1. Presale order
2. Group net order
3. Designated order
4. Member-at-the-takedown order

The highest priority is given to those orders that benefit the most members.

### Broker's Broker

Some municipal brokers specialize in trading only with institutional customers, banks and other municipal brokers, and not with the retail public. These firms are called *brokers' brokers* because their business consists in large part of helping other municipal broker-dealers place unsold portions of new bond issues.

## Payment and Delivery

After awarding an issue to a syndicate, the issuer has the bond certificates printed and finalizes any other legal matters. When the bonds are ready, the syndicate manager gives the syndicate members three business days' notice of the settlement date. On that date, the newly issued bonds are delivered to the underwriters with a final legal opinion, and the underwriters pay for the bonds on delivery.

**Confirmations of sales to customers.** At or before the completion of the transaction (settlement date), final confirmations are mailed to investors who purchased the bonds from the underwriters. The investors' confirmations disclose the purchase price and settlement date (if known) for the transaction. The investor must pay any interest that has accrued between the dated date and the settlement date. The underwriters then deliver the bonds, accompanied by the legal opinion, to the investors.

## Official Statement

Any broker-dealer involved in the sale of a new issue must furnish a final official statement to every customer who has purchased part of that new issue, including other broker-dealers. If the final official statement is not ready when the bonds are delivered, the dealer may send the preliminary official statement or may prepare and send a summary or an abstract of the official statement. When the final official statement is ready, however, the dealer must send it to customers and any industry member that requests it. At the latest, the official statement must be provided with the final confirmation.

### Analyzing the Official Statement

**Future financial needs.** The municipality might need to issue more debt if:

- its annual income is not sufficient to make the payments on its short-term (or floating) debt;
- principal repayments are scheduled too close together;
- sinking funds for outstanding term bonds are inadequate;
- pension liabilities are unfunded; or
- it plans to make more capital improvements soon.

Issuing more debt in the near future may result in a lower bond rating, which could cause the current issue to trade at a discount.

**The debt statement.** In the official statement is a debt statement providing additional information useful to municipal analysts. The estimated full valuation of taxable property, the estimated assessed value of property and the assessment percentage, and the estimated population are all included in the debt statement.

## Advertising

Abstracts and summaries of the official statement, offering circulars, reports, market letters, form letters, new issue advertisements and any other material designed for use in the public media are considered advertising. They must, therefore, be approved by a municipal securities principal or general securities principal of the dealer before use. The preliminary and final official statements are not considered advertising.

## The Broker-Dealer as Financial Adviser

A financial advisory relationship exists when a broker-dealer renders for a fee or other compensation financial advisory or consultant services to, or on behalf of, an issuer with respect to a new issue. This includes advice as to the structure, timing and terms and similar matters concerning the issue or issuer.

### Availability of an Official Statement

If a broker-dealer is responsible for preparing the final official statement for a new issue, the financial adviser must make a copy of that statement available to the broker-dealer selected as the manager of the underwriting promptly after the award is made and at least two days before the securities are delivered by the syndicate manager to the syndicate members.

# Questions

1. If a municipality appoints an underwriter to offer a new issue, the underwriting is

   A. negotiated
   B. a competitive bid
   C. proportionate
   D. an Eastern agreement

2. Which of the following new bond issues would most probably be purchased through competitive bidding?

   A. Corporate bonds
   B. General obligation bonds
   C. Income bonds
   D. Debentures

3. An official notice of sale would include all of the following EXCEPT the

   A. authority for sale
   B. date and time of sale
   C. amount of issue
   D. bond rating

4. A municipal dealer considering placing a bid in a competitive general obligation bond offering would obtain information from

   A. *The Yellow Sheets*
   B. *The Bond Buyer*
   C. *The Blue List*
   D. Standard & Poor's *Bond Guide*

5. Interested parties wishing to submit bids on competitive municipal underwritings can obtain bid worksheets through a service provided by

   A. *The Bond Buyer*
   B. *The Blue List*
   C. *Munifacts*
   D. Moody's

6. When evaluating the validity of a new municipal issue, the bond counsel examines

   I. municipal statutes
   II. the state constitution and amendments
   III. judicial edicts
   IV. the legislative authority of the issuer

   A. I and II only
   B. I, II and III only
   C. III and IV only
   D. I, II, III and IV

7. The manager of a municipal syndicate is a dealer that will

   A. act for the underwriting group
   B. take the largest position
   C. act for the issuing authority
   D. provide the legal opinion

8. In a competitive bid municipal underwriting, the completed bid form includes all of the following EXCEPT the

   A. reoffering scale
   B. bond interest rates
   C. premiums or discounts
   D. identity of the bidder

9. Which of the following statements is true of the good faith deposit of a competitively bid municipal offering?

   A. The deposit is returned by the issuer to the winning syndicate.
   B. The deposit is used to reduce the payment upon delivery of the bonds.
   C. The deposit is returned by the issuer to the underwriters if the underwriters suffer a loss as a result of syndicate operations.
   D. The deposit is treated as a portion of the settlement with the bond purchasers.

10. In a competitive bidding for a municipal bond to be issued at par, the underwriter will be selected on the basis of the

    A. refunding capabilities
    B. lowest interest rate offered
    C. highest dollar bid
    D. sinking fund provisions

11. A municipal syndicate account letter includes all of the following EXCEPT the

    A. final reoffering scale
    B. duration of the account
    C. participation of each member
    D. designation of the manager as the agent for the new issue underwriting

12. In a municipal securities underwriting, which of the following signs the agreement among underwriters?

    A. Members of the syndicate
    B. Issuer
    C. Bond counsel
    D. Trustee

13. The takedown in a municipal bond offering is the discount given to

    A. members of the syndicate
    B. nonmembers of the syndicate
    C. large institutional accounts
    D. members of the selling group

14. The date on which the interest on a new municipal issue will begin accruing is the

    A. filing date
    B. delivery date
    C. closing date
    D. dated date

15. All of the following are used to determine the bid for a municipal bond offering EXCEPT

    A. a good faith check
    B. yield
    C. maturity
    D. the type of bond

16. In an Eastern account, the broker-dealer is underwriting 200 bonds. If the firm sells its 200 bonds but other bonds remain unsold, it is liable for

    A. all of the unsold bonds
    B. none of the unsold bonds
    C. a maximum of 200 additional bonds
    D. a percentage of the unsold bonds equal to its percentage participation in the original allotment

17. A broker-dealer commits to $500,000 in bonds out of a total offering of $5 million in a Western syndicate. The broker-dealer sells $300,000 of the bonds. Of the total offering, $1 million of the bonds remain unsold. What is the syndicate member's remaining liability?

    A. $100,000
    B. $200,000
    C. $300,000
    D. $1,000,000

18. The issuer appoints the underwriter if the underwriting is

    A. negotiated
    B. competitive
    C. Eastern
    D. Western

19. The trust indenture of a revenue bond will show all of the following EXCEPT

    A. reoffering yields
    B. application of flow of funds
    C. discrimination covenant
    D. rate covenant

20. In a gross revenue pledge, which of the following is paid first?

    A. Debt service
    B. Operation and maintenance
    C. Surplus
    D. Debt service reserve

21. When an authority sets aside money for additions and improvements, this is what type of fund?

    A. Renewal and replacement
    B. Sinking
    C. Operations and maintenance
    D. Surplus

22. When a municipality is allocating funds from a revenue-producing facility under a net revenue pledge, the first priority is to

    A. pay operations and maintenance
    B. pay debt service, including principal and interest
    C. establish a reserve for retirement of bonds
    D. accumulate a surplus for expansion of the facility

# Answers

1. **A.** In a negotiated underwriting, the issuer selects an underwriter and negotiates the terms of the offering with that firm. In a competitive bid underwriting, the issuer selects the firm that offers the most attractive terms.

2. **B.** Municipalities are usually required to sell general obligation bonds on a competitive bid basis.

3. **D.** The official notice of sale is provided by the issuer. The bond rating is determined by rating companies.

4. **B.** *The Bond Buyer* contains public notices of invitations to bid, the 30-day visible supply, the placement ratio, etc.

5. **A.** *The Bond Buyer* provides bid worksheets.

6. **D.** The legal opinion examines all aspects of the validity of the bond, including its tax-exempt status, relevant statutes and the issuer's authority to issue the bond.

7. **A.** The manager of a municipal syndicate is the broker-dealer that acts with the issuer on behalf of the syndicate. The managing underwriter manages the entire underwriting process for the syndicate.

8. **A.** The completed bid form contains the yields and prices on the bonds according to the rates that the issuer will pay. It does not contain the reoffering scale—the prices at which the bonds will be sold to the public.

9. **B.** The good faith deposit is used to reduce the total price due to the issuer. Good faith deposits are returned to the syndicates that do not win the bid. Any loss incurred in the sale of the bonds is a loss to the underwriters; the deposit will not be returned by the issuer in such a case. The bond purchasers know nothing of the good faith deposit.

10. **B.** The issuer awards a competitive underwriting based on the lowest total cost to the issuer. The interest cost on the bonds is the cost to the issuer, and so bids are awarded to the syndicate that proposes the lowest coupons or yields.

11. **A.** The syndicate account letter identifies the syndicate manager and details terms of the syndicate agreement: duration of the account, participation and retention of each member, and priority of order allocation. The syndicate letter does not include the reoffering scale.

12. **A.** The issuer, the bond counsel and the trustee are not concerned with the agreement among underwriters. The agreement among underwriters is a document signed by members of the syndicate.

13. **A.** Takedown is the discount given to a syndicate member that buys bonds from the syndicate. The concession is a discount given to a nonmember that buys from a member.

14. **D.** The dated date is the date on which interest begins to accrue.

15. **A.** The bid on a municipal bond issue is determined by the type of bond, maturity dates and yields on the scale. The good faith check is for an amount stipulated by the issuer—usually a percentage of the offering.

16. **D.** An Eastern account is undivided. Each broker-dealer is responsible for the same percentage of unsold bonds as its percentage of participation in the offering.

17. **B.** A Western account is divided. The broker-dealer is responsible only for the bonds it is committed to sell. The broker-dealer committed to sell $500,000 in bonds but sold only $300,000; it is responsible for the remaining $200,000 in bonds.

18. **A.** In a negotiated offering, the underwriter and the issuer negotiate an agreement.

19. **A.** The trust indenture is the contract under which the revenue bond is issued. It lists the responsibilities of the issuing authority, including the application of funds, the covenant (or promise) not to discriminate and the rate covenant, which is a promise to charge rates sufficient to pay debt service.

20. **A.** Under a gross revenue pledge, debt service is the first item paid. The more common net revenue pledge applies gross revenues first to operations and maintenance and then pays debt service out of the remaining net revenues.

21. **D.** The word "authority" tells you that this is a revenue bond. An authority that issues a revenue bond establishes an operations and maintenance fund to meet expenses of operating and maintaining the facility, a sinking fund for debt service payment, a debt service reserve fund to ensure availability of money to pay debt service for a given period (typically one year), a renewal and replacement fund to cover major repairs or replacement of equipment, a reserve maintenance fund to cover extraordinary repair or maintenance expenses and a surplus fund to meet expenses not covered by other funds.

22. **A.** Under a net revenue pledge, the first obligation is to pay operations and maintenance. The remaining funds (the net revenues) are applied to bond interest, the sinking fund, the debt service reserve fund, the renewal and replacement fund, the reserve maintenance fund and the surplus fund—in that order. Under a gross revenue pledge, the first priority is to pay debt service.

# Municipal Trading and Taxation

## Quotations

"Quotation" means any bid for or offer of municipal securities. Any indication of interest or solicitation by a municipal broker-dealer (such as "bid wanted" or "offer wanted") would be considered a quotation request.

**Bona fide.** If a broker-dealer gives, distributes or publishes a quotation for a security, that quote must be bona fide. For a quote to be considered bona fide, the dealer must be prepared to trade the security at the price specified in the quote and under the conditions and restrictions (if any) accompanying the quote.

A quotation may take into consideration such other factors as the broker-dealer's inventory position and any anticipated movement of the market.

### Types of Quotations

- **Workable indication.** The bid price at which a dealer states its willingness to purchase securities from another dealer is called a workable indication.
- **Nominal (subject) quotation.** A dealer that offers a nominal (or subject) quotation intends only to indicate an approximate market value for a security. Nominal quotations are provided for informational purposes only and are permitted if the quote is clearly labeled as such.

**Holding a quote.** A municipal securities dealer may quote a bond price that is firm for a limited period of time. For example, the dealer may give a quote that is firm for one hour with five-minute recall. Within that hour, if another interested buyer asks the dealer for a quote on the same bond, he is given an **out-firm quote**. An out-firm quote signifies that the dealer has given out a firm quote to another buyer. The dealer may then call the first buyer back and give him five minutes to confirm his order or lose his right to buy the bond at the price quoted.

### Customer Communications

**Recommendations.** Municipal securities brokers and dealers are required to make reasonable and suitable recommendations to customers. These reasonableness and suitability tests apply to discretionary accounts as well as to other accounts, and they specifically prohibit **churning**—increasing commissions through excessive trading.

**Disclosure of participation in an underwriting.** A broker-dealer cannot enter a transaction for a customer in any security that the broker-dealer is helping to underwrite or in which it has a financial interest. The broker-dealer can effect a transaction in such a security only if it discloses this potential conflict of interest at or before the completion of the transaction.

## Confirmations

Customers must receive a written confirmation of each municipal securities transaction they have entered. The confirmation must describe the security accurately.

**Dollar bonds.** Municipal revenue bonds traded on a dollar basis (percentage of par) rather than on a YTM basis are commonly called *dollar bonds*. Dollar bonds usually are term bonds and most are callable prior to maturity.

### Disclosing Yield

- A confirmation for a trade effected on the basis of dollar price include that price and indicate the lowest potential yield (yield to premium call, to par option or to maturity) the customer might receive.
- A confirmation for a trade involving callable securities must include a statement indicating that the yield shown may be affected by the exercise of a call provision and that informa-

tion concerning the call provision will be provided by the broker-dealer upon request.
- If the bond is sold at a premium, the broker-dealer must show the bond's yield to the first call date, which is generally a yield lower than any other.

### Required Information on Confirmations

Confirmations must also include the following information:

- in agency transactions, the name of the party on the other side of the transaction and the source and amount of any commission (the name of the other party must be disclosed on request if it is not listed on the confirmation);
- the dated date if it affects the interest calculation;
- the first interest payment date if payments are not semiannual;
- whether the securities are fully registered, registered as to principal only or available in book-entry form; and
- whether the securities are called or prerefunded, as well as the date of maturity fixed by the call notice and the amount of the call price.

## Taxation of Municipal Issues

Municipal bonds are usually priced and offered for sale at a **yield to maturity** (**YTM**—called a **basis quote**). YTM is the total return on that investment per year and takes into account both the interest paid and the premium added to (or discount subtracted from) the par value.

### Adjusting the Cost Basis of Debt Securities

**Municipal bond bought at a premium.** A municipal bond at a premium (whether an original issue premium bond or a bond bought on the secondary market) must have the amount of the premium **amortized** over the life of the bond.

- Losses on bonds held to maturity and redeemed at par are not deductible.
- If the bond is sold before it matures, its cost basis must be adjusted by the amount of the amortized premium.

For example, an investor bought a Kenosha Harbor Authority bond at 108 when the bond had 16 years to maturity. Seven years later, the investor sold the bond at 105. To determine the investor's adjusted cost basis, first calculate the annual amount of the amortized premium. The $80 premium is amortized over 16 years; thus, the annual amortization amount is $80 divided by 16, which equals $5. Because the investor sold the bond after seven years, only $35 (7 × $5) of the premium was amortized. The adjusted cost basis is the investor's original price of $1,080 minus the $35 amortized premium, which equals $1,045. The investor sold the bond for $1,050, resulting in a $5 capital gain.

**Original issue discount.** When a municipal bond is issued at a price lower than par value (for example, a zero-coupon municipal bond), the difference between the discounted purchase price and the par value received at maturity is additional tax-free income.

- If an **original issue discount** (**OID**) bond is sold before it matures, the cost basis of the bond is adjusted by **accreting** the amount of the discount on a straight-line basis.
- If an OID bond is held until maturity, 100% of the discount will have been accreted and the investor will have no taxable capital gain.

**Secondary market discount.** The cost basis of a municipal bond issued at par or at a premium and bought at a discount in the secondary market is not adjusted.

- If the bond is held to maturity, the investor will realize a capital gain.
- If the bond is sold again in the secondary market, the gain or loss is determined by the difference between the bond's purchase price and sale price.

## Tax Benefits

Tax exemption is limited to **public purpose bonds**, and is not granted to any private activity bond.

Investors considering the purchase of a tax-exempt bond should compare its yield with the yields of other securities, including those that are not tax exempt. Because of the tax savings, the tax-free bond may be more attractive than a taxable bond with a higher interest rate.

- The higher the investor's tax bracket, the more the investor gains from the tax exemption.
- To determine a bond's tax-equivalent yield, divide the tax-free yield (yield to maturity) by 100% *less* the investor's tax rate:

$$\frac{\text{Tax-free yield}}{100\% - \text{Tax rate}} = \text{Tax-equivalent yield}$$

As an example, assume that two investors, one in a 15% tax bracket and one in a 30% tax bracket, are considering purchasing $10,000 worth of a new municipal issue with a coupon of 7%. Corporate bonds with similar maturities and ratings are currently being issued at 8.5%. What would the tax-equivalent yield of this municipal issue be for each investor?

The investor in the 15% tax bracket would receive a tax-equivalent yield of 8.2%. To calculate this, divide 7% by 100% minus his tax rate of 15%, or 7% divided by 85%, which equals 8.2%. The municipal bond would not be a good choice for this investor because he could get a higher rate of return by investing in corporates.

The investor in the 30% tax bracket would receive a tax-equivalent yield of 10% (7% divided by 100% minus his 30% tax rate, or 7% divided by 70%, which equals 10%) and, therefore, would receive a higher after-tax yield from the municipal.

## Bond Swaps

**Bond swapping** is a technique used by investors in bonds to generate current tax losses, improve yields or quality, or extend the maturity of their portfolios. The investor swaps by selling bonds that she already holds and replacing them with other bonds that better meet her investment objectives.

To create a tax loss with a bond swap, an investor can sell bonds she holds at a loss while simultaneously purchasing bonds similar to those she sold. For example, the investor might be holding 20 AA Kenosha, WI GO 6.5s of 2018 that she bought at par and that are now selling for 96. She could do a bond swap and lock in a capital loss by selling these and purchasing 20 AA Racine, WI GO 6.5s of 2020 at 95 as a replacement. The result of the swap would be a tax loss of $40 per bond in exchange for bonds with the same coupon and a slightly longer maturity.

To avoid having a legitimate bond swap classified as a wash sale by the IRS (in which case the loss would be disallowed for tax purposes), the replacement bonds purchased must differ in some significant respect from those sold. The IRS will not consider a bond swap a wash sale if the new bonds represent a change in:

- issuer
- maturity date
- rating
- coupon

# Questions

1. Which of the following best describe *municipal dollar bonds*?

   I. Term
   II. Serial
   III. Series
   IV. Callable

   A. I and II
   B. I and IV
   C. II and IV
   D. III and IV

2. All of the following describe term bonds EXCEPT that they

   A. mature entirely on a single date
   B. are called *dollar bonds*
   C. are not callable
   D. are quoted at a percentage of par

3. On what basis are municipal serial bonds quoted?

   A. Yield to maturity
   B. Discount yield
   C. Current yield
   D. Dollar price basis

4. What term describes the excess of the purchase price over the par value of a municipal bond?

   A. Spread
   B. Discount
   C. Premium
   D. Reallowance

5. A common feature shared by almost all revenue bonds is that they are

   A. issued at an original discount
   B. callable
   C. double-barreled
   D. serial bonds rather than term bonds

6. If interest rates rise, municipal bond prices should

   A. rise
   B. decline
   C. fluctuate
   D. stay the same

7. A customer purchases a public purpose municipal bond at $900 in the primary market. The bond matures in ten years. All of the following statements regarding the purchase are true EXCEPT that the

   A. interest is exempt from federal income tax
   B. customer will have no gain or loss if the bond is held to maturity
   C. customer will realize a capital gain of $100
   D. customer will not have to pay tax on the accrued discount each year

8. Which agency has the ultimate authority for determining the amount of the discount on original issue discount municipal bonds?

   A. IRS
   B. FRB
   C. SEC
   D. MSRB

9. A customer buys $100,000 of newly issued municipal bonds at a price of 105. The bonds mature in five years at par. Two years later, the customer sells the bonds at 95. What is the customer's loss for tax purposes?

   A. $3,000
   B. $5,000
   C. $8,000
   D. $10,000

10. A public purpose municipal bond is purchased at a discount in the secondary market at 90. The face amount is $10,000 and the bond has ten years to maturity. The bond is sold for 97 after five years. What is the taxable gain?

   A. $0
   B. $200
   C. $700
   D. Capital gains on municipal bonds are not taxable.

11. A customer buys a new issue municipal bond at $1,060 with an eight-year maturity. After four years, he sells the bond. What is the unamortized premium?

   A. $20
   B. $24
   C. $30
   D. $36

12. An investor purchases a 20-year municipal bond at $10 over par and sells the bond ten years later at 103. The investor has a

   A. loss of $20
   B. loss of $7
   C. loss of $2
   D. gain of $25

13. Interest expense incurred to purchase which of the following types of securities is NOT federally tax deductible?

   A. Corporate bonds
   B. Treasury securities
   C. Municipal bonds
   D. Common stocks

14. A financial institution buys $90,000 of 8%, 20-year revenue bonds. For book purposes, the institution uses straight-line accretion, but for tax purposes the institution uses cost. The bonds are sold after three years for $99,000. What will be the taxable gain?

   A. $3,000
   B. $5,000
   C. $7,500
   D. $9,000

15. A taxpayer in the 30% bracket would net the highest aftertax income from a

   A. 5% municipal bond
   B. 5 1/2% T bill
   C. 6% income bond
   D. 6 1/2% corporate bond

16. The current yield of a municipal bond

   A. is the annual interest divided by the market price
   B. reflects the time until maturity
   C. reflects the interest paid since issuance
   D. includes capital gains as well as interest payments

17. A municipal securities dealer buys $500,000 of 6% bonds at par and immediately reoffers the bonds. Under MSRB rules, which two of the following would most likely be considered bona fide quotes?

   I. 4.10 net
   II. 5.8 less 1/2
   III. 101
   IV. 108

   A. I and III
   B. I and IV
   C. II and III
   D. II and IV

18. According to the terms of the trust indenture, funds for the retirement of municipal revenue bonds would be deposited in what type of fund?

   A. Construction
   B. Maintenance
   C. Sinking
   D. Reserve

19. On January 1, 1996, a municipality publishes a notice that it has deposited sufficient U.S. government securities with the trustee to pay interest and principal on outstanding bonds maturing in the year 2000. This is termed
    A. refinancing
    B. refunding
    C. prerefunding
    D. replacement

# Answers

1. **B.** Municipal dollar bonds are term bonds quoted at a percentage of par. These quotes, unlike quotes made on a yield basis, are easily converted into dollars. Most term bonds are callable prior to maturity. Serial bonds are quoted on a yield basis and can also be callable.

2. **C.** All bonds in a term bond issue mature on the same date. They are known as *dollar bonds* because, unlike other municipal issues, they are quoted at a percentage of par rather than at yield. Issuers of term bonds create sinking funds to allow them to call bonds and repay the principal before maturity.

3. **A.** Municipal serial bonds are quoted on a yield-to-maturity basis.

4. **C.** When a bond is trading at a price greater than $1,000 par value, it is trading at a premium. "Spread" is the difference between the bid and ask prices. "Discount" describes a bond trading at less than par. "Reallowance" refers to the compensation of nonsyndicate members for their role in the sale of a new municipal bond issue.

5. **B.** Almost all revenue bonds are callable. If revenue exceeds projections, the excess funds can be used to pay off some of the bonds. To ensure that the bonds are available for purchase, they are issued with a call provision.

6. **B.** An inverse relationship exists between interest rates and bond prices. As current market interest rates rise, bond prices fall. As current market interest rates fall, bond prices rise.

7. **C.** The discount on OID bonds must be accreted annually. For municipals, this amount is nontaxable because the interest income on municipals is federally tax-exempt. If the bond is held to maturity, the entire discount is accreted, and the bond is valued at par; therefore, there is no gain or loss.

8. **A.** The IRS would ultimately decide the discount on an OID bond because the discount must be accreted annually and is treated as interest income. As the discount is accreted, the adjusted cost basis of the bond is increased, which changes the capital gain or loss that would be realized each year if the bond were sold.

9. **C.** The premium on a municipal bond must be amortized. The five-point premium on a five-year bond will reduce the cost basis by one point per year. After two years, the bonds purchased at $105,000 will be written down to $103,000. If the bonds are sold at $95,000, the tax loss is $8,000 ($103,000 – $95,000).

10. **C.** Because the municipal bond was bought at a discount in the secondary market, there is no requirement to accrete the discount. The bond is valued at cost ($9,000) for tax purposes. If the bond is sold for $9,700, the taxable gain is $700.

11. **C.** New issue municipal bonds purchased at a premium must amortize the premium on a straight-line basis. Thus, this bond has a $60 premium and an eight-year maturity so that $7.50 of the premium must be deducted from the bond's cost basis each year ($60 ÷ 8 = $7.50). After four years, $30 of the $60 premium will have been amortized ($7.50 × 4 = $30), leaving only $30 unamortized.

12. **D.** The bond is purchased $10 over par at 101. The premium must be amortized on a straight-line basis over the remaining life of the bond. Ten years later, the adjusted basis of the bond will be $1,005. One-half of the $10 premium will have been amortized. The sale price of $1,030 less the adjusted basis of $1,005 will result in a gain of $25.

13. **C.** Because the income generated by the bond is tax-free, the IRS does not allow taxpayers to deduct for interest expense incurred in the purchase of municipal bonds.

14. **D.** Because the institution only accretes the bond for its books, while it values the bond at cost for tax purposes, the tax cost is $90,000. If the bonds are sold for $99,000, the taxable gain is $9,000. Remember, you do not accrete secondary market discount municipal bonds for tax purposes. Only new issue discount municipal bonds must be adjusted.

15. **A.** Municipal bonds are exempt from federal taxation and in most cases from taxation by the state in which they are issued. Income bonds, corporate bonds and T bills are fully taxed. This particular investor would be taxed at the 30% level. The equivalent yield on a corporate bond would be 7.14% (5% ÷ 70%).

16. **A.** Current yield on a bond is the annual interest received divided by the bond's market price. It does not include capital gains or the number of years remaining until maturity, which are considered in the yield to maturity compensation.

17. **C.** Under MSRB rules, markups that dealers charge on bonds must be fair and reasonable, with the dealer considering the security's availability, its judgment of the current market and the fact that it is entitled to a reasonable profit on the trade. Of the quotes given, two represent small markups and two represent very large markups. Because the bonds were bought at par, a quote of 101 is a more reasonable markup than a quote of 108. Because the bonds have a 6% coupon, a quote of 5.8% less 1/2 a point is a more reasonable quote than a quote of 4.10 net.

18. **C.** The question defines a sinking fund—a fund set aside for the accumulation of money needed to retire a bond issue at maturity.

19. **C.** The question defines prerefunded or advance-refunded bonds, which are sometimes called *escrowed* bonds.

# Analysis of Municipal Securities

**General obligation bonds.** When analyzing GOs, investors assess the municipality's ability to raise enough tax revenue to pay off its debt.

**Revenue bonds.** With revenue bonds (as with corporate bonds), investors evaluate the likelihood that a specific facility will generate sufficient revenue to cover its operational costs and pay back the debt.

## General Obligation Bonds

**General wealth of the community.** GOs can be analyzed for safety by examining a community's:

- property values
- retail sales per capita
- diversity of industry in its tax base

The issuer's taxing power should enable it to continue making principal and interest payments through all but the most unusual economic circumstances.

**Debt limits.** The state constitution and a municipality's articles of incorporation will usually limit the dollar amount of GOs that a city may issue and have outstanding. This is a city's **constitutional debt limit.**

A state constitution or city charter can also limit the purposes for which a city may issue bonds. The citizens of a municipality control the GO debt of the city. Because their taxes will service such debt, voters must approve each issue through referendum.

**Overlapping debt.** Overlapping (**coterminous**) debt occurs when issuers can draw tax revenues from the same source. A municipality's share of any debt issued by its political subdivisions is part of overlapping debt.

**Income of the municipality.** Real property taxes are the principal income of counties, school districts and cities. City income can include fines, license fees, assessments, city sales taxes, hotel taxes, city income taxes, utility taxes and any city personal property tax. The largest source of city income is normally the tax on real property.

Income and sales taxes are major sources of state income.

**Ad valorem taxes.** Property taxes are based on a property's assessed valuation, which is a percentage of the estimated market value. An increase in assessed values is generally considered to be an indicator of a community's good health.

Because the real property tax is based on the value of the property, it is said to be an ad valorem (or **per value**) tax. GOs, backed by the power to tax and seize property, are considered safer than revenue bonds of the same issuer and, therefore, can be issued with a lower interest rate.

### Municipal General Obligation Debt Ratios

The ability of a community to meet its debt obligations and eventually retire its debt can be estimated by calculating mathematical ratios based on the information in the debt statement and other documents. Some of the more commonly used ratios include the following:

- net debt to assessed valuation;
- net debt to estimated valuation;
- debt per capita;
- debt service to annual revenues;
- debt trend;
- collection ratio;
- coverage ratio:
  - a coverage of 2:1 is considered adequate for a typical municipal revenue bond;
  - a coverage of 5:4 (125%) is considered adequate for utility revenue bonds; and
- taxes per person or per capita.

## Revenue Bonds

Revenue bonds are rated according to the potential of a facility to generate money to service the bond debt. When assessing the quality of revenue bonds, an investor should consider the following factors:

- economic justification
- competing facilities
- sources of revenue
- call provisions
- flow of funds

### Applications of Revenues

In most cases, a **net revenue pledge** is used, and the first payments cover operating and maintenance expenses. The remaining funds, or **net revenues**, are used to pay debt service and other expenses.

If the issuer does not need to commit any revenues to operating and maintenance expenses first, the first disbursements go directly to debt service. When debt service is paid first, the flow of funds is called a **gross revenue pledge**.

The projected **flow of funds** is found in the feasibility statement, which presents the underwriter's assessment of the feasibility of financial projections. Excess revenues that are received are usually segregated and placed in the **general reserve**. From the general reserve the funds can then be transferred as needed, such as to a sinking fund or other account.

### Flow of Funds in a Net Revenue Pledge

In a net revenue pledge, the gross revenues are usually deposited in the **gross revenue fund** (or general reserve) and then disbursed in the following order:

1. operations and maintenance
2. debt service account
3. debt service reserve fund
4. reserve maintenance fund
5. renewal and replacement fund
6. surplus fund

## Other Sources of Information for Municipal Bond Analysis

### Interest Rate Comparisons

A **bond appraisal** is an approximate valuation of a bond that is based on the current market prices of similar bonds.

### Municipal Bond Insurance

Issuers of municipal bonds can insure the principal and interest payments on their securities by purchasing insurance from the investor-owned Municipal Bond Investors Assurance Corp. (MBIA) or AMBAC Indemnity Corporation (AMBAC).

# Questions

1. A qualitative analysis of a general obligation bond that is to be issued would take into consideration all of the following factors EXCEPT the

   A. tax base of the community
   B. economic character of the community
   C. dollar denominations of the bonds to be issued
   D. makeup of the community's population

2. Which of the following is NOT considered when evaluating municipal revenue bond credit risk?

   A. Competing facilities
   B. Quality of management
   C. Coverage ratios
   D. Interest rate movements

3. A bond analyst checking a general obligation municipal bond will examine the

   I. past performance of the payment of interest
   II. per capita income of the citizens
   III. population growth of the area
   IV. industrial development of the area

   A. I, II and III only
   B. I, II and IV only
   C. II, III and IV only
   D. I, II, III and IV

4. A municipal bond issue would be nonrated when the

   A. municipality's credit is not good
   B. municipality's debt is too small to be rated
   C. amount of the issue is too small to be rated
   D. municipality has an outstanding bond in default

5. The number of times by which the annual net revenues of a facility exceed the annual interest charges and principal payments is called the

   A. working capital ratio
   B. dividend payout ratio
   C. debt service coverage ratio
   D. collection ratio

6. All of the following would be considered when analyzing an airport revenue bond issue EXCEPT

   A. energy costs
   B. per capita debt
   C. passenger traffic trends
   D. tourism in the area

7. Which of the following would a customer examine to evaluate the credit quality of a new municipal security?

   A. Official statement
   B. Legal opinion
   C. Prospectus
   D. Trust indenture

8. In analyzing the general obligation debt of a municipality, which of the following is LEAST important?

   A. Direct debt
   B. Authorized debt
   C. Matured debt
   D. Overlapping debt

9. The city of Bondville (population 10,000) has just issued $1 million in general obligation bonds and already has an outstanding debt of $2 million. The city is located in a municipal county with $1,500,000 in debt outstanding, most of which is funded from ad valorem taxes. Bondville makes up 70% of the county. What is the net direct debt per capita of Bondville?

   A. $150
   B. $300
   C. $405
   D. $450

10. All of the following would indicate deteriorating credit conditions EXCEPT an increase in

A. bankruptcies
B. consumer debt
C. bond defaults
D. assessed valuations

11. A corporation owns a building with an estimated market value of $400,000. How much tax will be due if the county assesses the building at $200,000 and applies a 10 mill tax rate?

A. $200
B. $400
C. $2,000
D. $4,000

12. The debt of other districts for which the residents of a municipal district may also be responsible is what kind of debt?

A. Funded
B. Floating
C. Overlapping
D. Unsecured

13. If a municipal issuer is in financial difficulty, which of the following could insure payment of principal and interest on the municipality's outstanding debt?

I. MBIA
II. AMBAC
III. SIPC
IV. FDIC

A. I and II only
B. I, II and III only
C. III and IV only
D. I, II, III and IV

# Answers

1. **C.** The dollar denomination of bonds to be issued has no bearing on a GO bond analysis. The tax base, economic character and population makeup would all be considered.

2. **D.** Interest rate movements have no bearing on determining the quality of revenue bond issues.

3. **D.** The past payment record indicates the reliability of earnings. Per capita income, population growth and industrial development all indicate how large a source of tax revenue backs the bond.

4. **B.** The size of the municipality does not count, but the size of the debt outstanding for a municipality does. A municipality with a small amount of debt will not have enough activity in those debt instruments to warrant a rating by a rating agency.

5. **C.** The debt service coverage ratio shows the number of times that interest and principal can be paid with net revenues.

$$\frac{\text{Annual earnings for debt service}}{\text{Annual interest charges + Principal payment}}$$

$= \text{Debt service coverage}$

6. **B.** Airport revenue bonds are paid off by revenues from the facility; therefore, an analyst would consider passenger traffic trends, tourism and energy costs. Per capita debt is a measure used in analyzing GO issues.

7. **A.** The official statement is an offering document that discloses material information on a new issue of municipal securities. Because it commonly includes information concerning the purpose of the issue, how the securities will be repaid and the financial, economic and social characteristics of the issuer, it is an appropriate place to review the creditworthiness of an issue. The legal opinion reviews the legality of the issue (including certain legal exemptions). A prospectus is the document that provides material information about a

nonexempt security being publicly distributed. The trust indenture is the basic bond contract between the issuer and the trustee that represents the bondholders.

8. **C.** Debt that has already matured is meaningless in evaluating a municipality's debt load.

9. **B.** The direct debt of Bondville is $3 million divided by 10,000 residents, which equals $300 direct debt per capita.

10. **D.** When credit conditions deteriorate, bankruptcies rise, bond defaults increase and consumer debt increases (answers A, B and C). An increase in assessed valuation (property value) would indicate a strengthening economy.

11. **C.**

| | |
|---|---|
| $200,000.00 | Assessed value |
| × .01 | .001 × 10 mill tax rate |
| $ 2,000.00 | |

12. **C.** Districts, counties and cities may have overlapping debt; a state does not.

13. **A.** MBIA and AMBAC insure municipal bonds.

# Municipal Securities Rules and Regulations

## The Securities Acts of 1933 and 1934

Municipal and government securities are exempt from the registration requirements of the Securities Act of 1933. Municipal issuers, underwriters, brokers and dealers are, however, always subject to the 1934 act's antifraud provisions.

## Municipal Securities Rulemaking Board

The MSRB is an independent self-regulatory organization (SRO) established by the Securities Acts Amendments of 1975. The act of 1975 requires underwriters and dealers of securities to protect the interests of investors (as well as themselves), be ethical in offering advice and be responsive to complaints and disputes.

The MSRB is the organization that makes rules pertaining to the issuance and trading of municipal securities.

**Rule enforcement**. The MSRB does not have the authority to enforce the rules it makes. The rules that pertain to broker-dealers are enforced on its behalf by the NASD and SEC, and the comptroller of the currency enforces MSRB rules that pertain to national banks. Neither the MSRB nor the SEC has any authority over municipal issuers.

### MSRB General Rules

It is the rep's responsibility to be familiar with the content of the MSRB's rules.

**Rule G-1**. The MSRB regulates separately identifiable divisions of banks that act as municipal securities dealers. Rule enforcement for a bank municipal dealer is carried out by bank regulators.

**Rule G-2**. Associated persons of municipal securities dealers must meet the MSRB's standards of professional qualifications.

**Rule G-3**. All associated persons of a municipal dealer except clerical persons must be registered with the MSRB. A person functioning as a supervisor must register as a municipal securities principal.

A person who is new to the municipal securities industry may not engage in any municipal securities business with the public during the required 90-day apprenticeship period (although he may engage in transactions with other municipal dealers). The apprentice can receive a salary during this time, but cannot receive a commission for transactions.

**Rule G-4**. The MSRB statutorily disqualifies from membership brokers, dealers and representatives if they have been expelled or suspended from any securities exchange or another SRO, if they have been convicted of any securities-related crime or if they have violated any part of any securities legislation.

**Rule G-5**. Anyone engaged in the municipal securities business must follow the rules of the SEC, any SRO to which they belong and the MSRB.

**Rule G-6**. Municipal securities broker-dealers must maintain fidelity bonds for all of its employees.

**Rule G-7**. A municipal broker-dealer must obtain information about its associated persons; most of the required information is contained on the associated person's complete Form U-4.

**Rule G-8**. Municipal securities dealers must maintain books and records of virtually all communications relating to municipal securities business, with the exception of internal memorandums.

**Rule G-9**. A municipal securities firm must keep on file for the life of the firm the records establishing the firm as a legal entity. Customer records (including written customer complaints) and general ledgers are kept for six years. All other records are kept for three years.

**Rule G-10**. Any time a municipal securities firm receives a complaint from a customer, the firm must record the complaint in a complaint file and deliver a copy of the MSRB's investor brochure to that customer.

**Rule G-11**. During the offering period of a new issue of municipal securities, the syndicate must establish a priority for allocating orders and the conditions that might allow a change in priority.

**Rule G-12**. Settlement of transactions between municipal securities firms must comply with the MSRB's uniform practices. Regular way settlement is the third business day after the trade date. For cash trades, settlement is on the trade date. To meet the requirements of good delivery, the bond certificate must be in good condition (any mutilated certificates must be validated), with the proper signatures, all unpaid coupons and the legal opinion attached.

**Rule G-13**. Municipal broker-dealers can publish quotations only for bona fide bids or offers. Nominal quotes (informational only) are permissible if they are identified as such.

**Rule G-14**. Municipal securities broker-dealers may publicize reports of trades only if the trades actually took place.

**Rule G-15**. Confirmations of trades must be sent or given to customers at or before the completion of the transaction. Confirms must include the following information:

- name, address and telephone number of the broker-dealer;
- customer's name;
- detailed description of the security, including issuer, interest rate and maturity, whether it is callable, etc.;
- trade date and time of execution;
- settlement date;
- CUSIP number (if any);
- yield and dollar price;
- amount of accrued interest;
- extended principal amount (the total principal of all securities covered by the confirmation);
- total dollar amount (the extended principal plus any accrued interest);
- capacity in which the firm does the trade (broker or dealer): if it is an agency transaction (broker), the name of the person on the other side of the trade must be given, if requested, and the amount of commission must be disclosed;
- dated date if it affects the interest calculation and the first interest payment date;
- level of registration of the security (fully registered, registered as to principal only or book-entry);
- whether the bonds are called or prerefunded; and
- any other special fact about the security traded (ex-legal trade, federally taxable, odd denominations, etc.).

**Rule G-16**. A municipal securities broker-dealer must undergo periodic compliance examinations.

**Rule G-17**. Municipal securities broker-dealers may not engage in deceptive, dishonest or unfair practices.

**Rule G-18**. Municipal securities dealers must make an effort to obtain fair and reasonable prices for customers.

**Rule G-19**. Municipal securities reps may not recommend municipal securities to a customer if the rep has not obtained suitability information from the customer. For an unsolicited transaction to be accepted, the customer initiating the trade must have a specific municipal security in mind. Discretionary accounts must be approved in advance and reviewed frequently by a principal.

**Rule G-20**. Municipal securities firms are prohibited from giving gifts valued at more than $100 to any person other than their own employees. Gifts of occasional meals or tickets to sporting events or concerts are permitted.

**Rule G-21**. Municipal securities firms must not publish false or misleading advertisements, and each advertisement must be approved in advance by a principal of the firm. Preliminary official statements and official statements are not considered advertising.

**Rule G-22**. Clients must be informed if a control relationship exists between a municipal firm and an issuer. A control relationship is defined as one in which the broker or dealer controls, is controlled by or is under common control with the issuer of the security or a person other than the issuer who is obligated, directly or indirectly, with respect to debt service on the security.

**Rule G-23**. A financial advisory relationship between a municipal securities dealer and an issuer must be set forth in writing and must be disclosed to purchasers of that issuer's securities.

**Rule G-24**. Confidential customer information (such as a list of an issuer's bondholders) may not be used for the firm's own financial gain.

**Rule G-25**. Municipal securities firms and their representatives may not misuse securities or money held for another person. They must not guarantee a customer against loss, nor share in the profits or losses of a customer's account (although joint accounts in a private capacity are allowed).

**Rule G-26**. A transfer of a customer's account to another broker-dealer must be completed promptly.

**Rule G-27**. A municipal securities principal must review and approve all new customer accounts, all municipal securities transactions and all correspondence.

**Rule G-28**. A municipal securities firm opening an account for an employee of another municipal securities firm must give written notice to the employing firm and send duplicate confirmations of transactions.

**Rule G-29**. Every municipal securities broker-dealer's office must have a copy of the MSRB's regulations available for customer inspection.

**Rule G-30**. Markups and commissions charged by municipal securities firms must be fair and reasonable, and may take into account all characteristics of the trade.

**Rule G-31**. A municipal securities broker-dealer may not solicit business from an investment company based on the broker-dealer's record of sales of the investment company's shares.

**Rule G-32**. When a new issue of municipal securities is delivered to a customer, a copy of the official statement must accompany or precede the delivery. If it is not yet completed, a preliminary official statement is acceptable.

**Rule G-33**. Accrued interest on municipal bonds is calculated based on a 360-day year with 30-day months.

**Rule G-34**. A managing underwriter of a new issue of municipal securities is responsible for having CUSIP numbers assigned to the issue.

**Rule G-35**. Arbitration settles disputes between member firms, between members and transfer agents and between members and banks. Customers may request to settle a dispute through arbitration.

**Rule G-36**. A final official statement for a new issue of municipal securities must be filed with the MSRB within ten days after the issue is awarded to the underwriter.

**Rule G-37**. Employees of municipal securities firms may contribute up to $250 to public officials responsible for awarding municipal securities business. Gifts of over $250 disqualify the firm from underwriting securities of that issuer. All gifts must be reported to the MSRB.

**Rule G-38**. Municipal securities dealers must have written agreements with consultants and disclose consulting arrangements to issuers and to the MSRB.

# Questions

1. Which of the following are NOT directly regulated by the MSRB?

   A. Bank dealers
   B. Issuers of municipal bonds
   C. Broker-dealers that deal in municipal bonds
   D. Federal Reserve Board

2. Which of the following statements are true?

   I. The MSRB was formed as a result of the Securities Exchange Act of 1934.
   II. The MSRB is a self-regulating organization.
   III. The MSRB does not enforce its own rules.
   IV. The MSRB controls the over-the-counter market.

   A. I and II
   B. I and III
   C. II and III
   D. II and IV

3. The MSRB is responsible to

   A. the NASD
   B. the SEC
   C. the NYSE
   D. no one, because it is a self-regulatory organization

4. Municipal securities issuers and dealers are subject to which of the following?

   I. Antifraud provisions under Rule 10b-5 of the Securities Exchange Act of 1934
   II. Issuer reporting requirements to the Securities and Exchange Commission under the Securities Exchange Act of 1934
   III. Prospectus delivery requirements to purchasers of new issues under the Securities Act of 1933

   A. I only
   B. I and II only
   C. II and III only
   D. I, II and III

5. Which of the following enforce(s) the rules of the MSRB?

   I. Comptroller of the Currency
   II. FDIC
   III. Federal Reserve Board

   A. I only
   B. II only
   C. II and III only
   D. I, II and III

6. A municipal securities principal at a bank is in charge of supervising all of the following EXCEPT

   A. writing legal opinions
   B. processing trades in municipal securities
   C. maintaining municipal securities records
   D. bank employees involved in municipal transactions

7. Which of the following statements about MSRB rules is true?

   A. The FDIC enforces MSRB rules governing brokerage firms.
   B. A broker expelled by the NYSE would not be disqualified by the MSRB.
   C. MSRB rules do not allow representatives to receive part of a client's profits instead of a commission.
   D. The MSRB has adopted the 5% markup policy.

8. An MSRB dealer opens an account for a customer. The dealer should ask about the customer's

   I. tax status
   II. investment objectives
   III. financial background
   IV. education

   A. I and II only
   B. I, II and III only
   C. II only
   D. I, II, III and IV

9. The municipal principal must approve all orders in writing taken for the account of

   I. individuals
   II. trust departments
   III. insurance companies
   IV. commercial banks

   A. I only
   B. I, II and III only
   C. III and IV only
   D. I, II, III and IV

10. According to the MSRB, if a customer wishes to purchase municipal bonds when the registered representative feels that the trade would be unsuitable, the trade

    A. may be executed if approved by the MSRB
    B. may be executed if the customer directs that it be done
    C. may be executed only if the customer has previous trading experience
    D. cannot be executed

11. Advertising related to municipal securities must be approved by which of the following?

    A. MSRB
    B. SEC
    C. Municipal securities principal
    D. General securities principal

12. A municipal dealer that receives an advisory fee from a client must, according to MSRB rules, notify the client in writing of

    A. the credit rating of any security recommended
    B. any financial interest the dealer may have in an underwriting of a security recommended for purchase
    C. the yearly trading range of any security recommended for purchase
    D. all of the above

13. According to MSRB rules, under which of the following conditions may a municipal dealer share in the profits of a customer's account?

    A. If the dealer effected the transaction for the customer
    B. If the dealer receives compensation on an offsetting transaction
    C. If a written guarantee is signed by the customer
    D. Under no circumstances

14. According to MSRB rules, one municipal dealer must notify another municipal dealer if relatives of employees of the second municipal dealer wish to open an account. Which of the following would trigger the notification requirement?

    A. Twenty-five-year-old daughter of an employee
    B. Spouse of an employee
    C. Aunt of an employee
    D. Son-in-law of an employee

15. Under MSRB rules, all of the following would be considered advertisements EXCEPT

    A. offering circulars
    B. market letters
    C. official statements
    D. summaries of official statements

16. According to the MSRB, a control relationship would exist between a municipal broker-dealer and an issuer when

    A. senior officers of the municipal dealer live in the municipality
    B. the firm recently completed a negotiated underwriting for the municipality
    C. an officer of the underwriter is in a position of authority over the issuer of the municipal bonds
    D. the dealer has an inventory of the issuer's bonds that are trading at a premium

17. MSRB rules would treat as "material"

    A. a gift of less than $50
    B. World Series tickets valued at $75
    C. reminder advertising valued at $25
    D. vintage wine valued at $125

18. A municipal bond is issued with five years of call protection. The bonds are callable after that date with a scale of declining premiums. The bond has been prerefunded and the proceeds of the refunding issue deposited in an escrow account and invested in direct federal debt issues. The bonds are sold at a dollar price, so the confirmation must show the

    A. lowest yield to maturity or yield to call
    B. yield to the maturity date established by the refunding
    C. yield to the longer call with the lower resulting yield
    D. yield to the longer call with the higher resulting yield

19. MSRB rules prohibit municipal securities firms from engaging in which of the following activities with investment companies?

    A. Accepting a presale order for a new municipal issue
    B. Hiring investment company officers
    C. Soliciting municipal transactions from the investment company as compensation for shares sold of the investment company
    D. Any transactions in municipal securities by investment companies

20. According to MSRB rules, all of the following is required customer account information EXCEPT the

    A. tax ID or Social Security number
    B. age and birth date
    C. name and address of employer
    D. signature of the municipal securities representative or general securities representative introducing the account and of a municipal securities principal or general securities principal indicating acceptance of the account

21. A registered representative qualified to sell only municipal securities may solicit orders for which of the following?

    I. Sewer and water revenue bonds
    II. General obligation bonds
    III. Municipal unit investment trusts
    IV. Open-ended municipal bond funds

    A. I and II only
    B. I and III only
    C. II and IV only
    D. I, II, III and IV

22. The first action to be taken by a municipal securities dealer upon receipt of a customer complaint is to

    A. notify the examining regulatory authority
    B. submit to arbitration
    C. refund any money to the customer making the complaint
    D. accept the complaint and record the action taken

23. Municipal bonds are MOST suitable for

    A. individual retirement accounts
    B. corporations in the maximum tax bracket
    C. pension plans
    D. individuals in the 15% tax bracket

24. Which of the following is the LEAST important factor contributing to the diversification of a municipal bond portfolio?

    A. Maturity
    B. Issuer location
    C. Denomination
    D. Quality

# Answers

1. **B.** Because municipal bond issues are exempt from registration with the SEC, neither the SEC nor the MSRB has any direct authority over the issuers of municipal securities.

2. **C.** The MSRB was formed as a result of the Securities Acts Amendments of 1975. It is a self-regulatory organization but does not enforce its own regulations. Regulations are enforced by another SRO (such as the NASD), which has authority over the municipal dealer. Although municipal bonds are sold in the over-the-counter market, the MSRB does not control that market; the NASD does.

3. **B.** It is true that the MSRB is a self-regulatory organization but it still is responsible to the SEC. The MSRB was formed to carry out the wishes of the SEC.

4. **A.** Municipal securities are exempt under the acts of 1933 and 1934. However, the 1934 act specifically states that its provisions for fraud pertain to municipal dealers and issuers. The issuer-reporting requirements of the SEC (such as annual and quarterly reports) apply to corporate issuers, not to municipal issuers. Prospectus delivery rules apply only to corporate issuers, not to municipal issuers.

5. **D.** The Comptroller of the Currency enforces MSRB rules in national banks. The Federal Reserve Board enforces the rules in nonnational banks that are members of the Federal Reserve System. The FDIC enforces MSRB rules for nonnational banks that are not members of the Federal Reserve System. The NASD and NYSE supervise member firms' compliance with MSRB rules.

6. **A.** An independent bond counsel writes legal opinions for the issuer of a municipal security. The municipal securities principal at a bank would have no authority over this aspect of municipal bond underwriting.

7. **C.** Registered representatives cannot share in the profits of a client's account. The rep can receive compensation only from the firm.

8. **B.** In opening an account for a customer, municipal rules limit the dealer to asking about tax status, investment objectives and financial background.

9. **D.** The municipal principal is required to approve all orders on a timely basis.

10. **D.** If a customer wishes to purchase a security that the registered representative feels is unsuitable, the trade may not be entered. The MSRB prohibits a rep from making an unsuitable recommendation; unless the customer names a specific issue, the rep is considered to be making a recommendation.

11. **C.** Municipal advertising must be approved by a municipal principal prior to first use.

12. **B.** Because a municipal bond dealer must always act in the best interests of the client, it must disclose to the client any personal interest it may have in a recommended security.

13. **D.** A representative may only share in the profits of an account owned jointly with another person. Even then, the rep may share in profits only to the extent of his interest in the account.

14. **B.** The rules governing opening accounts for other securities professionals apply to the immediate family members of those professionals. The immediate family member in this instance speaks of a financial unit. The spouse of the employee would be automatically in that family unit. A twenty-five-year-old offspring is not likely to be supported by the municipal employee, nor is the son-in-law. If they were, they also would be subject to the reporting requirements.

15. **C.** MSRB rules consider all forms of mass public communication to be advertising, except listings of dealer inventories, official statements and preliminary official statements.

16. **C.** The officer of the broker-dealer has control over both the broker-dealer and the issuer. This could open doors for possible manipulation, which is why the control relationship is forbidden.

17. **D.** The word "material" indicates that an *excessive* gift cannot be given by a municipal firm to employees of another municipal firm. The dollar value the MSRB considers "material" is $100. The vintage wine valued at $125 exceeds this limit.

18. **B.** The bond has been refunded. The money is in the escrow account. The outstanding bonds will be called as soon as possible. With these conditions, the date and the price at which the bonds will be called are known. The maturity date is established by the refunding. The yield that is to be shown on the confirmation is the yield to call established by that refunding.

19. **C.** The idea behind the municipal antireciprocal rule is that investment companies should not attempt to induce municipal broker-dealers to sell shares of the fund. This could be done if the investment company ran its portfolio trades only through those broker-dealers that sold the most fund shares. This practice is prohibited under MSRB rules. Of course, presale orders for new municipal issues may be accepted and transactions between investment companies and municipal broker-dealers are allowed. (Otherwise, how could the fund's portfolio be traded?)

20. **B.** The age or birth date is not required customer information.

21. **A.** Persons licensed to sell only municipal securities must limit their activities to securities issued by municipal issuers, the federal government and government agencies; sewer and water revenue bonds and general obligation bonds are securities of municipal issuers. Municipal bond mutual funds or investment trusts are investment company securities; sale of these securities requires either a general securities or an investment company/variable contracts representative license.

22. **D.** Upon receipt of a customer complaint, accept the complaint, record the action taken, put

it in a complaint file and respond; record the response.

23. **B.** The tax-exempt status of municipal bonds makes them especially appealing to two types of investors: individuals in high tax brackets and corporations in the maximum tax bracket. Because pension and profit-sharing plans are exempt from current federal income tax, they usually do not invest in municipals. For the same reason, municipal bonds are not suitable for IRAs. Tax-deferred plans prefer the higher rates associated with corporate and government bonds.

24. **C.** Bond denominations have no bearing on the diversification of a portfolio. Obviously, maturity, issuer location and quality are all important factors to consider when diversifying a portfolio.

# 16 Option Contracts

## Introduction to Options

An option is a **contract** between two people. The purchaser of the contract has paid money for the *right* to buy or the *right* to sell securities. The purchaser is also called the *holder*, the *buyer*, or *long the option*. The seller of the option contract, on the other hand, has accepted money for taking on an *obligation*. The seller is also called the *writer*, or *short the option*.

The option seller *must* buy or *must* sell the specified security if asked to do so by the option's buyer. A stock option contract represents an agreement between two people to buy or sell a round lot of stock.

### Calls and Puts

There are two types of options: calls and puts.

- A **call option** gives the holder the *right to call* a security away from someone else.
- A **put option** gives the holder the *right to put* a security to someone else.

A *call* is the right to *buy* a set amount of a specific investment instrument at a set price for a set period of time. A *put* is the right to *sell* a set amount of a specific investment instrument at a set price for a set period of time.

### Disposing of an Option

The holder of an option contract can:

- **exercise** the option
- let the option **expire**
- **sell** the option

### Underlying Instruments

Options are available on the following underlying instruments:

- corporate stock;
- broad- and narrow-based indexes;
- Treasury bonds, Treasury notes and Treasury bills; and
- major foreign currencies.

### Summary of Long and Short Positions

- A **long call** position represents the **right to buy** the underlying security.
- A **short call** position represents the **obligation to sell** the underlying security.
- A **long put** position represents the **right to sell** the underlying security.
- A **short put** position represents the **obligation to buy** the underlying security.

## Options Terminology

The following is a summary of some basic options terms:

- **Option**. A contract giving the buyer the right to buy or sell a security (such as stock) and requiring the writer to sell or buy the underlying item if the option buyer chooses to exercise the contract.
- **Call**. The right to buy stock (or another underlying security) at a specified price for a limited time.
- **Call buyer**. An investor who pays a premium for an option contract and receives the right to buy, during a specified time, the underlying security at the specified price.
- **Call writer**. An investor who receives a premium and takes on, for a specified time, the obligation to sell the underlying security at the specified price at the call buyer's discretion.
- **Covered**. The position of an options investor who owns an asset that guarantees the ability to perform if the option contract is exercised.
- **Naked** (or **uncovered**). The position of an options investor who writes a call or a put on a security he does not own.
- **Put**. The right to sell stock (or another underlying instrument) at a specified price for a limited time.
- **Put buyer**. An investor who pays a premium for an option contract and has, for a specified time, the right to sell the underlying security at the specified price.
- **Put writer**. An investor who receives a premium and takes on, for a specified time, the obligation to buy the underlying security at the specified price at the put buyer's discretion.
- **Strike price** (or **exercise price**). The price at which the underlying security will be sold if the option buyer exercises his rights in the contract.
- **Expiration date**. The specified date on which the option becomes worthless and the buyer no longer has the rights specified in the contract.
- **Premium**. The cash price that the option buyer pays to the option writer.
- **Underlying security**. The securities that are bought or sold when an option is exercised, or on which an option is based.

# Questions

1. Angus Bullwether is long 10 ABC Jul 50 calls. Identify the three choices he can make regarding his option position.

______________________________

______________________________

______________________________

Questions 2 through 6 are about Karen Kodiak's option position: Karen is long 10 ABC Jul calls at 4 1/2.

2. How many options does Karen own?

______________________________

3. What is the name of the underlying instrument?

______________________________

4. Does the contract give Karen the right to buy or sell stock?

______________________________

5. What is the total premium Karen paid for her position?

______________________________

6. How many shares of stock will change hands if Karen exercises her option?

______________________________

7. Which of the following investors will purchase stock if the option is exercised?

   I. Owner of a call
   II. Owner of a put
   III. Writer of a call
   IV. Writer of a put

   A. I and II
   B. I and IV
   C. II and III
   D. III and IV

8. Which of the following investors will sell stock if the option is exercised?

   I. Owner of a call
   II. Owner of a put
   III. Writer of a call
   IV. Writer of a put

   A. I and II
   B. I and IV
   C. II and III
   D. III and IV

## Answers

1. Exercise the option.
   Let the option expire.
   Trade the option in a closing sale.

2. 10.

3. ABC common stock.

4. Buy. A call is the right to buy stock.

5. $4,500. 4 1/2 × 100 shares per contract × 10 contracts = $4,500.

6. 1,000. 100 shares per contract × 10 contracts.

7. **B.** A call owner has the right to purchase stock from a call writer. A put writer has the obligation to purchase stock if a put buyer chooses to exercise the option.

8. **C.** A put owner acquires the right to sell stock by exercising the option. A call writer undertakes the obligation to sell stock if a call owner exercises the option.

# Equity Options

## The Option Contract

**Exercise prices.** An option's exercise price is the price at which the owner of the contract will be entitled to buy (or sell) the underlying security and the price at which the seller has an obligation to deliver (or purchase) that security.

If the advance or decline of the price of the underlying stock warrants it, the Options Clearing Corporation (OCC) will create new options with different strike prices.

The number immediately below the option's name (or abbreviation) in a printed quote is the price at which the underlying stock closed the day before. The fractional numbers listed under the headings "Calls—Last" and "Puts—Last" are the prices (or premiums) at which those individual option contracts closed the previous day.

If an "r" appears instead of a fractional dollar figure for a premium, the option was not traded that day. If an "s" appears, no option contract is currently being offered at that strike price.

**Expiration dates.** The OCC standardizes the expiration dates of listed options. Each class of listed options has a set of four expiration months (known as a **cycle**). An option might have expiration dates of January, April, July and October (**JAJO**); February, May, August and November (**FMAN**); or March, June, September and December (**MJSD**). Each option contract must expire on the preset option expiration day in one of those months.

### Type, Class and Series

- **Type**. There are two types of options: calls and puts.
- **Class**. All options of the same type on the same underlying security are considered as being of the same class.
- **Series**. All options of the same class, exercise price and expiration month are in the same series.

### Four Basic Options Transactions

**Long options.** The owner of an option is said to have a long position. This investor has paid money in the form of a premium to obtain the rights specified in the option contract.

- The investor with a **long call** has the right to *purchase* the underlying security at the strike price at any time through the expiration date.
- The investor with a **long put** has the right to *sell* the underlying security at the strike price until the expiration date.

**Short options.** The seller of an option has a short position. This investor receives a premium.

- The investor who is **short a call** is obligated to *sell* the underlying security at the strike price to the person who is long the call if the option is exercised by the expiration date. The writer receives the premium.
- The investor who is **short a put** is obligated to *buy* the underlying security at the strike price at any time through the expiration date if the put owner exercises the option. The put writer receives the premium.

## How the Options Market Functions

**Exchange-traded.** Options on stock (and some other securities) trade in both exchange and OTC markets. Exchange-traded options (also known as **listed** options) have standardized strike prices and expiration dates.

**Settlement.** Options can be traded between 9:30 am and 4:10 pm EST every business day the exchanges are open until the day before the option is set to expire. Transactions in listed options settle on the next business day.

**Listing requirements.** In order to qualify for trading on a listed options exchange, the security underlying the option contract must meet minimum requirements in the following:

- number of shares outstanding
- number of stockholders
- annual trading volume
- market price

**Delisting.** A market will delist an option if the underlying security falls below the minimum listing requirements by a significant percentage (for example, if the security's market price closes below $5 for six months).

**Order book official. Order book officials (OBOs)** or **board brokers** ensure that the exchange auction process runs smoothly. The OBOs and board brokers keep track of limit orders and maintain orderly markets; they cannot trade for their own accounts.

## Options Clearing Corporation

- The OCC is the entity that standardizes option contracts, guarantees performance of the contracts and issues options.
- On exchange-traded options, the standardized strike prices and expiration months are determined by the OCC.
- The market determines the premiums of OCC-issued, standardized options.
- Options are issued by the OCC the day after the order is executed *without a certificate.* The investor's proof of ownership of an option is the trade confirmation and any brokerage account statement she receives.

### Closing Options Positions

The OCC provides investors with a ready means of closing open option positions.

- An investor in options can close an open position by selling back a long option or buying back a short one in the secondary market.
- The investor long an option closes the position by entering a closing sale of an identical contract.
- The investor who is short an option closes the position by making a closing purchase of an identical contract.
- When an investor closes a position, the OCC takes the opposite side of the trade.

### OCC Options Disclosure Document

- The OCC publishes an options disclosure document called *Characteristics and Risks of Standardized Options*, which outlines the risks and rewards associated with investing in options.
- An investor must receive this document from the broker-dealer prior to or at the same time as the investor receives approval for options trading.
- The disclosure document must accompany any options sales literature a client is sent.
  - Sales literature, according to the options exchanges, does not include material that is strictly educational.
- If the OCC issues a revised disclosure document, the customer must receive a copy no later than with the next confirmation of an options trade.

**Options agreement.** A broker-dealer must obtain from any customer who intends to invest in options a signed options agreement within 15 days of approving the account for trading. In this agreement, a customer states that she has read the options disclosure document and agrees to abide by the position limits and other rules of options trading. The OCC also publishes a prospectus with information that is not in the options disclosure document. This prospectus must be made available to investors upon request.

## Option Contract Adjustments

**Cash dividends.** The OCC does not adjust the strike price of standardized options for ordinary cash dividends.

**Stock splits.** Options are adjusted for stock splits, reverse stock splits, stock dividends and rights offerings. When a stock splits, so does the option. Some stock splits do not work out to even round lots. In that case, the number of shares represented by the contracts cannot be divided into round lots, so the OCC adjusts the number of shares in the contract.

**Reverse splits.** Every once in a while, a corporation will choose either to increase the value or reduce the number of its outstanding shares or to increase the earnings per share by declaring a reverse split.

**Stock dividends.** If a company declares a stock dividend, the OCC can adjust the strike price, the number of shares in the contract or both as it deems necessary.

**Rounding.** Adjustments to exercise prices are rounded to the nearest eighth, and adjustments in the number of underlying shares are rounded down to the next whole share.

## Position and Exercise Limits

The exchanges limit the number of options that an individual investor can control on the same side of the market. The exchanges frequently adjust these limits, and as of May 1996 investors are limited to the following number of equity option contracts on the same side of the market:

- 25,000 contracts—options on the most heavily traded stocks
- 10,500 contracts—options on heavily traded stocks
- 7,500 contracts—options on less heavily traded stocks
- 4,500 contracts—options on the least heavily traded stocks

Under the exercise limits system, investors may not exercise more than the allowed number of contracts within *five consecutive business days*. For stock options, the exercise limit is the same as the position limit.

## Expiration and Exercise

The key option expiration times and dates are as follows:

- 4:10 pm EST (3:10 pm CST) on the third Friday of the month of expiration—listed equity options cease trading.
- 5:30 pm EST on the third Friday of the month of expiration—options can no longer be exercised by their holders.
- 11:59 pm EST on the Saturday following the third Friday of the expiration month—options expire.

**Automatic exercise.** In the absence of instructions to the contrary, the OCC will automatically exercise certain in-the-money contracts owned by public customers that are 3/4ths of a point in the money and any contracts owned by member firms that are 1/4th of a point in the money will be automatically exercised.

**Assignment of exercise.** The exercised party (the writer) must either deliver the stock in three business days (for a call) or buy the stock in three business days (for a put).

When an option owner notifies the OCC that he wants to exercise his option, the OCC randomly selects a firm to which it assigns the exercise. The assignment of the exercise notice to one of its customers by the broker-dealer may be done randomly or on a FIFO basis. It may not be assigned on the basis of who has the largest position or who can best afford it.

## Long-term Equity Options

Long-term equity options (such as the CBOE's Long-term Equity AnticiPation Securities, or LEAPS®) differ from traditional equity options in that they have a longer expiration. Expirations of up to 39 months are authorized, but currently available LEAPS expire within two and one-half years.

One LEAPS contract covers 100 shares of the underlying security. LEAPS are available as calls or puts. The premium tends to be greater than that of a traditional option because of the longer term and thus greater time value.

**Taxation.** The seller of a LEAPS option has a short-term gain in the amount of the premium received. The buyer of a LEAPS option can maintain the position for up to two and one-half years; therefore, any gains or losses are normally long term.

# Questions

Use the options table in Figure 1 to answer questions 1 through 5.

1. What is the closing price of All Swel stock?

    ______________________________

2. The number 30 appears to the right of "ALFA Inc." What does the number signify?

    ______________________________

3. What is the closing premium of the ALF Jan 35 calls?

    ______________________________

4. What does the small letter *r* mean?

    ______________________________

**Figure 1**

**CHICAGO BOARD**

| Option & NY Close | Strike Price | Calls-Last | | | Puts-Last | | |
|---|---|---|---|---|---|---|---|
| | | Jan | Feb | Mar | Jan | Feb | Mar |
| Adm Fam | 40 | 1 3/8 | 3 5/8 | r | 3/16 | 7/8 | 1 1/4 |
| 41 1/8 | 45 | 1/2 | 1 1/2 | 2 1/8 | 3 7/8 | r | 5 1/4 |
| 41 1/8 | 50 | r | 3/8 | 5/8 | s | s | 12 |
| ALFA, Inc. | 30 | 7 7/8 | 9 1/8 | 11 | r | r | 1/8 |
| 37 7/8 | 35 | 3 1/8 | 4 1/2 | 6 3/4 | r | 1/4 | 1/8 |
| 37 7/8 | 40 | 3/4 | 1 5/8 | 3 | 3/4 | 7/8 | r |
| All Swel | 25 | 1/4 | 1 3/8 | 2 | 1/8 | 1 | 1 5/8 |
| 25 1/4 | 30 | r | 1/8 | 7/8 | 3 3/4 | 4 5/8 | 7 |
| Bulln Bar | 20 | r | r | r | r | r | 7/8 |
| 24 | 22 1/2 | 1 | r | r | r | r | r |
| 24 | 25 | 5/16 | 1 | 2 1/4 | r | r | 2 5/8 |

Total call vol 1,240,086 Call open int 3,038,532
Total put vol 105,755 Put open int 941,395

r - Not Traded. s - No Option.

5. How much would an investor pay for an option granting the right to buy 100 shares of Bulln Bar stock at $25 per share before the expiration date in March?

______________________________

6. Who or what issues a listed option?

   A. Member firm of the option writer
   B. Exchange on which the option is purchased
   C. Investor who writes the option
   D. Options Clearing Corporation

7. An investor buys 1 DWQ Apr 70 call at 5, giving him the right to buy 100 shares of DWQ at $70 per share. Which aspect of the transaction is not set or standardized by the OCC?

   A. Contract size of 100 shares
   B. Premium of 5
   C. Exercise price of 70
   D. Expiration date in April

8. All of the following are characteristics of nonstandardized options EXCEPT

   A. negotiated exercise prices
   B. active secondary trading
   C. premiums determined by the market
   D. negotiated expiration dates

Choose from the following list of options to answer questions 9 through 11.

   A. COD Jul 60 put at 3
   B. MCS Jul 45 put at 2
   C. MCS Aug 50 put at 4
   D. MCS Aug 50 call at 5

9. ___ Which of the options, if any, are of the same type?

10. ___ Which of the options, if any, are of the same class?

11. ___ Which of the options, if any, are of the same series?

12. It would be fair and equitable for a brokerage firm to assign an option exercise notice to which of the following customers?

   A. Customer with the largest open position in that option
   B. Customer who first wrote that option
   C. Either A or B
   D. Neither A nor B

The OCC sets standard expiration dates and exercise times for all listed options. Use the July calendar below to answer questions 13 through 15 concerning an MCS Jul 40 call option: in each case, write the time of day, day of the week and date.

| July | | | | | | |
|---|---|---|---|---|---|---|
| S | M | T | W | T | F | S |
| | | | | | | 1 |
| 2 | 3 | 4 | 5 | 6 | 7 | 8 |
| 9 | 10 | 11 | 12 | 13 | 14 | 15 |
| 16 | 17 | 18 | 19 | 20 | 21 | 22 |
| 23 | 24 | 25 | 26 | 27 | 28 | 29 |
| 30 | 31 | | | | | |

13. What is the deadline for selling the call in the open market?

______________________________

14. What is the deadline for exercising the call?

______________________________

15. When does the option expire?

______________________________

16. A customer first discusses options trading with a registered representative on July 3rd. On July 7th the customer is approved for trading listed options and on July 12th he enters the first trade. Using the July calendar, on which of the following dates must the customer receive an options disclosure document?

A. July 3rd
B. July 7th
C. July 12th
D. July 13th

# Answers

1. 25 1/4. The closing price of the underlying stock is listed under the stock's name.

2. 30. This is the strike price of the option.

3. 3 1/8 ($312.50).

4. The option did not trade.

5. $225. 2 1/4 per share × 100 shares.

6. **D.** The OCC issues all listed options.

7. **B.** The OCC sets standard exercise prices and expiration dates for all listed options, but the premiums that buyers pay for options are determined by the market.

8. **B.** Unlike listed options, unlisted options do not trade continuously in an organized secondary market. Trades are negotiated between individuals.

9. **A, B, C.** All are puts.

10. **B, C.** Both are MCS puts.

11. None. Options of the same series are the same class, expiration date and strike price.

12. **B.** Firms can choose one of two methods: random; and first in, first out (Answer B).

13. 4:10 pm Eastern time on Friday, July 21st. Note that July has five Saturdays and only four Fridays. This is why the rule reads "the business day immediately preceding the Saturday that follows the third Friday of the expiration month."

14. 5:30 pm EST on Friday, July 21st.

15. 11:59 pm EST on Saturday, July 22nd.

16. **B.** The OCC disclosure document must precede or accompany approval for trading listed options.

# Option Trading and Strategies

### Value of an Option

The option buyer hopes that the option's price in the market will increase. The premium of an option changes as:

- the market price of the underlying security moves;
- the intrinsic value of the option increases or decreases; and
- the time remaining until the option's expiration date grows shorter.

An option is **in-the-money** whenever it is worth exercising.

- A call is in-the-money when the stock's market price exceeds the option's strike price.
  - An AFB 25 call is in-the-money by seven points if the price of AFB stock is 32.
- A put is in-the-money when the stock price is less than the strike price.
  - An AFB 25 put is in-the-money by four points if AFB stock is at 21.

An option is **out-of-the-money** when it is not worth exercising.

- A call is out-of-the-money when the stock price is below the exercise price.
  - A TCY 50 call is not worth exercising if TCY is available at a market price of 40.
- A put is out-of-the-money when the stock price is above the exercise price.
  - A TCY 50 put is not worth exercising if TCY can be sold in the market for 60.

An option is **at-the-money** when the underlying stock is trading exactly at the exercise price of the option.

### Intrinsic Value

If an option is in-the-money, its premium will reflect the potential profit to be made if it is exercised. This profit potential is known as *intrinsic value.*

- Intrinsic value is the difference between the option's strike price and the underlying stock's price.
- A call option has intrinsic value when the price of the underlying stock is above the option's exercise price.
  - When AFB is trading at 24, a call with a strike price of 20 is in-the-money and has an intrinsic value of $4 per share.
- A put option has intrinsic value when the price of the underlying stock is below the option's exercise price.
  - When TCY is trading at 42, a put with a strike price of 50 is in-the-money and has an intrinsic value of $8.
- An out-of-the-money option has no intrinsic value.

### Time Value

The amount an investor is willing to pay above an option's intrinsic value in order to buy and hold that option for the time remaining until the option expires is the *time value.*

- As the option's expiration date approaches, the time value tends to diminish.
- On the last trading day before expiration, the time value is gone and the premium usually equals the intrinsic value.
- To find the time value of an option, calculate the intrinsic value and subtract it from the premium.
  - If an AFB 80 call is trading for 6 1/4 when AFB stock is selling for 84, the premium represents both time and intrinsic value. Subtracting the strike price of 80 from the stock's market price of 84 yields $4 per share of intrinsic value in the premium. If that $4 of intrinsic value is subtracted from the premium of 6 1/4, you find that the premium for the AFB 80 call contains $2 1/4 per share of time value.

### Investor Outlook

- **Bullish** indicates optimism that a security or the market is going up.
- **Bearish** indicates pessimism, the belief that a security or the market is going down.

## Buying Calls

A **call option** is:

- the right to buy
- 100 shares
- of a specific stock
- at a specific price
- for a specific period of time

If John buys 1 AFB Apr 40 call for 2, that option gives him:

- the right to buy
- 100 shares
- of AFB
- at the strike price of $40 per share
- at any time before the option expires in April

John paid a premium of $200 (the "2" in the quote indicates a premium of $2 per share times the 100 shares the contract represents). If John decides not to exercise his option before it expires, he loses the entire $200 premium he paid for the option.

When John buys 1 AFB Apr 40 call at 2, he does so in anticipation that the price of the underlying stock will go up between now and April. If he is right and AFB is trading higher than $40 (at $46, for example) near the end of March, he can still purchase 100 shares for $4,000 by exercising his call. Because the market value of those shares at 46 is $4,600, John has profited. The right to make that purchase cost him $200, the premium he paid for his call option. If he is wrong and the price of the stock drops below 40, he will either let the option expire (if it has become worthless) or try to sell it to someone else to recoup at least some of the premium he paid.

Options are wasting assets; the passage of time depletes their value. If an option is allowed to expire unexercised, the buyer loses 100% of the premium he paid at the opening transaction.

### Objectives of Call Buyers

Call buyers are bullish on the underlying stock.

- **Speculation**. The most common reason for buying calls is to speculate with as little cash outlay as possible.

If AFB is trading at $60 ($6,000 per round lot of 100 shares) and an AFB 60 call is trading at 5 ($500 per contract), the investor can buy either the call or the stock. If she buys the stock and its price goes up to $80 a share within six months, she makes a $2,000 profit, a 33% return on the original $6,000 investment. The same movement in the stock will make the AFB 60 call worth at least its intrinsic value of 20 ($2,000). If the investor chooses instead to buy the AFB 60 call for $500, she can realize a $1,500 profit ($2,000 less the $500 premium), a 300% return on her $500 investment.

If the stock price falls, the investor risks the entire $6,000 purchase price. The option owner can also lose her entire investment, but a $500 loss is small in comparison to a $6,000 loss.

- **Deferring a decision**. An investor can buy calls on a stock, effectively locking in a purchase price until the option expires. This allows him to defer his buying decision until near the expiration date of the option.
- **Diversifying holdings**. With limited funds, an investor can buy calls on several stocks and possibly profit from any rise in the option premiums.

### Gain, Loss and Breakeven

- **Maximum gain**. There is no limit on the potential gains available to call owners because there is no limit on a rise in stock price.
- **Maximum loss**. Investors risk losing 100% of the premium paid.
- **Breakeven point**. An investor will break even when the market price is equal to the sum of the strike price and the premium paid.

## Writing Calls

An investor writes a call in the belief that the stock will stay the same or drop in price.

If the market price goes up, the stock can be **called away** from the call writer. That is, the call buyer might make the call writer deliver the stock at the option's strike price when the market price is considerably higher. An investor who writes 1 AFB Apr 40 call at 2 can be called upon to deliver 100 shares of AFB stock to the call buyer any time until the expiration date of the contract. The writer will receive $4,000 if that happens (the strike price of $40 per share times 100 shares), in addition to the premiums she has already been paid.

The potential loss of call writing is unlimited because there is no limit to how high the stock's price can rise.

### Objectives of Call Writers

Call writers are bearish on the underlying stock.

- **Speculating on a decline in a stock**. By writing calls on a stock, an investor can profit if the stock's price falls below the strike price. The investor earns the amount of the premiums, although he takes the risk that the stock's price will increase and the call will be exercised against him.
- **Increasing returns**. By writing calls that are slightly out-of-the-money on a stock he owns (covered call writing), an investor stands a good chance of keeping the premiums he receives without having to deliver the stock. Once the expiration date of an option has passed, the investor is free to write another call against his stock and receive another premium.
- **Locking in a sale price**. If an investor has already made a profit in a stock she holds and is interested in selling it, she can write a call at a strike price that will lock in that profit.

### Gain, Loss and Breakeven

- **Maximum gain**. The writer's gain is limited to the amount of the premium originally received.
- **Maximum loss**. There is no limit on an investor's potential loss.
- **Breakeven point**. An investor will break even when the market price is equal to the sum of the strike price and the premium received.

## Buying Puts

A **put option** is:

- the right to sell
- 100 shares
- of a specific stock
- at a specific price
- for a specific period of time

Put buyers expect that the underlying security will drop in price during the life of the option. If this happens, the investor can exercise the put option and sell the stock at a strike price that is higher than the market price of the stock.

The risk for put buyers is the same as the risk for call buyers. The owner may lose the entire amount invested in the premium.

### Objectives of Put Buyers

Put buyers are bearish on the underlying stock.

- **Speculating on a decline in a stock**. A put buyer can profit from a decline in the price of a stock that he does not own. If the investor does not want to buy and sell a stock, he could sell the put and profit from any increased premium if the price of the stock drops.
- **Deferring a decision**. An investor can buy puts on a stock, effectively locking in a sale price until the option expires. This allows him to defer his selling decision until near the expiration date of the option.

### Gain, Loss and Breakeven

- **Maximum gain**. The investor's maximum gain is the strike price of the option less the premium he paid.
- **Maximum loss**. A put buyer's maximum potential loss is the premium she paid. This will occur at any market price above the strike price.
- **Breakeven point**. The put buyer will break even when the market price is equal to the difference between the strike price and the premium paid.

## Writing Puts

Investors who write puts on stocks are bullish. They assume much greater risks than put buyers.

- Put buyers stand to lose only the premium paid if they are wrong.
- Put writers' losses are potentially far greater than the premiums they receive—they could be forced to pay a high price for a stock that is essentially worthless.

### Objectives of Put Writers

Put writers are bullish on the underlying stock.

- **Generating a large return**. The premium a put buyer is willing to pay for the put option is the return the put writer wants. They hope the puts they sell expire unexercised so they can keep the premiums. Put writers benefit from the diminishing time value of the options they sell.
- **Buying stock below its current price**. Put writers consider short puts a good way to buy stock cheap because the premium received, in effect, reduces the cost of the stock when the stock is put to them in an exercise.

### Gain, Loss and Breakeven

- **Maximum gain**. The put writer's maximum gain is the premium.
- **Maximum loss**. A put seller's maximum loss occurs if the stock price drops to zero. The maximum loss is the exercise price minus the premium received in the opening transaction.
- **Breakeven point**. The put seller will break even when the market price is equal to the difference between the strike price and the premium received.

## Summary of Breakevens, Gains and Losses

You may find it helpful to observe the following patterns:

- The breakeven point is the same for the long and short positions.
- The maximum loss when buying an option is the premium paid.
- The maximum gain when writing an option is the premium received.
- The writer's potential loss is the buyer's potential gain (and vice versa).

# Questions

Use the following information and chart to answer questions 1 through 3. $45 calls on COD have an intrinsic value and are in-the-money by $3. The market value of the COD stock ($48) is greater than the strike or exercise price of the call option by $3. The 45 calls have a $3 intrinsic value regardless of the expiration date. The 45 calls with the December expiration have $1 of time value. Time value is the premium on the option less the option's intrinsic value.

| Option & NY Close | Strike Price | Calls—Last Dec | Jan | Feb |
|---|---|---|---|---|
| XYZ | 45 | 4 | 6 | 7 |
| 48 | 50 | 1 1/2 | 3 1/2 | 4 1/2 |

1. What is the time value of the COD Jan 45 calls?

 ______________________

2. What is the time value of the COD Feb 45 calls?

 ______________________

3. With the market value of COD at 48, the $50 calls are out-of-the-money and have no intrinsic value. The market value is less than the exercise price. What is the time value of the COD 50 calls that expire in each of the following months?

 a. December ______________

 b. January ______________

 c. February ______________

4. A call is in-the-money when the market price of the underlying stock is

 A. equal to the strike price
 B. more than the strike price
 C. less than the strike price
 D. more than it was at the previous day's close

5. COD stock is trading at 25 3/4. COD Jul 25 calls are trading at a premium of 2. What is the intrinsic value of these calls?

 A. $0
 B. $75
 C. $125
 D. $200

6. COD stock is trading at 25 3/4. COD Jul 25 calls are trading at a premium of 2. What is the time value of the Jul 25 calls?

 A. $0
 B. $75
 C. $125
 D. $200

7. John buys 1 MCS Jul 70 call at 2 1/2 when the market is at 71. As time passes, the market price of MCS remains stable at 71. The premium, therefore, will probably

 A. stay the same
 B. go up
 C. go down
 D. exhibit extreme volatility

8. Adam buys 1 MCS 50 call at 4. What is the risk on this position?

 A. Loss of $400
 B. Loss of $500
 C. Loss of $5,000
 D. An unlimited amount

**Figure 2**

**CHICAGO BOARD**

| Option & NY Close | Strike Price | Calls-Last | | | Puts-Last | | |
|---|---|---|---|---|---|---|---|
| | | Jan | Feb | Mar | Jan | Feb | Mar |
| Adm Fam | 40 | 1 3/8 | 3 5/8 | r | 3/16 | 7/8 | 1 1/4 |
| 41 1/8 | 45 | 1/2 | 1 1/2 | 2 1/8 | 3 7/8 | r | 5 1/4 |
| 41 1/8 | 50 | r | 3/8 | 5/8 | s | s | 12 |
| ALFA, Inc. | 30 | 7 7/8 | 9 1/8 | 11 | r | r | 1/8 |
| 37 7/8 | 35 | 3 1/8 | 4 1/2 | 6 3/4 | r | 1/4 | 1/8 |
| 37 7/8 | 40 | 3/4 | 1 5/8 | 3 | 3/4 | 7/8 | r |
| All Swel | 25 | 1/4 | 1 3/8 | 2 | 1/8 | 1 | 1 5/8 |
| 25 1/4 | 30 | r | 1/8 | 7/8 | 3 3/4 | 4 5/8 | 7 |
| Bulln Bar | 20 | r | r | r | r | r | 7/8 |
| 24 | 22 1/2 | 1 | r | r | r | r | r |
| 24 | 25 | 5/16 | 1 | 2 1/4 | r | r | 2 5/8 |

Total call vol 1,240,086 Call open int 3,038,532
Total put vol 105,755 Put open int 941,395

r - Not Traded. s - No Option.

Use the options table in Figure 2 to answer questions 9 through 14.

9. What is the time value of the ALFA 35 calls that expire in

   a. January? ____________________

   b. February? ____________________

   c. March? ____________________

10. What is the maximum gain a writer can earn and the maximum loss a writer can suffer by writing an option on each of the following ALFA 35 calls?

| | | Max. Gain | Max. Loss |
|---|---|---|---|
| a. | Jan | ________ | ________ |
| b. | Feb | ________ | ________ |
| c. | Mar | ________ | ________ |

11. What is the maximum gain a writer of the Mar 45 Adm Fam calls can earn?

    ____________________

12. What is the intrinsic value of the Feb 25 All Swel calls?

    ____________________

13. What is the time value of the Feb 25 All Swel calls?

    ____________________

14. What is the most a writer of the Jan 30 ALFA calls can lose?

    ____________________

In questions 15 through 21, identify each situation by using the following terms:

A. Buying calls
B. Buying puts
C. Writing calls
D. Writing puts

15. ___ John sells 1 ABC Nov 45 put at 2 1/2.

16. ___ Belle receives a $400 premium for 1 Oct XYZ put.

17. ___ John has the obligation to buy 100 shares of ABC at 50 if the option is exercised.

18. ___ Adam has the right to sell 100 shares of MNO at 60 any time between July and October.

19. ___ Karen is long 1 ZYX Apr 30 put.

20. ___ Belle pays $225 for the option to buy 100 shares of ZYX at 25.

21. ___ Karen must sell 100 shares of PQR at 25 on demand; she owns 500 shares of PQR.

22. Which of the following investors are bearish?

I. Buyer of a call
II. Writer of a call
III. Buyer of a put
IV. Writer of a put

A. I and II
B. I and IV
C. II and III
D. III and IV

In questions 23 through 29, indicate whether you think the position would be taken by an investor who is a bull or an investor who is a bear.

23. ___ Long 1 XYZ Jul 60 put

24. ___ Short 1 XYZ Oct 60 put

25. ___ Buy 10 MNO Jul 35 puts

26. ___ Sell 10 ABC Jan calls

27. ___ Write 1 ABC call

28. ___ Buy 1 JKL call

29. ___ Write 10 KLM puts

30. Belle tells her broker that she thinks the price of ABC is going to go up, but currently she does not have the money to buy 100 shares. By which methods could she use options to profit from a rise in the stock's price?

I. Buy calls on ABC
II. Write calls on ABC
III. Buy puts on ABC
IV. Write puts on ABC

A. I and II
B. I and IV
C. II and III
D. II and IV

In questions 31 through 36, refer back to Figure 2 and indicate whether the option is in-, at- or out-of-the-money.

31. ___ Adm Fam Mar 45 puts

32. ___ Adm Fam Feb 50 calls

33. ___ ALFA Jan 40 calls

34. ___ Bulln Bar Mar 20 puts

35. ___ All Swel Feb 25 puts

36. ___ All Swel Jan 25 calls

37. All of the following are objectives of call buyers EXCEPT

A. speculating for profit on the rise in price of stock
B. delaying a decision to buy stock
C. hedging a long stock position against falling prices
D. diversifying holdings

# Answers

1. $3. $6 premium minus $3 intrinsic value equals $3 of time value.

2. $4. $7 premium minus $3 intrinsic value equals $4 of time value.

3. a. $1 1/2.
   b. $3 1/2.
   c. $4 1/2. The option has no intrinsic value; its premium, in each case, is all time value—the more time, the more value. Investors believe the market value has more chance of being greater than the strike price in January or February than in December.

4. **B.** Options are in-the-money when they are worth exercising. Calls are worth exercising when the strike price is less than the market price of the underlying stock.

5. **B.** The intrinsic value of an option is the amount that the option is in-the-money. When COD is trading at 25 3/4, the calls with a strike price of 25 are in-the-money by 3/4, which is $.75 a share, or $75 for all 100 shares of the underlying stock.

6. **C.** The time value is the premium minus the intrinsic value. The premium is 2 (or $200) and the intrinsic value is $75; $200 – $75 = $125.

7. **C.** Remember that options are wasting assets. As the expiration date approaches, the option's time value diminishes. Time, therefore, is against the option owner. In this case, the intrinsic value stays the same because the stock price remains stable at 71. (Intrinsic value for a call is the difference between the strike price and the market price—if the strike price is lower.)

8. **A.** The call buyer's risk is the amount of the premium paid for the option. If the call expires, the owner receives no return on investment.

9. a. $25 (or 1/4). The premium is 3 1/8. The intrinsic value is the market value of the underlying stock (37 7/8) minus the strike price (35), or 2 7/8. The time value is the premium minus the intrinsic value, or 3 1/8 minus 2 7/8, which equals 1/4.
   b. $162.50 (or 1 5/8). Premium (4 1/2) minus intrinsic value (2 7/8) equals time value (1 5/8).
   c. $387.50 (or 3 7/8). Premium (6 3/4) minus intrinsic value (2 7/8) equals time value (3 7/8).

10. a. $312.50; unlimited. The maximum gain a writer can earn is the premium received—in this case, 3 1/8 (or $312.50). The maximum loss a call writer can suffer is unlimited.
    b. $450; unlimited
    c. $675; unlimited

11. 2 1/8. The premium received is the maximum gain. The premium is 2 1/8 per share or $212.50 per contract.

12. $25. The intrinsic value is the market value of the underlying security minus the exercise price of the option: or 25 1/4 minus 25, which is 1/4.

13. 1 1/8. The Feb 25s are trading at 1 3/8, or $137.50 per contract. The intrinsic value as calculated in the preceding question is 1/4 (or $25). Time value is equal to the premium minus the intrinsic value—in this case, 1 3/8 minus 1/4, which is 1 1/8, or $1.125 per share.

14. A call writer has a potentially unlimited loss.

15. **D.** *Writing* is the same as *selling.*

16. **D.** The writer (or seller) receives the premium.

17. **D.** Writers undertake obligations; buyers acquire rights. A put writer is obligated to buy stock from a put owner, who exercises the option.

18. **B.** The put buyer has the right to sell stock to a put writer, who is obligated to buy that stock.

19. **B.** *Buying, owning* and *being long* are synonymous.

20. **A.** Call buyers have the right, or option, to buy stock from call writers.

21. **C.** Call writers must sell stock to call buyers, who exercise their options.

22. **C.** Remember that diagonal positions (those positions that are total opposites—Buys vs. Sells and Puts vs. Calls) are on the same side of the market.

23. Bear. Put owners have the right to sell stock by exercising their options. The lower the market price of the underlying stock, the more you profit from the right to sell stock at a price fixed by the option.

24. Bull. When the market price goes up, put owners will sell stock in the market rather than exercise their options. Put writers, therefore, will not have to take delivery of stock. The options will expire, and the writers will keep the premium received.

25. Bear.

26. Bear. The seller of a call receives a premium and is obligated to sell the underlying stock if a call buyer exercises the option. When the market price of the stock falls, call owners will be more likely to buy at the market price than to exercise their options to purchase stock at the strike price.

27. Bear. *Writing* means the same as *selling*.

28. Bull. Call buyers have the right to buy stock from call writers. The more the market price of the stock rises, the more attractive is the fixed strike price of the option.

29. Bull. *Writing* a put is the same as *shorting* a put.

30. **B.** The bullish strategies are buying calls and writing puts.

31. In-the-money.

32. Out-of-the-money.

33. Out-of-the-money.

34. Out-of-the-money.

35. Out-of-the-money.

36. In-the-money.

37. **C.** The right to purchase more shares of stock does not provide a hedge against falling prices.

# Multiple Option Strategies

## Risks and Rewards of Multiple Option Strategies

The following are a few general rules that apply to positions involving more than one option.

- Option buyers risk 100% of the premium paid.
- Put writers risk paying the exercise price for a worthless stock put to them by an option owner.
- Call writers who have not established an offsetting position take an unlimited risk.
- Multiple option strategies provide at least partial protection in the event the price of the underlying stock does not move in the direction the investor expects.

## Spreads

A spread is the purchase of one option and sale of another option of the same class.

- A call spread is a long call and short call.
- A put spread is a long put and short put.

### Types of Spreads

- **Price spread**. When the two options in a spread differ only in strike price, the investor has established a price spread (or vertical spread).
- **Time spread**. When the two options differ only in expiration date, the investor has established a time (or calendar or horizontal) spread.
- **Diagonal spread**. When the options differ in both price and time, the investor has established a diagonal spread because a line connecting these two options on an options quotation table would appear diagonal.

### Maximum Gains, Losses and Breakeven Points

- A person anticipating a market rise would open a bullish spread. Bulls buy calls and call spreads. Bulls sell puts and put spreads.
- A person anticipating a market decline would open a bearish spread. Bears buy puts and put spreads. Bears sell calls and call spreads.
- An investor whose opening option transactions result in money flowing into his account begins with a net credit. Because opening a credit spread makes the investor money initially, the investor is said to have *sold the spread.*
- An investor whose opening option transactions result in money flowing out of his account begins with a net debit. Because opening a debit spread costs the investor money initially, the investor is said to have *bought the spread.*

**Rules of thumb for risk and reward on spreads**. Following are the rules that you need to remember to determine gains, losses and breakeven points for spreads.

- Credit spreads
  - Maximum gain: the initial credit
  - Maximum loss: the difference between the strike prices minus the credit
- Debit spreads
  - Maximum gain: the difference between the strike prices minus the debit
  - Maximum loss: the initial debit
- Breakeven points
  - Call spreads: CAL—Calls Add to the Lower
  - Put spreads: PSH—Puts Subtract from the Higher

### Debit Call Spreads

**Investor objectives**. When a bullish investor establishes a debit call spread, she buys the call with the low strike price and sells the call with the high strike price.

A bullish investor buys a call or call spread because she expects that its net market value will increase along with the underlying stock's price. If it does, she can exercise the long option of the spread and buy stock below the market price. If the short option is exercised against her, she will be able to deliver the stock she just bought and keep the difference between the strike prices.

- **Maximum gain.** The investor will realize her maximum gain any time the stock's market price is at or above the strike price of the higher option. The maximum gain is the difference between the two prices, minus the net premium.
- **Maximum loss.** If the stock's price falls to or below the strike price of the lower option, both calls will expire worthless. The maximum loss on any debit spread is the net premium.
- **Breakeven.** Breakeven occurs when the stock's market price is above the lower strike price by the amount of the net premium. The breakeven point on a call spread is the lower strike price plus the net premium. (Remember: **C**alls **A**dd to the **L**ower—**CAL**.)

### Debit Put Spreads

**Investor objectives.** A bearish investor buys a put or put spread because he expects that the spread's net market value will increase as the underlying stock's price decreases.

- **Maximum gain.** The investor will realize his maximum gain any time the stock's market price is at or below the strike price of the lower option. The maximum gain is the difference between the two prices, minus the net premium.
- **Maximum loss.** If the stock's price rises to or above the strike price of the higher option, both puts will expire worthless. The maximum loss on a debit spread is the net premium.
- **Breakeven.** Breakeven occurs when the stock's market price is below the higher strike price by the amount of the net premium. The breakeven point on a put spread is the higher strike price minus the net premium. (Remember: **P**uts **S**ubtract from the **H**igher—**PSH**.)

### Credit Call Spreads

**Investor objectives.** Bearish investors sell calls and call spreads because they expect the underlying stock's price to go down.

- **Maximum gain.** The maximum gain on a credit call spread is the net premium. The maximum gain will occur when the stock price is at or below the *lower* strike price.
- **Maximum loss.** The maximum loss on a credit call spread is the difference between strike prices less the net premium. This occurs when the stock's price is at or above the higher strike price.
- **Breakeven.** The breakeven point will be the lower strike price plus the net premium. (Remember: **C**alls **A**dd to the **L**ower—**CAL**.)

### Credit Put Spreads

**Investor objectives.** Bullish investors sell puts and put spreads because they expect the stock's price to go up.

- **Maximum gain.** The maximum gain on a credit put spread is the net premium. This occurs when the stock price is at or above the higher strike price.
- **Maximum loss.** The maximum loss on a credit put spread is the difference between strike prices minus the net premium. This occurs when the stock's market price is at or below the lower strike price.
- **Breakeven.** The breakeven point on a put spread is the higher strike price minus the net premium. (Remember: **P**uts **S**ubtract from the **H**igher—**PSH**.)

### Spread Between Premiums

- **Credit spreads.** Investors with credit spreads want the spread between premiums to narrow. The spread between the premiums of two options *narrows* if both premiums decrease, which will happen if both options become worthless. Investors in credit spreads keep the credit received initially if the options become worthless.
- **Debit spreads.** Investors with debit spreads want the spread between premiums to *widen*. The widest the spread will ever be on the expiration date is the same as the difference between the two strike prices.

## Straddles and Combinations

### Long Straddles

**Investor objectives.** A long straddle is the purchase of a call and a put on the same stock with the same strike price and expiration date. Straddles are used by investors who think a stock's price is going to be volatile, but are not sure which direction the price will take.

- **Maximum gain.** The maximum gain for a long straddle is the maximum gain for the call.
- **Maximum loss.** The maximum loss is the entire premium if the options expire at-the-money.
- **Breakeven.** A long straddle breaks even when the stock price is equal to the strike price plus or minus the net debit.

### Short Straddles

**Investor objectives.** A short straddle is the sale of a call and a put on the same stock with the same strike price and expiration date. The straddle writer believes the stock price will not change much and will *not* move outside the breakeven points.

- **Maximum gain.** The maximum potential gain for a short straddle is the initial premiums received.
- **Maximum loss.** The maximum loss for a short straddle is the maximum loss for the short call.
- **Breakeven.** A short straddle breaks even when the stock price is equal to the strike price plus or minus the net credit.

### Long Combinations

A long combination is the purchase of a call and a put on the same stock at different strike prices or expirations. Long combinations are usually cheaper to establish than long straddles because most long combinations are established when both contracts are out-of-the-money.

As an example, when AFB is at $66, an investor could purchase 1 AFB Apr 70 call at 3 and 1 AFB Apr 65 put at 2 to create a long combination. The 70 call is 4 points out-of-the-money, and the 65 put is 1 point out-of-the-money. The combined premiums of $500 reflect the time value of the two options because neither has any intrinsic value at this point.

- **Maximum gain.** The maximum gain is the maximum potential gain of the call.
- **Maximum loss.** The customer will lose money if the stock price remains between 65 and 70. The maximum loss on a long combination is the premiums paid.
- **Breakeven.** The breakeven points for a long combination are the call strike price plus the total premiums, and the put strike price minus the total premiums.

### Short Combinations

A short combination is the sale of a call and a put on the same stock at different strike prices or expirations. Short combinations are used when no movement is expected in the market.

- **Maximum gain.** The writer collects the premiums and keeps them if both sides expire unexercised.
- **Maximum loss.** The maximum loss is the unlimited loss potential of the short call.

- **Breakeven.** The breakeven points for a short combination are the call strike price plus the total premiums, and the put strike price minus the total premiums.

## Using Options to Protect a Position

### Long Stock and Short Calls (Covered Call Writing)

**Objectives of covered call writers.** Covered call writers reduce the downside risk of long stock positions by the dollars they receive in premiums from selling the call, and the long stock position gives the call writer something to deliver if the call is exercised against him.

- **Rate of return.** If the buyer of the call option never exercises the call against the covered call writer, the writer will never have to deliver stock at the exercise price. He will keep any premium received, which will increase his return on his stock position.
- **Partial protection.** An investor long a stock can write calls to offset some of the downside risks of the stock with the premiums she receives for the options.

### Long Stock and Long Puts

- **Insurance to hedge against price declines.** If an investor owns stock, she can hedge her downside risk by purchasing puts at (or close to) the purchase price. By doing so, the investor has the option to sell the stock she holds long by exercising the puts if the market price of the stock ever goes below the strike price. No matter how far the stock declines, she can sell it for the exercise price of the puts.

### Short Stock and Long Calls

- **Insurance to hedge a short stock position.** "Shorting" stock means selling stock that the investor does not own, but has borrowed in order to sell and must eventually replace. Because there is no limit on how high the price can go, there is no limit on the short seller's loss potential. Because of the risk, some investors hedge their short stock positions by purchasing call options. Purchasing a call limits an investor's risk to the difference between the strike price of the call (plus the premium) and the price he received for the borrowed stock. The purchase of the call reduces the overall profit potential on the short position by the amount of the premium.

### Short Stock and Short Puts

A customer with a short stock position may partially hedge the short position by selling short a put at the same price. If the stock rises in value, the investor is partially protected by the amount of money received in premium.

### Ratio Call Writing

If the owner of 100 shares of AFB writes 2 AFB Jul 30 calls at 3 against the stock, the customer has established one covered position and one uncovered position. The call options were written on a 2-to-1 (2:1) ratio against the stock. If 3 calls were written against 100 shares, the ratio would be 3 to 1 (3:1). Ratio writing is used to increase premium income by the owner of the stock. The ratio writer is subject to the same risks and gains as a covered writer on the covered position and as a naked writer on the uncovered position(s). Ratio writing is also known as **variable hedging**.

# Questions

In questions 1 through 6, identify the positions described by indicating one of the following terms.

A. Price spread
B. Long straddle
C. Time spread
D. Short straddle
E. Diagonal spread
F. Combination

1. ___ Buy 1 QRS May 40 call; sell 1 QRS May 50 call.

2. ___ Buy 1 QRS May 40 call; buy 1 QRS May 40 put.

3. ___ Buy 1 QRS Aug 40 call; sell 1 QRS Dec 40 call.

4. ___ Buy 1 DOH May 30 call; buy 1 DOH Jul 40 put.

5. ___ Write 1 DOH Jan 30 call; write 1 DOH Jan 40 put.

6. ___ Buy 1 DOH Mar 35 call; write 1 DOH Jun 45 call.

7. Which two of the following are spreads?

   I. Long 1 DOH May 40 call; short 1 DOH May 50 call
   II. Long 1 DOH May 40 call; long 1 DOH May 50 call
   III. Long 1 DOH Aug 40 call; short 1 DOH May 40 call
   IV. Long 1 DOH Aug 40 call; short 1 DOH Aug 50 put

   A. I and II
   B. I and III
   C. II and III
   D. II and IV

8. Angus Bullwether sells an DOH Mar 35 call. To establish a straddle, he would

   A. sell an DOH Mar 35 call
   B. buy an DOH Mar 35 put
   C. sell an DOH Mar 35 put
   D. buy an DOH Mar 40 call

9. Angus buys 1 DOH Nov 70 put and sells 1 DOH Nov 60 put when DOH is selling for 65. This position is a

   A. bull spread
   B. bear spread
   C. combination
   D. straddle

10. ACM issues a news release that your customer believes will strongly affect the market price of ACM stock. Your customer is not, however, sure whether the effect will be positive or negative. In this situation, which of the following strategies would be best?

    A. Buy a call
    B. Write a call
    C. Write a straddle
    D. Buy a straddle

11. All of the following are credit spreads EXCEPT to

    A. write 1 Nov 35 put and buy 1 Nov 30 put
    B. buy 1 Apr 40 call and write 1 Apr 30 call
    C. buy 1 Jul 50 call and write 1 Jul 60 call
    D. buy 1 Jan 50 put and write 1 Jan 60 put

In questions 12 through 19, identify which are bull spreads and which are bear spreads.

12. Write 1 Nov 35 put; buy 1 Nov 30 put.

    ______________________

13. Buy 1 Jan 70 call; write 1 Jan 75 call.

    ______________________

14. Write 1 Apr 30 call; buy 1 Apr 40 call.

_______________

15. Write 1 Dec 45 put; buy 1 Dec 60 put.

_______________

16. Buy 1 Jul 50 call; write 1 Jul 60 call.

_______________

17. Buy 1 Dec 45 put; write 1 Dec 40 put.

_______________

18. Write 1 Jan 60 put; buy 1 Jan 50 put.

_______________

19. Buy 1 May 25 put; write 1 May 20 put.

_______________

20. In which of the following cases would the investor want the spread to widen?

    I. Buy 1 May 30 put; write 1 May 25 put.
    II. Write 1 Apr 45 put; buy 1 Apr 55 put.
    III. Buy 1 Nov 65 put; write 1 Nov 75 put.
    IV. Buy 1 Jan 40 call; write 1 Jan 30 call.

    A. I and II
    B. I and IV
    C. II and III
    D. III and IV

21. Belle Charolais purchases 2 QRS Jul 30 calls at 2 and 2 QRS Jul 30 puts at 2 1/2. She will break even when the price of the underlying stock is

    I. 25 1/2
    II. 27 1/2
    III. 32
    IV. 34 1/2

    A. I and IV
    B. II and III
    C. III
    D. IV

In questions 22 through 25, calculate the breakeven points on each position.

22. Buy 1 QRS Jan 40 call at 2 3/8; write 1 QRS Jan 45 call at 7/8.

_______________

23. Buy 1 DOH Apr 30 put at 3 3/8; write 1 DOH Apr 35 put at 5 7/8.

_______________

24. Write 1 MCS Dec 50 call at 5 1/4; buy 1 MCS Dec 55 call at 2.

_______________

25. Write 2 DWQ Apr 30 calls at 2 1/4; write 2 DWQ Apr 30 puts at 2 1/8.

_______________

Use the following information to answer questions 26 through 28. Karen Kodiak writes 1 QRS Apr 50 call at 4 and buys 1 QRS Apr 40 call at 8 when QRS is trading at 47.

26. If both calls expire unexercised, what will be Karen's gain or loss?

    A. $400 loss
    B. $600 gain
    C. $700 loss
    D. $1,100 gain

27. Excluding commissions, the breakeven point on Karen's position is

    A. 40
    B. 44
    C. 46
    D. 50

28. What will Karen's profit be if the underlying stock is trading at $52 at expiration?

    A. $200
    B. $400
    C. $600
    D. $800

In questions 29 through 32, indicate the maximum possible gain and the maximum possible loss for each spread.

29. Write 1 COD Oct 30 call at 3 3/16; buy 1 COD Oct 40 call at 1/16.

    Max. gain: ____________________

    Max. loss: ____________________

30. Buy 1 COD Jan 40 put at 6 1/2; write 1 COD Jan 30 put at 2 1/8.

    Max. gain: ____________________

    Max. loss: ____________________

31. Buy 1 COD Oct 80 call at 8; write 1 COD Oct 90 call at 2 3/4.

    Max. gain: ____________________

    Max. loss: ____________________

32. Write 1 COD Jan 130 call at 26 3/4; buy 1 COD Jan 140 call at 19 1/2.

    Max. gain: ____________________

    Max. loss: ____________________

Use the following information to answer questions 33 and 34. Adam writes an Apr 60 call on DWQ stock at 7 and covers the option by purchasing 100 shares of the underlying stock at $55 per share.

33. What is the initial cost of this covered call?

    ____________________

34. What is the breakeven point on Adam's position?

    ____________________

35. What is the breakeven point if you buy 100 TIP at 53 and sell 1 TIP 50 call for 7 1/2?

    ____________________

36. What is the breakeven point if you buy 100 MTN at 58 1/4 and sell 1 MTN 60 call at 6 1/2?

    ____________________

Use the following information to answer questions 37 through 41. An investor buys 100 MTN at 58 1/4 and sells 1 MTN 55 call for 7.

37. What is the price received when selling the stock at the exercise price?

______________________________

38. What are the dollar proceeds from the call?

______________________________

39. What would be the sale proceeds from the sale of the stock if the option is exercised?

______________________________

40. What was the cost of the stock?

______________________________

41. What is the maximum profit potential?

______________________________

42. Adam is short 100 shares of MTN and wants a hedge against a rise in the market price of the stock. What should be his strategy?

______________________________

43. Angus buys 500 shares of MTN. What strategy would provide insurance against a drop in the stock's market value?

______________________________

In questions 44 through 47, identify the option strategy that might help the investor achieve the specified goal.

A. Sell covered calls.
B. Sell naked calls.
C. Sell puts.

44. ___ Karen thinks GHI is going to drop sharply in price. What could she do if she wants to make a speculative profit on that drop, and is willing to take considerable risk?

45. ___ Angus owns 100 shares of GHI stock. He is worried that the price may drop but does not want to sell his stock. How could he partially ensure against falling market prices?

46. ___ Belle owns a large block of GHI. How could she generate extra income from her stock?

47. ___ How could Karen buy GHI common stock at a price below the market?

Use the following information to answer questions 48 through 50. Max Leveridge is long 100 shares of This Can't Be Sushi (TCB) at 51. He establishes a short straddle on TCB with a strike price of 50. The premium on the call is 3 1/4 and the premium on the put is 2 1/4.

48. What is Max's maximum gain on the position?

A. 2 1/4
B. 3 1/4
C. 5 1/2
D. 4 1/2

49. What is Max's maximum loss on the position?

    A. 45 1/2
    B. 47 3/4
    C. 51
    D. 95 1/2

50. What is Max's breakeven point on the position?

    A. 47 3/4
    B. 50 1/4
    C. 55 1/2
    D. 56 1/2

51. Which of the following is the riskiest options position?

    A. Covered call writing
    B. Uncovered call writing
    C. Writing puts
    D. Buying puts

52. All of the following are suitable objectives for a covered call writer EXCEPT

    A. hedging a long stock position
    B. increasing return on a long stock position
    C. speculating that a stock will not rise in price
    D. buying stock below the market

# Answers

1. **A.** The most common spread, and the one you're most likely to see on the Series 7 exam, is the price spread, in which the two options have the same expiration date but different exercise prices.

2. **B.** The investor is long a call and long a put with the same strike price and expiration date; this is a long straddle.

3. **C.** Also called a *horizontal* or *calendar* spread, a time spread involves two options with different expiration dates.

4. **F.** A combination is similar to a straddle in that the investor buys or sells a call and a put. With a combination, however, the strike prices, expiration dates or both are different.

5. **F.** The investor is selling a call and a put with different strike prices.

6. **E.** Both the expiration date and the price are different.

7. **B.** Choices I and III fit the definition of a call spread because each includes one long and one short option of the same type with either different strike prices (choice I) or different expiration dates (choice III). Choice II involves options of the same type but both are long. Choice IV involves options of different types.

8. **C.** Straddles involve options of different types, but either both options must be long or both must be short. They must have the same expiration date and strike price.

9. **B.** This put spread is established at a debit, because the investor pays more for the 70 put than he receives for the 60 put. Bears buy puts and put spreads.

10. **D.** If the stock goes either up or down sharply, your customer will profit from owning a straddle.

11. **C.** The lower the strike price, the more expensive the call option. The higher the strike price, the more expensive the put option. Because the investor has purchased the more expensive option with the lower strike price, this is a debit spread.

12. Bull spread. This is a put credit spread. The investor receives more for the Nov 35 put than she pays for the Nov 30 put. Bulls sell put spreads. The put with the higher strike price is more likely to be in-the-money as the market falls.

13. Bull spread. This is a call debit spread. Bulls buy calls. A lower strike price call is more likely to be in-the-money as the market rises.

14. Bear spread. This is a call credit spread. Bears sell calls.

15. Bear spread. This is a put debit spread. Bears buy puts. The 60 put is worth more because it has a higher strike price.

16. Bull spread. This is a call debit spread. Bulls buy calls.

17. Bear spread. This is a put debit spread. Bears buy puts.

18. Bull spread. This is a put credit spread. Bulls sell puts.

19. Bear spread. This is a put debit spread. Bears buy puts.

20. **A.** Choices I and II are debit spreads. An investor wants a debit spread to widen. As the distance between the premiums increases, the investor's potential profit also increases. This is because the investor intends to sell the option with the higher premium and buy back the option with the lower premium and, therefore, wants the selling price of one to be as much above the buying price of the other as possible.

21. **A.** Belle buys calls and puts with the same strike price and expiration date, so the position is a straddle. Straddles have two breakeven points—the strike price plus and minus the sum of the two premiums.

22. 41 1/2. Because this is a call spread, you find the breakeven point by adding the initial debit of 1 1/2 to the lower strike price: 40 + 1 1/2 = 41 1/2.

23. 32 1/2. This is a put spread established at a credit of 2 1/2. To find the breakeven point on a put spread, subtract the initial credit or debit from the higher strike price. (PSH: Puts Subtract from Higher). In this case, subtract the credit of 2 1/2 from the higher strike price of 35.

24. 53 1/4. To find the breakeven point on this call credit spread, add the initial credit of 3 1/4 to the lower strike price of 50.

25. 25 5/8, 34 3/8. A straddle, whether long or short, has two breakeven points: the strike price plus and minus the sum of the premiums paid or received. In this case, the sum of the premiums received for the two short options is 4 3/8, and the strike price is 30. At any stock price greater than 34 3/8 or less than 25 5/8, the investor who wrote this straddle will lose money.

26. **A.** If both options expire unexercised, Karen will lose her original investment in the position—a $400 debit derived from buying a call for $800 and selling one for $400.

27. **B.** Remember CAL: add the original debit of 4 to the lower strike price of 40 to find the breakeven point of 44.

28. **C.** At any stock price equal to or greater than the higher strike price of 50, Karen realizes her maximum gain—the difference between the strike prices minus the initial debit: 10 – 4 = 6, or $600 on the 100 shares in the contract.

29. Max. gain: $312.50. The maximum potential gain on a credit spread is the initial credit.

Max. loss: $687.50. The maximum potential loss on a credit spread is the difference between the strike prices minus the initial credit: 10 – 3 1/8 = 6 7/8; 6 7/8 × 100 shares = $687.50.

30. Max. gain: $562.50. The maximum gain on a debit spread is the difference between the strike prices minus the initial debit: 10 – 4 3/8 = 5 5/8; 5 5/8 × 100 shares = $562.50.

Max. loss: $437.50. The maximum loss on a debit spread is the initial debit.

31. Max. gain: $475. The maximum gain on a debit spread is the difference between the strike prices minus the initial debit: 10 – 5 1/4 = 4 3/4; 4 3/4 × 100 shares = $475.

Max. loss: $525. The maximum loss on a debit spread is the initial debit.

32. Max. gain: $725. The maximum gain on a credit spread is the initial credit received.

Max. loss: $275. The maximum loss on a credit spread is the difference between the strike prices minus the initial credit: 10 – 7 1/4 = 2 3/4; 2 3/4 × 100 shares = $275.

33. $4,800. The total debit for the position is $4,800. Adam pays $55 a share for 100 shares ($5,500) and receives $700 for writing the call: $5,500 – $700 = $4,800.

34. Adam pays $4,800 for his position—equivalent to $48 per share for the stock. Therefore, when the stock is trading for $48, he can sell it for $4,800 and break even. At that price, the call expires worthless. If the stock price rises to more than 60, the call will be in-the-money. Even if Adam's call is exercised, however, he will receive $60 per share ($6,000 for 100 shares) and make money on his position.

35. 45 1/2. 53 – 7 1/2 = 45 1/2. He paid 53 for the stock and offset the cost by selling a call for 7 1/2.

36. 51 3/4. 58 1/4 – 6 1/2 = 51 3/4.

37. $5,500. Remember, the call is exercisable at 55.

38. $700. The premium of $7 per share on a 100-share contract yields $700 to the writer.

39. $6,200. The strike price of 55 plus the premium of 7, times 100 shares.

40. $5,825. This is $58.25 per share.

41. $375. The stock was purchased at 58 1/4. If the market goes up, the call will be exercised. The stock will be delivered at the exercise price of $55 plus the premium received on the call, for sale proceeds of $62 per share. The net profit, therefore, will be 3 3/4 per share (62 – 58 1/4).

42. Buy calls. Short sellers are bearish. They have borrowed and sold stock; they must replace the borrowed shares. If they need to buy those shares in the market, they want the market price to fall, not rise. A call option provides insurance against a rising market price because it gives the owner the right to buy stock at the predetermined exercise price.

43. Buy puts or sell calls. Puts lock in a selling price for the underlying stock. Angus knows, therefore, that he can always sell his stock at the exercise price of the put, no matter how far the market may drop. The bearish put position is a hedge against losses on the bullish stock position. Selling calls would provide only a partial hedge against falling prices, to the amount of the premium received for writing the call.

44. **B.** Sell naked calls. Because Karen is willing to take a risk, she can write naked calls. If the stock price drops, she will keep the premium. If it does not drop, she risks having to buy stock at a high market price to deliver at the exercise price.

45. **A.** Sell covered calls. The covered call writer buys stock and, at the same time, writes a call on it. If the stock price drops, the investor will keep the option premium; that amount of money will compensate, to a degree, for loss on the long stock position.

46. **A.** Sell covered calls. The premiums received for writing the calls increase the yield from the position.

47. **C.** Sell puts. If a writer sells a put with an exercise price near the current market price and if the stock is put to writer, the effective cost of the stock is the strike price minus the premium. That effective cost may be less than the market price at the time the put is sold.

48. **D.** When trying to determine the maximum gain, maximum loss or breakeven, it is the underlying stock position (the long-term investment) that counts. In order to determine Max's profit, loss or breakeven, you have to make the assumption that he will close out his position at that point. This is the easiest way to calculate the net value of all account debits and credits.

In this problem, we are dealing initially with 100 shares of stock purchased at 51, a 50 call sold at 3 1/4 and a 50 put sold at 2 1/4. Our starting position, then, is a net debit of 51 and a net credit of 5 1/2. Now we must determine what will happen as the stock price moves up or down.

At any stock price exceeding 50, the put will expire worthless and the call will be exercised. If the call is exercised at 50, Max will lose $100 on the stock (cost basis of 51 minus the selling price of 50) but will still realize a net gain of $450 (net credit of 5 1/2 minus the 1-point loss). No matter how high the stock's price rises, the maximum gain on this position is $450.

49. **D.** If the stock falls to less than 50, the call will expire worthless but the put will be exercised and Max will have to buy another 100 shares. To determine his loss if this happens, assume that Max will sell the 100 shares put to him at the market, and then net that loss first against the credit he received for selling the straddle and then against his cost basis in the original 100-share investment.

As an example, assume that TCB goes to 45. The call will expire, and the put will be exercised against Max at 50. Max will have to buy the 100 shares at 50 and then sell those shares at 45, taking a 5-point loss on the stock. The net credit he received for the straddle (5 1/2) will offset the loss on the stock put to him, leaving him with a 1/2-point credit. This 1/2-point credit is then applied against the 6-point loss he faces on his original 100 shares (cost basis of 51 minus the 45 market value). At a market price of 45, Max realizes a 5 1/2-point loss.

If TCB goes to 0, Max will be put the 100 shares at 50 and be unable to sell them at 0, taking a 50-point loss on the stock. The net credit he received for the straddle (5 1/2) will only slightly offset the loss on the stock put to him, leaving him with a 44 1/2-point loss. This 44 1/2-point loss is then added to the 51-point loss he faces on his original 100 shares (cost basis of 51 minus the 0 market value). At a market price of 0, Max's maximum loss is 95 1/2 points.

50. **A.** In this breakeven problem, Max must be concerned not only with the possible loss on his long TCB position, but also on a second 100 shares of stock that will be put to him if the price of the stock drops to less than 50. To determine Max's breakeven, the first step is to calculate the average cost basis of these two positions. To do this we take the cost basis of his long stock (he purchased it at 51), add the cost basis of the stock that will be put to him (at a strike price of 50) and then divide that number by two to get his average cost basis. 51 + 50 = 101; 101 ÷ 2 = 50 1/2.

The next step is to apply the net premium against the two stock positions in the same way. Max's net premium for writing this straddle is 5 1/2 (3 1/4 for the call and 2 1/4 for the put). Because we are dealing with two stock positions, this premium must cover potential losses on both. To calculate the amount of protection this net premium offers, divide the premium by 2. 5 1/2 ÷ 2 = 2 3/4. Each position has downside protection of 2 3/4 points.

Finally, we can establish the breakeven for the entire strategy by subtracting the average downside protection (2 3/4 points) from the average cost basis for the stock (50 1/2). 50 1/2 – 2 3/4 = 47 3/4. Max's breakeven will occur at a stock price of 47 3/4.

To prove this, assume the stock drops to 47 3/4. Max would have a loss of 3 1/4 points on his long stock position (51 – 47 3/4). In addition, he is now obligated to buy another 100 shares at $50 per share and sell it at 47 3/4, a loss of 2 1/4. His total loss is 5 1/2 points (3 1/4 + 2 1/4). This loss is exactly covered by the 5 1/2 points in premiums he received for writing the straddle.

Here is a summary of the steps we took to find Max's breakeven point:

1. Find the average cost basis: (51 + 50) ÷ 2 = 50 1/2.
2. Find the average premium protection: 5 1/2 ÷ 2 = 2 3/4.
3. Subtract the average protection from the average cost basis: 50 1/2 – 2 3/4 = 47 3/4.

51. **B.** Uncovered call writing is very risky and can produce potentially unlimited losses.

52. **D.** A covered call writer has taken on the obligation to sell stock if the call is exercised, not to buy stock.

# Introduction to Nonequity Options

## Index Options

**Broad-based indexes.** Broad-based indexes are designed to reflect the movement of the whole market. Options are available on, among others, the:

- S&P 100 Index (ticker symbol OEX);
- S&P 500 Index (ticker symbol SPX);
- AMEX Major Market Index (ticker symbol XMI); and
- *Value Line* Index.

**Narrow-based indexes.** Narrow-based indexes track the movements of market segments, such as a group of stocks in one industry or a specific type of investment. Narrow-based indexes include the Technology Index and the Gold/Silver Index.

**Options on indexes.** Index options make it possible for investors to profit from the swings in the market or to hedge against losses that market movement can cause in individual stock positions.

**Multiplier.** Each index has been assigned a multiplier that is used to convert the listed strike prices and the premiums into dollars. For the S&P 100 Index (OEX), the multiplier is 100. An OEX Jun 380 call at 12 is worth $38,000 (380 × 100) and would cost an investor a premium of $1,200.

**Call options.** A call on an index gives its owner:

- the right to receive,
- in cash,
- the option's intrinsic value (the amount by which the call's strike price is below the index's market value),
- at an assigned time on the day of exercise.

Assume that the value of the OEX is 386.24 at the close of today's trading. The May 380 calls give call owners the right to receive the difference between 380 and 386.24, the value at the close. Because of the multiplier of 100, that amounts to $624. The writer of a call, if the option were exercised today, would owe that amount.

**Put options.** A put on an index gives its owner:

- the right to receive,
- in cash,
- the option's intrinsic value (the amount by which the put's strike price is above the index's market value),
- at the close on the day of exercise.

An OEX May 390 put, if exercised during a day when the market closed at 386.24, for example, would bring in $376 for its owner (390 – 386.24 = 3.76; 3.76 × 100 = $376). The writer of the option is obligated to pay $376.

**Exercise settlement.** Index option writers deliver cash. In the preceding example, the writer of the OEX 390 put would have delivered $376 in cash.

The amount that a writer must pay if exercised is based on the closing value for the S&P 100 that day, not on the value at the time of exercise. Settlement occurs one business day after exercise.

**Index option strategies.** An investor can:

- profit by speculating correctly on an upturn in the market;
- profit by speculating correctly on a downturn in the market; or
- hedge against changes in the market.

**Position and exercise limits.** For index options the:

- position limit is 25,000 contracts on the same side of the market; and
- exercise limit is 15,000 contracts in five days on the same side of the market.

### Capped Index Options

In a capped index option, a "capped" price set by the exchange triggers exercise of the option.

- The **cap interval** is set at 30 points above the strike price for a call and 30 points below the strike price for a put.
  - If the OEX index is currently 359.68, capped calls on the OEX would be listed

with a strike price of 360 and a capped price of 390, while capped puts would be listed with a strike price of 360 and a capped price of 330.

- A capped index option is exercised automatically when the index hits or goes through the capped price.
- Capped index options on both the S&P 100 and the S&P 500 are traded on the CBOE.

## Interest Rate Options

Interest rate options allow investors to profit from fluctuations in interest rates (and debt security prices) and to hedge the risks created by those fluctuations.

**Investor objectives.** Investors in interest rate options hope to:

- profit from changes in the prices of debt securities (caused by fluctuations in interest rates); or
- hedge existing portfolios of debt securities against price declines caused by increased interest rates.

The typical investor tends to be an institution rather than an individual.

Options on debt securities respond to changes in the price of the underlying security. A decrease in the interest paid on newly issued bonds will cause the prices of existing bonds that pay higher interest rates to increase. An increase in the interest paid on newly issued bonds will cause the prices of existing bonds that pay lower interest rates to decrease.

### Treasury Bills

- The underlying instrument for calls and puts on T bills is the most current 13-week (91-day) Treasury bill.
- The U.S. Treasury auctions 13-week T bills once a week.
- One T bill option represents $1 million worth of some future issue of 13-week bill.
- The deliverable bills are those issued during the week of settlement, not the one current when the option is written.
- To turn a T bill premium quote into a dollar figure, multiply it by $2,500.
  - The premium is an annualized percentage of the face value, $1 million. Although 1% of $1 million is $10,000, the T bill's life span is 13 weeks, just one-fourth of a 52-week year. Annualized, therefore, each point equals $2,500 (one-fourth of $10,000). An investor interested in purchasing a T bill call quoted at a premium of .5 could expect to pay $1,250.

### Treasury Notes and Bonds

- An option on either a note or a bond represents a specific underlying security with a face value of $100,000.
- Upon exercise, the owner of a put or the writer of a call must deliver a note or bond from that particular issue.
- Strike prices for notes and bonds are quoted at a percentage of face value.
  - For example, a call on an 8 7/8% bond has a strike price of 102. The owner of the call can exercise the option to purchase the bond for 102% of face value, which is $102,000 (plus accrued interest).
- One point of premium equals 1% of the note's or bond's face value, or $1,000.
  - A point of premium represents 1% of the face value, which equals $1,000. Each fraction of a point represents 1/32nd of $1,000, which equals $31.25. A premium of 1:30, therefore, represents a dollar price of $1,000 plus 30 times $31.25, which equals $1,937.50.

**Hedging with long call positions.** An investor who fears that long-term bond interest rates will head down and thus wants to lock in high current rates can purchase calls.

**Hedging with long put positions.** As a hedge against rising interest rates (and falling note prices), investors can buy puts.

### Yield-based Options

Yield-based options trade on the CBOE and are available on the most recently issued Treasury debt securities, namely:

- 13-week Treasury bill
- 5-year and 10-year Treasury note
- 30-year Treasury bond

Investors use yield-based options:

- to speculate on the direction of interest rates; or
- to hedge against interest rate risk.

**Characteristics.** Yield-based options have the following characteristics:

- a contract size multiplier of $100 (for example, a premium of 3 1/8 equals $312.50);
- settlement in cash rather than in delivery of the underlying security;
- a strike price that reflects the annualized yield to maturity of the underlying security (for example, a strike price of 65 is equal to a yield of 6.5% times a multiplier of 10); and
- an "exercise settlement value," meaning the current yield on the underlying security, multiplied by 10.

Whereas *prices* of debt securities have an *inverse* relationship to interest rates, their *yields* have a *direct* relationship. When interest rates go up, yields go up. Thus, when an investor believes interest rates are going up, she might buy calls on the yields of debt securities.

## Foreign Currency Options

**Currency exchange.** Investors trade foreign currency options (FCOs) for two reasons:

- they hope to profit from fluctuating exchange rates; and
- they want to hedge against the risks arising from fluctuating exchange rates.

**Currency risk.** The risk in monetary exchange arises from fluctuations in the exchange rate.

**Characteristics.** Foreign currency options have the following characteristics:

- The Philadelphia Stock Exchange facilitates the trading of options on foreign currencies.
- Underlying each FCO is an arbitrary amount of foreign money as set by the exchange.
- The strike price of the option is set at a certain amount of U.S. money.
- Each option contract represents the right to buy or sell the foreign currency for the specified amount of U.S. money.
- The owner of an FCO can lock in a certain exchange rate for a certain time.

**Underlying currencies.** Options are available on several foreign currencies, including British pounds, Canadian dollars, German marks, French francs, Japanese yen and Swiss francs.

**Price of the underlying currency.** Exchange rates are quoted in U.S. cents per unit of the underlying currency, with two exceptions: French francs trade in 1/10ths of a cent per franc; Japanese yen trade in 1/100ths of a cent per yen.

**Contract sizes.** Each FCO contract represents a specified number of units of the underlying foreign currency. For example, buying one call on British pounds represents the right to buy 31,250 British pounds at the specified exchange rate.

**Expiration date and last trading day.** All FCOs expire on the Friday preceding the third Wednesday of the month. Trading ceases at 1:30 pm EST on the expiration date.

**Position and exercise limits.** On the PHLX, position and exercise limits are 100,000 contracts on the same side of the market.

### Exercise Settlement

- **American system.** The PHLX uses the American exercise system (**American style**), which allows owners to exercise their options at any time up to and including the last business day before expiration. When an FCO is exercised, the owner of the put or writer of the call must deliver the currency of the country of origin.

- **European system**. The European exercise system (**European style**), by contrast, allows the option owner to exercise the option only during a specified period prior to its expiration (typically from one to five business days).

# Questions

1. The OEX and Major Market Indexes are examples of which of the following?

   A. Broad-based indexes
   B. Narrow-based indexes

Use the following information to answer questions 2 and 3. On November 4th, Angus Bullwether writes an OEX Jun 220 put at 6.

2. The maximum potential gain on Angus's position is

   ______________________________

3. Angus will achieve the maximum gain on his position if, on the expiration date, the OEX closes at what price?

   ______________________________

4. Karen Kodiak writes an XMI 450 call at 13. The market closes that day at 462.34. Karen will break even on her short call if, on the expiration date, the index closes at which of the following prices?

   A. 437
   B. 450
   C. 462.34
   D. 463

Use the following information to answer questions 5 through 7. Adam establishes a spread by purchasing an OEX Jul 285 call and writing a Jul 280 call.

5. Is his position a credit spread or a debit spread?

______________________________

6. Does Adam want his spread to widen or narrow?

______________________________

7. The index closes at 280 on expiration date. Does Adam realize his maximum gain or maximum loss?

______________________________

Calculate the breakeven point for the positions in questions 8 through 10.

8. Karen sells 1 OEX 285 call at 5. She will break even when the index is at

______________________________

9. Belle is long 10 470 puts on the AMEX Major Market Index. She initially paid an aggregate premium of $6,000. Her breakeven point comes with the index at

______________________________

10. Adam writes a spread on the PHLX Gold/Silver Index. He is long 1 Dec 105 put at 1 3/4 and short 1 Dec 110 put at 4 3/8. The breakeven point on this credit spread is an index value of

______________________________

11. An investor is long 10,000 OEX calls. How many OEX puts can the investor purchase?
    A. 5,000
    B. 15,000
    C. 25,000
    D. Any number

12. Armand A. Legge owns a large, diversified portfolio of stocks. While he is confident that his securities are well selected for the long term, he is concerned that he may be subject to market risk in the short run. What positions could he take in index options to hedge against a downturn in the market?

______________________________

13. Belle Charolais is bullish on the market. If she buys 1 Jul 490 call on the XMI, which of the following options might she write to create a debit spread?
    I. Jul 485 call
    II. Jul 480 call
    III. Jul 500 call
    IV. Jul 505 call

    A. I
    B. I and II
    C. II, III and IV
    D. III and IV

**Figure 3**

**Foreign Currency Options**
**Philadelphia**

Friday, January 18th, 1994

| Option & Underlying | Strike Price | Calls—Last Feb | Calls—Last Mar | Calls—Last Jun | Puts—Last Feb | Puts—Last Mar | Puts—Last Jun |
|---|---|---|---|---|---|---|---|
| 50,000 Australian Dollars—cents per unit. | | | | | | | |
| ADollr | 77 | r | r | r | 0.35 | r | r |
| 79.56 | 78 | r | r | r | r | r | 0.67 |
| 31,250 British Pounds—cents per unit. | | | | | | | |
| BPound | 165 | r | 14.10 | r | r | r | r |
| 179.44 | 170 | r | 9.40 | r | r | r | r |
| 179.44 | 175 | 5.10 | r | r | r | 1.70 | 3.80 |
| 179.44 | 177 1/2 | 3.15 | 3.90 | r | r | 2.40 | r |
| 6,250,000 Japanese Yen—100ths of a cent per unit. | | | | | | | |
| JYen | 73 | 1.92 | 2.45 | r | 0.48 | 0.79 | r |
| 74.68 | 74 | 1.40 | 1.95 | 3.0 | 0.75 | 1.15 | r |
| 74.68 | 75 | 0.95 | 1.48 | r | 1.34 | r | 2.20 |

Total call vol 13,389 Call open int 365,373 r - not traded s - no option offered
Total put vol 9,154 Put open int 353,817 Last is premium (purchase price)

14. In reading the foreign currency option quotes in Figure 3, you find that the exchange rate for British pounds is listed as 179.44. What does this mean?

    A. One U.S. dollar is equivalent to 17.944 pounds.
    B. One U.S. dollar is equivalent to 1.7944 pounds.
    C. One pound is equivalent to 1.7944 U.S. dollars.
    D. One pound is equivalent to 179.44 U.S. cents.

15. Your client owns a portfolio of blue chip stocks. She informs you that she believes that the securities will provide good, long-term appreciation but she is fearful that the market will decline over the short term. Which index options strategy should you recommend that will protect against the expected decline and still allow for long-term capital appreciation?

    A. Buy puts
    B. Buy calls
    C. Sell covered puts
    D. Sell covered calls

16. An investor exercises 1 PHLX Jan 40 call on the deutsche mark. The aggregate exercise price for this option is which of the following? (Each contract is for 62,500 DM.)

    A. $5,000
    B. $25,000
    C. $40,000
    D. $50,000

## Answers

1. **A.** Broad-based indexes attempt to reflect the status of the market as a whole, not the status of particular market segments.

2. $600. The potential gain on a short option is the premium received on the opening transaction.

3. 220. At (or above) the strike price of 220. At this price and above, the put expires worthless, and Angus keeps the premium he received for writing the option.

4. **D.** To break even, Karen must lose an amount equal to her initial gain—13 points. This will occur if her short call is in-the-money by 13 points and she is assigned an exercise.

5. Credit. Adam sold the call with the lower strike price. The lower the strike price of a call, the higher the premium. So he received more for his short call than he paid for his long one. He has a credit spread.

6. Narrow. The investor who opens a credit spread wants the spread between premiums to narrow. At best, both premiums become zero, and there is no spread between them. The writer keeps the net premium received.

7. Gain. As the writer of a bear credit spread, Adam wants the price of the index to drop until the calls expire worthless, and he keeps the initial credit.

8. 290. Strike price of 285 plus the premium of 5. The writer of a call is bearish and does not want the index to go up. If the index is greater than the strike price, the call may be exercised against the writer.

9. 464. Strike price of 470 minus the premium of 6 ($6,000 ÷ 10 contracts ÷ 100 shares per contract). Long puts are bearish; the writer wants the index value to go down.

10. 107 3/8. Remember, PSH: Puts Subtract from Higher. Here you subtract the initial credit of 2 5/8 from the higher strike price of 110, for a breakeven point of 107 3/8.

11. **C.** The position limit of 25,000 contracts applies to options on the same side of the market. Long calls and long puts are on opposite sides of the market.

12. Armand is bullish in the long term and wants insurance against losses in a bear market. He needs options that will be profitable in a bear market; therefore, he can buy puts or sell calls.

13. **D.** If Belle sold either a 500 call or a 505 call, she would have a debit spread because she has purchased the more expensive call—the one with a lower strike price. Belle would create a credit spread by selling the 480 call or the 485 call. Because they have lower strike prices, they would be more expensive than the 490 call.

14. **D.** The exchange rate refers to U.S. cents per British pound. 179.44 cents is $1.7944.

15. **A.** Because your client is long the stock, her position would be hurt by a drop in the market. To hedge against that risk, she must take an option position that appreciates in value as the market declines: long puts or short calls. Because your client also wishes to benefit from any appreciation, the long put is the better hedging vehicle. If the market averages increase, the put position would lose only the premium, and your client could still gain on her stocks.

16. **B.** Deutsche marks are quoted in cents per underlying currency unit. A 40 deutsche mark call represents a price of 40 cents per unit, or $.40 times 62,500 deutsche marks for a total exercise price of $25,000.

# Tax Rules for Options

## Taxable Option Events

Options are capital assets. Trading them involves capital gains and losses rather than ordinary income.

- **Call or put option expires**. An option that expires unexercised results in a capital loss for the person who paid the premium to buy it.
- **Call or put position is closed**. The tax effects of a closing purchase or sale are as follows:
  - A **capital gain** will result if the sale price of the option is greater than the purchase price.
  - A **capital loss** will result if the sale price is less than the purchase price of the option.
- **Call option is exercised**. The premium on the option affects the cost basis if the stock is being purchased or the sale proceeds if the stock is being sold. The total cost basis for the stock is the strike price plus the premium on the call. The sale proceeds equal the strike price *plus* the call premium.
- **Put option is exercised**. When a put is exercised, the premium of the option is subtracted from the cost basis (or sale proceeds) of the stock.

## Effect of Options on Stock Holding Periods

**Long stock and long a put**. The IRS has ruled that the purchase of a put on stock held twelve months or less automatically caps that stock's holding period at twelve months. Thus, any gain on that stock will be treated as short term.

- If the stock was held more than twelve months before the purchase of the put, the holding period is unaffected.
- If the investor has held stock for twelve months or less, buys a put and then sells that put in a closing transaction, the holding period of that stock (capped at twelve months at the purchase of the put) begins anew as of the closing date of the put sale.

**Long stock and short a call**. The IRS has ruled that the sale of a call that is deep in-the-money (a deep in-the-money call is one that has a strike price at least 10% below the current market value of the stock) automatically caps the holding period on stock held twelve months or less at twelve months. Thus, any gain on that stock will be treated as short term.

- Writing a call that is only slightly in-the-money (a strike price less than 10% below the current market value of the stock) also caps the holding period at twelve months, but in the event a closing purchase of a call is entered, the holding period of the stock resumes.
- If the stock was held more than twelve months before the sale of the call, the holding period is unaffected.

## Nonequity Options

One tax characteristic of nonequity options is unique. Investors holding nonequity option positions on December 31st are taxed as if the option positions were closed out.

# Questions

1. In September, an investor sells 2 AMF Jan 60 puts at 3. If the investor buys the 2 puts back at 4 1/2, the result for tax purposes is a

   A. $150 capital gain
   B. $150 capital loss
   C. $300 capital gain
   D. $300 capital loss

2. In September, an investor sells 2 AMF Jan 60 puts at 3. If the 2 AMF Jan 60 puts expire in January, what are the tax consequences for the seller?

   A. $600 gain realized in September
   B. $600 loss realized in September
   C. $600 gain realized in January
   D. $600 loss realized in January

3. On January 1st, an investor buys 1 FLB Apr 50 call at 4 and 1 FLB Apr 50 put at 2 1/2. Both options expire unexercised. What are the tax consequences for the investor?

   A. $150 net capital gain
   B. $150 net capital loss
   C. $400 gain on the call, $250 gain on the put
   D. $400 loss on the call, $250 loss on the put

4. Clara Bullock buys 1 FLB Oct 50 call at 3. She exercises the option to buy 100 shares when the market is at 60. What is the cost basis of the 100 shares?

   A. $5,000
   B. $5,300
   C. $6,000
   D. $6,300

5. A customer writes 1 Jul 50 put at 7. The put is exercised when the market price is 40. For tax purposes, what is the effective cost basis of the stock put to the seller?

   A. 40
   B. 43
   C. 50
   D. 57

# Answers

1. **D.** The closing cost of $900 minus $600 opening sale proceeds equals a $300 loss.

2. **C.** Expiration of a short option generates a gain at the time the option expires.

3. **D.** In a straddle, the options are treated separately for tax purposes. The investor has a $400 capital loss on the call and a $250 capital loss on the put.

4. **B.** The cost basis of the 100 shares is the total amount the investor spent to acquire them. She paid $300 to purchase the call option. When she exercised the call, she purchased 100 shares of FLB at $50 per share, for a total price of $5,000. The cost basis therefore is $5,300.

5. **B.** The cost basis is 50 (the price at which the writer must buy) minus 7 (the premium the writer was paid), or $43 per share.

# 17 Investment Company Products

## Investment Company Offerings

Investment companies operate and invest the pooled funds of investors as a single large account jointly owned by every shareholder in the company. Investment companies are **portfolio intermediaries.**

### The Investment Company Act of 1940

The act of 1940 states:

". . . investment companies are affected with a national public interest in that:

- the securities they issue constitute a significant percentage of all securities publicly offered;
- their process of issuing redeemable securities and their redemption of those securities is continuous; and
- the investing, reinvesting and trading by investment companies constitutes a significant percentage of all transactions in the securities markets of the nation."

### Types of Investment Companies

#### Face-amount Certificate Companies

A face-amount certificate is:

- a contract between an investor and an issuer,
- in which the issuer guarantees a payment of a **stated** (or **fixed**) sum,
- to the investor,
- at some set date in the future.

If the investor chooses to pay for the certificate in a lump sum, the investment is known as a **fully paid face-amount certificate.**

A typical face-amount certificate contract will require the investor to make 20 semiannual payments of $1,000 each over a period of ten years. In return, the company will guarantee that, at the end of ten years, it will return to the investor $25,000.

#### Unit Investment Trusts

A UIT is an investment company organized under a trust indenture. UITs:

- do not have a board of directors;
- do not employ an investment adviser;
- do not actively manage their own portfolios (trade securities);
- function as holding companies for their investors;
- typically purchase an investment portfolio consisting of fixed-income securities; and
- sell redeemable shares (also known as **units** or **shares of beneficial interest**) in this portfolio of securities. Each share represents the

ownership of an *undivided interest* in the underlying portfolio.

Once any of the securities in a UIT's portfolio are sold, mature, or are otherwise liquidated, the proceeds must be distributed.

### Management Investment Companies

Management investment companies actively *manage* a portfolio of securities in accordance with the investment objectives stated in their prospectuses.

### Closed-end Investment Companies

A closed-end investment company's capitalization is fixed. Closed-end investment companies are permitted to issue bonds and preferred stock as well as common stock.

Closed-end investment companies are more commonly known as **publicly traded funds**. After the stock is distributed, anyone who wants to buy or sell shares does so in the secondary market (either on an exchange or OTC). Supply and demand determine the price the investor will receive or will have to pay for shares. The **bid** price and the **ask** price reflect the open market's current valuation of their shares.

### Open-end Investment Companies

- An open-end investment company (or **mutual fund**) registers an open offering with the SEC.
- The open-end investment company can raise an unlimited amount of investment capital by continuously issuing new shares.
- When investors liquidate their holdings in a mutual fund, the fund's capital shrinks.
- The shares that an open-end investment company sells are known as **redeemable securities**.

Investors place their buy and sell orders directly with the investment company's underwriters (broker-dealers).

- Investors buy shares from the company at the public offering price (POP).
- Investors sell their shares back to the company at their net asset value (NAV).
- For each share an investor sells back (or redeems) the company will send the investor her proportionate share of the company's net assets.

### Diversified and Nondiversified

**Diversified.** Diversification is a combination risk management technique and investment approach. But not all investment companies feature diversified portfolios. An investment company will qualify as a diversified investment company if it meets the following **75-5-10** test:

- *75%* of total assets must be invested in securities issued by companies *other than the investment company itself* or its affiliates.
- No more than *5%* of total assets can be invested *in any one corporation's* securities.
- No more than *10%* of an outside corporation's *voting class securities* (common stock) can be owned by the investment company.

**Nondiversified.** A nondiversified investment company, on the other hand, is any company that fails to meet one or more of these criteria.

# Questions

1. "Mutual fund" is a popular name for

   A. all investment companies
   B. open-end investment companies
   C. closed-end investment companies
   D. a company that invests pooled funds

2. Which of the following are covered under the Investment Company Act of 1940?

   I. Unit investment trusts
   II. Face-amount companies
   III. Open-end management companies
   IV. Closed-end management companies

   A. I and II only
   B. I, III and IV only
   C. III and IV only
   D. I, II, III and IV

3. What kind of investment company has no provision for redemption of outstanding shares?

   A. Open-end company
   B. Closed-end company
   C. Unit investment trust
   D. Mutual fund

4. Diversified management companies must be invested so that

   I. they own no more than 5% of the voting stock of a single company
   II. no more than 5% of their assets are invested in any one company
   III. they own no more than 10% of the voting stock of any one company
   IV. if they own more than 25% of a target company, they do not vote the stock

   A. I and II
   B. I, II and IV
   C. II and III
   D. II, III and IV

5. Which type of mutual fund is sold at net asset value?

   A. Open-end
   B. Closed-end
   C. Front-end load
   D. No-load

6. All of the following statements about diversified and nondiversified investment companies are true EXCEPT that

   A. a nondiversified company is any management company not classified as a diversified company
   B. to be considered diversified, an investment company must invest 75% of its total assets in cash, receivables or securities
   C. both diversified and nondiversified companies are examples of management companies
   D. to be considered a nondiversified company, an investment company must invest the majority of its total assets in one industry

7. The Investment Company Act of 1940 regulates all of the following EXCEPT

   A. face-amount certificates
   B. holding companies
   C. closed-end funds
   D. unit investment trusts

8. Which of the following statements describe open-end investment companies?

   I. Shares are redeemable on demand at the net asset value.
   II. Shares are always sold by prospectus.
   III. Only a limited number of shares are offered.
   IV. Shares are sold on securities exchanges.

   A. I and II only
   B. I and III only
   C. III and IV only
   D. I, II, III and IV

9. According to the Investment Company Act of 1940, an investment company with a fixed portfolio, redeemable shares and no management fee is classified as a

   A. face-amount certificate company
   B. management company
   C. unit investment trust
   D. closed-end investment company

10. All of the following terms describe a fixed unit investment trust EXCEPT

   A. liquidity
   B. manageability
   C. redeemability
   D. classification as an investment company

11. Open-end investment companies, but not closed-end investment companies

   I. can make continuous offerings of shares provided the original registration statement and prospectus are periodically updated
   II. can be listed on registered national exchanges
   III. always redeem their shares
   IV. can issue only common stock

   A. I, II and III
   B. I and III
   C. I, III and IV
   D. II and IV

# Answers

1. **B.** The term "mutual fund" is synonymous with "open-end investment company."

2. **D.** All are covered under the act of 1940. Unit investment trusts, face-amount and management investment companies are all mentioned in this act. Remember, both open-end and closed-end management companies are management investment companies.

3. **B.** The closed-end company does not redeem shares that it issues. The closed-end company has a fixed capitalization and, like regular corporations, outstanding shares trade on the open market.

4. **C.** A diversified investment company:

- must have at least 75% of its assets invested in cash, securities or both;
- may own no more than 10% of the voting stock of a company; and
- may have no more than 5% of its total assets invested in one company.

5. **D.** A no-load fund is sold at NAV with no sales charges. A closed-end company may trade at NAV, but market price does not necessarily correlate with the NAV.

6. **D.** A nondiversified investment company does not meet one or more of the requirements of a diversified company. There are many diversified investment companies that invest primarily in a single industry.

7. **B.** Holding companies are subject to the Holding Company Act, a federal act distinct and separate from the Investment Company Act of 1940. Under the act of 1940, investment companies are divided into three major classifications: face-amount certificates, unit investment trusts and management companies (including closed-end companies and open-end investment companies).

8. **A.** Only choices I and II are true. Open-end investment companies must be prepared to

redeem shares at net asset value. Open-end investment companies continually issue new shares that are sold by prospectus. Unlike open-end investment companies, closed-end investment companies issue a limited number of shares that may be sold on an exchange.

9. **C.** Unlike unit investment trusts, which issue redeemable securities, face-amount certificate companies issue installment certificates with guaranteed principal and interest. A unit investment trust has a diversified portfolio that, once established, does not change. Therefore, it cannot be called a "management company." A closed-end investment company is a type of management company.

10. **B.** A unit investment trust is one of the three major types of investment companies. Because it is a fixed, redeemable portfolio of securities, it is not managed.

11. **C.** Open-end investment companies, but not closed-end investment companies, can make continuous offerings of shares, can redeem their shares and can issue only common stock.

# Characteristics of Mutual Funds

## The Mutual Fund Concept

- Each investor in the mutual fund's portfolio owns an **undivided interest** in the portfolio.
- All investors in the open-end fund are mutual participants; no one investor has a preferred status over any other investor.
- Mutual funds issue only one class of common share.
- No preferred class of shares or debt can be issued.
- Each investor shares mutually with other investors in gains and distributions derived from the investment company portfolio.
- Investors can purchase fractional shares.

## Advantages to Investors

- Mutual funds offer *guaranteed marketability*.
  - An open-end mutual fund must redeem shares presented to it by investors at the NAV within seven days.
- Investment decisions for the funds are made by full-time professional advisers.
- Mutual fund shares offer a greater degree of diversification than most private investors are able to achieve independently.
- A mutual fund's shares are held by a **custodian**, which ensures safekeeping.
- The investor has the ability to invest almost any sum because investment companies continuously offer full and fractional shares.
- Most funds allow a **minimum investment**, often $500 or less, to open an account. Once an account is open, many funds allow additional investment for as little as $25.
- The investment company may allow investments at reduced sales charges by offering **breakpoints**. The investor may also qualify for breakpoints through a statement (letter) of intention or rights of accumulation.
- The fund may provide for **reinstatement** of investment.
- The investor retains **voting rights** similar to those rights extended to common stockholders.
- Many funds offer **automatic reinvestment** of capital gains distributions and dividend distributions without a sales charge.
- The investor is able to **liquidate** a portion of his holding without disturbing the balance or diversification of the investment.
- Each year the fund must distribute to the investor a **Form 1099B** explaining taxability of distributions.

## Investment Objectives

An investment company's objective must be clearly stated in the investment company's prospectus and can be changed only by a majority vote of the fund's outstanding shares.

The investor should shop around to find a mutual fund with an objective similar to his own.

### Diversified Common Stock Funds

Growth funds:

- invest in equity securities of companies expected to increase in value more rapidly than the overall market.

Income funds:

- stress current yield or income; and
- may sacrifice safety of principal for increased potential income.

Combination funds:

- may attempt to combine the objectives of growth and current yield by diversifying its portfolio among companies showing long-term growth potential and companies currently paying high dividends.

### Specialized (Sector) Funds

Sector funds normally invest a minimum of 25% of their assets in their specialties or industries.

- **Special situation funds** buy for their portfolios securities of companies that may benefit from a change within the company or in the economy.

### Balanced Funds

Balanced funds attempt to combine the objectives of growth and income by investing in different vehicles; to do so, they:

- invest in stocks for appreciation and bonds for income payments; and
- balance their investments between preferred stock and bonds.

### Asset Allocation Funds

Asset allocation funds attempt to provide a consistent return for the investor; to do so, they:

- split investments between stocks, bonds and money-market instruments or cash; and
- switch the percentage holdings in each asset category according to the performance, or expected performance, of that group.

### Bond Funds

Bond funds seek income as a primary investment objective.

- **Junk bond funds** seek capital appreciation by investing in lower rated issues at high interest rates.

### Tax-free (Tax-exempt) Bond Funds

Tax-free bond funds seek income exempt from federal income tax.

- **Municipal bond funds** and **tax-exempt money-market funds** are common types of tax-exempt funds.

### U.S. Government and Agency Security Funds

These funds seek current income and maximum safety.

### Index Funds

An index fund attempts to mirror a market index, such as the S&P 500. The fund manager:

- buys and sells the securities in the fund portfolio in such a way that the portfolio maintains the same type and weightings of stock as the selected index; and
- does not attempt to beat the performance of the underlying index by actively managing the portfolio.

### Money-market Funds

Money-market funds are usually open-end investment companies, sold without a sales charge or liquidation fee, that offer:

- draft- (check-) writing privileges;
- a low expense ratio, usually limited to a management fee of .5% of net assets;
- a stable net asset value of $1.00 per share;
- a share in a portfolio of money-market instruments that have:
  - high interest rates
  - short maturities;
- payment of interest rates that:
  - are not fixed or guaranteed
  - change as frequently as daily; and
- earned interest that is:
  - computed daily
  - credited to customers' accounts monthly

## Comparing Mutual Funds

Before making a mutual fund investment, the investor should:

- define a personal investment objective
- scrutinize each potential investment

When choosing among funds that match the investor's objective, a few factors should be considered.

- **Performance**. The fund must disclose its returns over good years and bad, as well as how effectively it has achieved its stated investment objective.
- **Sales loads**. The fund's distributor receives a sales charge, which is subtracted from the amount of money the customer invests in the fund.
- **Expense ratio**. The ratio of total fund expenses to average net assets indicates whether fund operating expenses significantly reduce investor returns.
- **Taxation**. Mutual fund investors pay taxes on income distributions and on capital gains distributions; gains may be short-term or long-term based on the length of time the security is held in the portfolio.
- **Portfolio turnover**. The percentage of the fund's portfolio that is traded annually affects investor returns; a high turnover rate means the investor is likely to realize short-term capital gains each year the fund is held.

# Questions

1. Money-market funds usually offer which of the following?

   I. Daily interest calculations
   II. Check-writing privileges
   III. No-load funds
   IV. Long-term growth potential

   A. I and II
   B. I, II and III
   C. I, II and IV
   D. II, III and IV

2. The Investment Company Act of 1940 requires that redemption of mutual fund shares be made within how many days of tender?

   A. 5
   B. 7
   C. 10
   D. 30

3. An investor purchases shares in a sector fund. Which of the following statements describe this investment?

   I. The fund invests in a particular industry.
   II. The fund's objective is current income rather than capital growth.
   III. The fund invests primarily in common stocks.
   IV. The companies in which the fund invests must be within a specific region of the United States.

   A. I and II
   B. I and III
   C. II and III
   D. III and IV

4. Mr. Smith is interested in investing in an open-end investment company. His objective is high current yield, but he is uncomfortable with high risks. His registered representative should recommend what type of fund?

   A. Oil industry
   B. Balanced
   C. Growth
   D. Income

5. The greatest expense of an open-end investment company is

   A. the management fees
   B. salaries
   C. overhead
   D. custodial fees

6. The greatest cost in operating a money-market fund is

   A. custodial fees
   B. brokerage fees
   C. management fees
   D. overhead

# Answers

1. **B.** Money-market funds are made up of short-term, high-yield debt instruments, are sold no-load, calculate interest daily and offer check-writing privileges. Because their purpose is to provide income, money-market funds usually offer limited growth.

2. **B.** The Investment Company Act of 1940 requires that payment be made within seven days of receiving a redemption order.

3. **B.** Sector funds concentrate their investments in common stocks in a specific industry. Most industry funds seek capital growth rather than current income. An industry fund is not limited by geographic area.

4. **B.** An income fund provides current income rather than capital growth, with above-average risk. Balanced funds are less risky than the other investments listed and are, therefore, the appropriate choice. Oil industry funds and growth funds are not appropriate for Mr. Smith because of the high degree of risk.

5. **A.** The management fee is a mutual fund's greatest expense.

6. **C.** Management fees are the greatest cost of operating money-market funds.

# Investment Company Registration

A company must register as an investment company with the SEC if:

- the company is in the business of investing, reinvesting, owning, holding or trading in securities; or
- 40% or more of the company's assets are invested in securities.

## Registration of Investment Companies

An investment company is not allowed to issue securities to the public unless it has:

- private capitalization (seed money) of at least $100,000;
- 100 investors; and
- clearly defined investment objectives.

**Open-end investment companies**:

- may issue only one class of security;
- are permitted to borrow from banks;
- cannot issue preferred stock or bonds; and
- may borrow money as long as the company's asset-to-debt ratio is not less than 3-to-1.

### SEC Registration and Public Offering Requirements

An investment company must provide the following information in its registration form:

- the type of investment company it intends to be;
- any plans the company has to raise money by borrowing;
- the company's intention (if any) to concentrate its investments in a single industry;
- any plans for investing in real estate or commodities;
- conditions under which investment policies may be changed by a vote of the shareholders;
- the full names and addresses of each affiliated person; and
- a description of the business experience of each officer and director during the preceding five years.

Exempt from registration as investment companies are:

- underwriters and brokers;
- banks, insurance companies and bank investment advisory accounts;
- mortgage bankers;
- security holders protective committees; and
- real estate investment trusts (REITs).

### Continuous Public Offering Securities

- Shares must be sold by prospectus only.
- The financial information contained in the prospectus must be dated not more than 16 months prior to the sale.

In contrast, only the initial public offering of a closed-end company is sold with a prospectus.

### Registration Statement—Prospectus

Every prospectus must print the following disclaimer on its front cover:

> These securities have not been approved or disapproved by the Securities and Exchange Commission nor has the commission passed upon the accuracy or adequacy of this prospectus. Any representation to the contrary is a criminal offense.

## Securities Issued by Investment Companies

### Common Stock (Equity Securities)

- Shares of common stock represent an undivided interest in the company's portfolio.
- The investor's interest in the portfolio is proportionate to the number of shares owned.

- Open-end companies are not allowed to issue senior securities, such as bonds and preferred stock, but are permitted to borrow from banks.

### Bonds (Debt Securities)

- A closed-end investment company is permitted to issue debt securities.
- A closed-end investment company may issue either bonds or debentures, provided that, after they have been issued, the company maintains an asset-to-debt coverage ratio of at least 300%.

### Preferred Stock (Equity Securities)

- A closed-end investment company is permitted to issue preferred stock.

## Restrictions on Operations

### Functions and Activities of Investment Companies

Mutual funds are prohibited from:

- making securities purchases on margin;
- selling securities short;
- participating in joint investment or trading accounts; or
- acting as distributor of its own securities, except through an underwriter.

If the fund intends to engage in these activities, it must specifically disclose the fact and the extent to which it plans to engage in these activities in its prospectus.

## Changes in the Registration Statement

### Shareholders' Right to Vote

Changes that would require a majority vote of the shares outstanding include:

- changes in **borrowing** by open-end companies;
- **issuing or underwriting** other securities;
- purchasing or underwriting **real estate**;
- making **loans**;
- change of **subclassification**;
- change in **sales load policy**;
- change in the **nature of the business**; and
- change in **investment policy**.

# Questions

1. Shareholders of mutual funds have all of the following rights EXCEPT

    I. voting rights
    II. proxies
    III. receiving semiannual reports
    IV. preemptive rights

    A. I and II
    B. I, II and III
    C. II and IV
    D. IV

2. The Investment Company Act of 1940 states that

    A. it is unnecessary for the prospectus to disclose the management fee
    B. open-end companies may issue common stock only
    C. an investment company must have $5 million capital before its securities can be offered to the public
    D. no more than 50% of the board of directors of an investment company may be officers or employees of the company or investment advisers to the company

3. According to the Investment Company Act of 1940, borrowing by an open-end investment company

    A. is prohibited
    B. is permitted, but only by issuing bonds
    C. is limited to 33% of its net assets
    D. must conform to the 20-to-1 rule

4. According to the Investment Company Act of 1940, an investment company

    A. owns investment securities exceeding 50% of its total assets, excluding government securities
    B. is engaged primarily in investing in and trading securities, has a net worth in excess of $100,000 and has 40% or more of the value of its total assets in investment securities
    C. has a net invested worth of $100,000 and its outstanding securities are beneficially owned by more than 100 persons
    D. is engaged primarily in investing or trading in securities, defined as 50% or more of a company's total invested assets

## Answers

1. **D.** Shareholders of mutual funds have all of the rights mentioned except a preemptive right—the right for existing shareholders to maintain a proportionate ownership in the company. Other rights include approval of changes in investment objectives and approval of the investment advisory agreement.

2. **B.** The prospectus must state the management fee. An investment company needs only $100,000 and 100 investors in order to offer itself to the public. No more than 60% of the board of directors can be made up of officers or employees of the company. Open-end companies may issue only one class of equity—common stock.

3. **C.** The 1940 act limits borrowing. Any investment company must have 300% asset coverage, which means borrowing is limited to 33% of the net assets.

4. **B.** An investment company, as broadly defined in the 1940 act, is a company engaged primarily in the business of investing, reinvesting or trading in securities. It must have net worth in excess of $100,000 and own investment securities in an amount exceeding 40% of its total assets.

# Management of Investment Companies

## Board of Directors

- **Elections.** The shareholders of a management investment company must approve the election of the fund's board members, as well as any additions or replacements to the board.
- **Vacancies.** Vacancies that occur after the initial election may be filled in any legal manner as long as at least two thirds of the directors have been elected by the shareholders.
- **Noninterested persons.** At least 40% of the directors must be independent (noninterested persons).
- **Interested persons.** No more than 60% of the board members may be interested persons, including attorneys on retainer, accountants and any persons employed in similar capacities with the company.

## Investment Adviser

The board contracts with an outside **investment adviser** (portfolio manager). The adviser is responsible for:

- investing the cash and securities held in the fund's portfolio;
- implementing investment strategy;
- clearly identifying the tax status of any distribution made to shareholders as a result of activity in the fund's portfolio; and
- managing the day-to-day trading of the portfolio.

Investment advisers earn management fees for their services, typically a set annual percentage (such as .5% of the portfolio asset value being managed) which is paid from the net assets of the fund.

The **act of 1940** requires:

- a written contract, which must be approved initially by a vote of the shareholders; and
- that the advisory contract has a *maximum life of two years*, after which time it may be extended on a year-to-year basis by the annual approval of the directors and/or a majority vote of the shares.

The **contract** must also include:

- a precise description of all compensation to be paid the investment adviser;
- a provision that the contract may be terminated by the board of directors or by a majority vote of the shares with 60 days' notice;
- the requirement that any such assignment be approved by the shareholders of the investment company; and
- the requirement that any amendment or renewal of the advisory contract be approved by a majority of the noninterested (independent) directors.

## Affiliated Persons

Anyone who could have any type of control over an investment company's operations is called an affiliated person, including:

- anyone with 5% or more of the outstanding voting securities of the investment company;
- any corporation in which the investment company holds 5% or more of its outstanding securities;
- any person (an individual or a corporate entity) controlled in whole or in part by the investment company;
- all officers, directors, partners and employees of the investment company; and
- the investment adviser.

## Interested Persons

All of the following are considered interested persons:

- person associated with the investment company, its investment adviser or its principal underwriter, including the immediate families of any affiliated person;
- person employed by the investment company, the investment adviser or the principal underwriter;
- person who, within the last two years, has acted as legal counsel to any affiliated person;
- broker-dealer registered under the Securities Exchange Act of 1934; and
- any other person deemed to be interested by the SEC because of business dealings with the company, its investment adviser or its principal underwriter.

The directors of an investment company are specifically excluded from the definition of an interested person.

### Restrictions

An affiliated or interested person is prohibited from:

- borrowing money from the investment company; or
- selling any security or other property to the investment company or to any company controlled by the investment company.

## Custodian

The bank or broker-dealer performs an important safekeeping role as custodian of the company's securities and cash and receives a fee for its services (which, like the adviser's fee, is paid from the net assets of the fund).

## Transfer Agent (Customer Services Agent)

The functions of the transfer agent include:

- issuing and redeeming fund shares
- handling name changes for the fund
- sending out customer confirmations
- sending out fund distributions

## Underwriter

The underwriter (often called the *sponsor* or *distributor*) markets fund shares, prepares sales literature and, in return, receives a percentage of the sales charge paid by the client. The underwriter's compensation is part of the sales load paid by the customer when shares are purchased. Sales fees are not part of the fund's expenses.

The underwriter (distributor) of funds receives a fee for selling and promoting the fund shares to the public. This fee is in the form of a sales charge added to the share's NAV when sales are made to the public.

## Information Distributed to Investors

Shareholders must receive financial reports at least semiannually containing:

- the investment company's balance sheet;
- a valuation of all securities in the investment company's portfolio on the date of the balance sheet (a portfolio list);
- the investment company's income statement;
- a complete statement of all compensation paid to the board of directors and to the advisory board; and
- a statement of the total dollar amount of securities purchased and sold during the period.

## Questions

1. The custodian of a mutual fund usually does which of the following?
   A. Approves changes in investment policy.
   B. Holds the cash and securities of the fund and performs clerical functions.
   C. Manages the fund.
   D. Does cleaning and related duties on the fund's properties.

2. Investment company financial statements are sent to shareholders
   A. monthly
   B. quarterly
   C. semiannually
   D. annually

3. The role of a mutual fund's underwriter is to
   A. hold the fund's assets and perform clerical responsibilities
   B. administer and supervise the investment portfolio
   C. market shares
   D. provide investment advisory services

4. When a bank is serving as the custodian of a mutual fund, it always
   A. manages the portfolio
   B. signs all margin agreements
   C. holds the cash and securities and performs other clerical functions
   D. serves as the distributor of the fund and manages interactions with other underwriters

5. Typically, the largest single expense of a mutual fund is the
   A. custodian fee
   B. registration fee
   C. management fee
   D. brokerage fee

## Answers

1. **B.** The main functions of the custodian, usually a commercial bank, are to hold the fund's cash and assets for safekeeping and to perform related clerical duties. The custodian may also issue and redeem customer shares, send out customer confirmations and hold customer shares.

2. **C.** Investment company financial statements must be sent to shareholders at least semiannually.

3. **C.** The underwriter markets the fund's shares. Answer A is the responsibility of the custodian, answer B is the responsibility of the fund, and answer D is the responsibility of the manager.

4. **C.** The primary function of a mutual fund's custodian bank is to safeguard the physical assets of the fund, hold the cash and securities and perform other purely clerical functions. It does not manage the portfolio or serve in a selling capacity for the fund.

5. **C.** Typically, the largest single expense for a mutual fund is the management fee—the fee paid to the management company for buying and selling securities and managing the portfolio. A typical annual fee is 1/2 of 1% of the portfolio's asset value.

# Mutual Fund Marketing, Pricing and Valuation

## Methods of Marketing Mutual Fund Shares

There are several methods a fund may employ to distribute its shares to investors:

- fund to underwriter to dealer to investor;
- fund to underwriter to investor;
- fund to underwriter to plan company to investor; and
- fund to investor.
  - If an open-end investment company distributes shares to the public directly—that is, without the services of a distributor—and the fund offers its shares for sale at no load the fund is called a **no-load fund**. The fund pays all sales expenses.

### Sales at the Public Offering Price

Any sale of fund shares to a *customer* (a member of the general public who is *not* a member of the NASD) must be made at the **public offering price**.

## Determining the Value of Mutual Fund Shares

### Net Asset Value per Share

- **NAV**. NAV is the price on which sales of new shares to investors is based.
- **POP**. Public offering price (ask price) is equal to the NAV (bid price) plus a sales charge.
- **Liquidation price**. The liquidation price is always equal to the current NAV.
- **NAV per share**. The NAV per share is determined by dividing the total net assets by the number of shares outstanding.

$$\text{Assets (Cash + Current value of securities)} - \text{Liabilities} = \text{NAV of fund}$$

$$\frac{\text{NAV of fund}}{\text{Number of shares outstanding}} = \text{NAV per share}$$

### Changes in NAV

Events that may change a fund's NAV include:

- The NAV can change daily because of changes in the market value of the fund's portfolio.
- The appreciation or depreciation of portfolio assets is also called *unrealized gain* or *loss*. Gains (losses) are said to be unrealized until the fund actually sells the stock.

### Changes in NAV per Share

Events that may change a fund's NAV per share include:

- an **increase** in the NAV per share *if* portfolio securities increase in value or the portfolio receives income (interest on debt or dividends on stock) from the securities held in the portfolio;
- a **decrease** in the NAV per share if portfolio securities decrease in value or portfolio income or gain is paid out to shareholders (dividends or gains distributions); and

There is **no change** in the NAV per share if there is a sale (issuance) or redemption of fund shares or if there is a sale or purchase of portfolio securities (even if a previously unrealized gain or loss is realized).

## Sales Charges

The NASD prohibits its members from assessing sales charges *in excess of 8.5%* of the POP on mutual funds purchases by customers.

- Broker-dealers are free to charge lower rates *if they specify these rates in the prospectus,* but they must never charge more than the 8.5% maximum.

### Loads and Charges

- **Front-end loads** are the charges included in a fund's public offering price. The charges are added to the NAV of the shares at the time the investor purchases the shares. If a fund offers more than one sales load option, the shares sold with a front-end load are referred to as *Class A shares.*
- **Back-end loads** (contingent deferred loads) are those charged at the redemption of mutual fund shares or variable contracts. The sales load is a *declining percentage charge* that is reduced *annually* and that is applied to the proceeds of any shares sold in that year.
- **12b-1 asset-based fee**. Under section 12b-1, a company may collect a 12b-1 asset-based fee for promotion, sale or another activity in connection with the distribution of its shares. The fee is determined annually as a flat dollar amount or as a percentage of the company's average total NAV during the year.
  - **Misuse of no-load terminology**. A fund or contract that has a deferred sales charge or an asset-based 12b-1 fee may not be described as a no-load fund.

## Mutual Fund Pricing

### Pricing Management Company Shares

The formula for determining the POP of mutual fund shares is:

NAV + Sales charge = Offering price

The sales charge represents the money received by the underwriter for distributing fund shares. The basic formula for determining the sales charge on mutual fund shares is:

Offering price – NAV = Sales charge

To determine the POP, divide the NAV by the complement of the sales load (100% – SL%). The formula is as follows:

$$\frac{\text{Net asset value}}{100\% - \text{Sales charge }\%} = \text{POP}$$

### Computing the Sales Charge Percentage

When the NAV and the POP are known, the sales charge percentage included in the POP can be determined this way:

POP – NAV = Sales charge ($ amount)

$$\frac{\text{Sales charge (\$ amount)}}{\text{POP}} = \text{Sales charge }\%$$

For example, if the POP is $10.00 and the NAV is $9.15 per share, the sales charge percentage is calculated as follows:

$10.00 – $9.15 = $.85 Sales charge ($)

$.85 ÷ $10.00 = 8.5% Sales charge %

### Reductions in the Permitted Maximum Sales Charge

To qualify for the maximum 8 1/2% sales charge, the investment company must offer all of the following:

- **Automatic reinvestment**. Automatic reinvestment of income distributions at NAV (no sales charge) must be made available to any person who requests such reinvestment. The company does have the right to limit the availability of dividend reinvestment to holders of securities with a minimum stated value.
- **Lump-sum investments**. A scale of reduced sales charges must be offered for lump-sum investments;
- **Rights of accumulation**. Rights of accumulation must be made available to any person for a period of not less than ten years from the date of first purchase.

## Sales Charges and Quantity Discounts

Open-end investment companies encourage large investments by offering discounts. There may be one sales charge percentage for investing $500 and a different sales charge percentage for investing $100,000, so that the sales charge would be considerably less per dollar of investment for the person investing $100,000.

### Breakpoints

The schedule of discounts offered by a mutual fund is called the fund's *breakpoints.*

- Breakpoints are available to any person.
- Most investment companies consider a family unit to be one person (only minor children may be included in the family unit).
- Investment clubs or associations formed for the purpose of investing do not qualify for breakpoints.

The following is an example of a breakpoint schedule:

| Purchases | | Sales Cost |
|---|---|---|
| $1 to $9,999 | = | 8 1/2% |
| $10,000 to $24,999 | = | 7 1/2% |
| $25,000 to $49,999 | = | 7% |
| $50,000 plus | = | 6 1/2% |

### Statement of Intention (Letter of Intent)

With a letter of intent (LOI), a customer can indicate his intent to invest the additional funds necessary to reach the breakpoint at some time during the next 13 months.

- The LOI is a unilateral contract that is binding on the fund only.
- The customer must complete the investment in order to qualify for the reduced sales cost.
- The fund will hold the extra shares purchased from the reduced sales load in escrow.
- If the client deposits the money to complete the LOI, he receives the escrowed shares.
- Each investment is charged the appropriate sales load at the time of purchase.
- Appreciation and reinvested dividends do not count towards the contract amount.
- A fund often permits the client to sign a letter of intent as late as the 90th day after a purchase. The letter of intent is then backdated to the date of the original purchase. The LOI may be backdated by up to 90 days to include prior purchases, but may not cover more than 13 months in total.

### Rights of Accumulation

For the purpose of qualifying for breakpoints and reduced sales charges, the investment company will base the quantity of securities owned on:

- the current value of the securities at either NAV or POP;
- total purchases of such securities at the actual offering price; or
- the higher of current NAV or the total of purchases made to date (typically how it is valued).

### Combination Privilege

Funds that have the same principal underwriter may grant an investor the privilege of combining separate investments in two or more funds under the same management towards a breakpoint.

## Breakpoint Sales

The NASD prohibits registered reps making *breakpoint sales*, which is selling investment company shares in dollar amounts just below the point at which the sales charge is reduced *in order to make the higher commission.*

## Exchanges Within a Family of Funds

The advantage to the investor of making an exchange within a family of mutual funds is that it is often accomplished without incurring an additional sales charge.

- Any exchange of funds is considered a sale for tax purposes.
- Mutual funds may be purchased at NAV under a no-load exchange privilege.
- Any purchases may not exceed the proceeds generated by the sale (or redemption) of the other fund.
- The redemption may not involve a refund of sales charges.
- The sale (or exchange) must take place within 30 days after the redemption.

### Redemption of Fund Shares

Under the 1940 act, an open-end investment company must redeem shares tendered to it *within seven days* of receipt of a *written request* for redemption. The price at which shares are redeemed is the NAV, which must be calculated at least once per business day.

**Forward pricing.** The redemption price is the NAV next calculated after the investment company receives the redemption request (known as *forward pricing).*

# Questions

1. In order for a company to charge the maximum sales charge of 8 1/2%, it must offer all of the following EXCEPT
   A. automatic reinvestment of dividends and capital gains at NAV
   B. breakpoints
   C. automatic reinvestment at POP
   D. rights of accumulation

Use the following breakpoint schedule to answer questions 2 through 4.

| Purchases | Sales Cost |
|---|---|
| $1 to $9,999 | 8 1/2% |
| $10,000 to $24,999 | 7 1/2% |
| $25,000 to $49,999 | 7% |
| $50,000 to $99,999+ | 6 1/2% |

2. ArGood Mutual Fund has an NAV of $9.15 and a POP of $10. A customer wants to invest $30,000. How many shares of the fund will the customer receive?
   A. 2,951
   B. 3,000
   C. 3,049
   D. 3,279

3. A customer currently has $20,000 to invest but signs a letter of intent for $25,000. The NAV is $12 a share. What is the price the customer will pay per share?
   A. $12.00 plus a commission
   B. $12.90
   C. $12.97
   D. $12.97 for the first $20,000 and $12.90 for the remainder

4. An investor purchases an income fund for himself and deposits $5,000. He also purchases a growth fund for his minor child and deposits $20,000. Which of the following would represent his sales charges if both funds have the same management and breakpoints?

   I. $5,000 at 8 1/2%
   II. $20,000 at 7 1/2%
   III. $25,000 at 7%
   IV. $25,000 at 7 1/2%

   A. I and II
   B. III
   C. IV
   D. None of the above

5. A mutual fund is quoted at $16.56 NAV and $18.00 POP. The sales charge is

   A. 7 1/2%
   B. 7 3/4%
   C. 8%
   D. 8 1/2%

6. ACE Fund has an NAV per share of $9.20 and an 8% sales load. What is the dollar amount of the sales charge?

   A. $.60
   B. $.74
   C. $.80
   D. $10.00

7. A mutual fund has a 7% sales load, a 1 1/2% dealer concession and an NAV of $10.80. To determine the offering price, divide the NAV by

   A. 7%
   B. 8 1/2%
   C. .915
   D. .93

8. Redemption of a no-load fund may be made at the

   A. NAV minus the sales charge
   B. POP minus the sales charge
   C. NAV plus the sales charge
   D. NAV

9. A client owns 100 shares of a no-load mutual fund. When she redeems those shares, she will receive the net asset value

   A. plus a sales charge
   B. minus a redemption fee
   C. minus a sales charge
   D. minus both a redemption fee and a sales charge

10. Your client owns shares in an open-end investment company. The shares are currently quoted in the newspaper at $10 bid and $10.80 ask. Within the past twelve months, the investment company has distributed capital gains of $1.20 per share and dividends of $.60 per share. What is the current yield on your client's shares?

    A. 1.8%
    B. 5.0%
    C. 5.6%
    D. 6.0%

11. Ms. Bruin purchased mutual fund shares with a net asset value of $7.82 and an 8% sales charge. She paid a sales charge of

    A. $.68
    B. $.74
    C. $.80
    D. $.87

12. Klaus Bruin purchased mutual fund shares with a bid price of $15.50 and an 8% sales charge. At the time of his purchase, what was the price of his shares?

    A. $12.40
    B. $14.26
    C. $16.74
    D. $16.85

13. An open-end investment company receives a redemption request from an investor early in the day on Friday, June 23rd. The basis for the redemption price the investor receives is the

 A. net asset value on Friday, June 23rd
 B. net asset value on Monday, June 26th
 C. ask price on Friday, June 23rd
 D. ask price on Monday, June 26th

14. In reference to open-end investment companies, all of the following terms are synonymous EXCEPT

 A. bid price
 B. net asset value
 C. redemption price
 D. current price

15. Which of the following statements are true regarding a letter of intent and breakpoints?

 I. The letter of intent can be backdated a maximum of 30 days.
 II. The letter of intent is valid for 13 months.
 III. The investor is legally bound to meet the terms of the agreement.
 IV. The fund may hold shares in escrow.

 A. I and II
 B. II and III
 C. II and IV
 D. III and IV

16. Which of the following investors can take advantage of breakpoints?

 I. Individual
 II. Investment club
 III. Trust
 IV. Corporation

 A. I and II
 B. I, III and IV
 C. II, III and IV
 D. III and IV

17. The ACE Mutual Fund has an 8% sales load, a redemption fee of one-half of 1% and a current offering price of $10.70. If your customer redeemed 1,000 shares of the fund, he would receive

 A. $9,572.38
 B. $9,794.78
 C. $9,844
 D. $10,646.50

18. An investor purchasing 1,000 shares of a certain mutual fund that has a maximum sales charge of 8 1/2% and an NAV of $10.30 at the time of purchase will pay a total sales charge of (rounding to the nearest dollar)

 A. $88
 B. $96
 C. $875
 D. $957

19. The ArGood Mutual fund has a bid price of $9.15 and a sales charge of 8.5%. What is the price an investor will pay for each share of this fund? (Round to the nearest cent.)

 A. $8.37
 B. $9.93
 C. $10.00
 D. $10.76

# Answers

1. **C.** The maximum sales load is 8 1/2% *only* if the company offers rights of accumulation, breakpoints and automatic reinvestment at NAV, not at POP.

2. **C.** The offering price with a 7% sales charge is computed as follows: POP = NAV ÷ (100% – SC) = 9.15 ÷ (100% – 7%) = 9.15 ÷ .93 = $9.84. $30,000 ÷ $9.84 = 3,049 shares (rounded). Or, $30,000 – $2,100 (7%) = $27,900; $27,900 ÷ $9.15 (NAV) = 3,049 shares.

3. **B.** When the customer signs the letter of intent, she is entitled to the reduced sales load on the total amount of her investment. She has 13 months to complete the terms of the letter of intent. The offering price will be $12.90 (NAV of $12 ÷ 93%).

4. **B.** Investors are permitted to combine investments to reduce sales loads. This is true for a parent and minor child in two separate accounts as long as the investments are in the same family of funds.

5. **C.** The formula is sales cost divided by public offering price. The sales cost is the difference between NAV and POP, or $1.44 per share. $1.44 ÷ $18 = 8%.

6. **C.** If the fund has an NAV of $9.20 and a sales load of 8%, the offering price is $9.20 ÷ (100% – SC) = 9.20 ÷ .92 = $10.00. The sales charge is the 80-cent difference.

7. **D.** The formula used to determine the offering price is:

$$\frac{\text{NAV}}{100\% - \text{Sales charge}} = \text{POP}$$

The sales load and sales charge are synonymous and the dealer concession is part of that figure. 100% – 7% = 93%, or .93.

8. **D.** No-load funds are redeemed at net asset value. Mutual funds may also charge a redemption fee, which is subtracted from the NAV.

9. **B.** Mutual fund shares are redeemed at net asset value minus any redemption fee. Sales charges are paid when the shares are purchased, not on redemption.

10. **C.** In open-end investment companies, current yield is calculated as follows: Annual dividends divided by asked price equals yield. Your client would find the yield of his open-end investment company as follows: $.60 ÷ $10.80 = 0.0555 = 5.55% (5.6% rounded).

11. **A.** To find the dollar amount of the sales charge when you know the NAV and the sales charge percentage, calculate the complement of the sales charge by subtracting the sales charge from 100%. (100% – 8% = 92%.) Then divide the NAV by the complement of the sales charge to find the offering price ($7.82 ÷ .92 = $8.50, the offering price). The dollar amount of the sales charge is the offering price minus the NAV. $8.50 – $7.82 = $.68, the sales charge.

12. **D.** The terms "bid price" and "net asset value" are synonymous, and the terms "current price" and "offering price" are synonymous. Divide the bid price by the complement of the sales charge to find the current price: $15.50 ÷ .92 = $16.85.

13. **A.** When an investor redeems shares, the redemption price is based on the next computed NAV following the investment company's receipt of the redemption request. This is the NAV computed at the end of the day on which the company receives the request.

14. **D.** "Current price" is synonymous with "public offering price." Current price is not the same as bid price, net asset value or redemption price.

15. **C.** Only choices II and IV are true. Choice I is false because the letter of intent can be backdated 90 days. Choice III is false because the

investor is not required by law to satisfy the letter of intent although, in the case of default, she will pay a higher sales charge.

16. **B.** Breakpoint advantages are available only to "individuals." An investment club is not considered an individual, but trusts and corporations are.

17. **B.** The 1,000 shares have an offering price value of $10,700. The net asset value would be 92% of that amount, or $9,844. Then subtract 1/2 of 1% of $9,844 for the redemption fee, to arrive at a net figure of $9,794.78.

18. **D.** The 1,000 shares have a net asset value of $10,300. Divide that amount by the complement of 8 1/2% (100% ÷ 8.5% = 91.5%, or .915). The result is $11,257, which is the amount of the current offering price. The difference is $957.

19. **C.** To calculate the offering price when you know the bid price (the NAV) and the percentage of sales charge, divide the bid price ($9.15) by the complement of the sales charge (91.5%). This equals $10.00, the offering price.

# Mutual Fund Purchase and Withdrawal Plans

## Types of Mutual Fund Accounts

### Open Account

- The client will determine if fund share distributions are to be received in cash or reinvested.
- If the client elects to receive distributions in cash rather than reinvesting them, his proportionate interest in the mutual fund will be reduced each time a distribution is made.
- The client can make additional investments to an open account at any time and without limit as to dollar amount—that is, no such limit is set by law, although each fund may set its own minimums.

### Voluntary Accumulation Plan

- Allows the client to deposit regular periodic investments on a voluntary basis in preset amounts.
- May require a minimum initial purchase and minimum optional additional purchase amounts.
- Should the client miss a payment, the fund cannot penalize him.
- The plan may be discontinued at any time by the client.

### Periodic Payment Plans (Contractual Plans)

- The investor signs an agreement to invest an agreed upon dollar amount over a specified period of time.
- The agreement is binding on the company only; the investor cannot be held to the contract.
- The Investment Company Act of 1940 allows a maximum of 9% in sales charges by contractual plans.
- Some states do not allow the sale of contractual plans because of their high sales charges.
- Contractual plan companies are organized as **UITs**.
- The customer's units represent an undivided interest in the pool of underlying mutual fund shares.

### Front-end Load Plan

The seller is allowed to charge a maximum sales charge equal to 9% of the total payments as follows:

- Fifty percent of the total payments made during the first twelve months may be deducted and applied against total sales charges due over the life of the plan. The deduction must be applied evenly to twelve monthly payments.
- Over the remaining life of the plan, deductions for sales charges may be calculated in any reasonable manner.

### Spread Load Plan

- Over the *first four years* of the plan, *an average of 16%* of all payments made by the investor may be deducted and applied against the total sales charges called for over the life of the plan.
- In *each* of the *first four years*, the sales charge rate and dollar amount deducted for the year must be *uniformly applied* to each month's payment.
- The *deduction in any one year cannot exceed 20%* and the average over the four-year period cannot exceed 16%.

### Investor Right to Terminate a Plan

**Right of withdrawal (45-day free look).** The fund's custodian bank must furnish the investor with a written notice detailing the total sales charges that will apply over the life of the plan and must send that notice *within 60 calendar days* of the date a contractual plan certificate is issued to the customer.

The customer, if so inclined, may surrender the certificate and terminate the plan *within 45 days* from the mailing date of the custodian's written notice. If the customer does, in fact, surrender the certificate within that time, he is entitled to:

- a 100% refund of all sales charges paid to date; *plus*
- the current value of the investment.

**Right to refund (18-month partial refund period).** In a front-end load plan (but not in a spread-load plan), the right to refund provides that if a customer requests termination of a front-end load plan within the *first 18 months* from the issuance date of the periodic payment plan certificate, she is entitled to a refund of:

- all sales charges paid to date *in excess of 15% of the total (gross) payments* made to date; *plus*
- the current value of the investment, which is liquidated at current NAV (and may result in a profit or loss).

## Dollar Cost Averaging

Dollar cost averaging allows the investor to purchase more shares when prices are low and fewer shares when prices are high. In a fluctuating market, the average cost per share over a period of time will be lower for the investor than the average price of the shares for the same period.

## Withdrawal Plans

**Fixed dollar.** A client may request the withdrawal of a fixed amount of money periodically.

**Fixed percentage or fixed share.** Under a fixed-percentage or fixed-share withdrawal plan, either a fixed number of shares or a fixed percentage of the account will be liquidated each period.

**Fixed time.** Under a fixed-time withdrawal plan, clients liquidate their holdings over a fixed period of time.

- Withdrawal plans are not guaranteed.
- The registered rep may never promise the investor a guaranteed rate of return.
- The registered rep must stress to the investor that it is possible to exhaust the account by overwithdrawing.
- The registered rep must state that during a down market it is possible that the account will be exhausted if even a small amount is withdrawn.
- The registered rep must not use charts or tables unless the SEC specifically clears their use.

## Questions

1. In which of the following circumstances will dollar cost averaging result in an average cost per share that is lower than the average price per share?

   I. The price of the stock fluctuates over a period of time.
   II. A fixed number of shares is purchased regularly.
   III. A fixed dollar amount is invested regularly.
   IV. A constant dollar plan is maintained.

   A. I and II
   B. I and III
   C. I, III and IV
   D. II and III

2. What type of investment company is a contractual plan company?

   A. Unit investment trust
   B. Balanced fund
   C. Management company
   D. Closed-end fund

3. All of the following statements regarding dollar cost averaging are true EXCEPT that

   A. dollar cost averaging results in a lower average cost per share
   B. dollar cost averaging is not available to large investors
   C. more shares are purchased when prices are lower
   D. in sales literature, dollar cost averaging cannot be referred to as *averaging the dollar*

4. A contractual plan is MOST likely to be classified as a(n)

   A. closed-end investment company
   B. open-end investment company
   C. face-amount certificate
   D. unit investment trust

## Answers

1. **B.** Dollar cost averaging benefits the investor if the same amount is invested on a regular basis over a substantial period of time, during which the price of the stock fluctuates. A constant dollar plan (choice IV) is one in which the investor maintains a constant dollar value of securities in the investment portfolio.

2. **A.** A contractual plan is usually a unit investment trust; it is not a management company.

3. **B.** Dollar cost averaging is available to both small and large investors.

4. **D.** Contractual plans are usually unit investment trusts. Both closed-end and open-end investment companies are types of management companies, but a contractual plan is not. Face-amount certificates are a different classification of investment company.

# Mutual Fund Distributions and Taxation

## Distributions from Mutual Funds

**Dividend distributions**. Dividends are paid from the net investment income of the mutual fund.

**Net investment income** equals totals dividends received from common and preferred stock held in the portfolio plus all interest income received from bonds and other debt instruments minus fund operating expenses (adviser's fee, custodial fee, utilities, salaries, accounting costs and so on).

**Calculating fund yields**. Net investment income divided by the current offering price equals yield. All yield quotations must disclose the:

- general direction of the stock market for the period in question;
- NAV of the fund at the beginning and the end of the period; and
- percentage change in the fund's price during the period.

Current yield calculations may be based only on income distributions for the preceding twelve months.

Gains distributions may not be included in the yield calculations.

### Capital Gains Distributions

- Capital gains distributions are derived from the activities of the investment adviser trading securities held in the fund's portfolio.
- If the fund has held the stock for a period of at least one year, the gain is a long-term capital gain.
- Capital gains distributions (long term) may not be made more frequently than once per year.
- Any distribution of gains from an open-end investment company will be long term. Short-term gains are considered income distributions and will be identified and distributed as dividends.

**Selling dividends**. A registered representative may not encourage investors to purchase fund shares prior to a distribution because of the tax liability, and doing so is a violation of NASD rules known as **selling dividends**.

### Reinvestment of Dividend and Gains Distributions

Dividends may be systematically reinvested by customers at less than the POP, and can be used to purchase full and fractional shares as long as:

- shareholders who are not already participants in the reinvestment plan are given a separate opportunity to reinvest each dividend;
- the plan is described in the prospectus;
- the issuer of the securities bears no additional costs beyond those that would have been incurred in the normal payout of dividends; and
- all shareholders are notified of the availability of the dividend reinvestment plan at least once every year.

The following rules apply to distributions:

- The mutual fund may apply a reasonable charge against each dividend reinvestment.
- Whether the distributions are taken in cash or reinvested to purchase additional shares, they are taxable to the shareholders.
- Distributions from net investment income are taxed as ordinary income.
- Long-term capital gains are taxed at the ordinary income tax rate, up to a maximum rate of 28%.

**Source of distributions**. The fund must disclose the source and character of distributions, either from income or from capital transactions, as each distribution is made. Form 1099B is sent after the close of the year and details tax information related to distributions for the year.

### Realized Appreciation

A gain on the sale of portfolio securities is considered *realized appreciation* and is passed through to shareholders.

- If the fund held the security for a year or less, the gain is short-term and will appear as an income distribution on the shareholder's annual tax form.
- If the fund held the security for more than a year, the gain is long-term and will appear as a capital gain distribution on the shareholder's tax form.

### Unrealized Appreciation

If the fund's investment adviser decides to hold an appreciated security, the NAV of the fund shares increases to reflect the appreciated value. This increase in the value of the shares is considered *unrealized appreciation* and is not passed through to the shareholder. The shareholder incurs no tax liability if he does not sell his shares.

## Taxation of Mutual Funds

### Conduit (Pipeline) Theory

Triple taxation of investment income may be avoided if the open-end investment company qualifies under Subchapter M of the Internal Revenue Code (IRC). Subchapter M requires that the investment company distribute at least 90% of its net investment income to shareholders. If the company distributes less than 90%, the company is liable for tax on 100% of net investment income.

### Fund Share Liquidations to the Investor

**Cost base.** Cost base is the amount of money invested that has already been taxed. Upon liquidation, cost base represents a return of capital and is not subject to a tax liability. The difference between cost base and the current value of the investor's shares represents his taxable gain (or loss if cost base is greater than the current value of the shares).

**Valuing fund shares.** The cost base of mutual fund shares includes the total cost of the shares, including sales charges, plus any reinvested investment income and capital gains. The cost base is compared to the amount of money received from the sale of the shares. If the amount received is greater than the cost base, the investor will report a taxable gain. If the amount received is less than the cost base, the investor has a reportable loss.

Total value of fund shares − Cost base
= Taxable gain

### Accounting Methods

Should the investor decide to liquidate on a per-share basis, the calculation of cost base can be accomplished by electing one of three accounting methods: first in, first out (FIFO), share identification or average basis. If the investor fails to choose, the IRS assumes the investor is liquidating shares on a FIFO basis.

### Other Mutual Fund Taxation Considerations

**Withholding tax.** If an investor neglects or fails to include her tax ID number when purchasing mutual fund shares, the fund is required to withhold 31% of the distributions to the investor as a withholding tax.

**Cost basis of shares transferred.** The basis of property inherited is either stepped up or stepped down to its fair market value (FMV) at the date of the decedent's death.

**Taxation of investment returns.** The taxation of investment returns can be summarized as follows:

- Income distributions are taxed as ordinary income.
- Capital gains distributions are taxed as long-term capital gains.

**Exchanges within a family of funds.** The IRS considers a sale to have taken place and the customer has some tax liability under IRS regulations.

# Questions

1. Which of the following decides when a mutual fund goes ex-dividend?

   A. NASD
   B. NYSE
   C. SEC
   D. Board of directors of the fund

2. Klaus Bruin buys 100 shares of a mutual fund on December 28, 1984, for $4,000. He receives a capital gains distribution of $2.40 per share on March 6, 1985. He sells his 100 shares for $4,300 on June 19, 1985. For tax purposes, these transactions will result in

   A. a $240 capital gain
   B. a $300 capital gain
   C. a $540 capital gain
   D. $300 in ordinary income

3. The conduit theory

   A. is described in the Investment Company Act of 1940
   B. refers to a tax treatment available to investment companies
   C. was developed by the NASD
   D. is stated in the SEC statement of policy

Use the following information to answer questions 4 and 5. Last year, ACE Mutual Fund paid dividends of $1.50 per share and distributed 80 cents per share in capital gains. The fund has a bid price of $13.50 and an asked price of $14.20. An investor, who purchased shares in this fund nine months before the distributions, received $100 in eligible dividend income and $53 in capital gains.

4. If this is his only investment, the investor will

   I. not be required to pay any federal taxes on the dividend income
   II. be required to pay federal taxes at the ordinary income rate on the dividend income
   III. be required to pay tax on the $53 capital gain
   IV. not be required to pay capital gains tax on $53

   A. I and III
   B. I and IV
   C. II and III
   D. III and IV

5. What is the yield of the fund?

   A. 4.92%
   B. 10.00%
   C. 10.56%
   D. 16.20%

## Answers

1. **D.** The ex-date for a mutual fund is set by the board of directors.

2. **C.** Mr. Bruin will realize a $240 capital gain on the distribution and a $300 capital gain on the sale of the stock.

3. **B.** Regulated companies under Subchapter M of the IRS code are allowed to *pass through* income to beneficial owners without a tax at the fund level on the distributed income. This is known as *conduit* or *flow-through* of income and taxation.

4. **C.** This investor will pay taxes on the dividend income, and he will pay capital gains tax on the $53.

5. **C.** Divide the dividend of $1.50 by the asked price of $14.20.

# Real Estate Investment Trusts

A REIT pools capital in a manner similar to an investment company.

**Portfolio.** REIT portfolios are composed of professionally managed real estate holdings, typically either in direct ownership of income property or in mortgage loans.

**Pass-through of gains and income.** REITs allow gains, profits and income to pass through to investors.

**Organization.** REITs are organized as trusts or corporations where investors buy shares or certificates of beneficial interest either on stock exchanges or in the OTC market.

**Characteristics.** The following characteristics and rules apply to REITs:

- Shareholders receive dividends from investment income or capital gains distributions.
- The REIT investor cannot deduct operating or capital losses.
- Under the guidelines of Subchapter M of the Internal Revenue Code, a REIT can avoid being taxed as a corporation by receiving 75% or more of its income from real estate and distributing 95% or more of its taxable income to its shareholders (the distribution requirement for investment companies is 90%).

# 18 Retirement Planning

## Individual Retirement Accounts

### Participation in an IRA

Any taxpayer reporting earned income for a given tax year may participate in an IRA.

- Earned income is from the performance of personal services (as in a job) and not passive income (as from investments).
- The taxpayer may not participate if she has reached the age of 70 1/2 during the tax year.
- Contributions to an IRA may be made up to April 15th of the year following the tax year.

### IRA Contributions

The maximum annual IRA contribution that an employed individual can make is subject to the following limitations:

- for an individual account, 100% of earned income or $2,000, whichever is less; and
- for a spousal account, 100% of earned income or $2,250 (divided between two accounts), whichever is less.

The IRS allows an individual who has an unemployed spouse to contribute to a separate individual retirement account established for the nonworking spouse (known as a **spousal account**). The contribution may be divided between the two accounts in any way as long as the total contribution is not more than $2,250 and no more than $2,000 is contributed to either account.

The maximum contributions described may or may not be tax deductible, depending on whether the taxpayer is participating in an employer-sponsored retirement plan.

IRA owners are always *100% vested* in their contributions to their accounts.

**Participating (covered) employees.** If the taxpayer is eligible to participate in an employer-sponsored pension or profit-sharing plan, including a Keogh or simplified employee pension plan (SEP), the person's total earnings for the year will determine the extent to which self-funded, personal IRA contributions will be tax deductible.

### Excess Contributions

Annual IRA contributions in excess of the maximum are subject to a 6% penalty tax if the excess is not removed by the time the taxpayer files the tax return.

### IRA Investments

**Permissible investments.** IRA investments may include:

- stocks;
- bonds;
- UITs;
- mutual funds;

- limited partnerships;
- government securities;
- U.S. government-issued gold and silver coins; and
- annuities and many others.

Depending on where a person is in his earnings-cycle and how close his projected retirement date, growth-oriented stocks and mutual funds may be the best choice even though they carry with them the higher risks associated with investments in the stock market.

**Ineligible investments.** Investments considered ineligible for use in an IRA include:

- collectibles
- life insurance contracts

## IRA Rollovers

The following rules apply to rollovers:

- Rollovers must be completed within *60 calendar days* of the original funds' withdrawal from the qualified plan.
- Only the before-tax contributions and earnings of the account may be rolled over.
- Any tax-deferred portion not rolled over is considered a distribution and is subject to ordinary income tax.
- If an individual elects to roll over assets from a qualified plan to an IRA or other qualified plan (that is, she takes possession of the assets), the payor of the distribution must retain 20% of the distribution as a withholding tax. The option to forgo withholding is not available to the participant. If the individual elects a direct transfer, there is no withholding on the amount directly transferred.

## IRA Transfers

- In a *transfer* of funds between qualified retirement accounts, the account owner never actually takes physical possession of the funds.
- There is no limit to the number of times per year a person can transfer investments between qualified plans.

## IRA Withdrawals

IRA earnings are tax deferred until the money is received.

- Withdrawals may not begin without penalty before age 59 1/2 and must begin by April 1st of the year after the year in which the account owner reaches age 70 1/2.
- Withdrawals, except those that result from contributions made with aftertax dollars are taxable as ordinary income.
- Early withdrawals incur a 10% penalty unless they occur because of the individual's death or disability.
- A 50% penalty is applied to accounts not meeting minimum Internal Revenue Code (IRC) distribution requirements after age 70 1/2.

## Taxation on IRA Distributions

Taxpayers may elect to start receiving income from their IRAs:

- as early as age 59 1/2; or
- as late as the year after the year in which the taxpayer reaches age 70 1/2.

All distributions are treated as taxable income in the year in which received.

### IRA Abuses and Tax Penalties

Penalties will be levied by the IRS in the following cases:

- Excess contributions over the maximum annual limits will subject the taxpayer to a tax penalty of *6% of the excess amount.*

- Early withdrawals (prior to the minimum IRA disbursement age of 59 1/2) will be subject to an additional *tax penalty of 10%.*
- Failure to start distributions by April 1st of the year after the year in which the taxpayer reaches age 70 1/2 will cause the IRS to impose a *50% tax penalty.*

## Simplified Employee Pensions—SEP-IRAs

A SEP is a qualified plan that allows employers to contribute money to special SEP-IRAs set up for their employees.

- SEP contributions are not subject to current income tax.
- The sponsor may not discriminate.
- Participants are vested immediately.

**Eligibility**. An employee is eligible if he:

- is at least 21 years of age;
- has performed services for the employer during at least three of the immediately preceding five years; and
- has received at least $300 in compensation from the employer in the current year.

**Participation**. Every eligible employee must have a SEP-IRA.

- If an employee refuses to establish a SEP-IRA, the employer must establish an account in the name of that employee.

**Funding**. The employer can contribute from 0% to 15% of the employee's salary to the employee's SEP-IRA each year, up to a maximum of $30,000 per employee per year.

- The same percentage must be contributed for each employee.
- The employer contributes to her own SEP-IRA the same percentage of salary contributed to employee accounts.

**Vesting**. Participants in a SEP are fully vested immediately.

**Nondiscrimination**. All eligible employees must be covered and receive the same contribution percentage.

**Taxation**. Employer contributions are tax deductible to the employer.

Contributions are not taxable to the employee until withdrawn, and earnings in the account are tax deferred.

# Questions

1. The maximum allowable contribution to an IRA is

   A. $2,250 per individual account
   B. $2,000 per individual account
   C. $250 per individual account
   D. $0 because contributions to IRAs are no longer allowed

2. Premature distribution from an IRA is subject to a

   A. 5% penalty plus tax
   B. 6% penalty plus tax
   C. 10% penalty plus tax
   D. 50% penalty plus tax

3. Money can be rolled over from a qualified plan to an IRA

   A. every 60 days
   B. once a year
   C. at no time
   D. as directed by the customer

4. An individual with an IRA subsequently joins a corporation that covers the employee with a pension plan. What actions are taken regarding the IRA?

   A. The IRA must be made part of the pension plan.
   B. The IRA must be closed.
   C. The employee may continue to contribute to the IRA.
   D. The IRA is frozen.

5. What is the maximum permissible contribution to an IRA by an individual?

   A. $2,000
   B. $2,250
   C. $4,000
   D. 25% of one's earnings or $30,000, whichever is less

6. Your client, who is 50 years of age, wants to withdraw funds from her IRA. He asks you about the tax implications of early withdrawal. You should tell him the withdrawal will be taxed as

   A. ordinary income
   B. ordinary income plus a 10% penalty
   C. capital gains
   D. capital gains plus a 10% penalty

7. An individual who is less than age 70 1/2 is qualified to contribute to an IRA

   A. if he has earned income
   B. provided he is not covered by a pension plan through an employer
   C. provided he does not own a Keogh plan
   D. provided his income is between $40,000 and $50,000 if married and $25,000 and $35,000 if single

8. A client has just started her IRA. She will be vested

   A. immediately
   B. in two years
   C. in five years
   D. at age 70 1/2

9. Which of the following statements regarding IRAs is NOT true?

   A. IRA rollovers must be completed within 60 days of receipt of the distribution.
   B. Cash-value life insurance is a permissible IRA investment, but term insurance is not.
   C. The investor must be under 70 1/2 years of age to open and contribute to an IRA.
   D. Distributions may begin at age 59 1/2 and must begin by the year after the year in which the investor turns 70 1/2.

10. A client and his wife are going to make their annual contribution to their IRA. This year he earned $40,000 and his wife earned $45,000. How much may they contribute?

A. $2,000
B. $2,250
C. $4,000
D. $5,000

11. Under the Tax Reform Act of 1986, all of the following investments offer either full or partially tax-deductible contributions to individuals who meet eligibility requirements EXCEPT

A. IRAs
B. Keogh plans
C. variable annuities
D. none of the above

12. Which of the following individuals will NOT incur a penalty on an IRA withdrawal?

A. Man who has just become disabled
B. Woman who turned 59 a month before the withdrawal
C. Person, age 50, who decides on early retirement
D. Man in his early 40s who uses the money to buy a house

# Answers

1. **B.** Maximum contributions to an individual account are $2,000. Maximum contributions to a spousal account are $2,250.

2. **C.** The penalty for premature withdrawals from an IRA or a Keogh account is 10% plus normal income tax. Excess contribution penalty is 6%, while the 50% penalty applies after age 70 1/2.

3. **B.** A rollover is permitted once a year. Customers must accomplish this within 60 days after receipt of the distribution from a qualified plan.

4. **C.** Any individual who has earned income may continue to make contributions to his IRA even when covered by another pension plan.

5. **A.** Maximum contributions to an individual IRA account are $2,000 per year. Maximum contributions to a spousal account (where there is a nonworking spouse) are $2,250. Maximum contributions for a working couple are $4,000 ($2,000 each). Maximum contribution to a Keogh plan is 25% of annual income, up to a maximum of $30,000.

6. **B.** All withdrawals from IRAs are taxed at the individual's ordinary income tax rate at the time of withdrawal. Distributions taken before age 59 1/2 will incur an additional 10% penalty.

7. **A.** Any individual with earned income who is under the age of 70 1/2 may contribute up to $2,000 to an IRA. The deductibility of those contributions will be determined by that person's coverage under other qualified plans and by his level of income.

8. **A.** An account owner is *always* 100% vested in the value of her IRA.

9. **B.** Cash-value life insurance, term insurance and collectibles are not permissible investments in an IRA.

10. **C.** Because both the client and his wife had earned income, both are entitled to contribute 100% of that earned income, up to $2,000, to separate IRAs.

11. **C.** Contributions to variable annuities are made with aftertax dollars.

12. **A.** Early withdrawals, without penalty, are permitted only in the case of death or disability.

# Keogh (HR-10) Plans

Keogh plans are qualified plans. They are intended for self-employed persons and owner-employees of nonincorporated businesses or professional practices.

### Plan Eligibility

- **Owner-employee**. This term refers to sole proprietors who rely on their business for their livelihood.
- **Income must be earned**. Income must be earned income from personal services, not passive income from investments or other unearned sources.
- **Plan must be nondiscriminatory**. Owner-employees must provide for their full-time employees' retirement security under a Keogh plan in the same manner and to the same extent that the owner-employee's retirement security is provided.

### Contributions

- **Tax-deductibility**. The Keogh planholder is permitted to make tax-deductible *cash* contributions of up to 25% of income or $30,000, whichever is less.
- **Age limit**. A person may make contributions to a Keogh until he reaches age 70 1/2.
- **After-contribution income**. In computing the 25% contribution limit for a *business owner or self-employed person*, the limit is based on the owner's income remaining *after* the contribution is made.
  - The Keogh contribution limit for *employees* of a self-employed person is not subject to the after-contribution calculation.
  - For employees, the contribution limit is the lesser of 25% of gross income or $30,000.
  - The Keogh contributions of the employer and the employee must be the same percentage.
- **Nontax-deductible**. Keogh plan participants may make nondeductible contributions. The interest, dividends and growth attributable to such a nondeductible contribution accumulate tax-free until the owner withdraws them.

### Employee Eligibility

**Employee coverage**. Employee participation in an employer's Keogh plan is subject to the following employee eligibility rules:

- **Full-time employees**. All employees who receive compensation for at least 1,000 hours of work per year.
- **Tenured employees**. Employees who have completed one or more years of continuous employment or who have been employed continuously from the start-up date of the Keogh plan if less than three years have elapsed.
- **Adult employees**. Employees under the age of 21 can be excluded from Keogh plan coverage.

### Employee Vesting Requirements

An employee must be fully vested after five years of full-time service. A Keogh plan may elect an alternate schedule that allows for vesting to begin after the third year of employment and 100% vesting upon completion of seven years full-time service.

## Comparison of Qualified Retirement Plans

The principal similarities between Keoghs and IRAs are as follows:

- **Age limits**. Anyone under age 70 1/2 and who is otherwise eligible may make contributions.
- **Tax deferral of income contributed to plans**. Taxes are deferred on the amount of contribution until the individual begins to receive distributions.

- **Tax-sheltered.** Investment income from dividends, interest and capital gains is deferred until distribution.
- **Cash-only contributions.** An investor may contribute cash to a plan, but may not contribute stocks, bonds or other securities.
- **Distributions.** Retirement income distributions can begin as early as 59 1/2 or as late as the year after the year in which the taxpayer reaches 70 1/2. The tax penalties for early withdrawals or failure to start withdrawals are the same.
- **Penalties for early withdrawal.** The individual pays income tax on the total amount withdrawn during the year (including deductible and nondeductible contributions and earnings), plus a 10% penalty. Early withdrawals without penalty are permitted in the event of death or disability.
- **Rollovers and transfers.** Retirement benefits from IRAs and Keoghs may be rolled over once every twelve months. The rollover must be completed within 60 days. There is no annual limit on the number of direct transfers.
- **Available payout options.** Lump-sum distributions (which are eligible for five-year income averaging) or regular, periodic payouts are both permissible.
- **Beneficiary(ies).** Upon the planholder's death, payments are made to a beneficiary—rights to the cash and securities accumulated in the account do not end with the death of the owner.

# Questions

1. Which of the following may participate in a Keogh plan?

   I. Self-employed doctor
   II. Analyst who makes money giving speeches outside regular working hours
   III. Individual with a full-time job who has income from freelancing
   IV. Corporate executive who receives $5,000 in stock options from his corporation

   A. I only
   B. I and II only
   C. I, II and III only
   D. I, II, III and IV

2. Withdrawals from a Keogh plan may NOT be

   A. taxed as ordinary income
   B. taken in regular intervals
   C. taken as a lump sum and then averaged over five years for tax purposes
   D. received after age 59 1/2 without incurring a 10% penalty

3. Angus Bullwether has a salaried, full-time position, but his employer does not offer a company retirement plan. He also has his own clock repair business, which earns less than his salaried position. He wants to invest for his retirement. Which of the following investments is an option for Angus?

   A. An IRA if he does not have a Keogh plan
   B. A Keogh plan if he does not own an IRA
   C. Both an IRA and a Keogh plan
   D. An IRA, but not a Keogh because his self-employment is not his main source of income

4. Which of the following are characteristics of a Keogh plan?

    I. Dividends, interest and capital gains are tax deferred.
    II. Distributions after age 70 1/2 are tax free.
    III. Contributions are allowed for a non-working spouse.
    IV. Lump-sum distributions are allowed.

    A. I and II
    B. I and III
    C. I and IV
    D. II and III

5. All of the following factors influence the amount of money that can be contributed to a Keogh plan in one year EXCEPT

    A. the rules regarding maximum contributions
    B. whether the plan is qualified or non-qualified
    C. the amount of self-employment income
    D. whether the plan is defined benefit or defined contribution

6. Which of the following would disqualify a person from participation in a Keogh plan?

    A. She turned 70 eight months ago.
    B. She has a salaried position in addition to her self-employment.
    C. Her spouse has company-sponsored retirement benefits.
    D. She has an IRA.

# Answers

1. **C.** A person with self-employment income may deduct contributions to a Keogh plan.

2. **C.** The Tax Reform Act of 1986 repealed income averaging on lump-sum withdrawals for all taxpayers.

3. **C.** Because Angus has earned income, he is eligible to contribute to an IRA; and because he has self-employment income, he is also eligible to open and contribute to a Keogh plan.

4. **C.** All interest, dividends and capital gains accumulated in a Keogh are tax deferred until their withdrawal (which must begin between age 59 1/2 and the year after the year in which the account owner turns 70 1/2). The account owner may choose to take distributions in the form of regular income payments or as a single, lump-sum distribution.

5. **B.** Keogh plans, as defined by ERISA, are all qualified plans.

6. **A.** Keogh contributions can only be made *prior* to the date on which an individual turns 70 1/2.

# Corporate Retirement Plans

All corporate pension and profit-sharing plans must be established under a trust agreement.

- The trustee has a fiduciary responsibility towards the plan and the beneficial owners (the planholders).

## Defined Contribution Plan

Defined contribution plans include:

- profit-sharing plans
- money-purchase pension plans
- thrift plans
- 401K plans
- stock bonus plans

The plan provisions cover amounts going into the plan currently or the plan's current allocation. The future final accumulation or account balance depends on the total of the amounts contributed, interest and dividends earned and increase in value (asset appreciation).

Each year, the sponsoring employer may contribute on behalf of each plan participant the *lesser* of 25% of compensation or $30,000.

### Profit-sharing Plans

- Established and maintained by an employer to allow employees to participate in the profits of the business.
- Do not have to entail a definite predetermined contribution formula.
- Contributions can be made on a discretionary basis.
- Must have "substantial and recurring" contributions according to the Internal Revenue Code (IRC).

### Thrift and 401K Plans

- Employees direct the employer to contribute a percentage of salary towards retirement.
- Employers can make *matching contributions* up to a set percentage of the employee-directed contributions.
- Both the employee-directed basic and the employer's matching contributions are made pre-tax.

## Defined Benefit Plan

Defined benefit plans are designed to provide a specified benefit for their participants.

- The promised benefit is paid under the terms of the contract.
- Actuarial assumptions including mortality, turnover and interest rates help determine the appropriate current outlay necessary to fund the future benefits.
- The benefit may be expressed as a flat or fixed dollar amount paid monthly.
- The benefit may be based on a percentage of compensation.
- Amounts reasonable and necessary to provide such benefits are deductible by the employer.

## Distributions

### Payment of Benefits

Payouts are not limited by Social Security or any other payments received by the account owner.

### Taxation of Distributions

Distributions are taxed at the employee's ordinary income rate at the time of distribution.

# Nonqualified Corporate Retirement Plans

A nonqualified plan is an employee benefit provided by an employer that does not meet the standards required for qualified plan status under IRA or ERISA rules.

## Taxation

Contributions to nonqualified plans are not exempt from current income tax.

- Deferral of tax on plan earnings depends on the investment vehicle used to fund the plan.

## Types of Plans

Nonqualified corporate plans include:

- payroll deduction plans
- deferred compensation plans

**Deferred compensation plans**. These plans represent a *contractual agreement* between a firm and an employee by which the employee agrees to defer receipt of current compensation in favor of a payout at retirement. The agreement underlying a deferred compensation plan will usually include:

- list of the conditions and circumstances under which some or all of the benefits may be forfeited;
- statement to the effect that the employee is not entitled to any claim against the assets of the employer until retirement, death or disability; and
- disclaimer that the agreement may be void if the firm suffers a business failure or bankruptcy.

# Annuity Plans

An annuity is a contract between an individual and an insurance company, usually purchased for retirement income.

Owners of variable annuities have the right to vote on changes in investment policy and the right to vote for the investment adviser every two years. They may elect the board of managers, which oversees the management of the portfolio.

## Fixed Annuities

- Payment from a fixed annuity remains constant throughout the annuitant's life.
- The minimum return in a fixed annuity is guaranteed by the insurance company and no risk is borne by the annuitant.
- A fixed annuity is considered an insurance product.
- A salesperson must have an insurance license to sell fixed annuities.
- An investor with a fixed annuity risks loss of purchasing power because of inflation.

## Variable Annuities

- The money deposited in a variable annuity is invested primarily in a portfolio of equity securities.
- The annuitant participates in both the greater potential gain and the greater potential risk associated with equity securities.
- Payouts may vary considerably as the value of the annuity units fluctuates with the value of those securities.

### Separate Account

- Contributions made by investors to a variable annuity are kept in a separate account from the insurance company's general funds.
- If the funds are used to purchase securities directly, the separate account is considered a *management investment company.*
- If the funds are used to purchase shares in a mutual fund that is managed by someone other than the issuer of the variable annuity, the separate account is considered a *unit investment trust.*
- The value of the contract holder's investment in the separate account is an *undivided interest* in the securities held in the separate account, called *accumulation units.*

### Variable Annuity Payments

- Payments are determined by mortality tables and the value of the underlying securities in the annuitant's portfolio.
- Variable annuity plans do not guarantee the amount of payment because the insurance company does not (and cannot) guarantee the performance of the separate account.
- Initial payout is used to determine the number of annuity units in the account.
- Future payouts are determined by the fluctuating value of the annuity unit.

## Purchasing Annuities

**Accumulation stage**. The pay-in period for an annuity is known as the *accumulation stage.*

**Deferred annuities**. Annuities may be purchased with:

- **single premium/payment deferred annuity**—a lump-sum investment with payment of benefits deferred until the annuitant elects to receive them;
- **immediate annuity**—a lump-sum investment with immediate payment of benefits; and
- **periodic payment deferred annuity**—several smaller payments—known as *periodic payments*—over a period of time.

### Sales Charges on Variable Annuities

- **Periodic-payment annuity**
  - Maximum sales charge of 8.5% of the total payments made to the contract for the lesser of the payment period or twelve years.
- **Single-payment annuity**
  - Maximum sales charge must be related to the amount of the purchase payment.

## Annuity Payout Options

- **Life annuity/straight life**. Clients receive monthly benefit checks over their lifetime. There are no added options or benefits, and with this option, the annuitant receives the largest monthly payout.
- **Life annuity with period certain**. Clients receive payments for life, with a certain period of time guaranteed. If the investor dies before the expiration of the *period certain*, payments go to the annuitant's named beneficiary. If the annuitant lives beyond the period certain, payments continue until the annuitant's death.
- **Joint life with last survivor annuity**. The contract will continue to pay as long as one of the annuitants remains alive.

## Annuity Accounting

### Accumulation Units

- An accounting measure that represents the investor's share of ownership in the separate account.
- The unit value changes with the value of the securities held in the separate account and the total number of accumulation units outstanding.
- When the contract is annuitized, accumulation units are converted into annuity units.

### Annuity Units

- An annuity unit is a measure of value used only during the payout period of an annuitized contract.
- An accounting measure that determines the amount of each payment to the annuitant.
- The number of annuity units is calculated when the owner annuitizes the contract—that is, when payout begins.
- The value of the unit fluctuates with the value of the separate account portfolio.

### Assumed Interest Rate

The assumed interest rate (AIR) is a basis for projecting earnings for the variable annuity; it does not guarantee a rate of return.

- The higher the AIR, the higher the projected value of units and the greater the initial payment.
- The lower the AIR, the lower the projected value of units and the lower the initial payment.

**Fluctuating payments**. AIR is compared each month to the actual earnings achieved by the separate account, and the payout may increase, decrease or stay the same relative to the previous month's payout.

- If the realized rate of return in the current month is *higher than the AIR,* the current month's payout will be higher than the previous month's payout.
- If the realized rate of return in the current month is *lower than the AIR,* the current month's payout will be lower than the previous month's payout.
- If the realized rate of return in the current month is *equal to the AIR,* the current month's payout will be the same as the previous month's payout.

An AIR that is too high will result in subsequent payments that continually decrease because the projections are not met by actual portfolio performance.

An AIR that is too low will result in payments that will most likely continually increase as projected returns are surpassed.

## Taxation of Annuities

- Contributions to non-ERISA-qualified annuities are made with aftertax dollars.
- The amount of the contribution is not taxable when the account is annuitized.
- The money invested in an annuity represents the investor's cost base.
- Tax on interest received or capital growth of the contract is deferred until the owner withdraws money from the contract.
- On withdrawal, the amount in excess of the investor's cost base is taxed as ordinary income.
- If the investor receives a lump-sum withdrawal before age 59 1/2, the portion withdrawn is taxed as ordinary income and would be subject to an additional 10% penalty. The penalty does not apply, however, if the amount withdrawn is due to death or disability or is part of a life-income option plan with fixed payments.
- After age 59 1/2, taxes are payable on the earnings portion of the withdrawal only.

# Questions

1. In a variable annuity, total accumulation units are equal to

   A. the annuity's bookkeeping value
   B. the annuity owner's percentage of ownership of the separate account
   C. that portion of reinvested dividends
   D. the offering price

2. What has the greatest effect on the value of annuity units in a variable annuity?

   A. Changes in the Standard & Poor's index
   B. Cost-of-living index
   C. Fluctuations in the securities held in the portfolio
   D. Changes in stock market prices

3. Variable annuity salespeople must register with the

   I. SEC
   II. state banking commission
   III. NASD
   IV. state insurance commission

   A. I, II and III
   B. I and III
   C. I, III and IV
   D. II and IV

4. Holders of variable annuities receive the largest monthly payments under which of the following payout options?

   A. Life annuity
   B. Life annuity with period certain
   C. Joint and last survivor annuity
   D. All of the above

5. Changes in payments on a variable annuity will correspond most closely to fluctuations in the

   A. cost of living
   B. Dow Jones Industrial Average
   C. value of the underlying securities held in the separate account
   D. prime rate

6. The greatest effect on the value of the annuity unit in a variable annuity is caused by fluctuations in the

   A. prime rate
   B. Dow Jones Industrial Average
   C. value of the underlying securities in the portfolio
   D. actuarial rates

7. If Ms. Bullwether wants to sell variable annuities, she must be registered with the

   I. state banking commission
   II. NASD
   III. state annuity board
   IV. state insurance commission

   A. I and III
   B. I and IV
   C. II and III
   D. II and IV

8. Mr. Grizzly reaches age 65 and decides to retire. He wants to annuitize his annuity so that it will provide him with the maximum monthly income. You should recommend a

   A. joint and last survivor annuity
   B. life annuity with period certain
   C. life annuity
   D. unit refund annuity

9. Which of the following statements about an accumulation unit in a variable annuity is NOT true?

   A. An accumulation unit may also be called an annuity unit.
   B. An accumulation unit is the accounting measure that determines the owner's share of the separate account during the accumulation phase of a variable annuity.
   C. The current value of an accumulation unit determines the number of units each net payment purchases.
   D. Accumulation units are equal to the investor's percentage interest in the separate account times the number of accumulation units outstanding.

10. Mary Jones wants to purchase an annuity. She is concerned about protecting her purchasing power during her retirement. Her registered representative should recommend

   A. Series HH bonds
   B. fixed annuities
   C. variable annuities
   D. face-amount certificates

11. Which of the following statements regarding variable annuities are true?

   I. Variable annuities are classified as insurance products.
   II. Insurance companies keep variable annuity funds in separate accounts from other insurance products.
   III. Variable annuities can be purchased with a lump sum but are more commonly purchased with periodic payments.
   IV. Variable annuities offer the investor protection against capital loss.

   A. I and II
   B. I, II and III
   C. I and III
   D. II and IV

# Answers

1. **B.** Accumulation units in a plan are the owner's percentage interest in the separate account, similar to shares of a mutual fund.

2. **C.** Annuity unit price changes are based on changes of value of securities held in the separate account. This price change is a risk that is passed on to the investor in a variable annuity.

3. **C.** Variable annuity salespeople must be registered with the NASD and the state insurance commission. Registration with the NASD is *de facto* registration with the SEC. No registration is required with the state banking commission.

4. **A.** A life annuity guarantees payment for life to the contract holder. The period certain and survivor annuity have additional benefits that reduce monthly payments.

5. **C.** Variable annuities are based on investments held in the portfolio, which the insurance company segregates into the *separate account*. The value of the units will correspond to the changes in this account.

6. **C.** The performance of an annuity unit of a variable annuity is based on the fluctuating performance of the separate account of the insurance company. This separate account is composed of a portfolio of securities (stocks or bonds). The person who buys a variable annuity hopes that the value of that portfolio will increase so that the annuity payments can increase correspondingly.

7. **D.** A variable annuity is both a security and an insurance product. For this reason, a salesperson who wants to sell variable annuities must become licensed with both the NASD (to sell the security) and the state insurance commission (to sell the insurance product).

8. **C.** In a life annuity, clients receive monthly income checks until their death, at which time payments cease. This type of annuity provides the maximum monthly payment because there are no added options or benefits that reduce payouts.

9. **A.** An accumulation unit, as described in answers B, C and D, is not the same as an annuity unit. An annuity unit is the accounting measure that determines the amount of each payment during the payout period.

10. **C.** Variable annuities invest the separate fund in equities, so payout depends on the equities' performance. This provides some protection of purchasing power because equities generally increase more than the cost of living. The other three answers—Series HH bonds, fixed annuities and face-amount certificates—are fixed-income investments with no protection of purchasing power.

11. **B.** A variable annuity is both an insurance and a securities product. Choice IV is incorrect because the annuitant assumes the investment risk of a variable annuity and is not protected by the insurance company from capital losses.

# Qualified Annuity Plans

### Tax Advantages

Tax-sheltered annuity plans (TSAs) are entitled to the following tax advantages:

- **Income exclusion**. Contributions are excluded from the employee's gross income for that year.
- **Tax-free accumulation**. Earnings accumulate tax free and do not increase the participant's taxable income until the total dollars are withdrawn at retirement.

### Taxation of Distributions from a TSA

Distributions from a TSA must follow the same rules as all qualified plans.

### Investments

TSA plans may invest assets in any of the following vehicles:

- mutual funds
- stocks
- bonds
- CDs
- life insurance

## Eligibility Requirements

In order to be eligible to offer a TSA, the employer must qualify under either section 403(b) or 501(c)3 of the Internal Revenue Code, or must be classified as a church organization by the IRS.

### Public Educational 403(b) Institutions

These state-run educational systems include:

- elementary schools
- secondary schools
- colleges and universities
- medical schools

**Job classifications**. Individuals who are employed by the above school systems in the following job classifications may enroll in a TSA plan:

- teachers and other faculty members;
- administrators, managers, principals, supervisors and other members of the administrative staff;
- counselors;
- clerical staff and maintenance workers; and
- individuals who perform services for the institution, such as doctors or nurses.

### Tax-exempt 501(c)3 Organizations

Typical 501(c)3 organizations include:

- private colleges and universities
- trade schools
- parochial schools
- zoos and museums
- research and scientific foundations
- religious and charitable institutions
- private hospitals and medical schools

### Church Organizations

Eligible for a TSA plan are ordained ministers, priests or missionaries of the church. Clerical or administrative staff of a church organization are not eligible to participate in a TSA plan.

# Employee Retirement Income Security Act

ERISA guidelines for the regulation of retirement plans include:

- participation
- funding
- vesting
- communication
- nondiscrimination

ERISA does not require any employer to establish a pension plan for its workers.

Corporations usually choose to organize their plans under the standards set forth by ERISA because of the favorable tax treatment that both employer sponsors and employee plan participants are eligible for. The most important tax advantages for ERISA-qualified pension plans are:

- The employer is entitled to take a current income tax deduction for contributions made to the plan.
- The employees do not have to include in their current year's gross income any of their employer's contributions to their retirement plan. All contributions to the plan are tax deferred until they are distributed.
- Any income earned (or capital gains achieved) by the investments in the participant's account are not taxed to the plan participant until they are distributed or withdrawn.
- Distributions from the retirement plan may be eligible for special income and estate tax treatment at the time of withdrawal.
- Employees may voluntarily contribute to the plan, but their contributions are made with aftertax dollars; upon distribution, the contributions are returned tax free. Earnings from the plan are tax deferred.

# 19 Direct Participation Programs

## Characteristics of Limited Partnerships

### Partnerships and Limited Partnerships

Limited partnerships are direct participation programs (DPPs) that offer investors direct participation in the economic consequences of the business. They pass income, gains, losses, deductions and credits directly to investors.

Limited partnerships offer investors limited liability. Should the limited partnership default on its loans, investors could lose their entire investment but they are not personally liable for other partnership debts.

**Private placements and public offerings**. In a private placement limited partnership, a small number of limited partners (LPs) contribute large amounts of money. LPs tend to be wealthy investors with substantial investment experience.

In a public offering limited partnership, there are a larger number of investors, each of whom makes a relatively small contribution of capital to the business ($2,000 to $5,000 is a standard minimum contribution).

**Advantages and disadvantages of the limited partnership**. The DPP investor enjoys several advantages:

- an investment managed by others
- flow-through of income and certain expenses
- limited liability

The greatest disadvantage is lack of liquidity. Because the secondary market for DPPs is limited, investors who want to liquidate frequently cannot locate a buyer for their interests.

### Tax Reporting for Partnerships

Limited partnerships pass directly through to investors the economic benefits (growth and income) and tax consequences (allowable deductions and write-offs) of the business. Partnership losses are often apportioned among investors, enabling them to claim those losses as deductions on their personal tax forms. If the partnership's operations result in taxable income, that amount is divided proportionally among the partners.

Under current tax law, LPs are classified as passive investors: any income they receive from a partnership is passive income, and any loss passed through to them is a passive loss. An investor may use a tax loss from a partnership only to offset income from another passive investment. Passive losses can be carried forward to the next year and used to offset future passive income. Investors with no passive income in the year they receive passive losses cannot deduct the losses (neither stock dividends nor wages are classified as passive income).

## Forming a Limited Partnership

**Syndication and underwriting of limited partnerships.** The syndicator (or syndicate manager) is the individual or firm designated to work with the general partners (GPs) of a limited partnership. The syndicator's duties include preparing the paperwork needed to register the limited partnership with the SEC; organizing and overseeing the selling syndicate (and selling group); and promoting the partnership generally.

**Subscription agreement.** An investor interested in purchasing a limited partnership unit completes and signs a subscription agreement, which includes a statement of the investor's net worth and annual income and a power of attorney appointing the GP as the agent of the partnership. The subscription agreement, with the subscriber's money, is merely an offer to buy and becomes effective only when accepted and signed by the GP.

**Certificate of limited partnership.** The certificate of limited partnership includes the following information:

- partnership's name;
- partnership's business (e.g., to drill for oil or construct office buildings);
- principal place of business, often the GP's address;
- amount of time the partnership expects to be in business;
- size of each LP's investment and any additional investment expected;
- when each investor's contribution will be returned (if a time has been set);
- each LP's share of the profits or other compensation; and
- whether and under what conditions an LP can assign (sell or donate) an interest.

**Agreement of partnership.** The agreement of partnership is a contract that provides guidelines for operation of the partnership and describes the roles of the general and limited partners, including each party's rights and responsibilities.

## Dissolving a Limited Partnership

**Dissolution of partnership and settlement of accounts.** When the partnership dissolves, the GP must cancel the certificate of limited partnership and settle accounts in the following order:

1. secured lenders;
2. other creditors;
3. limited partners, first for their claims to a share of profits and second for their claims to a return of contributed capital; and
4. general partners, first for fees and other claims not involving profits or capital, second for a share of profits and third for capital return.

## Investors in a Limited Partnership

### General Partner

**Rights and responsibilities.** The GPs are the active investors in a limited partnership, and assume responsibility for all aspects of the partnership's operations. GPs assemble the investors' capital, select assets for investment and actively manage the business of the partnership after assets have been acquired. Like sole proprietors, GPs are involved in all of the partnership's decision making. The GP will:

- make decisions that bind the partnership;
- buy and sell property for the partnership;
- manage the partnership property and money;
- supervise all aspects of the partnership's business;
- receive compensation as specified in the partnership agreement; and
- maintain a 1% financial interest in the partnership.

GPs have unlimited liability and are, therefore, personally liable for all partnership business losses and debts.

**Restrictions on the activities of general partners.** The GP has a fiduciary relationship to the LPs. That is, the GP has been entrusted with the

LPs' capital and is morally and legally bound to use that capital in the investors' best interests. The GP is prohibited from:

- preventing the ordinary flow of partnership business;
- assigning or possessing partnership property for purposes other than those of the partnership;
- competing against the partnership for personal gain; or
- admitting new GPs or LPs or continuing the partnership after the loss of a GP unless specified in the agreement.

### Limited Partner

**Rights and responsibilities.** The basic obligation of the LP is to provide capital. The LP has the right to:

- receive returns as justified by the partnership's business;
- vote on the admission of a new GP;
- sue or remove the GP;
- petition a court to dissolve the partnership;
- vote on the sale or refinancing of partnership property; and
- inspect partnership books and records.

**Restrictions on the activities of limited partners.** Because LPs are passive investors, they assume no part of the management responsibilities or decision making and are, therefore, usually not held personally and individually liable for the general indebtedness of the partnership. An LP who exceeds legal boundaries by actively participating in business management may lose limited liability.

## Types of Limited Partnership Programs

### Real Estate Limited Partnerships

The primary benefit is strong growth potential through appreciation of property. Some partnerships distribute income too, and in many (but not all) real estate programs, cash distributions are sheltered from taxes by deductions for mortgage interest and depreciation.

**New construction.** A new construction program builds new property. The principal advantage of such a program is the potential for appreciation. Disadvantages to new construction are possible cost or time overruns, no established track record for new property, the difficulty of finding permanent financing and an inability to deduct current expenses during the construction period. Investments in new construction are more speculative than investments in existing property.

**Existing property.** Programs based on existing property with a track record are generally safer and more conservative than new construction programs. Potential disadvantages include greater maintenance or repair expenses than for new construction, expiring leases that may not be renewed and existing low-rent arrangements that may bring less revenue than desired.

**Raw land.** A limited partnership based on raw land is the most speculative type of real estate limited partnership, and has little to offer beyond appreciation potential—although this can be substantial.

### Oil and Gas Limited Partnerships

**Exploratory drilling.** Exploratory drilling programs (often called *wildcatting*) have a single objective—to locate undiscovered reserves of oil and gas. Exploratory drilling programs offer high risk and high reward.

The principal advantage of exploratory drilling programs is the write-off of intangible drilling costs (IDCs). These write-offs are generally taken the first year of operation. IDCs are the noncapitalized costs associated with drilling and sinking a well; they include wages, fuel, supplies, surveys and transportation of supplies and materials to the drilling site.

**Developmental drilling.** Developmental drilling programs target areas of proven reserves and plan new well drilling near existing fields. In general, there is less risk and less reward potential in developmental programs than there is in exploratory programs.

**Income programs.** Income programs, which invest in producing wells, are the least risky oil and gas investments. This type of oil and gas program would be appropriate for the investor whose goal is income. Income programs buy and market proven reserves of oil and gas. They do not explore or develop, nor do they pass on write-offs from IDCs.

### Equipment-leasing Limited Partnerships

Some DPPs purchase equipment that they then lease to other businesses on a long-term basis. Each investor receives a share of the income from the lease payments and a proportional share of operating expenses, interest expense and depreciation.

## Analysis and Evaluation of Direct Participation Programs

An investor should choose a limited partnership because:

- it appears to be a sound business venture (that is, it is economically viable);
- the general partner has demonstrated management ability and expertise in running similar programs;
- the program's objectives match the objectives of the investor, and will do so within a time frame that meets the investor's needs; and
- the startup costs and projected revenues are in line with the startup costs and revenues of similar, well-run ventures.

Investors considering a DPP should look at the offering documents to assess the economic soundness of the program. To gauge the possible success of a program, one should pay particularly close attention to the sponsor's track record and experience, as disclosed in the prospectus.

# 20 Key Facts and Figures

## How Many *Business* Days?

### Same Business Day

- The settlement date on cash transactions.

### One Business Day

- Regular way settlement on U.S. government securities.
- OCC settlement by broker-dealers for options transactions.

### Two Business Days

- The relationship of the normal ex-dividend date to the record date.
- The minimum period for seller's option contracts on U.S. government securities.

### Three Business Days

- Regular way settlement for securities other than U.S. governments.

### Four Business Days

- The minimum period for seller's option contracts on securities other than U.S. governments.

### Five Business Days

- The time within which cash account (nonmargin) purchases must be paid in full.
- The time within which Regulation T margin calls must be satisfied.

### Ten Business Days

- The maximum time allowed the seller to deliver certificates.
- The time within which the beneficial owner's shares will be represented if he has not responded prior to the stockholder's meeting.

## How Many *Calendar* Days?

### Seven Calendar Days

- The maximum time period for mutual funds to redeem shares tendered.

### Twenty Calendar Days

- The minimum time period between the filing date and the effective date (cooling-off period) of a security registration.
- The time period respondents may take to answer a simplified customer arbitration claim.

### Thirty Calendar Days

- The time that must elapse before termination as a registered rep is effective with the NASD unless accepted earlier by the Board of Governors.
- The number of days in any month when computing interest on debt securities other than U.S. governments.
- The IRS time period restriction on purchases to avoid wash sale designation (30 days before and 30 days after).

### Thirty-five Calendar Days

- The maximum time period for delivery on COD orders.

### Forty-five Calendar Days

- The maximum time period within which one can receive a 100% refund of sales charges on investment company contractual plans.

### Sixty Calendar Days

- The maximum length of a seller's option contract in a security.

### Ninety Calendar Days

- The length of time a cash account must be frozen for nonpayment.

## How Many *Months*?

### One Month

- The frequency with which statements must be mailed to active customers.

### Two Months

- The maximum time a registered rep can hold the mail of a customer who is traveling within the United States.

### Three Months

- The maximum time a registered rep can hold the mail of a customer who is out of the country.
- The length of time that a letter of intent can be backdated.

### Six Months

- The frequency with which investment companies must send reports to shareholders (semiannually).

### Twelve Months

- The frequency with which every publicly held firm and NYSE firm must be audited by an independent public accountant (annually).

### Thirteen Months

- The length of life of a letter of intent.

## How Many *Years*?

### Two Years

- The time fully paid restricted stock must be owned before selling under Rule 144.

### Three Years

- The length of time nonaffiliated persons must own fully paid for restricted stock before selling out under Rule 144 and be exempt from filing Form 144 and from the volume limits and current financial information requirements.

## Color Code that Paperwork!

Match the following color-coded terms with the definitions in questions 1 through 6.

A. Blue chip
B. *The Blue List*
C. Blue-sky
D. *Pink Sheets*
E. Red herring
F. *Yellow Sheets*

1. ___ Daily publication showing current offerings of municipal bond dealers

2. ___ Preliminary prospectus

3. ___ Nickname for state laws that regulate the securities industry

4. ___ Quote sheets that carry the wholesale prices between dealers for corporate bonds

5. ___ Well-established companies that have demonstrated the ability to pay dividends in both good times and bad

6. ___ Daily publication that shows wholesale quotations for over-the-counter stocks

**Answers:** 1. B; 2. E; 3. C; 4. F; 5. A; 6. D.

## Take a Letter!

Match the following securities regulations with the definitions in questions 1 through 3.

A. Reg A
B. Reg T
C. Reg U

1. ___ The securities regulation that exempts public offerings valued at less than $5 million from registration requirements

2. ___ The Federal Reserve Board regulation governing the amount of credit extended to clients by brokerage firms and dealers

3. ___ The Federal Reserve Board regulation governing the credit extended by banks for the purpose of securities transactions

**Answers:** 1. A; 2. B; 3. C

## Common Abbreviations

| | |
|---|---|
| ADR/ADS | American depositary receipt (share) |
| AE | account executive |
| AIR | assumed interest rate |
| AMBAC | AMBAC Indemnity Corporation |
| AMEX | American Stock Exchange |
| AMT | alternative minimum tax |
| AON | all or none |
| AP | associated person |
| APR | annual percentage rate |
| BA | banker's acceptance |
| BAN | bond anticipation note |
| BD | broker-dealer |
| BOT | bought |
| BSE | Boston Stock Exchange |
| BW | bid wanted |
| CBOE | Chicago Board Options Exchange |
| CBOT/CBT | Chicago Board of Trade |
| CD | certificate of deposit |
| CFTC | Commodities Futures Trading Commission |
| CHX | Chicago Stock Exchange |
| CLN | construction loan note |
| CMB | cash management bill |
| CME | Chicago Mercantile Exchange |
| CMO | collateralized mortgage obligation |
| CMV | current market value |
| COD | cash (collect) on delivery |
| COP | Code of Procedure |
| CPI | Consumer Price Index |
| CQS | Consolidated Quotation System |
| CR | credit balance (register) |
| CROP | compliance registered options principal |
| CSE | Cincinnati Stock Exchange |
| CUSIP | Committee on Uniform Securities Identification Procedures |
| CY | current yield |
| DBCC | District Business Conduct Committee |
| DEA | Designated Examining Authority |
| DFI | Dearborn Financial Institute, Inc. |
| DFPI | Dearborn Financial Publishing, Inc. |
| DJIA | Dow Jones Industrial Average |
| DJTA | Dow Jones Transportation Average |
| DJUA | Dow Jones Utility Average |
| DK | don't know |
| DNR | do not reduce |
| DPP | direct participation program |
| DR | debit balance (register) |
| DTC | Depository Trust Company |
| DVP | delivery vs. payment |
| EB | electronic book |
| EE | excess equity |
| EE | Series EE savings bond |
| EPS | earnings per share |
| EQ | equity |
| ERISA | Employee Retirement Income Security Act of 1974 |
| FAC | face amount certificate |
| FCA | Farm Credit Administration |
| FCO | foreign currency option |
| FCS | Farm Credit System |
| Fed | Federal Reserve System |
| FDIC | Federal Deposit Insurance Corporation |
| FHA | Federal Housing Administration |
| FHLB | Federal Home Loan Bank |
| FHLMC | Federal Home Loan Mortgage Corporation |
| FICB | Federal Intermediate Credit Bank |
| FIFO | first in, first out |
| FinOp | Financial and Operations Principal |
| FNMA | Federal National Mortgage Association |
| FOCUS | Financial and Operational Combined Uniform Single report |
| FOK | fill or kill |
| FOMC | Federal Open Market Committee |
| FRB | Federal Reserve Board |
| GNMA | Government National Mortgage Association |
| GDP | gross domestic product |
| GO | general obligation bond |
| GP | general partner |
| GTC | good till canceled |
| HH | Series HH savings bond |
| IDB | industrial development bond |
| IDR | industrial revenue bond |

| | |
|---|---|
| IO | interest-only CMO |
| IOC | immediate or cancel order |
| IPO | initial public offering |
| IRA | individual retirement account |
| IRC | Internal Revenue Code |
| IRR | internal rate of return |
| IRS | Internal Revenue Service |
| ITC | investment tax credit |
| JTIC | joint tenants in common |
| JTWROS | joint tenants with right of survivorship |
| LEAPS | Long-term Equity AnticiPation Securities |
| LIBOR | London Interbank Offered Rate |
| LIFO | last in, first out |
| LMV | long market value |
| LP | limited partner |
| MBIA | Municipal Bond Investors Assurance Corporation |
| MIG | Moody's investment grade |
| MPT | modern portfolio theory |
| MSRB | Municipal Securities Rulemaking Board |
| MV | market value |
| NASAA | North American Securities Administrators Association |
| NASD | National Association of Securities Dealers |
| Nasdaq | National Association of Securities Dealers Automated Quotation System |
| NAV | net asset value |
| NH | not held order |
| NIC | net interest cost |
| NL | no load |
| NNM | Nasdaq National Market |
| NSCC | National Securities Clearing Corporation |
| NYSE | New York Stock Exchange |
| OBO | order book official |
| OCC | Options Clearing Corporation |
| OID | original issue discount |
| ORS | order routing system |
| OS | official statement |
| OSJ | office of supervisory jurisdiction |
| OTC | over the counter |
| OW | offer wanted |
| PAC | planned amortization class CMO |
| PE | price-earnings ratio |
| PHLX | Philadelphia Stock Exchange |
| PO | principal-only CMO |
| POP | public offering price |
| PSE | Pacific Stock Exchange |
| RAN | revenue anticipation note |
| REIT | real estate investment trust |
| REMIC | real estate mortgage investment conduit |
| RIA | registered investment adviser |
| ROI | return on investment |
| ROP | registered options principal |
| RR | registered representative |
| RTFQ | read the full question |
| SEA | Securities Exchange Act of 1934 |
| SEC | Securities and Exchange Commission |
| SEP | simplified employee pension plan |
| SIA | Securities Industry Association |
| SIPC | Securities Investor Protection Corporation |
| SLD | sold |
| SLMA | Student Loan Marketing Association |
| SMA | special memorandum account |
| SMV | short market value |
| SOES | Small Order Execution System |
| SRO | self-regulatory organization |
| SROP | senior registered options principal |
| STRIPS | Separate Trading of Registered Interest and Principal of Securities |
| T+3 | trade date plus three days settlement |
| TAB | tax anticipation bill |
| TAC | targeted amortization class CMO |
| TAN | tax anticipation note |
| TCPA | Telephone Consumer Protection Act of 1991 |
| TIC | true interest cost |
| TRA | Tax Reform Act of 1986 |
| TSA/TDA | tax-sheltered (-deferred) annuity |
| UGMA/ UTMA | Uniform Gifts (Transfers) to Minors Act |
| UIT | unit investment trust |

| | |
|---|---|
| UPC | Uniform Practice Code |
| USA | Uniform Securities Act |
| VLI | variable life insurance |
| WD | when distributed |
| WI | when issued |
| YLD | yield |
| YTC | yield to call |
| YTM | yield to maturity |
| Z | zero |
| ZR | zero |

# References in *Review* for Q&A Exams

## Equity Securities

### 1. Corporate Ownership and Common Stock

1. Page 3
2. Page 1
3. Page 2
4. Page 1
5. Page 3
6. Page 1
7. Page 3
8. Page 3
9. Page 2
10. Page 1
11. Page 1
12. Page 2

### 2. Preferred Stock

1. Page 7
2. Page 7
3. Page 7
4. Page 7

### 3. Return on Investment

1. Page 10
2. Page 10
3. Page 10
4. Page 10
5. Page 10
6. Page 10
7. Page 10
8. Page 10

### 4. Transferability of Ownership

1. Page 13
2. Page 13
3. Page 13

### 5. Rights and Warrants

1. Page 15
2. Page 15
3. Page 16
4. Page 16
5. Page 16
6. Page 15
7. Page 15
8. Page 16
9. Page 16
10. Page 16
11. Page 16
12. Page 16
13. Page 16
14. Page 16

### 6. American Depositary Receipts

1. Page 19
2. Page 19
3. Page 19
4. Page 19

## Debt Securities

### 7. Characteristics of Bonds

1. Page 21
2. Page 23
3. Page 21
4. Page 23
5. Page 24
6. Page 22
7. Page 23
8. Page 21
9. Page 23
10. Page 22
11. Page 21
12. Page 22
13. Page 21
14. Page 21
15. Page 21
16. Page 22
17. Page 22
18. Page 21
19. Page 22
20. Page 22
21. Page 24
22. Page 24
23. Page 21

24. Page 24
25. Page 24
26. Page 22

**8. Bond Yields**

1. Page 30
2. Page 30
3. Page 30
4. Page 30
5. Page 30
6. Page 30
7. Page 28
8. Page 28
9. Page 28
10. Page 30
11. Page 28
12. Page 28
13. Page 30
14. Page 28
15. Page 28
16. Page 30
17. Page 30
18. Page 30
19. Page 30

## Corporate Debt Securities

**9. Characteristics of Corporate Bonds**

1. Page 36
2. Page 36
3. Page 36
4. Page 35
5. Page 36
6. Page 35
7. Page 36
8. Page 36
9. Page 35

**10. Convertible Securities**

1. Page 41
2. Page 42
3. Page 41
4. Page 41
5. Page 41
6. Page 41
7. Page 41
8. Page 40
9. Page 40
10. Page 40
11. Page 40
12. Page 41
13. Page 41
14. Page 40
15. Page 41
16. Page 40
17. Page 41
18. Page 41
19. Page 42
20. Page 40

## U.S. Government and Agency Securities

**11. Marketable Government Securities**

1. Page 45
2. Page 46
3. Page 45
4. Page 46
5. Page 45
6. Page 46
7. Page 45
8. Page 45
9. Page 45
10. Page 45
11. Page 45

**12. Nonmarketable Government Securities**

1. Page 49
2. Page 49
3. Page 49

**13. Agency Issues**

1. Page 52
2. Page 51
3. Page 51
4. Page 52
5. Page 52
6. Page 51
7. Page 52
8. Page 51
9. Page 51
10. Page 52
11. Page 53
12. Page 52
13. Page 52
14. Page 52
15. Page 52
16. Page 53
17. Page 51
18. Page 51
19. Page 52
20. Page 52
21. Page 52

## Money-market Securities and Interest Rates

**14. The Money Market**

1. Page 56
2. Page 56
3. Page 56
4. Page 56
5. Page 55
6. Page 56

7. Page 56
8. Page 56
9. Page 56
10. Page 56
11. Page 56
12. Page 56
13. Page 56
14. Page 55
15. Page 55
16. Page 55
17. Page 56
18. Page 56
19. Page 56
20. Page 56
21. Page 56

### 15. Interest Rates

1. Page 59
2. Page 59
3. Page 59
4. Page 59
5. Page 59
6. Page 59
7. Page 59
8. Page 59

### 16. Eurodollars and the Foreign Currency Markets

1. Page 61
2. Page 61
3. Page 61
4. Page 61
5. Page 61
6. Page 61
7. Page 61
8. Page 61
9. Page 61
10. Page 61
11. Page 61
12. Page 61
13. Page 61
14. Page 61
15. Page 61
16. Page 61
17. Page 61
18. Page 61

## Issuing Securities

### 17. The Regulation of New Issues

1. Page 66
2. Page 66
3. Page 66
4. Page 66
5. Page 66
6. Page 66
7. Page 67
8. Page 65
9. Page 66
10. Page 66
11. Page 66
12. Page 65
13. Page 66
14. Page 67
15. Page 66
16. Page 65
17. Page 67
18. Page 67
19. Page 67
20. Page 67
21. Page 66
22. Page 67
23. Page 65
24. Page 66
25. Page 65
26. Page 65

### 18. The Underwriting Process

1. Page 71
2. Page 72
3. Page 71
4. Page 72
5. Page 72
6. Page 70
7. Page 72
8. Page 72
9. Page 71
10. Page 71
11. Page 71
12. Page 71
13. Page 71
14. Page 72
15. Page 71
16. Page 72
17. Page 71
18. Page 70
19. Page 70
20. Page 72
21. Page 71

### 19. The Underwriting Syndicate

1. Page 74
2. Page 74
3. Page 74
4. Page 74
5. Page 74
6. Page 74
7. Page 74
8. Page 74
9. Page 74
10. Page 74
11. Page 74

**20. Types of Underwriting Commitments**

1. Page 76
2. Page 76
3. Page 76
4. Page 76
5. Page 76
6. Page 76
7. Page 76
8. Page 76
9. Page 76
10. Page 76
11. Page 76
12. Page 76
13. Page 76
14. Page 76
15. Page 76
16. Page 76
17. Page 76
18. Page 76

**21. Exemptions from the Securities Act of 1933**

1. Page 78
2. Page 79
3. Page 78
4. Page 78
5. Page 78
6. Page 78
7. Page 78
8. Page 78
9. Page 78
10. Page 78
11. Page 78
12. Page 78
13. Page 78
14. Page 78
15. Page 78
16. Page 78
17. Page 78
18. Page 78
19. Page 79
20. Page 78
21. Page 79
22. Page 78
23. Page 78
24. Page 78
25. Page 78
26. Page 79
27. Page 79

**22. Freeriding and Withholding: Hot Issues**

1. Page 81
2. Page 81
3. Page 81
4. Page 81
5. Page 81
6. Page 82
7. Page 81
8. Page 81
9. Page 81
10. Page 82
11. Page 81
12. Page 82
13. Page 82
14. Page 81
15. Page 82
16. Page 81
17. Page 81
18. Page 81
19. Page 81
20. Page 81
21. Page 81
22. Page 81
23. Page 81
24. Page 81

## Trading Securities

**23. The Regulation of Trading**

1. Page 86
2. Page 85
3. Page 86
4. Page 85
5. Page 85
6. Page 85

**24. Securities Markets and Broker-Dealers**

1. Page 88
2. Page 88
3. Page 88
4. Page 88
5. Page 88
6. Page 89
7. Page 89
8. Page 89
9. Page 88
10. Page 88
11. Page 89
12. Page 88
13. Page 88
14. Page 89
15. Page 89

**25. The New York Stock Exchange**

1. Page 91
2. Page 91
3. Page 91
4. Page 91
5. Page 91
6. Page 91

**26. The Specialist**

1. Page 95
2. Page 95

3. Page 95
4. Page 95
5. Page 95
6. Page 95

## 27. Types of Orders

1. Page 98
2. Page 98
3. Page 98
4. Page 97
5. Page 97
6. Page 97
7. Page 98
8. Page 97
9. Page 97
10. Page 97
11. Page 98
12. Page 97
13. Page 97
14. Page 97
15. Page 98
16. Page 97
17. Page 98
18. Page 98
19. Page 98
20. Page 98

## 28. Long and Short Sale Rules

1. Page 102
2. Page 102
3. Page 102
4. Page 102
5. Page 102
6. Page 102
7. Page 102
8. Page 102
9. Page 102
10. Page 102
11. Page 102
12. Page 102
13. Page 102

## 29. The Over-the-Counter Market

1. Page 104
2. Page 104
3. Page 104
4. Page 104
5. Page 104
6. Page 104
7. Page 104
8. Page 104
9. Page 104
10. Page 104

## 30. Quotations

1. Page 106
2. Page 106
3. Page 106
4. Page 106
5. Page 106
6. Page 106
7. Page 106
8. Page 106
9. Page 106
10. Page 106
11. Page 106

## 31. NASD 5% Markup Policy

1. Page 108
2. Page 108
3. Page 108
4. Page 108
5. Page 108
6. Page 108
7. Page 108
8. Page 108
9. Page 109
10. Page 108
11. Page 108
12. Page 108
13. Page 108
14. Page 108
15. Page 108
16. Page 108
17. Page 108
18. Page 108
19. Page 108
20. Page 108
21. Page 108
22. Page 108
23. Page 108
24. Page 108
25. Page 108

## 32. NASD Automated Quotation System

1. Page 111
2. Page 111
3. Page 111
4. Page 111
5. Page 111
6. Page 111
7. Page 111
8. Page 111
9. Page 112

## 33. Computerized Order Routing

1. Page 114
2. Page 114
3. Page 114
4. Page 114
5. Page 114
6. Page 114
7. Page 114
8. Page 114
9. Page 114
10. Page 114

**34. The Consolidated Tape**

1. Page 115
2. Page 115
3. Page 115
4. Page 115
5. Page 115
6. Page 115
7. Page 115
8. Page 115
9. Page 115
10. Page 116
11. Page 115
12. Page 115

## Customer Accounts

**35. New Accounts**

1. Page 123
2. Page 123
3. Page 123
4. Page 120
5. Page 123
6. Page 120
7. Page 120
8. Page 122
9. Page 120
10. Page 120
11. Page 120
12. Page 122
13. Page 123
14. Page 122
15. Page 123
16. Page 121
17. Page 120
18. Page 123
19. Page 123
20. Page 119
21. Page 121
22. Page 120
23. Page 121
24. Page 121
25. Page 123
26. Page 122
27. Page 122
28. Page 122
29. Page 122
30. Page 122
31. Page 122
32. Page 122
33. Page 122
34. Page 122
35. Page 121

**36. Types of Accounts**

1. Page 128
2. Page 129
3. Page 129
4. Page 128
5. Page 128
6. Page 128
7. Page 127
8. Page 130
9. Page 129
10. Page 128
11. Page 127
12. Page 128
13. Page 129
14. Page 129
15. Page 129
16. Page 127
17. Page 128
18. Page 129
19. Page 129
20. Page 129
21. Page 129
22. Page 128
23. Page 128
24. Page 128
25. Page 129
26. Page 127
27. Page 127
28. Page 128
29. Page 129

**37. Uniform Gifts to Minors Act Accounts**

1. Page 133
2. Page 133
3. Page 133
4. Page 133
5. Page 133
6. Page 133
7. Page 133
8. Page 133
9. Page 133
10. Page 133
11. Page 133
12. Page 133
13. Page 133
14. Page 133
15. Page 133
16. Page 133
17. Page 134
18. Page 133
19. Page 134
20. Page 133
21. Page 134

## Brokerage Office Procedures

**38. Brokerage Support Services**

1. Page 139
2. Page 139
3. Page 139
4. Page 139
5. Page 139
6. Page 139

7. Page 140
8. Page 140
9. Page 138
10. Page 138
11. Page 139
12. Page 139
13. Page 139
14. Page 139
15. Page 139
16. Page 137
17. Page 137
18. Page 140
19. Page 140
20. Page 138
21. Page 138
22. Page 137
23. Page 140
24. Page 138
25. Page 138
26. Page 140
27. Page 140
28. Page 138
29. Page 140

### 39. Accrued Interest Calculations

1. Page 146
2. Page 145
3. Page 145
4. Page 145
5. Page 145
6. Page 145
7. Page 145
8. Page 146
9. Page 145
10. Page 145
11. Page 145
12. Page 145
13. Page 145
14. Page 145
15. Page 145
16. Page 145
17. Page 146
18. Page 145
19. Page 146
20. Page 145

### 40. Rules of Good Delivery

1. Page 150
2. Page 149
3. Page 150
4. Page 150
5. Page 149
6. Page 150
7. Page 149
8. Page 149
9. Page 150
10. Page 149
11. Page 149
12. Page 150
13. Page 150
14. Page 149
15. Page 149
16. Page 149
17. Page 149
18. Page 150
19. Page 149
20. Page 149
21. Page 150
22. Page 149

## Margin Accounts

### 41. Extension of Credit in the Securities Industry

1. Page 153
2. Page 153
3. Page 153
4. Page 154
5. Page 153
6. Page 153
7. Page 154
8. Page 154
9. Page 154
10. Page 154
11. Page 154
12. Page 154
13. Page 154
14. Page 154
15. Page 154
16. Page 154
17. Page 154
18. Page 154

### 42. Margin Accounting

1. Page 156
2. Page 159
3. Page 159
4. Page 159
5. Page 159
6. Page 158
7. Page 159
8. Page 156
9. Page 156
10. Page 157
11. Page 155
12. Page 159
13. Page 155
14. Page 157
15. Page 155
16. Page 155
17. Page 155
18. Page 157
19. Page 159
20. Page 155
21. Page 158
22. Page 158
23. Page 158
24. Page 158
25. Page 158

26. Page 159
27. Page 157
28. Page 157
29. Page 157
30. Page 155
31. Page 155
32. Page 155
33. Page 155
34. Page 155
35. Page 155
36. Page 155
37. Page 159
38. Page 157
39. Page 157
40. Page 159
41. Page 159
42. Page 158
43. Page 157
44. Page 158
45. Page 159

### 43. Special Memorandum Account

1. Page 164
2. Page 165
3. Page 165
4. Page 165
5. Page 165
6. Page 165
7. Page 165
8. Page 165
9. Page 164
10. Page 164
11. Page 165
12. Page 165
13. Page 164
14. Page 164
15. Page 165

### 44. Pledging Customer Securities for Loans

1. Page 168
2. Page 168
3. Page 168
4. Page 168
5. Page 168
6. Page 168
7. Page 168
8. Page 168
9. Page 168

## Economics and Analysis

### 45. Economics

1. Page 172
2. Page 172
3. Page 171
4. Page 171
5. Page 172
6. Page 171
7. Page 171
8. Page 171
9. Page 171
10. Page 172
11. Page 173
12. Page 172
13. Page 173
14. Page 172
15. Page 172
16. Page 171
17. Page 171
18. Page 172
19. Page 172
20. Page 172
21. Page 172
22. Page 172

### 46. Government Economic Policy

1. Page 178
2. Page 178
3. Page 177
4. Page 177
5. Page 178
6. Page 179
7. Page 178
8. Page 178
9. Page 178
10. Page 178
11. Page 177
12. Page 178
13. Page 177
14. Page 178
15. Page 178
16. Page 178
17. Page 179
18. Page 178
19. Page 178
20. Page 178
21. Page 177

### 47. Technical Analysis

1. Page 181
2. Page 181
3. Page 181
4. Page 182
5. Page 181
6. Page 182
7. Page 182
8. Page 181
9. Page 181
10. Page 181
11. Page 182

### 48. Fundamental Analysis

1. Page 184
2. Page 184
3. Page 184
4. Page 184
5. Page 184
6. Page 184
7. Page 184
8. Page 184
9. Page 184
10. Page 184

### 49. Financial Statements

1. Page 186
2. Page 185
3. Page 186
4. Page 186
5. Page 186
6. Page 186
7. Page 185
8. Page 185
9. Page 185
10. Page 185
11. Page 186
12. Page 185
13. Page 185
14. Page 186
15. Page 186
16. Page 186
17. Page 185
18. Page 185
19. Page 185

### 50. Financial Ratios

1. Page 191
2. Page 191
3. Page 191
4. Page 190
5. Page 191
6. Page 191
7. Page 190
8. Page 190
9. Page 190
10. Page 191
11. Page 191
12. Page 191
13. Page 190
14. Page 190
15. Page 190
16. Page 191
17. Page 191

## Ethics, Suitability and Recommendations

### 51. Ethics in the Securities Industry

1. Page 196
2. Page 196
3. Page 196
4. Page 196
5. Page 197
6. Page 197
7. Page 197
8. Page 197
9. Page 197
10. Page 197
11. Page 197
12. Page 196
13. Page 197
14. Page 196
15. Page 196
16. Page 196
17. Page 196

### 52. Know Your Customer

1. Page 199
2. Page 200
3. Page 200
4. Page 199
5. Page 200
6. Page 199
7. Page 199
8. Page 199

### 53. Analyzing Financial Risks and Rewards

1. Page 202
2. Page 202
3. Page 202
4. Page 202
5. Page 202
6. Page 202
7. Page 202
8. Page 202
9. Page 202
10. Page 202
11. Page 202
12. Page 202

### 54. Portfolio Analysis

1. Page 205
2. Page 205
3. Page 205
4. Page 205
5. Page 205
6. Page 205
7. Page 205
8. Page 205
9. Page 205

### 55. Federal and State Taxation

1. Page 207
2. Page 209
3. Page 210
4. Page 208
5. Page 208
6. Page 208
7. Page 208
8. Page 208

9. Page 207
10. Page 207
11. Page 209
12. Page 208
13. Page 207
14. Page 207
15. Page 207
16. Page 209
17. Page 207
18. Page 210
19. Page 207
20. Page 208
21. Page 209
22. Page 207
23. Page 208
24. Page 208
25. Page 209
26. Page 208
27. Page 207
28. Page 209
29. Page 210
30. Page 210
31. Page 209
32. Page 209

## U.S. Government and State Rules and Regulations

### 56. Insider Trading Act of 1988

1. Page 213
2. Page 213
3. Page 213
4. Page 213

### 57. Securities Investor Protection Corporation

1. Page 214
2. Page 214
3. Page 214
4. Page 214
5. Page 214
6. Page 214
7. Page 214
8. Page 214
9. Page 214
10. Page 214
11. Page 214
12. Page 214
13. Page 214
14. Page 215
15. Page 214

### 58. Other Federal and State Legislation

1. Page 217
2. Page 217

## Other SEC and SRO Rules and Regulations

### 59. Registration and Regulation of Broker-Dealers

1. Page 221
2. Page 221

### 60. NASD Bylaws

1. Page 226
2. Page 224
3. Page 225
4. Page 224
5. Page 224
6. Page 225
7. Page 225
8. Page 223
9. Page 225
10. Page 225
11. Page 224
12. Page 225
13. Page 225
14. Page 225
15. Page 224
16. Page 226
17. Page 225
18. Page 225
19. Page 223
20. Page 224

### 61. Codes of Procedure and of Arbitration Procedure

1. Page 228
2. Page 228
3. Page 228
4. Page 229
5. Page 228
6. Page 229
7. Page 229
8. Page 228
9. Page 229
10. Page 228
11. Page 228
12. Page 229
13. Page 228
14. Page 228
15. Page 228
16. Page 229
17. Page 228
18. Page 228
19. Page 228
20. Page 229
21. Page 229
22. Page 229
23. Page 229
24. Page 228
25. Page 229

### 62. NYSE Constitution and Rules

1. Page 231
2. Page 231
3. Page 231
4. Page 231

### 63. Communications with the Public

1. Page 236
2. Page 236
3. Page 236
4. Page 234
5. Page 235
6. Page 234
7. Page 236
8. Page 236
9. Page 235
10. Page 234
11. Page 235
12. Page 235
13. Page 236
14. Page 234
15. Page 234
16. Page 236
17. Page 235
18. Page 235
19. Page 234
20. Page 236
21. Page 235
22. Page 234
23. Page 234
24. Page 235
25. Page 235
26. Page 237
27. Page 237
28. Page 236
29. Page 234
30. Page 235
31. Page 237
32. Page 237
33. Page 237
34. Page 237

## Municipal Securities

### 64. Municipal Bond Characteristics

1. Page 241
2. Page 240
3. Page 241
4. Page 241
5. Page 241
6. Page 241
7. Page 241
8. Page 242
9. Page 241
10. Page 241
11. Page 241
12. Page 241
13. Page 241
14. Page 240
15. Page 241
16. Page 241
17. Page 241
18. Page 241
19. Page 239
20. Page 239
21. Page 242
22. Page 241
23. Page 242
24. Page 239

### 65. Issuing Municipal Securities

1. Page 249
2. Page 248
3. Page 247
4. Page 247
5. Page 247
6. Page 247
7. Page 249
8. Page 248
9. Page 246
10. Page 248
11. Page 246
12. Page 246
13. Page 246
14. Page 249
15. Page 247
16. Page 246
17. Page 248
18. Page 247
19. Page 246
20. Page 246
21. Page 249
22. Page 249
23. Page 247
24. Page 249
25. Page 249
26. Page 250
27. Page 246
28. Page 250
29. Page 247

### 66. Municipal Trading and Taxation

1. Page 256
2. Page 255
3. Page 256
4. Page 255
5. Page 256
6. Page 255
7. Page 256
8. Page 257
9. Page 257
10. Page 256
11. Page 256
12. Page 257
13. Page 256

14. Page 256
15. Page 256
16. Page 257
17. Page 256
18. Page 256
19. Page 256
20. Page 256
21. Page 257
22. Page 255
23. Page 257
24. Page 255
25. Page 255
26. Page 256
27. Page 256
28. Page 255

### 67. Analysis of Municipal Securities

1. Page 262
2. Page 262
3. Page 262
4. Page 263
5. Page 263
6. Page 262
7. Page 262
8. Page 262
9. Page 262
10. Page 263
11. Page 263
12. Page 262
13. Page 262
14. Page 263
15. Page 262
16. Page 262
17. Page 262
18. Page 263
19. Page 262
20. Page 263
21. Page 262

### 68. Municipal Securities Rules and Regulations

1. Page 267
2. Page 267
3. Page 267
4. Page 268
5. Page 269
6. Page 267
7. Page 267
8. Page 268
9. Page 267
10. Page 268
11. Page 267
12. Page 267
13. Page 267
14. Page 269
15. Page 269
16. Page 267
17. Page 267
18. Page 269
19. Page 268
20. Page 269
21. Page 269
22. Page 269
23. Page 268
24. Page 268
25. Page 268
26. Page 268

## Option Contracts

### 69. Introduction to Options

1. Page 277
2. Page 277
3. Page 277
4. Page 277

### 70. Equity Options

1. Page 283
2. Page 283
3. Page 283
4. Page 283
5. Page 283
6. Page 283
7. Page 282
8. Page 282
9. Page 282
10. Page 282
11. Page 283
12. Page 283
13. Page 283
14. Page 281
15. Page 281
16. Page 283
17. Page 283
18. Page 283
19. Page 282
20. Page 283
21. Page 283
22. Page 283
23. Page 283
24. Page 283
25. Page 283
26. Page 283
27. Page 284
28. Page 284
29. Page 284

### 71. Option Trading and Strategies

1. Page 289
2. Page 289
3. Page 287
4. Page 288
5. Page 289
6. Page 288
7. Page 290

8. Page 290
9. Page 289
10. Page 289
11. Page 289
12. Page 287
13. Page 287
14. Page 287
15. Page 289
16. Page 290
17. Page 290
18. Page 289
19. Page 290
20. Page 288
21. Page 289
22. Page 290
23. Page 288
24. Page 287
25. Page 289
26. Page 289
27. Page 288
28. Page 288
29. Page 288
30. Page 289
31. Page 289
32. Page 289
33. Page 290
34. Page 290
35. Page 290
36. Page 290
37. Page 290
38. Page 290

### 72. Multiple Option Strategies

1. Page 296
2. Page 298
3. Page 297
4. Page 297
5. Page 297
6. Page 296
7. Page 299
8. Page 298
9. Page 299
10. Page 298
11. Page 297
12. Page 298
13. Page 296
14. Page 298
15. Page 298
16. Page 297
17. Page 298
18. Page 299
19. Page 299
20. Page 299
21. Page 298
22. Page 299
23. Page 298
24. Page 298

### 73. Introduction to Nonequity Options

1. Page 309
2. Page 309
3. Page 309
4. Page 309
5. Page 309
6. Page 309
7. Page 309
8. Page 309
9. Page 309
10. Page 309
11. Page 309
12. Page 309
13. Page 309
14. Page 310
15. Page 311
16. Page 310
17. Page 310
18. Page 311
19. Page 310
20. Page 311
21. Page 310
22. Page 311
23. Page 311
24. Page 311
25. Page 311
26. Page 309
27. Page 310
28. Page 310
29. Page 309

### 74. Tax Rules for Options

1. Page 316
2. Page 316
3. Page 316
4. Page 316
5. Page 316
6. Page 316
7. Page 316
8. Page 316
9. Page 316
10. Page 316
11. Page 316
12. Page 316
13. Page 316
14. Page 316
15. Page 316
16. Page 316
17. Page 316

## Investment Company Products

### 75. Investment Company Offerings

1. Page 320
2. Page 320
3. Page 320
4. Page 320
5. Page 319
6. Page 319

7. Page 320
8. Page 320
9. Page 319
10. Page 320
11. Page 320
12. Page 320
13. Page 320
14. Page 320
15. Page 320
16. Page 320
17. Page 320
18. Page 320
19. Page 320
20. Page 320
21. Page 320

### 76. Characteristics of Mutual Funds

1. Page 324
2. Page 325
3. Page 325
4. Page 324
5. Page 324
6. Page 325
7. Page 325
8. Page 325
9. Page 326
10. Page 325
11. Page 324
12. Page 324
13. Page 325
14. Page 324
15. Page 325
16. Page 325
17. Page 326
18. Page 324
19. Page 325
20. Page 325

### 77. Investment Company Registration

1. Page 329
2. Page 328
3. Page 328
4. Page 329
5. Page 328
6. Page 329
7. Page 329
8. Page 328
9. Page 329
10. Page 329
11. Page 329
12. Page 328
13. Page 328
14. Page 328
15. Page 328
16. Page 328
17. Page 328
18. Page 328
19. Page 328
20. Page 328
21. Page 328
22. Page 329

### 78. Management of Investment Companies

1. Page 333
2. Page 332
3. Page 332
4. Page 332
5. Page 332
6. Page 332
7. Page 332
8. Page 332
9. Page 333
10. Page 333
11. Page 333
12. Page 333
13. Page 333
14. Page 332
15. Page 332
16. Page 332
17. Page 333
18. Page 332
19. Page 332
20. Page 332
21. Page 332
22. Page 332
23. Page 333
24. Page 333
25. Page 332

### 79. Mutual Fund Marketing, Pricing and Valuation

1. Page 337
2. Page 336
3. Page 337
4. Page 335
5. Page 335
6. Page 338
7. Page 336
8. Page 335
9. Page 336
10. Page 338
11. Page 337
12. Page 337
13. Page 337
14. Page 337
15. Page 336
16. Page 337
17. Page 338
18. Page 335
19. Page 335
20. Page 338
21. Page 337
22. Page 338
23. Page 337
24. Page 337
25. Page 336

26. Page 335
27. Page 336
28. Page 337

### 80. Mutual Fund Purchase and Withdrawal Plans

1. Page 344
2. Page 343
3. Page 343
4. Page 344
5. Page 343
6. Page 344
7. Page 344
8. Page 343
9. Page 343
10. Page 344
11. Page 344
12. Page 344
13. Page 343
14. Page 343
15. Page 343
16. Page 344
17. Page 343
18. Page 344
19. Page 344
20. Page 343
21. Page 344

### 81. Mutual Fund Distributions and Taxation

1. Page 346
2. Page 346
3. Page 346
4. Page 346
5. Page 346
6. Page 346
7. Page 347
8. Page 346
9. Page 347
10. Page 347
11. Page 347
12. Page 347
13. Page 346
14. Page 347
15. Page 347
16. Page 346
17. Page 347
18. Page 347
19. Page 346
20. Page 347
21. Page 347
22. Page 347
23. Page 346

### 82. Real Estate Investment Trusts

1. Page 350
2. Page 350
3. Page 350
4. Page 350
5. Page 350

## Retirement Planning

### 83. Individual Retirement Accounts

1. Page 352
2. Page 352
3. Page 352
4. Page 351
5. Page 352
6. Page 352
7. Page 352
8. Page 351
9. Page 352
10. Page 351
11. Page 352
12. Page 352
13. Page 352
14. Page 352
15. Page 351
16. Page 351
17. Page 351
18. Page 351
19. Page 351
20. Page 351
21. Page 352
22. Page 351
23. Page 352
24. Page 351
25. Page 351
26. Page 352
27. Page 351
28. Page 351
29. Page 351
30. Page 352
31. Page 353
32. Page 353
33. Page 353
34. Page 353

### 84. Keogh (HR-10) Plans

1. Page 358
2. Page 357
3. Page 358
4. Page 357
5. Page 357
6. Page 357
7. Page 357
8. Page 357
9. Page 357
10. Page 357
11. Page 357
12. Page 357
13. Page 357
14. Page 357
15. Page 358
16. Page 357
17. Page 357
18. Page 357

19. Page 358
20. Page 357
21. Page 357
22. Page 357
23. Page 357
24. Page 357
25. Page 357
26. Page 358
27. Page 357

**85. Corporate Retirement Plans**

1. Page 360
2. Page 360
3. Page 360
4. Page 360
5. Page 360
6. Page 360
7. Page 360
8. Page 360
9. Page 360

**86. Nonqualified Corporate Retirement Plans**

1. Page 361
2. Page 361
3. Page 361
4. Page 361

**87. Annuity Plans**

1. Page 362
2. Page 363
3. Page 362
4. Page 364
5. Page 363
6. Page 362
7. Page 364
8. Page 364
9. Page 363
10. Page 363
11. Page 362
12. Page 364
13. Page 363
14. Page 364
15. Page 364
16. Page 363
17. Page 362
18. Page 362
19. Page 363
20. Page 363
21. Page 362
22. Page 363
23. Page 363
24. Page 363
25. Page 362
26. Page 364
27. Page 363
28. Page 363
29. Page 363
30. Page 364
31. Page 364

**88. Qualified Annuity Plans**

1. Page 367
2. Page 367
3. Page 367
4. Page 367

**89. ERISA**

1. Page 368
2. Page 368
3. Page 368
4. Page 368

## Direct Participation Programs

**90. Characteristics of Limited Partnerships**

1. Page 370
2. Page 370
3. Page 370
4. Page 371
5. Page 370
6. Page 370
7. Page 371
8. Page 371
9. Page 371
10. Page 372
11. Page 371
12. Page 371
13. Page 372
14. Page 372
15. Page 372

## Final Exams

**91. Final Exam One**

1. Page 52
2. Page 51
3. Page 210
4. Page 217
5. Page 46
6. Page 98
7. Page 191
8. Page 202
9. Page 140
10. Page 139
11. Page 336
12. Page 139
13. Page 207
14. Page 208
15. Page 22
16. Page 16
17. Page 16
18. Page 45
19. Page 45
20. Page 45
21. Page 45
22. Page 45

23. Page 56
24. Page 56
25. Page 97
26. Page 111
27. Page 89
28. Page 98
29. Page 98
30. Page 159
31. Page 120
32. Page 155
33. Page 120
34. Page 214
35. Page 350
36. Page 324
37. Page 325
38. Page 337
39. Page 108
40. Page 357
41. Page 350
42. Page 178
43. Page 171
44. Page 172
45. Page 172
46. Page 7
47. Page 81
48. Page 91
49. Page 46
50. Page 46
51. Page 350
52. Page 52
53. Page 52
54. Page 51
55. Page 52
56. Page 45
57. Page 267
58. Page 46
59. Page 59
60. Page 61
61. Page 56
62. Page 325
63. Page 24
64. Page 40
65. Page 81
66. Page 45
67. Page 66
68. Page 78
69. Page 78
70. Page 209
71. Page 122
72. Page 239
73. Page 145
74. Page 139
75. Page 150
76. Page 150
77. Page 92
78. Page 122
79. Page 106
80. Page 97
81. Page 372
82. Page 133
83. Page 196
84. Page 102
85. Page 128
86. Page 336
87. Page 209
88. Page 157
89. Page 36
90. Page 299
91. Page 209
92. Page 178
93. Page 52
94. Page 23
95. Page 157
96. Page 153
97. Page 172
98. Page 191
99. Page 191
100. Page 2
101. Page 311
102. Page 316
103. Page 36
104. Page 21
105. Page 22
106. Page 24
107. Page 23
108. Page 249
109. Page 249
110. Page 249
111. Page 122
112. Page 263
113. Page 257
114. Page 247
115. Page 247
116. Page 262
117. Page 247
118. Page 98
119. Page 24
120. Page 241
121. Page 240
122. Page 145
123. Page 191
124. Page 178
125. Page 178

## 91. Final Exam Two

1. Page 287
2. Page 108
3. Page 241
4. Page 263
5. Page 263
6. Page 257
7. Page 282
8. Page 281
9. Page 282
10. Page 311
11. Page 310
12. Page 309
13. Page 282
14. Page 311
15. Page 127

16. Page 22
17. Page 22
18. Page 28
19. Page 268
20. Page 214
21. Page 268
22. Page 289
23. Page 256
24. Page 240
25. Page 256
26. Page 205
27. Page 248
28. Page 247
29. Page 241
30. Page 240
31. Page 262
32. Page 263
33. Page 263
34. Page 240
35. Page 246
36. Page 241
37. Page 248
38. Page 263
39. Page 263
40. Page 157
41. Page 290
42. Page 21
43. Page 35
44. Page 121
45. Page 89
46. Page 370
47. Page 22
48. Page 102
49. Page 22
50. Page 269
51. Page 281
52. Page 181
53. Page 246
54. Page 256
55. Page 256
56. Page 45
57. Page 287
58. Page 256
59. Page 52
60. Page 123
61. Page 53
62. Page 53
63. Page 247
64. Page 269
65. Page 336
66. Page 247
67. Page 249
68. Page 127
69. Page 246
70. Page 248
71. Page 30
72. Page 246
73. Page 240
74. Page 246
75. Page 248
76. Page 249
77. Page 36
78. Page 23
79. Page 209
80. Page 256
81. Page 267
82. Page 255
83. Page 256
84. Page 102
85. Page 209
86. Page 246
87. Page 249
88. Page 181
89. Page 145
90. Page 179
91. Page 191
92. Page 36
93. Page 191
94. Page 178
95. Page 61
96. Page 61
97. Page 191
98. Page 190
99. Page 59
100. Page 178
101. Page 186
102. Page 191
103. Page 190
104. Page 191
105. Page 205
106. Page 191
107. Page 177
108. Page 30
109. Page 297
110. Page 297
111. Page 297
112. Page 120
113. Page 283
114. Page 250
115. Page 288
116. Page 283
117. Page 288
118. Page 128
119. Page 309
120. Page 309
121. Page 289
122. Page 296
123. Page 311
124. Page 311
125. Page 309

# Glossary

## A

**accredited investor** As defined in Rule 502 of Regulation D, any institution or individual meeting minimum net worth requirements for the purchase of securities qualifying under the Regulation D registration exemption.

An accredited investor is generally accepted to be one who:

- has a net worth of $1 million or more; or
- has had an annual income of $200,000 or more in each of the two most recent years (or $300,000 jointly with a spouse) and who has a reasonable expectation of reaching the same income level in the current year.

**accretion of bond discount** An accounting process whereby the initial cost of a bond purchased at a discount is increased annually to reflect the basis of the bond as it approaches maturity.

When a bond is bought at a discount, the IRS requires that a portion of the difference between the discounted purchase price and the face value be taxed each year until maturity even though the gain will not be realized until maturity. *See also* amortization of bond premium; basis.

**accrued interest** The interest that has accumulated since the last interest payment up to, but not including, the settlement date and that is added to the contract price of a bond transaction.

There are two methods for calculating accrued interest: the 30-day-month (360-day-year) method for corporate and municipal bonds, and the actual-calendar-days (365-day-year) method for government bonds. Income bonds, bonds in default and zero-coupon bonds trade without accrued interest (flat). *See also* flat.

**accumulation account** An account established to hold securities pending their deposit into a municipal securities unit investment trust.

**accumulation stage** The period during which contributions are made to an annuity account. *See also* accumulation unit.

**accumulation unit** An accounting measure used to determine an annuitant's proportionate interest in the insurer's separate account during the accumulation (deposit) stage of an annuity. *See also* accumulation stage; annuity unit; separate account.

**acid-test ratio** A measure of a corporation's liquidity, calculated by adding cash, cash equivalents, and accounts and notes receivable, and dividing the result by total current liabilities. It is a more stringent test of liquidity than current ratio. *Syn.* quick ratio. *See also* cash assets ratio; current ratio.

**acquisition fee** The total charges and commissions paid by any party in connection with the selection or purchase of property by a direct participation program. Included in the total is any real estate commission, acquisition expense, development fee, selection fee or construction fee of a similar nature. The fee is added to the basis in the asset for the purpose of depreciation and calculating gain or loss.

**adjusted basis** The value attributed to an asset or security that reflects any deductions taken on, or capital improvements to, the asset or security. Adjusted basis is used to compute the gain or loss on the sale or other disposition of the asset or security.

**adjusted gross income (AGI)** Earned income plus net passive income, portfolio income and capital gains. *See also* tax liability.

**administrator** (1) A person authorized by a court of law to liquidate the estate of an intestate decedent. (2) An official or agency that administers the securities laws of a state.

**ad valorem tax** A tax based on the value of real or personal property. Property taxes are the major source of revenues for local governing units. *See also* assessed value; mill rate.

**advance/decline line** A technical analysis tool representing the total of differences between advances and declines of security prices. The advance/decline line is considered the best indicator of market movement as a whole. *See also* breadth-of-market theory.

**advance refunding** Refinancing an existing municipal bond issue prior to its maturity or call date by using money from the sale of a new bond issue. The proceeds of the new bond issue are used to purchase government securities, and the municipality puts the principal and interest received from these securities into an escrow account; it then uses these funds to pay off the original bond issue at the first call date. *Syn.* prerefunding. *See also* defeasance; refunding.

**advertisement** Any promotional material designed for use by newspapers, magazines, billboards, radio, television, telephone recording, or other public medium where the firm has little control over the type of individuals being exposed to the material. *See also* sales literature.

**affiliate** (1) A person who directly or indirectly owns, controls or holds with power to vote 10% or more of the outstanding voting securities of a company. (2) With respect to a direct participation program, any person who controls, is controlled by or is under common control with the program's sponsor and includes any person who beneficially owns 50% or more of the equity interest in the sponsor. (3) Under the Investment Company Act of 1940, a person who has any type of control over an investment company's operations, which includes anyone with 5% or more of the outstanding voting securities of the investment company or any corporation of which the investment company holds 5% or more of outstanding securities. *See also* control person; insider.

**agency issue** A debt security issued by an authorized agency of the federal government. Such issues are backed by the issuing agencies themselves, not by the full faith and credit of the U.S. government (except GNMA and Federal Import Export Bank issues). *See also* government security.

**agency transaction** A transaction in which a broker-dealer acts for the accounts of others by buying or selling securities on behalf of customers. *See also* agent; broker; principal transaction.

**agent** (1) An individual or firm that effects securities transactions for the accounts of others. (2) A person licensed by a state as a life insurance agent. (3) A securities salesperson who represents a broker-dealer or issuer when selling or trying to sell securities to the investing public; this individual is considered an agent whether he actually receives or simply solicits orders. *See also* broker; broker-dealer; dealer; principal.

**aggressive investment strategy** A method of portfolio allocation and management aimed at achieving maximum return. Aggressive investors place a high percentage of their investable assets in equity securities and a far lower percentage in safer debt securities and cash equivalents, and pursue aggressive policies including margin trading, arbitrage and options trading. *See also* balanced investment strategy; defensive investment strategy.

**agreement among underwriters** The agreement that sets forth the terms under which each member of an underwriting syndicate will participate in a new issue offering and states the duties and responsibilities of the underwriting manager. *See also* syndicate; underwriting manager.

**agreement of limited partnership** The contract that establishes guidelines for the operation of a direct participation program, including the roles of the general and limited partners.

**allied member** A general partner of an NYSE member firm who is not an NYSE member, an owner of 5% or more of the outstanding voting stock of an NYSE member corporation or a principal executive director or officer of a member corporation. Allied members do not own seats on the NYSE.

**all or none order (AON)** An order that instructs the floor broker to execute the entire order in one transaction; if the order cannot be executed in its entirety, it is allowed to expire.

**all or none underwriting (AON)** A form of best efforts underwriting in which the underwriter agrees that if it is unable to sell all the shares (or a prescribed minimum), the issuer will cancel the offering. This type of agreement may be used when the issuer requires a minimum amount of capital to be raised; if the minimum is not reached, the securities sold and the money raised are returned. Commissions are not paid unless the offering is completed. *See also* underwriting.

**alternative minimum tax (AMT)** An alternative tax computation that adds certain tax preference items back into adjusted gross income. If the AMT is higher than the regular tax liability for the year, the regular tax and the amount by which the AMT exceeds the regular tax are paid. *See also* tax preference item.

**AMBAC Indemnity Corporation (AMBAC)** A corporation that offers insurance on the timely payment of interest and principal obligations of municipal securities. Bonds insured by AMBAC usually receive a AAA rating from rating services.

**American depositary receipt (ADR)** A negotiable certificate representing a given number of shares of stock in a foreign corporation; it is bought and sold in the American securities markets, just as stock is traded. *Syn.* American depositary share.

**American Stock Exchange (AMEX)** A private, not-for-profit corporation, located in New York City, that handles approximately one-fifth of all securities trades within the United States.

**AMEX** *See* American Stock Exchange.

**amortization** (1) The paying off of debt in regular installments over a period of time. (2) The ratable deduction of certain capitalized expenditures over a specified period of time.

**amortization of bond premium** An accounting process whereby the initial cost of a bond purchased at a premium is decreased to reflect the basis of the bond as it approaches maturity. *See also* accretion of bond discount.

**annual compliance review** The annual meeting that all registered representatives must attend, the purpose of which is to review compliance issues.

**annual ROI** The annual return on investment of a bond, which equals the annual interest either plus the prorated discount or minus the prorated premium.

**annuitant** A person who receives the distribution of an annuity contract.

**annuitize** To change an annuity contract from the accumulation (pay-in) stage to the distribution (pay-out) stage.

**annuity** A contract between an insurance company and an individual; it generally guarantees lifetime income to the individual on whose life the contract is based in return for either a lump sum or a periodic payment to the insurance company. The contract holder's objective is usually retirement income. *See also* deferred annuity; fixed annuity; immediate annuity; variable annuity.

**annuity unit** An accounting measure used to determine the amount of each payment during the distribution stage of an annuity. The calculation takes into account the value of each accumulation unit and such other factors as assumed interest rate and mortality risk. *See also* accumulation unit; annuity.

**appraisal** A written opinion of the value of a property prepared by an independent appraiser qualified to appraise that particular type of property.

**appreciation** The increase in value of an asset.

**arbitrage** The simultaneous purchase and sale of the same or related securities to take advantage of a market inefficiency. *See also* index arbitrage; market arbitrage; security arbitrage; special arbitrage account.

**arbitrageur** One who engages in arbitrage.

**arbitration** The arrangement whereby the Board of Arbitration of the NYSE, or a designated arbitration association, hears and settles disagreements between members, allied members, member organizations and their employees. Nonmembers who are in dispute with members or employees may submit voluntarily to arbitration.

**ask** An indication by a trader or a dealer of a willingness to sell a security or a commodity; the price at which an investor can buy from a broker-dealer. *Syn.* offer. *See also* bid; public offering price; quotation.

**assessed value** The value of a property as appraised by a taxing authority for the purpose of levying taxes. Assessed value may equal market value or a stipulated percentage of market value. *See also* ad valorem tax; mill rate.

**assessment** An additional amount of capital that a participant in a direct participation program may be called upon to furnish beyond the subscription amount. Assessments may be mandatory or optional and must be called within twelve months.

**asset** (1) Anything that an individual or a corporation owns. (2) A balance sheet item expressing what a corporation owns.

**asset allocation fund** A mutual fund that splits its investment assets among stocks, bonds and other vehicles in an attempt to provide a consistent return for the investor. *See also* mutual fund.

**assignee** A person who has acquired a beneficial interest in a limited partnership from a third party but who is neither a substitute limited partner nor an assignee of record.

**assignee of record** A person who has acquired a beneficial interest in a limited partnership and whose interest has been recorded on the books of the partnership and is the subject of a written instrument of assignment.

**assignment** (1) A document accompanying or part of a stock certificate that is signed by the person named on the certificate for the purpose of transferring the certificate's title to another person's name. (2) The act of identifying and notifying an account holder that an option held short in that account has been exercised by the option owner. *See also* stock power.

**associated person of a member (AP)** Any employee, manager, director, officer or partner of a member broker-dealer or other entity (issuer, bank, etc.), or any person controlling, controlled by or in common control with that member. *See also* registered representative.

**assumed interest rate (AIR)** The net rate of investment return required to be credited to a variable life insurance policy to ensure that at all times the variable death benefit equals the amount of the death benefit. The AIR forms the basis for projecting payments, but it is not guaranteed.

**at-the-money** The term used to describe an option when the underlying stock is trading precisely at the exercise price of the option. *See also* in-the-money; out-of-the-money.

**at-the-opening order** An order that specifies it is to be executed at the opening of the market or of trading in that security or else it is to be canceled. The order does not have to be executed at the opening price. *See also* market-on-close order.

**auction market** A market in which buyers enter competitive bids and sellers enter competitive offers simultaneously. The NYSE is an auction market.

**audited financial statement** A financial statement of a program, a corporation or an issuer (including the profit and loss statement, cash flow and source and application of revenues statement, and balance sheet) that has been examined and verified by an independent certified public accountant.

**authorized stock** The number of shares of stock that a corporation is permitted to issue. This number of shares is stipulated in the corporation's state-approved charter, and may be changed by a vote of the corporation's stock-holders.

**average** A price at a midpoint among a number of prices. Technical analysts frequently use averages as market indicators. *See also* index.

**average price** A step in determining a bond's yield to maturity. A bond's average price is calculated by adding its face value to the price paid for it and dividing the result by two.

## B

**B** Consolidated Tape market identifier for the Boston Stock Exchange.

**back away** The failure of an over-the-counter market maker to honor a firm bid and asked price; this violates the NASD Rules of Fair Practice.

**back-end load** A commission or sales fee that is charged upon the redemption of mutual fund shares or variable annuity contracts. It declines annually, to zero over an extended holding period—up to eight years—as described in the prospectus. *Syn.* contingent-deferred sales load. *See also* Class B Share; Class D share; front-end load; level load.

**balanced fund** A mutual fund whose stated investment policy is to have at all times some portion of its investment assets in bonds and preferred stock as well as in common stock in an attempt to provide both growth and income. *See also* mutual fund.

**balanced investment strategy** A method of portfolio allocation and management aimed at balancing risk and return; a balanced portfolio may combine stocks, bonds, packaged products and cash equivalents.

**balance of payments (BOP)** An international accounting record of all transactions made by one particular country with others during a certain time period; it compares the amount of foreign currency the country has taken in to the amount of its own currency it has paid out. *See also* balance of trade.

**balance of trade** The largest component of a country's balance of payments; it concerns the export and import of merchandise (not services). Debit items include imports, foreign aid, domestic spending abroad and domestic investments abroad. Credit items include exports, foreign spending in the domestic economy and foreign investments in the domestic economy. *See also* balance of payments.

**balance sheet** A report of a corporation's financial condition at a specific time.

**balance sheet equation** A formula stating that a corporation's assets equal the sum of its liabilities plus shareholders' equity.

**balloon maturity** A repayment schedule for an issue of bonds wherein a large number of the bonds come due at a prescribed time (normally at the final maturity date); a type of serial maturity. *See also* maturity date.

**banker's acceptance (BA)** A money-market instrument used to finance international and domestic trade. A banker's acceptance is a check drawn on a bank by an importer or exporter of goods and represents the bank's conditional promise to pay the face amount of the note at maturity (normally less than three months).

**bank guarantee letter** The document supplied by a commercial bank in which the bank certifies that a put writer has sufficient funds on deposit at the bank to equal the aggregate exercise price of the put; this releases the option writer from the option margin requirement.

**basis** The cost of an asset or security.

**basis point** A measure of a bond's yield, equal to 1/100th of 1% of yield. A bond whose yield increases from 5.0% to 5.5% is said to increase by 50 basis points. *See also* point.

**basis quote** The price of a security quoted in terms of the yield that the purchaser can expect to receive.

**bear** An investor who acts on the belief that a security or the market is falling or is expected to fall. *See also* bull.

**bear market** A market in which prices of a certain group of securities are falling or are expected to fall. *See also* bull market.

**best efforts underwriting** A new issue securities underwriting in which the underwriter acts as an agent for the issuer and puts forth its best efforts to sell as many shares as possible. The underwriter has no liability for unsold shares, unlike in a firm commitment underwriting. *See also* underwriting.

**beta coefficient** A means of measuring the volatility of a security or portfolio of securities in comparison with the market as a whole. A beta of 1 indicates that the security's price will move with the market. A beta greater than 1 indicates that the security's price will be more volatile than the market. A beta less than 1 means that it will be less volatile than the market.

**bid** An indication by an investor, a trader or a dealer of a willingness to buy a security or commodity; the price at which an investor can sell to a broker-dealer. *See also* offer; public offering price; quotation.

**bid form** The form submitted by underwriters in a competitive bid on a new issue of municipal securities. The underwriter states the interest rate, price bid and net interest cost to the issuer.

**blind pool** A direct participation program that does not state in advance all of the specific properties in which the general partners will invest the partnership's money. At least 25% of the proceeds of the offering are kept in reserve for the purchase of nonspecified properties.

**block trade** A trade so large that the normal auction market cannot absorb it in a reasonable time at a reasonable price. In general, 10,000 shares of stock or $200,000 worth of bonds would be considered a block trade.

**blotter** A book of original entry in which a broker-dealer records on a daily basis every transaction, movement of securities and cash receipt and disbursement.

**blue chip stock** The equity issues of financially stable, well-established companies that have demonstrated their ability to pay dividends in both good and bad times.

***Blue List, The*** A daily publication that lists current municipal bond offerings traded in the secondary market by banks and brokers nationwide.

**blue-sky** To register a securities offering in a particular state. *See also* blue-sky laws; registration by coordination; registration by filing; registration by qualification.

**blue-sky laws** The nickname for state regulations governing the securities industry. The term was coined in the early 1900s by a Kansas Supreme Court justice who wanted regulation to protect against "speculative schemes that have no more basis than so many feet of blue sky." *See also* Series 63; Uniform Securities Act.

**board of directors** (1) Individuals elected by stockholders to establish corporate management policies. A board of directors decides, among other issues, if and when dividends will be paid to stockholders. (2) The body that governs the NYSE; it is composed of 20 members who are elected for a term of two years by the NYSE general membership.

**Board of Governors** The body that governs the NASD; it is composed of 27 members elected by both the NASD general membership and by the Board itself.

**bona fide quote** An offer from a broker-dealer to buy or sell securities; it indicates a willingness to execute a trade under the terms and conditions accompanying the quote. *See also* firm quote; nominal quote; subject quote; workout quote.

**bond** A legal obligation of an issuing company or government to repay the principal of a loan to bond investors at a specified future date. Bonds are usually issued with a par value or face value of $1,000, representing the amount of money borrowed. The issuer promises to pay a percentage of the par value as interest on the borrowed funds. The interest payment is stated on the face of the bond at issue.

**bond anticipation note (BAN)** A short-term municipal debt security to be paid from the proceeds of long-term debt when it is issued.

**bond basis book** A reference book that gives yield-to-maturity tables for bonds, arranged according to coupon rates, times to maturity and prices.

**Bond Buyer indexes** Indexes of yield levels of municipal bonds, published daily by *The Bond Buyer.* The indexes are indicators of yields that would be offered on AA and A rated general obligation bonds with 20-year maturities and revenue bonds with 30-year maturities.

**bond counsel** An attorney retained by a municipal issuer to give an opinion concerning the legality and tax-exempt status of a municipal issue. *See also* legal opinion of counsel.

**bond fund** A mutual fund whose investment objective is to provide stable income with a minimal capital risk. It invests in income-producing instruments, which may include corporate, government or municipal bonds. *See also* mutual fund.

**bond interest coverage ratio** An indication of the safety of a corporate bond. It measures the number of times by which earnings before interest and taxes exceeds annual interest on outstanding bonds.

**bond quote** One of a number of quotations listed in the financial press and most daily newspapers that provide representative bid prices from the previous day's bond market. Quotes for corporate and government bonds are percentages of the bond's face value (usually $1,000). Corporate bonds are quoted in increments of 1/8th, where a quote of 99 1/8 represents 99.125% of par ($1,000), or $991.25. Government bonds are quoted in 1/32nds. Municipal bonds may be quoted on a dollar basis or on a yield-to-maturity basis. *See also* quotation; stock quote.

**bond rating** An evaluation of the possibility of default by a bond issuer, based on an analysis of the issuer's financial condition and profit potential. Bond rating services are provided by, among others, Standard & Poor's, Moody's Investors Service and Fitch Investors Service. *See also* Moody's Investors Service; Standard & Poor's Corporation.

**bond ratio** One of several tools used by bond analysts to assess the degree of safety offered by a corporation's bonds. It measures the percentage of the corporation's capitalization that is provided by long-term debt financing, calculated by dividing the total face value of the outstanding bonds by the total capitalization.

**bond swap** The sale of a bond and the simultaneous purchase of a different bond in a like amount. The technique is used to control tax liability, extend maturity or update investment objectives. *See also* wash sale.

**bond yield** The annual rate of return on a bond investment. Types of yield include nominal yield, current yield, yield to maturity, and yield to call. Their relationships vary according to whether the bond in question is at a discount, at a premium, or at par. *See also* current yield; nominal yield; yield to call; yield to maturity.

**book-entry security** A security sold without delivery of a certificate. Evidence of ownership is maintained on records kept by a central agency; for example, the Treasury keeps records of purchasers of Treasury bills. Transfer of ownership is recorded by entering the change on the books or electronic files. *See also* coupon bond; registered; registered as to principal only.

**book value per bond** A measure of the amount of producing assets behind each corporate bond, calculated by dividing net tangible assets by funded debt.

**book value per share** A measure of the net worth of each share of common stock. It is calculated by subtracting intangible assets and preferred stock from total net worth and then dividing the result by the number of shares of common outstanding.

**Boston Stock Exchange (BSE)** The third oldest stock exchange in the United States and the first exchange to provide membership to foreign broker-dealers. *See also* regional exchange.

**branch office** Any location identified by any means to the public as a place where a registered broker-dealer conducts business. *See also* office of supervisory jurisdiction.

**breadth-of-market theory** A technical analysis theory that predicts the strength of the market according to the number of issues that advance or decline in a particular trading day. *See also* advance/decline line.

**breakout** In technical analysis, the movement of a security's price through an established support or resistance level. *See also* resistance level; support level.

**breakpoint** The schedule of sales charge discounts offered by a mutual fund for lump-sum or cumulative investments.

**breakpoint sale** The sale of mutual fund shares in an amount just below the level at which the purchaser would qualify for reduced sales charges; this violates the NASD Rules of Fair Practice.

**broad-based index** An index that is designed to reflect the movement of the market as a whole. Examples include the S&P 100, the S&P 500, the

AMEX Major Market Index and the *Value Line* Composite Index. *See also* index; narrow-based index.

**broker** (1) An individual or firm that charges a fee or commission for executing buy and sell orders submitted by another individual or firm. (2) The role of a firm when it acts as an agent for a customer and charges the customer a commission for its services. *See also* agent; broker-dealer; dealer.

**broker-dealer (BD)** A person or firm in the business of buying and selling securities. A firm may act as both broker (agent) or dealer (principal) but not in the same transaction. Broker-dealers normally must register with the SEC, the appropriate SROs and any state in which they do business. *See also* agent; broker; dealer; principal.

**broker's broker** (1) A specialist executing orders for a commission house broker or another brokerage firm. (2) A floor broker on an exchange or a broker-dealer in the over-the-counter market executing a trade as an agent for another broker. *See also* correspondent broker-dealer.

**bucketing** Accepting customer orders without executing them immediately through an exchange. A "bucket shop" may use firm or other customer positions or orders to execute them, or may not execute them at all. Bucketing is an illegal activity

**bull** An investor who acts on the belief that a security or the market is rising or is expected to rise. *See also* bear.

**bull market** A market in which prices of a certain group of securities are rising or are expected to rise. *See also* bear market.

**business cycle** A predictable long-term pattern of alternating periods of economic growth and decline. The cycle passes through four stages: expansion, peak, contraction, and trough.

**business day** A day on which financial markets are open for trading. Saturdays, Sundays and legal holidays are not considered business days

**buyer's option** A settlement contract that calls for delivery and payment according to a number of days specified by the buyer. *See also* regular way; seller's option.

**buy-in** The procedure that the buyer of a security follows when the seller fails to complete the contract by delivering the security. The buyer closes the contract by buying the security in the open market and charging the account of the seller for transaction fees and any loss caused by changes in the markets. *See also* sell-out.

**buying power** The amount of fully margined securities that a margin client can purchase using only the cash, securities and special memorandum account balance and without depositing additional equity.

**buy stop order** An order to buy a security that is entered at a price above the current offering price and that is triggered when the market price touches or goes through the buy stop price.

## C

**C** Consolidated Tape market identifier for the Cincinnati Stock Exchange.

**call** (1) An option contract giving the owner the right to buy a specified amount of an underlying security at a specified price within a specified time. (2) The act of exercising a call option. *See also* put.

**callable bond** A type of bond issued with a provision allowing the issuer to redeem the bond prior to maturity at a predetermined price. *See also* call price.

**callable preferred stock** A type of preferred stock issued with a provision allowing the corporation to call in the stock at a certain price and retire it. *See also* call price; preferred stock.

**call buyer** An investor who pays a premium for an option contract and receives, for a specified time, the right to buy the underlying security at a specified price. *See also* call writer; put buyer; put writer.

**call date** The date, specified in the prospectus of every callable security, after which the issuer of the security has the option to redeem the issue at par or at par plus a premium.

**call loan rate** The rate of interest a brokerage firm charges its margin account clients on their debit balances.

**call money rate** The rate of interest a bank or lender charges brokerage firms on stock exchange collateral.

**call price** The price (usually a premium over the par value of the issue) at which preferred stocks or bonds can be redeemed prior to maturity of the issue.

**call protection** A provision in a bond indenture stating that the issue is noncallable for a certain period of time (five years, ten years, etc.) after the original issue date. *See also* call provision.

**call provision** The written agreement between an issuing corporation and its bondholders or preferred stockholders, giving the corporation the option to redeem its senior securities at a specified price before maturity and under specified conditions.

**call risk** The potential for a bond to be called before maturity, leaving the investor without the bond's current income. As this is more likely to occur during times of falling interest rates, the investor may not be able to reinvest his principal at a comparable rate of return.

**call spread** An option investor's position in which the investor buys a call on a security and writes a call on the same security but with a different expiration date, exercise price, or both.

**call writer** An investor who receives a premium and takes on, for a specified time, the obligation to sell the underlying security at a specified price at the call buyer's discretion. *See also* call buyer; put buyer; put writer.

**capital** Accumulated money or goods available for use in producing more money or goods.

**capital appreciation** A rise in the market price of an asset.

**capital asset** All tangible property, including securities, real estate and other property, held for the long term.

**capital contribution** The amount of a participant's investment in a direct participation program, not including units purchased by the sponsors.

**capital gain** The profit realized when a capital asset is sold for a higher price than the purchase price. *See also* capital loss; long-term gain.

**capitalization** The sum of a corporation's long-term debt, stock and surpluses. *See also* capital structure.

**capitalization ratio** A measure of an issuer's financial status that calculates the value of its bonds, preferred stock or common stock as a percentage of its total capitalization.

**capitalize** An accounting procedure whereby a corporation records an expenditure as a capital asset on its books instead of charging it to expenses for the year.

**capitalized expense** The cost of purchasing an asset that will benefit a business in the long term; examples include buildings, land, machinery and minerals.

**capital loss** The loss incurred when a capital asset is sold for a lower price than the purchase price. *See also* capital gain; long-term loss.

**capital market** The segment of the securities market that deals in instruments with more than one year to maturity—that is, long-term debt and equity securities.

**capital risk** The potential for an investor to lose all money invested owing to circumstances unrelated to the financial strength of the issuer. For example, derivative instruments such as options carry risk independent of the changing value of the underlying securities. *See also* derivative.

**capital structure** The composition of long-term funds (equity and debt) a corporation has as a source for financing. *See also* capitalization.

**capital surplus** The money a corporation receives in excess of the stated value of the stock at the time of first sale. *See also* par value.

**capped index option** A type of index option issued with a capped price at a set interval above the strike price (for a call) or below the strike price (for a put). The option is automatically exercised once the underlying index reaches the capped price. *See also* index option.

**capping** Placing selling pressure on a stock in an attempt to keep its price low or to move its price lower; this violates the NASD Rules of Fair Practice.

**cash account** An account in which the customer is required by the SEC's Regulation T to pay in full for securities purchased not later than two days after the standard payment period set by the NASD's Uniform Practice Code. *See also* margin account; Regulation T.

**cash assets ratio** The most stringent test of liquidity, calculated by dividing the sum of cash and cash equivalents by total current liabilities. *See also* acid-test ratio; current ratio.

**cash dividend** Money paid to a corporation's stockholders out of the corporation's current earnings or accumulated profits. All dividends must be declared by the board of directors.

**cash equivalent** A security that can be readily converted into cash; examples include Treasury bills, certificates of deposit and money-market instruments and funds.

**cash flow** The money received by a business minus the money paid out. Cash flow is also equal to net income plus depreciation or depletion.

**cash transaction** A settlement contract that calls for delivery and payment on the same day the trade is executed; payment is due by 2:30 pm EST (or within 30 minutes of the trade if made after 2:00 pm EST). *See also* regular way; settlement date.

**catastrophe call** The redemption of a bond by an issuer owing to disaster (for example, a power plant that has been built with proceeds from an issue burns to the ground). *See also* mandatory call; partial call.

**certificate of limited partnership** A legal document that provides creditors with such information as the term of the partnership, member contributions, sharing arrangements and provisions for changes in membership.

**change** (1) For an option or futures contract, the difference between the current price and the previous day's settlement price. (2) For an index or average, the difference between the current value and the previous day's market close. (3) For a stock or bond quote, the difference between the current price and the last trade of the previous day.

**chartist** A securities analyst who uses charts and graphs of the past price movements of a security to predict its future movements. *See also* technical analysis.

**Chicago Board Options Exchange (CBOE)** The self-regulatory organization with jurisdiction over all writing and trading of standardized options and related contracts listed on that exchange. Also, the first national securities exchange for the trading of listed options.

**Chicago Stock Exchange (CHX)** Regional exchange that provides a listed market for smaller businesses and new enterprises. In 1949 the exchange merged with the St. Louis, Cleveland and Minneapolis/St. Paul exchanges to form the Midwest Stock Exchange, but in 1993 the original name was reinstated. *See also* regional exchange.

**Chinese wall** A descriptive name for the division within a brokerage firm that prevents insider information from passing from corporate advisers to investment traders, who could make use of the information to reap illicit profits. *See also* Insider Trading and Securities Fraud Enforcement Act of 1988.

**churning** Excessive trading in a customer's account by a registered representative who ignores the customer's interests and seeks only to increase commissions; this violates the NASD Rules of Fair Practice.

**Cincinnati Stock Exchange (CSE)** In existence since 1885, this exchange operates the National Securities Trading System, the nation's only automated auction system for unlisted securities.

**class** Options of the same type (that is, all calls or all puts) on the same underlying security. *See also* series; type.

**Class A share** A class of mutual fund share issued with a front-end sales load. A mutual fund offers different classes of shares to allow investors to choose the type of sales charge they will pay. *See also* Class B share; Class C share; Class D share; front-end load.

**Class B share** A class of mutual fund share issued with a back-end load. A mutual fund offers different classes of shares to allow investors to choose the type of sales charge they will pay. *See also* back-end load; Class A share; Class C share; Class D share.

**Class C share** A class of mutual fund share issued with a level load. A mutual fund offers different classes of shares to allow investors to choose the type of sales charge they will pay. *See also* Class A share; Class B share; Class D share; level load.

**Class D share** A class of mutual fund share issued with both a level load and a back-end load. A mutual fund offers different classes of shares to allow investors to choose the type of sales charge they will pay. *See also* back-end load; Class A share; Class B share; Class C share; level load.

**classical economics** The theory that maximum economic benefit will be achieved if government does not attempt to influence the economy; that is, if businesses are allowed to seek profitable opportunities as they see fit.

**clearing agency** An intermediary between the buy and sell sides in a securities transaction that receives and delivers payments and securities. Any organization that fills this function, including a securities depository but not including a Federal Reserve Bank, is considered a clearing agency.

**clearing broker-dealer** A broker-dealer that clears its own trades as well as those of introducing brokers. A clearing broker-dealer can hold customers' securities and cash. *See also* introducing broker.

**close** (1) The price of the last transaction for a particular security on a particular day. (2) The midprice of a closing trading range.

**closed-end covenant** A provision of a bond issue's trust indenture stating that any additional bonds secured by the same assets must have a subordinated claim to those assets. *See also* junior lien debt; open-end covenant.

**closed-end investment company** An investment company that issues a fixed number of shares in an actively managed portfolio of securities. The shares may be of several classes; they are traded in the secondary marketplace, either on an exchange or over the counter. The market price of the shares is determined by supply and demand and not by net asset value. *See also* dual-purpose fund; mutual fund.

**closing date** The date designated by the general partners in a direct participation program as the date when sales of units in the program cease; typically the offering period extends for one year.

**closing purchase** An options transaction in which the seller buys back an option in the same series; the two transactions effectively cancel each other out and the position is liquidated. *See also* closing sale; opening purchase.

**closing sale** An options transaction in which the buyer sells an option in the same series; the two transactions effectively cancel each other out and the position is liquidated. *See also* closing purchase; opening sale.

**Code of Arbitration Procedure** The NASD's formal method of handling securities-related disputes or clearing controversies between members, public customers, clearing corporations or clearing banks. Such disputes involve violations of the Uniform Practice Code rather than the Rules of Fair Practice. Any claim, dispute or controversy between member firms or associated persons is required to be submitted to arbitration.

**Code of Procedure (COP)** The NASD's formal procedure for handling trade practice complaints involving violations of the Rules of Fair Practice. The NASD District Business Conduct Committee (DBCC) is the first body to hear and judge complaints. Appeals and review of DBCC decisions are handled by the NASD Board of Governors.

**coincident indicator** A measurable economic factor that varies directly and simultaneously with the business cycle, thus indicating the current state of the economy. Examples include nonagricultural employment, personal income and industrial production. *See also* lagging indicator; leading indicator.

**collateral** Certain assets set aside and pledged to a lender for the duration of a loan. If the borrower fails to meet obligations to pay principal or interest, the lender has claim to the assets.

**collateralized mortgage obligation (CMO)** A mortgage-backed corporate security; unlike pass-through obligations issued by FNMA and GNMA, its yield is not guaranteed and it does not have the backing of the federal government. These issues attempt to return interest and principal at a predetermined rate. *See also* tranche.

**collateral trust bond** A secured bond backed by stocks or bonds of another issuer. The collateral is held by a trustee for safekeeping.

**combination** An option position that represents a put and a call on the same stock at different strike prices, expirations or both.

**combination preferred stock** A type of preferred stock that combines two or more of the following preferred stock features: participating, cumulative, convertible, callable. *See also* preferred stock.

**combination privilege** A benefit offered by a mutual fund whereby the investor may qualify for a sales charge breakpoint by combining separate investments in two or more mutual funds under the same management.

**combined account** A customer account that has cash and long and short margin positions in different securities.

**commercial bank** An institution that is in the business of accepting deposits and making business loans. Commercial banks may not underwrite corporate securities or most municipal bonds. *See also* investment banker.

**commercial paper** An unsecured, short-term promissory note issued by a corporation for financing accounts receivable and inventories. It is usually issued at a discount reflecting prevailing market interest rates. Maturities range up to 270 days.

**commingling** (1) The combining by a brokerage firm of one customer's securities with another customer's securities and pledging them as joint collateral for a bank loan; unless authorized by the customers, this violates SEC Rule 15c2-1. (2) The combining by a brokerage firm of customer securities with firm securities and pledging them as joint collateral for a bank loan; this practice is prohibited. *See also* segregation.

**commission** A service charge assessed by an agent in return for arranging the purchase or sale of a security. A commission must be fair and reasonable, considering all the relevant factors of the transaction. *Syn.* sales charge. *See also* markup.

**commission house broker (CHB)** A member of an exchange who is eligible to execute orders for customers of a member firm on the floor of the exchange.

**Committee on Uniform Securities Identification Procedures (CUSIP)** A committee that assigns identification numbers and codes to all securities, to be used when recording all buy and sell orders.

**common stock** A security that represents ownership in a corporation. Holders of common stock exercise control by electing a board of directors and voting on corporate policy. *See also* equity; preferred stock.

**common stock ratio** One of several tools used by bond analysts to assess the degree of safety offered by a corporation's bonds. It measures the percentage of the corporation's total capitalization that is contributed by the common stockholders, and is calculated by adding the par value, the capital in excess of par and the retained earnings, and dividing the result by the total capitalization. *See also* bond ratio; preferred stock ratio.

**competitive bid underwriting** A form of firm commitment underwriting in which rival syndicates submit sealed bids for underwriting the issue. Competitive bidding normally is used to determine the underwriters for issues of general obligation municipal bonds, and is required by law in most states for general obligation bonds of more than $100,000. *See also* negotiated underwriting.

**completion of the transaction** As defined by the NASD, the point at which a customer pays any part of the purchase price to the broker-dealer for a security he has purchased or delivers a security that he has sold. If the customer makes payment to the broker-dealer before the payment is due, the completion of the transaction occurs when the broker-dealer delivers the security.

**concession** The profit per bond or share that an underwriter allows the seller of new issue securities. The selling group broker-dealer purchases the security from the syndicate member at the public offering price minus the concession. *Syn.* reallowance. *See also* takedown.

**conduit theory** A means for an investment company to avoid being taxed on net investment income distributed to shareholders. If a mutual fund acts as a conduit for the distribution of net investment income, it may qualify as a regulated investment company and be taxed only on the income retained by the fund.

**confidence theory** A technical analysis theory that measures the willingness of investors to take risks by comparing the yields on high-grade bonds to the yields on lower rated bonds.

**confirmation** A printed document that states the trade, settlement date and money due from or owed to a customer; it is sent or given to the customer on or before the settlement date. *See also* duplicate confirmation.

**Consolidated Quotation System (CQS)** A quotation and last-sale reporting service for NASD members that are active market makers of listed securities in the third market. It is used by market makers willing to stand ready to buy and sell securities for their own accounts on a continuous basis but that do not wish to do so through an exchange. Quotation display service is available for a fee to all Nasdaq subscribers, while quotation input service is available only to those members that are registered to do business in third market stocks.

**Consolidated Tape (CT)** A service of the New York Stock Exchange that delivers real-time reports of securities transactions to subscribers as they occur on the various exchanges.

The Tape distributes reports to subscribers over two different networks that the subscribers can tap into through either the high-speed electronic or the low-speed ticker lines. Network A reports transactions in NYSE-listed securities. Network B reports AMEX-listed securities transactions, as well as reports of transactions in regional exchange issues that substantially meet AMEX listing requirements.

**consolidation** The technical analysis term for a narrowing of the trading range for a commodity or security, considered an indication that a strong price move is imminent.

**constant dollar plan** A defensive investment strategy in which the total sum of money invested is kept constant, regardless of any price fluctuation in the portfolio. As a result, the investor sells when the market is high and buys when it is low.

**constant ratio plan** An investment strategy in which the investor maintains an appropriate ratio of debt to equity securities by making purchases and sales to maintain the desired balance.

**construction loan note (CLN)** A short-term municipal debt security that provides interim financing for new projects.

**constructive receipt** The date on which the Internal Revenue Service considers that a taxpayer receives dividends or other income.

**Consumer Price Index (CPI)** A measure of price changes in consumer goods and services used to identify periods of inflation or deflation.

**consumption** A term used by Keynesian economists to refer to the purchase by household units of newly produced goods and services.

**contra broker** The broker on the buy side of a sell order or on the sell side of a buy order.

**contraction** A period of general economic decline, one of the four stages of the business cycle. *See also* business cycle.

**contractionary policy** A monetary policy that decreases the money supply, usually with the intention of raising interest rates and combating inflation.

**contractual plan** A type of accumulation plan in which the investor agrees to invest a specific amount of money in the mutual fund during a specific time period. *See also* front-end load; mutual fund; voluntary accumulation plan.

**control (controlling, controlled by, under common control with)** The power to direct, or affect the direction of, the management and policies of a company, whether through the ownership of voting securities, by contract, or otherwise. Control is presumed to exist if a person, directly or indirectly, owns, controls, holds with the power to vote, or holds proxies representing more than 10% of a company's voting securities.

**control of securities** A term used to indicate the responsibilities of a broker-dealer with regard to securities in its possession. Under the SEC's customer protection rule, broker-dealers must maintain control procedures over customer funds and securities. Securities are considered under the control of, or in the possession of, a broker-dealer if they are in the broker-dealer's physical possession, are in an alternative location acceptable to the SEC, or are in transit for a period of time that does not exceed standards set by the SEC.

**control person** (1) A director, officer or other affiliate of an issuer. (2) A stockholder who owns at least 10% of any class of a corporation's outstanding securities. *See also* affiliate; insider.

**control security** Any security owned by a director, officer or other affiliate of the issuer or by a stockholder who owns at least 10% of any class of a corporation's outstanding securities. Who owns a security, not the security itself, determines whether it is a control security. *See also* Rule 144.

**conversion parity** Two securities, one of which can be converted into the other, of equal dollar value. The holder of a convertible security can calculate parity to help decide whether converting would lead to gain or loss.

**conversion price** The dollar amount of a convertible security's par value that is exchangeable for one share of common stock.

**conversion privilege** A feature added to a security by the issuer that allows the holder to change the security into shares of common stock; this makes the security attractive to investors and therefore more marketable. *See also* convertible bond; convertible preferred stock.

**conversion ratio** The number of shares of common stock per par value amount that the holder would receive for converting a convertible bond or preferred share.

**conversion value** The total market value of common stock into which a senior security is convertible. *See also* investment value.

**convertible bond** A debt security, usually in the form of a debenture, that can be exchanged for equity securities of the issuing corporation at specified prices or rates. *See also* debenture.

**convertible preferred stock** An equity security that can be exchanged for common stock at specified prices or rates. Dividends may be cumulative or noncumulative. *See also* cumulative preferred stock; noncumulative preferred stock; preferred stock.

**cooling-off period** The period (a minimum of 20 days) between the filing date of a registration statement and the effective date of the registration; in practice, the period varies in length.

**corporate account** An account held in the name of a corporation. The corporate agreement, signed when the account is opened, specifies which officers are authorized to trade in the account. In addition to standard margin account documents, a corporation must provide a copy of its charter and bylaws authorizing a margin account.

**corporate bond** A debt security issued by a corporation. A corporate bond typically has a par value of $1,000, is taxable, has a term maturity, and is traded on a major exchange.

**corporation** The most common form of business organization, in which the total worth of the organization is divided into shares of stock, each share representing a unit of ownership. A corporation is characterized by a continuous life span and the limited liability of its owners.

**CORR.** A message on the Consolidated Tape indicating an error in a previous report of a transaction. *See also* error report.

**correspondent broker-dealer** A broker-dealer that executes transactions for another broker-dealer in a market or locale in which the first broker-dealer has no office. *See also* broker's broker.

**cost basis** The price paid for an asset, including any commissions or fees, used to calculate capital gains or losses when the asset is sold.

**cost depletion** A method of calculating tax deductions for investments in mineral, oil or gas resources. The cost of the mineral-, oil- or gas-producing property is returned to the investor over the property's life by an annual deduction, which takes into account the number of known recoverable units of mineral, oil or gas to arrive at a cost-per-unit figure. The tax deduction is determined by multiplying the cost-per-unit figure by the number of units sold each year.

**cost of carry** All out-of-pocket costs incurred by an investor while holding an open position in a security, including margin costs, interest costs and opportunity costs.

**cost-push** Increasing costs of production, including raw materials and wages, that are believed to result in inflation. *See also* demand-pull.

**coterminous** A term used to describe municipal entities that share the same boundaries. For example, a municipality's school district and fire district may issue debt separately although the debt is backed by revenues from the same taxpayers. *See also* overlapping debt.

**coupon bond** A debt obligation with coupons representing semiannual interest payments attached; the coupons are submitted to the trustee by the holder to receive the interest payments. No record of the purchaser is kept by the issuer, and the purchaser's name is not printed on the certificate. *See also* book-entry security; registered; registered as to principal only.

**covenant** A component of a debt issue's trust indenture that identifies bondholders' rights and other provisions. Examples include rate covenants that establish a minimum revenue coverage for a bond; insurance covenants that require insurance on a project; and maintenance covenants that require maintenance on a facility constructed by the proceeds of a bond issue.

**coverage ratio** A measure of the safety of a bond issue, based on how many times earnings will cover debt service plus operating and maintenance expenses for a specific time period.

**covered call writer** An investor who sells a call option while owning the underlying security or some other asset that guarantees the ability to deliver if the call is exercised.

**covered put writer** An investor who sells a put option while owning an asset that guarantees the ability to pay if the put is exercised.

**credit agreement** A component of a customer's margin account agreement, outlining the conditions of the credit arrangement between broker and customer.

**credit balance (CR)** The amount of money remaining in a customer's account after all commitments have been paid in full. *See also* debit balance.

**creditor** Any broker or dealer, member of a national securities exchange, or person associated with a broker-dealer involved in extending credit to customers.

**credit risk** The degree of probability that a bond's issuer will default in the payment of either principal or interest.

**credit spread** A futures hedge position established when the premium received for the option sold exceeds the premium paid for the option bought. *See also* debit spread.

**crossing orders** Using one customer's order to fill a second customer's order for the same security on the opposite side of the market. This practice is permitted if the security is first offered to the exchange floor at a price one tick higher than the current bid; if there are no takers, the broker may cross the orders. Crossing orders is considered manipulative, however, if the transaction is not presented or recorded with the exchange.

**cum rights** A term describing stock trading with rights. *See also* ex-rights.

**cumulative preferred stock** An equity security that offers the holder any unpaid dividends in arrears. These dividends accumulate and must be paid to the holder of cumulative preferred stock before any dividends can be paid to the common stockholders. *See also* convertible preferred stock; noncumulative preferred stock; preferred stock.

**cumulative voting** A voting procedure that permits stockholders either to cast all of their votes for any one candidate or to cast their total number of votes in any proportion they choose. This results in greater representation for minority stockholders. *See also* statutory voting.

**current assets** Cash and other assets that are expected to be converted into cash within the next twelve months. Examples include such liquid items as cash and equivalents, accounts receivable, inventory and prepaid expenses.

**current liabilities** A corporation's debt obligations due for payment within the next twelve months. Examples include accounts payable, accrued wages payable and current long-term debt.

**current market value (CMV)** The worth of the securities in an account. The market value of listed securities is based on the closing prices on the previous business day. *See also* market value.

**current ratio** A measure of a corporation's liquidity; that is, its ability to transfer assets into cash to meet current short-term obligations. It is calculated by dividing total current assets by total current liabilities.

**current yield** The annual rate of return on a security, calculated by dividing the interest or dividends paid by the security's current market price. *See also* bond yield.

**CUSIP** *See* Committee on Uniform Securities Identification Procedures.

**custodial account** An account in which a custodian enters trades on behalf of the beneficial owner, often a minor. *See also* custodian.

**custodian** An institution or person responsible for making all investment, management and distribution decisions in an account maintained in the best interests of another. Mutual funds and contractual plan companies have custodians responsible for safeguarding certificates and performing clerical duties. *See also* mutual fund custodian; plan custodian.

**customer** Any person who opens a trading account with a broker-dealer. A customer may be classified in terms of account ownership, trading authorization, payment method or types of securities traded.

**customer agreement** A document that a customer must sign when opening a margin account with a broker-dealer; it allows the firm to liquidate all or a portion of the account if the customer fails to meet a margin call.

**customer statement** A document showing a customer's trading activity, positions and account balance. The SEC requires that customer statements be sent quarterly, but customers generally receive them monthly.

**cyclical industry** A fundamental analysis term for an industry that is sensitive to the business cycle and price changes. Most cyclical industries produce durable goods such as raw materials and heavy equipment.

## D

**dated date** The date on which interest on a new bond issue begins to accrue.

**day order** An order that is valid only until the close of trading on the day it is entered; if it is not executed by the close of trading, it is canceled.

**dealer** (1) An individual or firm that is engaged in the business of buying and selling securities for its own account, either directly or through a broker. (2) The role of a firm when it acts as a principal and charges the customer a markup or markdown. *Syn.* principal. *See also* broker; broker-dealer.

**debenture** A debt obligation backed by the general credit of the issuing corporation. *Syn.* unsecured bond. *See also* secured bond.

**debit balance (DR)** The amount of money a customer owes a brokerage firm. *See also* credit balance.

**debit spread** A futures hedge position established when the premium paid for the option bought exceeds the premium received for the option sold. *See also* credit spread.

**debt financing** Raising money for working capital or for capital expenditures by selling bonds, bills or notes to individual or institutional investors. In return for the money lent, the individuals or institutions become creditors and receive a promise to repay principal and interest on the debt. *See also* equity financing.

**debt security** A security representing a loan by an investor to an issuer such as a corporation, municipality, the federal government or a federal agency. In return for the loan, the issuer promises to repay the debt on a specified date and to pay interest. *See also* equity security.

**debt service** The schedule for repayment of interest and principal (or the scheduled sinking fund contribution) on an outstanding debt. *See also* sinking fund.

**debt service account** The account used to pay a municipal revenue bond's semiannual interest and principal maturing in the current year; it also serves as a sinking fund for term issues. *See also* flow of funds.

**debt service ratio** An indication of the ability of an issuer to meet principal and interest payments on bonds.

**debt service reserve fund** The account that holds enough money to pay one year's debt service on a municipal revenue bond. *See also* flow of funds.

**debt-to-equity ratio** The ratio of total long-term debt to total stockholders' equity; it is used to measure leverage.

**debt trend** A method of tracking whether certain municipal debt ratios are rising or falling in order to predict a municipality's or community's financial position in the coming years.

**declaration date** The date on which a corporation announces the amount, payment date and record date of an upcoming dividend.

**decreasing debt service** A schedule for debt repayment whereby the issuer repays principal in installments of equal size over the life of the issue. The amount of interest due therefore decreases and the amount of each payment becomes smaller over time. *See also* level debt service.

**deduction** An item or expenditure subtracted from adjusted gross income to reduce the amount of income subject to tax. *See also* tax credit.

**default** (1) The failure to pay interest or principal promptly when due. (2) The failure to perform on a futures contract as required by an exchange.

**defeasance** The termination of a debt obligation. A corporation or municipality removes debt from its balance sheet by issuing a new debt issue or creating a trust that generates enough cash flow to provide for the payment of interest and principal. *See also* advance refunding.

**defensive industry** A fundamental analysis term for an industry that is relatively unaffected by business cycles. Most defensive industries produce nondurable goods for which demand remains steady throughout the business cycle; examples include the food industry and utilities.

**defensive investment strategy** A method of portfolio allocation and management aimed at minimizing the risk of losing principal. Defensive investors place a high percentage of their investable assets in bonds, cash equivalents and stocks that are less volatile than average.

**deferred annuity** An annuity contract that delays payments of income, installments or a lump sum until the investor elects to receive them. *See also* annuity.

**deferred compensation plan** A nonqualified retirement plan whereby the employee defers receipt of current compensation in favor of a larger payout at retirement (or in the case of disability or death).

**deficiency letter** The SEC's notification of additions or corrections that a prospective issuer must make to a registration statement before the SEC will clear the offering for distribution.

**defined benefit plan** A qualified retirement plan that specifies the total amount of money that the employee will receive at retirement.

**defined contribution plan** A qualified retirement plan that specifies the amount of money that the employer will contribute annually to the plan.

**deflation** A persistent and measurable fall in the general level of prices. *See also* inflation; stagflation.

**delete information mode** A Consolidated Tape report from which certain information has been omitted in order to prevent the Tape from running late during periods of high market activity.

**delivery vs. payment (DVP)** A transaction settlement procedure in which securities are delivered to the buying institution's bank in exchange for payment of the amount due.

**demand** A consumer's desire and willingness to pay for a good or service. *See also* supply.

**demand deposit** A sum of money left with a bank (or borrowed from a bank and left on deposit) that the depositing customer has the right to withdraw immediately. *See also* time deposit.

**demand-pull** An excessive money supply that increases the demand for a limited supply of goods that is believed to result in inflation. *See also* cost-push.

**depletion** A tax deduction that compensates a business for the decreasing supply of the natural resource that provides its income (oil, gas, coal, gold or other nonrenewable resource). There are two ways to calculate depletion: cost depletion and percentage depletion. *See also* cost depletion; percentage depletion.

**depreciation** (1) A tax deduction that compensates a business for the cost of certain tangible assets. (2) A decrease in the value of a particular currency relative to other currencies.

**depreciation expense** A bookkeeping entry of a noncash expense charged against earnings to recover the cost of an asset over its useful life.

**depression** A prolonged period of general economic decline.

**derivative** An investment vehicle, the value of which is based on the value of another security. Futures contracts, forward contracts, options and CMOs are among the most common types of derivatives. Derivatives are generally used by institutional investors to increase overall portfolio return or to hedge portfolio risk.

**designated order** In a municipal bond underwriting, a customer order that is submitted by one syndicate member but that specifies more than one member to receive a percentage of the takedown. The size of the order establishes its priority for subscription to an issue. *See also* group net order; member-at-the-takedown order; presale order.

**devaluation** A substantial fall in the value of a currency as compared to the value of gold or to the value of another country's currency. *See also* revaluation.

**developmental drilling program** A limited partnership that drills for oil, gas or minerals in areas of proven reserves or near existing fields. *See also* exploratory drilling program; income program.

**diagonal spread** An option hedge position established by the simultaneous purchase and sale of options of the same class but with different exercise prices and expiration dates. *See also* spread.

**dilution** A reduction in earnings per share of common stock. Dilution occurs through the issuance of additional shares of common stock and the conversion of convertible securities.

**direct debt** The total of a municipality's general obligation bonds, short-term notes and revenue debt.

**direct participation program (DPP)** A business organized so as to pass all income, gains, losses and tax benefits to its owners, the investors; the business is usually structured as a limited partnership. Examples include oil and gas programs, real estate programs, agricultural programs, cattle programs, condominium securities and Subchapter S corporate offerings.

**discount** The difference between the lower price paid for a security and the security's face amount at issue. *See also* premium.

**discount bond** A bond that sells at a lower price than its face value. *See also* par value; premium bond.

**discount rate** The interest rate charged by the twelve Federal Reserve Banks for short-term loans made to member banks.

**discretion** The authority given to someone other than the beneficial owner of an account to make investment decisions for the account concerning the security, the number of shares or units, and whether to buy or sell. The authority to decide only timing or price does not constitute "discretion." *See also* limited power of attorney.

**discretionary account** An account in which the customer has given the registered representative authority to enter transactions at the rep's discretion.

**discretion exercised (DE)** The notation marked on an order placed for a discretionary account to indicate that the representative made the decision to trade. *See also* discretionary account.

**discretion not exercised (DNE)** The notation marked on an order placed for a discretionary account to indicate that the account owner made the decision to trade. *See also* discretionary account.

**disintermediation** The flow of money from low-yielding accounts in traditional savings institutions to higher yielding investments; typically, this occurs when the Fed tightens the money supply and interest rates rise.

**disposable income (DI)** The sum that people divide between spending and personal savings. *See also* personal income.

**distribution** Any cash or other property distributed to shareholders or general partners that arises from their interests in the business, investment company or partnership.

**diversification** A risk management technique that mixes a wide variety of investments within a portfolio, thus minimizing the impact of any one security on overall portfolio performance.

**diversified common stock fund** A mutual fund that invests its assets in a wide range of common stocks. The fund's objectives may be growth, income or a combination of both. *See also* growth fund; mutual fund.

**diversified investment company** As defined by the Investment Company Act of 1940, an investment company that meets certain standards as to the percentage of assets invested. These companies use diversification to manage risk. *See also* management company; nondiversified investment company; 75-5-10 test.

**divided account** *See* Western account.

**dividend** A distribution of the earnings of a corporation. Dividends may be in the form of cash, stock or property. All dividends must be declared by the board of directors. *See also* cash dividend; dividend yield; property dividend.

**dividend disbursing agent (DDA)** The person responsible for making the required dividend distributions to the broker-dealer's dividend department.

**dividend exclusion rule** An IRS provision that permits a corporation to exclude from its taxable income 70% of dividends received from domestic preferred and common stocks. The Tax Reform Act of 1986 repealed the dividend exclusion for individual investors.

**dividend payout ratio** A measure of a corporation's policy of paying cash dividends, calculated by dividing the dividends paid on common stock by the net income available for common stockholders. The ratio is the complement of the retained earnings ratio.

**dividends per share** The dollar amount of cash dividends paid on each common share during one year.

**dividend yield** The annual rate of return on a common or preferred stock investment. The yield is calculated by dividing the annual dividend by the purchase price of the stock. *See also* current yield; dividend.

**doctrine of mutual reciprocity** The agreement that established the federal tax exemption for municipal bond interest. States and municipalities do not tax federal securities or properties, and the federal government reciprocates by exempting local government securities and properties from federal taxation.

**dollar bonds** Municipal revenue bonds that are quoted and traded on a basis of dollars rather than yield to maturity. Term bonds, tax-exempt notes and New Housing Authority bonds are dollar bonds.

**dollar cost averaging** A system of buying mutual fund shares in fixed dollar amounts at regular fixed intervals, regardless of the price of the shares. The investor purchases more shares when prices are low and fewer shares when prices are high, thus lowering the average cost per share over time.

**donor** A person who makes a gift of money or securities to another; once the gift is donated, the donor gives up all rights to the gift. Gifts of securities to minors under the Uniform Gifts to Minors Act provide tax advantages to the donor. *See also* Uniform Gifts to Minors Act.

**do not reduce order (DNR)** An order that stipulates that the limit or stop price should not be reduced in response to the declaration of a cash dividend.

**don't know (DK)** A response to a confirmation received from a broker-dealer indicating a lack of information about, or record of, the transaction.

**double-barreled bond** A municipal security backed by the full faith and credit of the issuing municipality, as well as by pledged revenues. *See also* general obligation bond; revenue bond.

**Dow Jones averages** The most widely quoted and oldest measures of change in stock prices. Each of the four averages is based on the prices of a limited number of stocks in a particular category. *See also* average; Dow Jones Composite Average; Dow Jones Industrial Average; Dow Jones Transportation Average; Dow Jones Utilities Average.

**Dow Jones Composite Average (DJCA)** A market indicator composed of the 65 stocks that make up the Dow Jones Industrial, Transportation and Utilities Averages. *See also* average; Dow Jones Industrial Average; Dow Jones Transportation Average; Dow Jones Utilities Average.

**Dow Jones Industrial Average (DJIA)** The most widely used market indicator, composed of 30 large, actively traded issues of industrial stocks. *See also* average; Dow Jones Composite Average; Dow Jones Transportation Average; Dow Jones Utilities Average.

**Dow Jones Transportation Average (DJTA)** A market indicator composed of 20 transportation stocks. *See also* average; Dow Jones Composite Average; Dow Jones Industrial Average; Dow Jones Utilities Average.

**Dow Jones Utilities Average (DJUA)** A market indicator composed of 15 utilities stocks. *See also* average; Dow Jones Composite Average; Dow Jones Industrial Average; Dow Jones Transportation Average.

**down tick** *See* minus tick.

**Dow theory** A technical market theory that long-term trends in the stock market can be confirmed by analyzing the movements of the Dow Jones Industrial Average and the Dow Jones Transportation Average.

**dual-purpose fund** A closed-end investment company that offers two classes of stock: income shares and capital shares. Income shares entitle the holder to share in the net dividends and interest paid to the fund. Capital shares entitle the holder to profit from the capital appreciation of all the securities held by the fund. *See also* closed-end investment company.

**due bill** A printed statement showing the obligation of a seller to deliver securities or rights to the purchaser. A due bill is also used as a pledge to deliver dividends when the transaction occurs after the record date.

**due diligence** The careful investigation by the underwriters that is necessary to ensure that all material information pertinent to an issue has been disclosed to prospective investors.

**due diligence meeting** A meeting at which an issuing corporation's officials and representatives of the underwriting group present information on and answer questions about a pending issue of securities. The meeting is held for the benefit of brokers, securities analysts and institutional investors.

**duplicate confirmation** A copy of a customer's confirmation that a brokerage firm sends to an agent or an attorney if the customer requests it in writing. In addition, if the customer is an employee of another broker-dealer, SRO regulations may require a duplicate confirmation to be sent to the employing broker-dealer. *See also* confirmation.

## E

**earned income** Income derived from active participation in a trade or business, including wages, salary, tips, commissions and bonuses. *See also* portfolio income; unearned income.

**earnings per share (EPS)** A corporation's net income available for common stock divided by its number of shares of common stock outstanding.

**earnings per share fully diluted** A corporation's earnings per share calculated assuming that all convertible securities have been converted. *See also* earnings per share.

**Eastern account** A securities underwriting in which the agreement among underwriters states that each syndicate member will be responsible for its own allocation as well as for a proportionate share of any securities remaining unsold. *Syn.* undivided account. *See also* syndicate; Western account.

**economic risk** The potential for international developments and domestic events to trigger losses in securities investments.

**effective date** The date the registration of an issue of securities becomes effective, allowing the underwriters to sell the newly issued securities to the public and confirm sales to investors who have given indications of interest.

**efficient market theory** A theory based on the premise that the stock market processes information efficiently. The theory postulates that, as new information becomes known, it is reflected immediately in the price of stock and therefore stock prices represent fair prices.

**Employee Retirement Income Security Act of 1974 (ERISA)** The law that governs the operation of most corporate pension and benefit plans. The law eased pension eligibility rules, set up the Pension Benefit Guaranty Corporation and established guidelines for the management of pension funds. Corporate retirement plans established under ERISA qualify for favorable tax treatment for employers and participants.

**endorsement** The signature on the back of a stock or bond certificate by the person named on the certificate as the owner. Owners must endorse certificates when transferring them to another person. *See also* assignment.

**equipment-leasing limited partnership** A direct participation program that purchases equipment for leasing to other businesses on a long-term basis. Tax-sheltered income is the primary objective of such a partnership.

**equipment trust certificate** A debt obligation backed by equipment. The title to the equipment is held by an independent trustee (usually a bank), not the issuing company. Equipment trust certificates are generally issued by transportation companies such as railroads.

**equity (EQ)** (1) The ownership interest of common and preferred stockholders in a corporation. (2) In a margin or short account, equity equals what is owned minus what is owed. *See also* common stock; margin account; preferred stock.

**equity financing** Raising money for working capital or for capital expenditures by selling common or preferred stock to individual or institutional investors. In return for the money paid, the individuals or institutions receive ownership interests in the corporation. *See also* debt financing.

**equity interest** The legal right or title to a share in a business or property.

**equity option** A security representing the right to buy or sell common stock at a specified price within a specified time. *See also* nonequity option; option.

**equity security** A security representing ownership in a corporation or other enterprise. Examples of equity securities include:

- common and preferred stock;
- interests in a limited partnership or joint venture;
- securities that carry the right to be traded for equity securities, such as convertible bonds, rights and warrants; and
- put and call options on equity securities.

*See also* debt security.

**error report** A message on the Consolidated Tape correcting an error in a report on a previous trade. Any necessary correction is preceded by the letters "CORR." *See also* CORR.

**escrow agreement** The certificate provided by an approved bank that guarantees that the indicated securities are on deposit at that bank. An investor who writes a call option and can present an escrow agreement is considered covered and does not need to meet margin requirements.

**Eurobond** A long-term debt instrument of a government or corporation that is denominated in the currency of the issuer's country but is issued and sold in a different country.

**Eurodollar** U.S. currency held in banks outside the United States.

**excess equity (EE)** The value of money or securities in a margin account that is in excess of the federal requirement.

**excess margin securities** The securities in a margin account that are in excess of 140% of the account's debit balance. Such securities are available to the broker-dealer for debit balance financing purposes, but they must be segregated and earmarked as the customer's property.

**exchange** Any organization, association or group of persons that maintains or provides a marketplace in which securities can be bought and sold. An exchange does not have to be a physical place, and several strictly electronic exchanges do business around the world.

**exchange-listed security** A security that has met certain requirements and has been admitted to full trading privileges on an exchange. The NYSE, AMEX and regional exchanges set listing requirements for volume of shares outstanding, corporate earnings and other characteristics. Exchange-listed securities can be traded in the third market, the market for institutional investors.

**exchange market** All of the exchanges on which listed securities are traded.

**exchange offer** An offer to exchange one issuer's securities for those of another, often in conjunction with a corporate takeover.

**exchange privilege** A feature offered by a mutual fund allowing an investor to transfer an investment in one fund to another fund under the same sponsor without incurring an additional sales charge.

**ex-date** The first date on which a security is traded without entitling the buyer to receive distributions previously declared. *Syn.* ex-dividend date.

**ex-dividend date** *See* ex-date.

**executor** A person given fiduciary authorization to manage the affairs of a decedent's estate. An executor's authority is established by the last will of the decedent.

**exempt security** A security exempt from the registration requirements (although not from the antifraud requirements) of the Securities Act of 1933. Examples include U.S. government securities and municipal securities.

**exempt transaction** Transactions that do not trigger a state's registration and advertising requirements under the Uniform Securities Act. Examples of exempt transactions include:

- nonissuer transactions in outstanding securities (normal market trading);
- transactions with financial institutions;
- unsolicited transactions; and
- private placement transactions.

No transaction is exempt from the Uniform Securities Act's antifraud provisions.

**exercise** To effect the transaction offered by an option, right or warrant. For example, an equity call holder exercises a call by buying 100 shares of the underlying stock at the agreed-upon price within the agreed-upon time period.

**exercise price** The cost per share at which the holder of an option or a warrant may buy or sell the underlying security. *Syn.* strike price.

**ex-legal** A municipal issue that trades without a written legal opinion of counsel from a bond attorney. An ex-legal issue must be designated as such at the time of the trade. *See also* legal opinion of counsel.

**expansion** A period of increased business activity throughout an economy; one of the four stages of the business cycle. *See also* business cycle.

**expansionary policy** A monetary policy that increases the money supply, usually with the intention of lowering interest rates and combatting deflation.

**expense ratio** A ratio for comparing the efficiency of a mutual fund by dividing the fund's expenses by its net assets.

**expiration date** The specified date on which an option buyer no longer has the rights specified in the option contract.

**exploratory drilling program** A limited partnership that aims to locate and recover undiscovered reserves of oil, gas or minerals. These programs are considered highly risky investments. *See also* developmental drilling program; income program.

**ex-rights** Stock trading without rights. *See also* cum rights.

**ex-rights date** The date on or after which stocks will be traded without subscription rights previously declared.

**ex-warrants date** The date on or after which stocks will be traded without warrants previously declared.

## F

**face-amount certificate company (FAC)** An investment company that issues certificates obligating it to pay an investor a stated amount of money (the face amount) on a specific future date. The investor pays into the certificate in periodic payments or in a lump sum.

**Fannie Mae** *See* Federal National Mortgage Association.

**Farm Credit System (FCS)** An organization of 37 privately owned banks that provide credit services to farmers and mortgages on farm property. Included in the system are the Federal Land Banks, Federal Intermediate Credit Banks and the Banks for Cooperatives. *See also* Federal Intermediate Credit Bank.

**feasibility study** A due diligence investigation that determines whether a proposed municipal project will generate sufficient funds to cover operation of the project and debt service. A feasibility study is generally required before the issuance of a municipal revenue bond.

**Federal Deposit Insurance Corporation (FDIC)** The government agency that provides deposit insurance for member banks and prevents bank and thrift failures.

**federal funds** The reserves of banks and certain other institutions greater than the reserve requirements or excess reserves. These funds are available immediately.

**federal funds rate** The interest rate charged by one institution lending federal funds to another.

**Federal Home Loan Bank (FHLB)** A government-regulated organization that operates a credit reserve system for the nation's savings and loan institutions.

**Federal Home Loan Mortgage Corporation (FHLMC)** A publicly traded corporation that promotes the nationwide secondary market in mortgages by issuing mortgage-backed pass-through debt certificates. *Syn.* Freddie Mac.

**Federal Intermediate Credit Bank (FICB)** One of 12 banks that provide short-term financing to farmers as part of the Farm Credit System.

**Federal National Mortgage Association (FNMA)** A publicly held corporation that purchases conventional mortgages and mortgages from government agencies, including the Federal Housing Administration, Department of Veterans Affairs and Farmers Home Administration. *Syn.* Fannie Mae.

**Federal Open Market Committee (FOMC)** A committee that makes decisions concerning the Fed's operations to control the money supply. *See also* open-market operations.

**Federal Reserve Board (FRB)** A seven-member group that directs the operations of the Federal Reserve System. Board members are appointed by the president, subject to approval by Congress.

**Federal Reserve System** The central bank system of the United States. Its primary responsibility is to regulate the flow of money and credit. The system includes twelve regional banks, 24 branch banks and hundreds of national and state banks.

**fictitious quotation** A bid or an offer published before being identified by source and verified as legitimate. A fictitious quote may create the appearance of trading activity where none exists; this violates the NASD Rules of Fair Practice.

**fidelity bond** Insurance coverage required by the self-regulatory organizations for all employees, officers and partners of member firms to protect clients against acts of lost securities, fraudulent trading and check forgery. *Syn.* surety bond.

**fiduciary** A person legally appointed and authorized to hold assets in trust for another person and manage those assets for the benefit of that person.

**FIFO** *See* first in, first out.

**filing date** The day on which an issuer submits to the SEC the registration statement for a new securities issue.

**fill or kill order (FOK)** An order that instructs the floor broker to fill the entire order immediately; if the entire order cannot be executed immediately, it is canceled.

**final prospectus** The legal document that states the price of a new issue security, the delivery date, the underwriting spread and other material information. It must be given to every investor who purchases a new issue of registered securities. *Syn.* prospectus.

**firm commitment underwriting** A type of underwriting commitment in which the underwriter agrees to sell an entire new issue of securities. The underwriter acts as a dealer, pays the issuer a lump sum for the securities and assumes all financial responsibility for any unsold shares. *See also* underwriting.

**firm quote** The actual price at which a trading unit of a security (such as 100 shares of stock or five bonds) may be bought or sold. All quotes are firm quotes unless otherwise indicated. *See also* bona fide quote; nominal quote; workout quote.

**first in, first out (FIFO)** An accounting method used to assess a company's inventory, in which it is assumed that the first goods acquired are the first to be sold. The same method is used by the IRS to determine cost basis for tax purposes. *See also* last in, first out.

**fiscal policy** The federal tax and spending policies set by Congress or the president. These policies affect tax rates, interest rates and government spending in an effort to control the economy. *See also* monetary policy.

**fixed annuity** An insurance contract in which the insurance company makes fixed dollar payments to the annuitant for the term of the contract, usually until the annuitant dies. The insurance company guarantees both earnings and principal. *Syn.* guaranteed dollar annuity. *See also* annuity; variable annuity.

**fixed asset** A tangible, physical property used in the course of a corporation's everyday operations; it including buildings, equipment and land.

**fixed unit investment trust** An investment company that invests in a portfolio of securities in which no changes are permissible. *See also* nonfixed unit investment trust; unit investment trust.

**fixing** Trading in a new security for the purpose of stabilizing its price above the established public offering price; this practice is prohibited. *Syn.* pegging.

**flat** A term used to describe bonds traded without accrued interest; they are traded at the agreed-upon market price only. *See also* accrued interest.

**flat yield curve** A chart showing the yields of bonds with short maturities as equal to the yields of bonds with long maturities. *See also* inverted yield curve; normal yield curve; parallel shift; yield curve.

**floating debt** An obligation payable on demand or having a very short maturity.

**floor trader** An exchange member who executes transactions from the floor of the exchange only for his own account.

**flower bond** A type of Treasury bond issued with certain tax advantages that make it suitable for settling estate taxes after the investor's death. Flower bonds tend to trade at discounts due to their low coupon rates.

**flow of funds** The schedule of payments disbursed from the proceeds of a facility financed by a revenue bond. The flow of funds determines the order in which the operating expenses, debt service and other expenses are paid. Typically, the priority is (1) operations and maintenance, (2) debt service, (3) debt service reserve, (4) reserve maintenance, (5) renewal and replacement, (6) surplus. *See also* debt service account; debt service reserve fund.

**flow-through** A term that describes the way income, deductions and credits resulting from the activities of a business are applied to individual taxes and expenses as though each incurred the income and deductions directly. *See also* limited partnership.

**forced conversion** Market conditions created by a corporation to encourage convertible bondholders to exercise their conversion options. Often conversion is forced by calling the bonds when the market value of the stock is higher than the redemption price offered by the corporation. *See also* redemption.

**forced sell-out** The action taken when a customer fails to meet the deadline for paying for securities and no extension has been granted: the broker-dealer must liquidate enough securities to pay for the transaction.

**foreign associate** A non-U.S. citizen employed by an NASD member firm. Foreign associates are not subject to registration and licensing with the NASD. However, they must not engage in the securities business in any country or territory under the jurisdiction of the United States, nor do business with any U.S. citizen, national or resident alien.

**foreign currency** Money issued by a country other than the one in which the investor resides. Options and futures contracts on numerous foreign currencies are traded on U.S. exchanges.

**foreign currency option (FCO)** A security representing the right to buy or sell a specified amount of a foreign currency. *See also* option.

**foreign exchange rate** The price of one country's currency in terms of another currency.

**foreign limited representative** A person who is registered to sell securities in a foreign country and who has passed an examination attesting to knowledge of the laws and regulations necessary to conduct securities business in the United States.

**Form 8K** A legal document used to report events of consequence that occur in a corporation; such events include changes in control of the corporation or in its name, address, financial standing, board of directors or auditors.

**Form 10C** A legal document used by an issuer of securities quoted on Nasdaq to report a change in its name and changes of more than 5% in the amount of securities it has outstanding.

**Form 10K** An annual audited report that covers essentially all the information contained in an issuing company's original registration statement. A Form 10K is due within 90 days of year end.

**Form 10Q** A quarterly report containing a corporation's unaudited financial data. Certain nonrecurring events that arise during the quarterly period, such as significant litigation, must be reported. A Form 10Q is due 45 days after the end of each of the first three fiscal quarters.

**form letter** A sales letter whose contents are substantially identical to the contents of another sales letter. A form letter is subject to federal and NASD approval and filing requirements for sales literature. *See also* sales literature.

**forward pricing** The valuation process for mutual fund shares, whereby orders to purchase or redeem shares are executed at the price determined by the portfolio valuation calculated after the order is received. Portfolio valuations occur at least once per business day.

**401K plan** A tax-deferred defined contribution retirement plan offered by an employer.

**403B plan** A tax-deferred annuity retirement plan available to employees of public schools and certain nonprofit organizations.

**fourth market** The exchange where securities are traded directly from one institutional investor to another without the services of a brokerage firm, primarily through the use of INSTINET. *See also* INSTINET.

**fractional share** A portion of a whole share of stock. Mutual fund shares are frequently issued in fractional amounts. Fractional shares used to be generated when corporations declared stock dividends, merged or voted to split stock, but today it is more common for corporations to issue the cash equivalent of fractional shares.

**fraud** The deliberate concealment, misrepresentation or omission of material information or the truth, so as to deceive or manipulate another party for unlawful or unfair gain.

**Freddie Mac** *See* Federal Home Loan Mortgage Corporation.

**free credit balance** The cash funds in customer accounts. Broker-dealers are required to notify customers of their free credit balances at least quarterly.

**freeriding** Buying and immediately selling securities without making payment. This practice violates the SEC's Regulation T.

**freeriding and withholding** The failure of a member participating in the distribution of a hot issue to make a bona fide public offering at the public offering price. This practice violates the NASD Rules of Fair Practice. *See also* hot issue.

**front-end fee** The expenses paid for services rendered during a direct participation program's organization or acquisition phase, including front-end organization and offering expenses, acquisition fees and expenses, and any other similar fees designated by the sponsor.

**front-end load** A mutual fund commission or sales fee that is charged at the time shares are purchased. The load is added to the net asset value of the shares when calculating the public offering price. *See also* back-end load; Class A share; level load.

**frozen account** An account requiring cash in advance before a buy order is executed and securities in hand before a sell order is executed; the account holder has violated Reg T.

**full power of attorney** A written authorization for someone other than the beneficial owner of an account to make deposits and withdrawals and execute trades in the account. *See also* limited power of attorney.

**full trading authorization** An authorization, usually provided by a full power of attorney, for someone other than the customer to have full trading privileges in an account. *See also* limited trading authorization.

**fully registered bond** A debt issue that prints the name of the bondholder on the certificate. The issuer's transfer agent maintains the records and sends principal and interest payments directly to the investor. *See also* registered; registered as to principal only.

**fundamental analysis** A method of evaluating securities by attempting to measure the intrinsic value of a particular stock. Fundamental analysts study the overall economy, industry conditions and the financial condition and management of particular companies. *See also* technical analysis.

**funded debt** All long-term debt financing of a corporation or municipality; that is, all outstanding bonds maturing in five years or longer.

**funding** An ERISA guideline stipulating that retirement plan assets must be segregated from other corporate assets.

**funds statement** The part of a corporation's annual report that analyzes why working capital increased or decreased.

**fungible** Interchangeable owing to identical characteristics or value. A security is fungible if it can be substituted or exchanged for another security.

## G

**general account** The account that holds all of the assets of an insurer other than those in separate accounts. The general account holds the contributions paid for traditional life insurance contracts. *See also* separate account.

**general obligation bond (GO)** A municipal debt issue backed by the full faith, credit and taxing power of the issuer for payment of interest and principal. *See also* double-barreled bond; revenue bond.

**general partner (GP)** An active investor in a direct participation program who is personally liable for all debts of the program and who manages the business of the program. The GP's duties include: making decisions that bind the partnership; buying and selling property; managing property and money; supervising all aspects of the business; and maintaining a 1% financial interest in the partnership. *See also* limited partner.

**general partnership (GP)** An association of two or more entities formed to conduct a business jointly. The partnership does not require documents for formation, and the general partners are jointly and severally liable for the partnership's liabilities. *See also* limited partnership.

**generic advertising** Communications with the public that promote securities as investments but that do not make reference to a particular security.

**Ginnie Mae** *See* Government National Mortgage Association.

**Glass-Steagall Act of 1933** Federal legislation that forbids commercial banks to underwrite securities and forbids investment bankers to open deposit accounts or make commercial loans.

**good delivery** A term describing a security that is negotiable, in compliance with the contract of the sale and ready to be transferred from seller to purchaser.

**good faith deposit** A deposit contributed by each syndicate involved in a competitive bid underwriting for a municipal issue. The deposit ensures performance by the low bidder. The amount required to be deposited is stipulated in the official notice of sale sent to prospective underwriters; it is usually 2% to 5% of the bid.

**good till canceled order (GTC)** An order that is left on the specialist's book until it is either executed or canceled.

**goodwill** An intangible asset that represents the value that a firm's business reputation adds to its book value.

**Government National Mortgage Association (GNMA)** A wholly government-owned corporation that issues pass-through mortgage debt certificates backed by the full faith and credit of the U.S. government. *Syn.* Ginnie Mae.

**government security** A debt obligation of the U.S. government, backed by its full faith, credit and taxing power, and regarded as having no risk of default. The government issues short-term Treasury bills, medium-term Treasury notes and long-term Treasury bonds. *See also* agency issue.

**gross domestic product (GDP)** The total value of goods and services produced in a country in one year. It includes consumption, government purchases, investments, and exports minus imports.

**gross income** All income of a taxpayer, from whatever source derived.

**gross proceeds** The total of the initial invested capital in a direct participation program contributed by all of the original and additional limited partners.

**gross revenue pledge** The flow of funds arrangement in a municipal revenue bond issue indicating that debt service is the first payment to be made from revenues received. The pledge is contained in the trust indenture. *See also* net revenue pledge.

**gross revenues** All money received by a business from its operations. The term typically does not include interest income or income from the sale, refinancing or other disposition of properties.

**group net order** In a municipal bond underwriting, an order received by a syndicate member that is credited to the entire syndicate. Takedowns on these orders are paid to members according to their participation in the syndicate. *See also* designated order; member-at-the-takedown order; presale order.

**growth fund** A diversified common stock fund that has capital appreciation as its primary goal. It invests in companies that reinvest most of their earnings for expansion, research or development. *See also* diversified common stock fund; mutual fund.

**growth industry** An industry that is growing faster than the economy as a whole as a result of technological changes, new products or changing consumer tastes.

**growth stock** A relatively speculative issue believed to offer significant potential for capital gains; it often pays low dividends and sells at a high price-earnings ratio. *See also* price-earnings ratio.

**guaranteed bond** A debt obligation issued with a promise from a corporation other than the issuing corporation to maintain payments of principal and interest.

**guaranteed dollar annuity** *See* fixed annuity.

**guaranteed stock** An equity security, generally a preferred stock, issued with a promise from a corporation other than the issuing corporation to maintain dividend payments. The stock still represents ownership in the issuing corporation, but it is considered a dual security.

**guardian** A fiduciary who manages the assets of a minor or incompetent for the benefit of that person. *See also* fiduciary.

## H

**HALT** A message on the Consolidated Tape indicating that trading in a particular security has been stopped. *See also* trading halt.

**head and shoulders** On a technical analyst's trading chart, a pattern that has three peaks resembling a head and two shoulders. The stock price moves up to its first peak (the left shoulder), drops back, then moves to a higher peak (the top of the head), drops again but recovers to another, lower peak (the right shoulder). A head and shoulders top typically forms after a substantial rise and indicates a market reversal. A head and shoulders bottom (an inverted head and shoulders) indicates a market advance.

**hedge** An investment made in order to reduce the risk of adverse price movements in a security. Normally, a hedge consists of a protecting position in a related security. *See also* long hedge; short hedge.

**high** The highest price a security or commodity reaches during a specified period of time. *See also* low.

**holder** The owner of a security. *See also* long.

**holding company** A company organized to invest in and manage other corporations.

**holding period** A time period signifying how long a security is possessed by the owner. It starts the day after a purchase and ends on the day of sale.

**hold in street name** A securities transaction settlement and delivery procedure whereby a customer's securities are transferred into the broker-dealer's name and held by the broker-dealer. Although the broker-dealer is the nominal owner, the customer is still the beneficial owner. *See also* in-street-name account; transfer and hold in safekeeping; transfer and ship.

**horizontal spread** The purchase and sale of two options on the same underlying security and with the same exercise price but different expiration dates. *See also* spread.

**hot issue** A new issue that sells or is anticipated to sell at a premium over the public offering price. *See also* freeriding and withholding.

**HR-10 plan** *See* Keogh plan.

**hypothecation** Pledging to a broker-dealer securities bought on margin as collateral for the margin loan. *See also* rehypothecation.

## I

**identified security** The particular security designated for sale by an investor holding identical securities with different acquisition dates and cost bases. This allows the investor to control the amount of capital gain or loss incurred through the sale.

**immediate annuity** An insurance contract purchased for a single premium that starts to pay the annuitant immediately following its purchase. *See also* annuity.

**immediate family** A person who is supported financially by a person associated with the securities industry, including a parent, mother- or father-in-law, husband or wife, child or other relative.

**immediate or cancel order (IOC)** An order that instructs the floor broker to execute it immediately, in full or in part. Any portion of the order that remains unexecuted is canceled.

**income bond** A debt obligation that promises to repay principal in full at maturity. Interest is paid only if the corporation's earnings are sufficient to meet the interest payment and if the interest payment is declared by the board of directors. Income bonds are usually traded flat. *See also* flat.

**income fund** A mutual fund that seeks to provide stable current income by investing in securities that pay interest or dividends. *See also* mutual fund.

**income program** A limited partnership that buys and markets proven reserves of oil and gas: it buys the value of the oil in the ground. *See also* developmental drilling program; exploratory drilling program.

**income statement** The summary of a corporation's revenues and expenses for a specific fiscal period.

**index** A comparison of current prices to some baseline, such as prices on a particular date. Indexes are frequently used in technical analysis. *See also* average.

**index arbitrage** Trading a group of stocks in conjunction with stock index options or futures contracts in order to profit from incremental price differences. *See also* arbitrage.

**index option** A security representing the right to receive, in cash, the difference between the underlying value of a market index and the strike price of the option.The investor speculates on the direction, degree and timing of the change in the numerical value of the index. *See also* capped index option.

**indication of interest (IOI)** An investor's expression of conditional interest in buying an upcoming securities issue after the investor has reviewed a preliminary prospectus. An indication of interest is not a commitment to buy.

**individual retirement account (IRA)** A retirement investing tool for employed individuals that allows an annual contribution of 100% of earned income up to a maximum of $2,000. Some or all of the contribution may be deductible from current taxes, depending on the individual's adjusted gross income and coverage by employer-sponsored qualified retirement plans. *See also* Keogh plan; nonqualified retirement plan; qualified retirement plan; simplified employee pension plan.

**industrial development bond (IDB)** A debt security issued by a municipal authority, which uses the proceeds to finance the construction or purchase of facilities to be leased or purchased by a private company. The bonds are backed by the credit of the private company, which is ultimately responsible for principal and interest payments.

**inflation** A persistent and measurable rise in the general level of prices. *See also* deflation; stagflation.

**inflation risk** *See* purchasing power risk.

**initial margin requirement** The amount of equity a customer must deposit when making a new purchase in a margin account. The SEC's Regulation T requirement for equity securities is currently 50% of the purchase price. The NYSE and NASD's initial minimum requirement is a deposit of $2,000 but not more than 100% of the purchase price. *See also* margin; margin call.

**initial public offering (IPO)** The first sale of common stock by a corporation to the public. *See also* new issue market; public offering.

**in-part call** The redemption of a certain portion of a bond issue at the request of the issuer. *See also* in-whole call.

**inside information** Material information that has not been disseminated to, or is not readily available to, the general public.

**inside market** The best (highest) bid price at which an OTC stock can be sold, and the best (lowest) ask price at which the same stock can be bought in the interdealer market. *See also* affiliate; control person.

**insider** Any person who has or has access to material nonpublic information about a corporation. Insiders include directors, officers and stockholders who own more than 10% of any class of equity security of a corporation.

**Insider Trading and Securities Fraud Enforcement Act of 1988** Legislation that defines what constitutes the illicit use of nonpublic information in making securities trades and the liabilities and penalties that apply. *See also* Chinese wall; insider.

**INSTINET** An electronic securities order execution system, owned by Reuters Holdings PLC, that offers institutional investors a means of trading more than 15,000 U.S. and 5,000 global securities without using a broker-dealer or going through an exchange. INSTINET collects price quotations from exchange-based market makers and Nasdaq and displays the best bid and asked for each security. *See also* fourth market.

**institutional account** An account held for the benefit of others. Examples of institutional accounts include banks, trusts, pension and profit-sharing plans, mutual funds and insurance companies.

**institutional investor** A person or organization that trades securities in large enough share quantities or dollar amounts that it qualifies for preferential treatment and lower commissions. An institutional order can be of any size. Institutional investors are covered by fewer protective regulations because it is assumed that they are more knowledgeable and better able to protect themselves.

**in-street-name account** An account in which the customer's securities are held in the name of the brokerage firm, to facilitate payment and delivery. The customer remains the beneficial owner. *Syn.* street name account.

**insurance covenant** A provision of a municipal revenue bond's trust indenture that helps ensure the safety of the issue by promising to insure the facilities built. *See also* maintenance covenant; rate covenant.

**intangible asset** A property owned that is not physical, such as a formula, a copyright or goodwill. *See also* goodwill.

**intangible drilling cost (IDC)** In an oil and gas limited partnership, a tax-deductible cost; usually this is for a nonphysical asset, such as labor or fuel, which does not depreciate. The cost may be expensed in the year incurred, or deductions may be amortized over the life of the well.

**interbank market** An unregulated, decentralized international market in which the various major currencies of the world are traded.

**interest** The charge for the privilege of borrowing money, usually expressed as an annual percentage rate.

**interest rate option** A security representing the right to buy or sell government debt securities. The federal deficit has created a large market in securities that are sensitive to changes in interest rates; the investor can profit from fluctuations in interest rates and can hedge the risks created by the fluctuations.

**interest rate risk** The risk associated with investments relating to the sensitivity of price or value to fluctuation in the current level of interest rates; also, the risk that involves the competitive cost of money. This term is generally associated with bond prices, but it applies to all investments. In bonds, the price carries an interest risk because if bond prices rise, outstanding bonds will not remain competitive unless their yields and prices adjust to reflect the current market.

**interlocking directorate** Two or more corporate boards of directors that have individual directors who serve simultaneously on both boards. The concept is invoked in the Investment Company Act of 1940, which states that at least 40% of an investment company's board must remain independent from the operations of the investment company, and no more than 60% of the directors may be affiliated persons such as investment advisers, custodians or accountants.

**internal rate of return (IRR)** The investment yield required to make future cash flows exactly equal the initial capital investment.

**Internal Revenue Code (IRC)** The legislation that defines tax liabilities and deductions for U.S. taxpayers.

**Internal Revenue Service (IRS)** The U.S. government agency responsible for collecting most federal taxes and for administering tax rules and regulations.

**International Bank for Reconstruction and Development (IBRD)** The international organization that finances loans for building and improving infrastructure in developing countries. The loans are guaranteed by the government of the borrowing country. *Syn.* World Bank.

**interpolation** A method for determining a bond's price or yield when its actual price or yield falls between two numbers listed in a table in the bond basis book. *See also* bond basis book.

**interstate offering** An issue of securities registered with the SEC and sold to residents of states other than that in which the issuer does business.

**in-the-money** The term used to describe an option that has intrinsic value, such as a call option when the stock is selling above the exercise price or a put option when the stock is selling below the exercise price. *See also* at-the-money; intrinsic value; out-of-the-money.

**intrastate offering** An issue of securities exempt from SEC registration, available to companies that do business in one state and sell their securities only to residents of that same state. *See also* Rule 147.

**intrinsic value** The potential profit to be made from exercising an option. A call option is said to have intrinsic value when the underlying stock is trading above the exercise price. *See also* time value.

**introduced account** An account opened by an investment adviser or a broker-dealer acting on the behalf of its customers. The firm carrying the account receives full disclosure of the individual customers' account information and maintains records of statements and confirms for the individual customers. *Syn.* investment adviser's customer account. *See also* omnibus account.

**introducing broker (IB)** A broker-dealer that does not hold customers' money or securities; instead, it introduces customer accounts to a clearing broker-dealer, which handles all cash and securities for those accounts. *See also* clearing broker-dealer.

**inventory turnover ratio** A tool used by fundamental analysts to measure the efficiency of a company by determining how rapidly it is turning its inventory and accounts receivables into cash. *Syn.* efficiency ratio.

**inverted yield curve** A chart showing long-term debt instruments having lower yields than short-term debt instruments. *See also* flat yield curve; normal yield curve; parallel shift.

**investment adviser** (1) Any person who makes investment recommendations in return for a flat fee or percentage of assets managed. (2) For investment companies, the individual who has the daily responsibility of investing the cash and securities held in the fund's portfolio in accordance with objectives stated in the fund's prospectus.

**investment adviser representative** Any partner, officer, director or other individual associated with an investment adviser who gives investment advice, manages client portfolios, determines which investment recommendations should be given, sells investment advisory services, or supervises employees involved in any of these activities.

**Investment Advisers Act of 1940** Legislation governing who must register with the SEC as an investment adviser. *See also* investment adviser.

**investment adviser's customer account** *See* introduced account.

**investment banker** An institution in the business of raising capital for corporations and municipalities. An investment banker may not accept deposits or make commercial loans. *Syn.* investment bank. *See also* commercial bank.

**investment banking business** A broker, dealer or municipal or government securities dealer that underwrites or distributes new issues of securities as a dealer, or that buys and sells securities for the accounts of others as a broker.

**investment company** A company engaged in the business of pooling investors' money and trading in securities for them. Examples include face-amount certificate companies, unit investment trusts and management companies.

**Investment Company Act of 1940** Congressional legislation that regulates companies that invest and reinvest in securities. The act requires an investment company engaged in interstate commerce to register with the SEC.

**investment grade security** A security to which the rating services (Standard & Poor's, Moody's, etc.) have assigned a rating of BBB/Baa or above.

**investment objective** Any goal a client hopes to achieve through investing; examples include current income, capital growth and preservation of capital.

**investment pyramid** A portfolio strategy that allocates investable assets according to the relative safety of the investment. The base of the pyramid is composed of low-risk investments, the mid portion is composed of growth investments and the top of the pyramid is composed of speculative investments.

**investment value** The market price at which a convertible security (usually a debenture) would sell if it were not converted into common stock. *See also* conversion value; convertible bond; debenture.

**investor** The purchaser of an asset or security with the intent of profiting from the transaction.

**invitation for bids** A notice to securities underwriters soliciting bids for the issuing of a bond issue. These notices are published in *The Bond Buyer, Munifacts,* newspapers and journals.

**in-whole call** The redemption of a bond issue in its entirety at the option of the issuer, as opposed to its redemption based on a lottery held by an independent trustee. *See also* in-part call.

**IRA** *See* individual retirement account.

**IRA rollover** The reinvestment of assets that an individual receives as a distribution from a qualified tax-deferred retirement plan into an individual retirement account within 60 days of receiving the distribution. The individual may reinvest either the entire sum or a portion of the sum, although any portion not reinvested is taxed as ordinary income. *See also* individual retirement account; IRA transfer.

**IRA transfer** The direct reinvestment of retirement assets from the custodian of one qualified tax-deferred retirement plan to an individual retirement account. The account owner never takes possession of the assets, but directs that they be transferred directly from the existing plan custodian to the new plan custodian. *See also* individual retirement account; IRA rollover.

**issued stock** Equity securities authorized by the issuer's registration statement and distributed to the public. *See also* outstanding stock; treasury stock.

**issuer** (1) The entity, such as a corporation or municipality, that offers or proposes to offer its securities for sale. (2) The creator of an option: the issuer of an over-the-counter option is the option writer, and the issuer of a listed option is the Options Clearing Corporation.

There are two exceptions to the definition of issuer. In the case of voting-trust certificates or collateral-trust certificates, the issuer is the person who assumes the duties of depositor or manager. Also, there is considered to be no issuer for certificates of interest or participation in oil, gas, or mining titles or leases where payments are made out of production.

## *J*

**joint account** An account in which two or more individuals possess some form of control over the account and may transact business in the account. The account must be designated as either joint tenants in common or joint tenants with right of survivorship. *See also* joint tenants in common; joint tenants with right of survivorship.

**joint life with last survivor annuity** An annuity payout option that covers two or more people; the annuity payments continue as long as one of the annuitants remains alive.

**joint tenants in common (JTIC)** A form of joint ownership of an account whereby a deceased tenant's fractional interest in the account is retained by his estate. *See also* joint tenants with right of survivorship.

**joint tenants with right of survivorship (JTWROS)** A form of joint ownership of an account whereby a deceased tenant's fractional interest in the account passes to the surviving tenant(s). It is used almost exclusively by husbands and wives. *See also* joint tenants in common.

**joint venture** The cooperation of two or more individuals or enterprises in a specific business enterprise, rather than in a continuing relationship—as in a partnership.

**junior lien debt** A bond backed by the same collateral backing a previous issue and having a subordinate claim to the collateral in the event of default. *See also* closed-end covenant; open-end covenant.

## K

**Keogh plan** A qualified tax-deferred retirement plan for persons who are self-employed and unincorporated or who earn extra income through personal services aside from their regular employment. *Syn.* HR-10 plan. *See also* individual retirement account; nonqualified retirement plan; qualified retirement plan.

**Keynesian economics** The theory that active government intervention in the marketplace is the best method of ensuring economic growth and stability.

**know your customer rule** *See* Rule 405.

## L

**L** A category of the money supply that includes all of the components of M1, M2 and M3, in addition to all Treasury bills, savings bonds, commercial paper, bankers' acceptances and Eurodollar holdings of U.S. residents. *See also* M1; M2; M3; money supply.

**lagging indicator** A measurable economic factor that changes after the economy has started to follow a particular pattern or trend. Lagging indicators are believed to confirm long-term trends. Examples include average duration of unemployment, corporate profits and labor cost per unit of output. *See also* coincident indicator; leading indicator.

**last in, first out (LIFO)** An accounting method used to assess a corporation's inventory in which it is assumed that the last goods acquired are the first to be sold. The method is used to determine cost basis for tax purposes; the IRS designates last in, first out as the order in which sales or withdrawals from an investment are made. *See also* first in, first out.

**leading indicator** A measurable economic factor that changes before the economy starts to follow a particular pattern or trend. Leading indicators are believed to predict changes in the economy. Examples include new orders for durable goods, slowdowns in deliveries by vendors and numbers of building permits issued. *See also* coincident indicator; lagging indicator.

**lease rental bond** A debt security issued by a municipal authority to raise funds for new construction with the understanding that the finished structure will be rented to the authority and that the rental payments will finance the bond payments.

**legal list** The selection of securities determined by a state agency (usually a state banking or insurance commission) to be appropriate investments for fiduciary accounts such as mutual savings banks, pension funds and insurance companies.

**legal opinion of counsel** The statement of a bond attorney affirming that an issue is a municipal issue and that interest is exempt from federal taxation. Each municipal bond certificate must be accompanied by a legal opinion of counsel. *See also* ex-legal; qualified legal opinion; unqualified legal opinion.

**legislative risk** The potential for an investor to be adversely affected by changes in investment or tax laws.

**letter of intent (LOI)** A signed agreement allowing an investor to buy mutual fund shares at a lower overall sales charge, based on the total dollar amount of the intended investment. A letter of intent is valid only if the investor completes the terms of the agreement within 13 months of the time the agreement is signed. A letter of intent may be backdated 90 days.

**level debt service** A schedule for debt repayment whereby principal and interest payments remain essentially constant from year to year over the life of the issue. *See also* decreasing debt service.

**level load** A mutual fund sales fee charged annually based on the net asset value of a share. A 12b-1 asset-based fee is an example of a level load. *See* *also* back-end load; Class C share; Class D share; front-end load.

**Level One** The basic level of Nasdaq service; through a desktop quotation machine, it provides registered representatives with up-to-the-minute inside bid and ask quotations on hundreds of over-the-counter stocks. *See also* National Association of Securities Dealers Automated Quotation System.

**Level Two** The second level of Nasdaq service; through a desktop quotation machine, it provides up-to-the-minute inside bid and ask quotations and the bids and askeds of each market maker for a security. *See also* National Association of Securities Dealers Automated Quotation System.

**Level Three** The highest level of Nasdaq service; through a desktop quotation machine, it provides up-to-the-minute inside bid and ask quotations, supplies the bids and askeds of each market maker for a security and allows each market maker to enter changes in those quotations. *See also* National Association of Securities Dealers Automated Quotation System.

**leverage** Using borrowed capital to increase investment return.

**liability** A legal obligation to pay a debt owed. Current liabilities are debts payable within twelve months. Long-term liabilities are debts payable over a period of more than twelve months.

**LIBOR** *See* London Interbank Offered Rate.

**life annuity/straight life** An annuity payout option that pays a monthly check over the lifetime of the annuitant.

**life annuity with period certain** An annuity payout option that guarantees the annuitant a monthly check for a certain time period and thereafter until the annuitant's death. If the annuitant dies before the time period expires, the payments go to the annuitant's named beneficiary.

**life contingency annuity** An annuity payout option that provides a death benefit during the accumulation stage. If the annuitant dies during this period, a full contribution is made to the account, which is paid to the annuitant's named beneficiary.

**LIFO** *See* last in, first out.

**limited liability** The right of an investor to limit potential losses to no more than the amount invested. Equity shareholders, such as corporate stockholders and limited partners, have limited liability.

**limited partner (LP)** An investor in a direct participation program who does not participate in the management or control of the program and whose liability for partnership debts is limited to the amount invested in the program. *See also* general partner.

**limited partnership (LP)** An association of two or more partners formed to conduct a business jointly and in which one or more of the partners is liable only to the extent of the amount of money they have invested. Limited partners do not receive dividends but enjoy direct flow-through of income and expenses. *See also* flow-through; general partnership.

**limited partnership agreement** The contract between a partnership's limited and general partners that provides the guidelines for partnership operation and states the rights and responsibilities of each partner.

**limited power of attorney** A written authorization for someone other than the beneficial owner of an account to make certain investment decisions regarding transactions in the account. *See also* discretion; full power of attorney.

**limited principal** A person who has passed an examination attesting to the knowledge and qualifications necessary to supervise the business of a broker-dealer in a limited area of expertise. A limited principal is not qualified in the general fields of expertise reserved for a general securities principal; these include supervision of underwriting and market making and approval of advertising.

**limited representative** A person who has passed an examination attesting to the knowledge and qualifications necessary to sell certain specified investment products.

**limited tax bond** A general obligation municipal debt security issued by a municipality whose taxing power is limited to a specified maximum rate.

**limited trading authorization** An authorization, usually provided by a limited power of attorney, for someone other than the customer to have trading privileges in an account. These privileges are limited to purchases and sales; withdrawal of assets is not authorized. *See also* full trading authorization.

**limit order** An order that instructs the floor broker to buy a specified security below a certain price or to sell a specified security above a certain price. *See also* stop limit order; stop order.

**liquidation priority** In the case of a corporation's liquidation, the order that is strictly followed for paying off creditors and stockholders.

**liquidity** The ease with which an asset can be converted to cash in the marketplace. A large number of buyers and sellers and a high volume of trading activity provide high liquidity.

**liquidity ratio** A measure of a corporation's ability to meet its current obligations. The ratio compares current assets to current liabilities. *See also* acid-test ratio; current ratio.

**liquidity risk** The potential that an investor might not be able to sell an investment as and when desired.

**listed option** An option contract that can be bought and sold on a national securities exchange in a continuous secondary market. Listed options carry standardized strike prices and expiration dates. *See also* OTC option.

**listed security** A stock, bond or other security that satisfies certain minimum requirements and is traded on a regional or national securities exchange such as the New York Stock Exchange. *See also* over the counter.

**loan consent agreement** An optional contract between a brokerage firm and a margin customer that permits the firm to lend the margined securities to other brokers; the contract is part of the margin agreement.

**London Interbank Offered Rate (LIBOR)** The average of the interbank-offered interest rates for dollar deposits in the London market, based on the quotations at five major banks.

**long** The term used to describe the owning of a security, contract or commodity. For example, an owner of common stock is said to have a long position in the stock. *See also* short; short against the box.

**long hedge** Buying puts as protection against a decline in the value of a long securities or actuals position. *See also* hedge; short hedge.

**long straddle** An option investor's position that results from buying a call and a put on the same stock with the same exercise price and expiration month. *See also* short straddle; spread; straddle.

**long-term equity option** An option contract that has a longer expiration than traditional equity option contracts. The most common long-term equity option is the CBOE's Long-term Equity AnticiPation Security (LEAPS®).

**long-term gain** The profit earned on the sale of a capital asset that has been owned for more than twelve months. *See also* capital gain; capital loss; long-term loss; short-term capital gain.

**long-term loss** The loss realized on the sale of a capital asset that has been owned for more than twelve months. *See also* capital gain; capital loss; long-term gain; short-term capital loss.

**loss carryover** A capital loss incurred in one tax year that is carried over to the next or later years for use as a capital loss deduction. *See also* capital loss.

**low** The lowest price a security or commodity reaches during a specified time period. *See also* high.

## *M*

**M** Consolidated Tape market identifier for the Chicago Stock Exchange (formerly the Midwest Stock Exchange).

**M1** A category of the money supply that includes all coins, currency and demand deposits (that is, checking accounts and NOW accounts). *See also* L; M2; M3; money supply.

**M2** A category of the money supply that includes M1 in addition to all time deposits, savings deposits and noninstitutional money-market funds. *See also* L; M1; M3; money supply.

**M3** A category of the money supply that includes M2 in addition to all large time deposits, institutional money-market funds, short-term repurchase agreements and certain other large liquid assets. *See also* L; M1; M2; money supply.

**maintenance covenant** A provision of a municipal revenue bond's trust indenture that helps ensure the safety of the issue by promising to keep the facility and equipment in good working order. *See also* insurance covenant; rate covenant.

**Major Market Index (MMI)** A market indicator designed to track the Dow Jones industrials. It is composed of 15 of the 30 Dow Jones industrials and five other large NYSE-listed stocks. *See also* index.

**make a market** To stand ready to buy or sell a particular security as a dealer for its own account. A market maker accepts the risk of holding the position in the security. *See also* market maker.

**Maloney Act** An amendment enacted in 1938 to broaden Section 15 of the Securities Exchange Act of 1934. Named for its sponsor, the late Sen. Francis Maloney of Connecticut, the amendment provided for the creation of a self-regulatory organization for the specific purpose of supervising the over-the-counter securities market. *See also* National Association of Securities Dealers, Inc.

**management company** An investment company that trades various types of securities in a portfolio, in accordance with specific objectives stated in the prospectus. *See also* closed-end investment company; diversified investment company; mutual fund; nondiversified investment company.

**management fee** The payment to the sponsor of a direct participation program for managing and administering the program. The fee is capped at about 5% of the program's gross revenues.

**managing partner** The general partner of a direct participation program that selects the investments and operates the partnership.

**mandatory call** The redemption of a bond by an issuer authorized in the trust indenture and based on a predetermined schedule or event. *See also* catastrophe call; partial call.

**margin** The amount of equity contributed by a customer as a percentage of the current market value of the securities held in a margin account. *See also* equity; initial margin requirement; margin call; Regulation T.

**margin account** A customer account in which a brokerage firm lends the customer part of the purchase price of securities. *See also* cash account; Regulation T; special arbitrage account.

**margin call** The Federal Reserve Board's demand that a customer deposit a specified amount of money or securities when a purchase is made in a margin account; the amount is expressed as a percentage of the market value of the securities at the time of purchase. The deposit must be made within one payment period. *Syn.* T call. *See also* initial margin requirement; margin.

**margin maintenance call** A demand that a margin customer deposit money or securities when the customer's equity falls below the margin maintenance requirement set by the broker-dealer or by the NASD or NYSE.

**margin maintenance requirement** The minimum equity that must be held in a margin account, determined by the broker-dealer and by the NASD or NYSE. The amount of equity required varies with the type of security bought on margin, and the broker-dealer's house requirement is usually higher than that set by the NASD or NYSE.

**margin of profit ratio** A measure of a corporation's relative profitability. It is calculated by dividing the operating profit by the net sales.

**margin risk** The potential that a margin customer will be required to deposit additional cash if her security positions are subject to adverse price movements.

**margin security** A security that is eligible for purchase on margin, including any registered security, OTC margin stock or bond or Nasdaq National Market security. A firm is permitted to lend money to help customers purchase these securities, and may accept these securities as collateral for margin purchases. *See also* nonmargin security; OTC margin security.

**markdown** The difference between the highest current bid price among dealers and the lower price that a dealer pays to a customer.

**marketability** The ease with which a security can be bought or sold; having a readily available market for trading.

**market arbitrage** The simultaneous purchase and sale of the same security in different markets to take advantage of a price disparity between the two markets. *See also* arbitrage.

**market letter** A publication that comments on securities, investing, the economy or other related topics, and is distributed to an organization's clients or to the public. *See also* sales literature.

**market maker** A dealer willing to accept the risk of holding a particular security in its own account to facilitate trading in that security. *See also* make a market.

**market-on-close order** An order that specifies it is to be executed at, or as near as possible to, the close of the market or of trading in that security, or else it is canceled. The order does not have to be executed at the closing price. *Syn.* at-the-close order. *See also* at-the-opening order.

**market order** An order that is to be executed immediately at the best available price. A market order is the only order that guarantees execution. *Syn.* unrestricted order.

**market risk** The potential for an investor to experience losses owing to day-to-day fluctuations in the prices at which securities can be bought or sold. *See also* systematic risk.

**market value** The price at which investors buy or sell a share of common stock or a bond at a given time. Market value is determined by the interaction between buyers and sellers. *See also* current market value.

**market value on the trade date** The gross amount of a long purchase (including commissions) or the net proceeds of a short sale.

**markup** The difference between the lowest current offering price among dealers and the higher price a dealer charges a customer.

**married put** The simultaneous purchase of a stock and a put on that stock specifically identified as a hedge.

**matching orders** Simultaneously entering identical (or nearly identical) buy and sell orders for a security to create the appearance of active trading in that security. This violates the antifraud provisions of the Securities Exchange Act of 1934.

**material information** Any fact that could affect an investor's decision to trade a security.

**maturity date** The date on which a bond's principal is repaid to the investor and interest payments cease. *See also* balloon maturity; principal; serial bond; term maturity.

**member** (1) Of the New York Stock Exchange: one of the 1,366 individuals owning a seat on the Exchange. (2) Of the National Association of Securities Dealers: any broker or dealer admitted to membership in the Association.

**member-at-the-takedown order** In a municipal bond underwriting, a customer order submitted by one syndicate member, who will receive the entire takedown. Member-at-the-takedown orders receive the lowest priority when the securities of the issue are allocated. *See also* designated order; group net order; presale order.

**member firm** A broker-dealer in which at least one of the principal officers is a member of the New York Stock Exchange, another exchange, a self-regulatory organization, or a clearing corporation.

**membership** The members of the New York Stock Exchange, another exchange, a self-regulatory organization or a clearing corporation.

**merger** Combining two or more companies by offering the stockholders of one company securities in another company in exchange for the surrender of their stock. This falls under the purview of SEC Rule 145. *See also* Rule 145.

**Midwest Stock Exchange (MSE)** The former name of the Chicago Stock Exchange. *See also* Chicago Stock Exchange.

**mill rate** The tax per dollar of assessed value of property in a particular municipality, usually expressed in mills; one mill equals 1/10th of a cent ($.001). *See also* ad valorem tax; assessed value.

**mini-max underwriting** A form of best efforts underwriting in which the issuer sets a floor and a ceiling on the amount of securities to be sold. *See also* underwriting.

**minus tick** A security transaction's execution price that is below the previous execution price, by a minimum amount. A short sale may not be executed on a minus tick. *Syn.* down tick. *See also* plus tick; plus tick rule; short sale; tick; zero-minus tick.

**modern portfolio theory (MPT)** A method of choosing investments that focuses on the importance of the relationships among all of the investments in a portfolio rather than the individual merits of each investment. The method allows investors to quantify and control the amount of risk they accept and return they achieve.

**monetarist theory** An economic theory holding that the money supply is the major determinant of price levels and that therefore a well-controlled money supply will have the most beneficial impact on the economy.

**monetary policy** The actions of the Federal Reserve Board that determine the size and rate of growth of the money supply, which in turn affect interest rates. *See also* fiscal policy.

**money market** The securities market that deals in short-term debt. Money-market instruments are forms of debt that mature in less than one year and are very liquid. Treasury bills make up the bulk of the money-market instruments.

**money-market fund** A mutual fund that invests in short-term debt instruments. The fund's objective is to earn interest while maintaining a stable net asset value of $1.00 per share. Generally sold with no load, the fund may also offer draft-writing privileges and low opening investments. *See also* mutual fund.

**money supply** The total stock of bills, coins, loans, credit and other liquid instruments in the economy. It is divided into four categories—L, M1, M2 and M3—according to the type of account in which the instrument is kept. *See also* L; M1; M2; M3.

**Moody's Investors Service** One of the best known investment rating agencies in the United States. A subsidiary of Dun & Bradstreet, Moody's rates bonds, commercial paper, preferred and common stocks, and municipal short-term issues. *See also* bond rating; Standard & Poor's Corporation.

**moral obligation bond** A municipal revenue bond for which a state legislature has the authority, but no legal obligation, to appropriate money in the event the issuer defaults.

**mortgage bond** A debt obligation secured by a property pledge. It represents a lien or mortgage against the issuing corporation's properties and real estate assets.

**MSRB** *See* Municipal Securities Rulemaking Board.

**multiplier effect** The expansion of the money supply that results from a Federal Reserve System member bank's being able to lend more money than it takes in. A small increase in bank deposits generates a far larger increase in available credit.

**municipal bond** A debt security issued by a state, a municipality or other subdivision (such as a school, park, sanitary or other local taxing district) to finance its capital expenditures. Such expenditures might include the construction of highways, public works or school buildings.

**municipal bond fund** A mutual fund that invests in municipal bonds and operates either as a unit investment trust or as an open-end fund. The fund's objective is to maximize federally tax-exempt income. *See also* mutual fund; unit investment trust.

**Municipal Bond Investors Assurance Corp. (MBIA)** A public corporation offering insurance as to the timely payment of principal and interest on qualified municipal issues. Issues with MBIA insurance are generally rated AAA by Standard & Poor's.

**municipal broker's broker** A broker acting for another broker in trading municipal securities. The broker's broker does not take positions in a security or transact orders for the public. *See also* broker's broker.

**municipal note** A short-term municipal security issued in anticipation of funds from another source.

**Municipal Securities Rulemaking Board (MSRB)** A self-regulatory organization that regulates the issuance and trading of municipal securities. The Board functions under the supervision of the Securities and Exchange Commission; it has no enforcement powers.

***Munifacts*** A news wire service for the municipal bond industry; a product of *The Bond Buyer*.

**mutual fund** An investment company that continuously offers new equity shares in an actively managed portfolio of securities. All shareholders participate in the gains or losses of the fund. The shares are redeemable on any business day at the net asset value. Each mutual fund's portfolio is invested to match the objective stated in the prospectus. *See also* asset allocation fund; balanced fund; contractual plan; net asset value.

**mutual fund custodian** A national bank, stock exchange member firm, trust company or other qualified institution that physically safeguards the securities held by a mutual fund. It does not manage the fund's investments; its function is solely clerical. *See also* custodian; plan custodian.

## *N*

**N** Consolidated Tape market identifier for the New York Stock Exchange.

**naked** The position of an option investor who writes a call or a put on a security he does not own. *Syn.* uncovered.

**naked call writer** An investor who writes a call option without owning the underlying stock or other related assets that would enable the investor to deliver the stock should the option be exercised. *See also* naked put writer.

**naked put writer** An investor who writes a put option without owning the underlying stock or other related assets that would enable the investor to purchase the stock should the option be exercised. *See also* naked call writer.

**narrow-based index** An index that is designed to reflect the movement of a market segment, such as a group of stocks in one industry or a specific type of investment. Examples include the Technology Index and the Gold/Silver Index. *See also* broad-based index; index.

**NASD** *See* National Association of Securities Dealers, Inc.

**Nasdaq** *See* National Association of Securities Dealers Automated Quotation System.

**Nasdaq National Market (NNM)** The most actively traded over-the-counter stocks quoted on Nasdaq. Trades in these stocks are reported as they occur.

**Nasdaq 100** An index of the largest 100 nonfinancial stocks on Nasdaq, weighted according to capitalization.

**Nasdaq-OTC price indexes** Indexes of OTC-traded stocks, published by the NASD through Nasdaq.

**NASD Bylaws** The body of rules that describes how the NASD functions, defines its powers and determines the qualifications and registration requirements for brokers.

**NASD District Business Conduct Committee (DBCC)** A committee composed of up to twelve NASD members who each serve as administrator for one of the 13 local NASD districts. The DBCC has original jurisdiction for hearings and judging complaints.

**NASD 5% markup policy** A guideline for reasonable markups, markdowns and commissions for secondary over-the-counter transactions. According to the policy, all commissions on broker transactions and all markups or markdowns on principal transactions should equal 5% or should be fair and reasonable for that particular transaction.

***NASD Manual*** A publication that outlines NASD policies for regulating the over-the-counter market; included are the Rules of Fair Practice, the Uniform Practice Code and the Codes of Procedure and of Arbitration Procedure.

**NASDR** *See* NASD Regulation, Inc.

**NASD Regulation, Inc.** Branch of the NASD organized in 1996 to supervise member broker-dealers, enforce laws and ethical standards and mete out disciplinary action.

**NASD Rules of Fair Practice** Regulations designed to ensure that NASD member firms and their representatives follow fair and ethical trade practices when dealing with the public. The rules complement and serve as extensions of the Securities Act of 1933, the Securities Exchange Act of 1934 and the Investment Company Act of 1940.

**National Association of Securities Dealers, Inc. (NASD)** The self-regulatory organization for the over-the-counter market. The NASD was organized under the provisions of the 1938 Maloney Act. *See also* Maloney Act; Small Order Execution System.

**National Association of Securities Dealers Automated Quotation System (Nasdaq)** The nationwide electronic quotation system for up-to-the-minute bid and asked quotations on approximately 5,500 over-the-counter stocks.

**National Securities Clearing Corporation (NSCC)** An organization that acts as a medium through which member brokerage firms and exchanges reconcile accounts with each other.

**NAV** *See* net asset value.

**NAV of fund** The net total of a mutual fund's assets and liabilities; used to calculate the price of new fund shares.

**NAV per share** The value of a mutual fund share, calculated by dividing the total net asset value of the fund by the number of shares outstanding.

**negotiability** A characteristic of a security that permits the owner to assign, give, transfer or sell it to another person without the permission of a third party.

**negotiable certificate of deposit (CD)** An unsecured promissory note issued with a minimum face value of $100,000. It evidences a time deposit of funds with the issuing bank, and is guaranteed by the bank.

**negotiated underwriting** A form of underwriting agreement in which a brokerage firm consults with the issuer to determine the most suitable price and timing of a forthcoming securities offering. *See also* competitive bid underwriting.

**net asset value (NAV)** The value of a mutual fund share calculated once a day, based on the closing market price for each security in the fund's portfolio. It is computed by deducting the fund's liabilities from the total assets of the portfolio and dividing this amount by the number of shares outstanding. *See also* mutual fund.

**net capital (NC)** The amount of cash and assets readily convertible into cash that a broker-dealer owns in excess of its liabilities. The SEC sets net capital requirements to ensure that broker-dealers have enough money to deal responsibly with the investing public.

**net change** The difference between the closing price of a security on the trading day reported and the previous day's closing price. In over-the-counter transactions, the term refers to the difference between the closing bids.

**net current asset value per share** The calculation of book value per share that excludes all fixed assets. *See also* book value per share.

**net debt per capita** A measure of the ability of a municipality to meet its debt obligations; it compares the debt issued by the municipality to its property values.

**net debt to assessed valuation** A measure of the financial condition of a municipality; it compares the municipality's debt obligations to the assessed value of its property. *See also* net debt to estimated valuation.

**net debt to estimated valuation** A measure of the financial condition of a municipality; it compares the municipality's debt obligations to the estimated value of its property. *See also* net debt to assessed valuation.

**net direct debt** The amount of debt obligations of a municipality, including general obligation bonds and notes and short-term notes. Self-supported debt from revenue bond issues is not included in the calculation.

**net interest cost (NIC)** A means of evaluating the competitive bids of prospective bond underwriting syndicates. It calculates the coupon interest to be paid by each syndicate over the life of the bond. *See also* true interest cost.

**net investment income** The source of an investment company's dividend payments. It is calculated by subtracting the company's operating expenses from the total dividends and interest received from the securities in its portfolio.

**net investment return** The rate of return from a variable life insurance separate account. The cumulative return for all years is applied to the benefit base when calculating the death benefit.

**net proceeds** The amount of money received from a direct participation program offering less expenses incurred, such as selling commissions, syndicate fees and organizational costs.

**net revenue pledge** The flow of funds arrangement in a municipal revenue bond issue pledging that operating and maintenance expenses will be paid before debt service. The pledge is contained in the trust indenture. *See also* gross revenue pledge.

**net total debt** The sum of the debt obligations of a municipality, calculated by adding the municipality's net direct debt to its overlapping debt. *See also* net direct debt; overlapping debt.

**net worth** The amount by which assets exceed liabilities. *Syn.* shareholders' equity.

**new account form** Form that must be filled out for each new account opened with a brokerage firm. The form specifies, at a minimum, account owner, trading authorization, payment method and types of securities appropriate for the customer.

**new construction program** A real estate direct participation program that aims to provide capital appreciation from building new property.

**New Housing Authority bond (NHA)** A municipal special revenue bond backed by the U.S. government and issued by a local public housing authority to develop and improve low-income housing.

**new issue market** The securities market for shares in privately owned businesses that are raising capital by selling common stock to the public for the first time. *See also* initial public offering; secondary market.

**New York Stock Exchange (NYSE)** The largest stock exchange in the United States. It is a corporation, operated by a board of directors, and it is responsible for setting policy, supervising Exchange and member activities, listing securities, overseeing the transfer of members' seats on the Exchange and judging whether an applicant is qualified to be a specialist. *See also* Super Designated Order Turnaround System.

**New York Stock Exchange Composite Index** Index of common stocks listed on the NYSE, based on the price of each stock weighted by its total value of shares outstanding. *Syn.* NYSE Index.

**nine bond rule** An NYSE rule that requires orders for nine or fewer listed bonds to be sent to the floor of the NYSE before being traded in the over-the-counter market.

**no-load fund** A mutual fund whose shares are sold without a commission or sales charge. Shares are distributed directly by the investment company. *See also* mutual fund; net asset value; sales load.

**nominal owner** The person in whose name securities are registered if that person is other than the beneficial owner. This is the role of a brokerage firm when customer securities are registered in street name.

**nominal quote** A quotation on an inactively traded security that does not represent an actual offer to buy or sell but is given for informational purposes only. *See also* bona fide quote; firm quote; subject quote; workout quote.

**nominal yield** The interest rate stated on the face of a bond that represents the percentage of interest to be paid by the issuer on the face value of the bond. *See also* bond yield.

**nonaccredited investor** An investor not meeting the net worth requirements of Regulation D. Nonaccredited investors are counted for purposes of the 35-investor limitation for Regulation D private placements. *See also* accredited investor; private placement; Regulation D.

**nonaffiliate** A buyer of an unregistered public offering security who has no management or major ownership interest in the company being acquired. Nonaffiliates may sell this stock only after a specified holding period.

**noncompetitive bid** An order placed for Treasury bills in which the investor agrees to pay the average of the competitive bids and in return is guaranteed that the order will be filled.

**noncumulative preferred stock** An equity security that does not have to pay any dividends in arrears to the holder. *See also* convertible preferred stock; cumulative preferred stock; preferred stock.

**nondiscrimination** In a qualified retirement plan, a formula for calculating contributions and benefits that must be applied uniformly so as to ensure that all employees receive fair and equitable treatment. *See also* qualified retirement plan.

**nondiversification** A portfolio management strategy that seeks to concentrate investments in a particular industry or geographic area, in hopes of achieving higher returns. *See also* diversification.

**nondiversified investment company** A management company that does not meet the diversification requirements of the Investment Company Act of 1940. These companies are not restricted in the choice of securities or by the concentration of interest they have in those securities. *See also* diversified investment company; management company; mutual fund.

**nonequity option** A security representing the right to buy or sell an investment instrument other than a common stock at a specified price within a specified time period. Examples of such investment instruments include foreign currencies, indexes and interest rates. *See also* equity option;

foreign currency option; index option; interest rate option; option.

**nonfixed unit investment trust** An investment company that invests in a portfolio of securities and permits changes in the makeup of the portfolio. *See also* fixed unit investment trust; unit investment trust.

**nonissuer transaction** A securities trade that does not directly or indirectly benefit the issuer. Under the Uniform Securities Act, the proceeds of a nonissuer transaction go to the selling stockholder. Most nonissuer transactions are also called secondary transactions.

**nonmargin security** A security that must be purchased in a cash account, that must be paid for in full, and that may not be used as collateral for a loan. Examples include put and call options, rights, insurance contracts and new issues. *See also* margin security.

**nonqualified retirement plan** A corporate retirement plan that does not meet the standards set by the Employee Retirement Income Security Act of 1974. Contributions to a nonqualified plan are not tax deductible. *See also* qualified retirement plan.

**nonsystematic risk** The potential for an unforeseen event to affect the value of a specific investment. Examples of such events include strikes, natural disasters, introductions of new product lines and attempted takeovers. *See also* systematic risk.

**no-par stock** An equity security issued without a stated value.

**normal yield curve** A chart showing long-term debt instruments having higher yields than short-term debt instruments. *See also* flat yield curve; inverted yield curve; parallel shift; yield curve.

**note** A short-term debt security, usually maturing in five years or less. *See also* municipal note; Treasury note.

**not held order (NH)** An order that gives the floor broker discretion as to the price and timing of the order's execution. Not held orders are often entered for large amounts of a security.

**numbered account** An account titled with something other than the customer's name; the title might be a number, symbol or special title. The customer must sign a form designating ownership of the account.

**NYSE** *See* New York Stock Exchange.

## O

**odd lot** An amount of a security that is less than the normal unit of trading for that security. Generally, an odd lot is fewer than 100 shares of stock or five bonds. *See also* round lot.

**odd lot differential** The extra commission often charged when an odd lot order is executed on an exchange. Usually the charge is 12.5 cents (1/8th of a point) per share in addition to the broker's standard commission.

**odd-lot theory** A technical analysis theory based on the assumption that the small investor is always wrong. Therefore, if odd lot sales are up—that is, small investors are selling stock—it is probably a good time to buy.

**offer** (1) *See* ask. (2) Under the Uniform Securities Act, any attempt to solicit a purchase or sale in a security for value. *See also* bid; quotation; public offering price.

**offering circular** An abbreviated prospectus used by corporations issuing less than $5 million of stock. The SEC's Regulation A allows these offerings an exemption from the full registration requirements of the 1933 act. *See also* Regulation A.

**office of supervisory jurisdiction (OSJ)** The broker-dealer office responsible for supervising the activities of registered representatives and associated persons housed in that office and in other offices within the same region. The NASD requires a broker-dealer to assign these supervisory responsibilities to an office that carries out certain market making and customer service functions. *See also* branch office.

**Office of the Comptroller of the Currency (OCC)** The bureau of the U.S. Treasury Department that is responsible for issuing and enforcing regulations governing the investing and lending practices of the nation's banks.

**official notice of sale** The invitation to bid on a municipal bond issue; the invitation is sent to prospective underwriters and specifies, among other things, the date, time and place of sale, description of the issue, maturities, call provisions and amount of good faith deposit required.

**official statement (OS)** A document concerning a municipal issue that must be provided to every buyer. The document is prepared by the underwriter from information provided by the issuer; typically included are the offering terms, descriptions of the bonds and the issuer, the underwriting spread, fees received by brokers, initial offering price and tax status.

**oil and gas direct participation program** A direct participation program formed to locate new oil and gas reserves, develop existing reserves or generate income from producing wells. A high return is the primary objective of such a program. *Syn.* oil and gas limited partnership.

**oil depletion allowance** An accounting procedure that reduces the taxable portion of revenues from the sale of oil to compensate for the decreased supply of oil in the ground. Depletion is the natural resource counterpart of depreciation.

**omnibus account** An account opened in the name of an investment adviser or a broker-dealer for the benefit of its customers. The firm carrying the account does not receive disclosure of the individual customers' names or holdings and does not maintain records for the individual customers. *Syn.* special omnibus account. *See also* introduced account.

**OPD** A message on the Consolidated Tape announcing the initial transaction in a security for which the opening has been delayed.

**open-end covenant** A provision of a bond's trust indenture allowing the issuer to use the same collateral backing a bond as collateral for future bond issues. As a result, new creditors have the same claim on the collateral as existing creditors. *See also* closed-end covenant; junior lien debt.

**opening purchase** Entering the options market by buying calls or puts. *See also* closing sale; opening sale.

**opening sale** Entering the options market by selling calls or puts. *See also* closing purchase; opening purchase.

**open-market operations** The buying and selling of securities (primarily government or agency debt) by the Federal Open Market Committee to effect control of the money supply. These transactions increase or decrease the level of bank reserves available for lending.

**operating expenses** (1) The day-to-day costs incurred in running a business. (2) In an oil and gas program, any production or leasehold expense incurred in the operation of a producing lease, including district expense, direct out-of-pocket expenses for labor, materials and supplies and those shares of taxes and transportation charges not borne by overriding royalty interests.

**operating income** The profit realized from one year of operation of a business.

**operating ratio** The ratio of operating expenses to net sales; the complement to the margin of profit ratio.

**operations and maintenance fund** The account from which are paid current operating and maintenance expenses on a facility financed by a municipal revenue bond. *See also* flow of funds.

**option** A security that represents the right to buy or sell a specified amount of an underlying investment instrument—a stock, bond, futures contract, etc.—at a specified price within a specified time. The purchaser acquires a right, and the seller assumes an obligation.

**option agreement** The document a customer must sign within 15 days of being approved for options trading. In it the customer agrees to abide by the rules of the options exchanges and not to exceed position or exercise limits.

**option contract adjustment** An adjustment made automatically to the terms of an option on the ex-dividend date when a stock pays a stock dividend or if there is a stock split or a reverse split.

**options account** A customer account in which the customer has received approval to trade options.

**Options Clearing Corporation (OCC)** The organization that issues options, standardizes option contracts and guarantees their performance. The OCC made secondary trading possible by creating fungible option contracts.

**options disclosure document** A publication of the Options Clearing Corporation that outlines the risks and rewards of investing in options. The document must be given to each customer at the time of opening an options account, and must accompany any options sales literature sent to a customer.

**order book official (OBO)** The title given to a specialist or market maker employed on the Pacific, Philadelphia and Chicago Board Options exchanges.

**order memorandum** The form completed by a registered rep that contains customer instructions regarding the placement of an order. The memorandum contains such information as the customer's name and account number, a description of the security, the type of transaction (buy, sell, sell short, etc.) and any special instructions (such as time or price limits).

**ordinary income** Earnings other than capital gain.

**original issue discount bond (OID)** A corporate or municipal debt security issued at a discount from face value. The bond may or may not pay interest. The discount on a corporate OID bond is taxed as if accrued annually as ordinary income. The discount on a municipal OID bond is exempt from annual taxation; however, the discount is accrued for the purpose of calculating cost basis. *See also* zero-coupon bond.

**OTC margin security** A security that is not traded on a national exchange but that has been designated by the Federal Reserve Board as eligible for trading on margin. The Fed publishes a list of such securities. *See also* margin security.

**OTC market** The security exchange system in which broker-dealers negotiate directly with one another rather than through an auction on an exchange floor. The trading takes place over computer and telephone networks that link brokers and dealers around the world. Both listed and OTC securities, as well as municipal and U.S. government securities, are traded in the OTC market.

**OTC option** An option contract that is not listed on an exchange. All contract terms are negotiated between buyer and seller. *Syn.* nonstandard option. *See also* listed option.

**out-of-the-money** The term used to describe an option that has no intrinsic value, such as a call option when the stock is selling below the exercise price or a put option when the stock is selling above the exercise price. *See also* at-the-money; in-the-money; intrinsic value.

**outstanding stock** Equity securities issued by a corporation and in the hands of the public; issued stock that has not been reacquired by the issuer. *See also* treasury stock.

**overbought** A technical analysis term for a market in which more and stronger buying has occurred than the fundamentals justify. *See also* oversold.

**overlapping debt** A condition resulting when property in a municipality is subject to multiple taxing authorities or tax districts, each having tax collection powers and recourse to the residents of that municipality. *See also* coterminous.

**oversold** A technical analysis term for a market in which more and stronger selling has occurred than the fundamentals justify. *See also* overbought.

**over the counter (OTC)** The term used to describe a security that is traded through the telephone- and computer-connected OTC market rather than through an exchange. *See also* OTC market.

# P

**P** Consolidated Tape market identifier for the Pacific Stock Exchange.

**Pacific Stock Exchange (PSE)** The only SEC-registered stock exchange west of the Mississippi. It was registered in 1956, after merging four exchanges that served Los Angeles and San Francisco. *See also* regional exchange.

**parallel shift** An up or down movement in a yield curve of approximately the same percentage for all maturities. *See also* flat yield curve; inverted yield curve; normal yield curve.

**parity** In an exchange market, a situation in which all brokers bidding have equal standing and the winning bid is awarded by a random drawing. *See also* precedence; priority.

**parity price of common** The dollar amount at which a common stock is equal in value to its corresponding convertible security. It is calculated by dividing the convertible security's market value by its conversion ratio.

**parity price of convertible** The dollar amount at which a convertible security is equal in value to its corresponding common stock. It is calculated by multiplying the market price of the common stock by its conversion ratio.

**partial call** The redemption by an issuer of a portion of an outstanding bond issue prior to the maturity date. *See also* catastrophe call; mandatory call.

**participating preferred stock** An equity security that offers the holder a share of corporate earnings remaining after all senior securities have been paid a fixed dividend. The payment is made in addition to the fixed dividend stated on the certificate, and may be cumulative or noncumulative. *See also* convertible preferred stock; cumulative preferred stock; noncumulative preferred stock; preferred stock.

**participation** The provision of the Employee Retirement Income Security Act of 1974 requiring that in a qualified retirement plan all employees be covered within a reasonable time of their dates of hire.

**partnership** A form of business organization in which two or more individuals manage the business and are equally and personally liable for its debts.

**partnership account** An account that empowers the individual members of a partnership to act on the behalf of the partnership as a whole.

**par value** The dollar amount assigned to a security by the issuer. For an equity security, par value is usually a small dollar amount that bears no relationship to the security's market price. For a debt security, par value is the amount repaid to the investor when the bond matures, usually $1,000. *Syn.* principal. *See also* capital surplus; discount bond; premium bond.

**passive income** Earnings derived from a rental property, limited partnership or other enterprise in which the individual is not actively involved. Passive income therefore does not include earnings from wages or active business participation, nor does it include income from dividends, interest and capital gains. *See also* passive loss; unearned income.

**passive loss** A loss incurred through a rental property, limited partnership or other enterprise in which the individual is not actively involved. Passive losses can be used to offset passive income only, not wage or portfolio income. *See also* passive income.

**pass-through certificate** A security representing an interest in a pool of conventional, VA, Farmers Home Administration or other agency mortgages. The principal and interest payments are received by the pool and are passed through to the certificate holder. Payments may or may not be guaranteed. *See also* Federal National Mortgage Association; Government National Mortgage Association.

**pattern** A repetitive series of price movements on a chart used by a technical analyst to predict future movements of the market.

**payment date** The day on which a declared dividend is paid to all stockholders owning shares on the record date.

**payment period** As defined by the Federal Reserve Board's Regulation T, the period of time corresponding to the regular way settlement period, plus two business days.

**payroll deduction plan** A retirement plan whereby an employee authorizes a deduction from his check on a regular basis. The plan may be qualified, such as a 401K plan, or nonqualified.

**peak** The end of a period of increasing business activity throughout the economy, one of the four stages of the business cycle. *See also* business cycle.

**pegging** (1) Stabilizing a country's currency through its purchase or sale by the country's central bank. (2) *See* fixing.

**pension plan** A contract between an individual and an employer, labor union, government entity or other institution, which provides for the distribution of pension benefits at retirement.

**PE ratio** *See* price-earnings ratio.

**percentage depletion** A method of tax accounting for a direct participation program whereby a statutory percentage of gross income from the sale of a mineral resource is allowed as a tax-deductible expense. Percentage depletion is available to small producers only and not to purchasers of producing interests.

**person** As defined in securities law, an individual, corporation, partnership, association, fund, joint stock company, unincorporated organization, trust, government or political subdivision of a government.

**personal income (PI)** An individual's total earnings derived from wages, passive business enterprises and investments. *See also* disposable income.

**phantom income** In a limited partnership, taxable income that is not backed by a positive cash flow.

**Philadelphia Stock Exchange (PHLX)** Founded in 1790, the oldest stock exchange in the United States. Its three trading floors are devoted to equity securities, equity options and foreign currencies. *See also* regional exchange.

***Pink Sheets*** A daily publication compiled by the National Quotation Bureau and containing interdealer wholesale quotations for over-the-counter stocks. *See also Yellow Sheets.*

**placement ratio** A ratio compiled by *The Bond Buyer* indicating the number of new municipal issues that have sold within the last week.

**plan completion insurance** An insurance contract purchased by a contractual plan investor naming the plan custodian as beneficiary. In the event of the investor's death, the insurance proceeds are used to complete the contractual plan payments.

**plan custodian** An institution retained by a contractual plan company to perform clerical duties. The custodian's responsibilities include safeguarding plan assets, sending out customer confirmations and issuing shares. *See also* custodian; mutual fund custodian.

**plus tick** A security transaction's execution price that is above the previous execution price, by a minimum amount. *Syn.* up tick. *See also* minus tick; plus tick rule; tick; zero-plus tick.

**plus tick rule** The SEC regulation governing the market price at which a short sale may be made. No short sale may be executed at a price below the price of the last sale. *See also* minus tick;

short-exempt transaction; short sale; tick; zero-plus tick.

**point** A measure of a bond's price; $10 or 1% of the par value of $1,000. *See also* basis point.

**POP** *See* public offering price.

**portfolio income** Earnings from interest, dividends and other nonbusiness investments. *See also* earned income; passive income; unearned income.

**portfolio insurance** A method of hedging a portfolio of common stocks against market risk by selling stock index futures short. The technique is frequently used by institutional investors.

**portfolio manager** The entity responsible for investing a mutual fund's assets, implementing its investment strategy and managing day-to-day portfolio trading.

**position** The amount of a security either owned (a long position) or owed (a short position) by an individual or by a dealer. Dealers take long positions in specific securities to maintain inventories and thereby facilitate trading.

**position limit** The rule established by options exchanges that prohibits an investor from having a net long or short position of more than a specific number of contracts on the same side of the market.

**power of substitution** *See* stock power.

**Pr** A message on the Consolidated Tape indicating that the trade being reported is in a preferred stock.

**precedence** In an exchange market, the ranking of bids and offers according to the number of shares involved. *See also* parity; priority.

**preemptive right** The legal right of stockholders to maintain their proportionate ownership by purchasing newly issued shares before the new stock is offered to the public. *See also* right.

**preferred dividend coverage ratio** An indication of the safety of a corporation's preferred dividend payments. It is computed by dividing preferred dividends by net income.

**preferred stock** An equity security that represents ownership in a corporation. It is issued with a stated dividend, which must be paid before dividends are paid to holders of common stock. It generally carries no voting rights. *See also* callable preferred stock; convertible preferred stock; cumulative preferred stock; participating preferred stock; prior preferred stock.

**preferred stock fund** A mutual fund whose investment objective is to provide stable income with minimal capital risk. It invests in income-producing instruments such as preferred stock. *See also* bond fund.

**preferred stock ratio** One of several tools used by bond analysts to assess the safety of a corporation's bonds. It measures the percentage of the corporation's total capitalization that is composed of preferred stock by dividing the total face value of the preferred stock by the total capitalization.

**preliminary prospectus** An abbreviated prospectus that is distributed while an issuer's registration statement is being reviewed by the SEC. It contains the essential facts about the forthcoming offering except the underwriting spread, final public offering price and date on which the shares will be delivered. *Syn.* red herring.

**premium** (1) The amount of cash that an option buyer pays to an option seller. (2) The difference between the higher price paid for a security and the security's face amount at issue. *See also* discount.

**premium bond** A bond that sells at a higher price than its face value. *See also* discount bond; par value.

**prerefunding** *See* advance refunding.

**presale order** An order communicated to a syndicate manager prior to formation of the underwriting bid of a new municipal bond issue. If the syndicate wins the bid, the order takes the highest priority when orders are filled. *See also* designated order; group net order; member-at-the-takedown order.

**present value** The worth in today's terms of a future payment or stream of payments. It takes into account the time value of money by discounting the future value of an investment by an assumed compound interest rate.

**price-earnings ratio (PE)** A tool for comparing the prices of different common stocks by assessing how much the market is willing to pay for a share of each corporation's earnings. It is calculated by dividing the current market price of a stock by the earnings per share.

**price risk** The potential that the value of a currency or commodity will change between the signing of a delivery contract and the time delivery is made. The futures markets serve to manage price risk.

**primary offering** An offering in which the proceeds of the underwriting go to the issuing corporation, agency or municipality. The issuer seeks to increase its capitalization either by selling shares of stock, representing ownership, or by selling bonds, representing loans to the issuer.

**prime rate** The interest rate that commercial banks charge their prime or most creditworthy customers, generally large corporations.

**principal** (1) A person who trades for its own account in the primary or secondary market. (2) *See* dealer. (3) *See* par value.

**principal transaction** A transaction in which a broker-dealer either buys securities from customers and takes them into its own inventory or sells securities to customers from its inventory. *See also* agency transaction; agent; broker; dealer; principal.

**priority** In an exchange market, the ranking of bids and offers according to the first person to bid or offer at a given price. Therefore, only one individual or firm can have priority. *See also* parity; precedence.

**prior lien bond** A secured bond that takes precedence over other bonds secured by the same assets. *See also* mortgage bond.

**prior preferred stock** An equity security that offers the holder stock that has prior claim over other preferred stock in receipt of dividends and in distribution of assets in the event of liquidation. *See also* preferred stock.

**private placement** An offering of new issue securities that complies with Regulation D of the Securities Act of 1933. According to Regulation D, a security generally is not required to be registered with the SEC if it is offered to no more than 35 nonaccredited investors or to an unlimited number of accredited investors. *See also* Regulation D.

**profitability** The ability to generate a level of income and gain in excess of expenses.

**profitability ratio** One of several measures of a corporation's relative profit or income in relation to its sales. *See also* margin of profit ratio; return on equity.

**profit-sharing plan** An employee benefit plan established and maintained by an employer whereby the employees receive a share of the profits of the business. The money may be paid directly to the employee, deferred until retirement, or a combination of both approaches.

**program trading** A coordinated trading strategy involving the related purchases or sales of groups of stocks having a market value of $1 million or more. Program trading often involves arbitrage between the stock market and the futures market.

**progressive tax** A tax that takes a larger percentage of the income of high-income people than of low-income people; an example is the graduated income tax. *See also* regressive tax.

**property dividend** A distribution made by a corporation to its stockholders of securities it owns in other corporations or of its products. *See also* dividend.

**prospectus** *See* final prospectus.

**proxy** A limited power of attorney from a stockholder authorizing another person to vote on stockholder issues according to the first stockholder's instructions. In order to vote on corporate matters, a stockholder must either attend the annual meeting or must vote by proxy.

**prudent man rule** A legal maxim that restricts discretion in a fiduciary account to only those investments that a reasonable and prudent person might make.

**PSA prepayment model** A standard benchmark of prepayment speeds on mortgage loans, set forth by the Public Securities Association. Prices and interest rates of CMO securities are often based on these prepayment assumptions. *See also* Public Securities Association.

**public offering** The sale of an issue of common stock, either by a corporation going public or by an offering of additional shares. *See also* initial public offering.

**public offering price (POP)** (1) The price of new shares that is established in the issuing corporation's prospectus. (2) The price to investors for mutual fund shares, equal to the net asset value plus the sales charge. *See also* ask; bid; mutual fund; net asset value.

**public purpose bond** A municipal bond that is exempt from federal income tax as long no more than a 10% of the proceeds benefit private entities.

**Public Securities Association (PSA)** An organization of banks and broker-dealers that conduct business in mortgage-backed securities, money-market securities and securities issued by the U.S. government, government agencies and municipalities. *See also* PSA prepayment model.

**purchasing power risk** The potential that, due to inflation, a certain amount of money will not purchase as much in the future as it does today. *Syn.* inflation risk.

**put** (1) An option contract giving the owner the right to sell a specified amount of an underlying security at a specified price within a specified time. (2) The act of exercising a put option. *See also* call.

**put bond** A debt security requiring the issuer to purchase the security at the holder's discretion or within a prescribed time.

**put buyer** An investor who pays a premium for an option contract and receives, for a specified time, the right to sell the underlying security at a specified price. *See also* call buyer; call writer; put writer.

**put spread** An option investor's position in which the investor buys a put on a particular security and writes a put on the same security but with a different expiration date, exercise price, or both.

**put writer** An investor who receives a premium and takes on, for a specified time, the obligation to buy the underlying security at a specified price at the put buyer's discretion. *See also* call buyer; call writer; put buyer.

## Q

**qualified legal opinion** The statement of a bond attorney affirming the validity of a new municipal bond issue but expressing reservations about its quality. *See also* legal opinion of counsel; unqualified legal opinion.

**qualified retirement plan** A corporate retirement plan that meets the standards set by the Employee Retirement Income Security Act of 1974. Contributions to a qualified plan are tax deductible. *See also* individual retirement account; Keogh plan; nonqualified retirement plan.

**quick assets** A measure of a corporation's liquidity that takes into account the size of the unsold inventory. It is calculated by subtracting inventory from current assets, and it is used in the acid-test ratio. *See also* acid-test ratio.

**quick ratio** *See* acid-test ratio.

**quotation** The price being offered or bid by a market maker or broker-dealer for a particular security. *See also* ask; bid; bond quote; stock quote.

**quote machine** A computer that provides representatives and market makers with the information that appears on the Consolidated Tape. The information on the screen is condensed into symbols and numbers.

## R

**random walk theory** A market analysis theory that the past movement or direction of the price of a stock or market cannot be used to predict its future movement or direction.

**range** A security's low price and high price for a particular trading period, such as the close of a day's trading, the opening of a day's trading, or a day, month or year.

**rate covenant** A provision of a municipal revenue bond's trust indenture that helps ensure the safety of the issue by specifying the rates to be charged the user of the facility. *See also* insurance covenant; maintenance covenant.

**rating** An evaluation of a corporate or municipal bond's relative safety, according to the issuer's ability to repay principal and make interest payments. Bonds are rated by various organizations such as Standard & Poor's and Moody's. Ratings range from AAA or Aaa (the highest) to C or D, which represents a company in default.

**rating service** A company, such as Moody's or Standard & Poor's, that rates various debt and preferred stock issues for safety of payment of principal, interest or dividends. The issuing company or municipality pays a fee for the rating. *See also* bond rating; rating.

**raw land program** A real estate direct participation program that aims to provide capital appreciation by investing in undeveloped land.

**real estate investment trust (REIT)** A corporation or trust that uses the pooled capital of many investors to invest in direct ownership of either income property or mortgage loans. These investments offer tax benefits in addition to interest and capital gains distributions.

**real estate mortgage investment conduit (REMIC)** A corporation, trust or partnership that uses the pooled capital of many investors to invest in fixed portfolios of real estate mortgages. These investments offer tax benefits in addition to interest and capital gains distributions.

**real estate limited partnership** A direct participation program formed to build new structures, generate income from existing property or profit from the capital appreciation of undeveloped land. Growth potential, income distributions and tax shelter are the most important benefits of such a program.

**realized gain** The amount earned by a taxpayer when an asset is sold. *See also* unrealized gain.

**reallowance** *See* concession.

**recapitalization** Changing the capital structure of a corporation by issuing, converting or redeeming securities.

**recapture** The taxation as ordinary income of previously earned deductions or credits. Circumstances that may cause the IRS to require this tax to be paid include excess depreciation, premature sale of a asset or because a previous tax benefit is now disallowed.

**recession** General economic decline lasting from six to eighteen months.

**reclassification** The exchange by a corporation of one class of its securities for another class of its securities. This shifts ownership control among the stockholders and therefore falls under the purview of the SEC's Rule 145. *See also* Rule 145.

**record date** The date established by a corporation's board of directors that determines which of its stockholders are entitled to receive dividends or rights distributions.

**redeemable security** A security that the issuer redeems on the request of the holder. Examples include shares in an open-end investment company and Treasury notes.

**redemption** The return of an investor's principal in a security, such as a bond, preferred stock or mutual fund shares. By law, redemption of mutual fund shares must occur within seven days of receiving a request for redemption from the investor.

**redemption notice** A published announcement that a corporation or municipality is calling a certain issue of its bonds.

**red herring** *See* preliminary prospectus.

**reducing order** An order that reduces automatically to keep in step with the new price when a stock goes ex-dividend. Examples include buy limit orders, sell stop orders and sell stop limit orders.

**refinancing** Issuing equity, the proceeds of which are used to retire debt.

**refunding** Retiring an outstanding bond issue at maturity using money from the sale of a new offering. *See also* advance refunding.

**regional exchange** A stock exchange that serves the financial community in a particular region of the country. These exchanges tend to focus on securities issued within their regions, but also offer trading in NYSE- and AMEX-listed securities.

**registered** The term that describes a security that prints the name of the owner on the certificate. The owner's name is stored in records kept by the issuer or a transfer agent.

**registered as to principal only** The term used to describe a bond that prints the name of the owner on the certificate but that has unregistered coupons payable to the bearer. *See also* coupon bond; fully registered bond; registered.

**registered options principal (ROP)** The officer or partner of a brokerage firm who approves in writing accounts in which options transactions are permitted.

**registered principal** An associated person of a member firm who manages or supervises the firm's investment banking or securities business. This includes persons who train associated persons and who solicit business.

Unless the member firm is a sole proprietorship, it must employ at least two registered principals, one of whom must be registered as a general securities principal and one of whom must be registered as a financial and operations principal. If the firm does options business with the public, it must employ at least one registered options principal.

**registered representative (RR)** An associated person engaged in the investment banking or securities business. According to the NASD, this includes individuals who supervise, solicit or conduct business in securities and who train people to supervise, solicit or conduct business in securities.

Anyone employed by a brokerage firm who is not a principal and who is not engaged in clerical or brokerage administration is subject to registration and exam licensing as a registered representative. *See also* associated person of a member.

**registered trader** A member of an exchange who trades primarily for a personal account and at personal risk.

**registrar** The independent organization or part of a corporation responsible for accounting for all of the issuer's outstanding stock and certifying that its bonds constitute legal debt.

**registration by coordination** A process that allows a security to be sold in a state. It is available to an issuer who files for registration of the security under the Securities Act of 1933 and files duplicates of the registration documents with the state administrator. The state registration becomes effective at the same time the federal registration statement becomes effective.

**registration by filing** A process that allows a security to be sold in a state. Previously referred to as "registration by notification," it is available to an issuer who files for registration of the security under the Securities Act of 1933, meets minimum net worth and certain other requirements, and notifies the state of this eligibility by filing certain documents with the state administrator. The state registration becomes effective at the same time the federal registration statement becomes effective.

**registration by qualification** A process that allows a security to be sold in a state. It is available to an issuer who files for registration of the security with the state administrator, meets minimum net worth, disclosure and other requirements and files appropriate registration fees. The state registration becomes effective when the administrator so orders.

**registration statement** The legal document that discloses all pertinent information concerning an offering of a security and its issuer. It is submitted to the SEC in accordance with the requirements of the Securities Act of 1933, and forms the basis of the final prospectus that is distributed to investors.

**regressive tax** A tax that takes a larger percentage of the income of low-income people than of high-income people; examples include gasoline tax and cigarette tax. *See also* progressive tax.

**Reg T** *See* Regulation T.

**regular complaint procedure** The process for settling a charge or complaint under the NASD's Code of Procedure. *See also* Code of Procedure; summary complaint procedure.

**regular way** A settlement contract that calls for delivery and payment to occur a standard number of days after the date of the trade; the standard settlement cycle is established by the SEC. The type of security being traded determines the amount of time allowed for regular way settlement. *Syn.* standard securities settlement cycle. *See also* cash transaction; settlement date.

**regulated investment company** An investment company to which subchapter M of the Internal Revenue Code grants special status that allows the flow-through of tax consequences on a distribution to shareholders. If 90% of income is passed through to the shareholders, the company is not subject to tax on this income.

**Regulation A** The provision of the Securities Act of 1933 that exempts from registration small public offerings valued at no more than $5 million worth of securities issued during a twelve-month period.

**Regulation D** The provision of the Securities Act of 1933 that exempts from registration offerings sold to a maximum of 35 nonaccredited investors during a twelve-month period. *See also* private placement.

**Regulation T** The Federal Reserve Board regulation that governs customer cash accounts and the amount of credit that brokerage firms and dealers may extend to customers for the purchase of securities. Regulation T currently sets the loan value of marginable securities at 50% and the payment deadline at two days beyond regular way settlement. *Syn.* Reg T. *See also* Regulation U.

**Regulation U** The Federal Reserve Board regulation that governs loans by banks for the purchase of securities. Call loans are exempt from Regulation U. *See also* Regulation T.

**rehypothecation** The pledging of a client's securities as collateral for a bank loan. Brokerage firms may rehypothecate up to 140% of the value of their customers' securities to finance margin loans to customers. *See also* hypothecation.

**reinstatement privilege** A benefit offered by some mutual funds, allowing an investor to withdraw money from a fund account and then redeposit the money without paying a second sales charge.

**reinvestment** Using dividends, interest and capital gains earned in a mutual fund investment to purchase additional shares, rather than receiving the distributions in cash.

**reinvestment risk** The potential that a bond investor may not be able to reinvest interest income or principal in new bonds at the same rate of return.

**renewal and replacement fund** The account that is used to fund major renewal projects and equipment replacements financed by a municipal revenue bond issue. *See also* flow of funds.

**reoffering price** The price or yield at which a municipal security is sold to the public by the underwriters.

**repurchase agreement** A sale of securities with an attendant agreement to repurchase them at a higher price on an agreed-upon future date; the difference between the sale price and the repurchase price represents the interest earned by the investor. Repos are considered money-market instruments, and are used to raise short-term capital and as instruments of monetary policy. *See also* reverse repurchase agreement.

**reserve maintenance fund** The account that holds funds that supplement the general maintenance fund of a municipal revenue bond issue. *See also* flow of funds.

**reserve requirement** The percentage of depositors' money that the Federal Reserve Board requires a commercial bank to keep on deposit in the form of cash or in its vault.

**residual claim** The right of a common stockholder to corporate assets in the event that the corporation ceases to exist. A common stockholder may claim assets only after the claims of all creditors and other security holders have been satisfied.

**resistance level** A technical analysis term describing the top of a stock's historical trading range. *See also* breakout; support level.

**restricted account** A margin account in which the equity is less than the Regulation T initial requirement. *See also* equity; initial margin requirement; margin account; retention requirement.

**restricted security** An unregistered, nonexempt security acquired either directly or indirectly from the issuer, or an affiliate of the issuer, in a transaction that does not involve a public offering. *See also* holding period; Rule 144.

**retained earnings** The amount of a corporation's net income that remains after all dividends have been paid to preferred and common stockholders.

**retention** The percentage of a new issue that an underwriter holds to sell directly to its own customers. The securities that it underwrites but does not retain are turned back to the syndicate to be sold by the selling group.

**retention requirement** The provision of Regulation T that applies to the withdrawal of securities from a restricted account. The customer must deposit an amount equal to the unpaid portion of the securities being withdrawn, in order to reduce the debit balance. The retention requirement is the reciprocal of the initial margin requirement. *See also* restricted account.

**retirement account** A customer account established for the purpose of providing retirement funds.

**retiring bonds** Ending an issuer's debt obligation by calling the outstanding bonds, by purchasing bonds in the open market, or by repaying bondholders the principal amount at maturity.

**return on common equity** A measure of a corporation's profitability, calculated by dividing aftertax income by common shareholders' equity.

**return on equity** A measure of a corporation's profitability, specifically its return on assets, calculated by dividing aftertax income by tangible assets.

**return on investment (ROI)** The profit or loss resulting from a security transaction, often expressed as an annual percentage rate.

**revaluation** A change in the relative value of a country's currency owing to a decision by the country's government. *See also* devaluation.

**revenue anticipation note (RAN)** A short-term municipal debt security issued in anticipation of revenue to be received.

**revenue bond** A municipal debt issue whose interest and principal are payable only from the specific earnings of an income-producing public project. *See also* double-barreled bond; general obligation bond; municipal bond.

**reverse repurchase agreement** A purchase of securities with an attendant agreement to resell them at a higher price on an agreed-upon future date; the difference between the purchase price and the resale price represents the interest earned by the investor. The purchaser initiates the deal. *See also* repurchase agreement.

**reverse split** A reduction in the number of a corporation's shares outstanding that increases the par value of its stock or its earnings per share. The market value of the total number of shares remains the same. *See also* stock split.

**right** A security representing a stockholder's entitlement to the first opportunity to purchase new shares issued by the corporation at a predetermined price (normally less than the current market price) in proportion to the number of shares already owned. Rights are issued only for a short period of time, after which they expire. *See also* preemptive right; rights offering.

**right of accumulation** A benefit offered by a mutual fund that allows the investor to qualify for reduced sales loads on additional purchases according to the total dollar value of the fund account.

**rights agent** An agent of an issuing corporation who is responsible for maintaining current records of the names of the owners of rights certificates.

**rights offering** An issue of new shares of stock accompanied by the opportunity for each stockholder to maintain a proportionate ownership by purchasing additional shares in the corporation before the shares are offered to the public. *See also* right; standby underwriter.

**risk arbitrage** The purchase of stock in a company that is being acquired and the short sale of stock in the acquiring company, in order to profit from the anticipated increase in the acquired corporation's shares and decrease in the acquiring corporation's shares.

**riskless and simultaneous transaction** The buying or selling by a broker-dealer of a security for its own account so as to fill an order previously received from a customer. Although the firm is technically acting as a principal in the trade, the transaction is relatively riskless because the purchase and sale are consummated almost simultaneously.

**rollover** The transfer of funds from one qualified retirement plan to another qualified retirement plan; if this is not done within a specified time period, the funds are taxed as ordinary income.

**round lot** The normal unit of trading of a security, which is generally 100 shares of stock or five bonds. *See also* odd lot.

**RT** A message on the Consolidated Tape indicating a right.

**Rule 144** SEC rule requiring that persons who hold control or restricted securities may sell them only in limited quantities, and that all sales of restricted stock by control persons must be reported to the SEC by filing a Form 144, "Notice of Proposed Sale of Securities." *See also* control security; restricted security.

**Rule 145** SEC rule requiring that, whenever the stockholders of a publicly owned corporation are solicited to vote on or consent to a plan for reorganizing the corporation, full disclosure of all material facts must be made in a proxy statement or prospectus that must be in the hands of the stockholders before the announced voting date. *See also* merger; reclassification.

**Rule 147** SEC rule that provides exemption from the registration statement and prospectus requirements of the 1933 act for securities offered and sold exclusively intrastate.

**Rule 405** NYSE rule requiring that each member organization exercises due diligence to learn the essential facts about every customer. *Syn.* know your customer rule.

**Rule 415** SEC rule governing shelf offerings. The rule allows an issuer to sell limited portions of a new issue over a two-year period. *See also* shelf offering.

## S

**sale-leaseback** A method of raising cash by selling property to a buyer and then leasing it back from the buyer.

**sales charge** *See* commission.

**sales literature** Any written material distributed to customers or the public by a firm in a controlled manner. Examples include circulars, research reports, form letters, market letters, performance reports and text used for seminars. *See also* advertisement; form letter; market letter.

**sales load** The amount added to the net asset value of a mutual fund share to arrive at the offering price. *See also* mutual fund; net asset value; no-load fund.

**Sallie Mae** *See* Student Loan Marketing Association.

**savings bond** A government debt security that is not negotiable or transferable and that may not be used as collateral. *See also* Series EE bond; Series HH bond.

**scale** A list of each of the scheduled maturities in a new serial bond issue. The list outlines the number of bonds, maturity dates, coupon rates and yields.

**SEC** *See* Securities and Exchange Commission.

**secondary market** The market in which securities are bought and sold subsequent to their being sold to the public for the first time. *See also* new issue market.

**sector fund** A mutual fund whose investment objective is to capitalize on the return potential provided by investing primarily in a particular industry or sector of the economy.

**secured bond** A debt security backed by identifiable assets set aside as collateral. In the event that the issuer defaults on payment, the bondholders may lay claim to the collateral. *See also* debenture.

**Securities Act of 1933** Federal legislation requiring the full and fair disclosure of all material information about the issuance of new securities.

**Securities and Exchange Commission (SEC)** Commission created by Congress to regulate the securities markets and protect investors. It is composed of five commissioners appointed by the president of the United States and approved by the Senate. The SEC enforces, among other acts, the Securities Act of 1933, the Securities Exchange Act of 1934, the Trust Indenture Act of 1939, the Investment Company Act of 1940 and the Investment Advisers Act of 1940.

**Securities Exchange Act of 1934** Federal legislation that established the Securities and Exchange Commission. The act aims to protect investors by regulating the exchanges, over-the-counter market, extension of credit by the Federal Reserve Board, broker-dealers, insider transactions, trading activities, client accounts and net capital. *Syn.* act of 1934; Exchange Act.

**Securities Investor Protection Corporation (SIPC)** A nonprofit membership corporation created by an act of Congress to protect clients of brokerage firms that are forced into bankruptcy. Membership is composed of all brokers and dealers registered under the Securities Exchange Act of 1934, all members of national securities exchanges and most NASD members. SIPC provides customers of these firms up to $500,000 coverage for cash and securities held by the firms (although coverage of cash is limited to $100,000).

**security** Any piece of securitized paper that can be traded for value other than an insurance policy or a fixed annuity. Under the act of 1934, this includes any note, stock, bond, investment contract, debenture, certificate of interest in profit-sharing or partnership agreement, certificate of deposit, collateral trust certificate, preorganization certificate, option on a security, or other instrument of investment commonly known as a security.

Also categorized as securities are interests in oil and gas drilling programs, real estate condominiums and cooperatives, farmland or animals, commodity option contracts, whiskey warehouse receipts, multilevel distributorship arrangements, and merchandising marketing programs.

The federal courts have established that, if a person invests money in a common enterprise and is led to expect profits from the managerial efforts of the promoter or a third party, the investment is a security.

**security arbitrage** The simultaneous purchase and sale of related or convertible securities to take advantage of a price disparity between the two securities. *See also* arbitrage.

**segregation** Holding customer-owned securities separate from securities owned by other customers and securities owned by the brokerage firm. *See also* commingling.

**selection risk** The potential for loss on an investment owing to the particular security chosen performing poorly in spite of good overall market or industry performance.

**self-regulatory organization (SRO)** One of eight organizations accountable to the SEC for the enforcement of federal securities laws and the supervision of securities practices within an assigned field of jurisdiction. For example, the National Association of Securities Dealers regulates the over-the-counter market, the Municipal Securities Rulemaking Board supervises state and municipal securities and certain exchanges, such as the New York Stock Exchange and the Chicago Board Options Exchange, act as self-regulatory bodies to promote ethical conduct and standard trading practices.

**sell** To convey ownership of a security or other asset for money or value. This includes giving or delivering a security with or as a bonus for a purchase of securities, a gift of assessable stock, and selling or offering a warrant or right to purchase or subscribe to another security. Not included in the definition is a bona fide pledge or loan, or a stock dividend if nothing of value is given by the stockholders for the dividend.

**seller** *See* writer.

**seller's option** A settlement contract that calls for delivery and payment according to a number of days specified by the seller. *See also* buyer's option.

**selling away** An associated person engaging in private securities transactions without the knowledge and consent of the employing broker-dealer. This violates the NASD Rules of Fair Practice.

**selling dividends** (1) Inducing customers to buy mutual fund shares by implying that an upcoming distribution will benefit them; this practice is illegal. (2) Combining dividend and gains distributions in the calculation of current yield.

**selling group** Brokerage firms that help distribute securities in an offering but that are not members of the syndicate.

**sell-out** The procedure that the seller of a security follows when the buyer fails to complete the contract by accepting delivery of the security. The seller closes the contract by selling the security in the open market and charging the account of the buyer for transaction fees and any loss caused by changes in the market. *See also* buy-in.

**sell stop order** An order to sell a security that is entered at a price below the current market price and that is triggered when the market price touches or goes through the sell stop price.

**senior lien debt** A bond issue that shares the same collateral as is backing other issues but that has a prior claim to the collateral in the event of default.

**senior security** A security that grants its holder a prior claim to the issuer's assets over the claims of another security's holders. For example, a bond is a senior security over common stock.

**SEP** *See* simplified employee pension plan.

**separate account** The account that holds funds paid by variable annuity contract holders. The funds are kept separate from the insurer's general account, and are invested in a portfolio of securities that matches the contract holders' objectives. *See also* accumulation unit; annuity; general account.

**separately identifiable department or division** A department of a bank that engages in the business of buying or selling municipal securities under the direct supervision of an officer of the bank. Such a department is classified by the Municipal Securities Rulemaking Board as a municipal securities dealer, and must comply with MSRB regulations.

**Separate Trading of Registered Interest and Principal of Securities (STRIPS)** A zero-coupon bond issued and backed by the Treasury Department. *See also* zero-coupon bond.

**SEP-IRA** *See* simplified employee pension plan.

**serial bond** A debt security issued with a maturity schedule in which parts of the outstanding issue mature at intervals until the entire balance has been repaid. Most municipal bonds are serial bonds. *See also* maturity date; series bond.

**series** Options of the same class that have the same exercise price and the same expiration date. *See also* class; type.

**Series 6** The Investment Company/Variable Contract Products Limited Representative License, which entitles the holder to sell mutual funds and variable annuities and is used by many firms that sell primarily insurance-related products. The Series 6 can serve as the prerequisite for the Series 26 license.

**Series 7** The General Securities Registered Representative License, which entitles the holder to sell all types of securities products with the exception of commodities futures (which requires a Series 3 license). The Series 7 is the most comprehensive of the NASD representative licenses, and serves as a prerequisite for most of the NASD's principals examinations.

**Series 63** The Uniform Securities Agent State Law Exam, which entitles the successful candidate to sell securities and give investment advice in those states that require Series 63 registration. *See also* blue-sky laws; Uniform Securities Act.

**series bond** A debt security issued in a series of public offerings spread over an extended time period. All the bonds in the series have the same priority claim against assets. *See also* serial bond.

**Series EE bond** A nonmarketable, interest-bearing U.S. government savings bond issued at a discount from par. Interest on Series EE bonds is exempt from state and local taxes. *See also* savings bond; Series HH bond.

**Series HH bond** A nonmarketable, interest-bearing U.S. government savings bond issued at par and purchased only by trading in Series EE bonds at maturity. Interest on Series HH bonds is exempt from state and local taxes. *See also* savings bond; Series EE bond.

**settlement** The completion of a trade through the delivery of a security or commodity and the payment of cash or other consideration.

**settlement date** The date on which ownership changes between buyer and seller. Settlement provisions are standardized by the NASD's Uniform Practice Code. *See also* cash transaction; regular way.

**75-5-10 test** The standard for judging whether an investment company qualifies as diversified under the Investment Company Act of 1940. Under this act, a diversified investment company must have at least 75% of its total assets in cash, receivables or invested securities, no more than 5% of its total assets invested in the voting securities of any one company, and no single investment representing ownership of more than 10% of the outstanding voting securities of any one company. *See also* diversified investment company.

**shareholders' equity** *See* net worth.

**sharing arrangement** A method of allocating the responsibility for expenses and the right to share in revenues among the sponsor and limited partners in a direct participation program.

**shelf offering** An SEC provision allowing an issuer to register a new issue security without selling the entire issue at once. The issuer can sell limited portions of the issuer over a two-year period without reregistering the security or incurring penalties. See also Rule 415.

**short** The term used to describe the selling of a security, contract or commodity not owned by the seller. For example, an investor who borrows shares of stock from a broker-dealer and sells them on the open market is said to have a short position in the stock. *See also* long; short against the box.

**short against the box** The term used to describe the selling of a security, contract or commodity that the seller owns but prefers not to deliver; frequently this is done to defer taxation.

**short-exempt transaction** An exception to the SEC plus tick rule that allows a short sale in an arbitrage account even if the price is declining. *See also* plus tick rule.

**short hedge** Selling options or futures as protection against a decrease in the value of a long securities or actuals position. *See also* hedge; long hedge.

**short-interest theory** A technical analysis theory that examines the ratio of short sales to volume in a stock. Because the underlying stock must be purchased to close out the short positions, a high ratio is considered bullish.

**short sale** The sale of a security that the seller does not own, or any sale consummated by the delivery of a security borrowed by or for the account of the seller. *See also* plus tick rule.

**short straddle** An option investor's position that results from selling a call and a put on the same stock with the same exercise price and expiration month. *See also* long straddle; spread; straddle.

**short-term capital gain** The profit realized on the sale of an asset that has been owned for twelve months or less. *See also* capital gain; capital loss; long-term capital gain; short-term capital loss.

**short-term capital loss** The loss incurred on the sale of a capital asset that has been owned for twelve months or less. *See also* capital gain; capital loss; long-term capital loss; short-term capital gain.

**simplified employee pension (SEP) plan** A qualified retirement plan designed for employers with 25 or fewer employees. Contributions are made with before-tax dollars and earnings grow tax deferred. The contributions are made to the employee's SEP-IRA, which is an individual retirement account with a higher contribution limit. A SEP-IRA must be established for each employee eligible to participate in the SEP plan. *See also* individual retirement account.

**single account** An account in which only one individual has control over the investments and may transact business.

**sinking fund** An account established by an issuing corporation or municipality into which money is deposited regularly so that the issuer has the funds to redeem its bonds, debentures or preferred stock.

**SLD** A message on the Consolidated Tape indicating that the sale being reported was not reported on time and is therefore out of sequence.

**SMA** *See* special memorandum account.

**Small Order Execution System (SOES)** The automatic order execution system the NASD uses to facilitate the trading of public market and executable limit orders of 1,000 or fewer shares. Any Nasdaq or Nasdaq National Market security with at least one active SOES market maker is eligible for trading through SOES. SOES electronically matches and executes orders, locks in a price and sends confirms directly to the broker-dealers on both sides of the trade. *See also* National Association of Securities Dealers, Inc.

**sole proprietorship** A form of business organization in which a single owner has total control over the business, makes all managerial decisions and is personally liable for all debts of the business.

**solvency** The ability of a corporation both to meet its long-term fixed expenses and to have adequate money for long-term expansion and growth.

**special arbitrage account** A margin account for arbitrage transactions. These transactions are exempt from Reg T and short sale requirements. *See also* arbitrage; market arbitrage; risk arbitrage; security arbitrage.

**special assessment bond** A municipal revenue bond funded by assessments only on property owners who benefit from the services or improvements provided by the proceeds of the bond issue. *See also* revenue bond.

**specialist** A stock exchange member who stands ready to quote and trade certain securities either for his own account or for customer accounts. The specialist's role is to maintain a fair and orderly market in the stocks for which he is responsible. *See also* specialist's book.

**specialist's book** A journal in which a specialist records the limit and stop orders that he holds for execution. The contents of the journal are confidential. *See also* specialist.

**special memorandum account (SMA)** A notation on a customer's general or margin account indicating that funds are credited to the account on a memo basis; the account is used much like a line of credit with a bank. An SMA preserves the customer's right to use excess equity.

**special situation fund** A mutual fund whose objective is to capitalize on the profit potential of corporations in nonrecurring circumstances, such as undergoing reorganizations or being considered as takeover candidates.

**special tax bond** A municipal revenue bond payable only from the proceeds of a tax on certain items, rather than an ad valorem tax. *See also* revenue bond.

**speculation** Trading a commodity or security with a higher than average risk in return for a higher than average profit potential. The trade is effected solely for the purpose of profiting from it and not as a means of hedging or protecting other positions.

**speculator** One who trades a commodity or security with a higher than average risk in return for a higher than average profit potential. *See also* speculation.

**split offering** A public offering of securities that combines aspects of both a primary and a secondary offering. A portion of the issue is a primary offering, the proceeds of which go to the issuing corporation; the remainder of the issue is a secondary offering, the proceeds of which go to the selling stockholders. *See also* primary offering.

**sponsor** A person who is instrumental in organizing, selling, or managing a limited partnership.

**spousal account** A separate individual retirement account established for a nonworking spouse. Contributions to the account are made by the working spouse and grow tax-deferred until withdrawal. *See also* individual retirement account.

**spread** (1) In a quotation, the difference between the bid and the ask prices of a security. (2) An options position established by purchasing one option and selling another option of the same class but of a different series.

**spread order** A customer order specifying two option contracts on the same underlying security or commodity and a price difference between them. A spread order takes priority over equal but separate bids and offers.

**SRO** *See* self-regulatory organization.

**SROP** *See* senior registered options principal.

**S S** A symbol on the Consolidated Tape indicating that the stock in question sold in 10-share units.

**stabilizing** Bidding at or below the public offering price of a new issue security. Underwriting managers may enter stabilizing bids during the offering period to prevent the price from dropping sharply. *See also* fixing.

**stagflation** A period of high unemployment in the economy accompanied by a general rise in prices. *See also* deflation; inflation.

**Standard & Poor's Corporation (S&P)** A company that rates stocks and corporate and municipal bonds according to risk profiles and that produces and tracks the S&P indexes. The company also publishes a variety of financial and investment reports. *See also* bond rating; Moody's Investors Service; rating; Standard & Poor's 100 Stock Index; Standard & Poor's Composite Index of 500 Stocks.

**Standard & Poor's 100 Stock Index (S&P 100)** A value-weighted index composed of 100 blue chip stocks. The index is owned and compiled by Standard & Poor's Corporation. *See also* index; Standard & Poor's Corporation; Standard & Poor's Composite Index of 500 Stocks.

**Standard & Poor's Composite Index of 500 Stocks (S&P 500)** A value-weighted index that offers broad coverage of the securities market. It is composed of 400 industrial stocks, 40 financial stocks, 40 public utility stocks and 20 transportation stocks. The index is owned and compiled by Standard & Poor's Corporation. *See also* index; Standard & Poor's Corporation; Standard & Poor's 100 Index.

**standby underwriter** An investment banker that agrees to purchase any part of an issue that has not been purchased by current stockholders through a rights offering. The firm exercises the remaining rights, maintains a trading market in the rights, and offers the stock acquired to the public. *See also* rights offering.

**statutory disqualification** Prohibiting a person from associating with a self-regulatory organization because the person has been expelled, barred or suspended from association with a member of a self-regulatory organization; has had his registration suspended, denied or revoked by the SEC; has been the cause of someone else's suspension, barment or revocation; has been convicted of certain crimes; or has falsified an application or report that he is required to file with or on behalf of a membership organization.

**statutory voting** A voting procedure that permits stockholders to cast one vote per share owned for each position. The procedure tends to benefit majority stockholders. *See also* cumulative voting.

**stock ahead** The term used to describe the inability of a specialist to fill a limit order at a specific price because other orders at the same price were entered previously.

**stock certificate** Written evidence of ownership in a corporation.

**stock loan agreement** The document that an institutional customer must sign when the broker-dealer borrows stock from the customer's account; the document specifies the terms of the loan and the rights of both parties.

**stock power** A standard form that duplicates the back of a stock certificate and is used for transferring the stock to the new owner's name. A separate stock power is used if the registered owner of a security does not have the certificate available for signature endorsement. *Syn.* power of substitution. *See also* assignment.

**stock quote** A list of representative prices bid and asked for a stock during a particular trading day. Stocks are quoted in points, where one point equals $1, and 1/8ths of a point, where 1/8th equals 12.5 cents. Stock quotes are listed in the financial press and most daily newspapers. *See also* bond quote.

**stock split** An increase in the number of a corporation's outstanding shares that decreases the par value of its stock. The market value of the total number of shares remains the same. The proportional reductions in orders held on the books for a split stock are calculated by dividing the market price of the stock by the fraction that represents the split. *See also* reverse split.

**stop limit order** A customer order that becomes a limit order when the market price of the security reaches or passes a specific price. *See also* limit order; stop order.

**stop order** (1) A directive from the SEC that suspends the sale of new issue securities to the public when fraud is suspected or filing materials are deficient. (2) A customer order that becomes a market order when the market price of the security reaches or passes a specific price. *See also* limit order; market order; stop limit order.

**stopping stock** The method used by a specialist to guarantee that a customer order will be executed at a specific price.

**straddle** An option investor's position that results from buying a call and a put or selling a call and a put on the same security with the same exercise price and expiration month. *See also* long straddle; short straddle; spread.

**street name** *See* in-street-name account.

**strike price** *See* exercise price.

**stripped bond** A debt obligation that has been stripped of its interest coupons by a brokerage firm, repackaged and sold at a deep discount. It pays no interest but may be redeemed at maturity for the full face value. *See also* zero-coupon bond.

**Student Loan Marketing Association (SLMA)** A publicly owned corporation that purchases student loans from financial institutions and packages them for sale in the secondary market, thereby increasing the availability of money for educational loans. *Syn.* Sallie Mae.

**Subchapter S corporation** A small business corporation that meets certain requirements and is taxed as a partnership while retaining limited liability.

**subject quote** A securities quotation that does not represent an actual offer to buy or sell but is tentative, subject to reconfirmation by the broker-dealer. *See also* bona fide quote; firm quote; nominal quote; workout quote.

**subordinated debenture** A debt obligation, backed by the general credit of the issuing corporation, that has claims to interest and principal subordinated to ordinary debentures and all other liabilities. *See also* debenture.

**subscription agreement** A statement signed by an investor indicating an offer to buy an interest in a direct participation program. In the statement, the investor agrees to grant power of attorney to the general partner and to abide by the limited partnership agreement. The sale is finalized when the subscription agreement is signed by the general partner.

**subscription amount** The total dollar amount that a participant in a direct participation program has invested.

**suitability** A determination made by a registered representative as to whether a particular security matches a customer's objectives and financial capability. The rep must have enough information about each customer in order to make this judgment. *See also* Rule 405.

**summary complaint procedure** A process for settling a charge or complaint that is quicker and less formal than the NASD's regular complaint procedure. The maximum penalty imposed under the summary complaint procedure is $2,500 plus public censure. *See also* Code of Procedure; regular complaint procedure.

**Super Designated Order Turnaround System** The computerized trading and execution system used by the New York Stock Exchange. The system allows broker-dealers to choose the destinations of orders and the routes they will take; specialists or commission brokers executing the orders use the system to send reports back to the firms. Orders executed through the system are often confirmed back to the broker in less than 60 seconds. *See also* New York Stock Exchange.

**supervision** A system implemented by a broker-dealer to ensure that its employees and associated persons comply with the applicable rules and regulations of the SEC, the exchanges and the SROs.

**supply** The total amount of a good or service available for purchase by consumers. *See also* demand.

**supply-side theory** An economic theory holding that bolstering an economy's ability to supply more goods is the most effective way to stimulate economic growth. Supply-side theorists advocate income tax reduction insofar as this increases private investment in corporations, facilities and equipment.

**support level** A technical analysis term describing the bottom of a stock's historical trading range. *See also* breakout; resistance level.

**surety bond** *See* fidelity bond.

**surplus fund** An account that is used to pay a variety of a municipal revenue bond's expenses, including redeeming bonds, funding improvements and making tax payments. *See also* flow of funds.

**syndicate** A group of investment bankers formed to handle the distribution and sale of a security on behalf of the issuer. Each syndicate member is responsible for the sale and distribution of a portion of the issue. *See also* Eastern account; Western account.

**syndicate manager** *See* underwriting manager.

**systematic risk** The potential for a security to decrease in value owing to its inherent tendency to move together with all securities of the same type. Neither diversification nor any other investment strategy can eliminate this risk. *See also* market risk; nonsystematic risk.

# *T*

**T** Consolidated Tape market identifier for trades of exchange-listed securities executed over the counter.

**takedown** The discount from the public offering price at which a syndicate member buys new issue securities from the syndicate for sale to the public. *See also* concession.

**taxability** The risk of the erosion of investment income through taxation.

**taxable gain** The portion of a sale or distribution of mutual fund shares that is subject to taxation.

**tax and revenue anticipation note (TRAN)** A short-term municipal debt security to be paid off from future tax receipts and revenues.

**tax anticipation note (TAN)** A short-term municipal or government debt security to be paid off from future tax receipts.

**tax basis** The amount that a limited partner has invested in a partnership.

**tax credit** An amount that can be subtracted from a tax liability, often in connection with real estate development, energy conservation and research and development programs. Every dollar of tax credit reduces the amount of tax due, dollar for dollar. *See also* deduction.

**tax-equivalent yield** The rate of return a taxable bond must earn before taxes in order to equal the tax-exempt earnings on a municipal bond. This number varies with the investor's tax bracket.

**taxes per person** A measure of the tax burden of a municipality's population, calculated by dividing the municipality's tax receipts by its population.

**tax-exempt bond fund** A mutual fund whose investment objective is to provide maximum tax-free income. It invests primarily in municipal bonds and short-term debt.

**tax liability** The amount of tax payable on earnings, usually calculated by subtracting standard and itemized deductions and personal exemptions from adjusted gross income and then multiplying by the tax rate. *See also* adjusted gross income.

**tax preference item** An element of income that receives favorable tax treatment. The item must be added to taxable income when computing alternative minimum tax. Tax preference items include accelerated depreciation on property, research and development costs, intangible drilling costs, tax-exempt interest on municipal private purpose bonds, and certain incentive stock options. *See also* alternative minimum tax.

**tax-sheltered annuity (TSA)** An insurance contract that entitles the holder to exclude all contributions from gross income in the year they are made. Tax payable on the earnings is deferred until the holder withdraws funds at retirement. TSAs are available to employees of public schools, church organizations and other tax-exempt organizations.

**T bill** *See* Treasury bill.

**T bond** *See* Treasury bond.

**technical analysis** A method of evaluating securities by analyzing statistics generated by market activity, such as past prices and volume. Technical analysts do not attempt to measure a security's intrinsic value. *See also* chartist; fundamental analysis.

**Telephone Consumer Protection Act of 1991 (TCPA)** Federal legislation restricting the use of telephone lines for solicitation purposes. A company soliciting sales via telephone, facsimile or E-mail must disclose its name and address to the called party and must not call any person who has requested not to be called.

**tender offer** An offer to buy securities for cash or for cash plus securities.

**term maturity** A repayment schedule for a bond issue in which the entire issue comes due on a single date. *See also* maturity date.

**testimonial** An endorsement of an investment or service by a celebrity or public opinion influencer. The use of testimonials in public communications is regulated by the NASD.

**third market** The exchange where listed securities are traded in the over-the-counter market. Institutional investors are the primary users of the third market.

**third-party account** (1) A customer account for which the owner has given power of attorney to a third party. (2) A customer account opened by an adult naming a minor as beneficial owner. (3) A customer account opened for another adult; this type of account is prohibited.

**tick** A minimum upward or downward movement in the price of a security. *See also* minus tick; plus tick; plus tick rule.

**time deposit** A sum of money left with a bank (or borrowed from a bank and left on deposit) that the depositing customer has agreed not to withdraw for a specified time period or without a specified amount of notice. *See also* demand deposit.

**time value** The amount an investor pays for an option above its intrinsic value; it reflects the amount of time left until expiration. The amount is calculated by subtracting the intrinsic value from the premium paid. *See also* intrinsic value.

**timing risk** The potential for an investor to incur a loss as a result of buying or selling a particular security at an unfavorable time.

**T note** *See* Treasury note.

**tombstone** A printed advertisement that solicits indications of interest in a securities offering. The text is limited to basic information about the offering, such as the name of the issuer, type of security, names of the underwriters and where a prospectus is available.

**total capitalization** The sum of a corporation's long-term debt, stock accounts and capital in excess of par.

**trade comparison** The memorandum sent by both broker-dealers engaged on either side a trade; it confirms the details of the transaction. Comparison procedures are established by the NASD's Uniform Practice Code.

**trade confirmation** A printed document that contains details of a transaction, including the settlement date and amount of money due from or owed to a customer. It must be sent to the customer on or before the settlement date.

**trade date** The date on which a securities transaction is executed.

**trading authorization** *See* full trading authorization; limited trading authorization.

**trading halt** A pause in the trading of a particular security on one or more exchanges, usually in anticipation of a news announcement or to correct an order imbalance. During a trading halt, open orders may be canceled and options may be exercised. *See also* HALT.

**tranche** One of the classes of securities that form an issue of collateralized mortgage obligations. Each tranche is characterized by its interest rate, average maturity, risk level and sensitivity to mortgage prepayments. Neither the rate of return nor the maturity date of a CMO tranche is guaranteed. *See also* collateralized mortgage obligation.

**transfer agent** A person or corporation responsible for recording the names and holdings of registered security owners, seeing that certificates are signed by the appropriate corporate officers, affixing the corporate seal, and delivering securities to the new owners.

**transfer and hold in safekeeping** A securities buy order settlement and delivery procedure whereby the securities bought are transferred to the customer's name but are held by the broker-dealer. *See also* hold in street name; transfer and ship.

**transfer and ship** A securities buy order settlement and delivery procedure whereby the securities bought are transferred to the customer's name and are sent to the customer. *See also* hold in street name; transfer and hold in safekeeping.

**Treasury bill** A marketable U.S. government debt security with a maturity of less than one year. Treasury bills are issued through a competitive bidding process at a discount from par; there is no fixed interest rate. *Syn.* T bill.

**Treasury bond** A marketable, fixed-interest U.S. government debt security with a maturity of more than ten years. *Syn.* T bond.

**Treasury note** A marketable, fixed-interest U.S. government debt security with a maturity of between one and ten years. *Syn.* T note.

**Treasury receipt** The generic term for a zero-coupon bond issued by a brokerage firm and collateralized by Treasury securities held in escrow for the investor by a custodian.

**treasury stock** Equity securities that have been issued and repurchased by the issuing corporation from the public at the current market price. *See also* issued stock; outstanding stock.

**trendline** A tool used by technical analysts to trace a security's movement by connecting the reaction lows in an upward trend or the rally highs in a downward trend.

**trough** The end of a period of declining business activity throughout the economy, one of the four stages of the business cycle. *See also* business cycle.

**true interest cost (TIC)** A means of evaluating the competitive bids of prospective bond underwriting syndicates. Each syndicate provides a calculation of the coupon interest to be paid by the issuer over the life of the bond, taking into account the time value of money. *See also* net interest cost.

**trustee** A person legally appointed to act on behalf of a beneficiary.

**trust indenture** A legal contract between a corporation and a trustee that represents its bondholders that details the terms of a debt issue. The terms include the rate of interest, maturity date, means of payment and collateral.

**Trust Indenture Act of 1939** The legislation requiring that all publicly offered, nonexempt debt securities be registered under the Securities Act of 1933 and be issued under a trust indenture that protects the bondholders.

**12b-1 asset-based fees** A provision of the Investment Company Act of 1940 that allows a mutual fund to collect a fee for the promotion, sale or other activity connected with the distribution of its shares. The fee must be reasonable (typically 1/2 to 1% of net assets managed), up to a maximum of 8.5% of the offering price per share.

**two-dollar broker** An exchange member that executes orders for other member firms when their floor brokers are especially busy. Two-dollar brokers charge a commission for their services; the amount of the commission is negotiated.

**type** A term that classifies an option as a call or a put. *See also* class; series.

## *U*

**UGMA** *See* Uniform Gifts to Minors Act.

**uncovered** *See* naked.

**underlying securities** The futures or securities that are bought or sold when an option, right or warrant is exercised.

**underwriter** An investment banker that works with an issuer to help bring a security to the market and sell it to the public.

**underwriting** The procedure by which investment bankers channel investment capital from investors to corporations and municipalities that are issuing securities. *See also* all or none underwriting; best efforts underwriting; firm commitment underwriting; mini-max underwriting.

**underwriting compensation** The amount paid to a broker-dealer firm for its involvement in offering and selling securities.

**underwriting manager** The brokerage firm responsible for organizing a syndicate, preparing the issue, negotiating with the issuer and underwriters and allocating stock to the selling group. *Syn.* syndicate manager. *See also* agreement among underwriters; syndicate.

**underwriting spread** The difference in price between the public offering price and the price an underwriter pays to the issuing corporation. The difference represents the profit available to the syndicate or selling group.

**undivided account** *See* Eastern account.

**unearned income** Income derived from investments and other sources not related to employment services. Examples of unearned income include interest from a savings account, bond interest and dividends from stock. *See also* earned income; passive income; portfolio income.

**Uniform Gifts to Minors Act (UGMA)** Legislation that permits a gift of money or securities to be given to a minor and held in a custodial account that is managed by an adult for the minor's benefit. By transferring income and capital gains to a minor's name, they are taxed at a lower rate. *See also* Uniform Transfers to Minors Act.

**Uniform Practice Code (UPC)** The NASD policy that establishes guidelines for a brokerage firm's dealings with other brokerage firms.

**Uniform Securities Act (USA)** Model legislation for securities industry regulation at the state level. Each state may adopt the legislation in its entirety or it may adapt it (within limits) to suit its needs. *See also* blue-sky laws; Series 63.

**Uniform Transfers to Minors Act (UTMA)** Legislation adopted in some states that permits a gift of money or securities to be given to a minor and held in a custodial account that is managed by an adult for the minor's benefit until the minor reaches a certain age (not necessarily the age of majority). *See also* Uniform Gifts to Minors Act.

**unit** A share in the ownership of a direct participation program that entitles the investor to an interest in the program's net income, net loss and distributions.

**unit investment trust (UIT)** An investment company that sells redeemable shares in a professionally selected portfolio of securities. It is organized under a trust indenture, not a corporate charter. *See also* fixed unit investment trust; nonfixed unit investment trust.

**unqualified legal opinion** The statement of a bond counsel affirming the compliance of a new municipal bond issue with municipal statutes and tax regulations, and expressing no reservations about its validity. *See also* legal opinion of counsel; qualified legal opinion.

**unrealized gain** The amount by which a security appreciates in value before it is sold. Until it is sold, the investor does not actually possess the proceeds of the sale. *See also* realized gain.

**unsecured bond** *See* debenture.

**up tick** *See* plus tick.

**U.S. government and agency bond fund** A mutual fund whose investment objective is to provide current income while preserving safety of capital through investing in securities backed by the U.S. Treasury or issued by a government agency.

## V

***Value Line*** An investment advisory service that rates hundreds of stocks as to safety, timeliness and projected price performance. *See also Value Line* Composite Index.

***Value Line* Composite Index** A market index composed of 1,700 exchange and over-the-counter stocks. *See also* index; *Value Line*.

**variable annuity** An insurance contract in which at the end of the accumulation stage the insurance company guarantees a minimum total payment to the annuitant. The performance of a separate account, generally invested in equity securities, determines the amount of this total payment. *See also* accumulation stage; annuity; fixed annuity; separate account.

**vertical spread** The purchase and sale of two options on the same underlying security and with the same expiration date but with different exercise prices. *See also* spread.

**vesting** (1) An ERISA guideline stipulating that employees must be entitled to their entire retirement benefits within a certain period of time even if they are no longer with the employer. (2) The amount of time that an employee must work before retirement or benefit plan contributions made by the employer become the employee's property without penalty. The IRS and the Employee Retirement Income Security Act of 1974 set minimum requirements for vesting in a qualified plan.

**visible supply** (1) The disclosure, published in The Bond Buyer, of the total dollar amount of municipal securities known to be coming to market within the next 30 days. (2) All supplies of goods and commodities that are readily deliverable.

**volatility** The magnitude and frequency of changes in the price of a security or commodity within a given time period.

**volume of trading theory** A technical analysis theory holding that the ratio of the number of shares traded to total outstanding shares indicates whether a market is strong or weak.

**voluntary accumulation plan** A mutual fund account into which the investor commits to deposit amounts on a regular basis in addition to the initial sum invested.

**voting right** The right of a stockholder to vote for members of the board of directors and on matters of corporate policy—particularly the issuance of senior securities, stock splits and substantial changes in the corporation's business. A variation of this right is extended to variable annuity contract holders and mutual fund shareholders, who may vote on material policy issues.

**voting trust** A corporation that assumes common stock voting power of a second corporation for a limited time period, such as during a reorganization of the second corporation.

**voting trust certificate** A certificate issued in place of a stock certificate to stockholders of a corporation that is temporarily managed by a voting trust. The certificate represents all of the benefits of ownership except the power to vote. When the corporation resumes management of its own affairs, it replaces the voting trust certificate with a new stock certificate.

## W

**warrant** A security that gives the holder the right to purchase securities from the issuer of the warrant at a stipulated subscription price. Warrants are usually long-term instruments, with expiration dates years in the future.

**wash sale** Selling a security at a loss for tax purposes and, within 30 days before or after, purchasing the same or a substantially identical security. The IRS will disallow the claimed loss. *See also* bond swap.

**Western account** A securities underwriting in which the agreement among underwriters states that each syndicate member will be liable only for the sale of the portion of the issue allocated to it. *Syn.* divided account. *See also* Eastern account; syndicate.

**when issued contract** A trade agreement regarding a security that has been authorized but is not yet physically available for delivery. The seller agrees to make delivery as soon as the security is ready, and the contract includes provisions for marking the price to the market and for calculating accrued interest.

**when issued security (WI)** A securities issue that has been authorized and is sold to investors before the certificates are ready for delivery. Typically, such securities include new issue municipal bonds, stock splits and Treasury securities.

**W I** A message on the Consolidated Tape indicating that the trade being reported is in when issued stock or is trading when issued.

**Wilshire 5,000 Equity Index** A value-weighted market indicator composed of 5,000 exchange-listed and over-the-counter common stocks. It is the broadest measure of the market. *See also* index.

**withdrawal plan** A benefit offered by a mutual fund whereby a customer receives the proceeds of periodic systematic liquidation of shares in the account. The amounts received may be based on a fixed dollar amount, a fixed number of shares, a fixed percentage or a fixed period of time.

**workable indication** The price at which a municipal securities dealer is willing to purchase securities from another municipal dealer. The price may be revised if market conditions change.

**working capital** A measure of a corporation's liquidity; that is, its ability to transfer assets into cash to meet current short-term obligations. It is calculated by subtracting total current liabilities from total current assets.

**workout quote** A qualified quotation whereby a broker-dealer estimates the price on a trade that will require special handling owing to its size or to market conditions. *See also* bona fide quote; firm quote; nominal quote; subject quote.

**writer** The seller of an option contract. An option writer takes on the obligation to buy or sell the underlying security if and when the option buyer exercises the option. *Syn.* seller.

**WS** A message on the Consolidated Tape indicating that the trade being reported is for a warrant.

## Y

***Yellow Sheets*** A daily publication compiled by the National Quotation Bureau and containing interdealer wholesale quotations for over-the-counter corporate bonds. *See also Pink Sheets.*

**yield** The rate of return on an investment, usually expressed as an annual percentage rate. *See also* current yield; dividend yield; nominal yield; yield to call; yield to maturity.

**yield-based option** A security representing the right to receive, in cash, the difference between the current yield of an underlying U.S. government security and the strike price of the option. A yield-based option is used to speculate on or hedge against the risk associated with fluctuating interest rates; its strike price represents the anticipated yield of the underlying debt security.

**yield curve** A graphic representation of the actual or projected yields of fixed-income securities in relation to their maturities. *See also* flat yield curve; inverted yield curve; normal yield curve.

**yield to call (YTC)** The rate of return on a bond that accounts for the difference between the bond's acquisition cost and its proceeds, including interest income, calculated to the earliest date that the bond may be called by the issuing corporation. *See also* bond yield.

**yield to maturity (YTM)** The rate of return on a bond that accounts for the difference between the bond's acquisition cost and its maturity proceeds, including interest income. *See also* bond yield.

## Z

**zero-coupon bond** A corporate or municipal debt security traded at a deep discount from face value. The bond pays no interest; rather, it may be redeemed at maturity for its full face value. It may be issued at a discount, or it may be stripped of its coupons and repackaged. *See also* original issue discount bond; stripped bond.

**zero-minus tick** A security transaction's execution price that is equal to the price of the last sale but lower than the last different price. *See also* minus tick; plus tick; zero-plus tick.

**zero-plus tick** A security transaction's execution price that is equal to the price of the last sale but higher than the last different price. *See also* minus tick; plus tick; plus tick rule; zero-minus tick.

# Index


Account
  approval and acceptance, 120
  classification, 119
  documenting, 120
  member firm employee, 123
  mutual fund, 343-44
  new, 119-23
  ownership, 119
  records, 123
  SIPC coverage, 214
  transfers, 122-23
  types of, 127-30, 247
  UGMA, 133
Accounting methods, 347
Accreting, 256
Accrual bond CMOs, 52-53
Accrued interest, 145-46
  taxation, 208
Accumulation stage, 362
Accumulation units, 363
Acid-test ratio, 190
Active markets, 115
Additional bonds test, 241
Additional issue market, 70
Additional paid-in capital, 185
Adjustable-rate preferred, 7
ADRs, 19
Ad valorem taxes, 240, 262
Advance/decline line, 181
Advertisement, 234-37, 250
  new issue, 67
  SIPC membership, 215
Affiliated person, 78, 332
Aftermarket sales, 67
Agency issues, 21, 23, 51-53, 207-8, 325
Agent, 95
Aggressive investment strategies, 205
Agreement
  among underwriters, 247
  of partnership, 370
AIR, 363-64
All or none (AON), 76, 98
Alternative minimum tax (AMT), 209
Alternative order, 98
American depositary receipts (ADRs), 19
American exercise system, 311
Amortization, 256
AMT, 209
Annuity, 362-64
  accounting, 363-64
  payout options, 363
  qualified, 367
  units, 363
Antidilution agreement, 3
Antifraud regulations, 79
AON. *See* All or none
Arbitration, 92, 228-29, 231
Ask, 88, 106, 320
Asset allocation funds, 325
Asset coverage, 191
Assets, 185
  prior claim to, 7
  residual claims to, 3
  transfer of, 79
Assignment, 149
  of exercise, 283
Associated person, 82, 224
  private securities transaction, 196
  registration, 224
Assumed interest rate (AIR), 363-64
At-the-money, 287
At-the-opening, 98
Auction market, 91
Audited financial statements, 86
Authorized stock, 1
Authorizing resolution, 240
Automatic exercise, 283
Automatic reinvestment, 324, 336
Award resolution, 240

BA. *See* Bankers' acceptances
Back-end load, 336
Backing away, 106
Balanced funds, 325
Balanced investment strategies, 205
Balance of payments, 179
Balance sheet, 185
  customer's, 199
Balance of trade, 179
Balloon maturity, 21
Bankers' acceptances (BA), 56, 59
Banking Act, 65
*Barron's Confidence Index*, 182
Basis quote, 256
Bearer bonds, 22, 149
Beneficial owner, 127, 153
Beneficiaries, 358
Best efforts, 76
Beta coefficient, 205
Bid, 88, 106, 320
Bid forms (worksheets), 248
*Blue List, The*, 247
Blue-sky laws, 70, 71, 217
Board brokers, 282
Board of directors, 1, 10, 332
Bona fide quotation, 255
*Bond Buyer, The*, 24, 246, 247
Bonds
  certificate, 22
  characteristics of, 21-24

contract, 240
corporate, 35-36
counsel, 240, 246
funds, 325
rating and analyzing, 22-23
ratio, 190
redemption, 186
registration, 22
resolution, 240
shorting, 102
swaps, 257
traded flat, 140
yield, 23, 28-30
Book entry, 22, 45
Book value, 2, 191
Borrowing
from a customer, 196-97
limits, 168
Branch offices, 224
Breadth of the market, 181
Breakeven point, 288-90, 296-99
Breakout, 181
Breakpoint, 324, 337
Breakpoint sales, 196, 337
Broad-based indexes, 309
Broker-dealer
as financial adviser, 250
nature of business, 109
registration of, 223-24
role of, 89
Broker's broker, 249
Business accounts, 122
Business cycle, 171, 172-73
Buying power, 155, 159, 160
Buy stop order, 97

Call, 278
buyer, 278, 288
date, 29, 45
feature, 23, 241
money rate, 59
option, 277, 288, 309, 316
premium, 23
protection, 24, 29
risk, 202
writer, 278, 289
Callable preferred stock, 8
Cap interval, 309-10
Capital gains (losses), 208, 316, 346
Capitalization ratios, 190
Capital risk, 202
Capital structure, 185-86
Capped index options, 309-10
Capping, 197
Cash account, 120, 153
Cash assets ratio, 190
Cash deposit, nonrequired, 155
Cash dividends, 10, 282
Cash market, 61
Cash settlement, 139
Cash trades, 140
Cash withdrawals, 157, 165
Catastrophe clause, 241
CBOE, 223
CDs, 56-57
Certificate
of incumbency, 127
of limited partnership, 370
negotiability, 149-50
Certificates of deposit (CDs), 56-57
Charges for services performed, 138
Charting stocks, 181-82
Chicago Board Options Exchange (CBOE), 223
Chinese Wall doctrine, 213
Church organizations, 367
Churning, 196, 255
Circuit breaker rules, 91
Civil liabilities, 67, 213
Class of options, 281
Closed-end indentures, 35
Closed-end investment companies, 320
Closing transactions, 282
CMOs, 52-53
CMV, 157
Code of Arbitration Procedure, 223, 228-29
amendments to, 229
Code of Procedure, 223, 228
Coincident indicators, 172
Collateral trust bonds, 35
Collateralized mortgage obligations (CMOs), 52-53
Collateral trust bonds, 35
Combination funds, 324
Combination privilege, 337
Combinations, 298
Combined accounts, 159-60
Combined distribution, 70
Commercial paper, 56
Commingling, 168
Commissions, 89, 108
continuing, 224
Committee on Uniform Securities Identification Procedures (CUSIP), 13, 150
Common stock, 1-3
benefits and risks of, 3
ratio, 190
valuation of, 2
Communications
public, 234-37
untruths in, 67
Compensation, 128, 231
Competitive bid, 45, 246
underwritings, 76
Complaint
customer, 268
procedure, 228
Computerized order routing, 114
Concession, 248
Conduit theory, 347
Confidence theory, 182
Confirmations, 255-56
Conservators, 128
Consolidated (Ticker) Tape, 115-16
Consolidated Quotation System (CQS), 114
Consolidations, 78-79, 181
Constant dollar plan, 205
Constant dollars, 171
Constant ratio plan, 205
Constitutional debt limit, 262
Consumer Price Index (CPI), 172
Consumption, 173
Contingent orders, 98
Contraction, 171
Contract sizes, foreign currency options, 311
Contractual plan, 343
Control securities, 78
Conversion
parity, 41
price, 40
ratio, 40
value, 41
Convertible preferred stock, 8
Convertible securities, 40-42, 92, 186
Cooling-off period, 66, 71
Corporate
accounts, 127
analysis, 184

bonds, 35-37
book inspections, 3
convertible securities, 40-42
debt analysis, 191
ethics and responsibility, 195
issues, 23
money market issues, 55
ownership, 1-3
retirement plans, 360
securities underwriting, 70
taxes, 210
Cost basis
adjustment of, 208, 256
shares transferred, 347
Cost of goods sold, 186
Coterminous debt, 240, 262
Counter-cyclical industries, 184
Coupon bonds, 22
Covered, 278
Covered call writing, 299
CPI, 172
CQS, 114
Credit
agreement, 121
balance, 159
extension, 153-54
risk, 191, 202
Criminal penalties, 66, 197, 213
Cross lien, 168
Cum rights, 15
Cumulative preferred stock, 7
Cumulative voting, 2-3
Currency
exchange, 311
risk, 19, 311
Current assets, 185
Current liabilities, 185
Current market value, 157
Current ratio, 190
Current yield, 10, 28, 191
CUSIP number, 13, 150
Custodial accounts, 127-28, 129-30
Custodial trading authorization, 119
Custodian, 128, 133, 134, 324, 333
Custodian bank, 19
Customer, 85
accounts, 119-23
statements, 138
communications, 255
ethics, 195
investment outlook, 200
know your, 199-200
legal recourse of, 237
protection rule, 168
recommendations, 196-97, 235-36
securities, 168
sharing in account of, 197
Customer services agent, 333
Cycle, options, 281
Cyclical industries, 184

Dated date, 145
Day order, 97
DBCC, 228
Dealer, 89
inventory costs, 108
paper, 56
Death
of account holder, 129
of minor, custodian, donor, 134
Debentures, 35
Debt limits, 252
Debt ratio, 190, 262
Debt retirement, 23-24
Debt securities
characteristics of, 21-24
yields, 28-30
Debt service, 22
Debt statement, 249-50
Debt-to-equity ratio, 190
Declaration date, 139
Default risk, 202
Defensive industries, 184
Defensive investment strategies, 205
Deferred annuities, 362
Deferred compensation plans, 361
Defined benefit plans, 360
Defined contribution plans, 360
Deflation, 172
Delisting
options, 282
stock, 91
Delivery, 67, 119, 137, 249
Delivery vs. payment (DVP), 119
Demand deposit, 177
De minimis exemption, 224
Depreciation, 61, 185
Depressions, 171
Devaluation, 61-62
Developmental drilling, 371-72
Diagonal spread, 296
Direct paper, 56
Direct participation program, 369-72
Disciplinary action, 228, 231
Disclosure
markups, 109
underwriting participation, 255
Discount, 22
Discount bonds, 28, 29, 30
Discount rate, 59, 178
Discretionary accounts, 128-29
Discretionary trading authorization, 119, 129
Disintermediation, 179
Disproportionate allocation, 81-82
Distributions
corporate retirement plans, 360
IRAs and Keoghs, 358
mutual fund, 346-47
District Business Conduct Committee (DBCC), 228
Diversification, 205, 288, 320
Diversified common stock funds, 324
Divided account, 76, 247
Dividend(s), 10 , 186
cash, 10
disbursement, 139-40
disbursing agent, 139
distributions, 346
exclusions, 210
income, 208
payout ratio, 191
per share, 191
preferred stock and, 7
property, 10
record date, 140
reinvestment, 346
stock, 10
DNR, 98
Do not reduce (DNR) order, 98
Doctrine of reciprocal immunity (mutual reciprocity), 207, 239
Dollar bonds, 255
Dollar cost averaging, 205, 344
Donated securities, 133, 209
Donor, 134
Double-auction market, 88, 91
Double-barreled bonds, 241
Dow Jones averages, 181
Dow theory, 182
Due diligence, 71, 247-48
DVP, 119

Earned income, 207, 357
Earned surplus, 186
Earnings per share (EPS), 186, 191
Eastern account, 76, 247
Easy money, 173
Economic indicators, 172
Economics, 171-73
EE, 155
Effective date, 72
Employee
  ethics, 195
  IRA contribution, 351
  Keogh eligibility, 357
Employee Retirement Income Security Act (ERISA), 368
EPS. *See* Earnings per share
Equilibrium, 173
Equipment-leasing limited partnerships, 372
Equipment trust certificates, 35
Equity, 159
Equity options, 281-84
Equity securities, 328-29
  American depositary receipts, 19
  common stock, 1-3
  preferred stock, 7-8
ERISA, 368
Erroneous execution reports, 138
Error messages, 115
Escrow, 76
Estate taxes, 207
Ethics, 195-97
Eurobond, 61
Eurodollars, 61-62
European exercise system, 312
Eurosecurities, 61
Excess contribution, 351
Excess equity, 155-56
Excessive trading, 196, 255
Excess margin securities, 168
Excess reserves, 178
Exchange
  listed securities, 88
  listing requirements, 91
  market, 88
  offer, 141
  rates, 61-62
  short sale rules, 102
  stabilization fund, 61
  traded options, 281
Exchanges, 337-38, 347
Ex-dividend date, 16, 140
Executor, 127
Exempt securities, 78
Exempt transactions, 78
Exercise
  limits, 283, 309, 311
  option, 283
  price, 278, 281
  settlement, 309, 311-12
Existing property, 371
Ex-legal, 240, 246
Expansion, 171
Expense ratio, 326
Expiration date, 278, 281, 311
Exploratory drilling, 371
Ex-rights, 15
Extraordinary items, 186

Face-amount certificate company, 319
Face value, 45
Fail to deliver, 150
Fair dealing, 196
Family members, 81
Family of funds, 337-38, 347
FCOs, 311-12
Feasibility study, 248
Federal call, 154
Federal Farm Credit Bank, 51
Federal funds, 177-78
Federal funds rate, 59, 178
Federal Home Loan Bank (FHLB), 51
Federal Home Loan Mortgage Corporation (FHLMC), 51-52
Federal Intermediate Credit Banks (FICBs), 51
Federal National Mortgage Association (FNMA), 52
Federal Reserve Board (FRB), 177
FHLB, 51
FHLMC, 51-52
FICBs, 51
Fidelity bonds, 215
Fiduciary
  accounts, 127-28
  responsibility, 133-34
  trading authorization, 119
FIFO. *See* First in, first out
Fill or kill (FOK) order, 98
Final prospectus, 66, 72
Finance company paper, 56
Financial
  adviser, 250
  leverage, 186
  profile, 199
  ratios, 190-91
  risk, 202-3
  statements, 85-86, 185-86
Fingerprinting, 221
Firm commitment, 76, 248
Firm quote, 106
First in, first out (FIFO), 185, 347
Fiscal policy, 177, 179
Fixed annuities, 362
Fixed assets, 185
Fixed conversion, 40-41
Fixing, 72
Flat yield curve, 30
Flow of funds, 241, 263
Flower bonds, 46
FNMA, 52
FOK, 98
Forced conversion, 41-42
Forced sell-outs, 154
Foreign currency
  market, 61-62
  options, 311-12
Foreign securities, 19, 208
Form letters, 234
Form 1099B, 324, 346
45-day free look, 343-44
48-hour rule, 67
Forward market, 61
Forward pricing, 338
Forward trades, 61
401K plan, 360
Fourth market, 88
Fraudulent devices, 195
FRB. *See* Federal Reserve Board
Free credit balance, 138
Freeriding and withholding, 81-82
Front-end load, 336, 343
Front-running, 197
Frozen account, 139
Full Disclosure Act, 65
Full power of attorney, 128
Fully paid securities, 155, 168
Fully registered bonds, 22
Fundamental analysis, 184

GDP, 171
General obligation bonds, 239, 240-41, 262
General partners (GPs), 370-71

General reserve, 263
General securities representative license, 225
Generic advertising, 234
Gifted securities, 209
Gift tax, 207
Glass-Steagall Act of 1933, 65
GNMA, 52
GO. *See* General obligation bond
Good delivery, 149-50
 clearing rule, 149
Good faith deposit, 248
Good till canceled orders, 98
Government National Mortgage Association (GNMA), 52
GP, 370-71
Gross domestic product, 171
Gross revenue pledge, 263
Growth funds, 324
Growth industries, 184
Guaranteed bonds, 35
Guarantees, 197
Guardian, 127

Hedge, 299, 310
Holding a quote, 255
Holding period return, 202
Hold in street name, 119
Hot issues, 71, 81-82
House margin requirement, 158
HR-10 plans, 357-58
Hypothecation, 168
 agreement, 121

IDBs, 241
IDRs, 241
Illegal acts, 3
Immediate annuity, 362
Immediate or cancel orders, 98
Inactively traded stocks, 108
Income
 bonds, 36
 funds, 324
 programs, 372
 safety of, 191
Income statement, 186, 199
Income taxes, 207
Incompetence of account holder, 129
Indefeasible title, 133
Index arbitrage, 91
Index funds, 325
Index options, 309
Indication of interest, 66, 67, 235
Individual retirement accounts (IRAs)
 contributions to, 351
 participation in, 351
 rollovers, 352
 transfers, 352
 withdrawals, 352
Industrial development revenue bonds, 241
Industry analysis, 184
Inflation, 171-72
Inflation risk, 202
Inherited securities, 209
Initial margin requirement, 154, 155
Initial public offering (IPO), 70
Inside market, 88, 111
Inside market prices, 108
Insider Trading Act of 1988, 213
INSTINET, 88, 114
Insubstantiality, 82
Insurance covenant, 241
Interbank market, 61
Interdealer market, 88
Interdealer quote, 104
Interest
 bond, 21
 expense, 186
 income, 207-8
Interested persons, 332, 333
Interest-only CMOs (IOs), 52
Interest rate, 59, 179, 263
 options, 310
 risk, 202
Intermarket Trading System/Computer Assisted Execution System (ITS/CAES), 114
Internal rate of return, 203
International monetary factors, 179
In-the-money, 287
Intrastate offerings, 79
Intrinsic value, 287
Investment, 173
 grade bonds, 23
 intermediaries, 82
 recommendations, 196
 returns, 202-3, 347
 risks, 202
 value, 41
Investment adviser, 332
 registration of, 224
Investment banker, 70
Investment companies, 235
 management of, 332-33
 offerings, 319-20
 product recommendations, 236
 registration, 328-29
 types of, 319-20
Investment Company Act of 1940, 319, 332
IOC, 98
IOs, 52
IPO, 70
IRAs. *See* Individual retirement accounts, 351-53
Irrevocable gift, 133
Issued stock, 1
Issuer, 70
 bonds, 21
 convertible securities, 40
 exempt, 78
 money market securities, 55
 municipal securities, 239, 246-50
ITS/CAES, 114

Joint account, 127
Joint life with last survivor annuity, 363
Joint tenants in common (JTIC), 127, 129
Joint tenants with right of survivorship (JTWROS), 127, 129
JTIC. *See* Joint tenants in common
JTWROS. *See* Joint tenants with right of survivorship

Keogh plans, 357-58
Keynesian economics, 172-73

L, 177
Lagging indicators, 172
Last in, first out (LIFO), 185, 347
Leading indicators, 172
LEAPS, 283-84
Lease rental bonds, 241
Legal list, 128
Legal opinion, 150, 240, 246
Legal transfer items, 150
Legislative risk, 202
Letter of intent (LOI), 337
Leverage, 153, 190
Liabilities, 185

LIBOR, 59
Liens, 168
Life annuity/straight life, 363
Life annuity with period certain, 363
LIFO. *See* Last in, first out
Limited liability, 3
Limited ownership privileges, 7
Limited partner (LP), 371
Limited partnership, 369-72
  dissolution of, 370
  formation of, 370
Limited power of attorney, 128
Limited representative licenses, 225
Limited tax bonds, 240
Limit order book, 95
Limit orders, 97
Liquidation, 324
  priority, 36
  proceedings, 214
Liquidity, 23, 185
  collateralized mortgage obligations, 53
  money market accounts, 55
  ratios, 190
  risk, 202
Listed markets, 88
Listing
  requirements, options, 281-82
  requirements, stock, 91
  suspension or termination, 112
Load, 336
Loan consent agreement, 121
LOI, 337
London Interbank Offered Rate (LIBOR), 59
Long
  call, 277, 281, 310
  combinations, 298
  options, 281
  positions, 277
  put, 277, 281, 310
  sale, 102
  stock and long put(s), 299, 316
  stock and short call(s), 299, 316
  straddles, 298
Long-term equity options, 283-84
Long-term liabilities, 185
Long-term yield, 30
Losses avoided, 213
Low-priced stock, 159
LP, 369-72
Lump-sum accounts, 336

M1, M2, M3, 177
Mailing instructions, 120
Maintenance, 159
Maintenance covenant, 241
Maloney Act, 65, 217
Management investment companies, 320
Manipulative and deceptive practices, 195
Margin
  accounts, 120-21, 153
  agreement, 121
  expenses, 209
  maintenance call, 157
    short sales, 159
  of profit ratio, 190
  securities, 168
Marginal propensity to consume, 173
Market
  arbitrage, 92
  averages, 181
  convertible securities, 40
  identifier, 115
  order, 97
  risk, 202, 205
Marketability risk, 202
Marketable government securities, 45-46
Market maker, 88, 104
  registration, 114
  reports, 111
Market-on-close order, 98
Market value, 2, 155-58, 164
Markups, markdowns, 108-9
Maturities
  bond, 21
  date, 7
Mergers, 78-79
Mills, 240
Mini-max, 76
Minor, 134
Misleading information, 236
Misrepresentations, 197
Modern portfolio theory, 182
Monetary policy, 177-79
Money
  creation of, 177
  definition of, 177
Money market, 55-57
  funds, 325
  instruments, 55-56
Moral obligation bonds, 241
Moral suasion, 179
Mortgage bonds, 35
MPT, 182
MSRB. *See* Municipal Securities Rulemaking Board
Multiple option positions, 296-99
Multiplier effect, 178
Municipal securities, 23, 150, 208, 210, 242
  accrued interest, 145
  analysis of, 262-63
  characteristics, 239-42
  funds, 325
  insurance, 263
  legal limitations on, 240
  publications, 247
Municipal Securities Rulemaking Board, 223
  member firm employee accounts, 123
  rules, 267-69
*Munifacts*, 247
Mutual fund, 208, 320
  characteristics of, 324-26
  comparisons, 325-26
  distributions, 346-47
  marketing, 335-38
  pricing, 336
  types of, 343-44
  valuation, 335-38

Naked position, 278
Narrow-based indexes, 309
NASD. *See* National Association of Securities Dealers
*NASD Manual*, 223
Nasdaq, 104
  authorized securities, 111-12
  market maker requirements, 111
  National Market (NNM), 111-12
National Association of Securities Dealers (NASD), 70
  accounts for employees of other brokers, 123
  Automated Quotation, 104
  bylaws, 223-26
  5% markup policy, 108-9

hot issue violations, 82
margin maintenance requirements, 157
membership and registration, 223-24
public communication rules, 235-37
SOES, 114
NAV. *See* Net asset value
Negative yield curve, 30
Negotiability, 13
Negotiable CDs, 56-57
Negotiated market, 88, 104
Negotiated underwriting, 76, 246
Net asset value, 335, 336
Net income after taxes, 186
Net interest cost, 248
Net investment income, 346
Net price, 89
Net profit ratio, 190
Net revenue pledge, 263
Net sales, 186
New account form, 120
New accounts, 119-23
New construction, 371
New Housing Authority (NHA) bonds, 241
New issue
corporate, 70
regulation of, 65-67
worksheets, 247
New Issues Act, 65
New York Stock Exchange (NYSE), 91-92, 223
constitution and rules, 231
margin maintenance requirements, 157
member firm employee accounts, 123
Rule 405, 119
short sales minimum deposit, 158-59
SuperDot, 114
NHAs, 241
NIC, 248
Nine bond rule, 92
90-second reporting, 111
NNM, 111-12
No-load, 336
No-load fund, 335
Nominal owner, 153
Nominal quotation, 106, 255
Nominal yield, 28
Nonbranch offices, 224
Nondiversified management investment companies, 320
Nonequity options, 309-12, 316
Nonfinancial investment considerations, 199-200
Nonnegotiable CD, 56
Nonoperating income, 186
Nonqualified plans, 361
Nonsupported family members, 81
Nonsystematic risk, 205
Normal investment practice, 81
Normal yield curve, 30
Not held orders, 98
Notification, 196, 214
Numbered accounts, 122
NYSE. *See* New York Stock Exchange

OBO, 282
OCC. *See* Options Clearing Corporation
Odd-lot theory, 182
Offering, 65
terms of, 15
types of, 70
Official notice of sale, 246
Official statement, 240, 249-50
OID. *See* Original issue discount
Oil and gas limited partnerships, 371-72
Open account, 343
Open-end indentures, 35
Open-end investment companies, 320, 328
Open-market operations, 178
Operating expenses, 186
Operating profit, 186
Operating ratio, 190
Option, 278
account, 121
advertisements, 235
contract, 277-78, 281, 282
adjustments, 282-83
index, 309
terminology, 278
trading, 287-90
transactions, 281
Options Clearing Corporation, 282
Disclosure Document, 235, 282
Order
allocation, 249
book official (OBO), 282
memorandum, 137
processing, 137
types of, 97-98
Original issue discount, 209, 256
OS. *See* Official statement
OTC. *See* Over-the-counter market
Out-firm quote, 255
Out-of-the-money, 287
Outstanding stock, 1
Overdelivery, 149
Overlapping debt, 240, 262
Over-the-counter market, 88, 102, 104
Ownership, 1
transferability of, 13

PACs, 53
Paid-in surplus (capital), 2
Par bond, 28, 29, 30
Parity, 41, 91
Partially called bonds, 149
Participating preferred stock, 7-8
Partnership accounts, 127, 130
Partnerships, 369
Par value, 2
Passive income, 207
Payable date, 140
Payment, 119, 249
extensions for margin customers, 154
period, 139
Payout options, 358
PE ratio, 191
Peak, 171
Pegging, 61, 72
Penny stock, 2, 122
Penny Stock Reform Act of 1990, 122
Periodic payment deferred annuity, 362, 363
Periodic payment plans, 343
*Pink Sheets*, 104
Pipeline theory, 347
Placement ratio, 247
Planned amortization class CMOs, 53
Plus (up) tick, 97
Political risk, 202

Portfolio, 350
  analysis, 205
  income, 207
  management strategies, 205
  turnover, 326
POs, 52
Position limits, 283, 309, 311
Position trading, 89
Power of attorney, 122, 128, 129
Power of substitution, 149
Precedence, 91
Preemptive right, 3, 15
Preferred stock, 7-8, 329
  classes of, 7-8
  ratio, 190
Preliminary official statement, 240
Preliminary prospectus, 66, 67
Premium, 22, 278
  bond, 28-30
Prerefunding, 24
Present value, 203
Price
  levels, 171-72
  relationship to yield, 30
  spread, 296
Price-earnings (PE) ratio, 191
Pricing
  bonds, 22
  mutual fund, 336
  new issue, 71
  system, listed markets, 88
Primary market, 88
Primary offering, 65, 70
Prime paper, 56
Prime rate, 59
Principal, 95, 120
Principal-only CMOs, 52
Priority, 91
Prior lien bonds, 35
Prior preferred, 7
Private placements, 71, 78, 369
Private securities transactions, 196
Proceeds transactions, 108
Profitability ratios, 190
Profits gained, 213
Profit-sharing plan, 360
Program trading, 91
Progressive tax, 207
Property dividends, 10
Prospectus, 66-67, 328
  untruths in, 67
Prospectus Act, 65
Prosperity, 171
Protective covenants, 241
Proxy, 3, 140
  contest, 3
  department, 140
Prudent man rule, 128
Public educational 403(b) institutions, 367
Publicly traded funds, 320
Public offering, 71, 328
  private placements and, 369
Public offering price (POP), 74, 108, 335
Public purpose bonds, 257
Purchasing power risk, 202
Put, 278
  bonds, 24
  buyer, 278, 289-90
  option, 277, 309, 316
  writer, 278, 290

Qualifications
  examinations, 225
  investigation of, 224
Qualified annuity plans, 367
Qualified legal opinion, 240, 246
Qualified quotes, 106
Qualified plans, 357-58
Quantity discounts, 337
Quick assets, 190
Quotation, 95, 106, 255
  Consolidated Tape, 115-16
  requirements, 106
  spread and size, 106

Random walk theory, 182
Rate covenant, 241
Ratio writing, 299
Raw land, 371
Real estate investment trusts (REITs), 350
Real estate limited partnerships, 371
Realized appreciation, 347
Reallowances, 248
Receiver, 128
Recessions, 171
Recognized quotation, 106
Record date, 15
Recovery, 171
Recruitment advertising, 236
Red herring, 66
Redeemable securities, 320
Redemption, 23
  fund shares, 338
Reducing orders, 98
Refunding, 24
Registered as to principal only, 22
Registered bonds, 22, 149
Registered owner, 19
Registered representatives, 224-25
Registrar, 13
Registration, 221
  associated person, 224
  broker-dealer, 223-24
  by coordination, 71
  employee, 231
  exchanges, 85
  exemptions from, 224
  by filing, 71
  firms, 85
  ineligibility and disqualifications, 225-26
  investment adviser, 224
  investment company, 328-29
  market maker, 114
  municipal securities, 240
  NASD, 223-24
  principals, 225
  by qualification, 71
  securities, 65-67
  UGMA securities, 133
Regressive tax, 207
Regular way settlement, 138-39
Regulated investment company, 208
Regulation, 221
  interbank market, 61
  new issues, 65-67
  state, 217
  trading, 85-86
Regulation A, 78
Regulation D, 78
Regulation G, 179
Regulation T, 121, 153-54, 178
  call, 154
  initial margin, 160
  payment, 139
  retention requirement, 156
  short sales, 158-59
Regulation U, 179
Rehypothecation, 168
Reinstatement, 324
Reinvestment
  dividend, 346
  risk, 46, 202

REITs, 350
Reoffering yield (price), 246, 248
Repo, 55-56
Repurchase agreement, 55-56
Reserve requirement, 177, 178
Resistance level, 181
Restricted account, 81, 156-57, 159, 165
Restricted securities, 78
Retained earnings, 186
Retirement planning
  annuities, 362-64, 367
  corporate plans, 360-61
  ERISA, 368
  IRAs, 351-53
  Keoghs, 357-58
Return on investment, 10-11
Revaluation, 62
Revenue bonds, 239, 241, 262-63
Reversals, 181
Reverse repo, 56
Reverse repurchase agreement, 56
Reverse splits, 11, 283
Right(s), 15-16, 140
  of accumulation, 336, 337
  agent, 15
  characteristics of, 15
  issuance of, 16
  to refund, 344
  value of, 16
  of withdrawal, 343-44
Rising production, 173
Risk
  arbitrage, 92
  beyond underwriter's control, 76
  bondholders, 24
  investment, 202
  management, 205
  reinvestment, 46
  underwriter must assume, 76
Riskless and simultaneous transactions, 108
ROI. *See* Return on investment
Rollovers, 352, 358
Rounding, 283
Round lot, 149
Rule 15c2-1, 168
Rule 135a, 234
Rule 144, 78
Rule 144a, 78
Rule 145, 78-79
Rule 147, 79
Rule 405, 119
Rule 415, 70
Rule 506, 78
Rules G-1 to G-38, 267-69
Rules of Fair Practice, 223
Rules of good delivery, 149-50

Safety, 23
  collateralized mortgage obligations, 53
  debt securities, 191
  money market, 55
Sales
  charges, 335-36
  confirmations, 249
  by control persons, 78
  loads, 326
  to restricted accounts, 81
  supervision, hot issue, 82
  volume restrictions, 78
Sales literature, 234-37
Savings, 173
Savings bonds, 49
Seats, NYSE, 231
SEC. *See* Securities and Exchange Commission
Secondary market, 88
  discount, 209, 256
Secondary offering, 70
Secured bonds, 35
Securities, 78
  good condition of, 150
  markets, 70, 88
  receipt and delivery of, 137
  type of, 108
Securities Act of 1933, 65, 67, 267
  exemptions from, 78-79
Securities Exchange Act of 1934, 65, 79, 85-86, 221, 267
Securities and Exchange Commission (SEC), 66, 70, 85
  insider investigations, 213
  investment company registration, 328
  new issues and, 65-67
Securities Investor Protection Corporation (SIPC), 214-15
Selection risk, 202
Self-regulatory organization (SRO), 236
  margin maintenance requirement, 160
Seller's option contracts, 139
Selling
  away, 196
  concession, 248
  dividends, 196, 346
Selling group, 74
  agreement, 74
Sell order tickets, 102
Sell stop order, 97
Senior lien securities, 35
Separate account, 362
Separate customers, 214
SEP-IRAs, 353
Serial maturity, 21
Series
  bonds, 21
  of options, 281
Series 6, 225
Series 7, 225
Series 11, 225
Series 63, 225
Series EE bonds, 49
Series HH bonds, 49
Settlement
  date, 138
  options, 281
Shared account, 197
Shareholder's equity, 185
Shelf offering, 70
Short
  against the box, 159
  calls, 277, 281
  combinations, 298-99
  options, 281
  positions, 277
  puts, 277, 281
  sale, 102, 158-59
  stock and long calls, 299
  stock and short puts, 299
  straddles, 298
Shorting bonds, 102
Short-interest theory, 182
Short-term yield, 30
Signature, 123
  cards, 120
  guarantee, 149
Simplified customer arbitration, 229
Simplified employee pensions (SEP-IRAs), 353
Simplified industry arbitration, 229
Single accounts, 127, 129

Single premium (payment) deferred annuity, 362, 363
Sinking fund, 23, 241
SIPC, 214-15
Size, 95, 106, 111
SLMA, 52
SMA, 164-65
Small offerings, 78
Small Order Execution System, 114
SOES, 114
Specialist, 88, 95
Specialist's book, 95
Specialized (sector) funds, 325
Special memorandum account (SMA), 164-65
Special revenue bonds, 241
Special situation funds, 325
Special tax bonds, 241
Speculation, 62, 128, 288, 289
Split offering, 70
Spot market, 61
Spot trades, 61
Spousal account, 351
Spread, 106, 248, 296
  between premiums, 298
  breakdown of, 248
  load plan, 343
  types of, 296
SRO. *See* Self-regulatory organization
Stabilizing, 72
Stagflation, 172
Standard & Poor's 500, 181
Standby underwriting, 15, 71, 76
Stated (fixed) rate of return, 7
Statement of intention, 337
State securities regulations, 71, 217
Statute of limitations, 229
Statutory disqualification, 225-26
Statutory voting, 2
Sticky issue, 72
Stock
  ahead, 97
  certificate, 13
  classification, 1
  dividends, 10, 140, 283
  holding periods, 316
  power, 149
  same-day substitution of, 165
  splits, 10, 41, 98, 140, 186, 282-83
  withdrawals, 157
Stockholder, 70
  rights, 2-3
  subscription rights, 41
Stop limit order, 97
Stop order, 66, 97
Stopping stock, 95
Straddles, 298
Strike price, 278
STRIPS, 46
Student Loan Marketing Association, 52
Subject quotation, 106
Submission agreement, 229
Subordinated debentures, 35
Subscription agreement, 370
Subscription rights, 15-16, 41
Suitability, 196, 202
Summary complaint procedure, 228
Super Designated Order Turnaround (SuperDot), 114
SuperDot, 114
Support level, 181
Syndicate
  account, 248
  bid, establishment of, 248
  formation of, 71, 74, 247-48
  manager's fee, 248
Systematic risk, 202, 205

T+3, 138-39
TACs, 53
Takedown, 248
Targeted amortization class CMOs, 53
Taxation
  agency issues, 51
  annuities, 364
  collateralized mortgage obligations, 53
  corporate retirement plan distributions, 360
  federal and state, 207-10
  investment portfolios and, 207-9
  IRA distributions, 352-53
  LEAPS, 284
  limited partnership, 369
  municipal securities, 255-57
  mutual funds, 326, 347
  nonqualified plans, 361
  options, 316
  TSA distributions, 367
  UGMA, 134
  zero-coupon bonds, 36
Tax-exempt commercial paper, 242
Tax-exempt 501(c) organizations, 367
Tax-exempt interest income, 208
Tax-exempt money market funds, 325
Tax-free (tax-exempt) bond funds, 325
Tax preference items, 209
Tax-sheltered annuities (TSAs), 367
TCPA, 237
Technical analysis, 181-82
Technical market theories, 182
Telephone communications, 237
Telephone Consumer Protection Act of 1991 (TCPA), 237
Tender offers, 24, 140-41
Term bond, 21
Testimonials, 236
Third market, 88
30-day visible supply, 247
Thrift plan, 360
TIC, 248
Tight money, 173
Time deposit, 177
Times interest earned ratio, 191
Time spread, 296
Time value, 287
Timing risk, 202
Tombstone, 67, 234-35
Trade
  confirmations, 138
  settlement, 137-38
Trading
  authorization, 119, 122
  call's effect on, 24
  corporate bonds, 28-30
  foreign securities, 19
  halts, 88
  hours
    CQS, 114
    exchange, 88
    over-the-counter, 88
  interbank market, 61
  municipal, 255-57
  options, 287-90
  penny stock, 122
  regulation of, 85-86

Treasury bills, 45
Treasury bonds, 45
Treasury notes, 45
volume, 181
Tranche, 52
Transaction
restricted account, 156-57
settlement dates, terms, 138-39
trade settlement and, 137-38
Transfer, 231
agent, 13, 139, 333
and hold in safekeeping, 119
IRA, 352
procedures, 13
and ship, 119
Treasury bills, 45, 59, 310
Treasury bonds, 310
Treasury notes, 45, 310
Treasury receipts, 46
Treasury stock, 1
Trend, 181
Trendlines, 181
Trigger transactions, 97
Trough, 171
True interest cost, 248
Trustee, 36, 127
Trust indenture, 36-37, 65, 240
Trust Indenture Act of 1939, 36, 65, 217
Truth in Securities Act, 65
TSAs, 367
12b-1 asset-based fees, 336
Type, of options, 281

U-4, 224
UGMA. *See* Uniform Gifts to Minors Act
UIT, 319-20
Uncovered position, 278
Underdelivery, 149
Underlying currencies, 311
Underlying instruments, 277, 278
Underwriter, 70, 333
Underwriting
agreement, 74
commitments, 76
compensation, 74
fee, 248
limited partnership, 370
manager, 74
proceeds, 74
process, 70-72
standby, 15
syndicate formation, 71, 74, 247-48
time line for, 71-72
Undivided account, 76, 247
Undivided interest, 129, 320, 324
Uniform Gifts to Minors Act (UGMA), 128, 133-34
Uniform Practice Code, 223
Uniform Securities Act (USA), 217
U.S. government, 21
bonds, 145
securities, 23, 207
marketable, 45-46
nonmarketable, 49
Unit investment trust, 319-20
Units (shares) of beneficial interest, 319-20
Unqualified legal opinion, 240, 246
Unrealized appreciation, 347
Unsecured bonds, 335
Unsuitable trades, 202
USA, 217

Valuation, 61-62
common stock, 2
fund shares, 335, 347
options, 287
ratios, 191
*Value Line*, 181
Variable annuities, 362
payments, 362
sales charges, 363
Variable conversion, 40-41
Variable hedging, 299
Vesting, 357
Volume reports, 111
Voluntary accumulation plan, 343
Voting rights, 2, 324
Voting trust certificates, 3

Warrants, 16, 140
Wash sales, 209
Western account, 76, 247
When issued (WI), 15, 139, 154
WI. *See* When issued
Wilshire 5,000 Equity Index, 181
Withdrawal, 157
IRA, 352
penalties for early, 358
plans, 344
Withholding tax, 347
Workable indication, 255
Workout quote, 106

*Yellow Sheets*, 104
Yield
agency issues, 51
-based options, 311
bond, 28-30
collateralized mortgage obligations, 53
curve, 30
disclosure, 255-56
rating and, 23
Yield to call (YTC), 28-29
Yield to maturity (YTM), 28-29, 256
YTC, 29-30
YTM. *See* Yield to maturity

Zero-coupon bonds, 36
Z tranche CMOs, 52-53

## Notes

## Notes

## Notes

## Notes

## Notes